Give Me Five! English 6

TEACHER'S BOOK

Donna Shaw • Rob Sved

macmillan education

Macmillan Education
4 Crinan Street
London N1 9XW
A division of Springer Nature Limited

Companies and representatives throughout the world

Teacher's Book ISBN 978-1-380-02514-2
Teacher's Book Pack ISBN 978-1-380-02513-5

This edition published 2018
First edition entitled *High Five English!* published 2015 by Springer Nature Limited

Teacher's Edition credits:
Series concept design by Tom Cole
Page make up by emc design ltd
Cover design by Bigtop Design Limited
Cover photographs by Lisa Payne/ Springer Nature Limited

Authors' acknowledgements
The authors would like to thank everyone at Macmillan who has given help and advice throughout this project. Special thanks from Rob to Belén, Natalia, Xana and Pablo for all their inspiration. Special thanks from Donna to José, Elisa, Teresa and Marina for their encouragement and enthusiasm.

The publishers would like to thank the following teachers for their contribution to the project: Ana Postigo, CEIP Vicálvaro, Madrid; Beatriz García Vaquero, CEIP Mariano José de Larra, Madrid; Damián Quiralte Fresneda, CEIP Claudio Moyano, Madrid; Eamonn Healy, Colegio SEK Santa Isabel, Madrid; Elvira Robledo Gandarias, Colegio Ayalde, Loiu, Vizcaya; Francisco Javier Navarro Pineda, Colegio Tajamar, Madrid; Guiomar Yagüe Martínez, CEIP Celso Emilio Ferreiro, Móstoles, Madrid; Henar Del Gallo Muñoz, CEIP Cantos Altos, Collado Villalba, Madrid; Ignacio de la Puente Rodríguez, CEIP El Cantizal, Las Rozas, Madrid; Inmaculada Romero Fanego, CEIP Príncipes de Asturias, Pozuelo de Alarcón, Madrid; Laura Tenorio, CEIP Esperanza, Madrid; María del Rosario García Leal, CEIP Rufino Blanco, Madrid; Patricia Sanz, CEIP Félix Rodríguez de la Fuente, Coslada, Madrid; Silvia San José Paul, CEIP El Cantizal, Las Rozas, Madrid; Víctor Molinero Cuartango, CEIP Ciudad de Roma, Madrid; Virginia Escalona Monreal, CEIP La Encina, Las Rozas, Madrid; Laura Zarzuelo, Colegio Virgen de la Almudena, Collado Villalba, Madrid; Eugenio Domínguez, Colegio Virgen de la Almudena, Collado Villalba, Madrid; Silvia Díez de Rivera, Colegio Orvalle, Las Rozas, Madrid; Maite Crespo, Colegio Jesús Nazareno, Madrid; Rocío González, Colegio Jesús Nazareno, Madrid; Silvia Valderrama, CEIP Benito Pérez Galdós, Arganda del Rey, Madrid; Lilian Villafuerte, CEIP Rosa Chacel, Collado Villalba, Madrid; Cristina Baeza, CEIP Rosa Chacel, Collado Villalba, Madrid; Carlota Padovani, CEIP Vicálvaro, Madrid; Leyre, Alcalde CEIP Cortes de Cádiz, Madrid; María Andrés, Colegio Matter Inmaculata, Madrid.

Full acknowledgements for illustrations and photographs in the facsimile pages can be found in the Pupil's Book ISBN 978-1-380-01361-3 and the Activity Book ISBN 978-1-380-01381-1

Printed and bound in Great Britain by Ashford Colour Press Ltd

2022 2021 2020 2019 2018
10 9 8 7 6 5 4 3 2

Give Me Five! ENGLISH

TEACHER'S BOOK 6

Syllabus

Unit	Key Competences and Key Learning Outcomes	Contents
		Lexis
Starter Unit A new project	• Understand and act out a dialogue (Lesson 1) • Learn and practise how to use state verbs (Lesson 2) • Use the present passive to ask and say which languages are spoken in a country (Lesson 3) • Learn and practise how to use question tags in the present (Lesson 4) • Watch and understand a video (Video and 21st Century Skills) • Work with charts and graphic organisers (Lesson 2) • Complete a form (Lesson 3) • Analyse and apply rules for forming question tags in the present (Lesson 4) • Review vocabulary: things you see in a town or city (Lesson 1), state verbs (Lesson 2), countries and languages (Lesson 3) • Review and compare the present simple and present continuous (Lesson 2) • Set learning outcomes and reflect on learning (All lessons) • Think about the importance of protecting natural habitats (Lessons 1 and 4) • Understand that people can make a difference in their community (Lessons 3 and 4) • Work in pairs or small groups to practise and reinforce learning (All lessons) • Express personal opinions and preferences (Lessons 1 and 2) • Learn about global projects and how children around the world can communicate with each other (Lesson 3)	**Core vocabulary** • *block of flats, bridge, cycle path, department store, factory, hot-air balloon, skate park, stadium, statue, square, tunnel* **Other vocabulary** • *barn owl, bird's eye view, community, global project, in danger, make a difference, nest, nest box, online form, predator, species* • *Arabic, Chinese, Dutch, Gaelic, Japanese, Scots, Swedish* • *Belgium, China, Ecuador, Egypt, Mexico, Scotland, Sweden* **Recycled vocabulary** • *believe, climb, dislike, eat, go, know, prefer, swim, travel, want, work, understand; English, French, German, Spanish; USA, Japan; cat, countryside, dog, fox*
Unit 1 Travel trouble	• Name places, objects and verbs related to air travel (Lesson 1) • Use the past simple and past continuous with 'while' (Lesson 2) • Learn and practise verbs that are followed by an infinitive or a gerund (Lesson 4) • Learn words related to travel and tourism (Lesson 5) • Use verbs of the senses (Lesson 7) • Watch and understand a video (Video and 21st Century Skills) • Learn about the technology of solar energy and a solar-powered plane (Lesson 3) • Use the Pupil's App on Navio (All lessons) • Identify and practise saying the past simple verb ending -ed (Lesson 4) • Reflect on your own learning (Lesson 8) • Practise activity types found in the Cambridge Exams Practice: B1 Preliminary for Schools • Think about the importance of saving the planet's energy (Lesson 3) • Learn and practise how to make suggestions in a conversation (Lesson 8) • Work in pairs and small groups to practise and reinforce learning (All lessons) • Do a communication task (Lesson 5) • Think of ways to present balanced views (Video and 21st Century Skills) • Read and understand an article (Lesson 3) • Learn about Belgium (Lesson 3) • Read and write an eyewitness account (Lessons 6 and 7) • Sing a song (Lesson 8)	**Core vocabulary** • *arrivals, boarding pass, check-in desk, departures, flight attendant, hand luggage, land, passenger, queue, runway, take off, trolley* • *backpacker, guard, guest, lift, platform, reception, receptionist, ticket office, tourist information centre* **Extension vocabulary** • *announcement, board a plane, customs, fuel, gate, miss a flight; cash machine, lost property office, ticket barrier, waiting room* **Other vocabulary** • *explorer, first-class, fuel, international flight, lifeboat, nationality, porthole, steward, solar-powered plane* • *energy, exhibition, iceberg, solar panels* • *experience, fact, fictional, opinion, scene, senses; huge, nervous* • *maybe, perhaps* • *hold hands, imagine, promise, sink* **Recycled vocabulary** • *adventure, airport, bus journey, crash, hot-air balloon, lifejacket, orchestra, passport, ship, suitcase; battery, football team, poster, sign, smoke, stairs; agree, decide, feel, like, look, show, smell, smoke, sound, stop, suggest, taste, travel, try, walk around*

Competence in linguistic communication | Competence in mathematics, science and technology | Digital competence
Learning to learn | Social and civic competences | Sense of initiative and entrepreneurship | Cultural awareness and expression

Contents					Cross-curricular links
Structures	**Pronunciation**	**Sociocultural aspects**	**Culture around the world and Literacy**	**21st Century Skills**	
Core structures • *The children live in a big town, don't they?* • *Cats aren't predators, are they?* **Other structures** • *Which languages are spoken in (Scotland)? (English, Gaelic and Scots) are spoken in (Scotland).* **Recycled structures** • *You must be over seven years old to have a ride and children must be with an adult.* *There is / isn't a (stadium). There are (two squares). There aren't any (bridges). Is there a (skate park in our town)? Are there any (statues in our town)?* • *Which school do you go to?* *Are you ready then?* • Present simple affirmative, negative and question form • Present continuous affirmative, negative and question form		**Cooperative learning Skills** • Contributing ideas (Lessons 1–4) • Sharing ideas and opinions (Lessons 1–4) • Reflecting and setting goals (Lessons 1–4) • Checking learning (Lessons 1–4)		**Thinking skills** • Using a chart to categorise (Lesson 2); Memorising (Lesson 3); Completing a form (Lesson 3); Analysing and applying rules and patterns (Lesson 4)	
Core structures • *While I was (taking photos), he (agreed to sign a football). I (saw a hot-air balloon) while I was (walking to school).* • *I enjoyed (reading about Bertrand Piccard).* • *(Piccard) promised to (make his plane faster next time).* **Other structures** • *Can you remember what was happening at the station? The hot-air balloon looked like a floating ball. The ship stopped moving. I'm not sure. I suppose that they like to have new experiences.* **Recycled structures** • *What do you do to help save the planet's energy? Which poster idea would you choose? I'd choose the one about (different nationalities). You can't catch a bus here.*	• Past simple tense endings: /d/, /ɪd/, /t/	**Cooperative learning Skills** • Working together (Lessons 1-8) • Reflecting and setting goals (Lessons 1–8) • Collaborative speaking (Lesson 5) • Collaborative writing (Lesson 7) • Peer evaluation and feedback (Lesson 7) • Helping and encouraging (Lessons 1–8) • Expressing and respecting opinions (Lessons 1, 3, 6 and 8) **Values** • The importance of saving the planet's energy	**Culture around the world** • A solar-powered plane that landed in Belgium **Literacy** **Text type** • An eyewitness account (historical event; writing preparation) **Reading skills** • Predicting from pictures and context **Writing skills** • Using verbs of the senses	**21st Century Skills** • **Ways of thinking:** presenting balanced opinions and views **Thinking skills** • Categorising (lesson 1); Analysing and applying rules and patterns (Lessons 2 and 4); Discussing the importance of alternative energy (Lesson 3); Remembering and describing (Lesson 5); Seeing another person's point of view (Lesson 6); Planning, checking and correcting (Lesson 7); Evaluating (Lesson 8)	**Link to Science** • Solar energy **Arts and Crafts** • Proportion and head position in portraits

Syllabus

Unit	Key Competences and Key Learning Outcomes	Contents
		Lexis
Unit 2 Sports and hobbies	• Review and name sports and equipment (Lesson 1) • Practise using present perfect and past simple questions (Lesson 2) • Learn and practise how to use the present perfect (Lesson 4) • Review and name hobbies (Lesson 5) • Learn and practise how to use extreme adjectives (Lesson 7) • Watch and understand a video (Video and 21st Century Skills) • Find connections between words (Lessons 1 and 3) • Use the Pupil's App on Navio (All lessons) • Identify and practise using correct rhythm and stress in present perfect sentences (Lesson 4) • Reflect on your own learning (Lesson 8) • Practise activity types found in the Cambridge Exams Practice: B1 Preliminary for Schools • Understand the importance of controlling your temper (Lesson 3) • Learn how to initiate a conversation in a speaking task (Lesson 8) • Work in pairs or small groups to practise and reinforce learning (All lessons) • Do a communication task (Lesson 5) • Evaluate hobbies and abilities (Video and 21st Century Skills) • Read and understand information about a text (Lesson 3) • Learn about China (Lesson 3) • Read and write a magazine article (Lessons 6 and 7)	**Core vocabulary** • *archery, athletics, crash mat, fencing, gymnastics, hoop, martial arts, net, racket, rope, trampolining, water polo* • *belong to a sports club, collect cards, do circus skills, do needlework, do photography, go to drama class, make models, sing in a choir* **Extension vocabulary** • *bend, dive, score, serve, shoot, stretch, do gardening, do modern dance, do yoga, write blogs* **Other vocabulary** • *after-school club, karate, kitesurfing, kung fu, martial arts, shuttlecock, skipping, tug-of-war* • *bow, court, field, goal posts, leotard, mask, running track, sword, target* • *balance, concentrate, discipline, flexibility, powerful, self-confident, self-control, speed, strength* • *monk, temple* • *amazing, astonishing, brilliant, enormous, fantastic, fascinating, massive* • *Internet access, online games, social networking sites* **Recycled vocabulary** • *belt, champion, chess, school gym; get fit; hard-working*
Unit 3 Healthy habits	• Name different kinds of food (Lesson 1) • Learn and practise how to use 'too' and 'enough' with countable and uncountable nouns (Lesson 2) • Learn phrases related to keeping fit and healthy (Lesson 5) • Use connective words and phrases (Lesson 7) • Watch and understand a video (Video and 21st Century Skills) • Learn about making chocolate (Lesson 3) • Learn about healthy living and healthy eating (Lessons 5 and 6) • Use the Pupil's App on Navio (All lessons) • Identify and practise contracted forms: 'shouldn't', 'needn't', 'mustn't' (Lesson 4) • Reflect on your own learning (Lesson 8) • Practise activity types found in the Cambridge Exams Practice: B1 Preliminary for Schools • Learn about cooking and preparing food (Lesson 1) • Think about the importance of eating and celebrating together (Lesson 3) • Learn and practise how to ask questions in conversations (Lesson 8) • Work in pairs or small groups to practise and reinforce learning (All lessons) • Do a communication task (Lesson 5) • Collaborate to produce an exercise calendar (Video and 21st Century Skills) • Read and understand a story (Lesson 3) • Learn about Mexico (Lesson 3) • Read and write an argument text (Lessons 6 and 7) • Sing a song (Lesson 8)	**Core vocabulary** • *an avocado, beans, beef, a chilli pepper, cinnamon, corn, garlic, a lime, an onion, peanuts, prawns, turkey* • *do exercise, drink fizzy drinks, drink water, eat fruit and vegetables, eat junk food, go for walks, rest, spend time on the computer* **Extension vocabulary** • *blend, boil, chop, fry, mix, slice; eat sugary food, eat wholegrain bread, play sport regularly, watch a lot of TV* **Other vocabulary** • *cocoa, diet, fast food, pods, powder, saturated fat, spices, vanilla* • *dry, ground, roast, save time, water plants* • *addictive, bitter* • *all year round* • *keeping fit, eating healthily, rest, relaxation* **Recycled vocabulary** • *invite, wake up; doctor, hospital, volunteers; cheap, delicious, healthy; chocolate, salt, sugar; also, firstly, furthermore, however, on the one hand, on the other hand, secondly*

Competence in linguistic communication · Competence in mathematics, science and technology · Digital competence
Learning to learn · Social and civic competences · Sense of initiative and entrepreneurship · Cultural awareness and expression

Contents					Cross-curricular links
Structures	**Pronunciation**	**Sociocultural aspects**	**Culture around the world and Literacy**	**21st Century Skills**	
Core structures • *Have I / you / we / they ever (been sailing)? Yes, I / you / we / they have. No, I / you / we / they haven't.* • *Has he / she ever (done athletics)? Yes, he / she has. No, he / she hasn't.* • *When did I / you / he / she / we / they (go sailing)?* • *How long have I / you / we / they (played tennis)? I / You / We / They have (played tennis) for two years.* • *How long has he / she (studied French)? He / She has (studied French) since last year.* **Other structures** • *Why don't we talk about this picture first? What do you think about karate?* **Recycled structures** • *You need (a net and a ball). You must (pass the ball to your teammates and hit it over the net). You mustn't (hit it with your hand). Ross is mad about (flying). All five styles develop discipline and self-control. I prefer collecting stamps to cards. I'd rather collect stamps than cards. I think that Gisela is an amazing sportswoman. She came first in two races.*	• Rhythm and stress patterns in present perfect sentences	**Cooperative learning Skills** • Working together (Lessons 1–8) • Checking learning (Lessons 1–8) • Reflecting and setting goals (Lessons 1–8) • Collaborative writing (Lesson 7) • Peer evaluation (Lesson 7) • Initiating a conversation (Lesson 8) • Expressing and respecting opinions (Lessons 1, 3, 6 and 8) **Values** • The importance of controlling your temper	**Culture around the world** • Kung fu and the Shaolin monks in China **Literacy** **Text type** • A magazine article (non-chronological report; writing preparation) **Reading skills** • Scanning the text for key content **Writing skills** • Extreme adjectives for creating interest	**21st Century Skills** • **Living in the world:** achieving goals **Thinking skills** • Forming conceptual links and association (Lesson 1); Defining and describing (Lesson 1); Analysing and applying rules and patterns (Lesson 2, 4); Discussing and evaluating a martial art (Lesson 3); Comparing and contrasting (Lesson 5); Problem solving (Lesson 8); Evaluating (Lesson 8)	**Link to Science** • Protecting your body when you do sport **Arts and Crafts** • Representing movement
Core structures • *There are too many / aren't enough (tomatoes) this year.* • *There is too much / isn't enough (rain) at this time of year.* • *We need to make a cake. You needn't stop eating sugar completely.* • *You should go swimming this weekend. You shouldn't eat too many chocolate bars.* • *We must go shopping before the shops close. We mustn't be late.* **Other structures** • *Then they roasted and ground them. Some people argue that fast food is unhealthy. Some people say that we could use this time more effectively.* **Recycled structures** • *(Are) there any (tomatoes in guacamole)? How often do you (drink water)? I (drink water twice a day). Do you often eat fast food? The table is reserved for 1pm.*	• Contracted forms: 'shouldn't', 'needn't', 'mustn't'	**Cooperative learning Skills** • Working together (Lessons 1–8) • Reflecting and setting goals (Lessons 1–8) • Collaborative speaking (Lesson 5) • Collaborative writing (Lesson 7) • Peer evaluation and feedback (Lesson 7) • Helping and encouraging (Lessons 1–8) • Expressing and respecting opinions (Lessons 1, 3, 6 and 8) **Values** • The importance of eating and celebrating together	**Culture around the world** • The discovery of cocoa beans in Mexico **Literacy** **Text type** • An argument text (opinion piece; writing preparation) **Reading skills** • Scanning text for key information **Writing skills** • Using connective words and phrases	**21st Century Skills** • **Ways of working:** recording information and setting routines **Thinking skills** • Categorising (Lesson 1); Analysing and applying rules and patterns (Lesson 2 and 4); Discussing chocolate's history and its effects on health (Lesson 3); Thinking about healthy / unhealthy habits (Lesson 5); Seeing two sides of an argument (Lesson 6); Planning, checking and correcting (Lesson 7); Evaluating methods of keeping fit (Lesson 8)	**Link to Science** • Growing food and healthy eating **Arts and Crafts** • Scale and space

Syllabus

Unit	Key Competences and Key Learning Outcomes	Contents
		Lexis
Project 1: An energy proposal	• Learn and practise talking about renewable energy (Lesson 1) • Present your proposal to the class (Lesson 2) • Learn about different kinds of renewable energy (Lesson 1) • Think about your local area and its future (Lesson 2) • Research one type of renewable energy (Lesson 1) • Listen for specific information and complete notes (Lesson 1) • Reflect on what you have learnt and how you have worked together (Lesson 2) • Work in groups to design and write a digital presentation (Lesson 2) • Share information with your group (Lesson 1)	**Key vocabulary** • *advantages, coal, coast, disadvantages, electricity, electricity lines, gas, hydroelectric plants, impact, mountains, presentation, renewable energy, rivers, solar cells, wind, wind turbine* • *cheap, expensive, hydroelectric, solar, sunny, windy* • *face the north, produce, propose, ruin*
Unit 4 Creative kids	• Review and name different creative activities (Lesson 1) • Learn and practise how to use the past passive (Lesson 2) • Learn and practise how to ask and answer questions using the past passive (Lesson 4) • Review and name creative jobs (Lesson 5) • Practise using full stops, question marks and exclamation marks (Lesson 7) • Watch and understand a video (Video and 21st Century Skills) • Develop visual–spatial skills through describing different photos (Lesson 8) • Use the Pupil's App on Navio (All lessons) • Identify words that have the silent letter 'w' (Lesson 4) • Practise using the relative pronouns *who*, *that*, *which* and *where* when defining (Lesson 5) • Reflect on your own learning (Lesson 8) • Practise activity types found in the Cambridge Exams Practice: B1 Preliminary for Schools • Understand the importance of respecting other people's tastes (Lesson 3) • Show interest in other people by asking and answering questions about personal photos (Lesson 8) • Work in pairs or small groups to practise and reinforce learning (All lessons) • Do a communication task (Lesson 5) • Analyse forms of digital means for creative purposes (Video and 21st century Skills) • Read and understand a text (Lesson 3) • Learn about Japan (Lesson 3) • Read, write and draw a comic strip (Lessons 6 and 7) • Sing a song (Lesson 8)	**Core vocabulary** • *beads, clay, costume, create an animation, do ceramics, do origami, do traditional dancing, make a film, make jewellery, perform a play, puppet, stage* • *actor, composer, fashion designer, film director, graffiti artist, novelist, photographer, sound engineer* **Extension vocabulary** • *landscape, oil painting, portrait, sketch, still life, watercolour; hair stylist, illustrator, make-up artist, video game designer* **Other vocabulary** • *animated, anime, caption, character, comic books / strip, exclamation, manga, mood, sound effect, speech / thought bubble, story frame* • *odd sock* • *at the top / bottom, in the foreground / background / corner / middle, on the left / right* **Recycled vocabulary** • *funny; invite; boat trip, computer game; shadow puppets, sticks; kitten, monkey*

Competence in linguistic communication | Competence in mathematics, science and technology | Digital competence
Learning to learn | Social and civic competences | Sense of initiative and entrepreneurship | Cultural awareness and expression

Contents					Cross-curricular links
Structures	**Pronunciation**	**Sociocultural aspects**	**Culture around the world and Literacy**	**21st Century Skills**	
Key structures • *I'm going to find out some advantages and disadvantages of solar power.* • *Let's talk about solar power first.* • *What will the impact be on the environment?* • *What will the power be used for?* • *Where are you going to put it?* • *Why have you chosen it?*		**Cooperative learning Skills** • Sharing knowledge and information (Lessons 1 and 2) • Working together (Lesson 2)		**21st Century Skills** • Preparing a digital presentation about renewable energy in groups	**Link to Science** • Renewable energy **Arts and Crafts** • Baroque art
Core structures • *The puppet was / wasn't made last week.* • *The puppets were / weren't painted by the children.* • *When was (the picture painted)?* • *Who were (the songs sung) by?* **Other structures** • *I'm not very sure. I haven't got a clue. I've got no idea. I definitely know this one. I'm not certain. I'm sure I know the answer. Manga drawings are like comics that tell stories. Why have I only got odd socks?* **Recycled structures** • *If you pull hard enough, the tree will bend. Have you ever (made a film)? Yes, I have. No, I haven't. When did you do that? I've never (composed a song). How long have you (collected manga comic books)?*	• The silent letter 'w'	**Cooperative learning Skills** • Working together (Lessons 1–8) • Reflecting and setting goals (Lessons 1–8) • Collaborative writing (Lesson 7) • Peer evaluation (Lesson 7) • Showing interest (Lesson 8) • Praising and encouraging (Lesson 5) • Expressing and respecting opinions (Lessons 3 and 6) **Values** • The importance of respecting other people's tastes	**Culture around the world** • Japanese manga and anime **Literacy** **Text type** • A comic strip (a text to entertain; writing preparation) **Reading skills** • Using visual clues to support understanding **Writing skills** • Finishing a sentence	**21st Century Skills** • **Digital skills:** using digital media creatively **Thinking skills** • Forming conceptual links and associations (Lesson 1); Defining and describing (Lesson 1); Analysing and applying rules and patterns (Lessons 2 and 4); Discussing different forms of comic books (Lesson 3); Categorising (Lesson 4); divergent thinking (Lesson 6); Spatial thinking (Lesson 8); Evaluating creativity (Lesson 8)	**Link to Science** • Famous works of art, buildings and literature in the Spanish Golden Age **Arts and Crafts** • Expressive lines and colours

Syllabus

Unit	Key Competences and Key Learning Outcomes	Contents: Lexis
Unit 5 **Write it down!**	• Name different kinds of messages and communication (Lesson 1) • Learn words related to news articles (Lesson 5) • Use 'so' to connect sentences (Lesson 7) • Watch and understand a video (Video and 21st Century Skills) • Learn about deciphering hieroglyphic symbols (Lesson 3) • Learn about computer coding (Lesson 6) • Use the Pupil's App on Navio (All lessons) • Identify examples of reported speech in a dialogue (Lesson 2) • Practise saying sentences with 'would' and 'could' (Lesson 4) • Learn about adjectives with different endings (Lesson 5) • Identify features of a news article (Lesson 8) • Reflect on your own learning (Lesson 8) • Practise activity types found in the Cambridge Exams Practice: B1 Preliminary for Schools • Think about the importance of learning about civilisations from the past (Lesson 3) • Prepare a conversation about meeting a famous person (Lesson 8) • Work in pairs or small groups to practise and reinforce learning (All lessons) • Do a communication task (Lesson 5) • Do a collaborative assessment (Video and 21st Century Skills) • Read and understand a text (Lesson 3) • Learn about ancient Egypt and the Rosetta Stone (Lesson 3) • Read and write a newspaper article (Lessons 6 and 7)	**Core vocabulary** • *advert, blog post, brochure, cartoon, chat message, email, greetings card, leaflet, note, sign, sign language, text message* • *article, caption, fashion section, front page, headline, interview, reporter, review, sports news, world news* **Extension vocabulary** • *chat, design, email (v) post, text (v), type; breaking news, celebrity news, comments, local news* **Other vocabulary** • *characters, code, computer coding, hieroglyphics, letters, symbols* • *current affairs, film set, reporter, story-writing competition, website* • *keep up, look forward to, take turns, work it out* • *active, nervous, polite, professional, surprised, thrilled* • *ancient Egyptians / Greeks / Romans* **Recycled vocabulary** • *do homework, juggle, keep a blog, meet people, skate; engines, dance club, volunteers; excited, friendly, proud*
Unit 6 **Our future**	• Review and name different jobs (Lesson 1) • Learn and practise how to use modal verbs to make predictions about the future (Lesson 2) • Learn and practise how to use embedded questions (Lesson 4) • Review and name different life events (Lesson 5) • Review and practise how to use paragraphs (Lesson 7) • Watch and understand a video (Video and 21st Century Skills) • Compare and contrast life in the past and today (Lesson 6) • Use the Pupil's App on Navio (All lessons) • Identify and practise using rising and falling intonation patterns to express possibility and certainty (Lesson 4) • Practise sequencing words and events (Lesson 5) • Identify features of an informal letter (Lesson 7) • Reflect on your own learning (Lesson 8) • Practise activity types found in the Cambridge Exams Practice: B1 Preliminary for Schools • Understand the importance of being positive when there is a challenge (Lesson 3) • Share hopes and expectations for the future (Lessons 8) • Work in pairs or small groups to practise and reinforce learning (All lessons) • Do a communication task (Lesson 5) • Reflect on the use of robots in the future (Video and 21st Century Skills) • Read and understand a story (Lesson 3) • Learn about Scotland (Lesson 3) • Read and write a time capsule letter (Lessons 6 and 7) • Sing a song (Lesson 8)	**Core vocabulary** • *archaeologist, businessperson, computer technician, detective, electrician, graphic designer, physiotherapist, plumber, politician, security guard, tour guide, veterinary nurse* • *get married, get a job, go backpacking, go to university, have children, learn to drive, leave home, start a business* **Extension vocabulary** • *architect, author, editor, engineer, gardener, surgeon; be born, get married, move house, retire* **Other vocabulary** • *in (one year's) time, in (three months') time, next week, the day after tomorrow, this evening* • *ambition, challenge, cure, deaf, disease, fingertips, vibrations* • *arcade game, BMX bike, calculator, cassette, football training, percussion, time capsule, zero-gravity games* • *frustrated, positive* • *general description, opinion* **Recycled vocabulary** • *accommodation, brochure, entertainment; artist, astronaut, firefighter, musician, teacher; solar-powered*

Competence in linguistic communication · Competence in mathematics, science and technology · Digital competence
Learning to learn · Social and civic competences · Sense of initiative and entrepreneurship · Cultural awareness and expression

Contents					Cross-curricular links
Structures	**Pronunciation**	**Sociocultural aspects**	**Culture around the world and Literacy**	**21st Century Skills**	
Core structures • *He said (he was happy with the results).* • *He told me / He said (he liked oranges and apples).* • *She told me / She said (they weren't very good at tennis).* • *He said / He told me (it would rain tomorrow).* • *She said / She told me (they could read Arabic).* **Other structures** • *Darkness has always interested me so I wanted to write about it. It looks like a large piece of boring grey rock. It was so popular that they started a second group.* **Recycled structures** • *Which language does hamster come from? It comes from German. If you want to be a journalist, this is for you. How / When and where did it happen? What was she like? What's the name of your new film?*	• Sentences with 'would' and 'could'	**Cooperative learning Skills** • Working together (Lessons 1–8) • Reflecting and setting goals (Lessons 1–8) • Collaborative speaking (Lesson 5) • Collaborative writing (Lesson 7) • Peer evaluation and feedback (Lesson 7) • Helping and encouraging (Lessons 1–8) • Expressing and respecting opinions (Lessons 1, 3, 6 and 8) **Values** • The importance of learning about past civilisations	**Culture around the world** • Discovering the Rosetta Stone and the meaning of Egyptian hieroglyphics **Literacy** **Text type** • A newspaper article (text to inform; writing preparation) **Reading skills** • Skimming text to ascertain meaning **Writing skills** • Using 'so' to connect sentences	**21st Century Skills** • **Digital skills:** using digital media to research and present information **Thinking skills** • Assessing different ways of communicating (Lesson 1); Defining and describing (Lesson 1); Analysing and applying rules and patterns (Lesson 2 and 4); Giving an opinion on a story (Lesson 3); Organising the ideas in a newspaper article (Lesson 7); Planning, checking and correcting (Lesson 7); Evaluating (Lesson 8)	**Link to Science** • Discovering and decoding languages from the past **Arts and Crafts** • Contour lines
Core structures • *I will definitely be (an archaeologist). I probably won't be (a politician).* • *I may / might / could be (a chemist).* • *Do you think I / you / he / she / we / they will (be famous)?* **Other structures** • *When she was eight, Evelyn began studying the piano. I don't know. I don't think so. I'm not sure. I doubt it. You never know. I don't know the word for it, but (it's used for protecting your eyes). I imagine that life will be very different in the future.* **Recycled structures** • *I've played the guitar for four years. It was buried in (1980). A vet has to have a degree. A vet doesn't have to work at night. Do you (wear a uniform)? I hope that there aren't any wars.*	• Rising and falling intonation patterns with modal verbs of possibility and certainty	**Cooperative learning Skills** • Working together (Lessons 1–8) • Reflecting and setting goals (Lessons 1–8) • Expressing and respecting opinions (Lesson 3) • Collaborative writing (Lesson 7) • Peer evaluation (Lesson 7) • Showing interest in others (Lessons 2, 4, 5 and 8) • Praising and encouraging (Lesson 8) **Values** • The importance of being positive when there is a challenge	**Culture around the world** • The story of Evelyn Glennie, the Scottish musician **Literacy** **Text type** • An informal letter (information text; writing preparation) **Reading skills** • Comparing and contrasting information **Writing skills** • Using paragraphs	**21st Century Skills** • **Ways of thinking:** thinking in different ways **Thinking skills** • Forming conceptual links and associations (Lesson 1); Logical thinking (Lesson 1); Defining and describing (Lesson 1); Analysing and applying rules and patterns (Lessons 2 and 4); Sequencing (Lessons 5 and Review); Comparing and contrasting (Lesson 6); Spatial thinking (Lesson 8); Evaluating (Lesson 8)	**Link to Science** • Work: the three economic sectors; Sound energy: waves and vibrations **Arts and Crafts** • Perspective

Syllabus

Unit	Key Competences and Key Learning Outcomes	Contents Lexis
Project 2: Living on Mars	• Learn and practise how to talk about living on Mars (Lesson 1) • Present your design to the class (Lesson 2) • Learn about living on Mars (Lesson 1) • Think about designing a house to live in on Mars (Lesson 2) • Research one aspect of living on Mars (Lesson 1) • Listen for specific information and complete notes (Lesson 1) • Reflect on what you have learnt and how you have worked together (Lesson 2) • Work in groups to create a design (Lesson 2) • Share information with your group (Lesson 1)	**Key vocabulary** • *atmosphere, conditions, cooker, curved, dangerous, electricity, energy, generator, lights, oxygen, planets, plants, plastic, the Sun, spacesuit, temperature, ultraviolet rays, water* • *be made of, breathe, grow food, (to) heat, keep warm, melt the ice, protect*
Unit 7 Buying and selling	• Name words related to money and shopping (Lesson 1) • Learn and practise how to use comparative forms (Lesson 2) • Learn and practise how to use the first conditional (Lesson 4) • Learn words related to damaged objects (Lesson 5) • Use alliteration and rhyme to write slogans in advertising (Lesson 7) • Watch and understand a video (Video and 21st Century Skills) • Learn about comparing prices (Lessons 2 and 4) • Use the Pupil's App on Navio (All lessons) • Practise connected speech: linking sounds (Lesson 4) • Learn about adjectives with different endings: *-y*, *-ous*, *-ful* (Lesson 5) • Identify the text features of an advert (Lesson 7) • Reflect on your own learning (Lesson 8) • Practise activity types found in the Cambridge Exams Practice: B1 Preliminary for Schools • Learn about the importance of taking initiative (Lesson 3) • Practise how to give interesting answers in conversation (Lesson 8) • Work in pairs or small groups to practise and reinforce learning (All lessons) • Do a communication task (Lesson 5) • Think about buying and selling (Video and 21st century Skills) • Read and understand a text (Lesson 3) • Learn about the USA (Lesson 3) • Read and write an advert (Lessons 6 and 7) • Sing a song (Lesson 8)	**Core vocabulary** • *bank notes, cashier, coins, credit card, customer, moneybox, price tag, purse, receipt, save money, spend money, till* • *bent, cracked, faulty, loose, ripped, scratched, stained* **Extension vocabulary** • *cents, euros, pence, pounds, yen, yuan; crumpled, dented, shrunken, stretched* **Other vocabulary** • *bargain, business, craftspeople, salesperson, slogan, trade, quote* • *advertise, compare, complain, encourage, give advice / instructions, raise interest, (to) trade* • *dime, nickel, quarter* • *disappointed, fair, superstitious* • *fibreglass, plastic, polyester* • *waveboard* • *alliteration, rhyme* **Recycled vocabulary** • *big, expensive, old, remote-controlled, tall; boat, cotton, dollar, good / bad luck, kite, online, pocket money; receive*

- Competence in linguistic communication
- Competence in mathematics, science and technology
- Digital competence
- Learning to learn
- Social and civic competences
- Sense of initiative and entrepreneurship
- Cultural awareness and expression

Contents					Cross-curricular links
Structures	**Pronunciation**	**Sociocultural aspects**	**Culture around the world and Literacy**	**21st Century Skills**	
Key structures • *I'm going to find out how we could (breathe on Mars).* • *We need oxygen to breathe.* • *What would the house look like?* • *What would the house be made of?*		**Cooperative learning Skills** • Sharing knowledge and information (Lessons 1 and 2) • Working together (Lesson 2)		**21st Century Skills** • Designing a home on Mars in groups	**Link to Science** • Future technology **Arts and Crafts** • Modern art
Core structures • *I'm too old to play with teddies now.* • *He isn't old enough to buy a mobile phone.* • *My sister is (not) as tall as her friends.* • *If we buy Fairtrade products, it'll help the workers in poor countries.* • *If I finish my homework early, I'll play games on the computer.* • *If it doesn't rain, we'll play tennis.* • *If you don't buy a ticket, you won't win a prize.* • *What will you do if you miss the bus this afternoon?* **Other structures** • *Can I see your receipt? Would you like your money back?* **Recycled structures** • *Buy one now before we run out!* • *How much pocket money does Bella receive?* • *What would you sell at the sale?* • *How much would you sell it for?* • *They help them organise their production.*	• Features of connected speech: linking words	**Cooperative learning Skills** • Working together (Lessons 1–8) • Reflecting and setting goals (Lessons 1–8) • Collaborative speaking (Lesson 5) • Collaborative writing (Lesson 7) • Peer evaluation and feedback (Lesson 7) • Helping and encouraging (Lessons 1–8) • Expressing and respecting opinions (Lessons 1, 3, 6 and 8) **Values** • The importance of taking initiative	**Culture around the world** • How fair trade started in the USA **Literacy** **Text type** • An advert (text to persuade; writing preparation) **Reading skills** • Skimming text to ascertain meaning **Writing skills** • Using alliteration and rhyme in slogans	**21st Century Skills** • **Living in the world:** initiative and entrepreneurial skills **Thinking skills** • Defining and describing (Lesson 1); Analysing and applying rules and patterns (Lesson 2 and 4); Giving an opinion on a text (Lesson 3); Organising the ideas in an advert (Lesson 7); Planning, checking and correcting (Lesson 7); Evaluating (Lesson 8)	**Link to Science** • The economics of trade **Arts and Crafts** • Depth in landscapes

Syllabus

Unit	Key Competences and Key Learning Outcomes	Contents
		Lexis
Unit 8 Let's dream	• Name different activities on a tropical island (Lesson 1) • Learn and practise how to use the second conditional to talk about unlikely situations (Lesson 2) • Review and name unreal or unlikely experiences (Lesson 5) • Practise using personal pronouns and possessive adjectives (Lesson 7) • Watch and understand a video (Video and 21st Century Skills) • Sequence events (Lesson 6) • Use the Pupil's App on Navio (All lessons) • Practise saying the contracted form of 'would' (Lesson 4) • Reflect on your own learning (Lesson 8) • Identify the text features of a diary extract (Lesson 7) • Practise activity types found in the Cambridge Exams Practice: B1 Preliminary for Schools • Understand the importance of encouragement in groups (Lesson 3) • Practise agreeing and disagreeing with an opinion (Lesson 8) • Work in pairs or small groups to practise and reinforce learning (All lessons) • Do a communication task (Lesson 5) • Work as a team (Video and 21st century Skills) • Read and understand a story (Lesson 3) • Learn about Ecuador (Lesson 3) • Read and write a diary extract (Lessons 6 and 7)	**Core vocabulary** • *coral, boogie boarding, giant tortoise, hammock, have a nap, palm tree, sea kayaking, sea lion, scuba diving, shore, tropical fish, wildlife spotting* • *be invisible, be the president, get lost, have three wishes, meet a famous person, travel in space, travel back in time, win the lottery* **Extension vocabulary** • *dock, lagoon, reef, rock pool, sand dune, tide; lose your phone, find a wallet, see a robbery* **Other vocabulary** • *go sailing, climb a volcano, rescue* • *matches, stream, sun cream, tent, whale, lifeboat, shelter, sink, sunburnt, yacht* • *autobiographical, fictional, heading, reflection* • *anyone, anywhere, anything* **Recycled vocabulary** • *clean a beach, find, lose, meet, visit, win; adventure holiday, compass, desert island, environment, thirsty, hungry, weak; I, me, my, mine, our, ours, we, us*
Unit 9 School: past and future	• Name school equipment from the past and present (Lesson 1) • Learn and practise how to use 'used to' to talk about past habits (Lesson 2) • Compare and practise how to use 'will' and 'going to' to talk about the future (Lesson 4) • Review and name secondary school subjects and equipment (Lesson 5) • Practise using 'so' and 'because' (Lesson 7) • Watch and understand a video (Video and 21st Century Skills) • Use a Venn diagram to classify vocabulary (Lesson 1) • Read about science and technology (Lessons 1 and 3) • Use the Pupil's App on Navio (All lessons) • Practise the weak form of 'going to' (Lesson 4) • Reflect on your own learning (Lesson 8) • Practise activity types found in the Cambridge Exams Practice: B1 Preliminary for Schools • Understand the universal right for all children to an education (Lesson 3) • Work in pairs or small groups to practise and reinforce learning (All lessons) • Do a communication task (Lesson 5) • Analyse types of strong feelings (Video and 21st Century Skills) • Read and understand a story (Lesson 3) • Learn about Sweden (Lesson 3) • Read and write an advice column (Lessons 6 and 7) • Sing a song (Lesson 8)	**Core vocabulary** • *blackboard, canvas, chalk, easel, goggles, headphones, interactive whiteboard, laboratory, laptop, oil paints, overall, rows of desks* • *Chemistry, geometry set, Literature, locker, musical instrument, Physics, sports kit, timetable* **Extension vocabulary** • *absent, certificate, grades, present, register, report card, folder, highlighter pen, pendrive, stapler* **Other vocabulary** • *(to) award, be strict, carry rucksacks, impress, punish pupils, sit in rows, stay organised, work in silence* • *agony aunt column, ceremony, dynamite, homework diary, Nobel Prize, obituary, performing arts* • *anxious, bossy, sympathetic* **Recycled vocabulary** • *go shopping / to my grandparent's house / to secondary school; dream, tips; active, adventurous, boring, brave, friendly, helpful, important, shy*

Competence in linguistic communication · Competence in mathematics, science and technology · Digital competence · Learning to learn · Social and civic competences · Sense of initiative and entrepreneurship · Cultural awareness and expression

Contents					Cross-curricular links
Structures	**Pronunciation**	**Sociocultural aspects**	**Culture around the world and Literacy**	**21st Century Skills**	
Core structures • *If I lived in the Galapagos Islands, I would go wildlife spotting.* • *If I lived in the Galapagos Islands, I wouldn't climb a volcano.* • *I would go wildlife spotting if I lived in the Galapagos Islands.* • *Would you take water if you abandoned a boat? Yes, I would. No, I wouldn't.* • *What would you do if you were lost at sea? If I was lost at sea, I would make a sail for my boat.* **Other structures** • *I doubt it. It's very unlikely. You never know.* • *I think the (tent) would be a good idea. That's a good point. I see what you mean.* **Recycled structures** • *I wonder if I'll find a better place to live tomorrow. Milo and I love our cave. Would you like to visit the giant tortoise reserve? If I go shopping, I'll buy a T-shirt. While they were sailing towards the Galapagos Islands, their luck changed.*	• Contracted forms: 'would'	**Cooperative learning Skills** • Working together (Lessons 1–8) • Reflecting and setting goals (Lessons 1–8) • Encouraging (Lesson 5) • Empathising (Lesson 6) • Collaborative writing (Lesson 7) • Peer evaluation (Lesson 7) • Expressing and respecting opinions (Lessons 3, 6, 8) • Initiating a conversation (Lesson 8) **Values** • The importance of encouragement in groups	**Culture around the world** • How a couple were lost at sea for 117 days near the Galapagos Islands **Literacy** **Text type** • A diary extract (chronological account; writing preparation) **Reading skills** • Predicting content **Writing skills** • Using personal pronouns and possessive adjectives	**21st Century Skills** • **Ways of working:** working as a team **Thinking skills** • Listing and grouping vocabulary items (Lesson 1); Defining and describing (Lesson 1); Analysing and applying rules and patterns (Lesson 2 and 4); Predicting (Lesson 7 and Review); Problem solving (Lesson 8); Evaluating (Lesson 8)	**Link to Science** • Landscapes: coastlines, islands and volcanoes **Arts and Crafts** • Analogous colours
Core structures • *I / You / He / She / We / They used to (study History).* • *I / You / He / She / We / They didn't use to (play computer games).* • *Did I / you / he / she / we / they use to (have the Internet)? Yes, I / you / he / she / we / they did. No, I / you / he / she / we / they didn't.* • *I'm going to have lunch at two o'clock.* • *I'll answer the telephone. I think he'll pass the exam.* **Other structures** • *I'm nervous about / I'm excited about / I'm looking forward to / I'm worried about (going to secondary school). He feels (excited) about going to secondary school. Starting a new school is a big change.* **Recycled structures** • *Alfred Nobel was born in 1833. It's important to read your timetable. Gina is interested in making things. She isn't keen on very modern music. What's your favourite subject at school?*	• Features of connected speech: weak form of 'going to'	**Cooperative learning Skills** • Working together (Lessons 1–8) • Reflecting and setting goals (Lessons 1–8) • Expressing and respecting opinions (Lessons 3, 6) • Collaborative writing (Lesson 7) • Peer evaluation (Lesson 7) • Showing interest in others (Lessons, 1, 5, 8) • Praising and encouraging (Lesson 8) **Values** • The universal right for all children to an education	**Culture around the world** • The creation of the Nobel Prizes in Sweden **Literacy** **Text type** • An advice column (text to advise; writing preparation) **Reading skills** • Scanning for specific information **Writing skills** • Using 'so' and 'because' to talk about results and reasons	**21st Century Skills** • **Living in the world:** managing strong feelings **Thinking skills** • Forming conceptual links and associations (Lessons 1 and 8); Defining and describing (Lesson 1); Comparing and contrasting (Lesson 2); Analysing and applying rules and patterns (Lessons 2 and 4); Expressing cause and effect (Lesson 7); Problem solving (Lesson 8); Evaluating (Lesson 8)	**Link to Science** • Technology and progress in the Contemporary Age **Arts and Crafts** • Volume

Syllabus

Unit	Key Learning Outcomes	Contents
		Lexis
Project 3: Life in the past	• Write questions to find out about how people lived in the past (Lesson 1) • Present your virtual museum to the class (Lesson 2) • Research aspects of life in the past (Lesson 1) • Listen for specific information and complete notes (Lesson 1) • Reflect on what you have learnt and how you have worked together (Lesson 2) • Share knowledge about how people lived in the past (Lesson 1) • Work in groups to plan a virtual museum (Lesson 2) • Share information with your group (Lesson 1) • Learn about everyday life in the past (Lesson 1) • Find out about life in the past (Lesson 2)	**Key vocabulary** • *classroom, community, elderly, food, past, relative, travel* • *cricket, football, leapfrog, skipping ropes*
Festivals: Thanksgiving Day	• Write about different festival food in your country • Listen to and perform a poem about Thanksgiving Day • Learn about Thanksgiving Day traditions in the USA • Learn about Thanksgiving day food traditions around the world	**Key vocabulary** • *celebrate, harvest, marching bands, marshmalllows, parade, pecan nuts, seeds, squash, stuffing*
Festivals: Endangered Species Day	• Complete a reading and listening task about endangered species • Learn about endangered species • Think about how people can help endangered species • Learn about Endangered Species Day	**Key vocabulary** • *aquarium, block rivers, botanical gardens, build houses, climate change, destroy, disappear, endangered species, extinct, habitat, hunt, orang-utan, polar bears, pollute water, protect, survive, vaquita, wildlife refuge, zoo*

Competence in linguistic communication	Competence in mathematics, science and technology	Digital competence	Learning to learn	Social and civic competences	Sense of initiative and entrepreneurship	Cultural awareness and expression

Contents					Cross-curricular links
Structures	Pronunciation	Sociocultural aspects	Culture around the world and Literacy	21st Century Skills	
Key structures • *I'm going to write questions about (schools) in the past.* • *That's a good question. What / How about this?* • *What did he say about the games children used to play?*		**Cooperative learning Skills** • Sharing knowledge and information (Lessons 1 and 2) • Working together (Lesson 2)		**21st Century Skills** • Presenting information gathered on life in the past	**Link to Science** • Life in the 20th century **Arts and Crafts** • Art today
Key structures • *What special food do you eat during festivals?*		**Cooperative learning Skills** • Working together (Lesson 1)			
Key structures • *These are animals and plants that are in danger of disappearing completely from the world.*		**Cooperative learning Skills** • Working together (Lesson 1)			

Introduction to *Give Me Five!*

Give Me Five! is a six-level course for pupils who have an extended English timetable and are being taught at a faster pace. It is designed to develop pupils' communicative competences in a systematic and comprehensive manner.

With *Give Me Five!* 6, pupils …

- **develop multi-cultural understanding** by investigating nine different countries from around the world.
- **use new technologies and multimedia** as tools for learning.
- **develop their social and civic competences** through a hands-on cooperative project each term and the integration of collaborative tasks and strategies.
- **develop literacy skills** through a range of enjoyable and motivating real-world texts and a focus on the key reading and writing skills.
- **communicate confidently** through a wide variety of well supported speaking tasks.
- **participate fully** through a range of engaging activities such as stories, dialogues, games and problem solving tasks.
- **prepare for Cambridge Exams** through the systematic integration of exam practice material and a dedicated Exams Practice lesson in each unit.
- **develop their 21st century skills** through real-life videos and interesting tasks to practise and perfect the skills needed in the 21st century.
- **develop their thinking skills and multiple intelligences** through a variety of stimulating and challenging activities.
- **become independent and reflective learners** through the integration of learning-to-learn strategies and activities.
- **develop reading, writing, listening and speaking** in a balanced and integrative manner.
- **develop their oral fluency** through integrated practice of connected speech, stress, rhythm and intonation.
- **identify and talk about language patterns** and use them to personalise and be creative with new language.
- **link their learning to other areas in the curriculum** such as Science and Arts and Crafts.

Meet the characters in *Give Me Five! 6*

Callum, **Jess** and **Tom** are ten and eleven years old and they are friends and classmates. We first meet them at a traditional school fair where they release nine balloons as part of a balloon race. Each of the following units begins with news about where one of the balloons has landed and we are introduced to a child from that country. Callum, Jess and Tom are delighted to make nine new friends from around the world and to find out about life in the different countries.

Cooperative learning

Give Me Five! 6 incorporates a variety of **cooperative learning tasks and strategies** which require the pupils to work together in a structured way. Working in pairs and small groups has many benefits. The pupils are prepared to spend more time on the tasks, are motivated to produce more language and are more likely to use creative and logical thinking. Cooperative learning also helps develop a positive classroom environment as the pupils have a greater sense of belonging and learn to understand and value all the members of the group. Finally, cooperative tasks require the pupils to be active and more independent learners, building their self-confidence and their ability to cope with uncertainty and unpredictability.

Give Me Five! 6 provides many opportunities to use common and well-researched cooperative learning activities and strategies. A bank of these can be found below. There is also a simple, clearly staged **cooperative project** at the end of each term which provides the pupils with the opportunity to learn and practise **interpersonal skills** such as agreeing, disagreeing and negotiating roles and responsibilities.

In order to support the pupils when they work in pairs and groups, the teacher is provided with a set of **Talk role cards** (available in the Teacher's Resource Bank on Navio). These cards can be used to introduce and practise specific group skills and functions, such as recording information, organising materials or checking noise levels. They also encourage the pupils to take more responsibility for their actions and behaviour in the classroom. The different roles should be introduced one at a time and modelled by the teacher. As children become familiar with the role cards, the teacher can allocate different roles to pupils in the same group.

Cooperative learning activities and strategies bank

1 Three-step interview

The pupils work with a partner to ask and answer questions, e.g. about their preferences or their routines. Once they have completed the task, they turn to a new partner and report what their first partner has told them, e.g. *Peter loves skating.* This strategy can be used for personal questions, for example in some *Talk Partner* activities.

2 Think – write – pair – compare

Ask the pupils a question, e.g. **What water sports do you know?** Each pupil should think and write down their ideas. The pupils then share and compare their ideas with a partner or in a small group. Asking pupils to write down their ideas helps them to organise their thoughts and ensures full participation. This strategy can be used for brainstorming new vocabulary items.

3 Numbered heads

When the class is working in small groups, give each pupil a number (1–3). At the end of the task ask a question and say one of the numbers. The pupil with that number in each group should answer the question. Repeat the process with other questions, choosing a different number to answer each time. This strategy can be used when the pupils are planning and creating projects in small groups or when they are doing the review quiz in pairs at the end of the unit.

4 Round robin

Organise the class into small groups. Then ask an open-ended question. Each pupil should take turns to share their answer with their group. To prevent interruptions, give pupils a *talk token,* e.g. a rubber, to place on the table when they speak. Once they have done this, they cannot speak again until all their group's tokens are on the table. This strategy can be used, for example, when talking about values in Lesson 3 or in Lesson 8.

5 Board sharing

When pupils have discussed a question in small groups, ask them to choose their best answer. One pupil from each group should then write the information on the board. The class can then compare and discuss the different answers. This strategy can be used for brainstorming ideas or for making predictions, for example before reading the story in lesson 3.

6 Reading partners

Organise the class into pairs to read a text. The two pupils should take it in turns to read a section of the text, e.g. a paragraph, to each other. At the end of each section they should check each other's understanding. This strategy can be used, for example, after a class reading of the literacy texts in lessons 6 and 7.

21st Century learning

Give Me Five! 6 and 21st Century learning

Today's learners are growing up in a complex, changing world where an enormous amount of information is available at the touch of a button and where social media allows them to communicate with people all around the world. Technology is transforming the way we live and the way we learn. A key objective of *Give Me Five! 6* is to support learners in developing the necessary skills for the digital age. Apart from using digital technology, skills such as communicating and collaborating with others, thinking creatively and critically, and working to become a caring global citizen are an essential part of this course.

Give Me Five! 6 takes an integrated approach to the use of digital technology and the teaching of **digital skills**. In each unit there is a comprehensive set of digital practice material for the learner, helping them to become autonomous and digitally confident. Pupils are also supported in developing specific ICT skills. There are tips on how to use the Internet to find, select and present information, and there is a selection of projects with digital outcomes. Guided web quests also support pupils in using the Internet to explore new places around the world.

There are multiple opportunities for **communication** and **collaboration** in *Give Me Five! 6*. Learners are encouraged to work together to discover and build knowledge through quizzes and questionnaires, whole class discussions and a wide range of *Talk Partner* activities. Pupils also work with *Writing Partners* to plan, write and evaluate pieces of written work, and are encouraged to work cooperatively to review learning and reflect on progress at the end of each unit. Finally, there are structured cooperative projects which by providing opportunities for authentic communication, they encourage the development of interpersonal skills and enable learners to celebrate achievement.

Each unit of *Give Me Five! 6* provides a range of tasks to build the pupil's **critical and creative thinking skills.** These include problem-solving, evaluating information, and using imaginative thinking. The Video and 21st Century Skills lessons also focus on a selection of discrete thinking skills. They provide practical tips and thinking strategies.

The interconnectivity of the 21st Century and the increasing diversity of our communities mean that pupils need to learn how to respect and value other cultures. *Give Me Five! 6* provides learners with historical, geographical and cultural information about nine different places in the world. This rich content provides opportunities for **intercultural learning,** where learners identify cultural differences and similarities and build a positive attitude toward their own and other cultures.

Finally, a dedicated *Values* section in each unit supports learners in developing their **social and civic competencies** and helps them to make a positive difference in the world.

Video and 21st Century Skills lessons

Video generates interest and supports learners' listening skills by providing a clear visual context and model to practise speaking. It is also a flexible tool, allowing teachers to pause the recording or turn off the sound, and can be used as a stimulus for thinking, language practice and communication.

Each unit in *Give Me Five! 6* concludes with a Video and 21st Century Skills lesson. These video lessons help to build key 21st Century Skills, develop visual literacy and provide a springboard for authentic communication.

The stars of the videos are Amy and Max, the two children presenters of *Channel 21.* The children begin each programme by introducing a new topic and then share a selection of related video clips and interviews they have made. These visually rich videos bring images of the world into the classroom and offer insights into British culture. Amy and Max interview various people to find out about a diverse range of topics and proceed to show a video related to these topics. The children then discuss and highlight a 21st Century Skill in the material. This serves to contextualise the 21st Century Skill and show the learner how it is relevant in their learning and in their lives.

The 21st Century Skills selected for this level are the following:

Ways of thinking: these skills focus on critical and creative thinking and include developing your ideas (Unit 1) and being creative and original (Unit 6).

Ways of working: these skills focus on collaboration and communication and include making detailed comparisons (Unit 3) and being a leader (Unit 7).

Digital skills: these skills focus on researching and evaluating information and include researching a topic online (Unit 2), using technology to help us (Unit 4) and using a digital poster to persuade (Unit 8).

Living in the world: these skills focus on values, responsibility and cultural awareness and focus on protecting animals in danger (Unit 5).

Multiple Intelligences

According to the theory of **multiple intelligences**, each human being possesses a set of intelligences. As a consequence, learners have different needs, strengths and abilities in the classroom. In *Give Me Five!* seven key intelligences are highlighted:

Logical-mathematical intelligence

Activities and tasks that require the pupils to use mathematical and logical **thinking skills** are integrated into the material. These include **higher-order thinking skills** such as **problem solving**, **hypothesising** and **inferring**.

Intrapersonal intelligence

The pupils are encouraged to think about their **inner feelings**, **values** and **beliefs** through the values section in each unit. The use of discussion questions also help the pupils to develop and articulate their ideas.

Musical intelligence

The pupils are exposed to **songs** and **poems** in *Give Me Five! 6*. These help them to appreciate and produce **natural-sounding sounds**, **rhythm**, **stress** and **intonation**.

Interpersonal intelligence

A **values section** in each unit provides an opportunity for the pupils to reflect on their relationship with people around them and draws their attention to key **social and civic values and codes of conduct**.

Bodily-kinaesthetic intelligence

Physical expression is an important part of communication. The pupils are given the opportunity to develop fine motor skills by doing different tasks.

Visual-spatial intelligence

The dynamic design of *Give Me Five! 6* supports meaning and helps the pupils to **visualise contexts for language**. **Graphic organisers** help pupils form their own conceptual links and order new information.

Linguistic intelligence

The pupils are supported on their journey to becoming confident **and accurate speakers**, listeners, readers and writers of the English language. The pupils are given opportunities to use this language in a range of contexts.

Tips for teaching pupils with Special Educational Needs

Setting up the class and Working together

- Change the groupings regularly to make sure the SEN pupils have an opportunity to work with all their classmates.
- Make instructions clear and on a step-by-step basis. Check understanding by giving an example.
- Use positive classroom language. Say what you want pupils to do, not what you don't want them to do. For example say ***Look at the board*** not ***Don't keep turning round***.
- Develop a peer mentoring system to encourage pupils help each other and share skills.

Hearing Impaired (HI) pupils

- Write instructions on the board or highlight them on the IWB. Make sure you have your pupil's attention before you read out the instructions or speak.
- Seat your hearing impaired (HI) pupil facing and close to you to make lip reading and following instruction gestures easier.
- Assign or ask for a volunteer helper or note-taker to support the HI pupil.
- Give copies of the audioscripts for the pupil to follow.

Visually Impaired (VI) learners

- Say every word you write on the board and use realia to teach vocabulary. Realia allows the visually impaired pupils to use all their senses.
- *Give Me Five!* offers plenty of songs, stories and dialogues with lesson tips. Use the audio script for reading texts, stories, and example dialogues.
- Encourage other pupils to describe experiences and create an active and engaging learning environment.

Dyslexic learners

- For brainstorming activities, do the first few examples with the class. For writing activities at sentence level, provide the pupils with a model which can be done as a whole class first.
- Encourage the use of mind maps to illustrate, collate and organise vocabulary and ideas. Note-taking is a useful skill to help dyslexic pupils recognise keywords in listening and reading activities.
- Provide photocopies to allow pupils with dyslexia to mark the text or cut it and move it around. This allows for information to be processed in manageable chunks.

Key Competences and Key Learning Outcomes

The **Key Competences and Key Learning Outcomes** outline the **knowledge**, **skills** and **behaviour** that the pupils need to develop in order to achieve their full personal potential, participate in an effective and constructive way in society and become responsible and autonomous life-long learners.

Competence in linguistic communication: the ability to use language as an instrument to express and interpret concepts, facts, feelings and ideas in an appropriate and creative way.

Cultural awareness and expression: the ability to understand and appreciate different art and cultural forms.

Competence in mathematics, science and technology: the ability to develop and apply mathematical thinking to solve everyday problems and to use scientific knowledge to explain the natural world and understand the consequences of human action.

Sense of initiative and entrepreneurship: the ability to apply qualities and skills such as creativity, critical thinking and perseverance, and to plan and manage projects.

Digital competence: the ability to use digital technology confidently, critically and responsibly.

Social and civic competences: the ability to understand and appreciate diversity in society and to develop personal and interpersonal competences.

Learning to learn: the ability to organise one's own learning and work efficiently and autonomously as an individual or in a group.

How *Give Me Five! 6* develops the Key Competences and Key Learning Outcomes

Competence in linguistic communication

Give Me Five! 6 develops the pupils' linguistic skills in a systematic and integrative manner. The pupils learn to identify the meaning of words and phrases through working with **definitions**, **dialogues and stories**. The use of short **listening texts** helps them develop the ability to understand a range of communicative messages in everyday contexts.

The pupils have the opportunity to work intensively on key pronunciation features at sentence level, helping them **develop a clear and natural pronunciation**. The structured use of games, personalisation activities and problem-solving activities provide the pupils with frequent opportunities to communicate in the classroom and express their feelings and opinions in English.

A **cooperative project** each term also helps the pupils develop social competences and introduces language and strategies for working successfully in small groups.

Each unit of *Give Me Five! 6* has a **double-page literacy spread** which introduces the pupils to a variety of engaging real-world texts. **Reading strategies** are systematically introduced to support readers in understanding, responding to and reflecting on these texts, whilst an analysis of features such as the writer's purpose, audience and the informational content of a text help prepare pupils for writing. Discrete **writing skills** such as the use of time connectives, paragraphs or punctuation are also highlighted in the literacy lessons.

Competence in mathematics, science and technology

In *Give Me Five! 6* mathematical competence is developed in a number of ways. The pupils' understanding of **numbers, shapes, space and time** is reinforced and **language patterns** are identified and highlighted. The pupils also have the opportunity to work with **charts and diagrams**, and to do activities which require them to **solve problems**. Each unit of *Give Me Five! 6* is also **linked to an area of learning in the Science curriculum**, reinforcing key concepts and language across the curriculum.

Digital competence

Give Me Five! 6 uses **digital resources** as tools to support learning, familiarising the pupils with computer technology and showing them how technology can be used for learning purposes. The **Pupil's App on Navio** serves to consolidate class work and provide a **home-school link** by allowing the pupils to work independently outside the classroom. Within the classroom, the **Teacher's App on Navio** provide enhanced digital resources for presentation and practice, integrated audio and interactive activities.

Learning to learn

Give Me Five! 6 introduces a variety of **learning strategies** to help the pupils become more independent and reflective learners. Learning objectives are set at the beginning and are reviewed at the end of each lesson to check that the objectives have been met. The pupils are also encouraged to reflect on their learning and progress at the end of each unit through the use of a **self-evaluation task**. A Working with Words section in each unit introduces simple **strategies for recording, retrieving and extending vocabulary**. The use of writing criteria in the literacy lessons helps to develop pupils' **self-assessment skills**.

Finally, throughout *Give Me Five! 6* there is an emphasis on good learning habits and the importance of making an effort and being responsible for your work. Personal qualities such as self-confidence, initiative, curiosity, interest and creativity are also explicitly promoted, preparing pupils for life-long learning.

Social and civic competences

Developing the ability to understand how somebody else is feeling and knowing how to respond appropriately is an important objective of *Give Me Five! 6* and emphasis is placed on **positive classroom behaviour**. **Cooperative projects** provide the pupils with the language needed to engage effectively with others, whilst the integration of **collaborative activities and strategies** reinforces the importance of active participation, cooperation and respect and support for others.

A **values section** in each unit also encourages the pupils to reflect on their natural, social and cultural environment, integrating real-world topics such as saving the plant's energy, staying positive when facing a challenge and the importance of taking initiative.

Sense of initiative and entrepreneurship

Give Me Five! 6 develops a sense of initiative and entrepreneurship through the inclusion of **cooperative group tasks and projects**. These require the pupils to work in groups to plan and complete a task, such as designing a tourist attraction or organising a sightseeing trip. Working together to complete a task helps the pupils to take responsibility for their work and gain confidence in their abilities. Initiative is also encouraged through personalisation activities, problem-solving tasks and creative activities.

Cultural awareness and expression

In *Give Me Five! 6* the pupils are introduced to the real-world culture of nine different **countries around the world**. In addition to reading emails and text messages from children in these countries, there is an illustrated culture story in each unit which has been selected to be of **intrinsic interest** to the age group. Stories include the tragedy of Pompeii, the invention of Velcro and the history of a mythical beast.

Give Me Five! 6 also provides the opportunity to experience and appreciate a **range of art forms** such as songs, poems, literature, drawing, mime and performance and encourages the pupils to express their ideas, experiences and emotions through these mediums.

Give Me Five! 6 pupil components

Pupil's Book

This is a 128-page, full-colour book that contains a Starter Unit, nine thematic units, three cooperative projects and material for two festivals (Thanksgiving Day and Endangered Species Day). Each unit is divided into eight lessons and provides vocabulary input and practice, short dialogues to contextualise and practise language, grammar tables with guided questions to support inductive thinking. A Values task after the story encourages the pupils to discuss and reflect on personal, social or civic values. At the end of each unit there is a Video and 21st Century Skills lesson which supports the development of different skills. In addition, each unit contains opportunities for whole-class discussion, a selection of communicative activities, a pronunciation task to develop the pupils' fluency and an engaging two-page literacy spread. Material such as practice material for Cambridge English Young Learners exams, a grammar and vocabulary review section for each unit and a songs bank is provided at the back of the book.

Pupil's App on Navio

Powered By NAVIO

The Pupil's App on Navio is designed to accompany the course and provide extra practice in class or at home. Pupils can create avatars and then explore Navio's immersive worlds. Pupils complete game-based activities designed to practise and review the language and content learnt in class. As they do so, they earn rewards, points and badges. The App tracks pupils' progress so the teacher can see how they are doing and provide extra support where it is needed. The App also includes all the songs, stories and animations from the course so that pupils can review them at home and share them with their family. The access code for the Pupil's App can be found inside the front cover of the Pupil's Book.

Activity Book

This 136-page, write-in book works in tandem with the Pupil's Book to reinforce and extend language learning, support and develop reading and writing and provide further practice of the listening and speaking skills. Each unit comprises a variety of activities which are devised to engage and challenge the pupils, activate different intelligences, encourage creativity and allow the pupils to use language in a personal and meaningful way. At the end of each unit there is a full-page unit review and a Video and 21st Century Skills lesson. At the back of the Activity Book there is an additional full grammar and vocabulary practice section and material to support Study Skills lessons and extra Cambridge Exams Practice for each unit.

IDEAL WITH

BY ME

ByME Social Science Primary 6

ByME Natural Science Primary 6

ByME Arts and Crafts Primary 6

Grammar Goals 6

Give Me Five! 6 Teacher's components

Teacher's Book

This user-friendly, spiral-bound book provides teachers with as much or as little support as they need. The At a Glance Lesson Plans, illustrated with images of the Pupil's Book and Activity Book, clearly highlight the learning aims, key language, materials required, learning routines, key activities and a range of optional extra activities, including cross-curricular links. These are accompanied by Detailed Lesson Plans which provide complete and concise teaching notes for each activity and answer keys. Full audioscripts can be found at the back of the book. In addition, there is a Reflective Teacher page after certain units for documenting learning, noting ideas and planning actions.

Teacher's App on Navio

Powered By NAVIO

The Teacher's App on Navio offers one-stop access to all the many resources which accompany the course. **Tap and Teach Lessons** with **integrated audio and video** ensure that everything you need to teach each lesson is in one place. You can use the **Classroom Management tool** to award points for good behaviour or success in class, and track your pupils' marks and progress using the **Progress Tracker**. You'll find additional photocopiable resources in the **Teacher's Resource Bank** (see opposite) and **Test Generator**.

Class CDs

Four class CDs provide all the recorded material for the Pupil's Book and Activity Book. These include recordings of the key vocabulary, dialogues, pronunciation activities, stories, listening tasks, songs and Cambridge Exams Practice.

Flashcards

A set of 118 full-colour flashcards with photographs of the key vocabulary from Lesson 1 of each unit. Suggestions for using them are given in the Detailed Lesson Plans and in the Flashcards games bank on page 27.

Teacher's Resource Bank: course resources

The **Teacher's Resource Bank** located within the teacher's app on Navio, contains a wealth of resources that complement *Give Me Five!* In addition to providing downloads for all class audio and video, the resource bank contains:

- **Letters to parents:** an introductory letter, followed by a letter to present each unit.
- **Talk role cards:** a set of role cards to help develop teamwork and to encourage pupils to take responsibility for their work.

- **Vocabulary and Grammar worksheets:** to reinforce and extend the vocabulary and grammar syllabus.
- **Evaluation Rubrics:** one grid per unit to evaluate pupils' level of achievement of the Unit Key Competences and Key Learning Outcomes, as well as their cooperative learning skills.

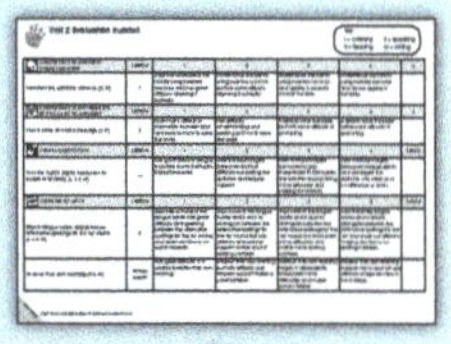

- **Tests:** a Diagnostic Test, Unit Tests, Term Tests and an End-of-Year Test with audio and Teacher's Notes including answer keys. Each test has a standard and a higher level version.

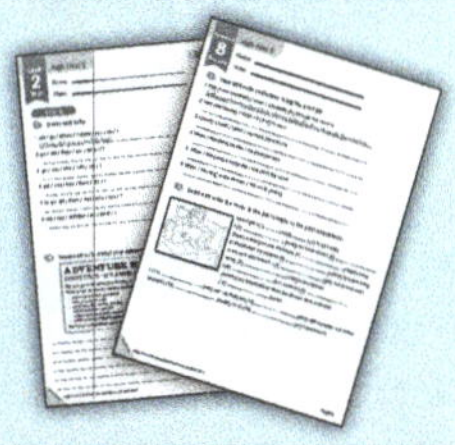

- **Word cards:** A set of 118 word cards. Suggestions for using them can be found in the Detailed Lesson Plans and in the Word cards games bank on page 27.

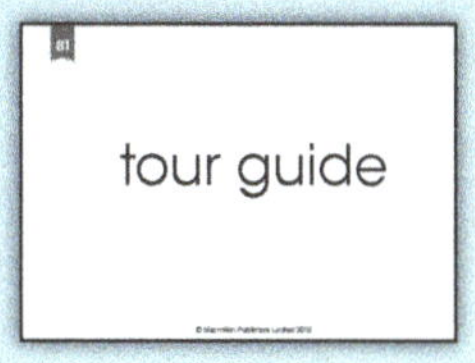

Teacher's Resource Bank: External Exams Resources

This section in the Teacher's Resource Bank supports teachers who are preparing their pupils for either one of the ***Trinity Graded Exams in Spoken English*** (Elementary Stage, Grade 6) or the ***Cambridge English Key for Schools (A2)***.

The external exams resources contain the following:

- **Videos** of children doing speaking practice.
- **Teacher's Notes** on how to exploit these videos in the classroom.
- Extra **Cambridge Exams practice material** and **practice tests** and **tips for teachers.**
- **Trinity Exam Practice Worksheets**
- Tips for preparing pupils for the exams and working with the Language Assistant.
- A set of **Trinity Exams Practice cards** for optional Trinity-type speaking practice at the start of each lesson.

Teacher's and Pupil's Apps on Navio

The Navio app which accompanies this course offers one-stop access to the huge range of resources that come with *Give Me Five! 6*. **Tap and Teach Lessons** enable you to move seamlessly between the book and digital components, and you can track your pupils' marks and review their progress using the **Progress Tracker**, and find additional resources in the **Resource Bank** and **Test Generator**.

Accessing the app

To access Navio:

1. Go to www.MacmillanNavio.com/givemefive
2. Follow the onscreen instructions

If you haven't got a Macmillan Education account, you need to create a profile. Then you can enter your access code and download the app for your device (see System Requirements: www.macmillannavio.com/system-requirements).

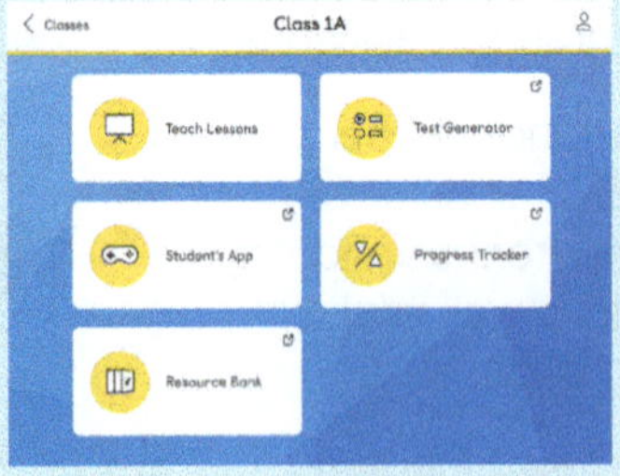

Setting up a class

You, or your school administrator, will need to set up a class and register pupils with their names and the email address of their parents or guardians. Once the class is created, login details can be given to parents. Parents can then log in to the Pupil's App and enter the access code from the inside cover of the Pupil's Book to access the 3D worlds and practice content.

Managing your downloads

Navio makes it easy to manage the storage space on your device, as you can control how much material you download at one time. Navio makes it clear how much storage space your chosen content will need. You can download the complete Teacher's and Pupil's Apps at once, or, if your device has limited storage capacity, you can choose to download only one or two units. And after you finish a unit, you can safely delete the content from your device. You won't lose your pupils' data, as this information is stored online.

Using the Progress Tracker

All the work your pupils complete in the app is recorded in the **Progress Tracker**. You can monitor the progress of a whole class or any individual pupil. Every activity in the App is mapped against the course Learning Outcomes and Skills, so you can easily identify where your pupils need extra support.

Teaching a lesson

Navio makes it easy to plan and teach your lessons with fully interactive **Tap and Teach Lessons** for every lesson in *Give Me Five! 6*. Go to your Class Dashboard and choose **Teach Lessons**. Find the lesson you want to teach and click to open it. Click on the **Toolbar** along the bottom of the screen to expand it to Thumbnail view. The Toolbar also contains the **Tap and Teach tools** you need to teach heads-up, whole-class activities, including a Timer, Pen tool and Mask tool.

Lessons follow the lesson plans in the Teacher's Book, and provide everything you need to teach from your device in one place. They include digital versions of all the activities in the Pupil's Book and Activity Book, with their answer keys. They also include all the audio and video you need for the lesson, as well as some extra tools such as digital Flashcards. All relevant pages from all three books are also provided so that you can project them in class, to help your pupils and to encourage heads-up participation.

When you teach, move through the lesson slide by slide using the arrows, or double click on a thumbnail to jump straight to a particular activity. If you prefer, you can **Filter activities** to customise the lesson so it includes only the content you want to teach.

Using the Rewards tool

Navio's new **Rewards tool** is a great way to keep your pupils engaged in class. Much more than just a record of attendance, you can also use it to award points for good behaviour or success in activities. You can even organise your class into teams, and you can award points to individuals, groups or the whole class at any time. When pupils earn points, they appear in the Pupil's App next time they log in, so parents can see their performance.

Pupil's App

As a teacher you can also access a version of the Pupil's App from the Class Dashboard. This has all the same content that your pupils can access at home, but your version is set in **Teacher Mode**. This means that all the activities and worlds are already unlocked, and the App does not record any marks to the Progress Tracker.

We recommend using Teacher Mode when pupils share devices to avoid mixing up pupils' grades and progress. However, if pupils have individual devices or are using the app at home, they should always log in with their own username and password. In this way they can earn points and badges, set up and customise their avatar and build a record of their progress in the Progress Tracker.

Flashcards and Word cards games bank

Flashcard games

1 *Keep talking*

Organise the class into teams. Show the class your first flashcard and elicit the vocabulary item. Then give the card to the first team and ask them to make a sentence about what is on the card, for example *It's yellow* (a banana). f the sentence is acceptable the team wins a point and the card is passed on to the next team who must think up another sentence, e.g. *It gives you light.* (A torch.) Continue the activity until the groups run out of things to say. Then repeat the procedure with another card.

2 *Chain game*

Hold up one of the flashcards (e.g. rock climbing) and say **Yesterday was a very busy day! I went rock climbing** … Give a different flashcard to another pupil (e.g. hiking). They have to say *Yesterday was a very busy day! I went rock climbing and I went hiking …* Keep handing out flashcards. The pupils continue to add new activities each time. When you start to hand out objects, the pupils can say *I took a torch*, etc.

Word card games

1 *Word card classification*

Use the word cards to organise and classify vocabulary items. You can use the cards to create a mind map, writing the name of the topic in the centre of the board and then asking the class to organise the word cards into sub-topics around the topic. You can also create Venn diagrams, for example classifying food into food groups according to whether it is eaten hot or cold, or organising activities on a line according to how boring or exciting they are.

2 *Mime the card*

Invite a pupil to come to the front of the room. Stand behind the pupil and show a word card to the rest of the class. The class mimes this activity or item and the pupil at the front should try to guess the word. Repeat the procedure with the other word cards, choosing a different pupil to come to the front of the class each time.

3 *Yes or No?*

Divide the class into teams. A pupil from one team to pick a word card from the lexical set and challenge the rest of their team to guess the word. Invite three different team members to ask yes/no questions, e.g. *Is it bigger than my hand? Can you see it in this room?* After three questions, a fourth pupil has to guess what it is.

Classroom games

1 *Opposites game*

Use this activity to practise opposites. Write a row of numbers (1–8) on the board and below it a row of letters (a-h). Explain that each number and each letter is an adjective. The pupils must find and match the opposite adjectives. Organise the class into two teams. The teams should take turns to say a number and letter. Read out the corresponding adjectives (below). If the adjectives are opposites, write them on the board and award the team a point. Then continue the game.

1 2 3 4 5 6 7 8
heavy strong noisy long
near hard rough expensive
A B C D E F G H
soft light far weak short
cheap smooth quiet

2 *Sharing sentences*

Use this activity to practise the past continuous and past simple tenses. Hand out a piece of paper to each pupil and ask them to fold the page in half (vertically). Then write a prompt for the first half of the sentence on the board ***I was … when …*** The pupils should copy and complete it, e.g. swimming, eating a pizza, on the left side of the paper. They should then fold the paper so you can only see the blank right side and pass it to a partner. Elicit different ways to complete the sentence using the past simple tense, e.g. *I saw a ghost.* The partners should write the second part of the sentence without looking at the first part and then pass it back for the original pupil to read. Repeat the procedure several times.

3 *No one can go to the cinema*

Use this activity to practise modal verbs of obligation. Invite a pupil to come to the front of the class and prompt them to ask another pupil *Can you go to the cinema with me?* Prompt the second pupil to give an excuse, e.g. *Sorry, I have to do my homework.* The first pupil should then say to a third pupil *(Pablo) has to do his homework. Can you go to the cinema with me?* Once again, the third pupil should give an excuse.

4 *Connections*

Explain to the pupils that you will go around the class asking them to say a word connected with the topic. If someone thinks that there isn't a connection, they can 'challenge' and the person who has said the word has to explain the connection to the topic. Repeat the activity with different topics.

5 *Freeze!*

Use this activity to practise the past continuous tense. Invite a pupil to come to the front of the class and close his / her eyes. Ask the rest of the class to stand up and mime doing an action. After the class have been miming for a few seconds say 3, 2, 1 ... FREEZE! The pupils should freeze in the middle of their action. Ask the pupil at the front of the class to open his / her eyes and identify what action each pupil was doing. The classmates sit down when the pupil guesses their actions correctly.

Using the Pupil's Book and Activity Book

Lesson 1

Clear objectives set the scene for learning and provide a suggestion for evaluation criteria.

Exciting and engaging photographs are used to activate the pupils' existing knowledge and encourage whole-class discussion.

Twelve items of vocabulary are introduced using **photographic flashcards** and **word cards**.

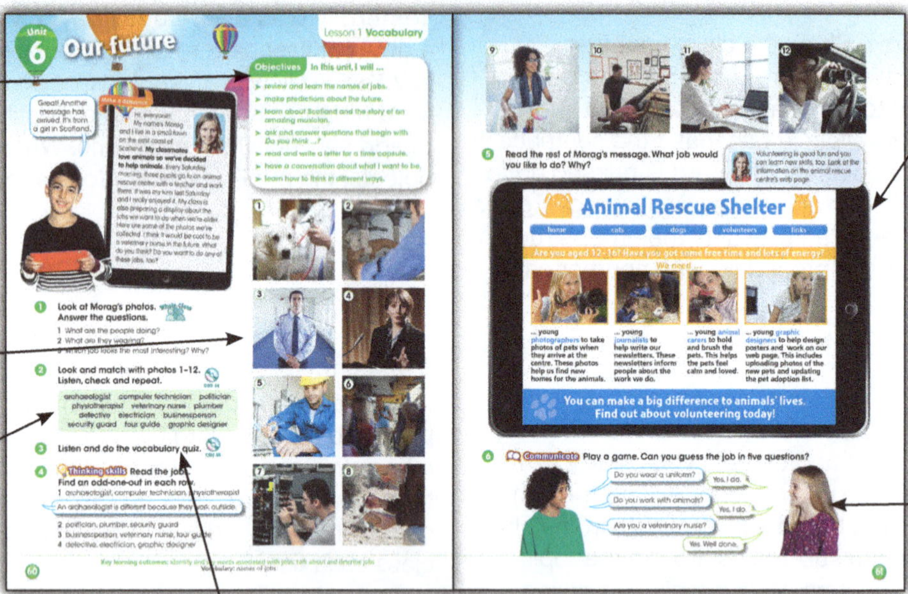

A **real-world reading text** helps contextualise new vocabulary and develop reading skills.

The pupils use a recycled structure to do a **personalised speaking task** in pairs.

A definitions **vocabulary quiz** reinforces understanding of the new vocabulary and develops listening skills.

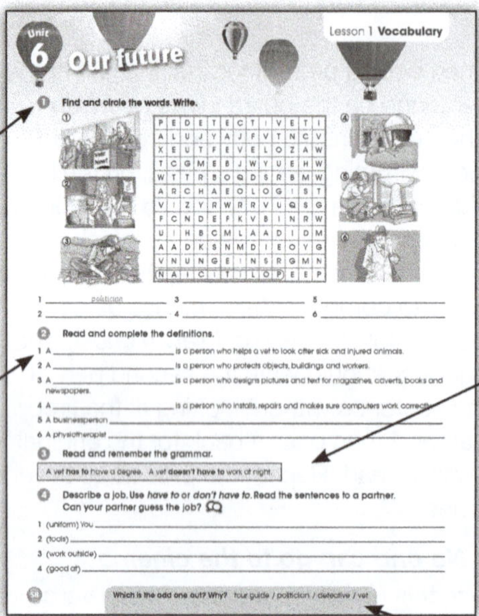

Fun, game-like activities **motivate the pupils to write** the new vocabulary items.

The pupils **practise reading and writing** definitions of the new vocabulary.

The pupils **review** a language structure and use it in a **personalised writing task**.

An odd-one-out activity on each Activity Book page allows children to have fun while developing **critical thinking skills**.

Digital resources

Teacher's Digital: Don't forget you can teach these lessons using the Teacher's App on Navio.

Pupil's Digital: Encourage your pupils to use the Pupil's App on Navio to practise the vocabulary from these lessons.

Powered By NAVIO

Lessons 2 and 3

A short text-message exchange places **grammar in a fun and familiar context**.

The **Grammar wall** highlights language patterns.

Think about grammar encourages the pupils to reflect on language.

The pupils work in pairs to do a **communicative speaking task** using the new grammar.

Thinking skills activities invite the pupils to activate previous knowledge before reading an exciting **factual** or **fictional** story with a **cultural** focus.

The story reinforces language introduced in Lessons 1 and 2 and previews language from Lesson 4.

Attractive and age-appropriate artwork and an exciting audio recording support the pupils' understanding of the story.

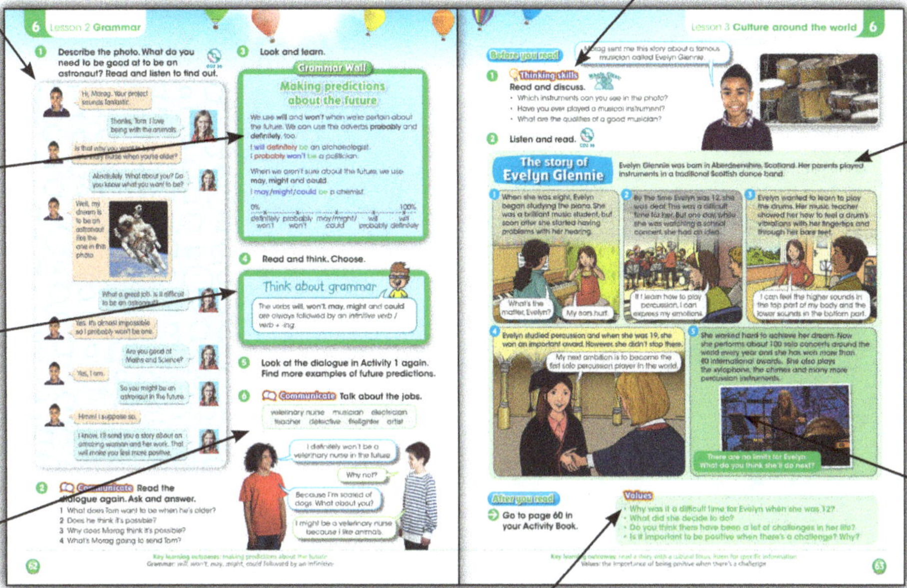

The *Give Me Five!* **Values** section encourages the pupils to reflect on the story and relate a personal, social or civic value to their own lives.

A varied range of activities give the pupils **practice in manipulating** the **form** of the new grammar.

Understanding of the content is consolidated through a listening activity type found in the **Cambridge English Key Test (KET)**.

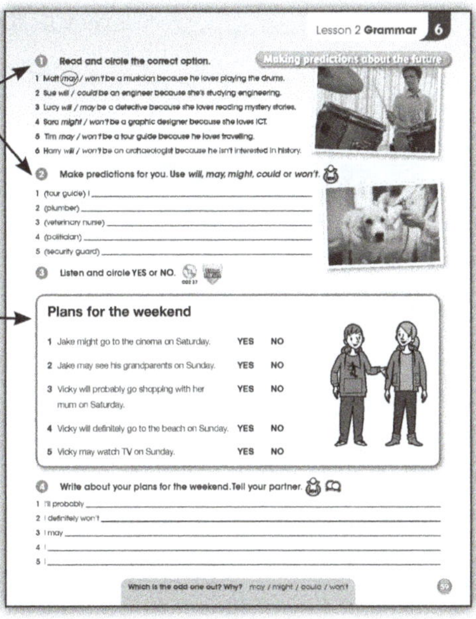

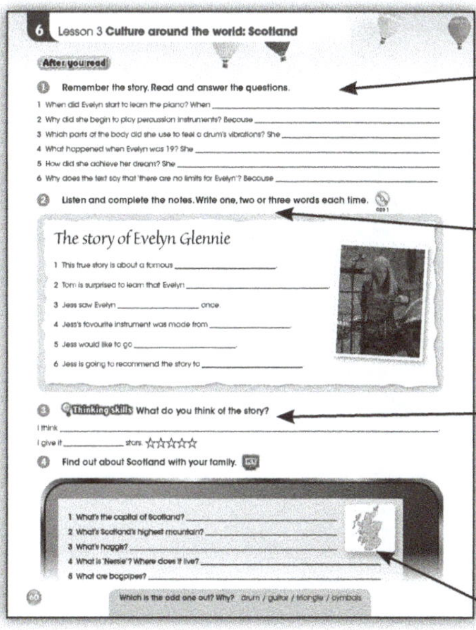

Activities check the pupils' understanding of the story.

Comprehension is reinforced through a listening activity.

The pupils are encouraged to give a **personal response** to the story.

A fun and motivating investigation task encourages pupils to develop their **digital skills**.

Digital resources

Teacher's Digital: Don't forget you can teach this lesson using the Teacher's App on Navio.

Pupil's Digital: Encourage your pupils to use the Pupil's App on Navio to practise the vocabulary from these lessons.

Powered By NAVIO

Using the Pupil's Book and Activity Book

Lessons 4 and 5

The pupils listen, read and act out a short dialogue which **contextualises new language**.

Between eight and ten new items of vocabulary are introduced and practised using **pictures** and **photos**.

The **Grammar wall** encourages the pupils to think analytically about new language.

Oral fluency is developed through practice of connected speech, stress, rhythm and intonation.

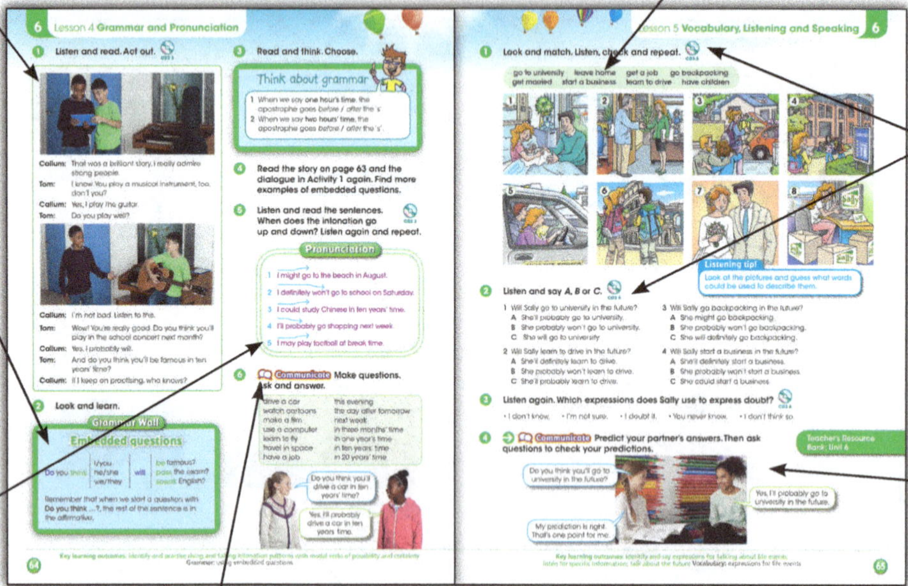

A listening task **prepares pupils for a communicative game**. The pupils listen for global and then specific comprehension.

The pupils play a communicative game in pairs. Each pupil has different information, providing the pupils with a genuine reason for speaking. The supporting material for these types of activities can be found on the Teacher's Resource Bank.

Communication icons indicate when the pupils have the opportunity to practise speaking in pairs. These activities build confidence and ensure full participation.

Reading and writing activities are **carefully staged** to build the pupils' confidence and ensure success.

Activities help consolidate and practise **pronunciation**.

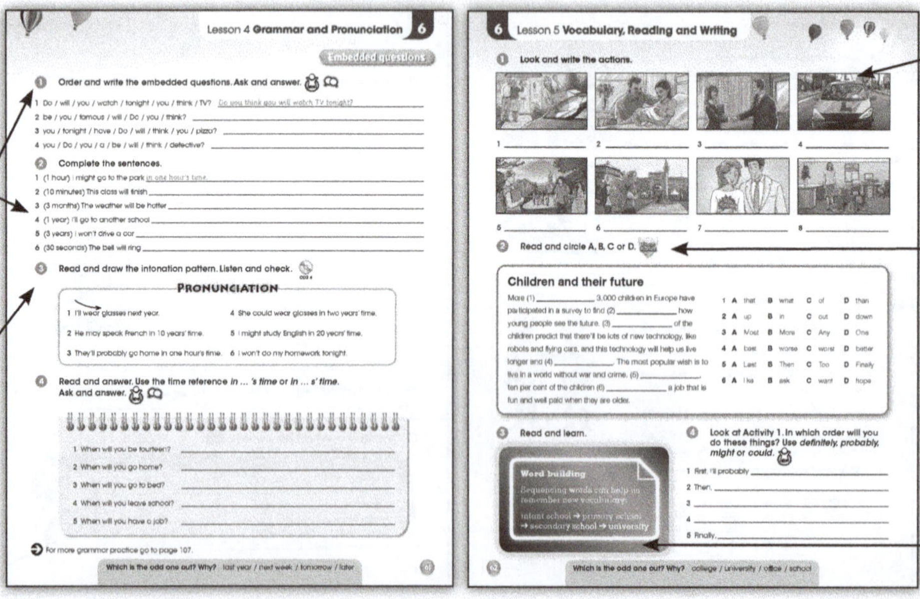

Activities encourage the pupils to recognise and practise the Lesson 5 vocabulary.

Understanding of the content is consolidated through a reading and writing activity type found in the **Cambridge English Key Test**.

The **Word building** section introduces and practises strategies for developing, recording and remembering vocabulary.

Digital resources

Teacher's Digital: Don't forget you can teach these lessons using the Teacher's App on Navio.

Pupil's Digital: Encourage your pupils to use the Pupil's App on Navio to practise the vocabulary from these lessons.

Powered By NAVIO

Lessons 6 and 7

The pupils are introduced to a wide **range of reading text types**. These are selected to **reflect the interests and experiences** of the age group and have an **authentic appearance** that will appeal to learners.

A variety of tasks help the pupils to understand the **purpose of a text**, **the intended audience** or what is **appropriate content**.

The **Before you read** activities help prepare the pupils to read. These include activating pupils' existing knowledge, exploiting visuals, asking questions to raise interest and making predictions.

The pupils are given the opportunity to communicate information and **express ideas**, **opinions**, **feelings and interpretations** of the text.

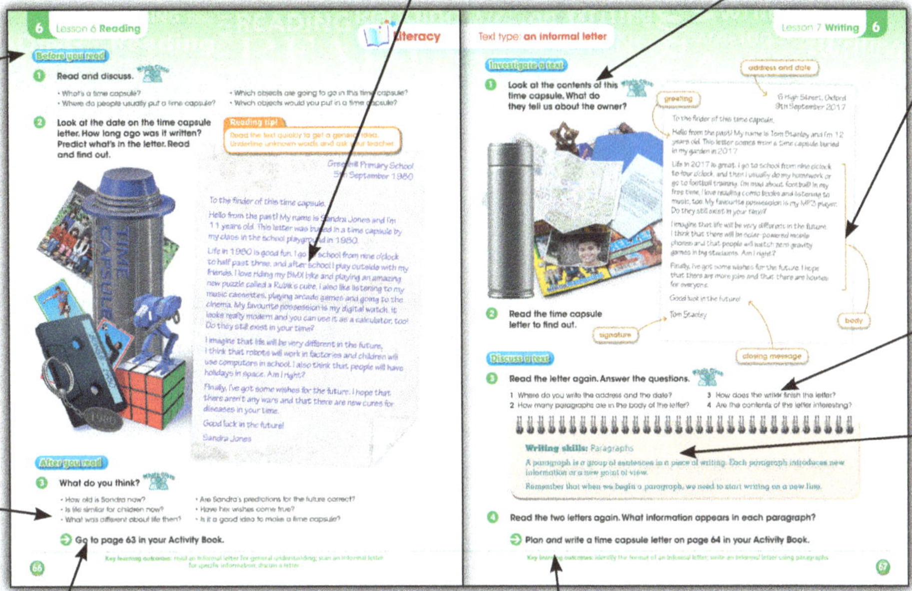

A shorter text provides a **writing model** for the pupils to follow.

Guided questions help the pupils **identify key text features** such as titles and captions.

The **Writing skills** section highlights a discrete writing skill such as time connectors.

The pupils are directed to the **After you read** activities in the Activity Book.

The pupils are directed to the Activity Book to prepare their piece of writing.

A range of activities reinforce and check the pupils' understanding of the literacy text.

Reading skills such as **skimming** and **scanning** are actively developed.

Understanding of the content is consolidated through a listening activity.

A variety of **enjoyable activities** allows the pupils to respond to the text in a personal and creative way.

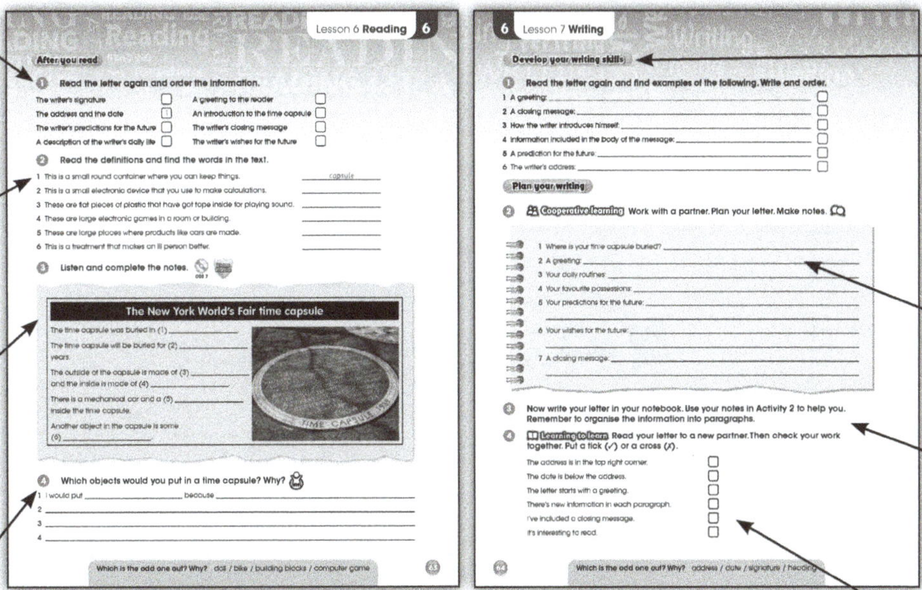

The pupils have the opportunity to practise and consolidate a discrete writing skill such as time connectors, adverbs of manner or the use of direct speech.

The pupils **work with a partner** to **plan**, **draft** and **revise** their writing.

Step-by-step instructions provide the pupils with plenty of support in the planning stage.

The pupils **share their work** with another student and use **self-assessment criteria** to check their work.

Digital resources

Teacher's Digital: Don't forget you can teach this lesson using the Teacher's App on Navio.

Pupil's Digital: Encourage your pupils to use the Pupil's App on Navio to practise the vocabulary from these lessons.

Powered By NAVIO

Using the Pupil's Book and Activity Book

Lesson 8, Review and Video and 21st Century Skills

There is a focus on the speaking skills needed for **external exams success** or real-life needs.

The pupils learn to communicate in different situations working on individual **presentation skills**, **conversation skills** or **cooperative speaking** tasks.

The pupils are encouraged to **reflect** upon their learning based on the **objectives** set at the beginning of the unit.

The pupils are directed to the Activity Book to do the **Unit Review**.

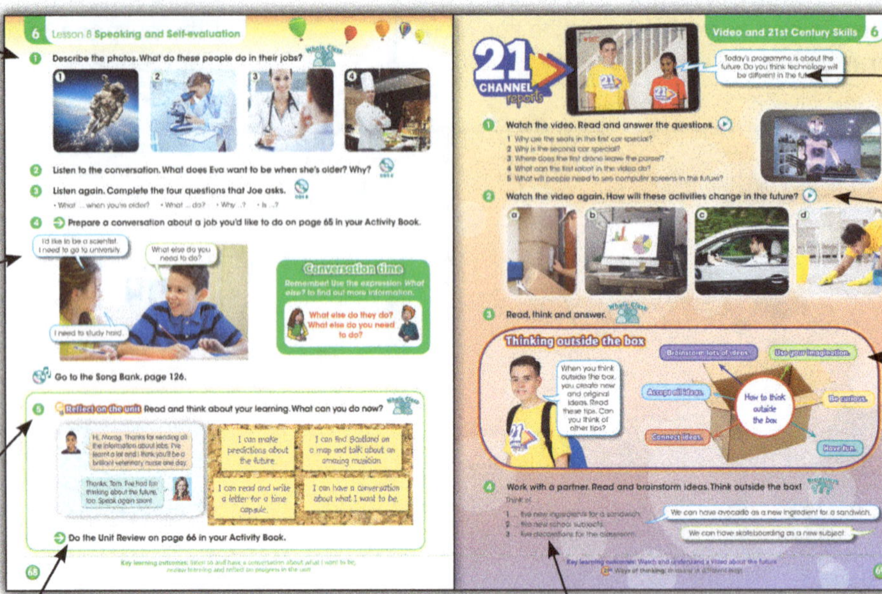

The children introduce the video lesson and spark the pupils' interest in a wide range of topics.

The pupils watch an engaging **video** related to the topic of the unit and 21st Century Skills.

Encouraging the pupils to be creative and original is a good way to practise **21st Century Skills**. Pupils are fostered to reflect on a different skill in each unit.

The pupils are directed to the Song Bank at the back of the Pupil's Book in Units 1, 3, 4, 6, 7 and 9.

Pupils are set fascinating tasks to promote the skills needed in the modern world.

A **framework** helps the pupils organise their ideas and select language for the speaking task.

The pupils are encouraged to organise their thoughts and ideas by making notes to **prepare a conversation** about a different topic in every unit.

The pupils reflect on their learning and set a **personal learning objective for the next unit**.

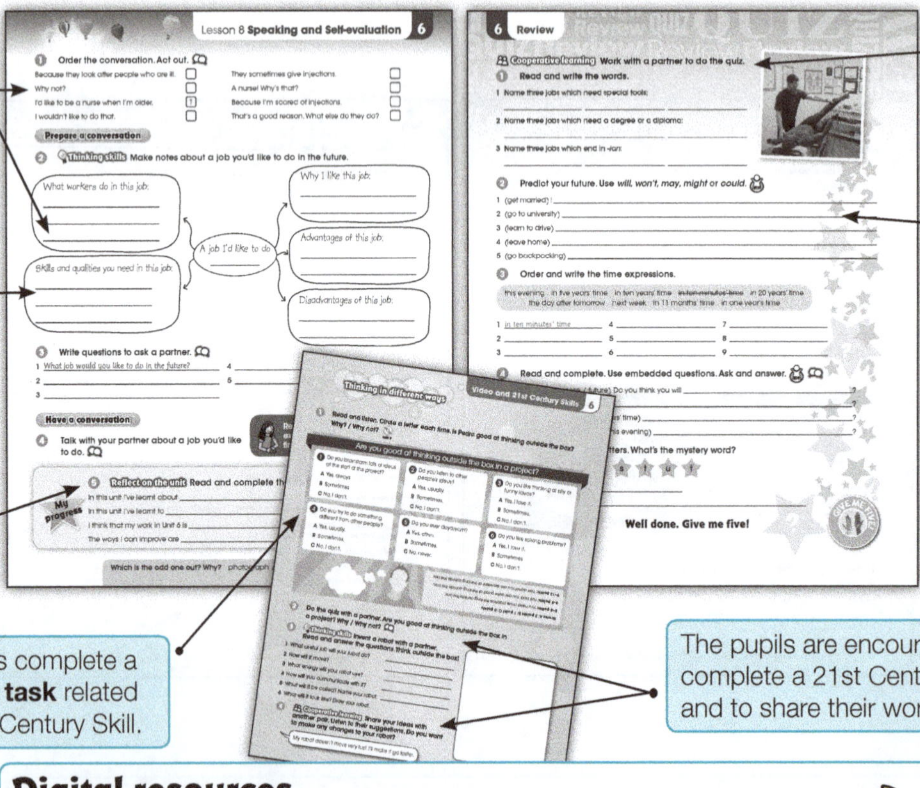

The pupils **work cooperatively** to check their learning.

A full page review **checks and reinforces** all of the unit vocabulary and grammar.

The pupils complete a **listening task** related to a 21st Century Skill.

The pupils are encouraged to complete a 21st Century Skills task and to share their work with a partner.

Digital resources

Teacher's Digital: Don't forget you can teach these lessons using the Teacher's App on Navio.

Pupil's Digital: Encourage your pupils to use the Pupil's App on Navio to practise the vocabulary from these lessons.

Powered By NAVIO

Using the projects

Give Me Five! 6 provides three fun and highly doable **projects**. An energy proposal (Term 1), Living on Mars (Term 2) and Life in the past (Term 3). These provide an opportunity for the pupils to **work cooperatively** in a structured way, building autonomy and promoting creativity.

The pupils have the opportunity to **share existing knowledge** about the topic.

A group investigation task develops the pupils' listening and **note-taking** skills.

Project tips help develop research and presentation and digital skills.

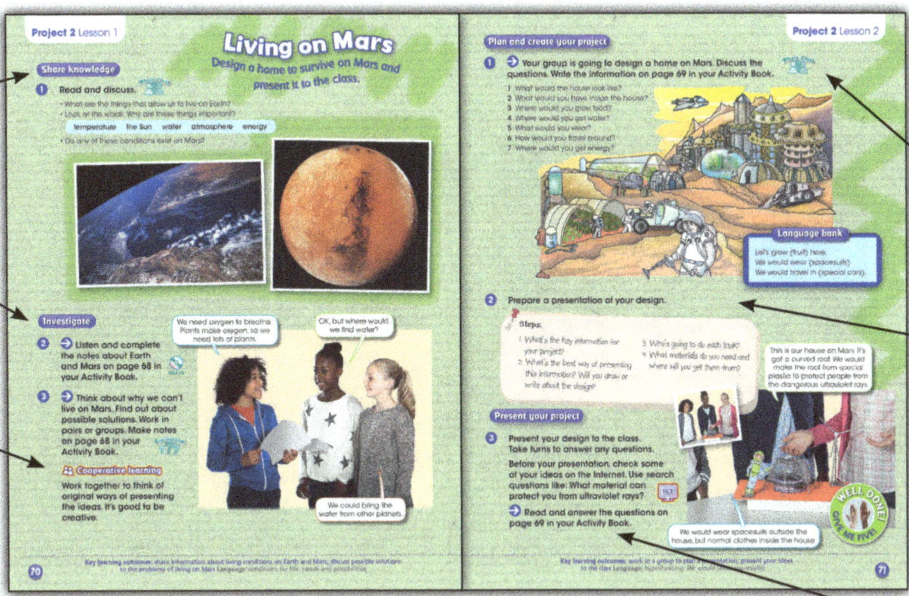

The pupils have an opportunity to work together to **plan and create** their project. Working together encourages the pupils to **talk meaningfully** about the task.

Tasks create **positive interdependence**. Each member's contribution is essential in order to complete the group's task.

The pupils have the opportunity to **reflect on what they have learnt** and their final piece of work.

The pupils develop their listening and **note-taking** skills.

The pupils also prepare their **investigation task** in the Activity Book.

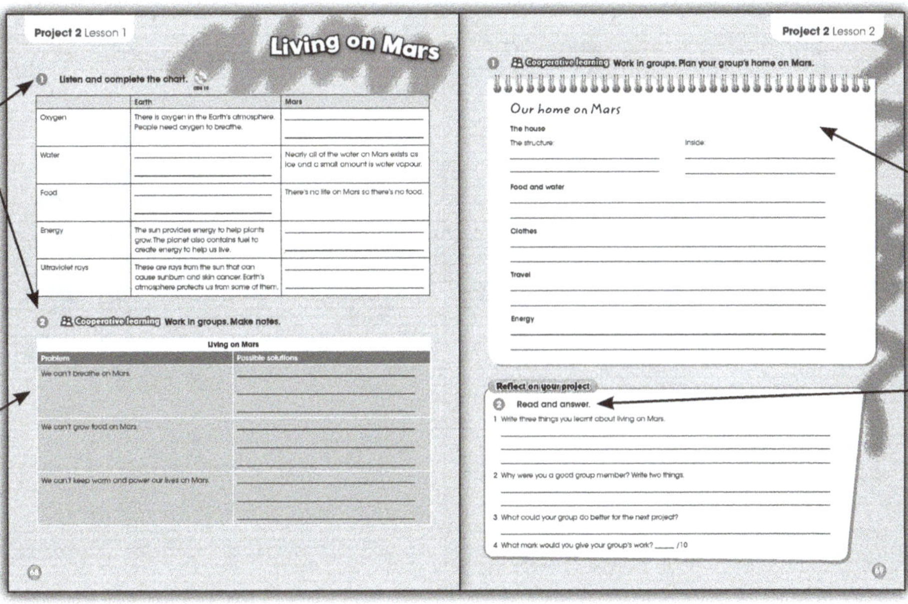

The pupils go to the Activity Book to **record their decisions** for the group task.

Thinking skills are developed by prompting the students to reflect about their findings and give an opinion.

Digital resources

Teacher's Digital: Don't forget you can teach this lesson using the Teacher's App on Navio.

Pupil's Digital: Encourage your pupils to use the Pupil's App on Navio to practise the vocabulary from these lessons.

Powered By NAVIO

Using the Exams Practice

The **Cambridge Exams Practice** section at the back of both the Pupil's Book and Activity Book introduces the pupils to the activity types found in the different parts of the three papers of the Cambridge English Key for Schools Tests: Listening, Reading and Writing and Speaking.

The nine Cambridge Exams Practice pages at the back of the Pupil's Book will help the pupils to **develop the necessary skills** to do the Reading and Writing papers.

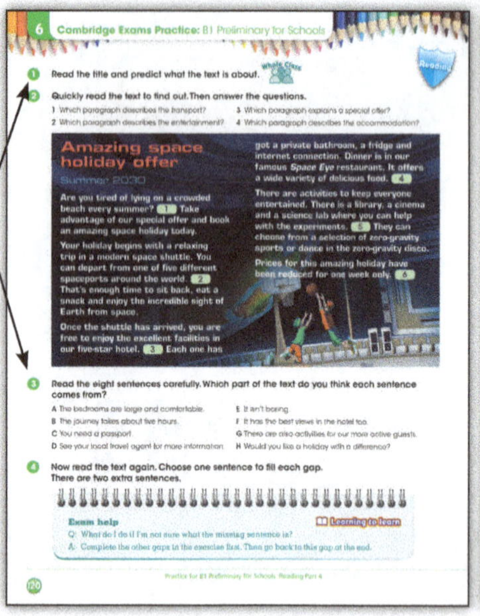

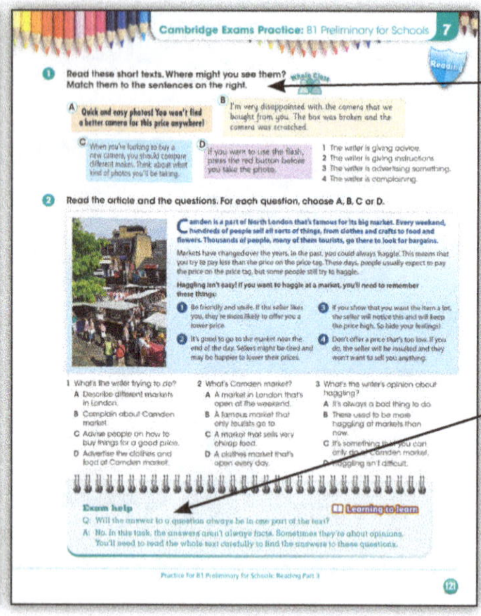

The pupils practise simple and effective **reading strategies** such as guessing the meaning of words or reading the clues to think of words.

An **Exam help** section supports the pupils by providing answers to common questions and concerns.

For further practice, watch the **External Exams Video** which you can find in the Teacher's Resource Bank.

The nine Cambridge Exams Practice pages at the back of the Activity Book will help the pupils to **develop the necessary skills** to do the Listening and Reading and Writing papers.

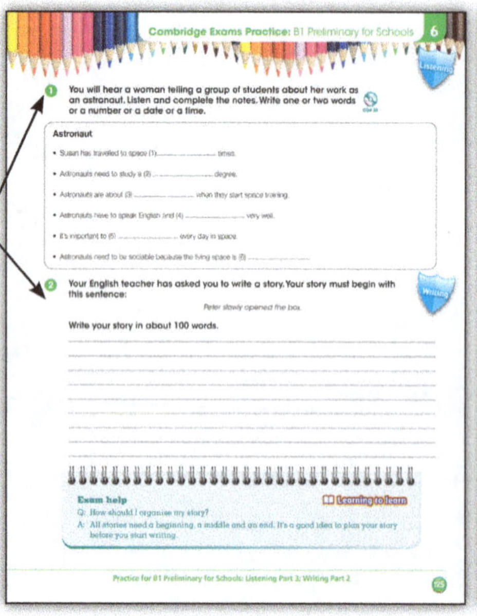

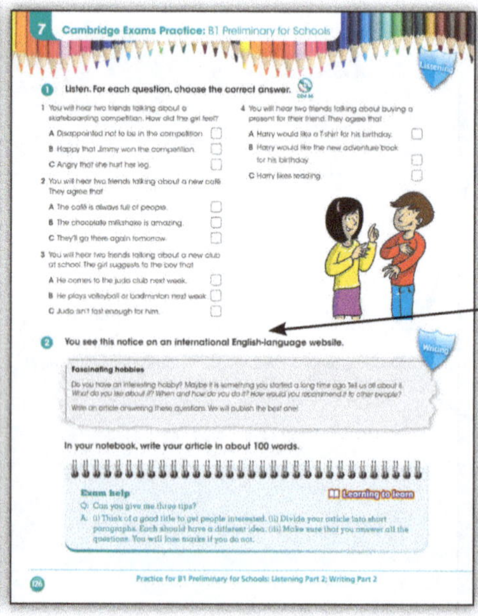

Pupils are encouraged to develop their reading and writing skills by practising activities found in the Reading and Writing papers.

Digital resources

Teacher's Digital: Don't forget you can teach these lessons using the Teacher's App on Navio.

Pupil's Digital: Encourage your pupils to use the Pupil's App on Navio to practise the vocabulary from these lessons.

Powered By NAVIO

Exams Practice

Give Me Five! 6 and the external exams

Give Me Five! 6 provides a wide range of material to support teachers who are preparing their pupils for the ***Cambridge English Key for Schools Test***. Reading, writing and listening activity types found in the ***Cambridge English Key for Schools Test*** are integrated into the material and both the Pupil's Book and the Activity Book end with a section full of Cambridge Exams Practice lessons. This material is adapted to match the linguistic and cognitive level of the pupils and language is systematically extended as the course progresses.

There is also the **External Exams Resources** which contain videos of children doing speaking practice, and provide detailed Teacher's Notes on how to exploit these videos in the classroom. The resources, which are part of the Teacher's Resource Bank, also include additional External exams practice material and practice tests for both the Cambridge English Key for Schools and the Trinity Graded Exam in Spoken English (Elementary Stage, Grade 6), and a set of Trinity Exams Practice cards.

Trinity Exams Practice cards

The **Trinity Exams Practice cards** are a set of downloadable and photocopiable cards. They can be used to build the pupils' confidence in asking and answering questions. On each card is a question based on the ***Trinity Graded Exam in Spoken English*** syllabus. These introduce questions from the Elementary Stage (Grade 6) and recycle questions from earlier grades. These cards should be printed out, laminated if possible and filed by unit. They can then be used during the Starting the lesson stage which systematically recycles language, transferring it to the pupils' long-term memory. For the Trinity Exams Practice cards routine, the teacher selects several cards from previous units. The teacher should choose a different set of cards for each lesson, and tricky questions and recent topics should be revisited more frequently. The teacher then uses the cards to practise asking and answering questions by doing one of the following suggested activities.

Trinity Exams Practice cards activity bank

1 Ask and answer in pairs

Ask the class to get into pairs. Then hold up one of the selected Trinity Exams Practice cards and ask the question. Invite a pupil to answer and repeat their answer for the class. The pupils then ask and answer the same question with their partner. Repeat the procedure with other cards.

2 Three-step interview

Follow the procedure for activity 1. When the pupils have asked and answered all the questions on the Trinity Exams Practice cards, ask them to get into different pairs. They should then share information about their first partner's responses.

3 Moving questions

Select eight Trinity Exams Practice cards and stick them on the board, writing a number (1–8) above each one. Organise the class into small groups of three or four. One pupil from each group should come to the board and read and memorise the first question. They should then return to the group and ask the question. Once everyone in the group has answered, a second pupil should repeat the procedure, reading and memorising the second question. Continue until all eight questions have been asked and answered.

4 Mix Pair Share

The pupils should move silently around the room. When you call out the word **pair**, they should form a pair with the person closest to them. The pupils who haven't found a partner should raise their hands to find each other. Read out a question on one of the Trinity Exams Practice cards and give the pupils a moment to think. The pupils then tell each other their answers. Encourage the pupils to keep talking as long as possible. When all the pupils have finished, repeat the procedure with other cards.

5 Card swap

Hand out a Trinity Exam Practice card to each pupil. The pupils should move silently around the room. When you call out the word **pair**, they should form a pair with the person closest to them. The pupils who haven't found a partner should raise their hands to find each other. The pupils should then take turns to ask and answer their question with their partners. When each pair has finished, the pupils should swap cards, find new partners and repeat the procedure. Stress the importance of giving complete answers to the different questions each time.

6 Card survey

Hand out a Trinity Exam Practice card to each pupil and explain that they are going to ask their question to six classmates. The pupils should move silently around the room. When you call out the word **pair**, they should form a pair with the person closest to them and ask their question. They may take notes as they listen to their partners' answers. When each pair has finished, the pupils should find new partners and repeat the procedure. At the end of the activity, ask different pupils to report their findings to the rest of the class.

7 Class question box

Make extra copies of the Trinity Exams Practice cards that you have practised in class. Laminate these, if possible, and store them in a class question box. Fast finishers can use these cards to review and practise language, working individually to write the answers in their notebooks or asking and answering the questions with a partner.

Using the Teacher's Book

The Teacher's Notes have a clear, user-friendly design, offering both an **At a Glance Lesson Plan** and a **Detailed Lesson Plan**. These mirror each other, enabling teachers to move between the two lesson plans with ease.

This box clearly shows the learning objectives, key active language and materials required for the lesson. The objectives are mapped to the **Key Competences and Key Learning Outcomes**.

The **At a Glance Lesson Plan** provides a brief overview of all the activities in the lesson, including **Starting** and **Ending the lesson activities** and **Extra activities**. Class audio references are also provided.

Fast forward icons indicate the **fast route** through for teachers who have shorter lessons or fewer hours of English.

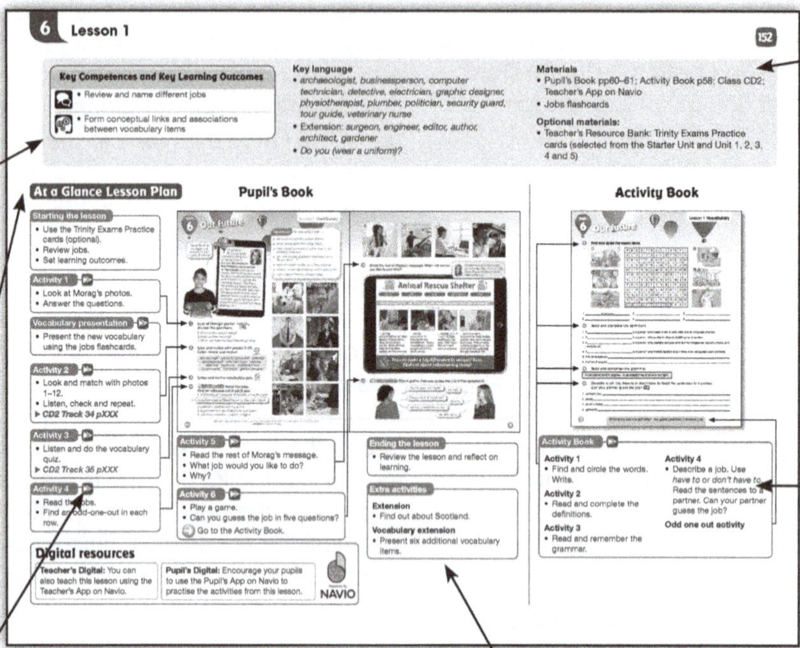

The required and optional materials for each lesson are included in the panel.

There is also a brief overview of the Activity Book activities.

Each lesson includes optional **Extra activities** to reinforce and extend learning. The **Vocabulary** extension suggests additional vocabulary to extend the lexical set.

The **Detailed Lesson Plan** provides more detailed **step-by-step instructions** for each activity.

The activities for **Starting the lesson** include optional use of the **Trinity Exams Practice cards** and set the learning objectives and outcomes of the lesson.

A clear layout and clear stages make the plan very easy to follow.

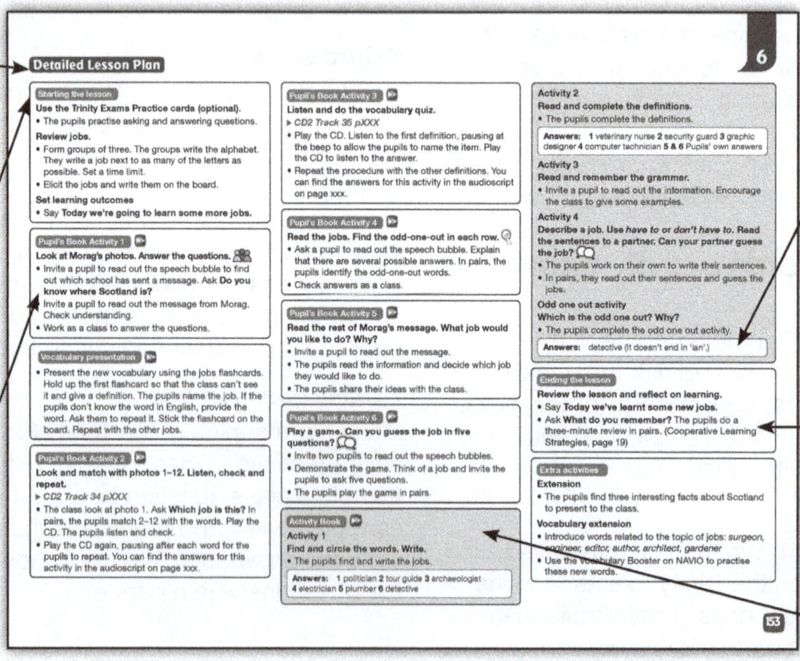

Answers are provided for most Pupil's Book and Activity Book activities.

The activities for **Ending the lesson** include reviewing the lesson and reflecting on learning.

Activity Book teaching notes always appear in a shaded box so they can be easily identified. The answers to the Activity Book tasks are also provided.

Unit S

A new project

Unit overview

Key Competences and Key Learning Outcomes

- Understand and act out a dialogue (Lesson 1)
- Learn and practise how to use state verbs (Lesson 2)
- Use the present passive to ask and say which languages are spoken in a country (Lesson 3)
- Use question tags to check information (Lesson 4)

- Read a poster and find information (Lesson 1)
- Work with charts and graphic organisers (Lesson 2)
- Complete a form (Lesson 3)
- Analyse rules for forming question tags (Lesson 4)

Learning to LEARN

- Review vocabulary: things you see in a town or city (Lesson 1), *there is / there are* (Lesson 1), countries and languages (Lesson 3)
- Review and compare present simple and present continuous (Lesson 2)

- Think about the importance of protecting natural habitats (Lessons 1 and 4)
- Understand that people can make a difference in their community (Lessons 3 and 4)

- Work in pairs or small groups to practise and reinforce learning (All lessons)

- Express personal opinions and preferences (Lessons 1 and 2)
- Learn about global projects (Lesson 3)
- Read and understand an information text about a balloon project in England (Lesson 4)

Vocabulary

Core vocabulary
block of flats, bridge, cycle path, department store, factory, hot-air balloon, skate park, stadium, statue, square, tunnel

Other vocabulary
barn owl, bird's eye view, community, global project, in danger, make a difference, nest, nest box, online form, predator, species; Arabic, Chinese, Dutch, Gaelic, Japanese, Scots, Swedish; Belgium, China, Ecuador, Egypt, Mexico, Scotland, Sweden

Recycled vocabulary
believe, climb, dislike, eat, go, know, prefer, swim, travel, want, work, understand; English, French, German, Spanish; USA, Japan; cat, countryside, dog, fox

Structures

Core structures
Are there any (statues in our town)? Yes, there are (a few statues in our town). She usually (plays tennis on Saturday morning). Today (she's waiting to have a ride in the hot-air balloon). The children live in a big city, don't they? Cats aren't predators, are they?

Other structures
Which languages are spoken in (Scotland)? (English, Gaelic and Scots) are spoken in (Scotland).

Recycled structures
You must be over seven years old to have a ride and children must be with an adult. Which school do you go to? Are you ready then? There is / isn't a (stadium). There are (two squares). There aren't any (bridges). Is there a (skate park in our town)? Are there any (statues in our town)?
Present simple affirmative, negative and question form; Present continuous affirmative, negative and question form

Thinking skills

Using a chart to categorise (Lesson 2); Memorising (Lesson 3); Completing a form (Lesson 3); Analysing and applying rules and patterns (Lesson 4)

Cooperative learning

Contributing ideas (Lessons 1–4); Sharing ideas and opinions (Lessons 1–4); Reflecting and setting goals (Lessons 1–4); Checking learning (Lessons 1–4)

Key Competences and Key Learning Outcomes

- Understand and act out a dialogue
- Review and learn things you see in a town or city
- Set learning outcomes and reflect on learning
- Think about the importance of protecting natural habitats
- Express personal opinions and preferences

Key language

- *block of flats, bridge, cycle path, department store, factory, hot-air balloon, skate park, stadium, statue, square, tunnel*
- *You must be over seven years old to have a ride and children must be with an adult. Which school do you go to? Are you ready then? There is / isn't a (stadium). There are (two squares). There aren't any (bridges). Is there a (skate park in our town)? Are there any (statues in our town)?*

Materials

- Pupil's Book pp4–5; Activity Book p2; Class CD1; Teacher's App on Navio
- Teacher's Resource Bank: Course character flashcards

At a Glance Lesson Plan

Pupil's Book

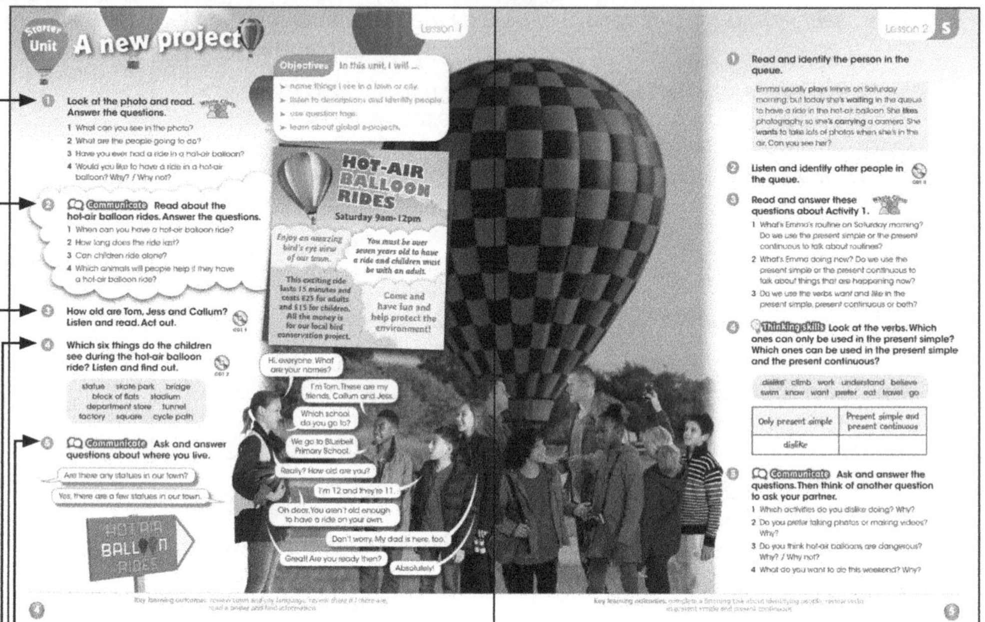

Starting the lesson

- Remember the course book characters.
- Set learning outcomes.

Activity 1

- Look at the photo and read.
- Answer the questions.

Activity 2

- Read about the hot-air balloon rides.
- Answer the questions.

Activity 3

- How old are Tom, Jess and Callum?
- Listen and read. Act out.
- ▶ *CD1 Track 1 p275*
- Act out.

Activity 4

- Which six things do the children see during the hot-air balloon ride?
- Listen and find out.
- ▶ *CD1 Track 2 p275*

Activity 5

- Ask and answer questions about where you live.

Go to the Activity Book.

Ending the lesson

- Review the lesson and reflect on learning.

Extra activity

Extension

- Create an alphabet list of things you see in a town or city.

Activity Book

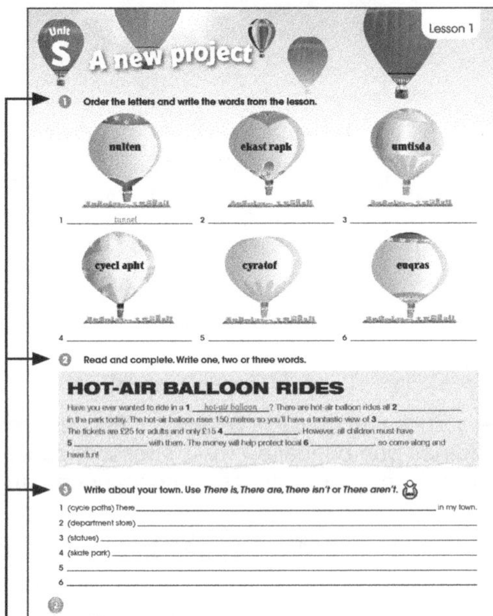

Activity Book

Activity 1

- Order the letters and write the words from the lesson.

Activity 2

- Read and complete. Write one, two or three words.

Activity 3

- Write about your town. Use *There is*, *There are*, *There isn't* or *There aren't*.

Digital resources

Teacher's Digital: You can also teach this lesson using the Teacher's App on Navio.

Pupil's Digital: Encourage your pupils to use the Pupil's App on Navio to practise the activities from this lesson.

Powered By NAVIO

Starting the lesson

Remember the course book characters.

- Introduce *Give Me Five! 6* to the class. Ask the pupils to describe the cover.
- If the pupils previously used *Give Me Five! 5*, encourage them to name and describe the three characters, Tom, Jess and Callum, using the course character flashcards. Ask the pupils to explain what the balloon race was. (*The children released some helium balloons at a school fair. Each balloon had a question attached to it. The balloons floated to different countries. The children who found the balloons then contacted Tom, Jess and Callum and answered their questions.*)

Set learning outcomes.

- Say **Today we're going to meet Tom, Jess and Callum and we're going to find out about where they live.**

Pupil's Book Activity 1

Look at the photo and read. Answer the questions.

- Focus the pupils on the photo on pages 4–5. Encourage them to describe what they can see in detail.
- Invite a pupil to read out each question. Answer as a class.

Pupil's Book Activity 2

Read about the hot-air balloon rides. Answer the questions.

- Ask **How much is the ride for children? What time do the rides begin? What can you see from the balloon?** Encourage the pupils to scan the text for the information.
- The pupils read the text on their own.
- They answer the questions with a partner. They can do this orally or in their notebooks.

Answers: **1** On Saturday **2** 15 minutes **3** No, they can't **4** Local birds

Pupil's Book Activity 3

How old are Tom, Jess and Callum? Listen and read. Act out.

▶ ***CD1 Track 1 p275***

- Ask the pupils if they know how old the course characters are.
- Play the CD. The pupils listen and read the dialogue to discover the ages. Confirm that the children are 12 and 11 years old.
- Check understanding. Ask **Can the children have a ride on their own? Who's going to ride with them?**
- Play the CD again, pausing after each sentence for the pupils to repeat.
- The pupils practise the dialogue in pairs.

Pupil's Book Activity 4

Which six things do the children see during the hot-air balloon ride? Listen and find out.

▶ ***CD1 Track 2 p275***

- Read the words as a class.
- Play the CD. The pupils listen and name the six things that the children can see.

Answers: stadium, skate park, square, statue, block of flats, bridge

Pupil's Book Activity 5

Ask and answer questions about where you live.

- Invite two pupils to read out the speech bubbles.
- If necessary, quickly review how to express quantity, i.e. a / an, some, a lot of, a few, not many, not any.
- The pupils ask and answer questions in pairs.

Activity Book

Activity 1

Order the letters and write the words from the lesson.

- Invite a pupil to order the letters to form the first word.
- The pupils work on their own to order and write the other words.

Answers: **1** tunnel **2** skate park **3** stadium **4** cycle path **5** factory **6** square

Activity 2

Read and complete. Write one, two or three words.

- Read out the text, pausing when there is a gap. The pupils listen and think about the missing words.
- The pupils work in pairs to complete the text.

Answers: **1** hot-air balloon **2** morning **3** our / the town **4** for children **5** an adult **6** birds

Activity 3

Write about your town. Use *There is, There are, There isn't* or *There aren't*.

- Invite a pupil to read and complete the first sentence.
- The pupils write the remaining sentences.

Ending the lesson

Review the lesson and reflect on learning.

- Say **Today we've found out about where Tom, Jess and Callum live.**
- Ask **What do you remember?** The pupils do a three-minute review in pairs. (Cooperative Learning Strategies, page 19)

Extra activity

Extension

- In groups, the pupils create an alphabet list of things and places that you can see in a town or city.

Key Competences and Key Learning Outcomes

- Learn and practise how to use state verbs
- Work with a chart to categorise verbs
- Set learning outcomes and reflect on learning
- Review and compare the present simple and the present continuous
- Express personal opinions and preferences

Key language

- *believe, climb, dislike, eat, go, know, prefer, swim, travel, want, work, understand*
- Present simple affirmative, negative and question form; Present continuous affirmative, negative and question form

Materials

- Pupil's Book pp4–5; Activity Book p3; Class CD1; Teacher's App on Navio
- Teacher's Resource Bank: Things I see in a town or city word cards

At a Glance Lesson Plan

Pupil's Book

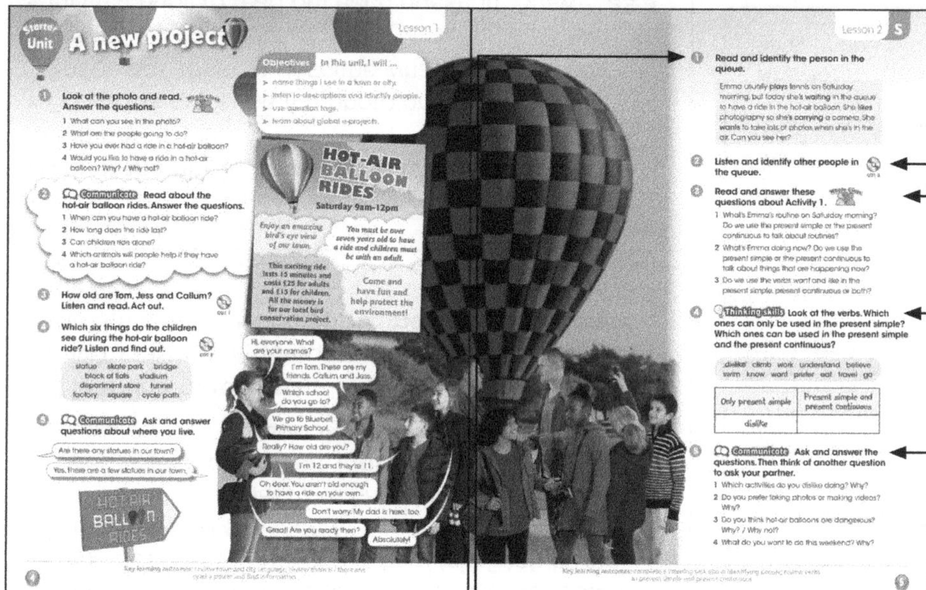

Starting the lesson

- Review things I see in a town or city.
- Set learning outcomes.

Activity 1

- Read and identify the person in the queue.

Activity 2

- Listen and identify other people in the queue.

▶ *CD1 Track 3 p275*

Activity 3

- Read and answer these questions about Activity 1.

Activity 4

- Look at the verbs. Which ones can only be used in the present simple?
- Which ones can be used in both the present simple and the present continuous?

Activity 5

- Ask and answer the questions.
- Then think of another question to ask your partner.

Go to the Activity Book.

Ending the lesson

- Review the lesson and reflect on learning.

Extra activity

Reinforcement

- Identify the untrue fact.

Digital resources

Teacher's Digital: You can also teach this lesson using the Teacher's App on Navio.

Pupil's Digital: Encourage your pupils to use the Pupil's App on Navio to practise the activities from this lesson.

Powered By NAVIO

Activity Book

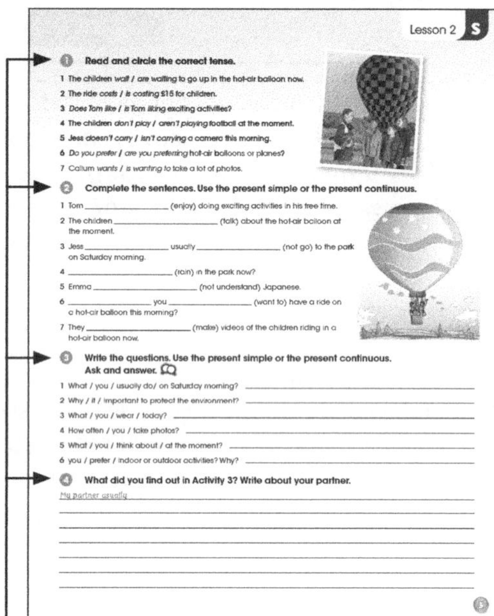

Activity Book

Activity 1

- Read and circle the correct tense.

Activity 2

- Complete the sentences. Use the present simple or the present continuous.

Activity 3

- Write the questions. Use the present simple or the present continuous. Ask and answer.

Activity 4

- What did you find out in Activity 3? Write about your partner.

Detailed Lesson Plan

Starting the lesson

Review things I see in a town or city.

- Stick the places in a town or city word cards on the board.
- Invite one pupil to come up to the board. The class help the pupil to alphabetically order the cards in 90 seconds.

Set learning outcomes.

- Say **Today we're going to remember and compare the present simple and the present continuous tenses.**

Pupil's Book Activity 1

Read and identify the person in the queue.

- Invite a pupil to read out the description.
- The pupils work on their own to identify the person in the picture.
- The pupils check their answer with a partner.
- Check the answer as a class.

Pupil's Book Activity 2

Listen and identify other people in the queue.

▶ ***CD1 Track 3 p275***

- Play the CD, pausing after the first description.
- Invite a pupil to identify the person in the picture. Encourage the pupils to explain their answer, rather than pointing, e.g. *It's the (girl) who's (at the front of the queue).*
- Repeat the procedure with the remaining descriptions.

Pupil's Book Activity 3

Read and answer these questions about Activity 1.

- Read the information as a class. Prompt the pupils to answer the questions.
- Highlight that we use the present simple to talk about routines or if something is generally true. We use the present continuous when something is happening at the time of speaking. Highlight that some verbs are only used in the present simple (state verbs).
- If you wish, review the form of the two tenses on the board.

Pupil's Book Activity 4

Look at the verbs. Which ones can only be used in the present simple? Which ones can be used in both the present simple and the present continuous?

- Copy the chart onto the board. Demonstrate how to classify the verbs by checking if it is possible to form the present continuous or not.
- The pupils copy the chart into their notebooks. In pairs, they classify the verbs. Encourage the pupils to add other verbs they know to their charts.
- Check answers as a class.

Answers: **Only present simple** dislike, understand, believe, know, want, prefer **Present simple and present continuous** climb, work, swim, eat, travel, go

Pupil's Book Activity 5

Ask and answer the questions. Then think of another question to ask your partner.

- Invite different pairs of pupils to ask and answer the questions. Highlight that the main verb is a state verb each time.
- In pairs, the pupils ask and answer the questions. They then think of another question to ask their partner.

Activity Book

Activity 1

Read and circle the correct tense.

- The pupils read and circle the correct form of the verb in each sentence.

Answers: **1** are waiting **2** costs **3** Does Tom like **4** aren't playing **5** isn't carrying **6** Do you prefer **7** wants

Activity 2

Complete the sentences. Use the present simple or the present continuous.

- The pupils write the correct form of the verb in each sentence.

Answers: **1** enjoys **2** are talking **3** doesn't, go **4** Is it raining **5** doesn't understand **6** Do, want to **7** are making

Activity 3

Write the questions. Use the present simple or the present continuous. Ask and answer.

- The pupils write the questions, using the correct form of the verb each time.
- In pairs, the pupils ask and answer the questions.

Answers: **1** What do you usually do on Saturday morning? **2** Why is it important to protect the environment? **3** What are you wearing today? **4** How often do you take photos? **5** What are you thinking about at the moment? **6** Do you prefer indoor or outdoor activities? Why?

Activity 4

What did you find out in Activity 3? Write about your partner.

- The pupils use the answers to Activity 3 to write about their partners.
- Invite different pupils to read out their sentences to the class.

Ending the lesson

Review the lesson and reflect on learning.

- Say **Today we've remembered and compared the present simple and the present continuous tenses.**
- Ask **What do you remember?** The pupils do a three-minute review in pairs. (Cooperative Learning Strategies, page 19)

Extra activity

Reinforcement

- Ask the pupils to write four sentences about their weekend routines. Three of these sentences should be true and one should be untrue.
- The pupils take turns to read out their sentences. The rest of the class should try to identify the untrue sentence.

Key Competences and Key Learning Outcomes

- Use the present passive to ask and say which languages are spoken in a country
- Complete a form
- Set learning outcomes and reflect on learning
- Review and learn the names of countries and languages
- Understand that people can make a difference in their community
- Learn about global projects and how children around the world can communicate

Key language

- *Arabic, Belgium, China, Chinese, Dutch, Ecuador, Egypt, English, French, Gaelic, German, global project, Japan, Japanese, make a difference, Mexico, online form, Scotland, Scots, Spanish, Sweden, Swedish, USA*
- *Which languages are spoken in (Scotland)? (English, Gaelic and Scots) are spoken there.*

Materials

- Pupil's Book p6; Activity Book p4; Class CD1; Teacher's App on Navio

Optional materials

- World map

At a Glance Lesson Plan

Pupil's Book

Starting the lesson

- Review names of countries in English.
- Set learning outcomes.

Activity 1

- Listen and read.

▶ *CD1 Track 4 p275*

- Answer the questions.

Activity 2

- Quickly read about the schools in the *Make a difference* project.
- How many schools are in Europe?
- Where are the other schools?

Activity 3

- Play a memory game in pairs.
- Ask and answer.

Go to the Activity Book.

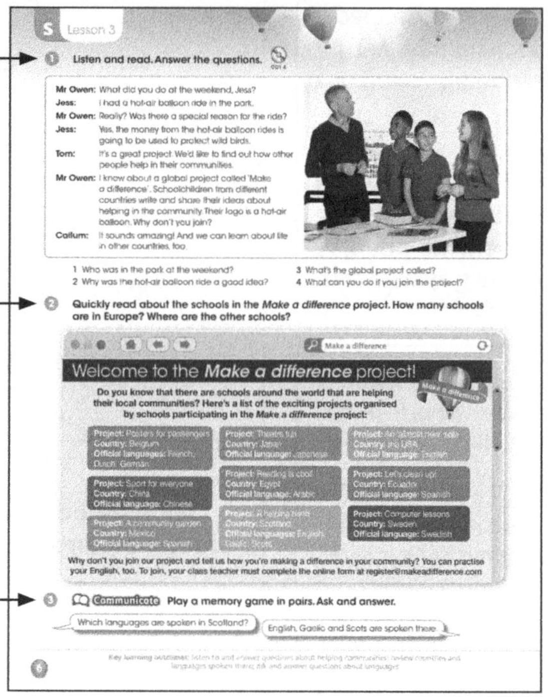

Ending the lesson

- Review the lesson and reflect on learning.

Extra activity

Extension

- Do more research on world languages.

Activity Book

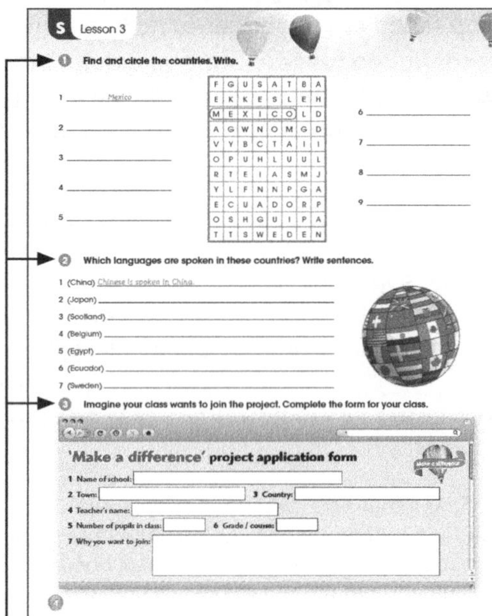

Activity Book: After you read

Activity 1

- Find and circle the countries. Write.

Activity 2

- Which languages are spoken in these countries? Write sentences.

Activity 3

- Imagine your class wants to join the project. Complete the form for your class.

Digital resources

Teacher's Digital: You can also teach this lesson using the Teacher's App on Navio.

Pupil's Digital: Encourage your pupils to use the Pupil's App on Navio to practise the activities from this lesson.

Powered By NAVIO

Starting the lesson

Review names of countries in English.

- Elicit the names of the continents. Write them as headings on the board. (*Europe, Asia, Africa, the Americas, Australia / Oceania, Antarctica.*)
- As a class, the pupils write the countries they know in each continent. Allocate a class scribe to write the words. Remind the pupils that there are no countries in Antarctica.
- If you have a world map, ask the pupils to find the different countries. They can share any information they know about the different places.

Set learning outcomes.

- Say **Today we're going to learn the names of more countries and find out which languages are spoken there.**

Pupil's Book Activity 1

Listen and read. Answer the questions.

▸ ***CD1 Track 4 p275***

- Prompt the class to describe the photo.
- Play the CD. The pupils listen and read the dialogue.
- In pairs, they read the questions and find the answers in the dialogue.

Answers: **1** Jess **2** The money is going to be used to protect wild birds. **3** Make a difference **4** You can write and share ideas about helping the community.

Pupil's Book Activity 2

Quickly read about the schools in the *Make a difference* project. How many schools are in Europe? Where are the other schools?

- Read the instructions as a class. Ask the pupils to quickly scan the text and find the answers.
- The pupils then read the text on their own.
- Check understanding. Confirm that there are three schools in Europe. The other schools are in Japan, the USA, China, Egypt, Ecuador and Mexico.
- Encourage the pupils to give their opinion on the project.

Pupil's Book Activity 3

Play a memory game in pairs. Ask and answer.

- Invite two pupils to read out the speech bubbles to demonstrate the activity.
- Quickly review the present passive form. Remind the pupils that we use the passive when we don't need to know who does the action.
- Give the class one minute to memorise the information about countries and languages.
- (Books closed.) Ask **Which language is spoken in (China)?** The pupils answer.
- The pupils play the memory game in pairs.

Activity Book

Activity 1

Find and circle the countries. Write.

- The pupils find and circle the countries in the puzzle. They write the words.

Answers: **1** Mexico **2** Ecuador **3** Sweden **4** Egypt **5** China **6** Scotland **7** Belgium **8** Japan **9** USA

Activity 2

Which languages are spoken in these countries? Write sentences.

- The pupils write sentences. They refer to the information in the Pupil's Book if necessary.

Answers: **1** Chinese is spoken in China. **2** Japanese is spoken in Japan. **3** English, Gaelic and Scots are spoken in Scotland. **4** Dutch, French and German are spoken in Belgium. **5** Arabic is spoken is Egypt. **6** Spanish is spoken in Ecuador. **7** Swedish is spoken in Sweden.

Activity 3

Imagine your class wants to join the project. Complete the form for your class.

- Read out the information as a class. Check understanding.
- In pairs, the pupils complete the form.
- Invite different pupils to read out their answers to item 7.

Ending the lesson

Review the lesson and reflect on learning.

- Say **Today we've learnt the names of other countries and found out which languages are spoken there.**
- Ask **What do you remember?** The pupils do a three-minute review in pairs. (Cooperative Learning Strategies, page 19)

Extra activity

Extension

- Connect to a children's website to discover interesting facts about countries and world languages, such as www.childrensuniversity.manchester.ac.uk/interactives/languages/words/map.

Key Competences and Key Learning Outcomes

- Learn and practise how to use question tags in the present
- Analyse and apply rules for forming question tags in the present
- Set learning outcomes and reflect on learning
- Think about the importance of protecting natural habitats
- Understand that people can make a difference in their community

Key language

- *barn owl, cat, community, countryside, dog, fox, in danger, nest, nest box, predator, species*
- *The children live in a big town, don't they? Cats aren't predators, are they?*

Materials

- Pupil's Book p7; Activity Book p5; Teacher's App on Navio

Optional materials

- Dice

At a Glance Lesson Plan

Pupil's Book

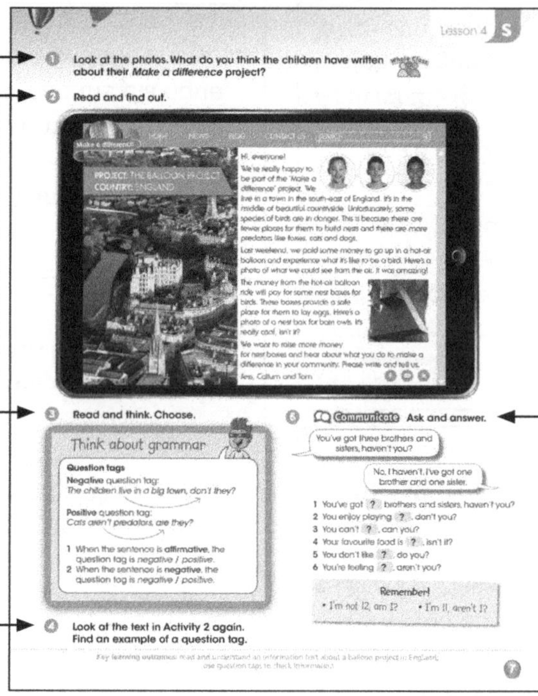

Starting the lesson
- Review countries and languages.
- Set learning outcomes.

Activity 1
- Look at the photos.
- What do you think the children have written about their *Make a difference* project?

Activity 2
- Read and find out.

Activity 3
- Read and think.
- Choose.

Activity 4
- Look at the text in Activity 2 again.
- Find an example of a question tag.

Activity 5
- Ask and answer.
- Go to the Activity Book.

Ending the lesson
- Review the lesson and reflect on learning.

Extra activity

Reinforcement
- Play a question tag game.

Activity Book

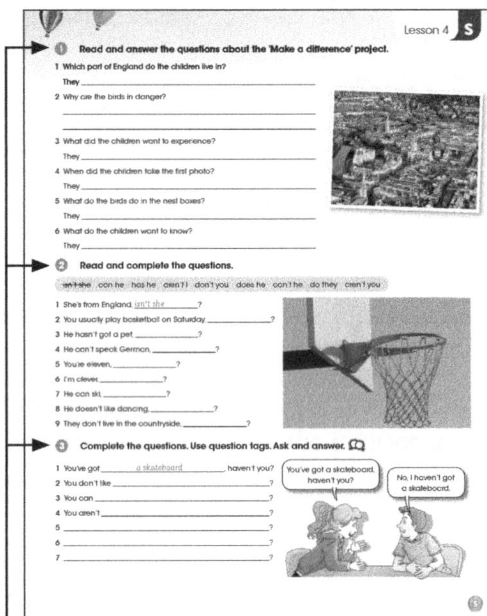

Activity Book

Activity 1
- Read and answer the questions about the 'Make a difference' project.

Activity 2
- Read and complete the questions.

Activity 3
- Complete the questions. Use question tags. Ask and answer.

Digital resources

Teacher's Digital: You can also teach this lesson using the Teacher's App on Navio.

Pupil's Digital: Encourage your pupils to use the Pupil's App on Navio to practise the activities from this lesson.

Powered By NAVIO

Starting the lesson

Review countries and languages.

- Organise the class into pairs. Challenge the pupils to remember where the schools in the *Make a difference* project are. The pupils quickly write the nine countries in their notebooks.
- Review the languages that are spoken in each country.

Set learning outcomes.

- Say **Today we're going to read a report from the *Make a difference* project and we're going to learn how to use mini-questions called question tags.**

Pupil's Book Activity 1

Look at the photos. What do you think the children have written about their *Make a difference* project?

- Explain that Tom, Jess and Callum's class has written about the *Make a difference* project.
- Describe the photos as a class. Encourage the pupils to make predictions about the content of the text.

Pupil's Book Activity 2

Read and find out.

- Read the text to find out if the pupils' predictions in Activity 1 were correct.
- Check understanding. Ask **Where do the children live? Why are some birds in danger? What are nest boxes?**

Pupil's Book Activity 3

Read and think. Choose.

- Read the information as a class.
- In pairs, the pupils discuss and complete each sentence (*1 negative, 2 positive*).
- Check answers as a class.

Pupil's Book Activity 4

Look at the text in Activity 2 again. Find an example of a question tag.

- In pairs, the pupils find an example of a question tag in the text.

Pupil's Book Activity 5

Ask and answer.

- Invite two pupils to read out the speech bubbles.
- Elicit possible ways of completing the different questions. Prompt different pupils to give their answers.
- In pairs, the pupils ask and answer the questions.

Activity Book

Activity 1

Read and answer the questions about the 'Make a difference' project.

- Read out the first question. Invite a pupil to answer it.
- The pupils read and answer the remaining questions.

Answers: **1** live in the south east of England. **2** Because foxes, cats and dogs hunt the birds and there are fewer places for them to build nests. **3** wanted to experience what it's like to be a bird. **4** took the first photo when they were in the air. **5** lay eggs. **6** want to know what other children do to make a difference in their communities.

Activity 2

Read and complete the questions.

- The pupils write the question tags.
- Check answers as a class.

Answers: **1** isn't she **2** don't you **3** has he **4** can he **5** aren't you **6** aren't I **7** can't he **8** does he **9** do they

Activity 3

Complete the questions. Use question tags. Ask and answer.

- Invite a pupil to read out the first sentence. Elicit other ways of completing it. Repeat the procedure with the other sentences.
- The pupils write the sentences.
- The pupils then work in pairs to ask and answer the questions.

Ending the lesson

Review the lesson and reflect on learning.

- Say **Today we've read a report from the *Make a difference* project and we've learnt how to use question tags.**
- Ask **What do you remember?** The pupils do a three-minute review in pairs. (Cooperative Learning Strategies, page 19)

Extra activity

Reinforcement

- Write the following list on the board: *1 aren't I? 2 haven't you? 3 doesn't he? 4 can she? 5 do you? 6 is she?*
- Demonstrate how to play the Question tag game. Throw the dice and look at the corresponding question tag on the board. Then invent a statement which matches the tag, e.g. **2 You've got a cat, haven't you?**
- Repeat the procedure several times.
- Organise the class into groups of three. Give each group a dice. The pupils take turns to roll the dice and invent a matching statement. The rest of the group decides if the statement is correct.
- Check answers as a class.

Date: ____________________ **Unit:** __________

1 What did my pupils learn in this unit?

2 How did my pupils work? (✓)

individually ☐ in pairs ☐ in small groups ☐

in large groups ☐ as a class ☐

3 Which key competences did my pupils develop? Give a score from 1 to 5 (5 being the highest).

- Competence in linguistic communication ☐
- Competence in mathematics, science and technology ☐
- Digital competence ☐
- Learning to learn ☐
- Social and civic competences ☐
- Sense of initiative and entrepreneurship ☐
- Cultural awareness and expression ☐

4 Which lessons / activities were the most successful and why?

5 Which lessons / activities did my pupils find the most difficult and why?

6 What did I try in the classroom for the first time? How did it go?

7 Which resources did I find most useful? (including webpages)

8 What could I do differently next time I teach this unit?

Unit 1 Travel trouble

Unit overview

Key Competences and Key Learning Outcomes

- Name places, objects and verbs related to air travel (Lesson 1)
- Use the past continuous and the past simple with 'while' (Lesson 2)
- Learn and practise verbs that use the infinitive or gerund (Lesson 4)
- Learn words related to travel and tourism (Lesson 5)
- Learn verbs of the senses (Lesson 7)
- Review tenses for talking about future plans (Lesson 8)
- Watch and understand a video (Video and 21st Century Skills)

- Learn about solar energy and flight (Lesson 3)

- Use the Pupil's App on Navio
- Investigate Belgium

- Read for specific information (Lesson 1)
- Order events chronologically (Lesson 6)
- Review learning and reflect on progress in the unit (Lesson 8)
- Practise activity types found in the Cambridge Exams: B1 Preliminary for Schools

- Talk about how to make travellers in an airport feel happier (Lesson 1)
- Understand the importance of saving the planet's energy (Lesson 3)
- Learn and practise how to make suggestions in a conversation (Lesson 8)

- Work in pairs and small groups to practise and reinforce learning (All lessons)
- Do a communication task (Lesson 5)
- Think about ways to present balanced views (Video and 21st Century Skills)

- Read an article (Lesson 3)
- Learn about Belgium (Lesson 3)
- Read and write an eyewitness account (Lessons 6 and 7)
- Sing a song (Lesson 8)

Vocabulary

Core vocabulary
arrivals, boarding pass, check-in desk, departures, flight attendant, hand luggage, land, passenger, queue, runway, take off, trolley; backpacker, guard, guest, lift, platform, reception, receptionist, ticket office, tourist information centre

Extension vocabulary (optional)
announcement, board a plane, customs, fuel, gate, miss a flight, ticket barrier, lost property office, waiting room, cash machine

Other vocabulary
explorer, first-class, fuel, international flight, lifeboat, nationality, porthole, steward, solar-powered plane; energy, exhibition, iceberg, solar panels; experience, fact, fictional, opinion, scene, senses; huge, nervous; maybe, perhaps; hold hands, imagine, promise, sink; cable cars, trams, rickshaws, monorail

Recycled vocabulary
adventure, airport, bus journey, crash, hot-air balloon, lifejacket, orchestra, passport, ship, suitcase; battery, football team, poster, sign, smoke, stairs; agree, decide, feel, like, look, show, smell, sound, stop, suggest, taste, travel, try, walk around

Structures

Core structures
While I was (taking photos), he (agreed to sign a football). I (saw a hot-air balloon) while I was (walking to school). I enjoyed (reading about Bertrand Piccard). (Piccard) promised to (make his plane faster next time).

Other structures
Can you remember what was happening at the station? The hot-air balloon looked like a floating ball. The ship stopped moving. I'm not sure. I suppose that they like to have new experiences.

Recycled structures
What do you do to help save the planet's energy? Which poster idea would you choose? I'd choose the one about (different nationalities). You can't catch a bus here.

Pronunciation

Past simple tense endings: /d/, /ɪd/, /t/

Literacy

Text type: an eyewitness account (historical event; writing preparation)
Reading skills: predicting from pictures and context
Writing skills: using verbs of the senses

Culture ... around the world

A solar-powered plane that landed in Belgium

21st Century Skills

Ways of thinking: Presenting balanced opinions and views

Thinking skills

Categorising (Lesson 1); Analysing and applying rules and patterns (Lessons 2 and 4); Discussing the importance of alternative energy (Lesson 3); Remembering and describing (Lesson 5); Seeing another person's point of view (Lesson 6); Planning, checking and correcting (Lesson 7); Evaluating (Lesson 8)

Cooperative learning

Working together; Reflecting and setting goals; Helping and encouraging (Lessons 1–8); Collaborative speaking (Lesson 5); Collaborative writing (Lesson 7); Peer evaluation and feedback (Lesson 7); Expressing and respecting opinions (Lessons 1, 3, 6 and 8)

Values

The importance of saving the planet's energy

Cross-curricular links

Links to Science
Using a compass
Suggested Arts and Crafts concepts
Proportion in portraits

Key Competences and Key Learning Outcomes

- Name places, objects and verbs related to air travel
- Review and practise using 'would' to talk about hypothetical situations
- Read a message for specific information
- Talk about how to make travellers in airports feel happier

Key language

- *arrivals, boarding pass, check-in desk, departures, flight attendant, hand luggage, land, passenger, queue, runway, take off, trolley; adventure, airport, exhibition, fact, hold hands, nationality, passport, poster, show, suitcase, travel*
- Extension: *announcement, board a plane, customs, fuel, gate, miss a flight*
- *Which poster idea would you choose? I'd choose the one about (different nationalities).*

Materials

- Pupil's Book pp8–9; Activity Book p6; Class CD1; Teacher's App on Navio
- Air travel flashcards

Optional materials

- Teacher's Resource Bank: Trinity Exams Practice cards (from the Starter Unit)

At a Glance Lesson Plan

Starting the lesson

- Use the Trinity Exams Practice cards (optional).
- Review types of transport.
- Set learning outcomes.

Activity 1

- Look at the photos Julie has sent.
- Answer the questions.

Vocabulary presentation

- Present the new vocabulary using the air travel flashcards.

Activity 2

- Look and match with photos 1–12.
- Listen, check and repeat.

▶ *CD1 Track 5 p275*

Activity 3

- Listen and do the vocabulary quiz.

▶ *CD1 Track 6 p275*

Activity 4

- Think about travelling. Copy the chart.
- Complete it with things you put in your hand luggage and things you put in your suitcase.

Pupil's Book

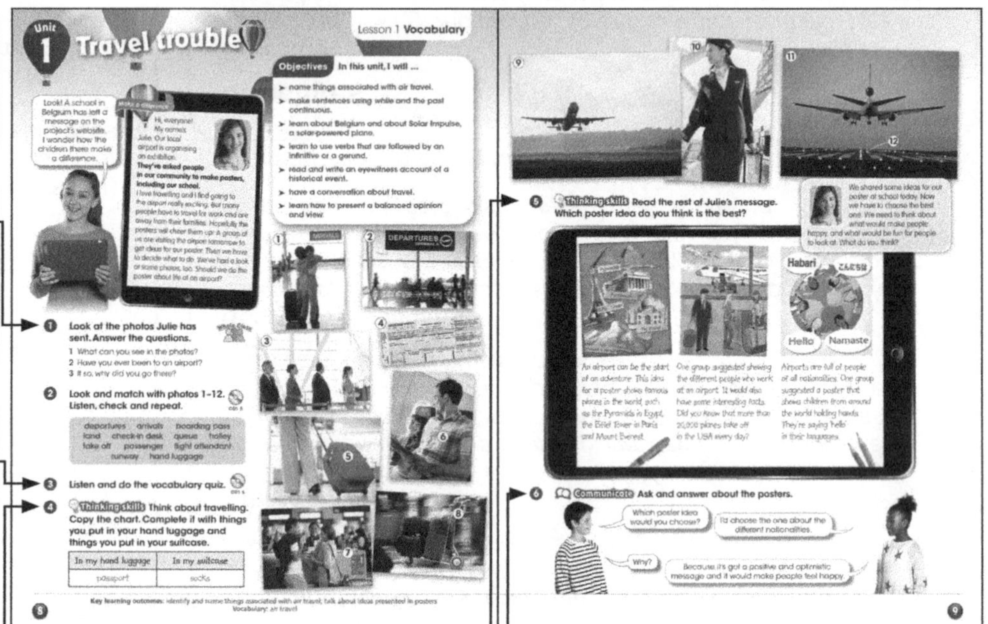

Activity 5

- Read the rest of Julie's message.
- Which poster idea do you think is the best?

Activity 6

- Ask and answer about the posters.
- Go to the Activity Book.

Ending the lesson

- Review the lesson and reflect on learning.

Extra activities

Extension

- Find out about Belgium.

Vocabulary extension

- Present six additional vocabulary items.

Activity Book

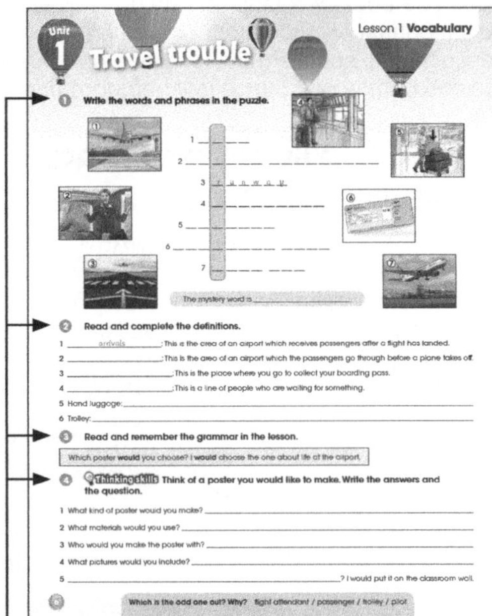

Activity Book

Activity 1

- Write the words and phrases in the puzzle.

Activity 2

- Read and complete the definitions.

Activity 3

- Read and remember the grammar in the lesson.

Activity 4

- Think of a poster you would like to make. Write the answers and the question.

Odd one out activity

Digital resources

Teacher's Digital: You can also teach this lesson using the Teacher's App on Navio.

Pupil's Digital: Encourage your pupils to use the Pupil's App on Navio to practise the activities from this lesson.

Powered By NAVIO

Starting the lesson

Use the Trinity Exams Practice cards (optional).
- The pupils practise asking and answering questions.

Review types of transport.
- In groups, the pupils note as many types of transport as they can. Check ideas as a class.

Set learning outcomes
- Say **Today we're going to learn words that are connected to one kind of transport.**

Pupil's Book Activity 1

Look at the photos Julie has sent. Answer the questions.
- Invite a pupil to read out the speech bubble to find out which school has sent a message. Ask **Do you know where Belgium is?**
- Invite a pupil to read out the message from Julie. Check understanding.
- Work as a class to answer the questions.

Vocabulary presentation
- Stick the air travel flashcards on the board. Point to the first one and elicit the word. For objects, ask **When do you use (a boarding pass)?** For places, ask **What can you find (at departures)?** For verbs, say **This plane is (taking off). Is it going up or down?** Repeat with the other flashcards.

Pupil's Book Activity 2

Look and match with photos 1–12. Listen, check and repeat.

▶ *CD1 Track 5 p275*
- Ask the pupils to look at photo number 1. Ask **What's this?** In pairs, the pupils match 2–12 with the words.
- Play the CD. The pupils listen and check. Play the CD again, pausing after each word for the pupils to repeat. You can find the answers for this activity in the audioscript on page 275.

Pupil's Book Activity 3

Listen and do the vocabulary quiz.

▶ *CD1 Track 6 p275*
- Play the CD. Listen to the first definition, pausing at the beep to allow the pupils to name the item. Play the CD to listen to the answer.
- Repeat the procedure with the other definitions. You can find the answers for this activity in the audioscript on page 275.

Pupil's Book Activity 4

Think about travelling. Copy the chart. Complete it with things you put in your hand luggage and things you put in your suitcase.
- Explain that the pupils should think of things they would take on a plane.
- The pupils work in pairs to complete each column.
- Check answers as a class.

Pupil's Book Activity 5

Read the rest of Julie's message. Which poster idea do you think is the best?
- Invite a pupil to read out the message. The pupils read the information and choose the best poster.
- The pupils share their ideas with the class, but they don't give their reasons at this stage.

Pupil's Book Activity 6

Ask and answer about the posters.
- Invite two pupils to read out the speech bubbles.
- The pupils talk about their poster choices, giving reasons for their choices.

Activity Book

Activity 1

Write the words and phrases in the puzzle.
- The pupils write the words and find the mystery word.

Answers: **1** land **2** flight attendant **3** runway **4** passenger **5** trolley **6** boarding pass **7** take off **Mystery word:** airport

Activity 2

Read and complete the definitions.
- The pupils complete the definitions.

Answers: **1** arrivals **2** departures **3** check-in desk **4** queue **5 & 6** Pupils' own answers

Activity 3

Read and remember the grammar in the lesson.
- Invite a pupil to read out the information. Explain that they are not really choosing a poster, so the situation is imaginary. This is why they use *would*.

Activity 4

Think of a poster you would like to make. Write the answers and the question.
- Read out the questions as a class. The pupils complete the answers and the missing question.
- Invite a pupil to read out the sentences. Then ask another pupil to do the same.

Odd one out activity

Which is the odd one out? Why?
- The pupils complete the odd one out activity

Answers: trolley (The others are people.)

Ending the lesson

Review the lesson and reflect on learning.
- Say **Today we've learnt words connected to air travel**.
- Ask **What do you remember?** The pupils do a three-minute review in pairs. (Cooperative Learning Strategies, page 19)

Extra activities

Extension
- The pupils use the Internet to find information about Belgium.

Vocabulary extension
- Present six additional air travel words: *announcement, board a plane, customs, fuel, gate, miss a flight*.
- Use the Vocabulary Booster on NAVIO to practise these new words.

Key Competences and Key Learning Outcomes

- Listen to and read a dialogue
- Use the past continuous and past simple with 'while' to talk about an action interrupting a longer action in the past

LEARN
- Identify examples of the past continuous and past simple in the dialogue

Key language

- *airport, football team, solar-powered plane*
- *While I was (taking photos), he (agreed to sign a football). I (saw a hot-air balloon) while I was (walking to school).*

Materials

- Pupil's Book p10; Activity Book p7; Class CD1; Teacher's App on Navio
- Teacher's Resource Bank: Air travel word cards

Optional materials

- Teacher's Resource Bank: Trinity Exams Practice cards (selected from the Starter Unit)

At a Glance Lesson Plan

Pupil's Book

Starting the lesson

- Use the Trinity Exams Practice cards (optional).
- Review air travel vocabulary.
- Set learning outcomes.

Activity 1

- Describe the photo.
- Why do you think Julie talks about this team?
- Read and listen to find out.

▶ *CD1 Track 7 p275*

Activity 2

- Read the dialogue again.
- Which sentence is true?

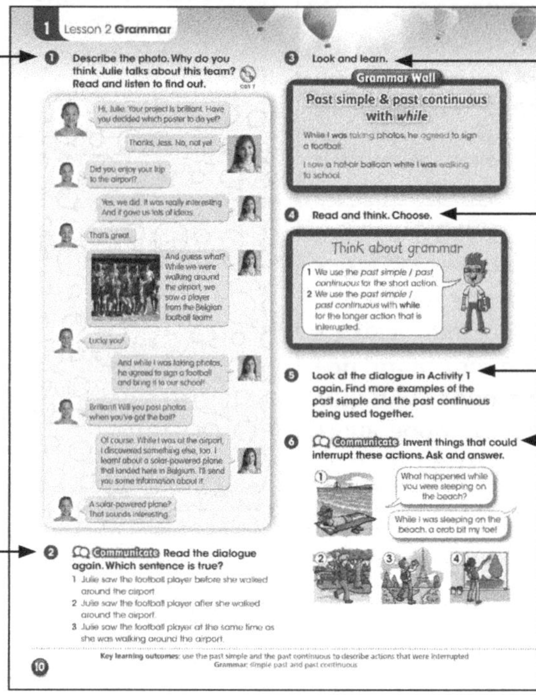

Activity 3

- Look and learn – Grammar wall

Activity 4

- Read and think.
- Choose.

Activity 5

- Look at the dialogue in Activity 1 again.
- Find more examples of the past simple and the past continuous being used together.

Activity 6

- Invent things that could interrupt these actions.
- Ask and answer.

Go to the Activity Book.

Ending the lesson

- Review the lesson and reflect on learning.

Extra activity

Reinforcement

- Make nonsense sentences with *while*.

Activity Book

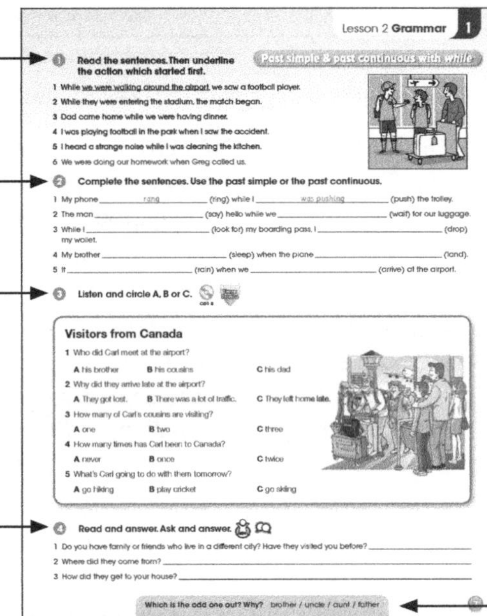

Activity Book

Activity 1

- Read the sentences. Then underline the action which started first.

Activity 2

- Complete the sentences. Use the past simple or the past continuous.

Activity 3

- Listen and circle A, B or C.

▶ *CD1 Track 8 p276*

Activity 4

- Read and answer. Ask and answer.

Odd one out activity

Digital resources

Teacher's Digital: You can also teach this lesson using the Teacher's App on Navio.

Pupil's Digital: Encourage your pupils to use the Pupil's App on Navio to practise the activities from this lesson.

Powered By NAVIO

Starting the lesson

Use the Trinity Exams Practice cards (optional).
- The pupils practise asking and answering questions.

Review air travel vocabulary.
- Organise the pupils into groups of four. Give each group an air travel word card. The pupils write a definition for that word.
- Each group reads out the definitions. The class guesses the words.

Set learning outcomes.
- Say **Today we're going to learn how to talk about actions in the past.**

Pupil's Book Activity 1

Describe the photo. Why do you think Julie talks about this team? Read and listen to find out.

▶ *CD1 Track 7 p275*
- Prompt the pupils to describe what they can see in the photo. Ask **Do you know what the sport is? Which team is it? Why do you think Julie talks about them?**
- Play the CD. The pupils listen and read the dialogue. Confirm that it is the Belgium football team and that Julie sees a player at the airport.

Pupil's Book Activity 2

Read the dialogue again. Which sentence is true?
- In pairs, the pupils read the dialogue again and identify the true sentence. (*Sentence 3.*)

Pupil's Book Activity 3

Look and learn – Grammar wall
- Read the information on the Grammar wall as a class.
- Use questions to encourage the pupils to think about form and identify patterns. Ask **Which action started first: taking photos or agreeing to sign a ball? Which tense is the past continuous? Which tense is the past simple?**

Pupil's Book Activity 4

Read and think. Choose.
- Focus the pupils' attention on the Think about grammar box. Read out the sentences as a class. The pupils discuss and complete the sentences in pairs.
- Check answers as a class (*1 past simple 2 past continuous*).

Pupil's Book Activity 5

Look at the dialogue in Activity 1 again. Find more examples of the past simple and the past continuous being used together.
- In pairs, the pupils find the example in the dialogue.

Pupil's Book Activity 6

Invent things that could interrupt these actions. Ask and answer.
- Ask the pupils to describe picture 1. Then invite two pupils to read out the speech bubbles.
- In pairs, the pupils look at the pictures and invent things that could interrupt the actions. They make sentences.

Activity Book

Activity 1

Read the sentences. Then underline the action which started first.
- The pupils read each sentence and then look at the two actions. They underline the one that started first.
- In pairs, the pupils complete the activity.

Answers: **1** We were walking around the airport. **2** They were entering the stadium. **3** We were having dinner. **4** I was playing football. **5** I was cleaning the kitchen. **6** We were doing our homework.

Activity 2

Complete the sentences. Use the past simple or the past continuous.
- The pupils complete the sentences with past simple or past continuous forms of the verbs in brackets.

Answers: **1** rang, was pushing **2** said, were waiting **3** was looking for, dropped **4** was sleeping, landed **5** was raining, arrived

Activity 3

Listen and circle A, B or C.

▶ *CD1 Track 8 p276*
- Ask the class to quickly read the questions. Then play the CD. The pupils listen.
- Play the CD again. The pupils choose the correct letter for each question.

Answers: **1** B **2** A **3** B **4** A **5** B

Activity 4

Read and answer. Ask and answer.
- The pupils read and answer the questions about people in their family.
- In pairs, they ask and answer the questions.

Odd one out activity

Which is the odd one out? Why?
- The pupils complete the odd one out activity.

Answers: aunt (The others are male.)

Ending the lesson

Review the lesson and reflect on learning.
- Say **Today we've learnt how to talk about one action interrupting another action in the past using 'while'.** Elicit one or two examples from the pupils.
- Ask **What do you remember?** The pupils do a three-minute review in pairs. (Cooperative Learning Strategies, page 19)

Extra activities

Reinforcement
- Organise the class into two groups. Write *While I _(A)_, _(B)_* on the board. Pairs in Group A think of actions that are continuous. Pairs in Group B think of actions that could interrupt. Give an example, e.g. **While I was reading a comic, a lion jumped through the window.**
- Ask a pupil from Group A and a pupil from Group B to read out their sentence parts. See if they make sense. Repeat with other pairs. Then as a class choose the best sentence.

Key Competences and Key Learning Outcomes

- Read an article with confidence and fluency
- Learn about solar energy and flight
- Use the Internet to investigate Belgium
- Think about the importance of saving the planet's energy
- Learn about Belgium

Key language

- *battery, energy, explorer, fuel, imagine, international flight, nervous, promise, solar panels*
- *What do you do to help save the planet's energy?*

Materials

- Pupil's Book p11; Activity Book p8: Class CD1; Teacher's App on Navio

Optional materials

- Teacher's Resource Bank: Trinity Exams Practice cards (selected from the Starter Unit)

At a Glance Lesson Plan

Pupil's Book

Starting the lesson

- Use the Trinity Exams Practice cards (optional).
- Review words related to air travel.
- Set learning outcomes.

Activity 1: Before you read

- Read and discuss.

Activity 2

- Listen and read.

▶ *CD1 Track 9 p276*

Go to the Activity Book.

***Give Me Five!* values**

- Read and discuss.

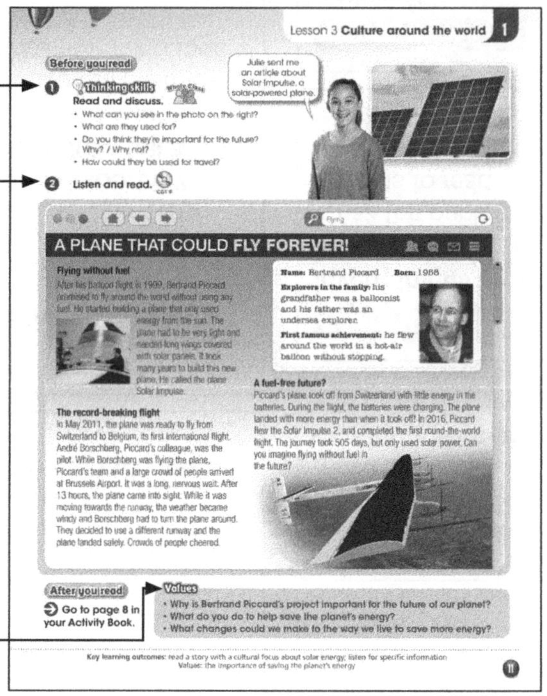

Ending the lesson

- Review the lesson and reflect on learning.

Extra activity

Extension

- Research other objects powered by solar panels.

Activity Book

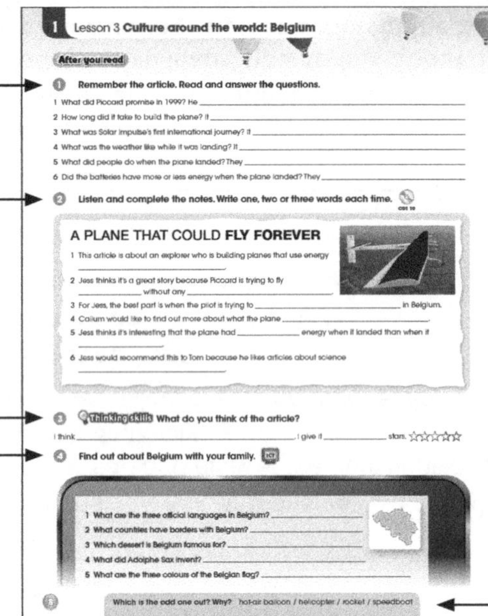

Activity Book: After you read

Activity 1

- Remember the article. Read and answer the questions.

Activity 2

- Listen and complete the notes. Write one, two or three words each time.

▶ *CD1 Track 10 p276*

Activity 3

- What do you think of the article?

Activity 4

- Find out about Belgium with your family.

Odd one out activity

Digital resources

Teacher's Digital: You can also teach this lesson using the Teacher's App on Navio.

Pupil's Digital: Encourage your pupils to use the Pupil's App on Navio to practise the activities from this lesson.

Powered By NAVIO

Starting the lesson

Use the Trinity Exams Practice cards (optional).

- The pupils practise asking and answering questions.

Review words related to air travel.

- Ask the pupils to think about what they might do if they were going to go on a plane. Ask different pupils to give a sentence, in the order that they might happen. Give the first sentence: **I entered the airport with my suitcase.** Encourage the pupils to use the vocabulary they have learnt.

Set learning outcomes.

- Say **Today we're going to read an article about solar energy and planes.**

Pupil's Book Activity 1: Before you read

Read and discuss.

- Read the questions as a class. Encourage the pupils to share information about where they have seen solar panels. Ask them to give their opinions on the importance of solar panels.

Pupil's Book Activity 2

Listen and read.

▶ ***CD1 Track 9 p276***

- Play the CD. The pupils follow in their books.
- Ask questions to check understanding.

Suggested comprehension questions:

- Fact box: **What kind of family does Bertrand Piccard come from?** (*A family of explorers.*)
- Paragraph 1: **What was the plane like?** (*Very light with long wings covered with solar panels.*) **What was the plane called?** (*Solar Impulse.*)
- Paragraph 2: **Between which two countries was its first international flight?** (*Switzerland and Belgium.*) **Who was waiting at Brussels Airport?** (*Piccard's team and a large crowd of people.*) **How long was the journey?** (*13 hours.*) **What was the weather like in Belgium?** (*Windy.*)
- Paragraph 4: **What happened to the batteries during the flight?** (*They were charging.*)

Activity Book: After you read

Activity 1

Remember the article. Read and answer the questions.

- Read out the first question. Invite a pupil to answer it.
- The pupils read and answer the remaining questions.

Answers: **1** promised to fly around the world without using any fuel. **2** took **12** years. **3** was from Switzerland to Belgium. **4** was windy. **5** cheered. **6** had more energy.

Activity 2

Listen and complete the notes. Write one, two or three words each time.

▶ ***CD1 Track 10 p276***

- Read out the notes as a class. Ask the pupils to guess the missing words.
- Play the CD without pausing. The pupils listen and complete as much information as possible.
- Play the CD again, pausing after each piece of key information to check the answer.

Answers: **1** from the sun **2** planes, fuel **3** land **4** looks like **5** more, took off **6** and technology

Activity 3

What do you think of the article?

- The pupils write their opinion and give a rating.
- Invite different pupils to share their opinions.

Activity 4

Find out about Belgium with your family. ICT

- Read out the questions about Belgium. Ask **Where can you find out this information?** (*Internet, library, asking friends and family.*) The pupils complete the activity at home.
- If you prefer to do this activity in the class, connect to a children's website which has information about Belgium, such as www.sciencekids.co.nz/sciencefacts/countries/belgium.html.
- Read out the questions. As a class, the pupils find and write the answers.

Answers: **1** French, Dutch, German **2** Luxemburg, Netherlands, France, Germany **3** waffles **4** the saxophone **5** red, yellow, black

Odd one out activity

Which is the odd one out? Why?

- The pupils complete the odd one out activity.

Answers: speedboat (It doesn't travel in the air.)

***Give Me Five!* values**

Read and discuss.

- Read out the questions and discuss them as a class.
- Explain that the planet's resources, like oil and gas, will not last forever. Planes use a lot of fuel so it is important to look for other ways to power them. Encourage the pupils to think about other ways of saving energy.

Ending the lesson

Review the lesson and reflect on learning.

- Say **Today we've read some information about solar energy and using it to fly.**
- Ask **What do you remember?** The pupils do a three-minute review in pairs. (Cooperative Learning Strategies, page 19)

Extra activity

Extension

- Ask **Do you know of other things that are solar-powered?** (*Calculators, radio, car, outdoor lamps, etc.*)
- In groups, the pupils research something that is solar-powered. They present the information to the class.

Key Competences and Key Learning Outcomes

- Act out a short dialogue in pairs
- Learn and practise verbs that use the infinitive or a gerund
- Identify and practise the sounds of the *-ed* ending for past simple verbs

Key language

- *agree, decide, imagine, like, stop, suggest, try*
- *I enjoyed (reading about Bertrand Piccard). (Piccard) promised to (make his plane faster next time).*

Materials

- Pupil's Book p12; Activity Book p9, Class CD1; Teacher's App on Navio

Optional materials

- Teacher's Resource Bank: Trinity Exams Practice cards (selected from the Starter Unit)

At a Glance Lesson Plan

Pupil's Book

Starting the lesson

- Use the Trinity Exams Practice cards (optional).
- Review the article from Lesson 3.
- Set learning outcomes.

Activity 1

- Listen and read.
- ▶ *CD1 Track 11 p276*
- Act out.

Activity 2

- Look and learn – Grammar wall

Activity 3

- Read and think.
- Choose.

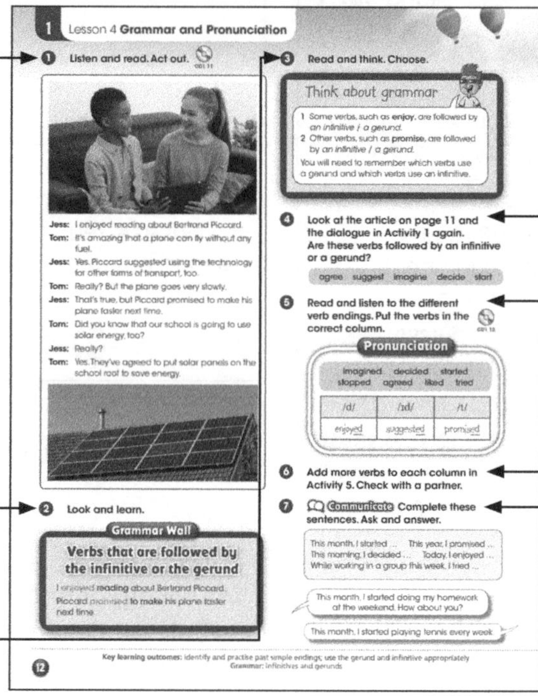

Activity 4

- Look at the article on page 11 and the dialogue in Activity 1 again.
- Are these verbs followed by an infinitive or a gerund?

Activity 5

- Read and listen to the different verb endings.
- ▶ *CD1 Track 12 p276*
- Put the verbs in the correct column.

Activity 6

- Add more verbs to each column in Activity 5.
- Check with a partner.

Activity 7

- Complete these sentences.
- Ask and answer.
- Go to the Activity Book.

Ending the lesson

- Review the lesson and reflect on learning.

Extra activities

Reinforcement

- Play noughts and crosses with verbs.

Activity Book

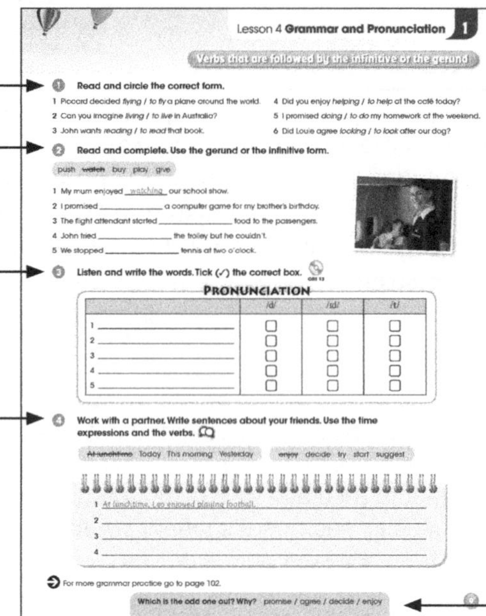

Activity Book

Activity 1

- Read and circle the correct form.

Activity 2

- Read and complete. Use the gerund or the infinitive form.

Activity 3

- Listen and write the words. Tick (✓) the correct box.

▶ *CD1 Track 13 p276*

Activity 4

- Work with a partner. Write sentences about your friends. Use the time expressions and the verbs.

Odd one out activity

Digital resources

Teacher's Digital: You can also teach this lesson using the Teacher's App on Navio.

Pupil's Digital: Encourage your pupils to use the Pupil's App on Navio to practise the activities from this lesson.

Powered By NAVIO

Starting the lesson

Use the Trinity Exams Practice cards (optional).

- The pupils practise asking and answering questions.

Review the article from Lesson 3.

- Ask yes/no questions about the article from Lesson 3.

Set learning outcomes.

- Say **Today we're going to learn about verbs that are followed by another verb.**

Pupil's Book Activity 1

Listen and read. Act out.

▶ *CD1 Track 11 p276*

- The pupils look at the photos. Ask **What are Tom and Jess doing in the first photo?**
- Play the CD. The pupils listen and read the dialogue. Check understanding.
- Play the CD again, pausing after each sentence for the pupils to repeat.
- The pupils practise the dialogue in pairs.

Pupil's Book Activity 2

Look and learn – Grammar wall

- Read the information on the Grammar wall as a class.
- Encourage the pupils to think about the difference between the verbs that follow 'enjoyed' and 'promised'. Ask **What kind of verb follows enjoyed / promised?** (*A gerund / an infinitive.*)

Pupil's Book Activity 3

Read and think. Choose.

- Focus the pupils' attention on the Think about grammar box. The pupils discuss and complete the sentences in pairs.
- Check answers as a class (*1 a gerund 2 an infinitive*).

Pupil's Book Activity 4

Look at the article on page 11 and the dialogue in Activity 1 again. Are these verbs followed by an infinitive or a gerund?

- In pairs, the pupils find examples of the verbs and decide if they are followed by an infinitive or a gerund.

Pupil's Book Activity 5

Read and listen to the different verb endings. Put the verbs in the correct column.

▶ *CD1 Track 12 p276*

- Play the CD. Elicit the three different sounds. Ask the pupils to put the verbs in the correct column.

Answers: /d/ enjoyed, imagined, agreed, tried
/ɪd/ suggested, decided, started
/t/ promised, stopped, liked

Pupil's Book Activity 6

Add more verbs to each column in Activity 5. Check with a partner.

- Ask the pupils to add more verbs to each column. They check with a partner. Then ask different pupils to write the verbs on the board.

Pupil's Book Activity 7

Complete these sentences. Ask and answer.

- Invite two pupils to read the speech bubbles.
- The pupils work on their own to complete the prompts. In pairs, they ask and answer about their sentences.

Activity Book

Activity 1

Read and circle the correct form.

- The pupils work on their own or in pairs to complete each sentence.

Answers: **1** to fly **2** living **3** to read **4** helping **5** to do **6** to look

Activity 2

Read and complete. Use the gerund or the infinitive form.

- The pupils complete the sentences.

Answers: **1** watching **2** to buy **3** giving **4** to push **5** playing

Activity 3

Listen and write the words. Tick (✓) the correct box.

▶ *CD1 Track 13 p276*

- Play the CD. The pupils listen and write the words.
- Play the CD again. The pupils tick the correct boxes.

Answers: **1** liked /t/ **2** stopped /t/ **3** enjoyed /d/ **4** suggested /ɪd/ **5** promised /t/

Activity 4

Work with a partner. Write sentences about your friends. Use the time expressions and the verbs.

- In pairs, the pupils make true sentences.

Odd one out activity

Which is the odd one out? Why?

- The pupils complete the odd one out activity.

Answers: enjoy (It's followed by a gerund.)

Ending the lesson

Review the lesson and reflect on learning.

- Say **Today we've talked about verbs followed by gerunds and verbs followed by infinitives.**
- Ask **What do you remember?** The pupils do a three-minute review in pairs. (Cooperative Learning Strategies, page 19)

Extra activity

Reinforcement

- Draw a noughts and crosses grid on the board. Write a verb in each square.
- Divide the class into two teams. Team A chooses a square and makes a sentence with the verb and a gerund or an infinitive. If it is correct, they win the square. Repeat with Team B. The team with three squares in a row wins.

Vocabulary Extension

- Present six additional words related to travel: *ticket barrier, trolley, lost property office, waiting room, cash machine*
- Use the Vocabulary Booster on NAVIO to practise these new words.

Key Competences and Key Learning Outcomes

- Learn words related to travel and tourism
- Practise activity types found in the Cambridge Exams: B1 Preliminary for Schools
- Learn how prepositions can be used to change the meaning of verbs
- Listen for gist and specific information
- Do a communication task

Key language

- *backpacker, guard, guest, lift, platform, reception, receptionist, ticket office, tourist information centre*
- Extension: *ticket barrier, lost property office, waiting room, cash machine*
- *Can you remember what was happening at the station?*

Materials

- Pupil's Book p13; Activity Book p10; Class CD1; Teacher's App on Navio

Optional materials

- Teacher's Resource Bank: Trinity Exams Practice cards (selected from the Starter Unit)

At a Glance Lesson Plan

Pupil's Book

Starting the lesson

- Use the Trinity Exams Practice cards (optional).
- Review verbs followed by a gerund or an infinitive.
- Set learning outcomes.

Activity 1

- Look and match.
- Listen, check and repeat.
- ▶ *CD1 Track 14 p277*

Activity 2

- Listen and say *A, B or C*.
- ▶ *CD1 Track 15 p277*

Activity 3

- Listen again.
- ▶ *CD1 Track 15 p277*
- Which of these verbs can you hear in the past continuous?

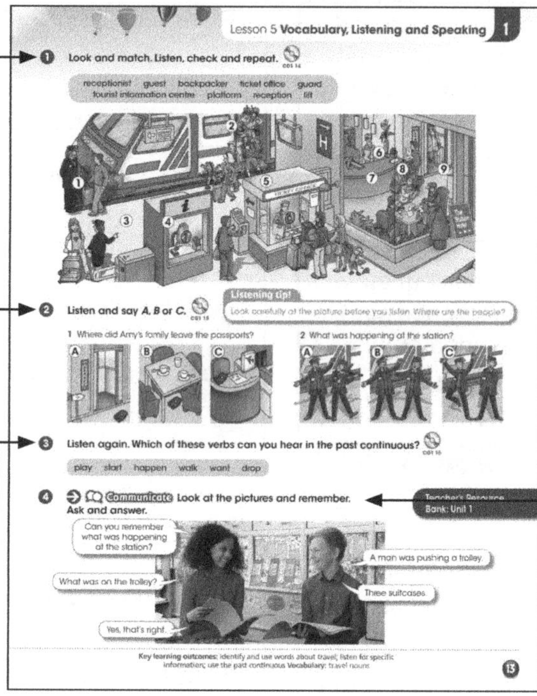

Activity 4

- Look at the pictures and remember.
- Ask and answer. (Teacher's Resource Bank: Unit 1).

Ending the lesson

- Review the lesson and reflect on learning.

Extra activities

Reinforcement

- Play a description game.

Vocabulary extension

- Present four additional vocabulary items.

Digital resources

Teacher's Digital: You can also teach this lesson using the Teacher's App on Navio.

Pupil's Digital: Encourage your pupils to use the Pupil's App on Navio to practise the activities from this lesson.

Powered By NAVIO

Activity Book

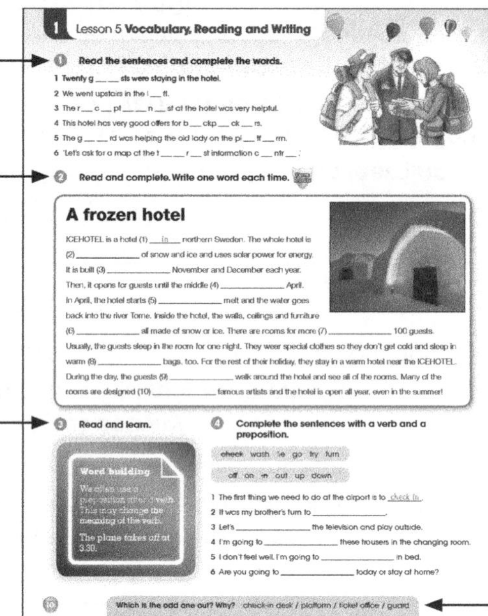

Activity Book

Activity 1

- Read the sentences and complete the words.

Activity 2

- Read and complete. Write one word each time.

Activity 3

- Read and learn.

Activity 4

- Complete the sentences with a verb and a preposition.

Odd one out activity

Detailed Lesson Plan

Starting the lesson

Use the Trinity Exams Practice cards (optional).

- The pupils practise asking and answering questions.

Review verbs followed by a gerund or an infinitive.

- Ask questions and invite the pupils to answer you in complete sentences. Ask **What did you decide to do this morning? What do you enjoy doing at the weekend? Have you promised to do anything recently? Have you agreed to do anything this weekend?**

Set learning outcomes.

- Say **Today we're going to learn some more travel words and we're going to do a communication task.**

Pupil's Book Activity 1

Look and match. Listen, check and repeat.

▶ ***CD1 Track 14 p277***

- In pairs, ask the pupils to match the words they know with the numbers in the picture.
- Play the CD. The pupils listen and check.
- Play the CD again, pausing after each word or phrase for the pupils to repeat. You can find the answers for this activity in the audioscript on page 277.

Pupil's Book Activity 2

Listen and say *A, B* or *C*.

▶ ***CD1 Track 15 p277***

- Invite a pupil to describe the first three pictures. Read Listening tip! as a class.
- Play the CD. The pupils listen and identify the correct picture.
- Repeat the procedure with the second set of pictures. Ask more questions about the texts if you have time, e.g. **In number 1, what did they do at the cafe? In number 2, who started to dance?**

Answers: **1** A **2** B

Pupil's Book Activity 3

Listen again. Which of these verbs can you hear in the past continuous?

▶ ***CD1 Track 15 p277***

- Invite a pupil to read out the verbs. Ask one pupil to give an example of 'play' in the past continuous.
- Play the CD again. The pupils listen and identify the verbs in the past continuous.

Answers: happen, walk, play

Pupil's Book Activity 4

Look at the pictures and remember. Ask and answer (Teacher's Resource Bank: Unit 1).

- Explain that the pupils are going to play a memory game. Invite a pair to read out the speech bubbles.
- Organise the class into pairs (A and B).
- Invite two pupils to demonstrate the activity. Pupil A will look at a picture for a minute. Pupil B will ask questions to see how much he / she can remember. Then the pupils swap roles and repeat.
- Ask the pupils to do the activity in pairs.

Activity Book

Activity 1

Read the sentences and complete the words.

- Ask the pupils to read the sentences and complete the words. All of the missing letters are vowels.

Answers: **1** guests **2** lift **3** receptionist **4** backpackers **5** guard, platform **6** tourist, centre

Activity 2

Read and complete. Write one word each time.

- The pupils look at the photo. Ask **What is it?** (*A hotel made of ice.*) **What would it be like?**
- The pupils complete the gaps with one word only.

Answers: **1** in **2** made **3** in **4** of **5** to **6** are **7** than **8** sleeping **9** can **10** by

Activity 3

Read and learn.

- Read the information as a class. Encourage the pupils to think of other examples.

Activity 4

Complete the sentences with a verb and a preposition.

- The pupils work in pairs or on their own to complete the sentences.

Answers: **1** check in **2** wash up **3** turn off **4** try on **5** lie down **6** go out

Odd one out activity

Which is the odd one out? Why?

- The pupils complete the odd one out activity.

Answers: check-in desk (You don't find it at a railway station.)

Ending the lesson

Review the lesson and reflect on learning.

- Say **Today we've learnt more travel words and we've done a communication task.**
- Ask **What do you remember?** The pupils do a three-minute review in pairs. (Cooperative Learning Strategies, page 19)

Extra activity

Reinforcement

- Define one of the words that the pupils have learnt, e.g. **This person works in a hotel.** Ask the pupils to guess the word. (*Receptionist.*)
- In pairs, the pupils write definitions for the words on Pupil's Book page 13. They then read out the definitions for other pupils to guess.

Vocabulary Extension

- Present additional words related to travel: *ticket barrier, lost property office, waiting room, cash machine*
- Use the Vocabulary Booster on Navio to practise these new words

Key Competences and Key Learning Outcomes

- Practise language to talk about historical events
- Do pre-reading tasks to predict content and raise interest
- Read a text for general understanding
- Order events chronologically
- Share what you know about this type of text
- Read an eyewitness account of the sinking of the Titanic
- Give an opinion on the text

Key language

- *fictional, first-class, huge, iceberg, lifeboat, lifejacket, orchestra, porthole, sink, steward*
- *The ship stopped moving.*

Materials

- Pupil's Book p14; Activity Book p11; Class CD1; Teacher's App on Navio

Optional materials

- Teacher's Resource Bank: Trinity Exams Practice cards (selected from the Starter Unit)

At a Glance Lesson Plan

Pupil's Book

Starting the lesson

- Use the Trinity Exams Practice cards (optional).
- Review travel vocabulary.
- Set learning outcomes.

Activity 1: Before you read

- Read and discuss.

Activity 2

- Look at the pictures.
- Who do you think is telling the story?
- Read and find out.

Activity 3: After you read

- What do you think?
- Go to the Activity Book.

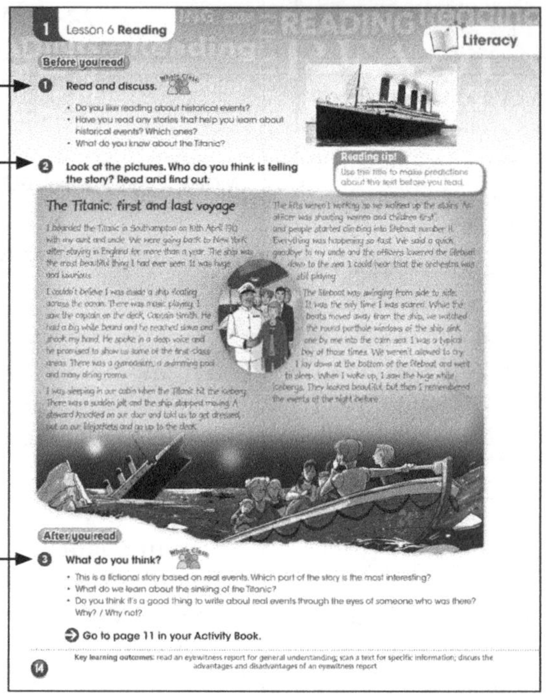

Ending the lesson

- Review the lesson and reflect on learning.

Extra activity

Extension

- Role play a meeting between the boy and the captain.

Activity Book

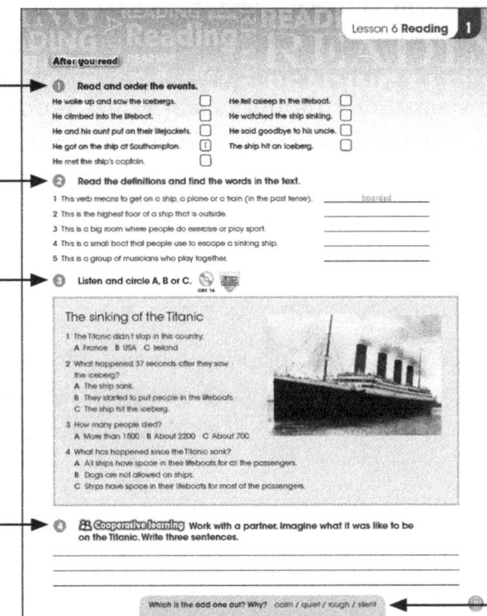

Activity Book: After you read

Activity 1

- Read and order the events.

Activity 2

- Read the definitions and find the words in the text.

Activity 3

- Listen and circle A, B or C.

▶ *CD1 Track 16 p277*

Activity 4

- Work with a partner. Imagine what it was like to be on the Titanic. Write three sentences.

Odd one out activity

Digital resources

Teacher's Digital: You can also teach this lesson using the Teacher's App on Navio.

Pupil's Digital: Encourage your pupils to use the Pupil's App on Navio to practise the activities from this lesson.

Powered By NAVIO

Detailed Lesson Plan

Starting the lesson

Use the Trinity Exams Practice cards (optional).

- The pupils practise asking and answering questions.

Review travel vocabulary.

- Divide the class into three groups. One group is 'planes', the next group is 'trains' and the final group is 'ships'.
- Say words that are related to one or more of these categories (or to none of these categories). The pupils who think the word is related to their category put up their hands.

Set learning outcomes.

- Say **Today we're going to read a story about the Titanic.**

Pupil's Book Activity 1: Before you read

Read and discuss.

- Read the questions as a class. Prompt the pupils to answer in as much detail as possible.

Pupil's Book Activity 2

Look at the pictures. Who do you think is telling the story? Read and find out.

- Describe and discuss the pictures of the boy and the captain, and the lifeboat and the sinking ship. Encourage the pupils to predict who is telling the story. Then read the story to find out.
- Confirm that the story is told in the first person and it is through the eyes of the boy.

Pupil's Book Activity 3: After you read

What do you think?

- Read the first sentence as a class. Make sure the pupils understand that the event is real, but the account is fictional. It is based on research so it seems true. Prompt the pupils to give answers to the questions, encouraging them to explain their answer each time.

Activity Book: After you read

Activity 1

Read and order the events.

- Read the sentences as a class. The pupils work on their own to put the sentences in the order of the story.

Answers: 9, 6, 4, 1, 2, 8, 7, 5, 3

Activity 2

Read the definitions and find the words in the text.

- The pupils work in pairs or on their own to write the words, using the text in the Pupil's Book to help them.

Answers: **1** boarded **2** deck **3** gymnasium **4** lifeboat **5** orchestra

Activity 3

Listen and circle A, B or C.

▶ *CD1 Track 16 p277*

- Read the questions as a class. As you read the questions encourage the pupils to predict the answers.
- Play the CD. The pupils listen and choose the answers. They check their answers with a partner.
- Play the CD again, pausing after each piece of information. The pupils complete and check their answers.

Answers: **1** B **2** C **3** A **4** A

Activity 4

Work with a partner. Imagine what it was like to be on the Titanic. Write three sentences.

- Ask the pupils to imagine that they were on the Titanic before it sank. They write three sentences to describe the ship.

Odd one out activity

Which is the odd one out? Why?

- The pupils complete the odd one out activity.

Answers: rough (All of the others are related to calmness.)

Ending the lesson

Review the lesson and reflect on learning.

- Say **Today we've read a historical text.**
- Ask **What do you remember?** The pupils do a three-minute review in pairs. (Cooperative Learning Strategies, page 19)

Extra activity

Extension

- Ask the pupils to look again at the text in the Pupil's Book. They imagine the meeting between the boy and Captain Smith. The pupils work in pairs to create a short dialogue (about eight lines) between the captain and the boy. They then present the dialogue to the class.

Key Competences and Key Learning Outcomes

- Learn and practise how to use verbs of the senses
- Identify the text features of an eyewitness account
- Use criteria to check your writing
- Share and discuss your writing with a partner
- Write an eyewitness account of a historical event

Key language

- *feel, hot-air balloon, look, scene, senses, smell, smoke, sound, taste*
- *The hot-air balloon looked like a floating ball.*

Materials

- Pupil's Book p15; Activity Book p12; Teacher's App on Navio

Optional materials

- Teacher's Resource Bank: Trinity Exams Practice cards (selected from the Starter Unit)

At a Glance Lesson Plan

Pupil's Book

Starting the lesson

- Use the Trinity Exams Practice cards (optional).
- Review the account from Lesson 6.
- Set learning outcomes.

Activity 1: Investigate a text

- Look at these headlines.
- When do you think the events happened?
- Imagine being there.
- What would you see, hear and feel?
- Which of these events is described in Activity 2?

Activity 2

- Read the account to find out if you guessed correctly.

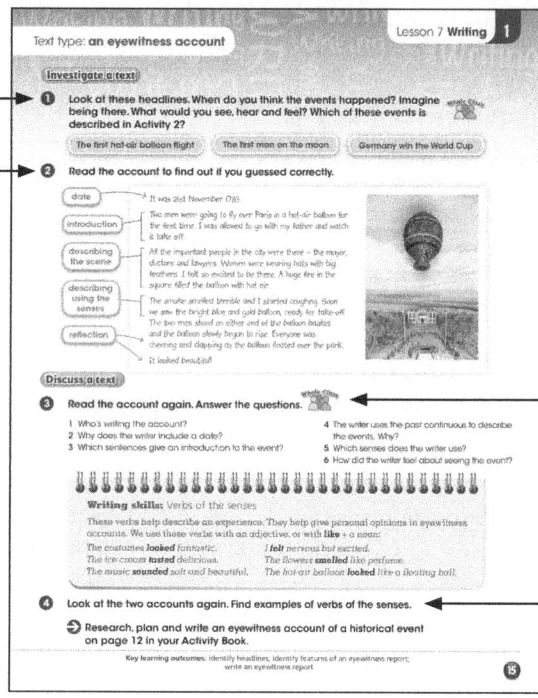
Lesson 7 Writing 1

Text type: an eyewitness account

Investigate a text

1 Look at these headlines. When do you think the events happened? Imagine being there. What would you see, hear and feel? Which of these events is described in Activity 2?

The first hot-air balloon flight | The first man on the moon | Germany win the World Cup

2 Read the account to find out if you guessed correctly.

Discuss a text

3 Read the account again. Answer the questions.

Writing skills: Verbs of the senses

4 Look at the two accounts again. Find examples of verbs of the senses.

Research, plan and write an eyewitness account of a historical event on page 12 in your Activity Book.

Activity 3: Discuss a text

- Read the account again.
- Answer the questions.

Writing skills

- Read about verbs of the senses.

Activity 4

- Look at the two accounts again.
- Find examples of verbs of the senses.
- Go to the Activity Book.

Ending the lesson

- Review the lesson and reflect on learning.

Extra activity

Extension

- Describe objects, places and experiences.

Digital resources

Teacher's Digital: You can also teach this lesson using the Teacher's App on Navio.

Pupil's Digital: Encourage your pupils to use the Pupil's App on Navio to practise the activities from this lesson.

Powered By NAVIO

Activity Book

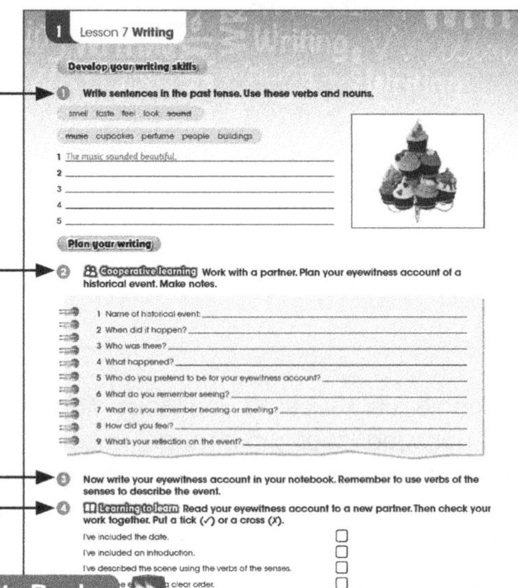
1 Lesson 7 Writing

Develop your writing skills

1 Write sentences in the past tense. Use these verbs and nouns.

Plan your writing

2 Cooperative learning Work with a partner. Plan your eyewitness account of a historical event. Make notes.

3 Now write your eyewitness account in your notebook. Remember to use verbs of the senses to describe the event.

4 Learning to learn Read your eyewitness account to a new partner. Then check your work together. Put a tick (✓) or a cross (✗).

Activity Book

Activity 1: Develop your writing skills

- Write sentences in the past tense. Use these verbs and nouns.

Activity 2: Plan your writing

- Work with a partner. Plan your eyewitness account of a historical event. Make notes.

Activity 3

- Now write your eyewitness account in your notebook.

Remember to use verbs of the senses to describe the event.

Activity 4

- Read your eyewitness account to a new partner. Then check your work together. Put a tick (✓) or a cross (✗).

Odd one out activity

Starting the lesson

Use the Trinity Exams Practice cards (optional).

- The pupils practise asking and answering questions.

Review the account from Lesson 6.

- Ask the pupils to remember verbs in the past tense that were used in the eyewitness account from Lesson 6. Write them on the board.
- Then ask the pupils to make sentences about the Titanic using these verbs.

Set learning outcomes.

- Say **Today we're going to write about a historical event as an eyewitness account.**

Pupil's Book Activity 1: Investigate a text

Look at these headlines. When do you think the events happened? Imagine being there. What would you see, hear and feel? Which of these events is described in Activity 2?

- Ask the pupils to look at the headlines. In pairs, they imagine what it would be like being in each place.
- In pairs, the pupils report back to the class.
- Then ask the pupils to look at the text and predict which of the three events is being described.

Pupil's Book Activity 2

Read the account to find out if you guessed correctly.

- The pupils read the account and check the answer.

Pupil's Book Activity 3: Discuss a text

Read the account again. Answer the questions.

- Read and discuss the questions as a class. Highlight that a good eyewitness account will describe the scene clearly and use the senses to make it feel like the reader is there.

Writing skills

- Read about verbs of the senses.
- Encourage the pupils to think of other adjectives that could be used in the example sentences.

Pupil's Book Activity 4

Look at the two accounts again. Find examples of verbs of the senses.

- The pupils look at the accounts in Lessons 6 and 7 to find examples of verbs of the senses.

Activity Book

Activity 1: Develop your writing skills

Write sentences in the past tense. Use these verbs and nouns.

- The pupils write sentences.

Answers: **1** The music sounded beautiful. **2** The cupcakes tasted (adjective). **3** The perfume smelt (adjective). **4** The people felt (adjective). **5** The buildings looked (adjective).

Activity 2: Plan your writing

Work with a partner. Plan your eyewitness account of a historical event. Make notes.

- Read out the notes as a class. Check understanding.
- In pairs, the pupils choose an event and make notes about it. The event could be one that they have learnt about at school, or a more recent event that they know about.
- **Note:** the pupils will need time to research the event. If you have computers in the classroom, they can do this in class time. Alternatively, they can investigate and complete the notes as homework.

Activity 3

Now write your eyewitness account in your notebook. Remember to use verbs of the senses to describe the event.

- The pupils write their account in their notebooks.

Activity 4

Read your eyewitness account to a new partner. Then check your work together. Put a tick (✓) or a cross (✗).

- Read through the statements as a class.
- Organise the class into new partners. One pupil reads aloud their text. The other pupil listens. The pupils work together to decide if the text fulfils the criteria and tick the corresponding boxes. The pupils can add, improve or correct the text at this stage.
- The pupils swap roles.

Odd one out activity

Which is the odd one out? Why?

- The pupils complete the odd one out activity.

Answers: happy (It isn't a verb of the senses.)

Ending the lesson

Review the lesson and reflect on learning.

- Say **Today we've read an eyewitness account about the first hot-air balloon ride in France and we've written an eyewitness account.**
- Ask **What do you remember?** The pupils do a three-minute review in pairs. (Cooperative Learning Strategies, page 19)

Extra activity

Extension

- Ask the pupils to write down four things: an item of food, a place near where they live, a song or a piece of music, and a person they know. For each one, the pupils write sentences using the verbs of the senses with adjectives. Encourage them to use different adjectives where possible.

Key Competences and Key Learning Outcomes
• Review tenses for talking about future plans
• Prepare and practise speaking activity types found in Cambridge Exams: B1 Preliminary for Schools • Reflect on learning and progress • Listen to a text for general and specific information
• Learn and practise how to make suggestions in a conversation

Key language
- *abroad, coast*
- *Have you ever been abroad?*

Materials
- Pupil's Book p16; Activity Book pp13–14; Class CD1; Teacher's App on Navio

Optional materials
- Teacher's Resource Bank: Trinity Exams Practice cards (selected from the Starter Unit)

At a Glance Lesson Plan

Pupil's Book

Starting the lesson
- Use the Trinity Exams Practice cards (optional).
- Review holiday language.
- Set learning outcomes.

Activity 1
- Look at the photos.
- What do they show?
- How are they different?

Activity 2
- Listen to the conversation.
- ▶ *CD1 Track 17 p277*
- Has Alec ever been abroad?

Activity 3
- Listen again.
- ▶ *CD1 Track 17 p277*
- Complete the five questions that Ella asks.

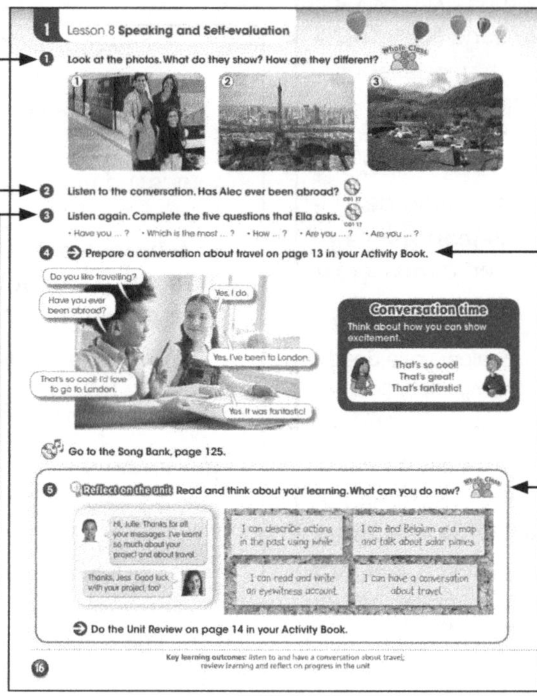

Activity 4
- Prepare a conversation about travel on page 13 in your Activity Book.
- Go to the Activity Book.

Song
- ▶ *CD4 Track 16 p296*
- ▶ *CD4 Track 17 p296 (optional karaoke version)*

Activity 5
- Read and think about your learning.
- What can you do now?

Ending the lesson
- Review the lesson and reflect on learning.

Activity Book

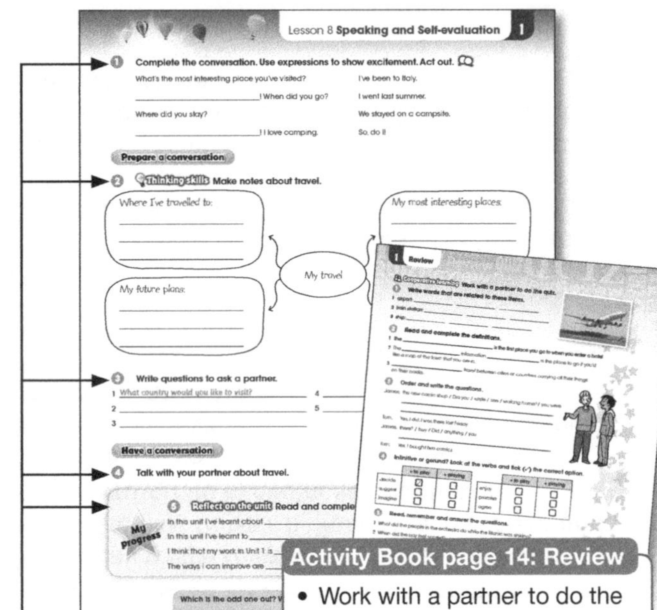

Activity Book page 14: Review
- Work with a partner to do the quiz.

Activity Book

Activity 1
- Complete the conversation. Use expressions to show excitement. Act out.

Activity 2
- Make notes about travel.

Activity 3
- Write questions to ask a partner.

Activity 4
- Talk with your partner about travel.

Activity 5 My progress
- Read and complete the sentences.

Odd one out activity

Digital resources

Teacher's Digital: You can also teach this lesson using the Teacher's App on Navio.

Powered By NAVIO

Starting the lesson

Use the Trinity Exams Practice cards (optional).

- The pupils practise asking and answering questions.

Review holiday language.

- Invite a pupil to the front of the class. Ask the pupil to think of a holiday destination. Prompt the class to ask closed questions to find out where it is and how they can get there. If necessary, write prompts on the board. When the class guesses correctly, repeat with another pupil.

Set learning outcomes.

- Say **Today we're going to learn and practise how to have a conversation about travelling and we're going to think about our learning.**

Pupil's Book Activity 1

Look at the photos. What do they show? How are they different?

- The pupils describe the three photos.

Pupil's Book Activity 2

Listen to the conversation. Has Alec ever been abroad?

▶ ***CD1 Track 17 p277***

- Explain that Alec and Ella are talking about travelling. Play the CD. Ask the pupils which place Alec has been to.
- Play the CD again. The pupils complete the notes.

Answers: Yes, he's been to Scotland and France.

Pupil's Book Activity 3

Listen again. Complete the five questions that Ella asks.

▶ ***CD1 Track 17 p277***

- The pupils complete the sentences.

Answers: Have you ever been abroad? Which is the most interesting place you've visited? How did you get there?Are you going anywhere this summer? Are you camping or staying in a hotel?

Pupil's Book Activity 4

Prepare a conversation about travel on page 13 in your Activity Book.

- Ask students what questions they would ask each other about travelling to another country or to another place.
- Direct them to Activity Book, page 13.

Activity Book

Activity 1

Complete the conversation. Use expressions to show excitement. Act out.

- In pairs, pupils complete the sentences and then act out.

Activity 2

Make notes about travel.

- The pupils complete the notes about themselves.

Activity 3

Write questions to ask a partner.

- Pupils write questions about travel to ask each other.

Activity 4

Talk with your partner about travel.

- In pairs, the pupils have a conversation about travel using the questions from Activity 3. One pupil asks the questions and the partner answers. They then swap roles.

Song

Read and discuss the questions.

- Go to the Song Bank on page 125.

▶ ***CD4 Track 16 p296***

▶ ***CD4 Track 17 p296 (optional karaoke version)***

Pupil's Book Activity 5

Read and think about your learning. What can you do now?

- Read the messages as a class. Then look back through the unit and prompt the pupils to identify other things they have learnt / done.

Activity Book

Activity 5: My progress

Read and complete the sentences.

- Read out the sentences. Encourage the pupils to think of different ways of completing them.
- The pupils complete the sentences.

Odd one out activity

- The pupils complete the odd one out activity.

Answers: hotel (It isn't a piece of camping equipment.)

Ending the lesson

Review the lesson and reflect on learning.

- Say **Today we've learnt and practised how to have a conversation about travelling and we've thought about our learning. What have you learnt?**

Activity Book page 14: Review

Work with a friend to do the quiz.

- Organise the class into pairs. Explain that they are going to work together to do a quiz. Set a time limit for the pupils to do this (10–15 minutes). Stress that the pupils are not competing with each other.
- Read out the six tasks that the pupils have to complete. Check understanding. Then say **Ready, steady … Go!**
- Correct the answers as a class.

Answers: **2 1** reception **2** tourist, centre **3** Backpackers **3** Did you see the new comic shop while you were walking home? Did you buy anything there? **4 + to play** decide, promise, agree **+ playing** suggest, imagine, enjoy **5 1** They played music. **2** When the lifeboats were lowered into the water and they were swinging from side to side. **6** iceberg, a large piece of ice floating in the ocean

Key Competences and Key Learning Outcomes

- Watch and understand a video about different transport
- Think of ways to present balanced views
- Use balanced opinions to discuss a project about transport

Key language

- *cable car, cycle rickshaw, monorail, motorbike, underground*
- *Cycle rickshaws are good for the environment. Yes, but they only carry one or two people.*

Materials

- Pupil's Book p17; Activity Book p15; Class CD1; Teacher's App on Navio
- Teacher's Resource Bank: Talk cards

Optional materials

- Teacher's Resource Bank: Trinity Exams Practice cards (selected from the Starter Unit)

At a Glance Lesson Plan

Pupil's Book

Starting the lesson

- **Think-Pair-Share** Review after school activities.
- Set learning outcomes and use the talk cards.

Activity 1

- Before you watch.
- Watch the video.

Unit 1 video p300

- Read and say *true* or *false*.
- Correct the false sentences.

Activity 2

- Match the words to the pictures.
- Which form of transport does Amy mention in the video?

Activity 3

- Read, think and answer.

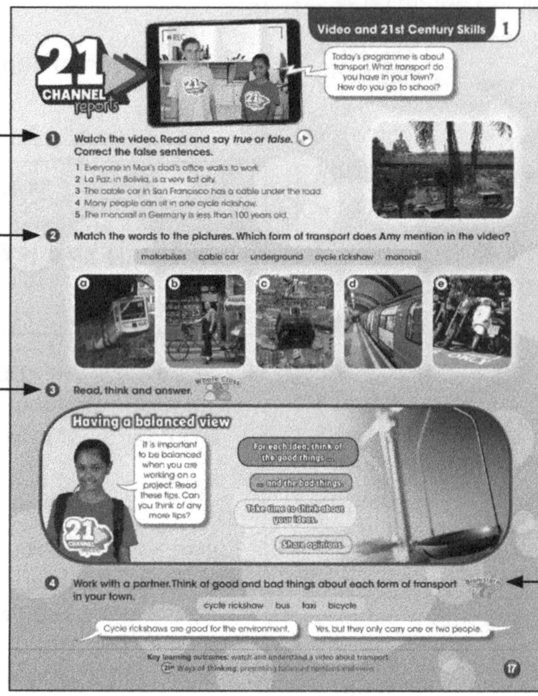

Activity 4

- Work with a partner.
- Think of good and bad things about each form of transport in your town.

Go to the Activity Book.

Ending the lesson

- Review the lesson and reflect on learning.

Extra activity

- Describe a type of transport for your partner to guess.

Activity Book

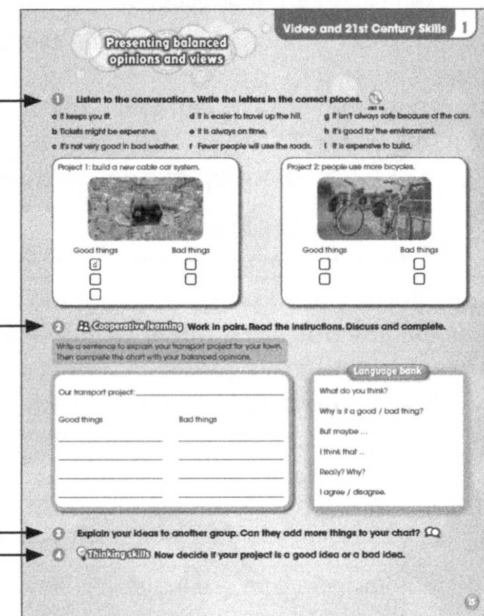

Activity Book

Activity 1

- Listen to the conversations. Write the letters in the correct places.

▶ *CD1 Track 18 p277*

Activity 2

- Work in pairs. Read the instructions. Discuss and complete.

Activity 3

- Explain your ideas to another group. Can they add more things to your chart?

Activity 4

- Now decide if your project is a good or bad idea.

Digital resources

Teacher's Digital: You can also teach this lesson using the Teacher's App on Navio.

Pupil's Digital: Encourage your students to use the Pupil's App on Navio to practise the activities from this lesson.

Powered By NAVIO

Starting the lesson

Think-Pair-Share Review types of transport in a city.

- Ask **How many different types of transport can you think of?** The class thinks silently for a minute.
- Then the pupils work with a Talk Partner to name different types of transport.
- Invite different Talk Partners to say a different type of transport. Write the name on the board.
- Finally, repeat the procedure, asking different pairs of Talk Partners each time, until all the ideas have been recorded.

Set learning outcomes and use the talk cards.

- Say **Today we're going to watch a video and then talk about different types of transport.**
- Explain to pupils that in every unit they will watch a TV programme called Channel 21, which is presented by two children called Max and Amy. Each video will cover a different topic.

Pupil's Book Activity 1

Before you watch

- Look at the photo of Max and Amy and explain that these are the presenters of Channel 21.
- Read the speech bubble to pupils. Ask **What transport do you have in your town?** Elicit responses from a number of pupils.
- Ask **How do you go to school?** Elicit responses from a number of pupils.
- Read the questions in Activity 1. Explain that students have to say true or false.

Watch the video. Read and say true or false. Correct the false sentences. *p300*

- Watch Part 1.
- Ask a pupil to read out sentence 1. Ask the class whether they think the sentence is true or false. Repeat with sentences 2–5.
- Play Part 2. Students work in pairs. They correct the false sentences.

Answers: **1** F **2** F **3** T **4** F **6** F
1 They go by bike, bus, drive a car, scooter or walk.
2 It isn't flat. **4** One person can sit in a rickshaw.
5 More than 100 years old.

Pupil's Book Activity 2

Match the words to the pictures. Which form of transport does Amy mention in the video?

- Ask what forms of transport pupils remember from the video.
- Ask them to look at item 1 and tell you what form of transport it is.
- Pupils work in pairs to complete the activity.

Answers: **a** monorail **b** cycle rickshaw **c** cable car **d** underground **e** motorbikes

Pupil's Book Activity 3

Read, think and answer.

- Tell pupils that Amy and Max talk about how important it is to have a balanced view when working on a project. Ask what points Amy and Max present.
- Pupils work in pairs to read and think about each point. Ask why each point is important and how it can help them with their project.
- Ask if they can think of any more ideas.

Pupil's Book Activity 4

Work with a partner. Think of good and bad things about each form of transport in your town.

- Pupils work in pairs.
- Ask if they can think of any more ideas.
- Invite different Talk Partners to present their idea to the class.

Activity Book

Activity 1

Listen to the conversations. Write the letters in the correct places.

▶ *CD1 Track 18 p277*

- Ask **How do you get to school?** Elicit answers and write them on the board.
- Then ask what good and bad things these ways of getting to school have.
- Have pupils read the sentences and guess where they might go.
- Play the CD and complete the activity.

Answers: Project 1. Good things: d, e, f Bad things: b, i
Project 2. Good things: a, h Bad things: c, g

Activity 2

Work in pairs. Read the instructions. Discuss and complete.

- Explain that pupils will do a project on transport in their town.
- Pupils work in small groups. Remind them to try and have a balanced view and to implement Max's and Amy's points on how to work on a project.
- Refer pupils to the language bank. Explain these phrases can help them communicate with each other.

Activity 3

Explain your ideas to another group.
Can they add more things to your chart?

- Have groups share their charts and exchange ideas.
- Ask some groups to present their work to the class.

Activity 4

Now decide if your project is a good idea or a bad idea.

- In their groups, pupils identify the good and bad points about their projects.

Ending the lesson

Review the lesson and reflect on learning.

- Say **Today we've watched a video about different forms of transport. What have we learnt about them?** The pupils do a three-minute review in pairs. (Cooperative Learning Strategies, page 19)

Extra activity

Reinforcement

- Invite a pupil to the front of the class. Have them describe a form of transport for the class to guess.
- Have pupils continue in small groups.

Date: ____________________ Unit: __________

1 What did my pupils learn in this unit?

____

____

____

____

2 How did my pupils work? (✓)

individually ☐ in pairs ☐ in small groups ☐

in large groups ☐ as a class ☐

3 Which key competences did my pupils develop? Give a score from 1 to 5 (5 being the highest).

- Competence in linguistic communication ☐
- Competence in mathematics, science and technology ☐
- Digital competence ☐
- Learning to learn ☐
- Social and civic competences ☐
- Sense of initiative and entrepreneurship ☐
- Cultural awareness and expression ☐

4 Which lessons / activities were the most successful and why?

____

____

____

____

5 Which lessons / activities did my pupils find the most difficult and why?

____

____

____

____

6 What did I try in the classroom for the first time? How did it go?

____

____

____

____

7 Which resources did I find most useful? (including webpages)

____

____

____

____

____

____

8 What could I do differently next time I teach this unit?

____

____

____

____

Unit 2

Sports and hobbies

Unit overview

Key Competences and Key Learning Outcomes

- Review and name sports and equipment (Lesson 1)
- Practise using 'must' and 'need' to talk about sports (Lesson 1)
- Practise using the present perfect (Lessons 2 and 4)
- Review and name hobbies (Lesson 5)
- Practise expressing preferences
- Use extreme adjectives (Lesson 7)
- Watch and understand a video (Video and 21st Century Skills)

- Find connections between words (Lessons 1 and 3)

- Use the Pupil's App on Navio
- Investigate China

- Listen for general and specific information (Lessons 3 and 5)
- Practise rhythm and stress patterns in present perfect sentences (Lesson 4)
- Identify parts of an article (Lesson 7)
- Review learning and reflect on progress in the unit (Lesson 8)
- Practise activity types found in the Cambridge Exams: B1 Preliminary for Schools

- Understand the importance of controlling your temper (Lesson 3)
- Learn and practise how to initiate a conversation (Lesson 8)

- Work in pairs or small groups to practise and reinforce learning (All lessons)
- Do a communication activity (Lesson 5)
- Evaluate hobbies and abilities (Video and 21st Century Skills)

- Read a text (Lesson 3)
- Learn about China (Lesson 3)
- Read and write a magazine article (Lessons 6 and 7)

Vocabulary

Core vocabulary
archery, gymnastics, fencing, athletics, water polo, trampolining, martial arts, net, rope, racket, hoop, crash mat; sing in a choir, do circus skills, collect cards, belong to a sports club, go to drama class, do photography, do needlework, make models

Extension vocabulary (optional)
bend, dive, score, serve, shoot, stretch, do gardening, do yoga, do athletics, do modern dance, write blogs

Other vocabulary
after-school club, karate, kitesurfing, kung fu, martial arts, shuttlecock, skipping, tug-of-war; bow, court, field, goal posts, leotard, mask, running track, sword, target; balance, concentrate, discipline, flexibility, powerful, self-confident, self-control, speed, strength; monk, temple; amazing, astonishing, brilliant, enormous, fantastic, fascinating, massive; Internet access, online games, social networking site; tournaments

Recycled vocabulary
belt, champion, chess, school gym; get fit; hard-working

Structures

Core structures
Have I / you / we / they ever (been sailing)? Yes, I / you / we / they have. No, I / you / we / they haven't. Has he / she ever (done athletics)? Yes, he / she has. No, he / she hasn't. When did I / you / he / she / we / they (go sailing)? How long have I / you / we / they (played tennis)? I / You / We / They have (played tennis) for two years. How long has he / she (studied French)? He / She has (studied French) since last year.

Other structures
Why don't we talk about this picture first? What do you think about karate?

Recycled structures
You need (a net and a ball). You must (pass the ball to your teammates and hit it over the net). You mustn't (hit it with your hand). All five styles develop discipline and self-control. I prefer collecting stamps to cards. I'd rather collect stamps than cards. I think that Gisela is an amazing sportswoman.

Pronunciation

Rhythm and stress patterns in present perfect sentences

Literacy

Text type: a magazine article (non-chronological report; writing preparation)
Reading skills: scanning the text for key content
Writing skills: extreme adjectives for creating interest

Culture ... around the world

Kung fu and the Shaolin monks in China

21st Century Skills

Living in the world: achieving goals

Thinking skills

Forming conceptual links and associations (Lesson 1); Defining and describing (Lesson 1); Analysing and applying rules and patterns (Lessons 2, 4); Discussing and evaluating a martial art (Lesson 3); Comparing and contrasting (Lesson 5); Problem solving (Lesson 8); Evaluating (Lesson 8)

Cooperative learning

Working together (Lessons 1–8); Checking learning (Lessons 1–8); Reflecting and setting goals (Lessons 1–8); Collaborative writing (Lesson 7); Peer evaluation (Lesson 7); Initiating a conversation (Lesson 8); Expressing and respecting opinions (Lessons 1, 3, 6, 8)

Values

The importance of controlling your temper

Cross-curricular links

Links to Science
First aid techniques

Suggested Arts and Crafts concepts
Representing movement

Key Competences and Key Learning Outcomes

- Review and name sports and equipment
- Review and practise how to use 'must' and 'need' to talk about sports

- Find connections between words

Key language

- *archery, athletics, crash mat, fencing, gymnastics, hoop, martial arts, net, racket, rope, trampolining, water polo; bow, court, field, goal posts, leotard, mask, running track, sword, target*
- Extension: *bend, dive, score, serve, shoot, stretch*
- *You need (a net). You must (pass the ball to your teammates).*

Materials

- Pupil's Book pp18–19; Activity Book p16; Class CD1; Teacher's App on Navio
- Sports and equipment flashcards

Optional materials

- Teacher's Resource Bank: Trinity Exams Practice cards (selected from the Starter Unit and Unit 1)

At a Glance Lesson Plan

Pupil's Book

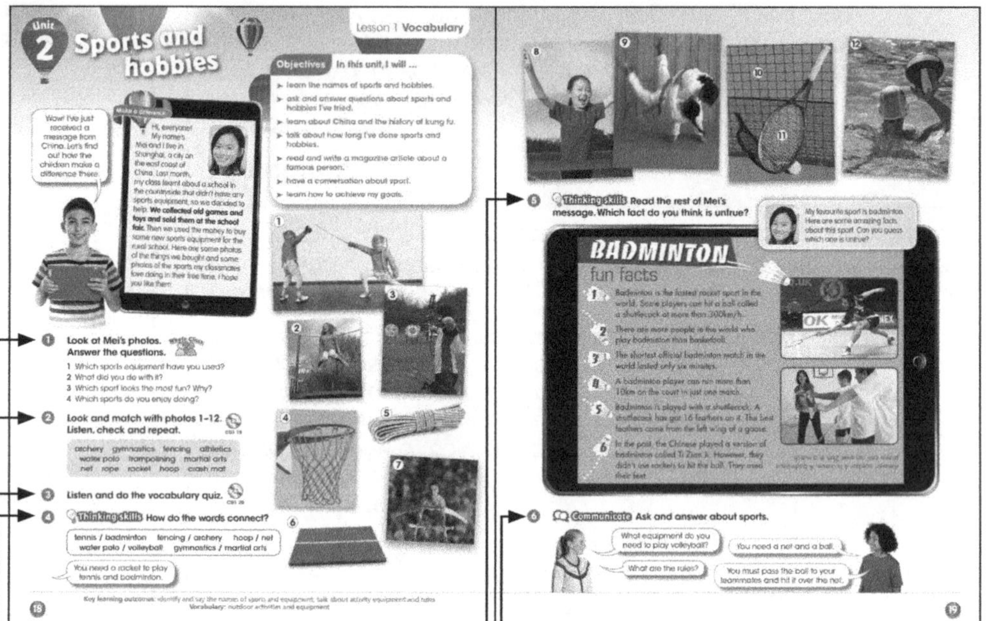

Starting the lesson
- Use the Trinity Exams Practice cards (optional).
- Review and classify sports.
- Set learning outcomes.

Activity 1
- Look at Mei's photos.
- Answer the questions.

Vocabulary presentation
- Present the new vocabulary using the sports and equipment flashcards.

Activity 2
- Look and match with photos 1–12.
- Listen, check and repeat.

▶ *CD1 Track 19 p277*

Activity 3
- Listen and do the vocabulary quiz.

▶ *CD1 Track 20 p278*

Activity 4
- How do the words connect?

Activity 5
- Read the rest of Mei's message.
- Which fact do you think is untrue?

Activity 6
- Ask and answer about sports.
- Go to the Activity Book.

Ending the lesson
- Review the lesson and reflect on learning.

Extra activities

Extension
- Find out about China.

Vocabulary extension
- Present six additional vocabulary items.

Activity Book

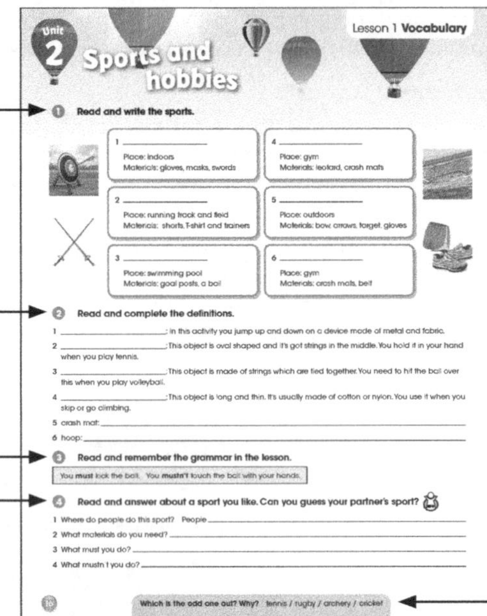

Activity Book

Activity 1
- Read and write the sports.

Activity 2
- Read and complete the definitions.

Activity 3
- Read and remember the grammar in the lesson.

Activity 4
- Read and answer about a sport you like. Can you guess your partner's sport?

Odd one out activity

Digital resources

Teacher's Digital: You can also teach this lesson using the Teacher's App on Navio.

Pupil's Digital: Encourage your pupils to use the Pupil's App on Navio to practise the activities from this lesson.

Powered By NAVIO

Detailed Lesson Plan

Starting the lesson

Use the Trinity Exams Practice cards (optional).

- The pupils practise asking and answering questions.

Review and classify sports.

- Say **Name five (team) sports.** The pupils brainstorm ideas in groups. The first group to finish reads out their list. Repeat with a new challenge, e.g. water sports, etc.

Set learning outcomes

- Say **Today we're going to remember and learn the names of sports and equipment.**

Pupil's Book Activity 1

Look at Mei's photos. Answer the questions.

- Invite a pupil to read out the speech bubble to find out which school has sent a message. Ask **Do you know where China is?**
- Invite a pupil to read out the message from Mei. Check understanding.
- Work as a class to answer the questions.

Vocabulary presentation

- Present the new vocabulary using the sports and equipment flashcards. Hold up the first flashcard and elicit / say the word. For equipment, ask **Which sport uses a (net)?** For sports, ask **What equipment do you need for (fencing)?** Stick the flashcard on the board. Repeat with the other flashcards.

Pupil's Book Activity 2

Look and match with photos 1–12. Listen, check and repeat.

▶ *CD1 Track 19 p277*

- Ask the pupils to look at photo number 1. Ask **What's this?** In pairs, the pupils match 2–12 with the words.
- Play the CD. The pupils listen and check. Play the CD again, pausing after each word for the pupils to repeat. You can find the answers for this activity in the audioscript on page 277.

Pupil's Book Activity 3

Listen and do the vocabulary quiz.

▶ *CD1 Track 20 p278*

- Play the CD. Listen to the first definition, pausing at the beep to allow the pupils to name the item. Play the CD to listen to the answer.
- Repeat the procedure with the other definitions. You can find the answers for this activity in the audioscript on page 278.

Pupil's Book Activity 4

How do the words connect?

- Explain that the pupils are going to think of connections between two words. Invite a pupil to read out the example. In pairs, the pupils complete the activity.
- Check answers as a class.

Pupil's Book Activity 5

Read the rest of Mei's message. Which fact do you think is untrue?

- Invite a pupil to read out the message. The pupils read the information and decide which fact is untrue.
- Check answers as a class.

Answers: 4 (A badminton player can run more than 2km.)

Pupil's Book Activity 6

Ask and answer about sports.

- Invite two pupils to read out the speech bubbles.
- The pupils talk about about the equipment and rules for different sports.

Activity Book

Activity 1

Read and write the sports.

- Read out the information for number 1. The class identifies the sport. The pupils complete the activity.

Answers: **1** fencing **2** athletics **3** water polo **4** gymnastics **5** archery **6** martial arts

Activity 2

Read and complete the definitions.

- The pupils complete the definitions.

Answers: **1** trampolining **2** racket **3** net **4** rope **5** you use this to fall on when doing karate **6** you throw a ball through this

Activity 3

Read and remember the grammar in the lesson.

- Invite a pupil to read out the information. Encourage the pupils to think of other sports rules.

Activity 4

Read and answer about a sport you like.
Can you guess your partner's sport?

- The pupils answer the questions.
- In pairs, the pupils read their sentences and guess the sport.

Odd one out activity

Which is the odd one out activity.

- The pupils complete the odd one out activity.

Answers: archery (It isn't played with a ball.)

Ending the lesson

Review the lesson and reflect on learning.

- Say **Today we've learnt the names of sports and equipment.**
- Ask **What do you remember?** The pupils do a three-minute review in pairs. (Cooperative Learning Strategies, page 19)

Extra activities

Extension

- The pupils find five facts about China to present to the class.

Vocabulary extension

- Present six additional sports words: *bend, dive, score, serve, shoot, stretch.*
- Use the Vocabulary Booster on NAVIO to practise these new words.

Key Competences and Key Learning Outcomes

- Listen to and read a dialogue
- Practise using the present perfect to talk about past activities
- Practise using the past simple to ask for specific information about past activities

- Identify examples of the present perfect and past simple in the dialogue

Key language

- *chess, kung fu, skipping, tug-of-war*
- *Have I / you / we / they ever (been sailing)? Yes, I / you / we / they have. No, I / you / we / they haven't.*
  Has he / she ever (done athletics)? Yes, he / she has. No, he / she hasn't. When did I / you / he / she / we / they (go sailing)?

Materials

- Pupil's Book p20; Activity Book p17; Class CD1; Teacher's App on Navio
- Teacher's Resource Bank: Sports and equipment word cards

Optional materials

- Teacher's Resource Bank: Trinity Exams Practice cards (selected from the Starter Unit and Unit 1)
- Dice

At a Glance Lesson Plan

Pupil's Book

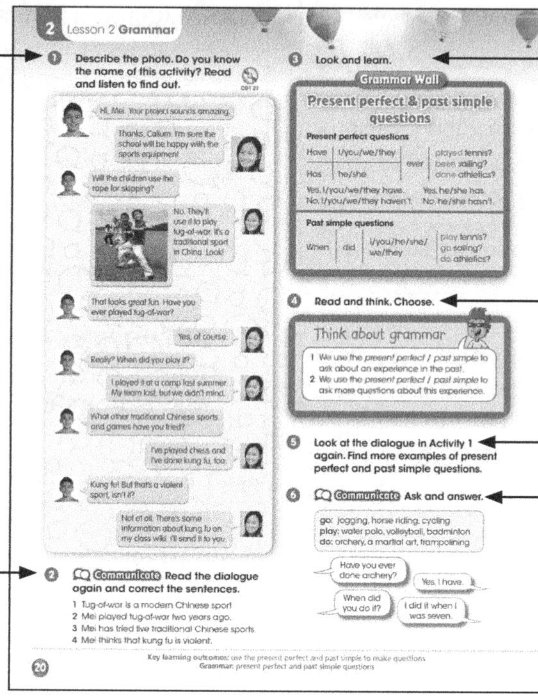
2 Lesson 2 Grammar

1 Describe the photo. Do you know the name of this activity? Read and listen to find out.

2 Communicate Read the dialogue again and correct the sentences.

3 Look and learn.

Grammar Wall — Present perfect & past simple questions

4 Read and think. Choose.

Think about grammar

5 Look at the dialogue in Activity 1 again. Find more examples of present perfect and past simple questions.

6 Communicate Ask and answer.

20

Starting the lesson
- Use the Trinity Exams Practice cards (optional).
- Review sports and equipment.
- Set learning outcomes.

Activity 1
- Describe the photo.
- Do you know the name of this activity?
- Read and listen to find out.

▶ *CD1 Track 21 p278*

Activity 2
- Read the dialogue again and correct the sentences.

Activity 3
- Look and learn – Grammar wall

Activity 4
- Read and think.
- Choose.

Activity 5
- Look at the dialogue in Activity 1 again.
- Find more examples of present perfect and past simple questions.

Activity 6
- Ask and answer.
- Go to the Activity Book.

Ending the lesson
- Review the lesson and reflect on learning.

Extra activity

Reinforcement
- Play a game with dice.

Activity Book

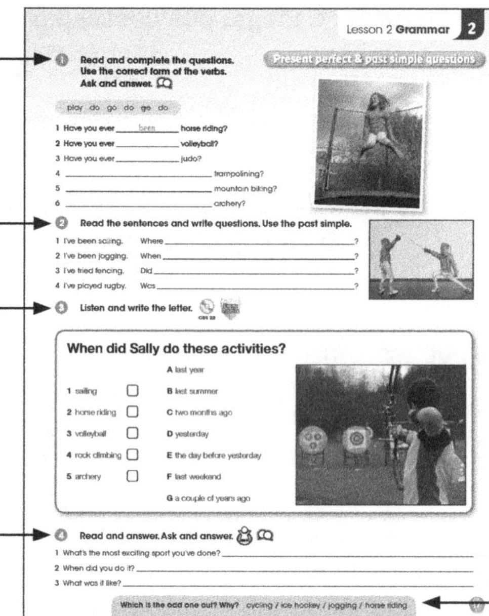
Lesson 2 Grammar 2

1 Read and complete the questions. Use the correct form of the verbs. Ask and answer.

2 Read the sentences and write questions. Use the past simple.

3 Listen and write the letter.

When did Sally do these activities?

4 Read and answer. Ask and answer.

Which is the odd one out? Why?

Activity Book

Activity 1
- Read and complete the questions. Use the correct form of the verbs. Ask and answer.

Activity 2
- Read the sentences and write questions. Use the past simple.

Activity 3
- Listen and write the letter.

▶ *CD1 Track 22 p278*

Activity 4
- Read and answer. Ask and answer.

Odd one out activity

Digital resources

Teacher's Digital: You can also teach this lesson using the Teacher's App on Navio.

Pupil's Digital: Encourage your pupils to use the Pupil's App on Navio to practise the activities from this lesson.

Powered By NAVIO

Starting the lesson

Use the Trinity Exams Practice cards (optional).

- The pupils practise asking and answering questions.

Review sports and equipment.

- Place the sports and equipment word cards face down on a desk. The pupils work in groups of three.
- Pupil 1 collects a word card and defines the word for their group. Pupil 2 says the word and Pupil 3 spells it. The pupils change roles. Repeat with a new word card.

Set learning outcomes

- Say **Today we're going to learn how to talk about the sports we've tried in the past.**

Pupil's Book Activity 1

Describe the photo. Do you know the name of this activity? Read and listen to find out.

▶ *CD1 Track 21 p278*

- Prompt the pupils to describe the photo. Ask them if they know what the activity is called.
- Play the CD. The pupils listen and read the dialogue. Confirm that the activity is tug-of-war.

Pupil's Book Activity 2

Read the dialogue again and correct the sentences.

- In pairs, the pupils correct the sentences. *(1 Tug-of-war is a traditional Chinese sport. 2 Mei played tug-of-war last summer. 3 Mei has tried two other traditional Chinese sports. 4 Mei thinks that kung fu isn't violent.)*

Pupil's Book Activity 3

Look and learn – Grammar wall

- Read the information on the Grammar wall as a class.
- Encourage the pupils to think about form and identify patterns. Say **The present perfect needs two verbs. Which is the first verb? What form is the second verb in?** Remind the pupils of the irregular verb list (Activity Book page 134).

Pupil's Book Activity 4

Read and think. Choose.

- Focus the pupils' attention on the Think about grammar box. The pupils complete the sentences in pairs.
- Check answers as a class (*1 present perfect 2 past simple*).

Pupil's Book Activity 5

Look at the dialogue in Activity 1 again. Find more examples of present perfect and past simple questions.

- In pairs, the pupils find examples of present perfect and past simple questions.

Pupil's Book Activity 6

Ask and answer.

- Invite two pupils to read out the speech bubbles to demonstrate the activity.
- In pairs, the pupils ask and answer questions.

Activity Book

Activity 1

Read and complete the questions. Use the correct form of the verbs. Ask and answer.

- The pupils complete the questions.
- Check answers as a class. In pairs, the pupils ask and answer the questions.

Answers: **1** been **2** played **3** done **4** Have you ever done **5** Have you ever been **6** Have you ever done

Activity 2

Read the sentences and write questions. Use the past simple.

- Remind the class that we use the past simple tense to ask for specific information about a past experience.
- Invite a pupil to complete and say the first question. The pupils complete the remaining questions.

Answers: **1** did you go sailing **2** did you go jogging **3** you like it **4** it fun

Activity 3

Listen and write the letter.

▶ *CD1 Track 22 p278*

- Ask the pupils to quickly read the notes. Then play the CD. The pupils listen and follow in their books.
- Play the CD again, pausing after each piece of key information. The pupils write the letter.

Answers: **1** A **2** G **3** D **4** B **5** C

Activity 4

Read and answer. Ask and answer.

- The pupils answer the questions. They then work in pairs to ask and answer the questions.

Odd one out activity

Which is the odd one out? Why?

- The pupils complete the odd one out activity.

Answers: ice hockey (It uses the verb 'play' the others use the verb 'go'.)

Ending the lesson

Review the lesson and reflect on learning.

- Say **Today we've learnt how to talk about the sports we've tried in the past.**
- Ask **What do you remember?** The pupils do a three-minute review in pairs. (Cooperative Learning Strategies, page 19)

Extra activity

Reinforcement

- Choose a pupil to throw a dice. The rest of the class shouldn't see the number on the dice.
- Ask **Have you ever (been horse riding)?** The pupil answers according to the number on the dice (1–3 = truth, 4–6 = false). If the answer is yes, ask more specific questions using the past simple. The class listens and decides if the answer is true or false.
- Repeat the procedure with different pupils. Prompt the class to ask questions.

Key Competences and Key Learning Outcomes

- Read information with confidence and fluency
- Use the Internet to investigate China
- Listen for general and specific information
- Understand the importance of controlling your temper
- Learn about China and the history of kung fu and Shaolin monks
- Express an opinion on the text

Key language

- *balance, discipline, flexibility, monk, powerful, self-control, speed, strength, temple*
- *All five styles develop discipline and self-control.*

Materials

- Pupil's Book p21; Activity Book p18; Class CD1; Teacher's App on Navio

Optional materials

- Teacher's Resource Bank: Trinity Exams Practice cards (selected from the Starter Unit and Unit 1)

At a Glance Lesson Plan

Pupil's Book

Starting the lesson

- Use the Trinity Exams Practice cards (optional).
- Review actions related to different sports.
- Set learning outcomes.

Activity 1: Before you read

- Read and discuss.

Activity 2

- Listen and read.

▶ *CD1 Track 23 p278*

Go to the Activity Book.

***Give Me Five!* values**

- Read and discuss.

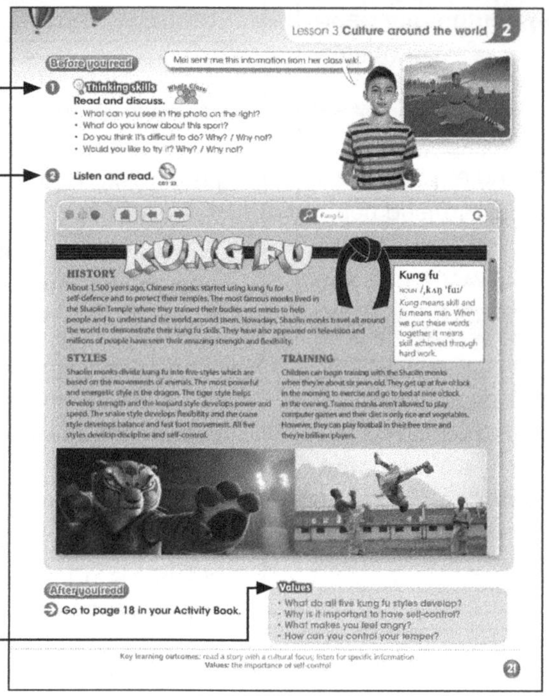

Ending the lesson

- Review the lesson and reflect on learning.

Extra activity

Extension

- Create sports similes.

Activity Book

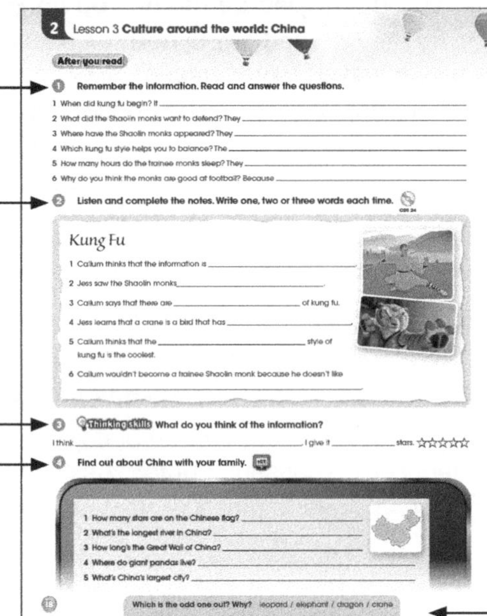

Activity Book: After you read

Activity 1

- Remember the information. Read and answer the questions.

Activity 2

- Listen and complete the notes. Write one, two or three words each time.

▶ *CD1 Track 24 p278*

Activity 3

- What do you think of the information?

Activity 4

- Find out about China with your family.

Odd one out activity

Digital resources

Teacher's Digital: You can also teach this lesson using the Teacher's App on Navio.

Pupil's Digital: Encourage your pupils to use the Pupil's App on Navio to practise the activities from this lesson.

Powered By NAVIO

Starting the lesson

Use the Trinity Exams Practice cards (optional).

- The pupils practise asking and answering questions.

Review actions related to different sports.

- The pupils brainstorm actions associated with different sports, e.g. football: kick, score, save, run, jump; volleyball: throw, hit, jump, dive, etc.

Set learning outcomes.

- Say **Today we're going to read some information about kung fu.**

Pupil's Book Activity 1: Before you read

Read and discuss.

- Read the questions as a class. Encourage the pupils to share information about the sport and to give their opinions.

Pupil's Book Activity 2

Listen and read.

▶ *CD1 Track 23 p278*

- Play the CD. The pupils follow in their books.
- Ask questions to check understanding.

Suggested comprehension questions:

- Dictionary box: **What does kung fu mean?** (*Skill through hard work.*)
- Paragraph 1: **When was kung fu first used?** (*About 1,500 years ago.*)
- Paragraph 2: **How many styles of kung fu do the Shaolin monks have?** (*Five styles.*)
- Paragraph 3: **What sport can the trainee monks play in their free time?** (*Football.*)

Activity Book: After you read

Activity 1

Remember the information. Read and answer the questions.

- Invite a pupil to answer the first question.
- The pupils work on their own or in pairs to answer the remaining questions.

Answers: **1** began 1,500 years ago. **2** wanted to defend their temples. **3** have appeared on television. **4** crane style helps you to balance. **5** sleep eight hours.

Activity 2

Listen and complete the notes. Write one, two or three words each time.

▶ *CD1 Track 24 p278*

- Read out the notes as a class. Ask the pupils to guess the missing words.
- Play the CD without pausing. The pupils listen and complete as much information as possible.
- Play the CD again, pausing after each piece of key information to check the answer.

Answers: **1** interesting **2** last year **3** five styles **4** long legs **5** dragon **6** getting up early

Activity 3

What do you think of the information?

- The pupils write their opinion and give a rating.
- Invite different pupils to share their opinions.

Activity 4

Find out about China with your family. ICT

- Read out the questions about China. Ask **Where can you find out this information?** (*Internet, library, asking friends and family.*) The pupils complete the activity at home.
- If you prefer to do this activity in class, connect to a children's website which has information about China, such as www.sciencekids.co.nz/sciencefacts/countries/china.html or http://kids.nationalgeographic.com/explore/countries/china.
- Read out the questions. The pupils work as a class to find and write the answers.

Answers: **1** five **2** the Yangtze river **3** 8,850km **4** in bamboo forests **5** Shanghai

Odd one out activity

Which is the odd one out? Why?

- The pupils complete the odd one out activity.

Answers: elephant (It isn't a kung fu style.)

***Give Me Five!* values**

Read and discuss.

- Read out the questions and discuss them as a class.
- Explain that it is normal to feel angry sometimes. Discuss how to recognise when we are angry, the importance of being able to talk about our feelings and the different strategies we can use to control our temper.

Ending the lesson

Review the lesson and reflect on learning.

- Say **Today we've read some information about kung fu.**
- Ask **What do you remember?** The pupils do a three-minute review in pairs. (Cooperative Learning Strategies, page 19)

Extra activity

Extension

- Review the five animals on which kung fu styles are based.
- Explain that we can describe a sports person by comparing their action with an animal. On the board write **He jumps like a …** Ask the pupils to complete it with an animal.
- Brainstorm other sports actions. In pairs, the pupils create other sports similes.

Key Competences and Key Learning Outcomes

- Act out a short dialogue in pairs
- Learn and practise using the present perfect to talk about how long you have done different activities
- Analyse and apply rules for using the present perfect with 'for' and 'since'
- Identify and practise using correct rhythm and stress in present perfect sentences

Key language

- *belt, concentrate, get fit, karate*
- *How long have I / you / we / they (played tennis)? I / You / We / They have (played tennis) for two years. How long has he / she (studied French)? He / She has (studied French) since last year.*

Materials

- Pupil's Book p22; Activity Book p19; Class CD1; Teacher's App on Navio

Optional materials

- Teacher's Resource Bank: Trinity Exams Practice cards (selected from the Starter Unit and Unit 1)

At a Glance Lesson Plan

Pupil's Book

Starting the lesson

- Use the Trinity Exams Practice cards (optional).
- Review sports and hobbies.
- Set learning outcomes.

Activity 1

- Listen and read.
- ▶ *CD1 Track 25 p279*
- Act out.

Activity 2

- Look and learn – Grammar wall

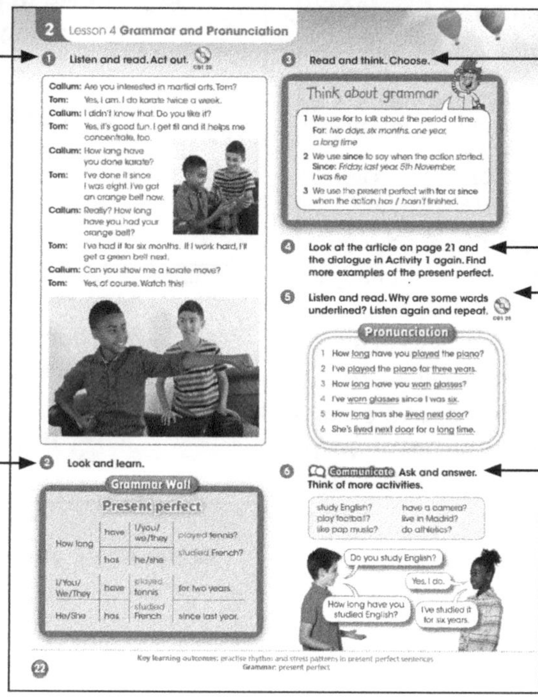

Activity 3

- Read and think.
- Choose.

Activity 4

- Look at the article on page 21 and the dialogue in Activity 1 again.
- Find more examples of the present perfect.

Activity 5

- Listen and read.
- ▶ *CD1 Track 26 p279*
- Why are some words underlined?
- Listen again and repeat.

Activity 6

- Ask and answer.
- Think of more activities.
- Go to the Activity Book.

Ending the lesson

- Review the lesson and reflect on learning.

Extra activities

Reinforcement

- Play a game with time expressions.

Activity Book

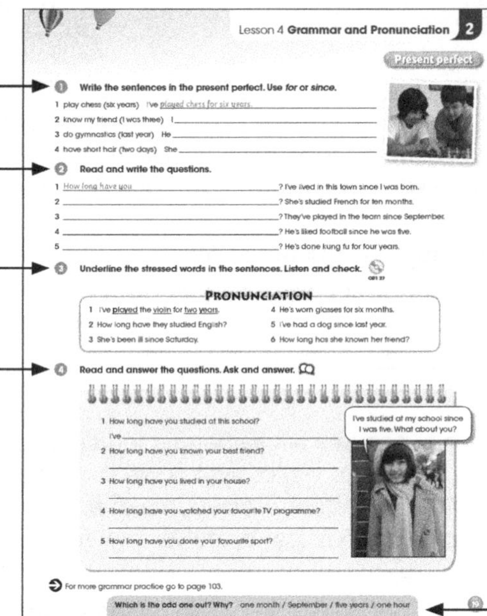

Activity Book

Activity 1

- Write the sentences in the present perfect. Use *for* or *since.*

Activity 2

- Read and write the questions.

Activity 3

- Underline the stressed words in the sentences. Listen and check.
- ▶ *CD1 Track 27 p279*

Activity 4

- Read and answer the questions. Ask and answer.

Odd one out activity

Digital resources

Teacher's Digital: You can also teach this lesson using the Teacher's App on Navio.

Pupil's Digital: Encourage your pupils to use the Pupil's App on Navio to practise the activities from this lesson.

Powered By NAVIO

Starting the lesson

Use the Trinity Exams Practice cards (optional).

- The pupils practise asking and answering questions.

Review sports and hobbies.

- Ask **Do you do any sports or hobbies?** Invite a pupil to answer. **What equipment do you use?**
- In pairs, the pupils have three minutes to tell each other about sports and hobbies they do.

Set learning outcomes

- Say **Today we're going to talk about how long we've done different sports and activities.**

Pupil's Book Activity 1

Listen and read. Act out.

▶ *CD1 Track 25 p279*

- The pupils look at the photos. Ask **What are Callum and Tom talking about in photo 1? What is Tom doing in photo 2?**
- Play the CD. Check understanding. Ask **What sport does Tom do? When did he begin it?**
- Play the CD again, pausing after each sentence for the pupils to repeat.
- The pupils practise the dialogue in pairs.

Pupil's Book Activity 2

Look and learn – Grammar wall

- Read the information on the Grammar wall as a class.
- Encourage the pupils to think about the difference between 'for' and 'since'. Ask **Do we use 'for' or 'since' if we say when the action started?** (*Since.*) Give examples, e.g. **since (last week)**. Ask **Do we use 'for' or 'since' if we say the period of time?** (*For.*) Give examples, e.g. **for (10 minutes)**.

Pupil's Book Activity 3

Read and think. Choose.

- Focus the pupils' attention on the Think about Grammar box. Read out the sentences as a class. The pupils complete the final sentence in pairs.
- Check answers as a class. (*3 hasn't*)

Pupil's Book Activity 4

Look at the article on page 21 and the dialogue in Activity 1 again. Find more examples of the present perfect.

- In pairs, the pupils find examples of the present perfect.

Pupil's Book Activity 5

Listen and read. Why are some words underlined? Listen again and repeat.

▶ *CD1 Track 26 p279*

- Play the CD, pausing after each sentence. The pupils identify that the underlined words are stressed.
- Play the CD again. The pupils listen and repeat.

Pupil's Book Activity 6

Ask and answer. Think of more activities.

- Invite two pupils to read out the speech bubbles. Then invite other pairs of pupils to have a similar exchange, using the different prompts.
- In pairs, the pupils ask and answer questions.

Activity Book

Activity 1

Write the sentences in the present perfect. Use *for* or *since*.

- Invite a pupil to read out the example.
- The pupils write the sentences.

Answers: **1** played chess for six years. **2** 've known my friend since I was three. **3** 's done gymnastics since last year. **4** 's had short hair for two days.

Activity 2

Read and write the questions.

- The pupils write the questions.

Answers: **1** lived in this town? **2** How long has she studied French? **3** How long have they played in the team? **4** How long has he liked football? **5** How long has he done kung fu?

Activity 3

Underline the stressed words in the sentences. Listen and check.

▶ *CD1 Track 27 p279*

- In pairs, the pupils underline the stressed words.
- Play the CD. The pupils listen and check.

Answers: **1** played, violin, two, years **2** long, studied, English **3** been, ill, Saturday **4** worn, glasses, six, months **5** had, dog, last, year **6** long, known, friend

Activity 4

Read and answer the questions. Ask and answer.

- The pupils write the answers to the questions.
- They ask and answer the questions in pairs.

Odd one out activity

Which is the odd one out? Why?

- The pupils complete the odd one out activity.

Answers: September (It isn't a period of time.)

Ending the lesson

Review the lesson and reflect on learning.

- Say **Today we've talked about how long we've done different sports and activities.**
- Ask **What do you remember?** The pupils do a three-minute review in pairs. (Cooperative Learning Strategies, page 19)

Extra activity

Extension

- The class stands up. Say different time expressions. The pupils stand for expressions used with 'for' and sit down for expressions used with 'since'.

Key Competences and Key Learning Outcomes

- Review and name hobbies
- Practise expressing preferences
- Practise activity types found in the Cambridge Exams: B1 Preliminary for Schools
- Learn how the suffixes *-er* and *-or* change some verbs to nouns
- Listen for gist and specific information
- Do a communication task

Key language

- *belong to a sports club, do circus skills, collect cards, go to drama class, do photography, do needlework, make models, sing in a choir*
- Extension: *do gardening, do yoga, do modern dance, write blogs*
- *I prefer collecting stamps to cards. I'd rather collect stamps than cards.*

Materials

- Pupil's Book p23; Activity Book p20; Class CD1; Teacher's App on Navio

Optional materials

- Teacher's Resource Bank: Trinity Exams Practice cards (selected from the Starter Unit and Unit 1)

At a Glance Lesson Plan

Pupil's Book

Starting the lesson

- Use the Trinity Exams Practice cards (optional).
- Review the present perfect with *for* or *since*.
- Set learning outcomes.

Activity 1

- Look and match.
- Listen, check and repeat.
- ▶ ***CD1 Track 28 p279***

Activity 2

- Listen and say *A*, *B* or *C*.
- ▶ ***CD1 Track 29 p279***

Activity 3

- Listen again.
- ▶ ***CD1 Track 29 p279***
- Which expressions do the children use to say what they prefer?

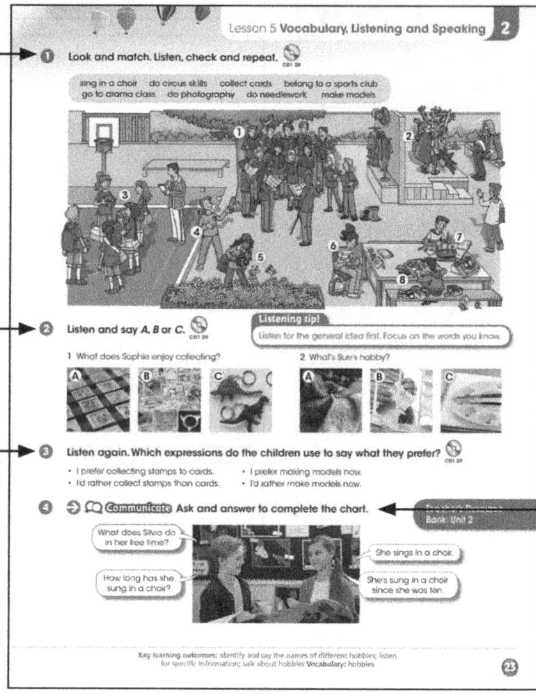

Activity 4

- Ask and answer to complete the chart (Teacher's Resource Bank: Unit 2).

Ending the lesson

- Review the lesson and reflect on learning.

Extra activities

Reinforcement

- Play a mime game.

Vocabulary Extension

- Present four additional vocabulary items.

Activity Book

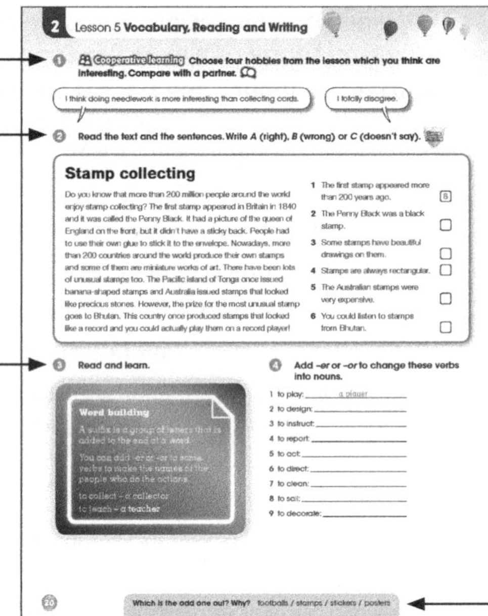

Activity Book

Activity 1

- Choose four hobbies from the lesson which you think are interesting. Compare with a partner.

Activity 2

- Read the text and the sentences. Write *A* (right), *B* (wrong) or *C* (doesn't say).

Activity 3

- Read and learn.

Activity 4

- Add *-er* or *-or* to change these verbs into nouns.

Odd one out activity

Digital resources

Teacher's Digital: You can also teach this lesson using the Teacher's App on Navio.

Pupil's Digital: Encourage your pupils to use the Pupil's App on Navio to practise the activities from this lesson.

Powered By NAVIO

Detailed Lesson Plan

Starting the lesson

Use the Trinity Exams Practice cards (optional).

- The pupils practise asking and answering questions.

Review the present perfect with *for* or *since*.

- Choose a pupil and say **Your (pencil case) is really cool. How long have you had it?** Prompt the pupil to answer with a full sentence using 'for' or 'since'. Repeat the procedure with other pupils.
- In pairs, the pupils ask and answer questions about each other's possessions.

Set learning outcomes

- Say **Today we're going to learn the names of some more hobbies and you're going to work together to complete a chart.**

Pupil's Book Activity 1

Look and match. Listen, check and repeat.

▶ *CD1 Track 28 p279*

- In pairs, ask the pupils to match the words they know with the numbers 1–8 in the picture.
- Play the CD. The pupils listen and check.
- Play the CD again, pausing after each phrase for the pupils to repeat. You can find the answers for this activity in the audioscript on page 279.

Pupil's Book Activity 2

Listen and say *A*, *B* or *C*.

▶ *CD1 Track 29 p279*

- Invite a pupil to describe the first three photos in the activity. Read Listening tip! as a class.
- Play the CD. The pupils listen and identify the correct photo.
- Repeat the procedure with the second set of photos.

Answers: **1** A **2** B

Pupil's Book Activity 3

Listen again. Which expressions do the children use to say what they prefer?

▶ *CD1 Track 29 p279*

- Invite a pupil to read out the four expressions.
- Play the CD again. The pupils listen and identify the expressions that the children use.

Answers: I'd rather collect stamps than cards. I prefer making models now.

Pupil's Book Activity 4

Ask and answer to complete the chart (Teacher's Resource Bank: Unit 2).

- Explain to the pupils that they are going to complete a chart. Invite two pupils to read out the speech bubbles.
- Organise the class into pairs (A and B). Refer to Teacher's Resource Bank: Unit 2 for material.
- Invite two pupils to demonstrate the activity. The rest of the class then do the same in their pairs.

Activity Book

Activity 1

Choose four hobbies from the lesson which you think are interesting. Compare with a partner.

- Draw the line on the board. Write *boring* and *brilliant* at either end.
- Ask a pupil to write one of the hobbies from Activity 1 in the Pupil's Book onto the line. The position will reflect how boring or interesting the pupil finds the hobby. Repeat the procedure with other hobbies.
- The pupils work on their own to complete the activity.
- Then invite two pupils to read out the speech bubbles. In pairs, the pupils compare the information on their lines.

Activity 2

Read the text and the sentences.
Write *A* (right), *B* (wrong) or *C* (doesn't say).

- Ask **Do you collect stamps?**
- Check understanding of text by asking questions. Pupils complete activity individually.

Answers: **1** B **2** C **3** A **4** B **5** C **6** A

Activity 3

Read and learn.

- Read the information as a class. Encourage the pupils to think of other examples.

Activity 4

Add *-er* or *-or* to change these verbs into nouns.

- The pupils work in pairs or on their own to make the nouns by adding -er or -or.

Answers: **1** a player **2** a designer **3** an instructor **4** a reporter **5** an actor **6** a director **7** a cleaner **8** a sailor **9** a decorator

Odd one out activity

Which is the odd one out? Why?

Answers: footballs (They aren't flat.)

Ending the lesson

Review the lesson and reflect on learning.

- Say **Today we've learnt the names of some hobbies and you've worked together to complete a chart.**
- Ask **What do you remember?** The pupils do a three-minute review in pairs.

Extra activities

Reinforcement

- In pairs, pupils mime a word for their partner to guess.

Vocabulary extension

- Present additional hobbies: *bend, dive, score, serve, shoot, stretch, do gardening, do yoga, do, do modern dance, write blogs.*
- Use the Vocabulary booster on NAVIO to practise these new words.

Key Competences and Key Learning Outcomes

- Practise talking about famous people
- Do pre-reading tasks to predict content and raise interest
- Read a text for general understanding
- Scan the text for key content
- Share what you know about this type of text
- Read a magazine article
- Give an opinion on the text

Key language

- *champion, hard-working, kitesurfing, self-confident*
- *I think that Gisela is an amazing sportswoman.*

Materials

- Pupil's Book p24; Activity Book p21; Class CD1; Teacher's App on Navio

Optional materials

- Teacher's Resource Bank: Trinity Exams Practice cards (selected from the Starter Unit and Unit 1)

At a Glance Lesson Plan

Pupil's Book

Starting the lesson

- Use the Trinity Exams Practice cards (optional).
- Review hobbies from Lesson 5.
- Set learning outcomes.

Activity 1: Before you read

- Read and discuss.

Activity 2

- Look at the photos.
- Why do you think this person is famous?
- Read and find out.

Activity 3: After you read

- What do you think?
- Go to the Activity Book.

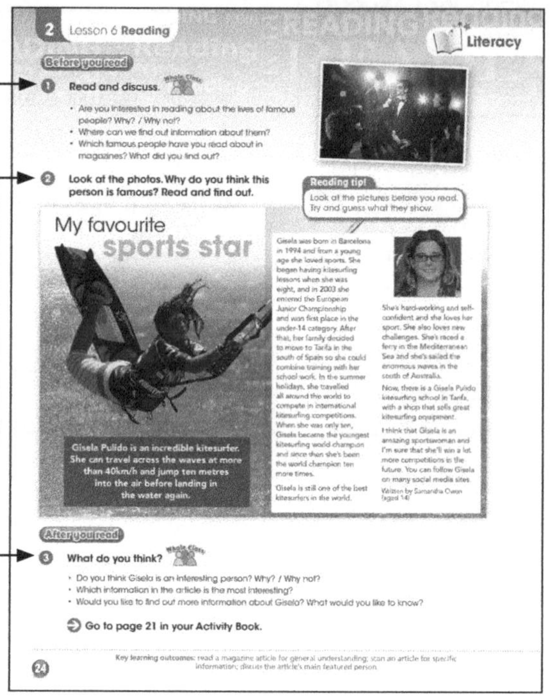
2 Lesson 6 Reading

Literacy

Before you read

1 Read and discuss.

2 Look at the photos. Why do you think this person is famous? Read and find out.

Reading tip!

My favourite sports star

Gisela Pulido is an incredible kitesurfer. She can travel across the waves at more than 40km/h and jump ten metres into the air before landing in the water again.

After you read

3 What do you think?

Go to page 21 in your Activity Book.

24

Ending the lesson

- Review the lesson and reflect on learning.

Extra activity

Extension

- Role play an interview with Gisela.

Activity Book

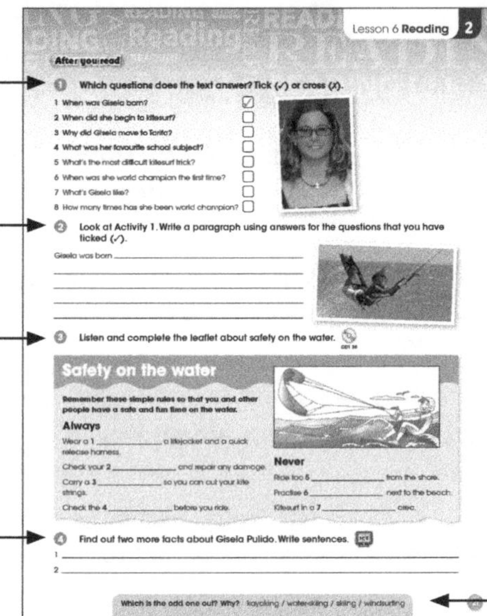
Lesson 6 Reading 2

After you read

1 Which questions does the text answer? Tick (✓) or cross (✗).

2 Look at Activity 1. Write a paragraph using answers for the questions that you have ticked (✓).

3 Listen and complete the leaflet about safety on the water.

Safety on the water

Always

Never

4 Find out two more facts about Gisela Pulido. Write sentences.

Which is the odd one out? Why?

Activity Book: After you read

Activity 1

- Which questions does the text answer? Tick (✓) or cross (✗).

Activity 2

- Look at Activity 1. Write a paragraph using answers for the questions that you have ticked (✓).

Activity 3

- Listen and complete the leaflet about safety on the water.

▶ *CD1 Track 30 p279*

Activity 4

- Find out two more facts about Gisela Pulido. Write sentences.

Odd one out activity

Digital resources

Teacher's Digital: You can also teach this lesson using the Teacher's App on Navio.

Pupil's Digital: Encourage your pupils to use the Pupil's App on Navio to practise the activities from this lesson.

Powered By NAVIO

Starting the lesson

Use the Trinity Exams Practice cards (optional).

- The pupils practise asking and answering questions.

Review hobbies from Lesson 5.

- In pairs, challenge the pupils to remember eight hobbies from Lesson 5. Then quickly review their ideas as a class.

Set learning outcomes.

- Say **Today we're going to read an article about an incredible sports person.**

Pupil's Book Activity 1: Before you read

Read and discuss.

- Read the questions as a class. Prompt the pupils to answer in as much detail as possible.

Pupil's Book Activity 2

Look at the photos. Why do you think this person is famous? Read and find out.

- Discuss the photos as a class. Encourage the pupils to predict why the person is famous. Then read the magazine article to find out.
- Confirm that Gisela is one of the best kitesurfers in the world and that she has been the world champion ten times.

Pupil's Book Activity 3: After you read

What do you think?

- Read the first two questions as a class. Prompt the pupils to give their opinions. Encourage them to give a reason each time.
- Then ask the pupils to think of more information that they would like to find out about Gisela.

Activity Book: After you read

Activity 1

Which questions does the text answer? Tick (✓) or cross (✗).

- Read the questions as a class. The pupils work on their own to identify which questions are answered in the text, consulting the magazine article in the Pupil's Book as they do so.

Answers: 1 ✓ 2 ✓ 3 ✓ 4 ✗ 5 ✗ 6 ✓ 7 ✓ 8 ✓

Activity 2

Look at Activity 1. Write answers for the questions that you have ticked (✓).

- The pupils work with a partner or on their own to answer questions 1, 2, 3, 6, 7 and 8 in Activity 1. They look for the answers in the Pupil's Book each time.

Answers: **1** Gisela was born in 1994. She began to kitesurf when she was eight. She moved to Tarifa so she could combine training with her schoolwork. She was world champion for the first time when she was ten. She's hard-working and self-confident. She's been world champion ten times.

Activity 3

Listen and complete the leaflet about safety on the water.

▶ *CD1 Track 30 p279*

- Read the safety rules as a class. Encourage the pupils to predict the missing words each time.
- Play the CD. The pupils listen and complete as much of the information as possible. They check their answers with a partner.
- Play the CD again, pausing after each piece of information. The pupils complete and check their answers.

Answers: **1** helmet **2** equipment **3** knife **4** weather **5** far **6** jumping **7** swimming

Activity 4

Find out two more facts about Gisela Pulido. Write sentences. ICT

- Ask the class to find out two more facts. The pupils can do this at home or in the classroom if you have an Internet connection.

Odd one out activity

Which is the odd one out? Why?

- The pupils complete the odd one out activity.

Answers: skiing (It isn't a water sport.)

Ending the lesson

Review the lesson and reflect on learning.

- Say **Today we've read an article about an incredible sports woman.**
- Ask **What do you remember?** The pupils do a three-minute review in pairs. (Cooperative Learning Strategies, page 19)

Extra activity

Extension

- Focus the class on the questions in Activity 1 of the Activity Book (page 21). Invite different pupils to change each question to the second person, i.e. *When were you born? When did you begin to kitesurf?*
- In pairs, the pupils role play an interview between a journalist and Gisela.

Key Competences and Key Learning Outcomes

- Learn and practise how to use extreme adjectives
- Identify the text features of a magazine article
- Use criteria to check your writing
- Share and discuss your writing with a partner
- Write a magazine article about a famous person

Key language

- *amazing, astonishing, brilliant, enormous, fantastic, fascinating, massive*
- *Ross is mad about (flying).*

Materials

- Pupil's Book p25; Activity Book p22; Teacher's App on Navio

Optional materials

- Teacher's Resource Bank: Trinity Exams Practice cards (selected from the Starter Unit and Unit 1)
- Photos of famous people

At a Glance Lesson Plan

Pupil's Book

Starting the lesson

- Use the Trinity Exams Practice cards (optional).
- Review describing famous people.
- Set learning outcomes.

Activity 1: Investigate a text

- Read the information.
- Write two open and two closed questions about Ross Lynch.

Activity 2

- Read the article.
- Does it answer your questions?

Activity 3: Discuss a text

- Read the article again.
- Answer the questions.

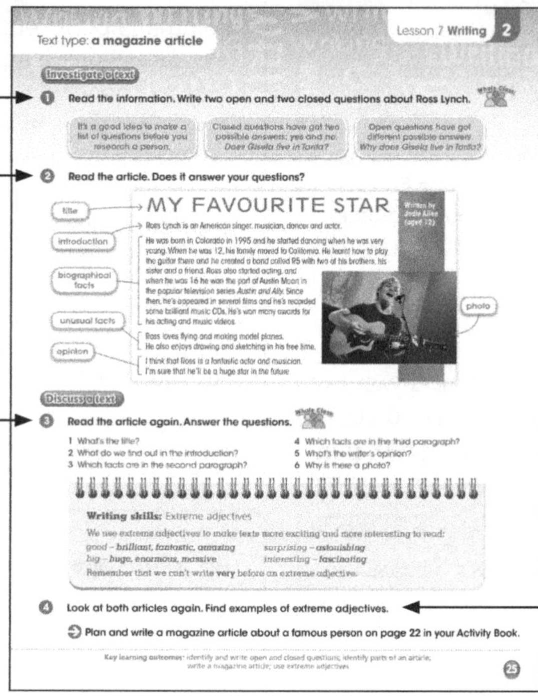

Writing skills

- Read about extreme adjectives.

Activity 4

- Look at both articles again.
- Find examples of extreme adjectives.
- Go to the Activity Book.

Ending the lesson

- Review the lesson and reflect on learning.

Extra activity

Extension

- Find three interesting facts about famous people.

Activity Book

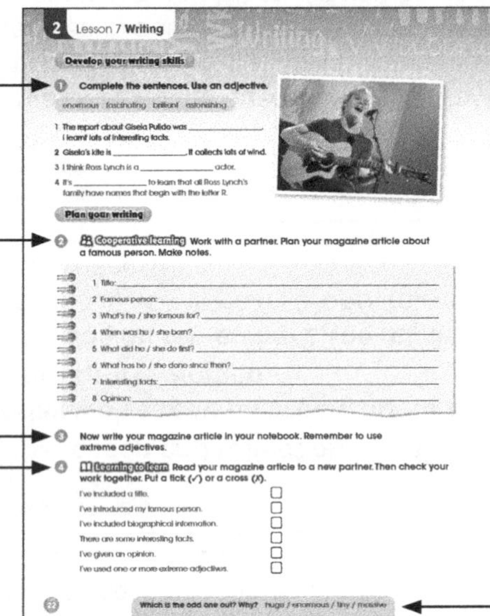

Activity Book

Activity 1: Develop your writing skills

- Complete the sentences. Use an adjective.

Activity 2: Plan your writing

- Work with a partner. Plan your magazine article about a famous person. Make notes.

Activity 3

- Now write your magazine article in your notebook. Remember to use extreme adjectives.

Activity 4

- Read your magazine article to a new partner. Then check your work together. Put a tick (✓) or a cross (✗).

Odd one out activity

Digital resources

Teacher's Digital: You can also teach this lesson using the Teacher's App on Navio.

Pupil's Digital: Encourage your pupils to use the Pupil's App on Navio to practise the activities from this lesson.

Powered By NAVIO

Starting the lesson

Use the Trinity Exams Practice cards (optional).

- The pupils practise asking and answering questions.

Review describing famous people.

- Think of a famous person that the pupils know. Describe the person's appearance, character and what he / she is famous for. The pupils try to name the person.
- If you have a photo of the person, show it to the class. Encourage the pupils to add any other information they know.
- Repeat the procedure with other famous people.

Set learning outcomes

- Say **Today we're going to read and write an article about a famous person.**

Pupil's Book Activity 1: Investigate a text

Read the information. Write two open and two closed questions about Ross Lynch.

- Read the information as a class.
- The pupils work in pairs to think of two open and two closed questions about Ross Lynch.
- Invite different pairs to read out their questions.

Pupil's Book Activity 2

Read the article. Does it answer your questions?

- The pupils read the magazine article. They check whether their questions are answered.

Pupil's Book Activity 3: Discuss a text

Read the article again. Answer the questions.

- Read and discuss the questions as a class. Highlight that a good article has a clear title and introduction, biographical facts and some interesting or unusual information. The writer should also give a personal opinion about the famous person.

Writing skills

- Read about using extreme adjectives.
- Encourage the pupils to say the adjectives in an exaggerated, emphatic way in order to highlight their extreme meaning, e.g. *amazing*, *enormous*.

Pupil's Book Activity 4

Look at both articles again. Find examples of extreme adjectives.

- The pupils look at the articles in Lessons 6 and 7 to find examples of extreme adjectives.

Activity Book

Activity 1: Develop your writing skills

Complete the sentences. Use an adjective.

- The pupils work on their own or in pairs to complete the sentences.

Answers: **1** fascinating **2** enormous **3** brilliant **4** astonishing

Activity 2: Plan your writing

Work with a partner. Plan your magazine article about a famous person. Make notes.

- Read out the notes as a class. Check understanding.
- In pairs, the pupils choose a famous person and make notes.
- **Note:** the pupils will need time to research their famous person. If you have Internet access in the classroom, they can do this in class time. Alternatively, they can complete the notes as homework.

Activity 3

Now write your magazine article in your notebook. Remember to use extreme adjectives.

- The pupils write their articles in their notebooks.

Activity 4

Read your magazine article to a new partner. Then check your work together. Put a tick (✓) or a cross (✗).

- Read through the statements as a class.
- Organise the class into new partners. One pupil reads aloud their text. The other pupil listens. The pupils work together to decide if the text fulfils the criteria and tick the corresponding boxes. The pupils can add, improve or correct the text at this stage.
- The pupils swap roles.

Odd one out activity

Which is the odd one out? Why?

- The pupils complete the odd one out activity.

Answers: tiny (It doesn't refer to something that is big.)

Ending the lesson

Review the lesson and reflect on learning.

- Say **Today we've read and written an article about a famous person.**
- Ask **What do you remember?** The pupils do a three-minute review in pairs. (Cooperative Learning Strategies, page 19)

Extra activity

Extension

- Ask the pupils to leave their notebooks on their desks so that other pupils can read their articles. The pupils then move around the class, reading the different articles. Each pupil should write down three interesting facts that they learn.

Key Competences and Key Learning Outcomes

- Practise expressions for making suggestions

- Prepare and practise speaking activity types found in Cambridge Exams: B1 Preliminary for Schools
- Review learning and reflect on progress
- Listen to a text for general and specific information

- Work in a group to choose equipment
- Learn and practise how to initiate a conversation in a speaking task

Key language

- *absolutely, match*
- *What sport do you play?*

Materials

- Pupil's Book p26; Activity Book pp23–24; Class CD1; Teacher's App on Navio

Optional materials

- Teacher's Resource Bank: Trinity Exams Practice cards (selected from the Starter Unit and Unit 1)

At a Glance Lesson Plan

Pupil's Book

Starting the lesson

- Use the Trinity Exams Practice cards (optional).
- Review sports and hobbies.
- Set learning outcomes.

Activity 1

- Describe the photos.
- Have you ever done these sports?

Activity 2

- Listen to the conversation.
- ▶ ***CD1 Track 31 p279***
- Which sports does James talk about?

Activity 3

- Listen again.
- ▶ ***CD1 Track 31 p279***
- Complete the four questions that Anna asks.

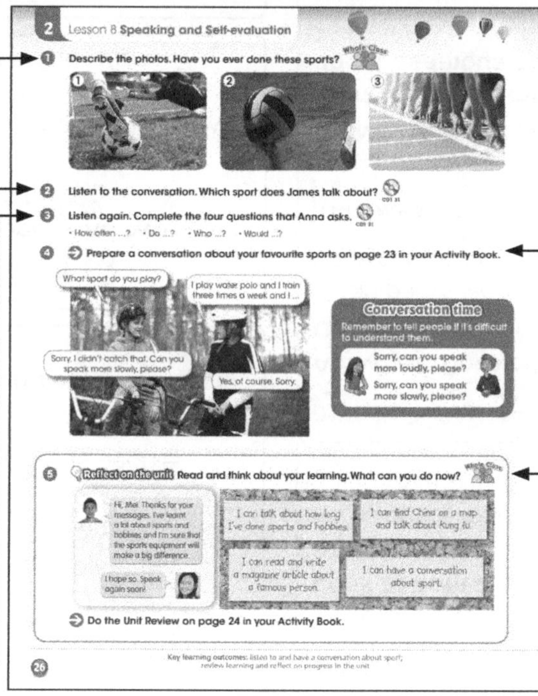

Activity 4

- Prepare a conversation about your favourite sports on page 23 in your Activity Book.
- Go to the Activity Book.

Activity 5

- Read and think about your learning. What can you do now?

Ending the lesson

- Review the lesson and discuss their favourite lesson.

Activity Book

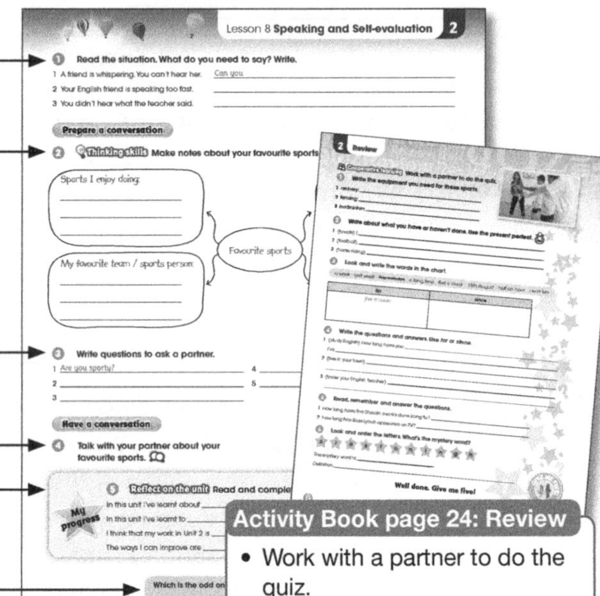

Activity Book page 24: Review

- Work with a partner to do the quiz.

Activity Book

Activity 1

- Read the situation. What do you need to say? Write.

Activity 2

- Make notes about your favourite sports.

Activity 3

- Write questions to ask a partner.

Activity 4

- Talk with your partner about your favourite sports.

Activity 5 My progress

- Read and complete the sentences.

Odd one out activity

Digital resources

Teacher's Digital: You can also teach this lesson using the Teacher's App on Navio.

Powered By NAVIO

Starting the lesson

Use the Trinity Exams Practice cards (optional).
- The pupils practise asking and answering questions.

Review sports and hobbies.
- Invite a pupil to the front of the class. Ask the pupil to think of a sport they enjoy.
- Prompt the rest of the class to ask questions to find out which sport it is. Prompt if necessary, e.g. *Do you need to wear / use (a helmet)? Do you do this activity (indoors)? Is it (a team sport)?*

Set learning outcomes.
- Say **Today we're going to learn and practise how to have a conversation about sport and we're going to think about our learning in this unit.**

Pupil's Book Activity 1

Describe the photos. Have you ever done these sports?
- Ask a volunteer pupil to describe one of the photos. Elicit from class what the sport is.
- Go through each picture and ask what sport it is.

Pupil's Book Activity 2

Listen to the conversation. Which sports does James talk about?

▶ ***CD1 Track 31 p279***
- Explain that pupils will hear a boy and a girl talking about sports.
- Play the CD, pausing when a sport is mentioned.

Answers: water polo, football, athletics

Pupil's Book Activity 3

Listen again. Complete the four questions that Anna asks.

▶ ***CD1 Track 31 p279***
- Ask pupils to try and finish the question openers.
- Play CD, pausing after each question for pupils to complete the answer.

Answers: How often do you play it? Do you ever watch any sports? Who's your favourite sports person? Would you like to try a new sport?

Activity Book

Activity 1

Read the situation. What do you need to say? Write.
- Read out the first sentence and elicit an answer.
- Invite pupils to read their sentences.

Answers: **1** Can you speak more loudly please? **2** Can you speak more slowly please? **3** Can you repeat that please?

Activity 2

Make notes about your favourite sports.
- Pupils work individually to complete the spidergram.
- Ask volunteers to read some of their sentences to the class.

Activity 3

Write questions to ask a partner.
- Explain that pupils have to make questions about sports for their partners.
- Ask pupils to say a few questions.
- Have pupils complete the activity.

Activity 4

Talk with your partner about your favourite sports.
- In pairs, pupils have a conversation about their favourite sports using the questions in Activity 3. Pupils swap roles.

Pupil's Book Activity 4

Prepare a conversation about your favourite sports on page 23 in your Activity Book.
- Ask pupils what type of questions they would ask their friends about sports.
- Refer pupils to the Conversation time box. Explain that we use these phrases if we can't hear or understand what someone is saying. Ask if they can think of any more sentences.
- Refer pupils to the Activity Book.

Pupil's Book Activity 5

Read and think about your learning. What can you do now?
- Read the messages as a class. Then look back through the unit and prompt the pupils to identify other things they have learnt / done.

Activity Book

Activity 5: My progress

Read and complete the sentences.
- Read out the sentences. Encourage the pupils to think of different ways of completing them.

Odd one out activity

Which is the odd one out? Why?

Answers: net (You don't hold it in your hand.)

Ending the lesson

Review the lesson and reflect on learning.
- Say **Today we've learnt and practised how to start a conversation and we've thought about our learning in this unit. What do you remember?**

Activity Book page 24: Review

Work with a partner to do the quiz.
- Organise the class into pairs. Explain that they are going to work together to do a quiz. Set a time limit for the pupils to do this (10–15 minutes). Stress that the pupils are not competing with each other.
- Read out the six tasks that the pupils have to complete. Check understanding. Then say **Ready, steady … Go!**
- The pupils work in their pairs to do the quiz. Ask the pupils who finish quickly to help another pair.
- Correct the answers as a class.

Answers: **1 1** bow, arrow **2** sword, mask **3** shuttlecock, racket **3 for** five minutes, a week, a long time, half an hour **since** last week, five o'clock, 16th August, I was ten **4 1** studied English? **2** How long have you lived in your town? **3** How long have you known your English teacher? **5 1** They've done kung fu for 1,500 years. **2** He's appeared on TV since he was 16. **6** astonishing, something that is extremely surprising

Key Competences and Key Learning Outcomes

- Watch and understand a video about hobbies
- Evaluate hobbies and abilities
- Understand the importance of persevering and working hard to achieve goals
- Understand what you are good at and what you need to improve on
- Understand the importance of having a positive attitude in the face of difficulty

Key language

- *belt, be patient, metronome, positive attitude, set a goal*
- *Maths is sometimes difficult for me. What about you? No, it's not difficult for me.*

Materials

- Pupil's Book p27; Activity Book p25; Class CD1; Teacher's App on Navio
- Teacher's Resource Bank: Talk cards

Optional materials

- Teacher's Resource Bank: Trinity Exams Practice cards (selected from the Starter Unit)

At a Glance Lesson Plan

Pupil's Book

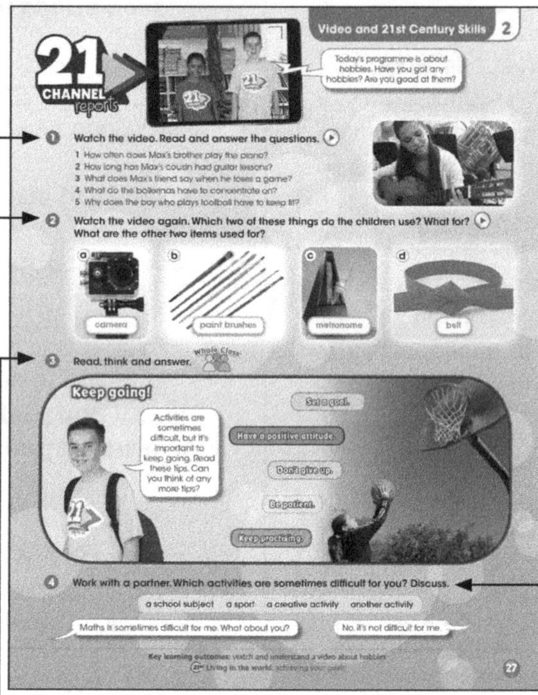
Video and 21st Century Skills 2

1 Watch the video. Read and answer the questions.

2 Watch the video again. Which two of these things do the children use? What for? What are the other two items used for?

camera · paint brushes · metronome · belt

3 Read, think and answer.

Keep going!

Set a goal. · Have a positive attitude · Don't give up. · Be patient. · Keep practising.

4 Work with a partner. Which activities are sometimes difficult for you? Discuss.

a school subject · a sport · a creative activity · another activity

Maths is sometimes difficult for me. What about you? · No, it's not difficult for me.

27

Starting the lesson

- **Think-Pair-Share.** Review hobbies.
- Set learning outcomes and use the talk cards.

Activity 1

- Before you watch.
- Watch the video.
- *Unit 2 video p300*
- Read and answer the questions.

Activity 2

- Watch the video again.
- *Video 2*
- Which two of these things do the children use?
- What for?
- What are the other two items used for?

Activity 3

- Read, think and answer.

Activity 4

- Work with a partner.
- Which activities are sometimes difficult for you?
- Discuss.
- Go to the Activity Book.

Ending the lesson

- Review the lesson and reflect on learning.

Extra activity

- Discuss why hobbies are good for you.

Activity Book

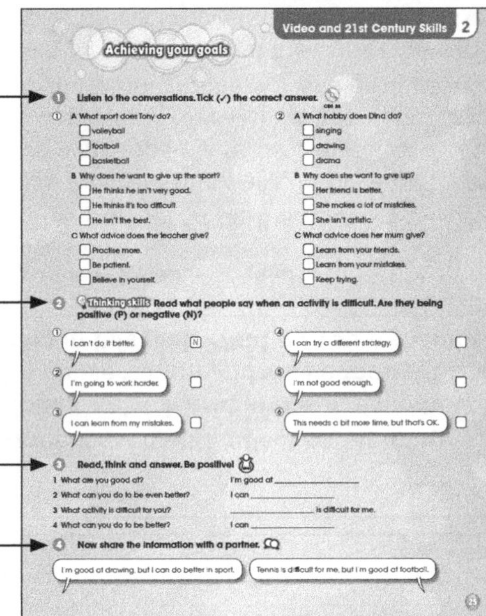
Video and 21st Century Skills 2

Achieving your goals

1 Listen to the conversations. Tick (✓) the correct answer.

2 Thinking skills Read what people say when an activity is difficult. Are they being positive (P) or negative (N)?

3 Read, think and answer. Be positive!

4 Now share the information with a partner.

Activity Book

Activity 1

- Listen to the conversations. Tick (✓) the correct answer.

▶ *CD1 Track 32 p279*

Activity 2

- Read what people say when an activity is difficult. Are they being positive (P) or negative (N)?

Activity 3

- Read, think and answer. Be positive!

Activity 4

- Now share the information with a partner.

Digital resources

Teacher's Digital: You can also teach this lesson using the Teacher's App on Navio.

Pupil's Digital: Encourage your pupils to use the Pupil's App on Navio to practise the activities from this lesson.

Powered By NAVIO

Starting the lesson

Think-Pair-Share. Review different types of hobbies.

- Ask **What hobbies do you do and when?** Elicit answers and write them on the board.
- Then the pupils work with a Talk Partner to name different types of hobbies.
- Invite different Talk Partners to say a different type of hobby.
- Finally, repeat the procedure, asking different pairs of Talk Partners each time, until all the hobbies have been recorded.

Set learning outcomes and use the talk cards.

- Say **Today we're going to watch a video and then talk about different types of hobbies.**
- Ask pupils if they remember who the presenters are (Max and Amy).
- Point to the talk cards to show the pupils the different ways they will be working in the lesson.

Pupil's Book Activity 1

Before you watch

- Ask pupils what type of hobbies they think Max and Amy will present in the lesson.
- Read the speech bubble to pupils. Ask **Are you good at your hobbies?** Elicit responses from a number of pupils.
- Read the questions in Activity 1. Explain that students have to answer them.

Watch the video. Read and answer the questions.
p300

- Watch Part 1.
- Ask a pupil to read out question 1. Ask the class for the answer. Repeat with all items.
- Play Part 2, pausing at each section for pupils to write the answer. Students work in pairs to answer the questions.

Answers: **1** He plays every day (for 15 minutes). **2** He's had lessons for five years. **3** He says it doesn't matter. **4** They have to concentrate on their steps. **5** Because he has to run a lot.

Pupil's Book Activity 2

Watch the video again. Which two of these things do the children use? What for? What are the other two items used for?

- Ask to tell you what types of hobbies the pupils remember from the video. Ask if they remember what equipment is used.
- Ask them to look at each item in the activity and tell you why it is used.
- Play the video pausing after each hobby. Ask which of the items can be used in each hobby and why.

Answers: **a** People who do photography can use this. **b** The model plane maker can use the paintbrushes to paint the planes. **c** The piano and guitar players can use the metronome to play music. It keeps to the beat. **d** People who do karate can use this. It shows what level they are at.

Pupil's Book Activity 3

Read, think and answer.

- Ask what points Amy and Max present.
- Pupils work in pairs to read and think about each point. Ask why each point is important and how it can help them when they do hobbies.
- Ask if they can think of any more ideas.

Pupil's Book Activity 4

Work with a partner. Which activities are sometimes difficult for you? Discuss.

- Pupils work in pairs to read and think about which activities are sometimes difficult for them.
- Invite different Talk Partners to present their idea to the class.

Activity Book

Activity 1

Listen to the conversations. Tick (✓) the correct answer.

▶ *CD1 Track 32 p279*

- Ask why they think people sometimes give up a hobby. Elicit answers and write them on the board.
- Then ask why people should always try hard before giving up.
- Explain they will listen to conversations about hobbies and different advice the children are given.
- Play the CD and complete the activity.

Answers: **1** A football **2** B He thinks he isn't very good. C Be patient. **2** A Drawing B She makes a lot of mistakes. C Learn from your mistakes.

Activity 2

Read what people say when an activity is difficult. Are they being positive (P) or negative (N)?

- Refer pupils to the first item. Elicit why this is negative (because the person saying it doesn't believe they can do better).
- In pairs, have pupils complete the activity. Elicit answers.

Answers: **1** N **2** P **3** P **4** P **5** N **6** P

Activity 3

Read, think and answer. Be positive!

- Go through each item and elicit ideas from different pupils.
- Pupils complete the activity individually.

Activity 4

Now share the information with a partner.

- In pairs, pupils read and discuss their information.
- Ask some pupils to present their opinions to the class.

Ending the lesson

Review the lesson and reflect on learning.

- Say **Today we've watched a video about different hobbies. What have we learnt about them?** Elicit the information from the pupils. The pupils do a three-minute review in pairs. (Cooperative Learning Strategies, page 19)

Extra activity

Reinforcement

- Have a class discussion on why hobbies are good for you. Write ideas on the board as they are presented.

Date: ____________ Unit: ____________

1 What did my pupils learn in this unit?

2 How did my pupils work? (✓)

individually ☐ in pairs ☐ in small groups ☐

in large groups ☐ as a class ☐

3 Which key competences did my pupils develop? Give a score from 1 to 5 (5 being the highest).

- Competence in linguistic communication ☐
- Competence in mathematics, science and technology ☐
- Digital competence ☐
- Learning to learn ☐
- Social and civic competences ☐
- Sense of initiative and entrepreneurship ☐
- Cultural awareness and expression ☐

4 Which lessons / activities were the most successful and why?

5 Which lessons / activities did my pupils find the most difficult and why?

6 What did I try in the classroom for the first time? How did it go?

7 Which resources did I find most useful? (including webpages)

8 What could I do differently next time I teach this unit?

Unit 3

Healthy habits

Unit overview

Key Competences and Key Learning Outcomes

- Name different kinds of food (Lesson 1)
- Use 'too' and 'enough' with countable and uncountable nouns (Lesson 2)
- Learn phrases related to keeping fit and healthy (Lesson 5)
- Use connective words and phrases (Lesson 7)
- Watch and understand a video (Video and 21st Century Skills)

- Learn about making chocolate (Lesson 3)
- Learn about healthy living and healthy eating (Lessons 5 and 6)

- Use the Pupil's App on Navio
- Investigate Mexico (Lesson 3)

- Practise saying contracted forms 'shouldn't', 'needn't', 'mustn't' (Lesson 4)
- Identify the text features of an argument (Lesson 7)
- Reflect on your own learning (Lesson 8)
- Practise activity types found in the Cambridge Exams: B1 Preliminary for Schools

- Learn about cooking and preparing food (Lesson 1)
- Think about the importance of eating and celebrating together (Lesson 3)
- Ask questions in a conversation (Lesson 8)

- Work in pairs or small groups to practise and reinforce learning (All lessons)
- Do a communication activity (Lesson 5)
- Collaborate to produce an exercise calendar (Video and 21st Century Skills)

- Read a story (Lesson 3)
- Learn about Mexico (Lesson 3)
- Read and write an argument text (Lessons 6 and 7)
- Sing a song (Lesson 8)

Vocabulary

Core vocabulary
an avocado, beans, beef, a chilli pepper, cinnamon, corn, garlic, a lime, an onion, peanuts, prawns, turkey; do exercise, drink fizzy drinks, drink water, eat fruit and vegetables, eat junk food, go for walks, rest, spend time on the computer

Extension vocabulary (optional)
blend, boil, chop, fry, mix, slice; eat sugary food, eat wholegrain bread, play a sport regularly, watch a lot of TV

Other vocabulary
cocoa, diet, fast food, pods, powder, saturated fat, spices, vanilla; dry, ground, roast, save time, water plants; addictive, bitter; all year round; keeping fit, eating healthily, rest, relaxation; marathon, cross-country

Recycled vocabulary
invite, wake up; doctor, hospital, volunteers; cheap, delicious, healthy; chocolate, salt, sugar; also, firstly, furthermore, however, on the one hand, on the other hand, secondly

Structures

Core structures
There are too many (tomatoes). There aren't enough (volunteers). There's too much (rain at this time of year). There isn't enough (sunlight). We should / must / need to (make a cake). You shouldn't / mustn't / needn't (stop eating sugar completely).

Other structures
Then they roasted and ground them. Some people argue that fast food is unhealthy. Some people say that we could use this time more effectively.

Recycled structures
(Are) there any (tomatoes in guacamole)? How often do you (drink water)? I (drink water twice a day). Do you often eat fast food? The table is reserved for 1pm.

Pronunciation

Contracted forms: 'shouldn't', 'needn't', 'mustn't'

Literacy

Text type: an argument text (opinion piece; writing preparation)
Reading skills: scanning text for key information
Writing skills: using connective words and phrases

Culture ... around the world

The discovery of cocoa beans in Mexico

21st Century Skills

Ways of working: Recording information and setting routines

Thinking skills

Categorising (Lesson 1); Analysing and applying rules and patterns (Lessons 2 and 4); Discussing chocolate's history and its repercussions on health (Lesson 3); Thinking about healthy or unhealthy habits (Lesson 5); Seeing two sides of an argument (Lesson 6); Planning, checking and correcting (Lesson 7); Evaluating methods of keeping healthy and fit (Lesson 8)

Cooperative learning

Working together (Lessons 1–8); Reflecting and setting goals (Lessons 1–8); Collaborative speaking (Lesson 5); Collaborative writing (Lesson 7); Peer evaluation and feedback (Lesson 7); Helping and encouraging (Lessons 1–8); Expressing and respecting opinions (Lessons 1, 3, 6 and 8)

Values

The importance of eating and celebrating together

Cross-curricular links

Links to Science
Nutrition
Suggested Arts and Crafts concepts
Scale and space

Key Competences and Key Learning Outcomes

- Name different kinds of food
- Review and practise using 'any' with countable and uncountable nouns
- Read a message for specific information
- Learn about cooking and preparing food

Key language

- *an avocado, beans, beef, a chilli pepper, cinnamon, corn, garlic, a lime, an onion, peanuts, prawns, turkey*
- Extension: *blend, boil, chop, fry, mix, slice*
- *(Are) there any (tomatoes in guacamole)?*

Materials

- Pupil's Book pp28–29; Activity Book p26; Class CD1; Teacher's App on Navio
- Food flashcards

Optional materials

- Teacher's Resource Bank: Trinity Exams Practice cards (from the Starter Unit and Units 1 and 2)

At a Glance Lesson Plan

Pupil's Book

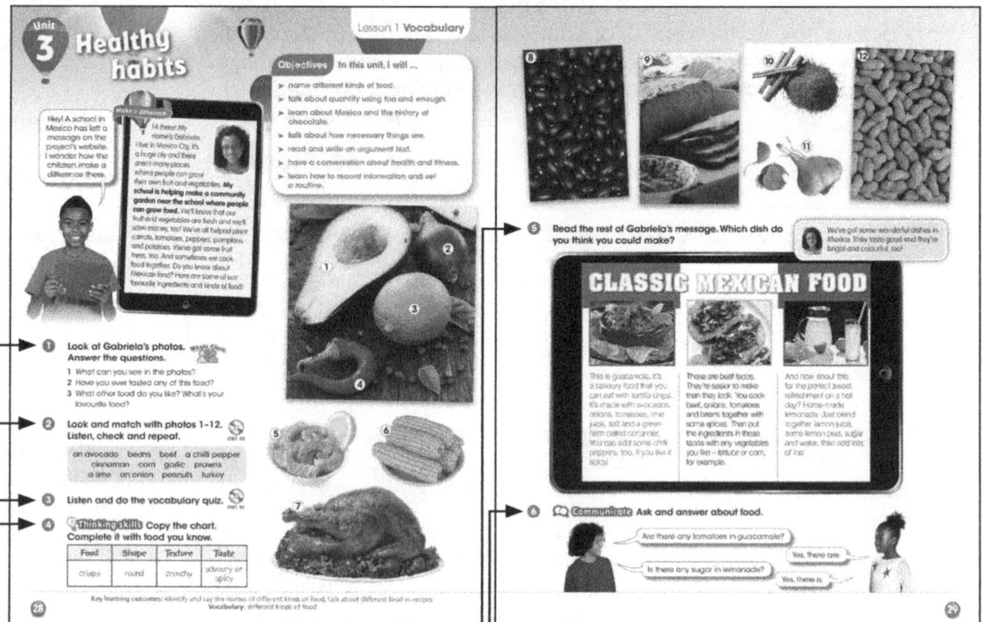

Starting the lesson

- Use the Trinity Exams Practice cards (optional).
- Review fruit and vegetables.
- Set learning outcomes.

Activity 1

- Look at Gabriela's photos.
- Answer the questions.

Vocabulary presentation

- Present the new vocabulary using the food flashcards.

Activity 2

- Look and match with photos 1–12.
- Listen, check and repeat.

▶ *CD1 Track 33 p280*

Activity 3

- Listen and do the vocabulary quiz.

▶ *CD1 Track 34 p280*

Activity 4

- Copy the chart.
- Complete it with food you know.

Activity 5

- Read the rest of Gabriela's message.
- Which dish do you think you could make?

Activity 6

- Ask and answer about food.

Go to the Activity Book.

Ending the lesson

- Review the lesson and reflect on learning.

Extra activities

Extension

- Find out about Mexico.

Vocabulary extension

- Present six additional vocabulary items.

Activity Book

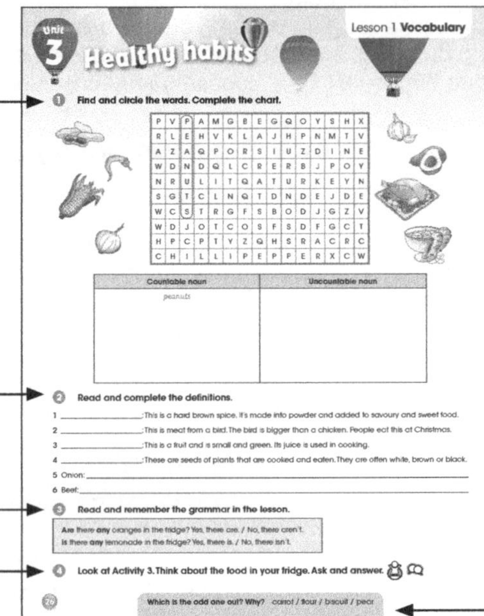

Activity Book

Activity 1

- Find and circle the words. Complete the chart.

Activity 2

- Read and complete the definitions.

Activity 3

- Read and remember the grammar in the lesson.

Activity 4

- Look at Activity 3. Think about the food in your fridge. Ask and answer.

Odd one out activity

Digital resources

Teacher's Digital: You can also teach this lesson using the Teacher's App on Navio.

Pupil's Digital: Encourage your pupils to use the Pupil's App on Navio to practise the activities from this lesson.

Powered By NAVIO

Starting the lesson

Use the Trinity Exams Practice cards (optional).
- The pupils practise asking and answering questions.

Review fruit and vegetables.
- In groups, challenge the pupils to write 15 different kinds of fruit and vegetables.
- Invite the group with the longest list to read it out. Other groups add their ideas.

Set learning outcomes.
- Say **Today we're going to learn words that are connected to food from Mexico.**

Pupil's Book Activity 1

Look at Gabriela's photos. Answer the questions.
- Invite a pupil to read out the speech bubble to find out which school has sent a message. Ask **Do you know where Mexico is?**
- Invite a pupil to read out the message from Gabriela. Check understanding.
- Work as a class to answer the questions.

Vocabulary presentation

- Present the new vocabulary using the food flashcards. Hold up the first flashcard and elicit / say the word. Ask **What kind of food is it? Fruit? Vegetable? Meat? Spice?** Stick the flashcards on the board, grouped according to the kind of food.

Pupil's Book Activity 2

Look and match with photos 1–12. Listen, check and repeat.

▶ *CD1 Track 33 p280*
- Ask the pupils to look at item 1 in the photo. Ask **What's this?** In pairs, the pupils match 1–12 with the words.
- Play the CD. The pupils listen and check. Play the CD again, pausing after each word for the pupils to repeat. You can find the answers for this activity in the audioscript on page 280.

Pupil's Book Activity 3

Listen and do the vocabulary quiz.

▶ *CD1 Track 34 p280*
- Play the CD. Listen to the first definition, pausing at the beep to allow the pupils to name the item. Play the CD to listen to the answer.
- Repeat the procedure with the other definitions. You can find the answers for this activity in the audioscript on page 280.

Pupil's Book Activity 4

Copy the chart. Complete it with food you know.
- Explain that the pupils are going to think of food items and adjectives to describe that food. The adjectives should describe the shape, texture or taste of the food.
- In pairs, the pupils copy and complete the chart.
- Check answers as a class.

Pupil's Book Activity 5

Read the rest of Gabriela's message. Which dish do you think you could make?
- Invite a pupil to read out the message. The pupils read the information and decide which food they could make.

Pupil's Book Activity 6

Ask and answer about food.
- Invite two pupils to read out the speech bubbles.
- Ask why 'are' is used in the first question but 'is' is used in the second.
- In pairs, the pupils ask and answer questions.

Activity Book

Activity 1

Find and circle the words. Complete the chart.
- The pupils write the words in the correct column.

Answers: **countable noun** peanuts, chilli pepper, onion, prawns, avocado **uncountable noun** corn, turkey, garlic

Activity 2

Read and complete the definitions.
- The pupils complete the definitions.

Answer: **1** cinnamon **2** turkey **3** lime **4** beans **5 & 6** Pupils' own answers

Activity 3

Read and remember the grammar in the lesson.
- Invite a pupil to read out the information. Check that the pupils understand what 'countable' and 'uncountable' mean.

Activity 4

Look at Activity 3. Think about the food in your fridge. Ask and answer.
- The pupils ask and answer questions about food in their fridge at home.

Odd one out activity

Which is the odd one out? Why?
- The pupils complete the odd one out activity

Answers: flour (It's uncountable.)

Ending the lesson

Review the lesson and reflect on learning.
- Say **Today we've learnt words for food that is connected with Mexico.**
- Ask **What do you remember?** The pupils do a three-minute review in pairs. (Cooperative Learning Strategies, page 19)

Extra activities

Extension
- The pupils find five facts about Mexico to present to the class. They can use the Internet.

Vocabulary extension
- Present six additional words related to food: *blend, boil, chop, fry, mix, slice.*
- Use the Vocabulary Booster on NAVIO to practise these new words.

Key Competences and Key Learning Outcomes

- Listen to and read a dialogue
- Learn and practise how to use 'too' and 'enough' with countable and uncountable nouns

- Identify examples of 'too' and 'enough' in the dialogue

Key language

- *all year round, volunteers, water plants*
- *There are too many / aren't enough (tomatoes) this year. There is too much / isn't enough (rain) at this time of year.*

Materials

- Pupil's Book p30; Activity Book 27; Class CD1; Teacher's App on Navio
- Teacher's Resource Bank: Food word cards

Optional materials

- Teacher's Resource Bank: Trinity Exams Practice cards (from the Starter Unit and Units 1 and 2)

At a Glance Lesson Plan

Pupil's Book

Starting the lesson

- Use the Trinity Exams Practice cards (optional).
- Review food vocabulary.
- Set learning outcomes.

Activity 1

- Describe the photo.
- What do you think Gabriela is talking about?
- Read and listen to find out.

▶ *CD1 Track 35 p280*

Activity 2

- Read and say *true* or *false*.
- Correct the false sentences.

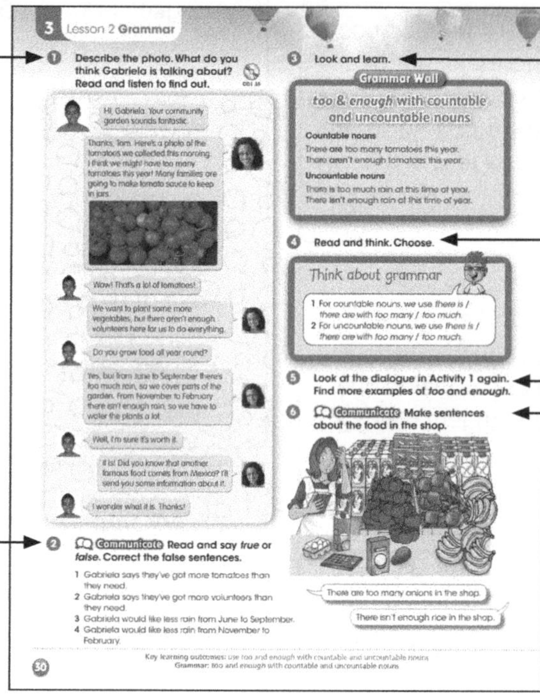

Activity 3

- Look and learn – Grammar wall

Activity 4

- Read and think.
- Choose.

Activity 5

- Look at the dialogue in Activity 1 again.
- Find more examples of *too* and *enough*.

Activity 6

- Make sentences about the food in the shop.

Go to the Activity Book.

Ending the lesson

- Review the lesson and reflect on learning.

Extra activity

Reinforcement

- Make sentences about what is in the classroom.

Activity Book

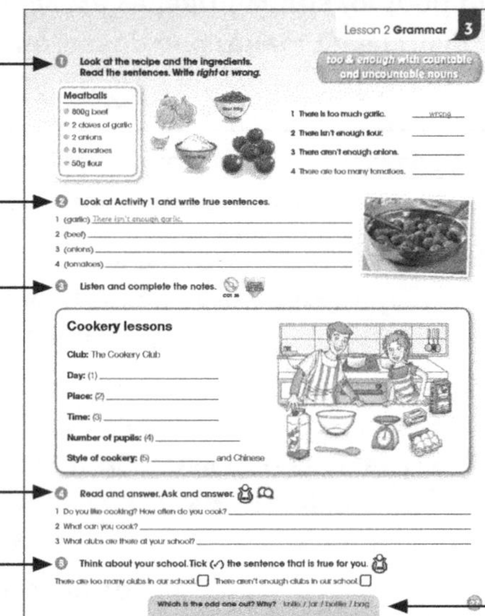

Activity Book

Activity 1

- Look at the recipe and the ingredients. Read the sentences. Write *right* or *wrong*.

Activity 2

- Look at Activity 1 and write true sentences.

Activity 3

- Listen and complete the notes.

▶ *CD1 Track 36 p280*

Activity 4

- Read and answer. Ask and answer.

Activity 5

- Think about your school. Tick (✓) the sentence that is true for you.

Odd one out activity

Digital resources

Teacher's Digital: You can also teach this lesson using the Teacher's App on Navio.

Pupil's Digital: Encourage your pupils to use the Pupil's App on Navio to practise the activities from this lesson.

Powered By NAVIO

Starting the lesson

Use the Trinity Exams Practice cards (optional).
- The pupils practise asking and answering questions.

Review food vocabulary.
- Give each group of four a food word card. The group writes a definition of that word.
- The groups read out the definitions for other groups to guess. Both groups get a point if the definition is guessed. The groups guessing get an extra point if they can spell the word.

Set learning outcomes.
- Say **Today we're going to learn how to talk about quantity – how much of something there is.**

Pupil's Book Activity 1

Describe the photo. What do you think Gabriela is talking about? Read and listen to find out.

▶ *CD1 Track 35 p280*

- Prompt the pupils to describe what they can see in the photo. Ask **What do you think she's talking about?**
- Play the CD. The pupils listen and read the dialogue. Confirm that she is talking about the tomatoes that they grow at the community garden.

Pupil's Book Activity 2

Read and say *true* or *false*.
Correct the false sentences.
- In pairs, the pupils decide which sentences are true and which are false. (*True: 1 and 3 False: 2 and 4.*)

Pupil's Book Activity 3

Look and learn – Grammar wall
- Read the information on the Grammar wall as a class.
- Use questions to encourage the pupils to think about form and identify patterns. Ask **Is 'enough' used with countable or uncountable nouns, or both?** (Both)

Pupil's Book Activity 4

Read and think. Choose.
- Focus the pupils' attention on the Think about grammar box. Read out the sentences as a class. The pupils discuss and complete the sentences in pairs.
- Check answers as a class (*1 there are, too many 2 there is, too much*).

Pupil's Book Activity 5

Look at the dialogue in Activity 1 again. Find more examples of *too* and *enough*.
- In pairs, the pupils find examples of 'too' and 'enough' in the dialogue.

Pupil's Book Activity 6

Make sentences about the food in the shop.
- Ask the pupils to describe the shop. Then invite two pupils to read out the speech bubbles.
- In pairs, the pupils make sentences about the shop. Invite different pupils to share their sentences with the class.

Activity Book

Activity 1

Look at the recipe and the ingredients. Read the sentences. Write *right* or *wrong*.
- The pupils look at the recipe and the ingredients. They read the sentences and write *right* or *wrong*.
- Check answers as a class.

Answers: **1** wrong **2** right **3** wrong **4** wrong

Activity 2

Look at Activity 1 and write true sentences.
- Ask a pupil to read the example.
- The pupils write true sentences about the ingredients.

Answers: **1** There isn't enough garlic. **2** There is too much beef. **3** There aren't enough onions. **4** There aren't enough tomatoes.

Activity 3

Listen and complete the notes.

▶ *CD1 Track 36 p280*

- Ask the pupils to read the notes. They think about the kind of words that go in the gaps. Then play the CD. The pupils listen.
- Play the CD again. The pupils complete the notes.

Answers: **1** Friday **2** Room 30 **3** 3.15 **4** 24 **5** Italian

Activity 4

Read and answer. Ask and answer.
- The pupils write answers to the questions. They then ask and answer the questions in pairs.

Activity 5

Think about your school. Tick (✓) the sentence that is true for you.
- The pupils read and tick a sentence.

Odd one out activity

Which is the odd one out? Why?
- The pupils complete the odd one out activity.

Answers: knife (You can't put things into it.)

Ending the lesson

Review the lesson and reflect on learning.
- Say **Today we've learnt how to talk about how much of something there is. We used 'too much', 'too many' and 'not enough'.**
- Ask **What do you remember?** The pupils do a three-minute review in pairs. (Cooperative Learning Strategies, page 19)

Extra activity

Reinforcement
- In pairs, the pupils write sentences about the classroom using 'too much', 'too many' and 'not enough'. Encourage them to be creative, e.g. *There isn't enough chocolate in the classroom.*
- Ask pairs to read out their sentences and correct them when necessary.

Key Competences and Key Learning Outcomes

- Read a story with confidence and fluency
- Learn about making chocolate
- Use the Internet to investigate Mexico
- Think about the importance of eating and celebrating together
- Learn about Mexico

Key language

- *bitter, chocolate, cocoa, delicious, dry, ground, pods, powder, spices, sugar, vanilla*
- *Then they roasted and ground them.*

Materials

- Pupil's Book p31; Activity Book p28; Class CD1; Teacher's App on Navio

Optional materials

- Teacher's Resource Bank: Trinity Exams Practice cards (from the Starter Unit and Units 1 and 2)

At a Glance Lesson Plan

Pupil's Book

Starting the lesson

- Use the Trinity Exams Practice cards (optional).
- Review words related to food.
- Set learning outcomes.

Activity 1: Before you read

- Read and discuss.

Activity 2

- Listen and read.

▶ *CD1 Track 37 p280*

Go to the Activity Book.

***Give Me Five!* values**

- Read and discuss.

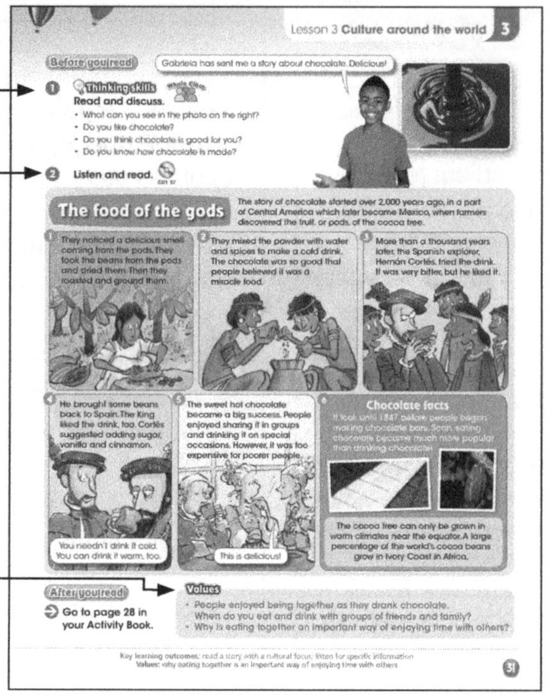

Ending the lesson

- Review the lesson and reflect on learning.

Extra activity

Extension

- Find out more about chocolate.

Activity Book

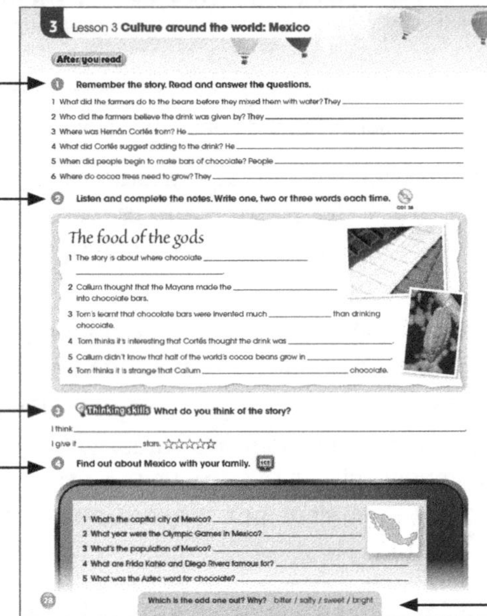

Activity Book: After you read

Activity 1

- Remember the story. Read and answer the questions.

Activity 2

- Listen and complete the notes. Write one, two or three words each time.

▶ *CD1 Track 38 p281*

Activity 3

- What do you think of the story?

Activity 4

- Find out about Mexico with your family.

Odd one out activity

Digital resources

Teacher's Digital: You can also teach this lesson using the Teacher's App on Navio.

Pupil's Digital: Encourage your pupils to use the Pupil's App on Navio to practise the activities from this lesson.

Powered By NAVIO

Starting the lesson

Use the Trinity Exams Practice cards (optional).

- The pupils practise asking and answering questions.

Review words related to food.

- Ask the pupils to think about the difference between sweet food and savoury food. Play a game. Start a chain of food. The first pupil says a sweet food and the next a savoury food and so on. The pupils cannot repeat a word that has already been said. Count the length of the chains to see which is the longest.

Set learning outcomes.

- Say **Today we're going to read about chocolate.**

Pupil's Book Activity 1: Before you read

Read and discuss.

- Read the questions as a class. The pupils share opinions about how healthy chocolate is and how it is made.

Pupil's Book Activity 2

Listen and read.

▶ ***CD1 Track 37 p280***

- Play the CD. The pupils follow in their books.
- Ask questions to check understanding.

Suggested comprehension questions:

- Introduction box: **Did the country of Mexico exist 2,000 years ago?** (*No, it didn't.*)
- Frame 1: **What three things did they do to the pods?** (*Dried them, roasted them and ground them.*)
- Frame 2: **Why did the farmers think it was food from the gods?** (*Because it tasted so good.*)
- Frame 3: **Who was Cortés?** (*A Spanish explorer.*)
- Frame 4: **What happened when Cortés took the beans to Spain?** (*The king of Spain liked the drink.*)
- Frame 5: **Did people drink chocolate every day?** (*No they didn't.*)
- Frame 6: **Which country grows a lot of the world's cocoa beans?** (*The Ivory Coast.*)

Activity Book: After you read

Activity 1

Remember the story. Read and answer the questions.

- Ask a pupil to read out the first question and answer it.
- The pupils read and answer the remaining questions.

Answers: **1** dried them, roasted them and ground them. **2** believed it was given by the gods. **3** was from Spain. **4** suggested adding sugar, vanilla and cinnamon. **5** began to make bars of chocolate in 1847. **6** need to grow near the equator.

Activity 2

Listen and complete the notes. Write one, two or three words each time.

▶ ***CD1 Track 38 p281***

- Read out the notes. Ask the pupils to guess the missing words.
- Play the CD without pausing. The pupils listen and complete as much information as possible.
- Play the CD again, pausing after each piece of key information to check the answer.

Answers: **1** came from **2** beans **3** later **4** too bitter **5** Ivory Coast **6** doesn't like

Activity 3

What do you think of the story?

- The pupils write their opinion and give a rating.
- Invite different pupils to share their opinions.

Activity 4

Find out about Mexico with your family. ICT

- Read out the questions about Mexico. Ask **Where can you find out this information?** (*Internet, library, asking friends and family.*) The pupils complete the activity at home.
- If you prefer to do this activity in class, connect to a children's website which has information about Mexico, such as www.sciencekids.co.nz/sciencefacts/countries/mexico.html.
- Read out the questions. The pupils work as a class to find and write the answers.

Answers: **1** Mexico City **2** 1968 **3** 122 million **4** painting **5** chocolate

Odd one out activity

Which is the odd one out? Why?

- The pupils complete the odd one out activity.

Answers: bright (It doesn't describe the taste of food.)

***Give Me Five!* values**

Read and discuss.

- Read out each question and discuss it as a class.
- Explain that eating food together is a tradition in many cultures. People do it for special occasions or sometimes just to enjoy being with others. Encourage the pupils to think about times when they enjoy eating with others. Ask them to think about why this is important.

Ending the lesson

Review the lesson and reflect on learning.

- Say **Today we've read about where chocolate came from.**
- Ask **What do you remember?** The pupils do a three-minute review in pairs. (Cooperative Learning Strategies, page 19)

Extra activity

Extension

- Ask the pupils to think about what else they would like to know about chocolate, e.g. *What is white chocolate?* In groups or pairs, the pupils write down two or three questions.
- Ask the pupils to give you ten questions. Write them on the board. Vote for the five questions that the class would most like to answer.
- Tell the pupils that they need to try and find out the answers to the questions before the next class. They write sentences in English.

Key Competences and Key Learning Outcomes

- Act out a short dialogue in pairs
- Learn and practise how to use modal verbs for obligation and lack of obligation
- Identify and practise contracted forms: 'shouldn't', 'needn't', 'mustn't'
- Think about rules at school

Key language

- *mobile phone, school uniform*
- *We need to make a cake. You needn't stop eating sugar completely. You should go swimming this weekend. You shouldn't eat too many chocolate bars. We must go shopping before the shops close. We mustn't be late.*

Materials

- Pupil's Book p32; Activity Book p29; Class CD1; Teacher's App on Navio

Optional materials

- Teacher's Resource Bank: Trinity Exams Practice cards (from the Starter Unit and Units 1 and 2)

At a Glance Lesson Plan

Pupil's Book

Starting the lesson

- Use the Trinity Exams Practice cards (optional).
- Review the story from Lesson 3.
- Set learning outcomes.

Activity 1

- Listen and read.

▶ ***CD1 Track 39 p281***

- Act out.

Activity 2

- Look and learn – Grammar wall

Activity 3

- Read and think.
- Choose.

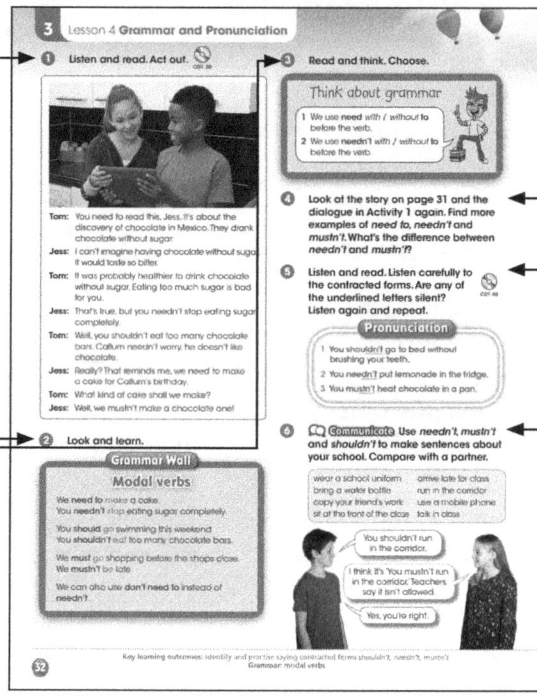
Lesson 4 Grammar and Pronunciation

1 Listen and read. Act out.

3 Read and think. Choose.

Think about grammar

4 Look at the story on page 31 and the dialogue in Activity 1 again. Find more examples of *need to*, *needn't* and *mustn't*. What's the difference between *needn't* and *mustn't*?

5 Listen and read. Listen carefully to the contracted forms. Are any of the underlined letters silent? Listen again and repeat.

Pronunciation

2 Look and learn.

Grammar Wall

Modal verbs

6 Communicate Use *needn't*, *mustn't* and *shouldn't* to make sentences about your school. Compare with a partner.

Activity 4

- Look at the story on page 31 and the dialogue in Activity 1 again.
- Find more examples of *need to*, *needn't* and *mustn't*.
- What's the difference between *needn't* and *mustn't*?

Activity 5

- Listen and read.

▶ ***CD1 Track 40 p281***

- Listen carefully to the contracted forms.
- Are any of the underlined letters silent?
- Listen again and repeat.

Activity 6

- Use *needn't*, *mustn't* and *shouldn't* to make sentences about your school.
- Compare with a partner.

Go to the Activity Book.

Ending the lesson

- Review the lesson and reflect on learning.

Extra activities

Reinforcement

- Write about a school without rules.

Activity Book

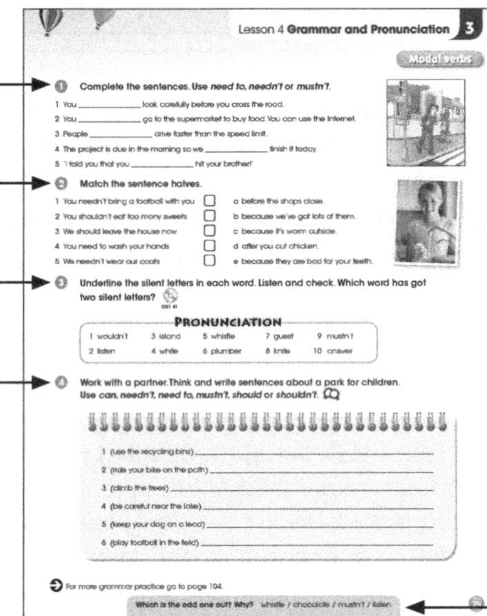
Lesson 4 Grammar and Pronunciation

Modal verbs

1 Complete the sentences. Use *need to*, *needn't* or *mustn't*.

2 Match the sentence halves.

3 Underline the silent letters in each word. Listen and check. Which word has got two silent letters?

PRONUNCIATION

4 Work with a partner. Think and write sentences about a park for children. Use *can*, *needn't*, *need to*, *mustn't*, *should* or *shouldn't*.

Activity Book

Activity 1

- Complete the sentences. Use *need to, needn't* or *mustn't*.

Activity 2

- Match the sentence halves.

Activity 3

- Underline the silent letters in each word. Listen and check. Which word has got two silent letters?

▶ ***CD1 Track 41 p281***

Activity 4

- Work with a partner. Think and write sentences about a park for children. Use *can*, *needn't*, *need to*, *mustn't*, *should* or *shouldn't*.

Odd one out activity

Digital resources

Teacher's Digital: You can also teach this lesson using the Teacher's App on Navio.

Pupil's Digital: Encourage your pupils to use the Pupil's App on Navio to practise the activities from this lesson.

Powered By NAVIO

Detailed Lesson Plan

Starting the lesson

Use the Trinity Exams Practice cards (optional).

- The pupils practise asking and answering questions.

Review the story from Lesson 3.

- Ask some yes/no questions about the story from Lesson 3.

Set learning outcomes.

- Say **Today we're going to learn how to talk about obligation.**

Pupil's Book Activity 1

Listen and read. Act out.

▶ *CD1 Track 39 p281*

- The pupils look at the photo. Ask **What are Tom and Jess talking about?**
- Play the CD. The pupils listen and read the dialogue. Check understanding.
- Play the CD again, pausing after each sentence for the pupils to repeat.
- The pupils practise the dialogue in pairs.

Pupil's Book Activity 2

Look and learn – Grammar wall

- Read the information on the Grammar wall as a class.
- Encourage the pupils to think about the difference between the sentences in each pair. Emphasise that modal verbs always go before the main verb. Explain that 'have to', 'need to' and 'must' all mean that it is necessary to do something.

Pupil's Book Activity 3

Read and think. Choose.

- Focus the pupils' attention on the Think about Grammar box. The pupils complete the sentences.
- Check answers as a class (*1 with 2 without*).

Pupil's Book Activity 4

Look at the story on page 31 and the dialogue in Activity 1 again. Find more examples of *need to*, *needn't* and *mustn't*. What's the difference between *needn't* and *mustn't*?

- In pairs, the pupils find the examples in the dialogue. Discuss the difference between 'needn't' and 'mustn't'. (*Needn't means there is no obligation to do something. Mustn't means there is an obligation not to do something.*)

Pupil's Book Activity 5

Listen and read. Listen carefully to the contracted forms. Are any of the underlined letters silent? Listen again and repeat.

▶ *CD1 Track 40 p281*

- Play the CD. The pupils listen to the sentences. Ask the pupils to say which of the underlined letters is not pronounced.
- Play the CD again. The pupils listen, check and repeat.

Answers: **1** l **2** no letter is silent **3** the first 't'

Pupil's Book Activity 6

Use *needn't*, *mustn't* and *shouldn't* to make sentences about your school. Compare with a partner.

- Ask two pupils to read out the speech bubbles.
- In pairs, the pupils make true sentences.
- Check answers as a class. Do the other pupils agree?

Activity Book

Activity 1

Complete the sentences. Use *need to*, *needn't* or *mustn't*.

- Invite a pupil to complete the first sentence with the correct modal verb.
- The pupils complete the remaining sentences.

Answers: **1** need to **2** needn't **3** mustn't **4** need to **5** mustn't

Activity 2

Match the sentence halves.

- The pupils match the sentence halves.

Answers: **1** b **2** e **3** a **4** d **5** c

Activity 3

Underline the silent letters in each word. Listen and check. Which word has got two silent letters?

▶ *CD1 Track 41 p281*

- The pupils underline the silent letter(s) in each word.
- Play the CD. The pupils check their answers.

Answers: **1** l **2** t **3** s **4** h **5** h, t **6** b **7** u **8** k **9** the first t **10** w

Activity 4

Work with a partner. Think and write sentences about a park for children. Use *can*, *needn't*, *need to*, *mustn't*, *should* or *shouldn't*.

- In pairs, the pupils write sentences about a park.
- Compare answers as a class. Choose a class set of park rules.

Odd one out activity

Which is the odd one out? Why?

- The pupils complete the odd one out activity.

Answers: chocolate (The 't' is silent in the other words.)

Ending the lesson

Review the lesson and reflect on learning.

- Say **Today we've talked about the words we use to express obligation.**
- Ask **What do you remember?** The pupils do a three-minute review in pairs. (Cooperative Learning Strategies, page 19)

Extra activity

Reinforcement

- In groups, the pupils write sentences using 'needn't' for a school without rules.
- The groups present their sentences to the class. Ask **What would a school like this be like?**

Key Competences and Key Learning Outcomes

- Learn phrases related to keeping fit and healthy
- Learn about healthy living and healthy eating
- Practise activity types found in the Cambridge Exams: B1 Preliminary for Schools
- Learn about antonyms
- Do a communication task

Key language

- *do exercise, drink fizzy drinks, drink water, eat fruit and vegetables, eat junk food, go for walks, rest, spend time on the computer*
- Extension: *eat sugary food, eat wholegrain bread, play sports regularly, watch a lot of TV*
- *How often do you (drink water)? I (drink water twice a day).*

Materials

- Pupil's Book p33; Activity Book p30; Class CD1 and CD2; Teacher's App on Navio

Optional materials

- Teacher's Resource Bank: Trinity Exams Practice cards (from the Starter Unit and Units 1 and 2)

At a Glance Lesson Plan

Pupil's Book

Starting the lesson

- Use the Trinity Exams Practice cards (optional).
- Review *must, mustn't, need to* and *needn't*.
- Set learning outcomes.

Activity 1

- Look and match.
- Listen, check and repeat.
- ▶ *CD1 Track 42 p281*

Activity 2

- Listen and say *A, B, C* or *D*.
- ▶ *CD2 Track 1 p281*

Activity 3

- Listen again.
- ▶ *CD2 Track 1 p281*
- What five questions does Alfie ask?

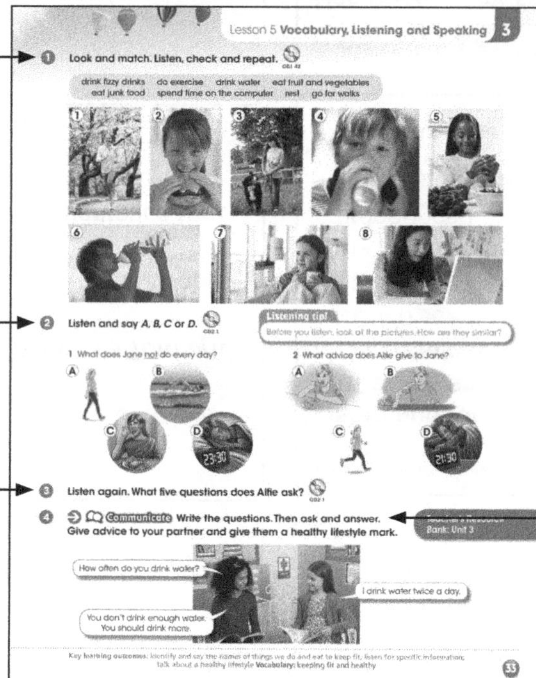

Activity 4

- Write the questions. Then ask and answer.
- Give advice to your partner and give them a healthy lifestyle mark (Teacher's Resource Bank: Unit 3).

Ending the lesson

- Review the lesson and reflect on learning.

Extra activity

Vocabulary extension

- Present four additional vocabulary items.

Activity Book

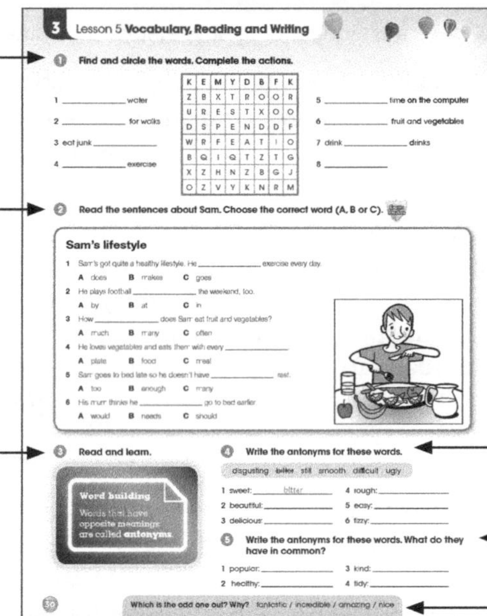

Activity Book

Activity 1

- Find and circle the words. Complete the actions.

Activity 2

- Read the sentences about Sam. Choose the correct word (A, B or C).

Activity 3

- Read and learn.

Activity 4

- Write the antonyms for these words.

Activity 5

- Write the antonyms for these words. What do they have in common?

Odd one out activity

Digital resources

Teacher's Digital: You can also teach this lesson using the Teacher's App on Navio.

Pupil's Digital: Encourage your pupils to use the Pupil's App on Navio to practise the activities from this lesson.

Powered By NAVIO

Starting the lesson

Use the Trinity Exams Practice cards (optional).

- The pupils practise asking and answering questions.

Review *must*, *mustn't*, *need to* and *needn't*.

- On the board, write *homework*, *bus*, *listen*, *eat*, *play football*, *wear a hat*.
- Ask the pupils to make sentences using *need to*, *needn't*, *must* or *mustn't*. They can write the sentences down first or they can suggest sentences orally.

Set learning outcomes

- Say **Today we're going to learn some phrases about being healthy and we're going to do a communication task.**

Pupil's Book Activity 1

Look and match. Listen, check and repeat.

▶ *CD1 Track 42 p281*

- In pairs, ask the pupils to match the phrases they know with the photos.
- Play the CD. The pupils listen and check.
- Play the CD again, pausing after each word or phrase for the pupils to repeat. You can find the answers for this activity in the audioscript on page 281.

Pupil's Book Activity 2

Listen and say *A*, *B*, *C* or *D*.

▶ *CD2 Track 1 p281*

- Invite a pupil to read the first question and describe the first four pictures. Read Listening tip! as a class.
- Play the CD. The pupils listen and identify the correct picture.
- Repeat the procedure with the second set of pictures. Ask more questions about the texts if you have time, e.g. **In number 1, when does Jane play hockey?** (*Every weekend.*) **In number 2, does Alfie think she gets enough exercise?** (*Yes.*)

Answers: **1** B **2** D

Pupil's Book Activity 3

Listen again. What five questions does Alfie ask?

▶ *CD2 Track 1 p281*

- Tell the pupils that they need to listen and note down the five questions that Alfie asks.
- Play the CD. The pupils make notes. Play the CD again if necessary.
- Check answers as a class.

Answers: How often do you do exercise? How often do you eat fruit and vegetables? How often do you drink fizzy drinks? How often do you eat junk food? How much sleep do you have?

Pupil's Book Activity 4

Write the questions. Then ask and answer. Give advice to your partner and give them a healthy lifestyle mark (Teacher's Resource Bank: Unit 3).

- Explain to the pupils that they are going to look at the six pictures and write questions. All of the questions will begin *How often do you*.
- Organise the class into pairs (A and B). Ask Pupils A to open their Activity Books at page 127 and Pupils B at page 128.
- Invite two pupils to demonstrate the activity. Pupil A asks questions and Pupil B answers. Then Pupil A gives Pupil B some advice. Pupil B writes it down. Then the pupils swap roles.
- Ask the pupils to do the activity in their pairs.

Activity Book

Activity 1

Find and circle the words. Complete the actions.

- Ask the pupils to read the phrases. They find and circle the words. They then complete the phrases.

Answers: **1** drink **2** go **3** food **4** do **5** spend **6** eat **7** fizzy **8** rest

Activity 2

Read the sentences about Sam. Choose the correct word (A, B or C).

- Pupils complete the gaps choosing A, B or C.

Answers: **1** A **2** B **3** C **4** C **5** B **6** C

Activity 3

Read and learn.

- Read the information as a class.

Activity 4

Write the antonyms for these words.

- The pupils write the antonyms.

Answers: **1** bitter **2** ugly **3** disgusting **4** smooth **5** difficult **6** still

Activity 5

Write the antonyms for these words. What do they have in common?

- The pupils write the correct antonyms.

Answers: **1** unpopular **2** unhealthy **3** unkind **4** untidy They are formed with the prefix 'un-'.

Odd one out activity

Which is the odd one out? Why?

- The pupils complete the odd one out activity.

Answers: nice (It isn't an extreme adjective.)

Ending the lesson

Review the lesson and reflect on learning.

- Say **Today we've learnt phrases about being healthy and we've done a communication task.**
- Ask **What do you remember?** The pupils do a three-minute review in pairs.

Extra activity

Vocabulary Extension

- Present four more words related to the topic: *watch a lot of TV, play a sport regularly, eat sugary food, eat wholegrain bread.*
- Use the Vocabulary booster on NAVIO to practise these new words.

Key Competences and Key Learning Outcomes
• Practise talking about healthy living
• Learn about healthy living and healthy eating
• Do pre-reading tasks to predict content and raise interest • Read a text for general understanding
• Learn about weighing up different sides of an argument

Key language

- *addictive, cheap, diet, fast food, healthy, salt, saturated fat, save time, sugar*
- *Some people argue that fast food is unhealthy.*

Materials

- Pupil's Book p34; Activity Book p31; Class CD2; Teacher's App on Navio

Optional materials

- Teacher's Resource Bank: Trinity Exams Practice cards (from the Starter Unit and Units 1 and 2)

At a Glance Lesson Plan

Pupil's Book

Starting the lesson

- Use the Trinity Exams Practice cards (optional).
- Review the health vocabulary from Lesson 5.
- Set learning outcomes.

Activity 1: Before you read

- Read and discuss.

Activity 2

- Look at the photos.
- What do you think the argument is about?
- Read and find out.

Activity 3: After you read

- What do you think?
- Go to the Activity Book.

Ending the lesson

- Review the lesson and reflect on learning.

Extra activity

Extension

- Have a debate.

Activity Book

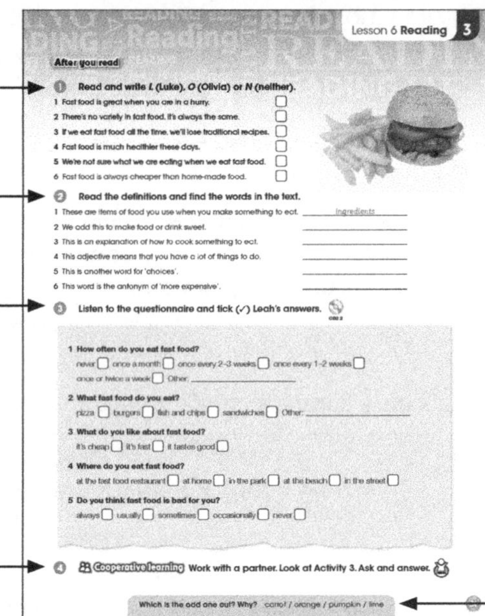

Activity Book: After you read

Activity 1

- Read and write *L* (Luke), *O* (Olivia) or *N* (neither).

Activity 2

- Read the definitions and find the words in the texts.

Activity 3

- Listen to the questionnaire and tick (✓) Leah's answers.

▶ ***CD2 Track 2 p281***

Activity 4

- Work with a partner. Look at Activity 3. Ask and answer.

Odd one out activity

Digital resources

Teacher's Digital: You can also teach this lesson using the Teacher's App on Navio.

Pupil's Digital: Encourage your pupils to use the Pupil's App on Navio to practise the activities from this lesson.

Powered By NAVIO

Starting the lesson

Use the Trinity Exams Practice cards (optional).

- The pupils practise asking and answering questions.

Review the health vocabulary from Lesson 5.

- In pairs, the pupils prepare definitions for a healthy activity and for an unhealthy activity.
- The pupils read out their definitions. The class guesses the activities.
- Continue until you have reviewed most of the health vocabulary from Lesson 5.

Set learning outcomes.

- Say **Today we're going to read two different opinions about one subject.**

Pupil's Book Activity 1: Before you read

Read and discuss.

- Read the questions as a class. Prompt the pupils to answer in as much detail as possible.

Pupil's Book Activity 2

Look at the photos. What do you think the argument is about? Read and find out.

- Ask the pupils to describe the photos of fast food. Encourage the pupils to predict what the two opinions are. Then read the text to find out.
- Confirm that the argument is about eating fast food. Luke argues that it is a bad thing while Olivia argues that it is a good thing.

Pupil's Book Activity 3: After you read

What do you think?

- Read the first question as a class. Encourage the pupils to look at the way the argument was told and not to think about their own opinions. Then ask the pupils which argument they agree with. Encourage them to explain their answers.
- In pairs, the pupils add arguments to each side. Ask the pupils to share their ideas with the class. Then discuss why it is good to give different opinions in an opinion piece.

Activity Book: After you read

Activity 1

Read and write *L* (Luke), *O* (Olivia) or *N* (neither).

- Read the sentences as a class. The pupils work on their own to write the correct letter. Ensure that the pupils understand that 'neither' means that the sentence does not relate to Luke or Olivia.

Answers: **1** O **2** L **3** L **4** O **5** L **6** N

Activity 2

Read the definitions and find the words in the texts.

- The pupils work with a partner or on their own to write the words. They use the text in the Pupil's Book to help them.

Answers: **1** ingredients **2** sugar **3** recipe **4** busy **5** options **6** cheaper

Activity 3

Listen to the questionnaire and tick (✓) Leah's answers.

▶ *CD2 Track 2 p281*

- Read the questions as a class. As you read the questions, encourage the pupils to predict the answers. Explain that this is a survey and sometimes more than one box can be ticked. Remind the pupils that they may also need to complete the 'Other' sections.
- Play the CD. The pupils listen and choose the answers. They check their answers with a partner.
- Play the CD again, pausing after each piece of information. The pupils complete and check their answers.

Answers: **1** once every 2–3 weeks **2** burgers, sandwiches, salad **3** it's fast, it tastes good **4** at home, the park **5** sometimes, important to have a varied diet

Activity 4

Work with a partner.

Look at Activity 3. Ask and answer.

- In pairs, the pupils ask the questions from Activity 3. One pupil asks all the questions and writes down the answers as notes. Then they swap roles.

Odd one out activity

Which is the odd one out? Why?

- The pupils complete the odd one out activity.

Answers: lime (It isn't orange.)

Ending the lesson

Review the lesson and reflect on learning.

- Say **Today we've read two sides of an argument about fast food.**
- Ask **What do you remember?** The pupils do a three-minute review in pairs. (Cooperative Learning Strategies, page 19)

Extra activity

Extension

- Organise the class into groups of four. Give each group a type of fast food.
- The pupils will debate the advantages and disadvantages of their given fast food within their group.
- In pairs, the pupils prepare their side of the mini-debate.
- When the pupils are ready, ask each group to speak for four minutes (two minutes for each side).
- At the end of each mini-debate, the class votes on which side gave a better argument.

Key Competences and Key Learning Outcomes
• Review and use connective words and phrases
• Identify the text features of an argument • Use criteria to check your writing
• Share and discuss your writing with a partner
• Write an argument text

Key language

- *also, firstly, furthermore, however, on the one hand, on the other hand, secondly, wake up*
- *Some people say that we could use this time more effectively.*

Materials

- Pupil's Book p35; Activity Book p32; Teacher's App on Navio

Optional materials

- Teacher's Resource Bank: Trinity Exams Practice cards (from the Starter Unit and Units 1 and 2)

At a Glance Lesson Plan

Pupil's Book

Starting the lesson

- Use the Trinity Exams Practice cards (optional).
- Review food items.
- Set learning outcomes.

Activity 1: Investigate a text

- Read and answer.

Activity 2

- Read the text and follow the two sides of the argument.

Activity 3: Discuss a text

- Read the argument text again.
- Answer the questions.

Writing skills

- Read about using connective words and phrases.

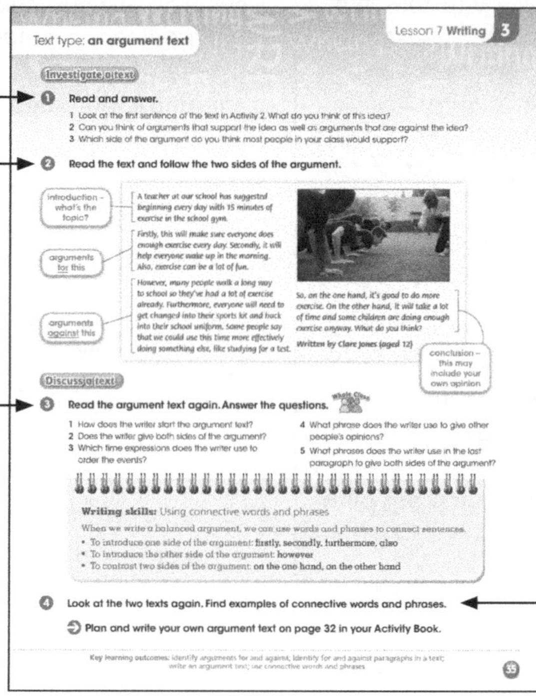

Text type: an argument text

Lesson 7 Writing 3

Investigate a text

1 Read and answer.

2 Read the text and follow the two sides of the argument.

Discuss a text

3 Read the argument text again. Answer the questions.

Writing skills: Using connective words and phrases

When we write a balanced argument, we can use words and phrases to connect sentences.

- To introduce one side of the argument: firstly, secondly, furthermore, also
- To introduce the other side of the argument: however
- To contrast two sides of the argument: on the one hand, on the other hand

4 Look at the two texts again. Find examples of connective words and phrases.

Plan and write your own argument text on page 32 in your Activity Book.

Activity 4

- Look at the two texts again.
- Find examples of connective words and phrases.

Go to the Activity Book.

Ending the lesson

- Review the lesson and reflect on learning.

Extra activity

Reinforcement

- Use connectives in a speaking task.

Digital resources

Teacher's Digital: You can also teach this lesson using the Teacher's App on Navio.

Pupil's Digital: Encourage your pupils to use the Pupil's App on Navio to practise the activities from this lesson.

Powered By NAVIO

Activity Book

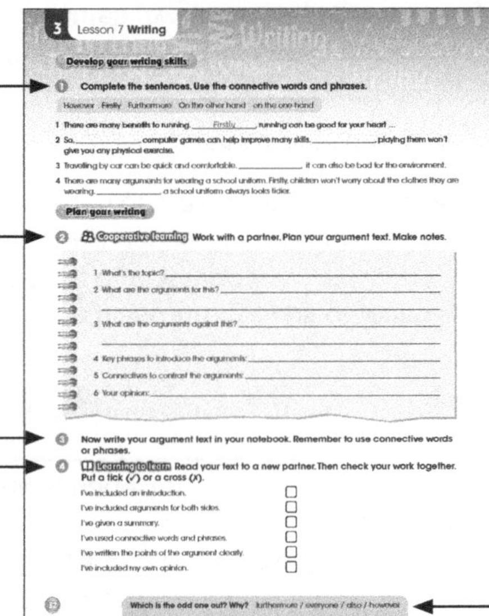

3 Lesson 7 Writing

Develop your writing skills

1 Complete the sentences. Use the connective words and phrases.

Plan your writing

2 Cooperative learning Work with a partner. Plan your argument text. Make notes.

3 Now write your argument text in your notebook. Remember to use connective words or phrases.

4 Learning to learn Read your text to a new partner. Then check your work together. Put a tick (✓) or a cross (✗).

Which is the odd one out? Why? furthermore / everyone / also / however

Activity Book

Activity 1: Develop your writing skills

- Complete the sentences. Use the connective words and phrases.

Activity 2: Plan your writing

- Work with a partner. Plan your argument text. Make notes.

Activity 3

- Now write your argument text in your notebook. Remember to use connective words or phrases.

Activity 4

- Read your text to a new partner. Then check your work together. Put a tick (✓) or a cross (✗).

Odd one out activity

Starting the lesson

Use the Trinity Exams Practice cards (optional).

- The pupils practise asking and answering questions.

Review food items.

- Write five food categories on the board *Grains and potatoes, Meat and fish, Fruit and vegetables, Fat and/or sugar, Milk and dairy food*. Give an example of a food item for each category.
- In pairs, ask the pupils to write one kind of food for each category. Check answers as a class. Write them on the board if they are correct.
- Continue until you have revised a good number of food items.

Set learning outcomes

- Say **Today we're going to read an argument text and then write our own argument texts.**

Pupil's Book Activity 1: Investigate a text

Read and answer.

- Ask the pupils to read the first sentence of the text. Invite them to give their opinions about the idea.
- Ask the pupils to think about the answers to the other two questions in pairs.
- Discuss their answers as a class. You could have a class vote and compare it to a class vote you have after reading the text.

Pupil's Book Activity 2

Read the text and follow the two sides of the argument.

- The pupils read the text.

Pupil's Book Activity 3: Discuss a text

Read the argument text again.
Answer the questions.

- Read and discuss the questions as a class. Confirm that the writer starts with an introduction explaining what the argument is about and then gives both sides of the argument. Then ask the pupils to identify expressions that order the events, that give both sides of the argument and that give other people's opinions. (*Firstly, secondly, also, furthermore; on the one hand, on the other hand; some people say.*)

Writing skills

- Read about using connective words and phrases.
- Focus on the pronunciation of 'furthermore' and 'however'. Both have three syllables. The stress on 'furthermore' is on the last syllable. The stress on 'however' is on the second.

Pupil's Book Activity 4

Look at the two texts again. Find examples of connective words and phrases.

- The pupils look at the texts again and identify examples of connective words and phrases.

Activity Book

Activity 1: Develop your writing skills

Complete the sentences. Use the connective words and phrases.

- The pupils work on their own or in pairs to complete the sentences.

Answers: **1** Firstly **2** on the one hand, On the other hand **3** However **4** Furthermore

Activity 2: Plan your writing

Work with a partner. Plan your argument text. Make notes.

- Read out the notes as a class. Check understanding.
- In pairs, the pupils think of an argument. You may need to give them some ideas.
- The pupils then work together to complete the notes.

Activity 3

Now write your argument text in your notebook. Remember to use connective words or phrases.

- The pupils write their argument text in their notebooks.

Activity 4

Read your text to a new partner. Then check your work together. Put a tick (✓) or a cross (✗).

- Read through the statements as a class.
- Organise the class into new partners. One pupil reads aloud their text. The other pupil listens. The pupils work together to decide if the text fulfils the criteria and tick the corresponding boxes. The pupils can add, improve or correct the text at this stage.
- The pupils swap roles.

Odd one out activity

Which is the odd one out? Why?

- The pupils complete the odd one out activity.

Answers: everyone (It isn't a connective word.)

Ending the lesson

Review the lesson and reflect on learning.

- Say **Today we've read an argument about exercise at school and written our own argument texts.**
- Ask **What do you remember?** The pupils do a three-minute review in pairs. (Cooperative Learning Strategies, page 19)

Extra activity

Reinforcement

- On the board, write an argument, e.g. *Children should cook at least one meal at home every week.* The pupils think of sentences for both sides of the argument.
- Go round the class asking for sentences agreeing with the argument. Each time, the pupils have to use a connective word, e.g. *Firstly*, *secondly* etc.
- Then say **Change**. The next pupil begins with *however* and says a sentence to support the other side of the argument. The following pupil also says a sentence to support this side of the argument. This continues until the pupils run out of ideas.

Key Competences and Key Learning Outcomes

- Review talking about healthy living
- Prepare and practise speaking activity types found in Cambridge Exams: B1 Preliminary for Schools
- Reflect on learning and progress
- Listen to a text for general and specific information
- Learn and practise how to ask questions in conversations

Key language
- *keeping fit, eating healthily, rest*
- *Do you think you're healthy? think you're healthy?*

Materials
- Pupil's Book p36; Activity Book pp33–34; Class CD2; Teacher's App on Navio

Optional materials
- Teacher's Resource Bank: Trinity Exams Practice cards (from the Starter Unit and Units 1 and 2)

At a Glance Lesson Plan

Pupil's Book

Starting the lesson
- Use the Trinity Exams Practice cards (optional).
- Review talking about health.
- Set learning outcomes.

Activity 1
- Describe the photos.
- What is the connection between them?

Activity 2
- Listen to the conversation.
- ▶ *CD2 Track 3 p281*
- How does Charlotte keep healthy?

Activity 3
- Listen again.
- ▶ *CD2 Track 3 p281*
- Complete the four questions that Finn asks.

Go to the Activity Book.

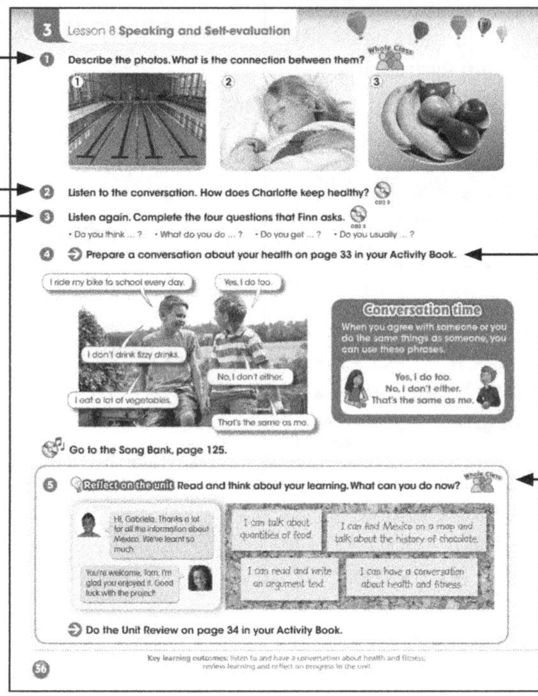

Activity 4
- Prepare a conversation about your health on page 33 in your Activity Book.

Go to the Activity Book.

Song
- ▶ *CD4 Track 18 p296*
- ▶ *CD4 Track 19 p296 (optional karaoke version)*

Activity 5
- Read and think about your learning.
- What can you do now?

Ending the lesson
- Review the lesson and reflect on learning.

Activity Book

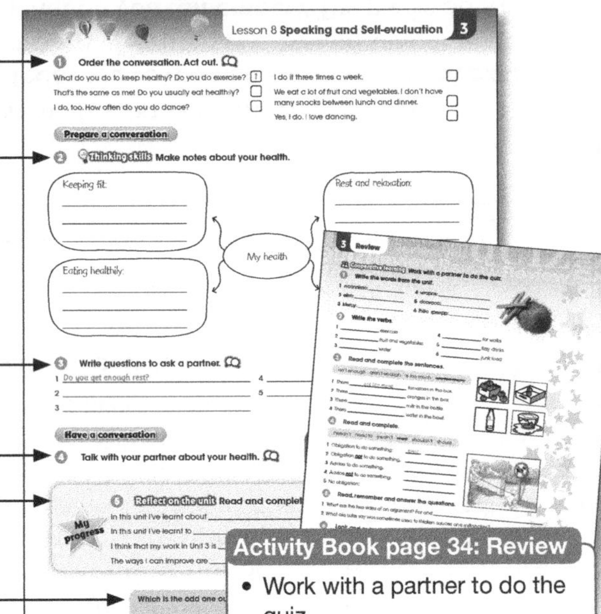

Activity Book page 34: Review
- Work with a partner to do the quiz.

Activity Book

Activity 1
- Order the conversation. Act out.

Activity 2
- Make notes about your health.

Activity 3
- Write questions to ask a partner.

Activity 4
- Talk with your partner about your health.

Activity 5
- Read and complete the sentences.

Odd one out activity

Digital resources

Teacher's Digital: You can also teach this lesson using the Teacher's App on Navio.

Powered By NAVIO

Detailed Lesson Plan

Starting the lesson

Use the Trinity Exams Practice cards (optional).

- The pupils practise asking and answering questions.

Review talking about health.

- Ask **What do you do to keep healthy?** One pupil replies. Invite that pupil to ask the question to another pupil. Continue until all have answered the question.

Set learning outcomes.

- Say **Today we're going to learn and practise how to have a conversation about health and fitness and we're going to think about our learning.**

Pupil's Book Activity 1

Describe the photos. What is the connection between them?

- The pupils describe the photos. Ask **Why are these photos connected to health and fitness?**

Pupil's Book Activity 2

Listen to the conversation. How does Charlotte keep healthy?

▶ *CD2 Track 3 p281*

- Explain that Charlotte is talking about health and fitness. The pupils listen and write as many answers as they can.

Answers: **Keeping fit** go swimming twice a week, ride a bike to school every day **Rest** goes to bed quite late **Eating healthily** fruit and vegetables every meal, balanced diet, not many sweets **Other** doesn't have fizzy drinks; eats chocolate twice a week

Pupil's Book Activity 3

Listen again. Complete the four questions Finn asks.

▶ *CD2 Track 3 p281*

- The pupils listen again and complete the questions. Check answers as a class.

Answers: Do you think you're healthy? What do you do to keep healthy? Do you get enough rest? Do you usually eat healthily?

Pupil's Book Activity 4

Prepare a conversation about your health on page 33 in your Activity Book.

- Organise the pupils into new pairs. The pupils have two conversations with their new partner in their Activity Books.

Song

Read and discuss the questions.

- Go to the Song Bank on page 125 to do the Pupil's Book song activities (see p243).

▶ *CD4 Track 18 p296*

▶ *CD4 Track 19 p296 (optional karaoke version)*

Activity Book

Activity 1

Order the conversation. Act out.

- The pupils complete the activity and act out.

Answers: 1, 5, 3, 4, 6, 2

Activity 2

Make notes about your health.

- The pupils complete the spidergram about themselves.

Activity 3

Write questions to ask a partner.

- Ask pupils what types of questions they'd like to ask and make notes on the board.
- Have pupils refer to Finn's questions to complete the activity if they like.

Activity 4

Talk with your partner about your health.

- In pairs, the pupils have a conversation using their notes from Activity 3 if they wish. Refer pupils to the Remember! box. Then they swap roles.

Pupil's Book Activity 5

Read and think about your learning. What can you do now?

- Read the messages as a class. Then look back through the unit and prompt the pupils to identify other things they have learnt / done.

Activity Book

Activity 5

Read and complete the sentences.

- Read out the sentences. Encourage the pupils to think of different ways of completing them.

Odd one out activity

Which is the odd one out? Why?

- The pupils complete the odd one out activity.

Answers: tour guide (It isn't a job connected with health.)

Ending the lesson

Review the lesson and reflect on learning.

- Say **Today we've learnt and practised how to have a conversation about health and fitness and we've thought about our learning in this unit.**
- Ask **What do you remember?** The pupils do a three-minute review in pairs.

Activity Book page 34: Review

Work with a partner to do the quiz.

- Organise the class into pairs. Explain that they are going to work together to do a quiz. Set a time limit for the pupils to do this (10–15 minutes). Stress that the pupils are not competing with each other.
- Read out the six tasks that the pupils have to complete. Check understanding. Then say **Ready, steady … Go!**
- The pupils work in their pairs to do the quiz. Ask the pupils who finish quickly to help another pair.
- Correct the answers as a class.

Answers: **1** **1** cinnamon **2** lime **3** turkey **4** prawns **5** avocado **6** chilli pepper **2** **1** do **2** eat **3** drink **4** go **5** drink **6** eat **3** **1** are too many **2** aren't enough **3** isn't enough **4** is too much **4** **1** must, need to **2** mustn't **3** should **4** shouldn't **5** needn't **5** **1** against **2** wood pulp **6** chocolate, a product made from cocoa

Key Competences and Key Learning Outcomes

- Watch and understand a video about keeping fit
- Collaborate to produce an exercise calendar
- Understand the importance of having a regular exercise routine
- Understand that recording information and setting a routine helps motivation

Key language

- *athletics club, cross country club, kilometres, marathon*
- *Do you do a lot of exercise? Yes, I like running. I do athletics every week.*

Materials

- Pupil's Book p37; Activity Book p35; Class CD1; Teacher's App on Navio
- Teacher's Resource Bank: Talk Cards

Optional materials

- Teacher's Resource Bank: Trinity Exams Practice cards (selected from the Starter Unit)

At a Glance Lesson Plan

Pupil's Book

Starting the lesson

- **Think-Pair-Share.** Review ways of keeping fit and its importance.
- Set learning outcomes.

Activity 1

- Before you watch
- Watch the video.
- *Unit 3 video p301*
- Read and say *true* or *false*.
- Correct the false sentences.

Activity 2

- Watch the video again.
- *Unit 3 video*
- What does Amy say about these different activities?

Activity 3

- Read, think and answer.

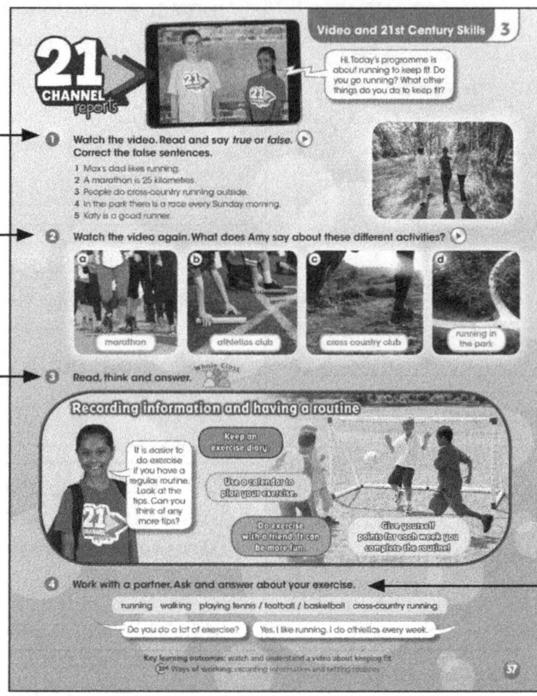

Activity 4

- Work with a partner.
- Ask and answer about your exercise.
- Go to the Activity Book.

Ending the lesson

- Review the lesson and reflect on learning.

Extra activity

- Discuss why keeping fit is good for you.

Activity Book

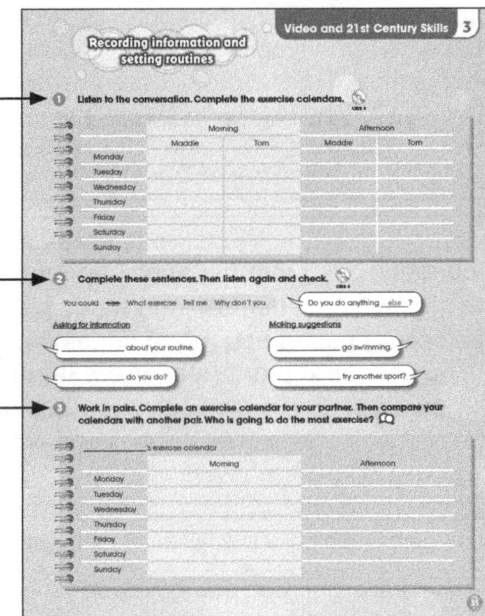

Activity Book

Activity 1 ▶
- Listen to the conversation. Complete the exercise calendars.

▶ *CD2 Track 4 p282*

Activity 2 ▶
- Complete these sentences. Then listen again and check.

Activity 3
- Work in pairs. Complete an exercise calendar for your partner. Then compare your calendars with another pair. Who is going to do the most exercise?

Digital resources

Teacher's Digital: You can also teach this lesson using the Teacher's App on Navio.

Pupil's Digital: Encourage your pupils to use the Pupil's App on Navio to practise the activities from this lesson.

Powered By NAVIO

Starting the lesson

Think-Pair-Share. Review different ways and the importance of keeping fit.

- Ask **How do you keep fit and why is it important?** Elicit answers and write them on the board.
- Pupils work with a Talk Partner to talk about different ways if keeping fit.
- Invite different Talk Partners to say a different ways of keeping fit.
- Finally, repeat the procedure, asking different pairs of Talk Partners each time, until all the answers have been recorded.

Set learning outcomes and use the talk cards.

- Say **Today we're going to watch a video and then talk about keeping fit.**
- Ask pupils if they remember who the presenters are (Max and Amy).
- Point to the talk cards to show the pupils the different ways they will be working in the lesson.

Pupil's Book Activity 1

Before you watch

- Ask pupils what types of activities to keep fit they think Max and Amy will present in the lesson.
- Read the speech bubble to pupils. Ask **Do you go running?** Elicit responses from a number of pupils.
- Read the statements in Activity 1. Explain that students have to answer them.

Watch the video. Read and and say *true* or *false*. Correct the false sentences. *p301*

- Watch Part 1.
- Ask a pupil to read out statement 1. Ask the class for the answer.
- Play Part 2, pausing at each section for pupils to answer. Pupils then work in pairs to answer the questions.

Answers: **1** F **2** F **3** T **4** F **5** T
1 Amy's aunt likes running.
2 A marathon is usually 40 kilometres.
4 There is a race every Saturday morning.

Pupil's Book Activity 2

Watch the video again. What does Amy say about these different activities?

- Ask pupils to tell you what they remember from the video. Ask if they remember types of running was mentioned.
- Ask them to look at each item in the activity and tell you what they remember about them.
- Play the second part of the video pausing after each form of running. Ask what Amy has said about these activities and if they found the information interesting.

Answers: **1** A marathon is about 40 kilometres and it's a long race. Amy wants to do a marathon one day.
2 The athletics club is at school and only in the summer.
3 The cross country club is outside in all weathers.
4 Every Saturday at half past nine, people run in the park.

Pupil's Book Activity 3

Read, think and answer.

- Tell pupils that in the last part of the video Amy and Max talk about how it's good to have a routine to help you keep fit. Ask what points they remember the Amy and Max present.
- Pupils work in pairs to read and think about each point. Ask why each point is important and how it can help them keep fit.
- Ask if they can think of any more ideas.

Pupil's Book Activity 4

Work with a partner. Ask and answer about your exercise.

- Ask pupils to look at the word box and say if they do any of the things in it to keep fit.
- Ask if there is anything else they do or would like to try.
- Encourage pupils to say why they should do their best to keep fit.

Activity Book

Activity 1

Listen to the conversation. Complete the exercise calendars.

▸ *CD2 Track 4 p282*

- Ask if they keep a diary of their daily routine.
- Explain they will listen to two kids talking about their exercise calendar which they have to complete.
- Play the CD and complete the activity.
- Ask if pupils have a similar exercise routine.

Answers: Maddie: Afternoon: Monday – swimming, Wednesday – football, Saturday – ride a bike // Tom: Afternoon: Tuesday – tennis, Thursday – running
Maddie: Morning: Saturday – cycling / Tom: Morning: Saturday: cycling, Sunday: running

Activity 2

Compete the sentences. Then listen again and check.

▸ *CD2 Track 4 p284*

- Have pupils complete the activity and check answers with their partners.
- Explain that these are examples of how to ask for information and how to make suggestions politely in a conversation.
- Ask if there are any other questions or suggestions they could add. Write answers on the board.

Answers: Asking for information: Tell me about your routine. What exercise do you do? Making suggestions: You could go swimming. Why don't you try another sport?

Activity 3

Work in pairs. Complete an exercise calendar for your partner. Then compare your calendars with another pair. Who is going to do the most exercise?

- Pupils complete the activity in pairs and present their calendars to the class.

Ending the lesson

Review the lesson and reflect on learning.

- Say **What have we learnt about keeping fit today?** The pupils do a three-minute review in pairs.

Extra activity

Reinforcement

- Place pupils in small groups and have them make a poster on different ways of keeping fit.
- Pupils present their work to the class.

Project 1: An energy report

Key Competences and Key Learning Outcomes

- Learn and practise how to talk about renewable energy
- Learn about different kinds of renewable energy
- Research one type of renewable energy
- Listen for specific information and complete notes
- Share information with your group

Key language

- *advantages, cheap, coal, disadvantages, electricity, expensive, gas, hydroelectric, mountains, renewable energy, rivers, solar, solar cells, sunny, wind, windy*
- *I'm going to find out some advantages and disadvantages of solar power. Let's talk about solar power first.*

Materials

- Pupil's Book p38; Activity Book p36; Class CD2; Teacher's App on Navio

At a Glance Lesson Plan

Pupil's Book

Starting the lesson
- Set learning outcomes.

Activity 1: Share knowlege
- Read and discuss.

Activity 2: Investigate
- Listen and complete the notes about renewable energy on page 36 in your Activity Book.

▶ *CD2 Track 5 p282*

Go to the Activity Book.

Activity 3: Share information
- What are the advantages and disadvantages of each source of renewable energy?
- Work in pairs or groups. Make notes on page 36 in your Activity Book.

Go to the Activity Book.

Ending the lesson
- Review the lesson and reflect on learning.

Extension activity
- Do further research on renewable energy.

Link to Science
- **Energy and electricity:** Renewable energy

Activity Book

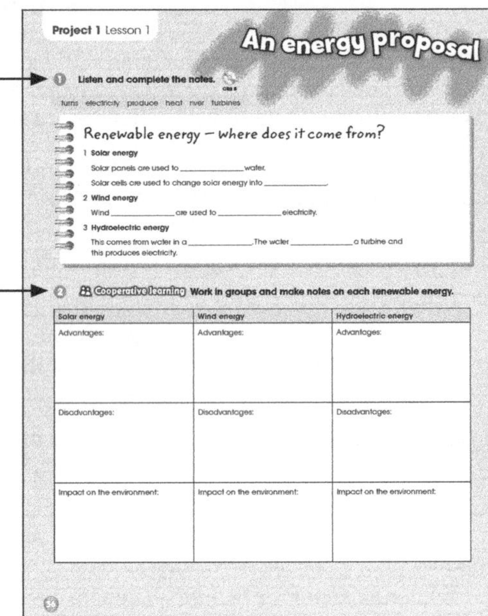

Activity Book

Activity 1
- Listen and complete the notes.

▶ *CD2 Track 5 p282*

Activity 2
- Work in groups and make notes on each renewable energy.

Digital resources

Teacher's Digital: You can also teach this lesson using the Teacher's App on Navio.

Pupil's Digital: Encourage your pupils to use the Pupil's App on Navio to practise the activities from this lesson.

Powered By NAVIO

Starting the lesson

Set learning outcomes.

- Say **Today we're going to begin a project.**
- Focus the group's attention on heading and sub heading.
- Ask pupils what type of energy they use in their homes.

Pupil's Book Activity 1: Share knowledge

Read and discuss.

- Read and discuss the question as a class.
- In pairs, the pupils match the words with the photos. Check answers as a class.
- Ask the final question. Ask the pupils what they think 'renewable' means.

Pupil's Book Activity 2: Investigate

Listen and complete the notes about renewable energy on page 36 in your Activity Book.

▶ *CD2 Track 5 p282*

- Read the instructions. Ask the pupils to open their Activity Books (page 36).

Activity Book

Activity 1

Listen and complete the notes.

▶ *CD2 Track 5 p282*

- Read the word box and the information as a class. Predict the first two answers.
- Play the CD. The pupils listen and complete the notes.
- Play the CD a second time, pausing after each piece of key information. The pupils give the answer each time.

Answers: **1** heat, electricity **2** turbines, produce **3** river, turns

Pupil's Book Activity 3: Investigate

What are the advantages and disadvantages of each source of renewable energy? Work in pairs or groups. Make notes on page 36 in your Activity Book.

- Read the rubric as a class. Organise the class into groups of three.
- Read the Cooperative learning rubric and remind pupils to apply it.
- Invite three pupils to read out the speech bubbles. Then ask the pupils to open their Activity Books on page 36. The pupils discuss and decide on their tasks. Each pupil in the group focuses on a different renewable energy.

Activity Book

Activity 2

Work in groups and make notes on each renewable energy.

- Explain the three sections in each column. Make it clear that the pupils should make notes and not write full sentences.
- If the pupils have access to the Internet, they can research the information online. Alternatively, they can use reference books.
- Invite pupils to share their ideas with the class.

Ending the lesson

Review the lesson and reflect on learning.

- Say **Today we've learnt about renewable energy.**
- Ask **What do you remember?** The pupils do a three-minute review in pairs. (Cooperative Learning Strategies, page 19)

Extension activity

- In their groups, the pupils use the Internet to find out more information. Ask them to find two interesting facts for each renewable energy.

Link to Science

- If you are studying the Science topic of energy, review the different forms of energy. Ask the pupils what forms of energy they can remember. (*light, sound, thermal, kinetic, electrical, chemical, nuclear*). Ask **Which forms of energy are used in this classroom and which others are used at home?**

Project 1: An energy report

Key Competences and Key Learning Outcomes

- Present your proposal to the class
- Think about your local area and its future
- Reflect on what you have learnt and how you have worked together
- Work in groups to design and write a digital presentation

Key language

- *coast, electricity lines, face the north, hydroelectric plants, impact, presentation, produce, propose, renewable energy, ruin, wind turbine*
- *What will the impact be on the environment? What will the power be used for? Where are you going to put it? Why have you chosen it?*

Materials

- Pupil's Book p39; Activity Book p37; Teacher's App on Navio
- Computer with digital presentation facilities

At a Glance Lesson Plan

Pupil's Book

Starting the lesson

- Set learning outcomes.

Activity 1: Plan and create your project

- In pairs or groups, propose a renewable energy for your community.
- Discuss the questions and write your answers on page 37 in your Activity Book.

Go to the Activity Book.

Activity 2

- Write and create a digital presentation of your proposal.

Activity 3: Present your project

- Present your proposal to the class.
- Take turns to answer any questions.

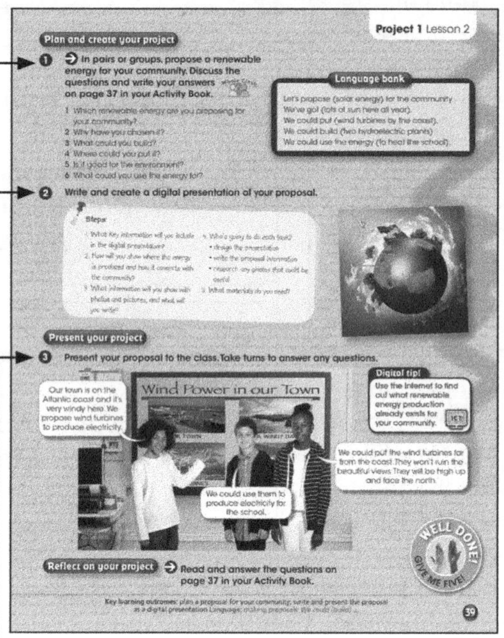

Ending the lesson

- Review the lesson and reflect on learning.

Reinforcement activity

- Make a class display of your work.

Digital resources

Teacher's Digital: You can also teach this lesson using the Teacher's App on Navio.

Pupil's Digital: Encourage your pupils to use the Pupil's App on Navio to practise the activities from this lesson.

Powered By NAVIO

Activity Book

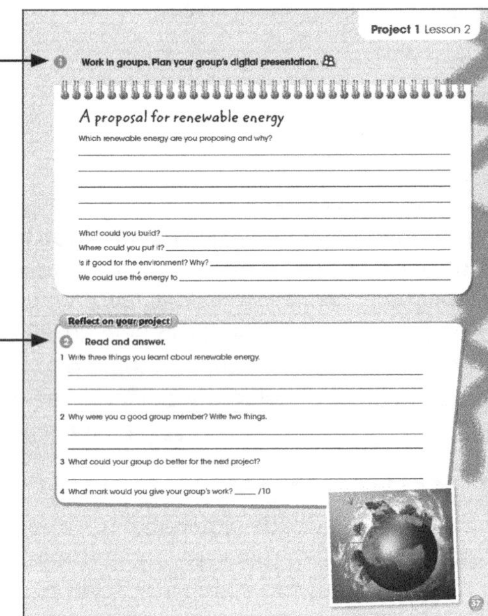

Activity Book

Activity 1

- Work in groups. Plan your group's digital presentation.

Activity 2

- Read and answer.

Starting the lesson

- Say **Today we're going to continue the project.** Prompt the pupils to tell you what they did in the last lesson.
- Highlight that the pupils will be working in small groups again. Prompt the pupils to tell you what they must do when they work in groups: listen, take turns, respect different opinions, etc.

Pupil's Book Activity 1: Plan and create your project

In pairs or groups, propose a renewable energy for your community. Discuss the questions and write your answers on page 37 in your Activity Book.

- Explain that the pupils are going to work in their groups to agree the answers to the questions.
- Focus the pupils on the Language bank. Encourage them to use these phrases to make suggestions to their group.

Activity Book

Activity 1

Work in groups. Plan your group's digital presentation.

- Explain that while the pupils are discussing the plans for their project, they should make notes. Ask a pupil to read out the questions.
- Give the pupils two minutes thinking time on their own. Then ask the groups to complete the notes.
- Go round the groups helping them make decisions about their project.

Pupil's Book Activity 2

Write and create a digital presentation of your proposal.

- Read out the steps as a class. Check understanding. Give and elicit examples for each task.
- The groups discuss their presentations and make notes of their decisions. Go round and answer questions.
- They then prepare the presentation. They can do this as a poster or as a digital presentation, or even present it in a different way if they wish.

Pupil's Book Activity 3: Present your project

Present your proposal to the class. Take turns to answer any questions.

- Focus the pupils on the photo. Encourage them to talk about what they can see. Ask **What is this group's proposal about? What can you see on the screen?**
- Ask three pupils to read out the speech bubbles.
- Invite different groups in turn to present their proposal to the rest of the class. Ensure that each pupil in the group participates in the presentation, but accept that some pupils may contribute more than others. At the end of each presentation, ask the group a question and encourage the rest of the class to think of questions they would like to ask. The group giving the presentation should answer the questions.
- At the end of the activity, ask the pupils to vote for the best proposal. Write the names of the different proposals on the board. Explain that the pupils can only vote for one proposal and they can't vote for their own group. Say the name of each proposal in turn. Ask the pupils to raise their hands if they think that one is the best. Do a quick hand count and write the number next to the proposal.

Activity Book: Reflect on your project

Activity 2

Read and answer.

- The pupils work in their groups to think about how they have worked, what they have learnt and what they have produced.
- They then complete the questions.
- The pupils share the information with the class.

Ending the lesson

Review the lesson and reflect on learning.

- Say **We've done a project about renewable energy.**
- Ask **What do you remember?** The pupils do a three-minute review in pairs. (Cooperative Learning Strategies, page 19)

Reinforcement activity

- Make a display of the pupils' work so that other classes can enjoy and learn from the work. You can print out parts of the presentations or pupils can make posters from the material. Digital presentations can also be uploaded onto the class or school web page.

Date: ______________ Unit: __________

1 What did my pupils learn in this unit?

2 How did my pupils work? (✓)

individually ☐ in pairs ☐ in small groups ☐

in large groups ☐ as a class ☐

3 Which key competences did my pupils develop? Give a score from 1 to 5 (5 being the highest).

- Competence in linguistic communication ☐
- Competence in mathematics, science and technology ☐
- Digital competence ☐
- Learning to learn ☐
- Social and civic competences ☐
- Sense of initiative and entrepreneurship ☐
- Cultural awareness and expression ☐

4 Which lessons / activities were the most successful and why?

5 Which lessons / activities did my pupils find the most difficult and why?

6 What did I try in the classroom for the first time? How did it go?

7 Which resources did I find most useful? (including webpages)

8 What could I do differently next time I teach this unit?

Unit 4

Creative kids

Unit overview

Key Competences and Key Learning Outcomes

- Review and name different creative activities (Lesson 1)
- Learn and practise how to use the past passive (Lesson 2)
- Review and name creative jobs (Lesson 5)
- Practise using punctuation (Lesson 7)
- Watch and understand a video (Video and 21st Century Skills)

- Analyse and apply rules for forming the past passive (Lesson 2)
- Develop visual–spatial skills through describing different photos (Lesson 8)

- Use the Pupil's App on Navio
- Investigate Japan (Lesson 3)

- Identify and classify words with the silent 'w' (Lesson 4)
- Practise using the relative pronouns 'who', 'that', 'which' and 'where' when defining (Lesson 5)
- Identify the text features of a comic strip (Lesson 7)
- Review learning and reflect on progress in the unit (Lesson 8)
- Practise activity types found in the Cambridge Exams: B1 Preliminary for Schools

- Understand the importance of respecting other people's tastes (Lesson 3)
- Ask and answer questions about creative activities (Lesson 8)

- Work in pairs or small groups to practise and reinforce learning (All lessons)
- Do a communication activity (Lesson 5)
- Analyse forms of digital means for creative purposes (Video and 21st Century Skills)

- Read a text (Lesson 3)
- Learn about Japan (Lesson 3)
- Read, write and draw a comic strip (Lessons 6 and 7)
- Sing a song (Lesson 8)

Vocabulary

Core vocabulary
beads, clay, costume, create an animation, do ceramics, do origami, do traditional dancing, make a film, make jewellery, perform a play, puppet, stage; actor, composer, fashion designer, film director, graffiti artist, novelist, photographer, sound engineer

Extension vocabulary (optional)
landscape, oil painting, portrait, sketch, still life, watercolour; hair stylist, illustrator, make-up artist, video game designer

Other vocabulary
animated, anime, caption, character, comic books / strip, exclamation, manga, mood, sound effect, speech / thought bubble, story frame; odd sock; at the top / bottom, in the foreground / background / corner / middle, on the left / right; designing, sides, to record

Recycled vocabulary
funny; invite; boat trip, computer game; shadow puppets, sticks; kitten, monkey

Structures

Core structures
The puppet was / wasn't made last week. The puppets were / weren't painted by the children. When was (the picture painted)? Who were (the songs sung) by?

Other structures
I'm not very sure. I haven't got a clue. I've got no idea. I definitely know this one. I'm not certain. I'm sure I know the answer. Manga drawings are like comics that tell stories. Why have I only got odd socks?

Recycled structures
If I pull hard enough, the tree will bend. Have you ever (made a film)? Yes, I have. No, I haven't. When did you do that? I've never (composed a song). How long have you (collected manga comic books)?

Pronunciation

The silent letter 'w'

Literacy

Text type: a comic strip (a text to entertain; writing preparation)
Reading skills: using visual clues to support understanding
Writing skills: finishing a sentence

Culture ... around the world

Japanese manga and anime

21st Century Skills

Using digital media creatively

Thinking skills

Forming conceptual links and associations (Lesson 1); Defining and describing (Lesson 1); Analysing and applying rules and patterns (Lessons 2 and 4); Discussing different forms of comic books (Lesson 3); Categorising (Lesson 4); Divergent thinking (Lesson 6); Spatial thinking (Lesson 8); Evaluating creativity (Lesson 8)

Cooperative learning

Working together (Lessons 1–8); Reflecting and setting goals (Lessons 1–8); Collaborative writing (Lesson 7); Peer evaluation (Lesson 7); Showing interest (Lesson 8); Praising and encouraging (Lesson 5); Expressing and respecting opinions (Lessons 3 and 6)

Values

The importance of respecting other people's tastes

Cross-curricular links

Links to Science
Goya
Suggested Arts and Crafts concepts
Expressive lines and colours

Key Competences and Key Learning Outcomes

- Review and name different creative activities
- Understand and act out a grammar dialogue
- Complete and practise a dialogue
- Listen for specific information

Key language

- *beads, clay, costume, create an animation, do ceramics, do origami, do traditional dancing, make a film, make jewellery, perform a play, puppet, stage*
- Extension: *landscape, oil painting, portrait, sketch, still life, watercolour*
- *Have you ever (made a film)?*

Materials

- Pupil's Book pp40–41; Activity Book p38; Class CD2; Teacher's App on Navio
- Creative activities flashcards

Optional materials

- Teacher's Resource Bank: Trinity Exams Practice cards (selected from the Starter Unit and Unit 1, 2 and 3)

At a Glance Lesson Plan

Pupil's Book

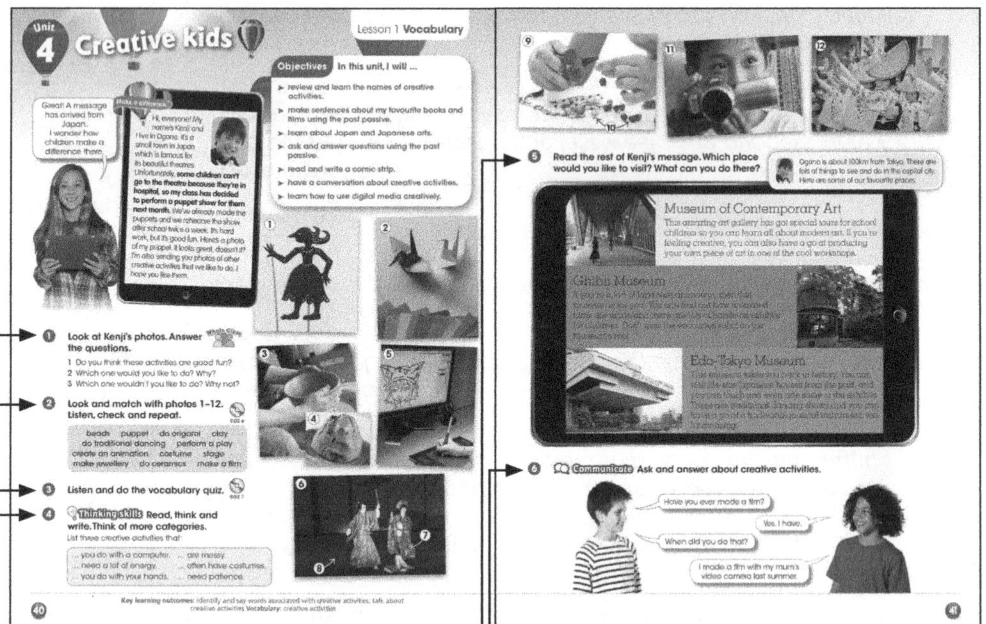

Starting the lesson
- Use the Trinity Exams Practice cards. (optional)
- Review materials in Arts and Crafts lessons.
- Set learning outcomes.

Activity 1
- Look at Kenji's photos.
- Answer the questions.

Vocabulary presentation
- Present the new vocabulary using the creative activities flashcards.

Activity 2
- Look and match with photos 1–12.
- Listen, check and repeat.

▶ *CD2 Track 6 p282*

Activity 3
- Listen and do the vocabulary quiz.

▶ *CD2 Track 7 p282*

Activity 4
- Read, think and write.
- Think of more categories.

Activity 5
- Read the rest of Kenji's message.
- Which place would you like to visit?
- What can you do there?

Activity 6
- Ask and answer about creative activities.

Go to the Activity Book.

Ending the lesson
- Review the lesson and reflect on learning.

Extra activities

Extension
- Find out about Japan.

Vocabulary extension
- Present six additional vocabulary items.

Activity Book

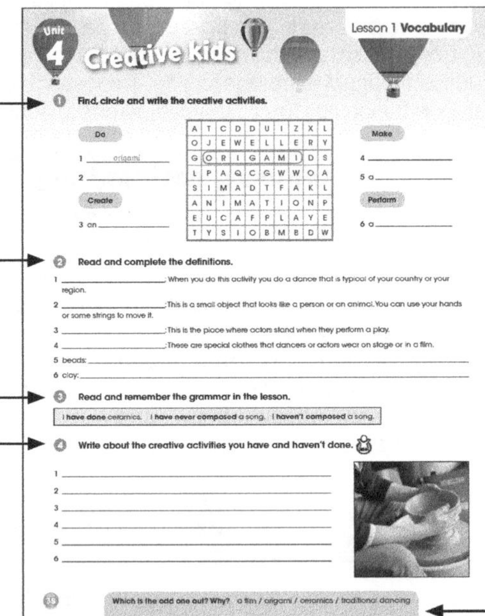

Activity Book

Activity 1
- Find, circle and write the creative activities.

Activity 2
- Read and complete the definitions.

Activity 3
- Read and remember the grammar in the lesson.

Activity 4
- Write about the creative activities you have and haven't done.

Odd one out activity

Digital resources

Teacher's Digital: You can also teach this lesson using the Teacher's App on Navio.

Pupil's Digital: Encourage your pupils to use the Pupil's App on Navio to practise the activities from this lesson.

Powered By NAVIO

Detailed Lesson Plan

Starting the lesson

Use the Trinity Exams Practice cards (optional).

- The pupils practise asking and answering questions.

Review materials in Arts and Crafts lessons.

- In groups, ask the pupils to think of ten materials they use when they do Arts and Crafts. The first group to finish reads out their list. Other groups add to the list.

Set learning outcomes.

- Say **Today we're going to learn the names of creative activities and materials you use to do them.**

Pupil's Book Activity 1

Look at Kenji's photos. Answer the questions.

- Invite a pupil to read out the speech bubble to find out which school has sent a message. Ask **Do you know where Japan is?**
- Invite a pupil to read out the message from Kenji. Check understanding.
- Work as a class to answer the questions.

Vocabulary presentation

- Present the new vocabulary using the creative activities flashcards. Show the first flashcard and elicit / say the word. For a piece of equipment or material, ask **What (is it) used for?** For an activity, ask **What do you need to do this activity?** Stick the flashcards on the board. Repeat with the other flashcards.

Pupil's Book Activity 2

Look and match with photos 1–12. Listen, check and repeat.

▶ *CD2 Track 6 p282*

- Ask the pupils to look at photo number 1. Ask **What's this?** In pairs, the pupils match 2–12 with the words. Play the CD. The pupils listen and check.
- Play the CD again, pausing after each word for the pupils to repeat. You can find the answers for this activity in the audioscript on page 282.

Pupil's Book Activity 3

Listen and do the vocabulary quiz.

▶ *CD2 Track 7 p282*

- Play the CD. Listen to the first definition, pausing at the beep to allow the pupils to name the item. Play the CD to listen to the answer.
- Repeat the procedure with the other definitions. You can find the answers for this activity in the audioscript on page 282.

Pupil's Book Activity 4

Read, think and write. Think of more categories.

- Read the instructions as a class.
- In pairs, the pupils list the creative activities.
- Check answers as a class.

Pupil's Book Activity 5

Read the rest of Kenji's message. Which place would you like to visit? What can you do there?

- Invite a pupil to read out the message. The pupils read the information about the museums in Tokyo.
- The pupils decide which place they would like to visit and then share their ideas with a partner.
- Finally, invite different pupils to share their ideas.

Pupil's Book Activity 6

Ask and answer about creative activities.

- Invite two pupils to read out the speech bubbles.
- The pupils ask and answer questions about the different creative activities they have done.

Activity Book

Activity 1

Find, circle and write the creative activities.

- The pupils find and circle the creative activities. They write each activity below the correct verb.

Answers: **1** origami **2** ceramics **3** animation **4** jewellery **5** film **6** play

Activity 2

Read and complete the definitions.

- The pupils complete the definitions.

Answers: **1** traditional dancing **2** puppet **3** stage **4** costume **5 & 6** Pupils' own answers

Activity 3

Read and remember the grammar in the lesson.

- Invite a pupil to read out the information. Encourage the pupils to give examples.

Activity 4

Write about the creative activities you have and haven't done.

- The pupils work on their own to write their sentences.

Odd one out activity

Which is the odd one out? Why?

- The pupils complete the odd one out activity.

Answers: a film (You use it with the verb 'make' not with the verb 'do'.)

Ending the lesson

Review the lesson and reflect on learning.

- Say **Today we've learnt the names of creative activities and materials you use to do them.**
- Ask **What do you remember?** The pupils do a three-minute review in pairs. (Cooperative Learning Strategies, page 19)

Extra activities

Extension

- The pupils find three interesting facts about Japan to present to the class.

Vocabulary extension

- Present six additional words relating to painting: *landscape, oil painting, portrait, sketch, still life, watercolour.*
- Use the Vocabulary Booster on NAVIO to practise these new words.

Key Competences and Key Learning Outcomes

- Listen to and read a dialogue
- Learn and practise how to use the past passive
- Identify examples of the past passive in the dialogue
- Analyse and apply rules for forming the past passive

Key language

- *compose, create, perform, record, shadow puppets, shine a light, sticks*
- *The puppet was / wasn't made last week. The puppets were / weren't painted by the children.*

Materials

- Pupil's Book p42; Activity Book p39; Class CD2; Teacher's App on Navio
- Teacher's Resource Bank: Creative activities word cards

Optional materials

- Teacher's Resource Bank: Trinity Exams Practice cards (selected from the Starter Unit and Units 1, 2 and 3)

At a Glance Lesson Plan

Pupil's Book

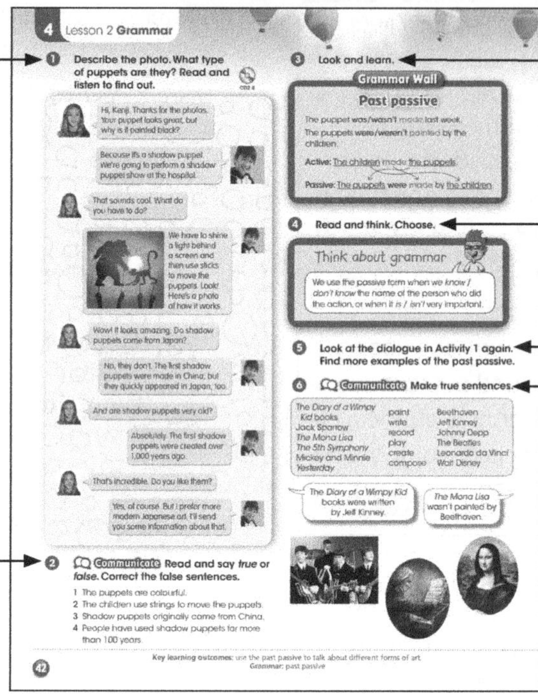

Starting the lesson

- Use the Trinity Exams Practice cards (optional).
- Review creative activities and materials.
- Set learning outcomes.

Activity 1

- Describe the photo.
- What type of puppets are they?
- Read and listen to find out.

▶ *CD2 Track 8 p283*

Activity 2

- Read and say *true* or *false*.
- Correct the false sentences.

Activity 3

- Look and learn – Grammar wall

Activity 4

- Read and think.
- Choose.

Activity 5

- Look at the dialogue in Activity 1 again.
- Find more examples of the past passive.

Activity 6

- Make true sentences.

Go to the Activity Book.

Ending the lesson

- Review the lesson and reflect on learning.

Extra activity

Reinforcement

- Play a memory game using the past passive.

Activity Book

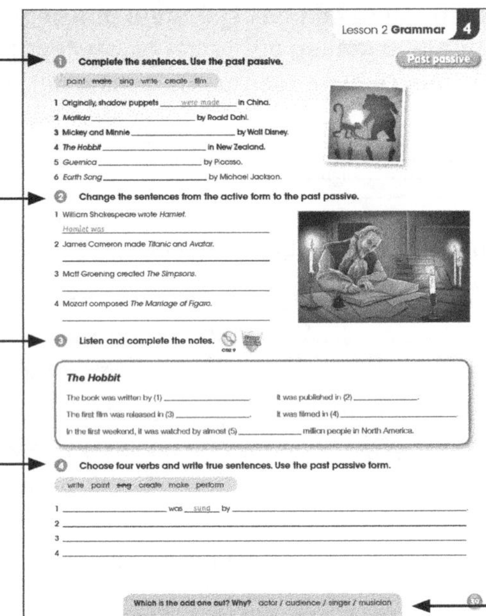

Activity Book

Activity 1

- Complete the sentences. Use the past passive.

Activity 2

- Change the sentences from the active form to the past passive.

Activity 3

- Listen and complete the notes.

▶ *CD2 Track 9 p283*

Activity 4

- Choose four verbs and write true sentences. Use the past passive form.

Odd one out activity

Digital resources

Teacher's Digital: You can also teach this lesson using the Teacher's App on Navio.

Pupil's Digital: Encourage your pupils to use the Pupil's App on Navio to practise the activities from this lesson.

Powered By NAVIO

Starting the lesson

Use the Trinity Exams Practice cards (optional).
- The pupils practise asking and answering questions.

Review creative activities and materials.
- Place the creative activities word cards face down on a desk. Organise the class into groups of three.
- Pupil 1 collects a word card and defines the word. Pupil 2 says the word and Pupil 3 spells it. The pupils swap roles. Repeat with a new word card.

Set learning outcomes.
- Say **Today we're going to talk about famous books, music, art and films.**

Pupil's Book Activity 1

Describe the photo. What type of puppets are they? Read and listen to find out.

▶ *CD2 Track 8 p283*
- Prompt the pupils to describe the photo. Ask **Do you know what these puppets are called?**
- Play the CD. The pupils listen and read the dialogue. Confirm that they are shadow puppets.

Pupil's Book Activity 2

Read and say *true* or *false*. Correct the false sentences.
- In pairs, the pupils decide if the sentences are true or false. They correct the false sentences. (*1 False. The puppets are black. 2 False. The children use sticks to move the puppets. 3 True 4 True*)

Pupil's Book Activity 3

Look and learn – Grammar wall
- Read the information on the Grammar wall as a class.
- Encourage the pupils to think about form and identify patterns. Say **The past passive needs two verbs. Which verb is the first verb? What form of the second verb do we use?**
- Remind the pupils that there is a list of irregular verbs at the back of their Activity Book (page 135).

Pupil's Book Activity 4

Read and think. Choose.
- Focus the pupils' attention on the Think about grammar box. Read out the sentences as a class. The pupils discuss and complete the sentences in pairs.
- Check answers as a class. (*don't know, isn't*)

Pupil's Book Activity 5

Look at the dialogue in Activity 1 again. Find more examples of the past passive.
- In pairs, the pupils find examples of the past passive.

Pupil's Book Activity 6

Make true sentences.
- Invite two pupils to read out the speech bubbles.
- Invite other pupils to make similar true sentences.
- In pairs, the pupils form their sentences.

Activity Book

Activity 1

Complete the sentences. Use the past passive.
- The pupils complete the sentences.

Answers: **1** were made **2** was written **3** were created **4** was filmed **5** was painted **6** was sung

Activity 2

Change the sentences from the active form to the past passive.
- Write the first sentence on the board. Demonstrate how to form the past passive.
- In pairs, the pupils change the remaining sentences.

Answers: **1** Hamlet was written by William Shakespeare. **2** Titanic and Avatar were made by James Cameron. **3** The Simpsons was created by Matt Groening. **4** The Marriage of Figaro was composed by Mozart.

Activity 3

Listen and complete the notes.

▶ *CD2 Track 9 p283*
- Read the notes as a class. Encourage the pupils to think about the kind of information that is missing.
- Play the CD. The pupils listen and complete the information. They check the answers with a partner.
- Play the CD again, pausing after each piece of key information. The pupils say the missing information.

Answers: **1** Tolkien **2** 1937 **3** 2012 **4** New Zealand **5** 11

Activity 4

Choose four verbs and write true sentences. Use the past passive form.
- In pairs, the pupils write sentences.
- Invite different pairs to read out their sentences.

Odd one out activity

Which is the odd one out? Why?
- The pupils complete the odd one out activity.

Answers: audience (They watch performances.)

Ending the lesson

Review the lesson and reflect on learning.
- Say **Today we've talked about famous books, music, art and films.**
- Ask **What do you remember?** The pupils do a three-minute review in pairs. (Cooperative Learning Strategies, page 19)

Extra activity

Reinforcement
- Write numbers 1–6 and letters A–F on the board. Organise the class into teams. Team A chooses a number and a letter. Read out the corresponding information (1 The Hobbit 2 Hamlet 3 Mona Lisa 4 Yesterday 5 Matilda 6 Micky Mouse; A The Beatles B Tolkien C Walt Disney D Shakespeare E Roald Dahl F Leonardo da Vinci). The team makes a true sentence in the past passive. If it is correct, they win a point. Repeat with Team B. The team with the most points wins.

Key Competences and Key Learning Outcomes

- Read a text with confidence and fluency
- Use the Internet to investigate Japan
- Listen for general and specific information
- Understand the importance of respecting other people's tastes
- Learn about Japan
- Express an opinion on a text

Key language

- *animated, anime, character, comic books, exaggerate, manga, mood, story frame*
- *Manga drawings are like comics that tell stories.*

Materials

- Pupil's Book p43; Activity Book p40; Class CD2; Teacher's App on Navio
- A sheet of scrap paper for each pupil

Optional materials

- Teacher's Resource Bank: Trinity Exams Practice cards (selected from the Starter Unit and Units 1, 2 and 3)

At a Glance Lesson Plan

Pupil's Book

Starting the lesson

- Use the Trinity Exams Practice cards (optional).
- Review the past passive.
- Set learning outcomes.

Activity 1: Before you read

- Read and discuss.

Activity 2

- Listen and read.

▶ *CD2 Track 10 p283*

Go to the Activity Book.

***Give Me Five!* values**

- Read and discuss.

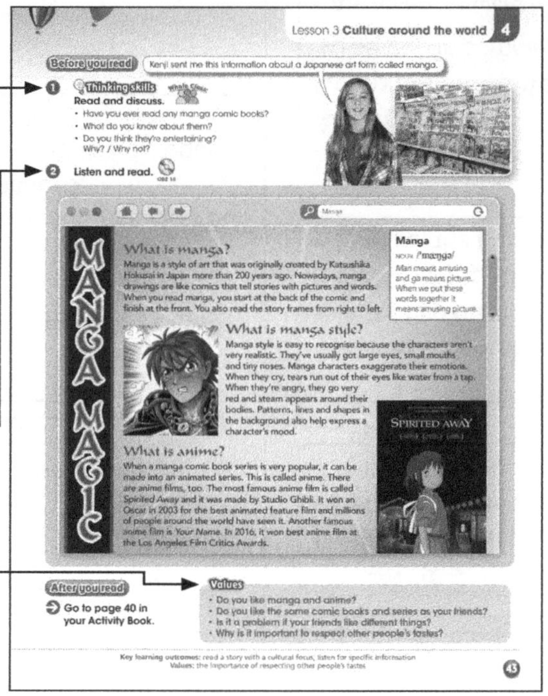

Ending the lesson

- Review the lesson and reflect on learning.

Extra activity

Extension

- Create your own manga character.

Activity Book

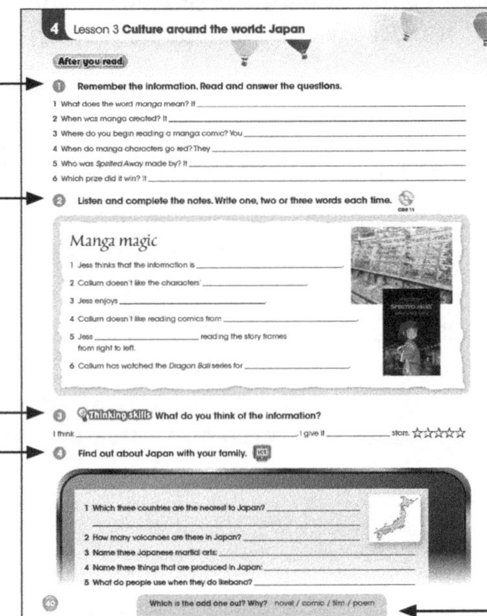

Activity Book: After you read

Activity 1

- Remember the information. Read and answer the questions.

Activity 2

- Listen and complete the notes. Write one, two or three words each time.

▶ *CD2 Track 11 p283*

Activity 3

- What do you think of the information?

Activity 4

- Find out about Japan with your family.

Odd one out activity

Digital resources

Teacher's Digital: You can also teach this lesson using the Teacher's App on Navio.

Pupil's Digital: Encourage your pupils to use the Pupil's App on Navio to practise the activities from this lesson.

Powered By NAVIO

Detailed Lesson Plan

Starting the lesson

Use the Trinity Exams Practice cards (optional).

- The pupils practise asking and answering questions.

Review the past passive.

- Explain to the class that they are going to be artists. Hand out scrap paper. Give the pupils three minutes to draw a self-portrait. The pupils mustn't write their names on their drawings. Collect the portraits.
- Show the first self-portrait. Say **Who was it drawn by?** The pupils can make three guesses, e.g. *It was drawn by (Paula).*
- Finally, the artist should raise his / her hand and say *It was drawn by me.*
- Repeat the procedure with other drawings.

Set learning outcomes.

- Say **Today we're going to read some information about a style of drawing from Japan.**

Pupil's Book Activity 1: Before you read

Read and discuss.

- Read the questions as a class. Encourage the pupils to share information about manga comic books. Ask them to give their opinions about these comic books.

Pupil's Book Activity 2

Listen and read.

▶ *CD2 Track 10 p283*

- Play the CD. The pupils follow in their books.
- Ask questions to check understanding.

Suggested comprehension questions:

- Paragraph 1: **Where does the story start in a manga comic book?** (*At the back of the book.*) **Do you read the left story frame or the right story frame first?** (*The right.*)
- Paragraph 2: **What do the characters look like in a manga cartoon?** (*They have large eyes, small mouths and tiny noses.*) **Why do the artists draw lines and shapes behind the characters?** (*To express a character's mood.*)
- Paragraph 3: **What is anime?** (*An animated series of a popular manga comic book.*)

Activity Book: After you read

Activity 1

Remember the information. Read and answer the questions.

- Read out the first question. Invite a pupil to answer it.
- The pupils read and answer the remaining questions.

Answers: **1** means funny picture. **2** was created more than 200 years ago. **3** begin at the back of the book. **4** go red when they are angry. **5** was made by Studio Ghibli. **6** won an Oscar.

Activity 2

Listen and complete the notes. Write one, two or three words each time.

▶ *CD2 Track 11 p283*

- Read out the notes. Ask the pupils to guess the missing words.
- Play the CD without pausing. The pupils listen and complete as much information as possible.
- Play the CD again, pausing after each piece of key information to check the answer.

Answers: **1** interesting **2** big eyes **3** drawing manga **4** from right to left **5** doesn't mind **6** three years

Activity 3

What do you think of the information?

- The pupils write their opinion and give a rating.
- Invite different pupils to share their opinions.

Activity 4

Find out about Japan with your family. ICT

- Read out the questions about Japan. Ask **Where can you find out this information?** (*Internet, library, asking friends and family.*) The pupils complete the activity at home.
- If you prefer to do this activity in the class, connect to a children's website which has information about Japan, such as www.sciencekids.co.nz/sciencefacts/countries/japan.html.
- Read out the questions. The pupils work as a class to find and write the answers.

Answers: **1** China, North Korea, South Korea **2** about 200 **3** karate, judo, sumo, jujitsu, aikido **4** cars, televisions, robots **5** flowers

Odd one out activity

Which is the odd one out? Why?

- The pupils complete the odd one out activity.

Answers: film (It isn't printed.)

Give Me Five! values

Read and discuss.

- Read out each question and discuss it as a class.
- Encourage the pupils to think of what life would be like if we all liked the same things. Then discuss the benefits of diversity.

Ending the lesson

Review the lesson and reflect on learning.

- Say **Today we've read some information about manga and anime.**
- Ask **What do you remember?** The pupils do a three-minute review in pairs. (Cooperative Learning Strategies, page 19)

Extra activity

Extension

- Quickly review what manga characters look like. Then ask the pupils to create their own manga character. The pupils draw their character and write a description.

Key Competences and Key Learning Outcomes

- Learn and practise how to ask and answer questions using the past passive
- Act out a short dialogue in pairs
- Analyse and apply rules for forming the past passive in a question
- Identify and classify words that have the silent letter 'w'

Key language

- *comic book, computer game*
- *When was (the picture painted)? Who were (the songs sung) by?*

Materials

- Pupil's Book p44; Activity Book p41; Class CD2; Teacher's App on Navio

Optional materials

- Teacher's Resource Bank: Trinity Exams Practice cards (selected from the Starter Unit and Units 1, 2 and 3)

At a Glance Lesson Plan

Pupil's Book

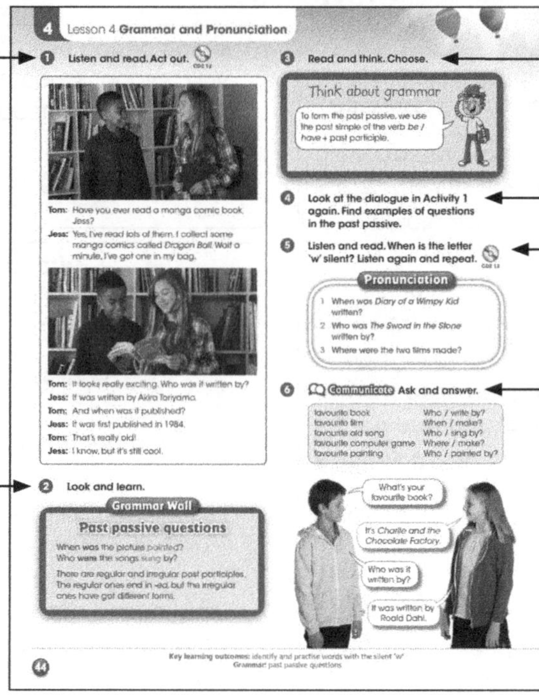

Starting the lesson

- Use the Trinity Exams Practice cards (optional).
- Review information about manga and anime.
- Set learning outcomes.

Activity 1

- Listen and read.
- ▶ *CD2 Track 12 p283*
- Act out.

Activity 2

- Look and learn – Grammar wall

Activity 3

- Read and think.
- Choose.

Activity 4

- Look at the dialogue in Activity 1 again.
- Find examples of questions in the past passive.

Activity 5

- Listen and read.
- When is the letter 'w' silent?
- ▶ *CD2 Track 13 p283*
- Listen again and repeat.

Activity 6

- Ask and answer.
- Go to the Activity Book.

Ending the lesson

- Review the lesson and reflect on learning.

Extra activities

Extension

- Make tongue twisters containing the letter 'w'.

Activity Book

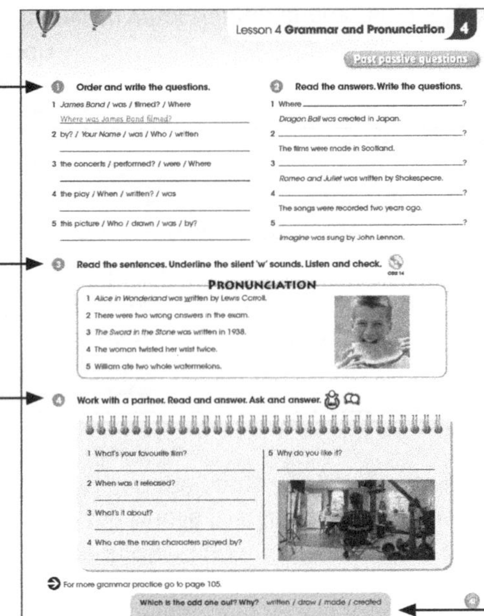

Activity Book

Activity 1

- Order and write the questions.

Activity 2

- Read the answers. Write the questions.

Activity 3

- Read the sentences. Underline the silent 'w' sounds. Listen and check.
- ▶ *CD2 Track 14 p283*

Activity 4

- Work with a partner. Read and answer. Ask and answer.

Odd one out activity

Digital resources

Teacher's Digital: You can also teach this lesson using the Teacher's App on Navio.

Pupil's Digital: Encourage your pupils to use the Pupil's App on Navio to practise the activities from this lesson.

Powered By NAVIO

Starting the lesson

Use the Trinity Exams Practice cards (optional).
- The pupils practise asking and answering questions.

Review information about manga and anime.
- Ask **How much information do you remember about manga and anime?**
- In pairs, the pupils quickly review what they learnt in Lesson 3. Share ideas as a class.

Set learning outcomes
- Say **Today we're going to practise asking and answering questions using the past passive.**

Pupil's Book Activity 1

Listen and read. Act out.

▸ *CD2 Track 12 p283*
- The pupils look at the photos. Ask **What are Tom and Jess talking about in photo (1)?**
- Play the CD. The pupils listen and read the dialogue. Check understanding. Ask **What does Jess collect?**
- Play the CD again, pausing after each sentence for the pupils to repeat.
- The pupils practise the dialogue in pairs.

Pupil's Book Activity 2

Look and learn – Grammar wall
- Read the information on the Grammar wall as a class. Draw attention to the word order in the question form.

Pupil's Book Activity 3

Read and think. Choose.
- Focus the pupils' attention on the Think about Grammar box. The pupils discuss and complete the sentence in pairs.
- Check answers as a class. (*be*)

Pupil's Book Activity 4

Look at the dialogue in Activity 1 again. Find examples of questions in the past passive.
- In pairs, the pupils find examples of questions in the past passive.

Pupil's Book Activity 5

Listen and read. When is the letter 'w' silent? Listen again and repeat.

▸ *CD2 Track 13 p283*
- The pupils read the sentences. They count the number of times the letter 'w' appears. (*12*)
- Play the CD, pausing after each sentence. The pupils identify when the letter 'w' is silent. (*Written, who, sword, two.*) Explain that 'wr' is always pronounced as 'r' (*written*), 'wh' is sometimes pronounced as 'h' (*who*) and sometimes 'w' isn't pronounced at all (*sword, two*).
- Play the CD again. The pupils listen and repeat.

Pupil's Book Activity 6

Ask and answer.
- Invite two pupils to read out the speech bubbles. Then invite other pairs to have a similar exchange.
- In pairs, the pupils ask and answer the questions.

Activity Book

Activity 1

Order and write the questions.
- Invite a pupil to read out the first question.
- The pupils order and write the remaining questions.

Answers: **1** Where was *James Bond* filmed? **2** Who was *Your Name* written by? **3** Where were the concerts performed? **4** When was the play written? **5** Who was this picture drawn by?

Activity 2

Read the answers. Write the questions.
- The pupils read the answers and write the questions.

Answers: **1** was Dragon Ball created? **2** Where were the films made? **3** Who was Romeo and Juliet written by? **4** When were the songs recorded? **5** Who was Imagine sung by?

Activity 3

Read the sentences. Underline the silent 'w' sounds. Listen and check.

▸ *CD2 Track 14 p283*
- In pairs, the pupils underline the silent 'w' sound.
- Play the CD. The pupils listen and check their answers.

Answers: **1** written **2** two, wrong, answers **3** sword, written **4** wrist **5** two, whole

Activity 4

Work with a partner. Read and answer. Ask and answer.
- Invite a pupil to read out and answer the first question.
- The pupils write the answers to the questions.
- Then they ask and answer the questions with a partner.

Odd one out activity

Which is the odd one out? Why?
- The pupils complete the odd one out activity.

Answers: draw (It isn't a past participle.)

Ending the lesson

Review the lesson and reflect on learning.
- Say **Today we've practised asking and answering questions using the past passive.**
- Ask **What do you remember?** The pupils do a three-minute review in pairs. (Cooperative Learning Strategies, page 19)

Extra activity

Extension
- Ask the pupils to brainstorm words with the 'w' sound.
- In groups, challenge the pupils to produce a tongue twister with as many 'w' sounds as possible. The tongue twister has to make sense.
- Invite the pupils to demonstrate their tongue twisters. The class decides which is the funniest / most difficult tongue twister.

Key Competences and Key Learning Outcomes

- Review and name creative jobs
- Practise using expressions to express certainty and uncertainty

- Practise activity types found in the Cambridge Exams: B1 Preliminary for Schools
- Practise using the relative pronouns *'who'*, *'that'*, *'which'* and *'where'* when defining
- Listen for gist and specific information

- Do a communication task

Key language

- *actor, composer, fashion designer, film director, graffiti artist, novelist, photographer, sound engineer*
- Extension: *hair stylist, illustrator, make-up artist, video game designer*
- *I'm not very sure. I haven't got a clue. I've got no idea. I definitely know this one. I'm not certain. I'm sure I know the answer.*

Materials

- Pupil's Book p45; Activity Book p42; Class CD2; Teacher's App on Navio

Optional materials

- Teacher's Resource Bank: Trinity Exams Practice cards (selected from the Starter Unit and Units 1,2 and 3)

At a Glance Lesson Plan

Pupil's Book

Starting the lesson

- Use the Trinity Exams Practice cards (optional)
- Review jobs.
- Set learning outcomes.

Activity 1

- Look and match.
- Listen, check and repeat.

▶ *CD2 Track 15 p283*

Activity 2

- Read and choose the correct answers.
- Listen and check.

▶ *CD2 Track 16 p284*

Activity 3

- Listen again.

▶ *CD2 Track 16 p284*

- Which five expressions do the children use to express certainty and uncertainty?

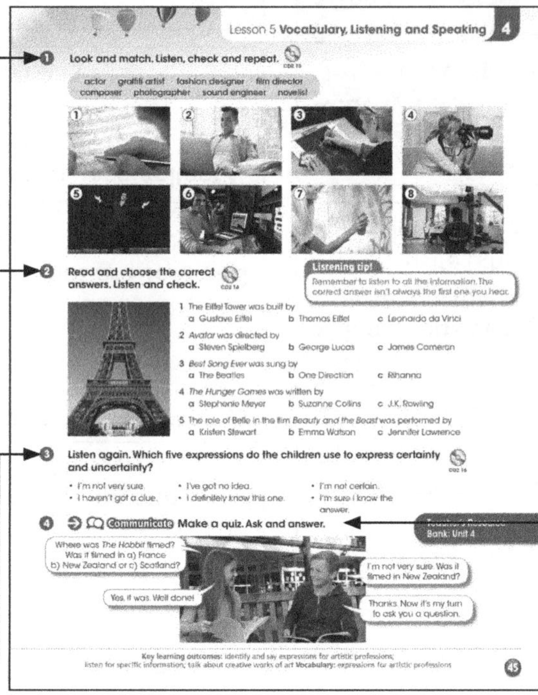

Activity 4

- Make a quiz.
- Ask and answer (Teacher's Resource Bank: Unit 4).

Ending the lesson

- Review the lesson and reflect on learning.

Extra activities

Extension

- Prepare a culture quiz.

Vocabulary Extension

- Present four additional vocabulary items.

Activity Book

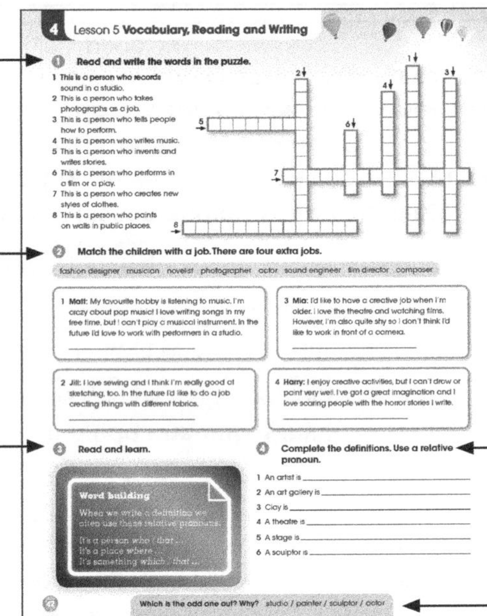

Activity Book

Activity 1

- Read and write the words in the puzzle.

Activity 2

- Match the children with a job. There are four extra jobs.

Activity 3

- Read and learn.

Activity 4

- Complete the definitions. Use a relative pronoun.

Odd one out activity

Digital resources

Teacher's Digital: You can also teach this lesson using the Teacher's App on Navio.

Pupil's Digital: Encourage your pupils to use the Pupil's App on Navio to practise the activities from this lesson.

Powered By NAVIO

Starting the lesson

Use the Trinity Exams Practice cards (optional).

- The pupils practise asking and answering questions.

Review jobs.

- Draw a Venn diagram on the board with two overlapping circles titled *Scientific* and *Artistic*. Elicit a scientific job, an artistic job and a job that is both scientific and artistic. Write the jobs in the diagram.
- The pupils copy the diagram into their notebooks. In pairs, they complete it with jobs that they know.
- Invite the pupils to share their ideas with the class. Write their jobs in the diagram on the board.

Set learning outcomes.

- Say **Today we're going to learn the names of some more creative jobs and you're going to prepare and do a quiz.**

Pupil's Book Activity 1

Look and match. Listen, check and repeat.

▶ *CD2 Track 15 p283*

- In pairs, ask the pupils to match the words they know with the photos.
- Play the CD. The pupils listen and check.
- Play the CD again, pausing after each job for the pupils to repeat. You can find the answers for this activity in the audioscript on page 283.

Pupil's Book Activity 2

Read and choose the correct answers. Listen and check.

▶ *CD2 Track 16 p284*

- Read Listening tip! as a class. Invite a pupil to read out the first sentence. Ask the pupil to choose the correct answer.
- Repeat the procedure with the other questions.
- Play the CD. The pupils listen and identify the correct answer each time.

Answers: **1** a **2** c **3** b **4** b **5** a

Pupil's Book Activity 3

Listen again. Which five expressions do the children use to express certainty and uncertainty?

▶ *CD2 Track 16 p284*

- Invite a pupil to read out the sentences for expressing certainty and uncertainty.
- Play the CD again. The pupils listen and identify the expressions that the children use.

Answers: I haven't got a clue. I'm not certain. I definitely know this one. I'm sure I know the answer. I've got no idea.

Pupil's Book Activity 4

Make a quiz. Ask and answer (Teacher's Resource Bank: Unit 4).

- Explain to the pupils that they are going to prepare and do a quiz like the one in Activity 2. Invite two pupils to read out the speech bubbles.
- Organise the class into pairs (A and B).
- The pupils complete their questions. If a pupil needs more support, ask him / her to work with a pupil who is preparing the same questions. Check the questions as a class.
- Then invite two pupils to demonstrate the activity. Pupil A asks a question. Encourage Pupil B to respond using the expressions of certainty and uncertainty.
- Ask the pupils to do the activity in their pairs.

Activity Book

Activity 1

Read and write the words in the puzzle.

- The pupils read each definition and write the creative jobs in the puzzle.

Answers: **1** sound engineer **2** photographer **3** film director **4** composer **5** novelist **6** actor **7** fashion designer **8** graffiti artist

Activity 2

Match the children with a job. There are four extra jobs.

- Read the list of creative jobs as a class.
- In pairs, the pupils read each description and choose a job that each child would like to do in the future. Remind pupils not to make a decision until they have read the complete description.
- Check answers as a class.

Answers: **1** sound engineer **2** fashion designer **3** film director **4** novelist

Activity 3

Read and learn.

- Read the information as a class. Encourage the pupils to complete the sentences.

Activity 4

Complete the definitions. Use a relative pronoun.

- The pupils complete the definitions.

Odd one out activity

Which is the odd one out? Why?

Answers: studio (It isn't a person.)

Ending the lesson

Review the lesson and reflect on learning.

- Ask **What do you remember about creative jobs?** The pupils do a three-minute review in pairs.

Extra activities

Extension

- In pairs, ask the pupils to prepare some culture quiz questions in the past passive and have three options. The questions can be about paintings, buildings, films, etc.
- The pupils take turns to ask their quiz questions to the class.

Vocabulary extension

- Present additional words related to artistic professions: *hair stylist, illustrator, make-up artist, video game designer, chef.*
- Use the Vocabulary Booster on NAVIO to practise these words.

Key Competences and Key Learning Outcomes

- Do pre-reading tasks to predict content and raise interest
- Read a text for general understanding
- Guess the meaning of words from context

- Discuss and share what you know about this type of text

- Read a comic strip
- Give an opinion on the text

Key language

- *comic strip, funny, kidnap, monkey, odd sock*
- *Why have I only got odd socks?*

Materials

- Pupil's Book p46; Activity Book p43; Class CD2; Teacher's App on Navio

Optional materials

- Teacher's Resource Bank: Trinity Exams Practice cards (selected from the Starter Unit and Units 1, 2 and 3)

At a Glance Lesson Plan

Pupil's Book

Starting the lesson

- Use the Trinity Exams Practice cards (optional).
- Review creative jobs.
- Set learning outcomes.

Activity 1: Before you read

- Read and discuss.

Activity 2

- Look at the title.
- What do you think happens in the comic strip?
- Read and find out.

Activity 3: After you read

- What do you think?
- Go to the Activity Book.

Ending the lesson

- Review the lesson and reflect on learning.

Extra activity

Extension

- Create a different ending for the comic strip.

Activity Book

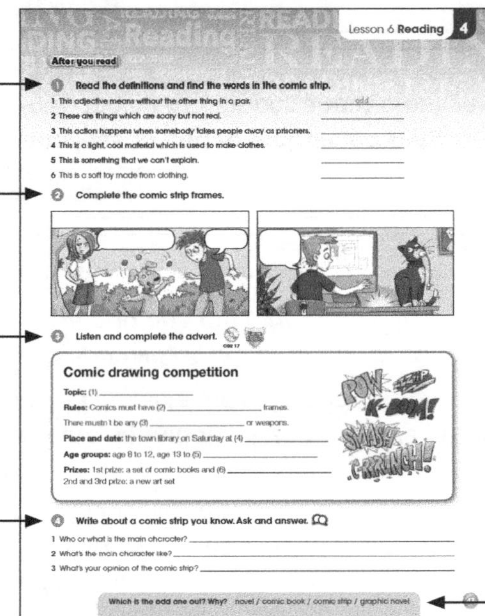

Activity Book: After you read

Activity 1

- Read the definitions and find the words in the comic strip.

Activity 2

- Complete the comic strip frames.

Activity 3

- Listen and complete the advert.

▶ *CD2 Track 17 p284*

Activity 4

- Write about a comic strip you know. Ask and answer.

Odd one out activity

Digital resources

Teacher's Digital: You can also teach this lesson using the Teacher's App on Navio.

Pupil's Digital: Encourage your pupils to use the Pupil's App on Navio to practise the activities from this lesson.

Powered By NAVIO

Starting the lesson

Use the Trinity Exams Practice cards (optional).

- The pupils practise asking and answering questions.

Review creative jobs.

- Challenge the pupils to remember the eight creative jobs from Lesson 5. Then quickly review the jobs as a class. Prompt the pupils to define each job.

Set learning outcomes

- Say **Today we're going to read a comic strip.**

Pupil's Book Activity 1: Before you read

Read and discuss.

- Read the questions as a class. Prompt the pupils to answer in as much detail as possible.
- Explain to the class that a comic strip is a short story told in drawings. It usually appears in newspapers or magazines.

Pupil's Book Activity 2

Look at the title. What do you think happens in the comic strip? Read and find out.

- Invite a pupil to read out the title of the comic strip. Ask the class to predict what the story will be about.
- The pupils read the story to find out.
- Check understanding. Ask **How many odd socks is Pat holding?** (*Two.*) **Where does he think they go first?** (*A big city.*) **What's his second idea?** (*Aliens kidnap them.*) **What's his third idea?** (*They're eaten up by a washing machine.*) **Who has the answer to the mystery?** (*His little sister.*) **Where are all the socks?** (*She made a sock monkey.*)

Pupil's Book Activity 3: After you read

What do you think?

- Read the first two questions as a class. Prompt the pupils to give their opinions.
- Then ask the pupils whether they have got good imaginations. Prompt them to hypothesise about where the missing socks go.

Activity Book: After you read

Activity 1

Read the definitions and find the words in the comic strip.

- Read the first definition and word. Ask the pupils to find the word in the comic strip.
- The pupils read the remaining definitions and find the words.

Answers: **1** odd **2** monsters **3** kidnap **4** cotton **5** mystery **6** sock monkey

Activity 2

Complete the comic strip frames.

- Invite a pupil to describe the first picture. Ask **How do the children feel? What are they thinking?** Repeat the procedure with the second picture.
- In pairs, the pupils write the accompanying speech bubbles.
- Invite different pairs of pupils to read out their work.

Activity 3

Listen and complete the advert.

▶ *CD2 Track 17 p284*

- Read the information as a class. Encourage the pupils to predict the missing words each time.
- Play the CD. The pupils listen and complete as much of the information as possible. They check their answers with a partner.
- Play the CD again, pausing after each piece of information. The pupils complete and check their answers.

Answers: **1** superheroes **2** six **3** fighting **4** 10 **5** 17 **6** DVDs

Activity 4

Write about a comic strip you know. Ask and answer.

- Ask the pupils to think of a comic strip they know and that they enjoy reading.
- Invite a pupil to read and answer the first question.
- The pupils write their answers to the questions.
- In pairs, the pupils ask and answer about the comic strips.

Odd one out activity

Which is the odd one out? Why?

- The pupils complete the odd one out activity.

Answers: novel (It doesn't have pictures.)

Ending the lesson

Review the lesson and reflect on learning.

- Say **Today we've read a comic strip.**
- Ask **What do you remember?** The pupils do a three-minute review in pairs. (Cooperative Learning Strategies, page 19)

Extra activity

Extension

- Quickly review what happened in the comic strip in the Pupil's Book. Then ask **How did the comic strip end? Can you think of a different ending?**
- In pairs, the pupils think of an alternative ending. Then they draw and write a new final frame. The pupils share their work with the rest of the class.

Key Competences and Key Learning Outcomes

- Practise using full stops, question marks and exclamation marks
- Identify the text features of a comic strip
- Use criteria to check your writing
- Share and discuss your writing with a partner
- Read, write and draw a comic strip

Key language

- *caption, exclamation, kitten, sound effect, speech bubble, thought bubble*
- *If I pull hard enough, the tree will bend.*

Materials

- Pupil's Book p47; Activity Book p44; Teacher's App on Navio
- Teacher's Resource Bank: Talk Cards

Optional materials

- Teacher's Resource Bank: Trinity Exams Practice cards (selected from the Starter Unit and Units 1, 2 and 3)

At a Glance Lesson Plan

Pupil's Book

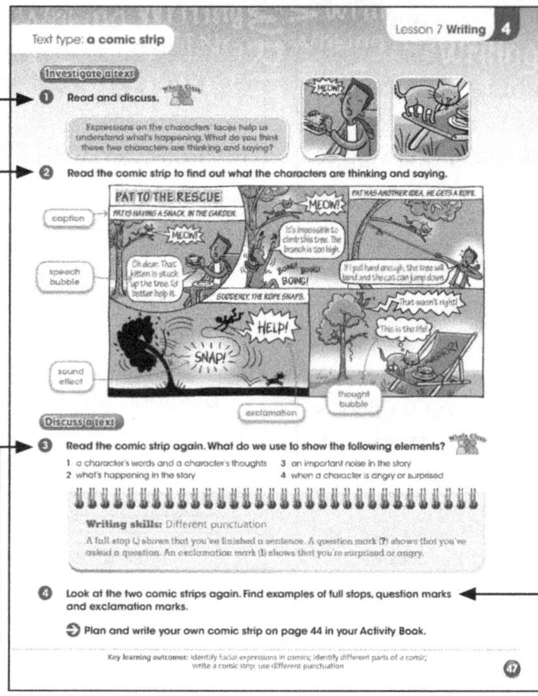
Text type: a comic strip

Investigate a text

1 Read and discuss.

2 Read the comic strip to find out what the characters are thinking and saying.

PAT TO THE RESCUE

Discuss a text

3 Read the comic strip again. What do we use to show the following elements?

4 Look at the two comic strips again. Find examples of full stops, question marks and exclamation marks.

Plan and write your own comic strip on page 44 in your Activity Book.

Starting the lesson

- Use the Trinity Exams Practice cards (optional).
- Review and learn common exclamations.
- Set learning outcomes.

Activity 1: Investigate a text

- Read and discuss.

Activity 2

- Read the comic strip to find out what the characters are thinking and saying.

Activity 3: Discuss a text

- Read the comic strip again.
- What do we use to show the following elements?

Writing skills

- Read about different punctuation.

Activity 4

- Look at the two comic strips again.
- Find examples of full stops, question marks and exclamation marks.
- Go to the Activity Book.

Ending the lesson

- Review the lesson and reflect on learning.

Extra activity

Extension

- Share your comic strips.

Activity Book

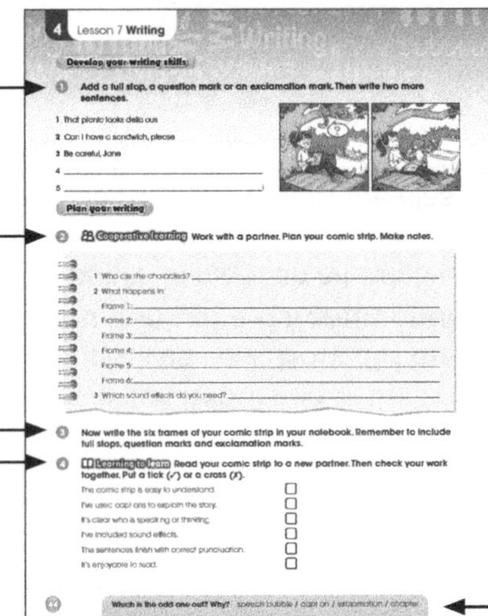
Lesson 7 Writing

Develop your writing skills

1 Add a full stop, a question mark or an exclamation mark. Then write two more sentences.

Plan your writing

2 Work with a partner. Plan your comic strip. Make notes.

3 Now write the six frames of your comic strip in your notebook. Remember to include full stops, question marks and exclamation marks.

4 Read your comic strip to a new partner. Then check your work together. Put a tick (✓) or a cross (✗).

Activity Book

Activity 1: Develop your writing skills

- Add a full stop, a question mark or an exclamation mark. Then write two more sentences.

Activity 2: Plan your writing

- Work with a partner. Plan your comic strip. Make notes.

Activity 3

- Now write the six frames of your comic strip in your notebook. Remember to include full stops, question marks and exclamation marks.

Activity 4

- Read your comic strip to a new partner. Then check your work together. Put a tick (✓) or a cross (✗).

Odd one out activity

Digital resources

Teacher's Digital: You can also teach this lesson using the Teacher's App on Navio.

Pupil's Digital: Encourage your pupils to use the Pupil's App on Navio to practise the activities from this lesson.

Powered By NAVIO

Starting the lesson

Use the Trinity Exams Practice cards (optional).

- The pupils practise asking and answering questions.

Review and learn common exclamations.

- Write a list of common exclamations on the board, e.g. *Help! Be careful! Come on! Oh no! Be quiet! Go away! Ouch! Wow! Hurray!*
- The pupils work in pairs to decide when you would use these exclamations.
- Check the pupils' ideas as a class.

Set learning outcomes

- Say **Today we're going to read and write a comic strip.**

Pupil's Book Activity 1: Investigate a text

Read and discuss.

- Read the information as a class.
- Invite the pupils to look at the characters' faces. Ask **What are the characters thinking? What do you think they're saying?**
- The pupils make predictions about what the characters are thinking and saying.

Pupil's Book Activity 2

Read the comic strip to find out what the characters are thinking and saying.

- The pupils read the comic strip to find out what the characters are thinking and saying.

Pupil's Book Activity 3: Discuss a text

Read the comic strip again. What do we use to show the following elements?

- Read and discuss the question as a class. Highlight features such as speech and thought bubbles, captions, sound effects and exclamations.

Writing skills

- Read about finishing a sentence using full stops, question marks and exclamation marks.

Pupil's Book Activity 4

Look at the two comic strips again. Find examples of full stops, question marks and exclamation marks.

- The pupils look at the comic strips in Lessons 6 and 7 to find examples of the different types of punctuation.

Activity Book

Activity 1: Develop your writing skills

Add a full stop, a question mark or an exclamation mark. Then write two more sentences.

- The pupils work on their own or in pairs to punctuate the three sentences.
- They then write their own sentences according to the punctuation given.

Answers: 1 . 2 ? 3 !

Activity 2: Plan your writing

Work with a partner. Plan your comic strip. Make notes.

- Read out the notes as a class. Check understanding.
- The pupils work in pairs to plan the story line of their comic strip. Remind them that the comic strip will need a beginning, a middle and an end.

Activity 3

Now write the six frames of your comic strip in your notebook. Remember to include full stops, question marks and exclamation marks.

- The pupils work in pairs to draw and write their comic strip in their notebooks.
- Remind the class to use a full stop, a question mark or an exclamation mark at the end of each sentence.

Activity 4

Read your comic strip to a new partner. Then check your work together. Put a tick (✓) or a cross (✗).

- Read through the statements as a class.
- Organise the class into new partners. One pupil reads aloud their comic strip. The other pupil listens. The pupils work together to decide if the comic strip fulfils the criteria and tick the corresponding boxes. The pupils can add, improve or correct the comic strip at this stage.
- The pupils swap roles.

Odd one out activity

Which is the odd one out? Why?

- The pupils complete the odd one out activity.

Answer: chapter (It isn't part of a comic strip.)

Ending the lesson

Review the lesson and reflect on learning.

- Say **Today we've read and written a comic strip.**
- Ask **What do you remember?** The pupils do a three-minute review in pairs. (Cooperative Learning Strategies, page 19)

Extra activity

Extension

- Ask the pupils to leave their notebooks on their desks so that other pupils can read their comic strips. The pupils move around the class, reading the comic strips. Each pupil chooses three comic strips that they enjoyed reading.

Key Competences and Key Learning Outcomes

- Learn about creative activities
- Develop visual–spatial skills through describing different photos
- Prepare and practise speaking activity types found in Cambridge Exams: B1 Preliminary for Schools
- Reflect on learning and progress
- Listen to a text for general and specific information
- Show interest in other people by asking and answering questions about creative activities

Key language

- *creative, doodles, virtual worlds, water park*
- *I'm impressed.*

Materials

- Pupil's Book p48; Activity Book pp45–46; Class CD2; Teacher's App on Navio

Optional materials

- Teacher's Resource Bank: Trinity Exams Practice cards (selected from the Starter Unit and Units 1,2 and 3)

At a Glance Lesson Plan

Pupil's Book

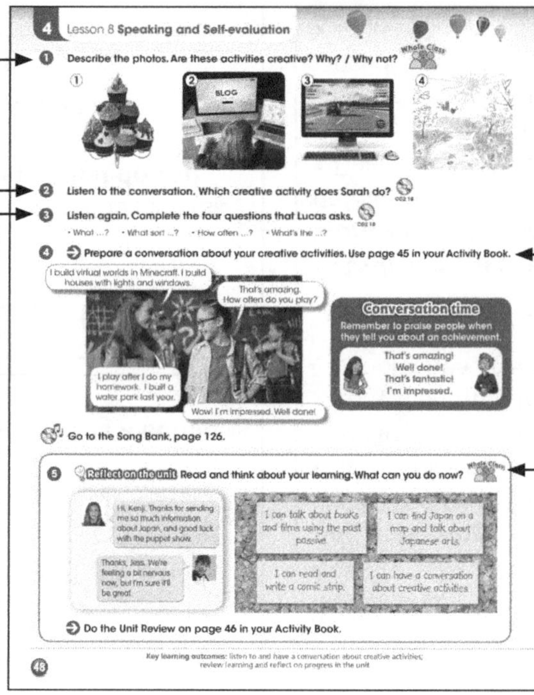

Starting the lesson

- Use the Trinity Exams Practice cards (optional).
- Review prepositions of location.
- Set learning outcomes.

Activity 1

- Describe the photos.
- Are these activities creative?
- Why? / Why not?

Activity 2

- Listen to the conversation.
- ▶ *CD2 Track 18 p284*
- Which creative activity does Sarah do?

Activity 3

- Listen again.
- ▶ *CD2 Track 18 p284*
- Complete the four questions that Lucas asks.

Go to the Activity Book.

Activity 4

- Prepare a conversation about your creative activities. Use page 45 in your Activity Book.

Go to the Activity Book.

Activity 5

- Read and think about your learning.
- What can you do now?

Song

- ▶ *CD4 Track 20 p297*
- ▶ *CD4 Track 21 p297 (optional karaoke version)*

Ending the lesson

- Review the lesson and reflect on learning.

Digital resources

Teacher's Digital: You can also teach this lesson using the Teacher's App on Navio.

Powered By NAVIO

Activity Book

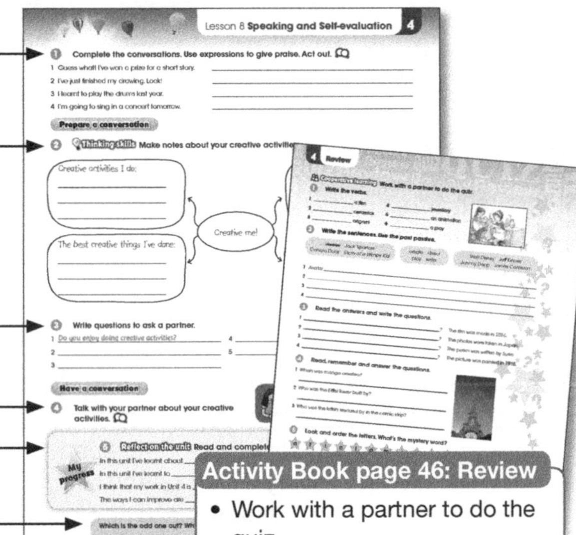

Activity Book page 46: Review

- Work with a partner to do the quiz.

Activity Book

Activity 1
- Complete the conversations. Use expressions to give praise. Act out.

Activity 2
- Make notes about your creative activities.

Activity 3
- Write questions to ask a partner.

Activity 4
- Talk with your partner about your creative activities.

Activity 5
- Read and complete the sentences.

Odd one out activity

Starting the lesson

Use the Trinity Exams Practice cards (optional).

- The pupils practise asking and answering questions.

Set learning outcomes.

- Say **Today we're going to listen to and have a conversation about creative activties and we're going to think about our learning in this unit.**

Pupil's Book Activity 1

Describe the photos. Are these activities creative? Why? / Why not?

- The pupils describe the photos and say in what way they are creative.

Pupil's Book Activity 2

Listen to the conversation. Which creative activity does Sarah do?

▶ ***CD2 Track 18 p284***

- Play CD for pupils to complete the activity.
- Check answers in pairs and then as a class.

Answers: builds virtual world on her computer

Pupil's Book Activity 3

Listen again. Complete the four questions that Lucas asks.

▶ ***CD2 Track 18 p284***

- Read the phrases and have pupils say if they remember how they finish.
- Play the CD again, pausing to allow the pupils to complete the activity.

Answers: **1** What creative activities do you do? **2** What sort of things do you build? **3** How often do you play Minecraft? **4** What's the best thing you've built?

Song

Read and discuss the questions.

- Go to the Song Bank on page 126 to do the Pupil's Book activities (see p244).

▶ ***CD4 Track 20 p297***

▶ ***CD4 Track 21 p297 (optional karaoke version)***

Activity Book

Activity 1

Complete the conversations. Use expressions to give praise. Act out.

- Pupils complete the activity on their own as they refer to the Conversation Time box.
- The pupils act out the conversation and then swap roles.

Activity 2

Make notes about your creative activities.

- Have pupils complete the activity and suggest they refer back to Lucas' question in Activity 3 of the Pupil's Book.

Activity 3

Write questions to ask a partner.

- Pupils ask each other the questions from Activity 2.

Activity 4

Talk with your partner about your creative activities.

- Refer pupils to the Remember! box. Ask how they feel when they are praised.
- Pupils discuss creative activities using their questions.

Pupil's Book Activity 4

Prepare a conversation about your creative activities. Use page 45 in your Activity Book.

- Pupils complete Activities 1 and 2 in their Activity Book.

Pupil's Book Activity 5

Read and think about your learning. What can you do now?

- Pupils look back through the unit and identify other things they have learnt / done.

Activity Book

Activity 5: My progress

Read and complete the sentences.

- Read out the sentences. Encourage the pupils to think of different ways of completing them.
- The pupils complete the sentences.

Odd one out activity

Which is the odd one out? Why?

- The pupils complete the odd one out activity.

Answers: the top (You don't use 'in' with it.)

Ending the lesson

Review the lesson and reflect on learning.

- Say **Today we've learnt and practised how to describe a photo and we've thought about our learning.**
- Ask **What do you remember?** The pupils do a three-minute review in pairs. (Cooperative Learning Strategies, page 19)

Activity Book page 46: Review

Work with a partner to do the quiz.

- Organise the class into pairs. Explain that they are going to work together to do a quiz. Set a time limit for the pupils to do this (10-15 minutes). Stress that the pupils are not competing with each other.
- Read out the five tasks that the pupils have to complete. Check understanding. Then say **Ready, steady … Go!**
- The pupils work in their pairs to do the quiz. Ask the pupils who finish quickly to help another pair.
- Correct the answers as a class.

Answers: **1 1** make **2** do **3** do **4** make **5** create **6** perform **2 1** Avatar was directed by James Cameron. **2** Jack Sparrow was played by Johnny Depp. **3** Donald Duck was created by Walt Disney. **4** Harry Potter was written by J.K.Rowling. **3 1** When was the film made? **2** Where were the photos taken? **3** Who was the poem written by? **4** When was the picture painted? **4 1** It was created more than 200 years ago. **2** It was built by Gustave Eiffel. **3** The kitten was rescued by Pat. **5** exclamation, punctuation used at the end of a sentence to show surprise or anger

Key Competences and Key Learning Outcomes

- Watch and understand a video about creative technology
- Consider and discuss how you have been and could be creative using technology
- Analyse forms of digital means for creative purposes

Key language

- *illustrator, tablet*
- *Have you ever created a photo story? Yes, I have. What was it like? It was really funny. I did it with my friends at school.*

Materials

- Pupil's Book p49; Activity Book p47; Class CD1; Teacher's App on Navio

Optional materials

- Teacher's Resource Bank: Trinity Exams Practice cards (selected from the Starter Unit)

At a Glance Lesson Plan

Pupil's Book

Starting the lesson

- **Think-Pair-Share.** Review ways of how we can use technology to create things.
- Set learning outcomes and use the talk cards.

Activity 1

- Before you watch.
- Watch the video.
- *Unit 4 video p301*
- Read and answer the questions.

Activity 2

- Watch the video again.
- *Unit 4 video*
- Which of these digital technologies do you see?
- Who uses it?

Activity 3

- Read, think and answer.

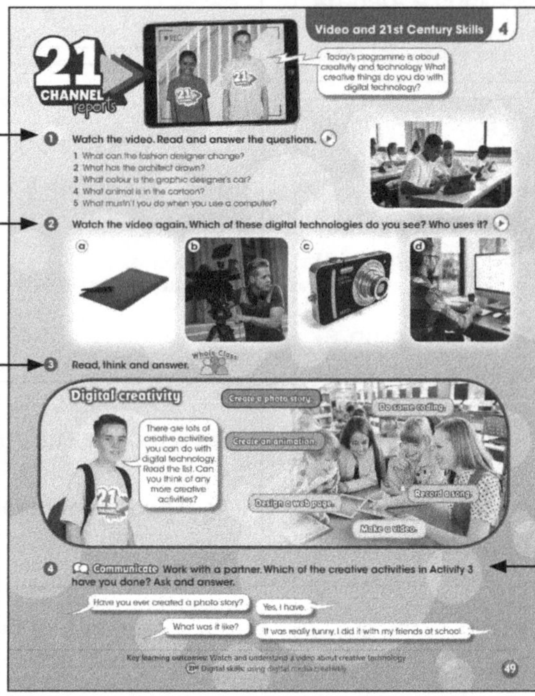

Activity 4

- Work with a partner.
- Which of the creative activities in Activity 3 have you done?
- Ask and answer.
- Go to the Activity Book.

Ending the lesson

- Review the lesson and reflect on learning.

Extra activity

- Poster about different types of technology pupils use daily.

Digital resources

Teacher's Digital: You can also teach this lesson using the Teacher's App on Navio.

Pupil's Digital: Encourage your pupils to use the Pupil's App on Navio to practise the activities from this lesson.

Powered By NAVIO

Activity Book

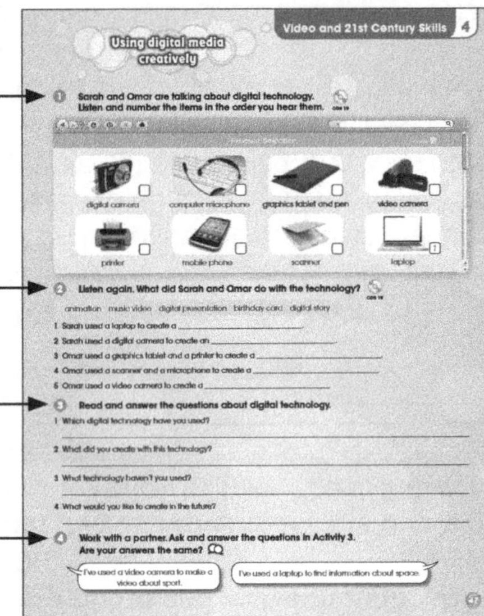

Activity Book

Activity 1

- Sarah and Omar are talking about digital technology. Listen and number the items in the order you hear them.
- *CD2 Track 19 p284*

Activity 2

- Listen again. What did Sarah and Omar do with the technology?

Activity 3

- Read and answer the questions about digital technology.

Activity 4

- Work with a partner. Ask and answer the questions in Activity 3. Are your answers the same?

Starting the lesson

Think-Pair-Share. Review ways of how we can use technology to create things.

- Ask **What form of technologies they have at home?** Elicit answers and write them on the board.
- Extend the discussion to talk about how they use the different types of technologies.
- Pupils work with a Talk Partner to talk about forms of technology they have at home and how they use it.
- Invite different Talk Partners to tell the class what they discussed with their partners.

Set learning outcomes and use the talk cards.

- Say **Today we're going to watch a video about creative technology.**
- Ask pupils if they remember who the presenters are (Max and Amy).
- Point to the talk cards to show the pupils the different ways they will be working in the lesson.

Pupil's Book Activity 1

Before you watch

- Ask pupils what they have learnt so far from the videos they have watched and what they expect to learn from today's video.
- Read the speech bubble to pupils. Elicit responses from a number of pupils.
- Ask which occupations they can think of that use technology and why.

Watch the video. Read and answer the questions.
p301

- Watch Part 1.
- Have students read the questions quietly.
- Play Part 2, pausing at each section for pupils to answer. Pupils then work in pairs to answer the questions.

Answers: **1** She can change colours. **2** A building in 3D. **3** It's **4** It's a fox. **5** You mustn't use it for too long.

Pupil's Book Activity 2

Watch the video again. Which form of digital technology do you see? Who uses it?

- Ask pupils to tell you what they remember from the video. Ask if they remember types of digital technologies mentioned.
- Ask them to look at each item in the activity and tell you which ones were used and why.
- Play the second part of the video for reinforcement.

Answers: **a** – a graphic designer, **b** – digital camera – film makers, **d** – computer – designers

Pupil's Book Activity 3

Read, think and answer.

- Tell pupils that in the last part of the video Amy and Max talk about how there are a lot of creative activities that can be done with technology. Ask what points they remember the Amy and Max present.
- Pupils work in pairs to read and think about each point. Ask if they have used technology to do any of these creative activities. Then ask if they can think of any more activities.

Pupil's Book Activity 4

Work with a partner. Which of the creative activities in Activity 3 have you done?
Ask and answer.

- Have pupils work in groups and keep notes about what technology they used.
- Pupils present their group's notes to the class.

Activity Book

Activity 1

Sarah and Omar are talking about digital technology. Listen and number the items in the order you hear them.

▸ *CD2 Track 19 p284*

- Look at each type of technology and ask what it does.
- Play the CD and complete the activity.

Answers: **1** laptop **2** mobile phone **3** digital camera **4** graphics tablet **5** printer **6** scanner **7** computer microphone **8** video camera

Activity 2

Listen again. What did Sarah and Omar do with the technology?

▸ *CD2 Track 19 p284*

- Have pupils complete the activity and check answers with their partners.
- Ask what else these things can be used for.

Answers: **1** digital presentation **2** animation **3** birthday card **4** digital story **5** music video

Activity 3

Read and answer the questions about digital technology.

- Pupils complete the activity quietly.

Activity 4

Work with a partner. Ask and answer the questions in Activity 3. Are your answers the same?

- In pairs pupils complete the activity.
- Have pupils swap pairs and repeat the activity.

Ending the lesson

Review the lesson and reflect on learning.

- Say **Today we've watched a video about using technology to be creative. What have we learnt ?** Elicit the information from the pupils. The pupils do a three-minute review in pairs. (Cooperative Learning Strategies, page 19)

Extra activity

Reinforcement

- Place pupils in small pairs and make a poster, similar to that in Activity 1.
- Extend the activity by having pupils write why they use them as well.
- Pupils present their work to the class.

Date: ______________________ Unit: ____________

1 What did my pupils learn in this unit?

2 How did my pupils work? (✓)

individually ☐ in pairs ☐ in small groups ☐

in large groups ☐ as a class ☐

3 Which key competences did my pupils develop? Give a score from 1 to 5 (5 being the highest).

- Competence in linguistic communication ☐
- Competence in mathematics, science and technology ☐
- Digital competence ☐
- Learning to learn ☐
- Social and civic competences ☐
- Sense of initiative and entrepreneurship ☐
- Cultural awareness and expression ☐

4 Which lessons / activities were the most successful and why?

5 Which lessons / activities did my pupils find the most difficult and why?

6 What did I try in the classroom for the first time? How did it go?

7 Which resources did I find most useful? (including webpages)

8 What could I do differently next time I teach this unit?

Unit 5

Write it down!

Unit overview

Key competences and learning outcomes

- Name different kinds of messages and communication (Lesson 1)
- Learn words related to news articles (Lesson 5)
- Review news vocabulary (Lesson 6)
- Use 'so' to connect sentences (Lesson 7)
- Watch and understand a video (Video and 21st Century Skills)

- Learn about deciphering hieroglyphic symbols (Lesson 3)
- Learn about computer coding (Lesson 6)

- Use the Pupil's App on Navio
- Investigate Egypt (Lesson 3)

- Identify examples of reported speech in a dialogue (Lesson 2)
- Identify and practise saying sentences with 'would' and 'could' (Lesson 4)
- Learn about adjectives with different endings (Lesson 5)
- Identify the text features of a newspaper article (Lesson 7)
- Review learning and reflect on progress in the unit (Lesson 8)
- Practise activity types found in the Cambridge Exams: B1 Preliminary for Schools

- Think about the importance of learning about civilisations (Lesson 3)
- Prepare a conversation about meeting a famous person (Lesson 8)

- Work in pairs or small groups to practise and reinforce learning (All lessons)
- Do a communication task (Lesson 5)
- Do a collaborative assessment (Video and 21st Century Skills)

- Read a text (Lesson 3)
- Learn about ancient Egypt (Lesson 3)
- Read and write a newspaper article (Lessons 6 and 7)

Vocabulary

Core vocabulary
advert, blog post, brochure, cartoon, chat message, email, greetings card, leaflet, note, sign, sign language, text message; article, caption, fashion section, front page, headline, interview, reporter, review, sports news, world news

Extension vocabulary (optional)
chat, design, post, type, write, text (v), email (v); local news, breaking news, celebrity news, comments

Other vocabulary
characters, code, computer coding, hieroglyphics, letters, symbols; current affairs, film set, reporter, story-writing competition, website; keep up, look forward to, take turns, work it out; active, nervous, polite, professional, surprised, thrilled; ancient Egyptians / Greeks / Romans, Wales, Welsh, deaf, translate, play

Recycled vocabulary
do homework, juggle, keep a blog, meet people, skate; engines, dance club, volunteers; excited, friendly, proud

Structures

Core structures
He said (he was happy with the results). He told me / He said (he liked oranges and apples). She told me / She said (they weren't very good at tennis). He said / He told me (it would rain tomorrow). She said / She told me (they could read Arabic).

Other structures
Darkness has always interested me so I wanted to write about it. It looks like a large piece of boring grey rock. It was so popular that they started a second group.

Recycled structures
Which language does (hamster) come from? It comes from (German). If you want to be a journalist, this is for you. How / When and where did it happen? What was she like? What's the name of your new film?

Pronunciation

Sentences with 'would' and 'could'

Literacy

Text type: a newspaper article (text to inform; writing preparation)
Reading skills: skimming text to ascertain meaning
Writing skills: using 'so' to connect sentences

Culture ... around the world

Discovering the Rosetta Stone and the meaning of Egyptian hieroglyphics

21st Century Skills

Digital Skills: using digital media to research and present information

Thinking skills

Assessing different ways of communicating (Lesson 1); Defining and describing (Lesson 1); Analysing and applying rules and patterns (Lessons 2 and 4); Giving an opinion on a story (Lesson 3); Organising the ideas in a newspaper article (Lesson 7); Planning, checking and correcting (Lesson 7); Evaluating (Lesson 8)

Cooperative learning

Working together (Lessons 1–8); Reflecting and setting goals (Lessons 1–8); Collaborative speaking (Lesson 5); Collaborative writing (Lesson 7); Peer evaluation and feedback (Lesson 7); Helping and encouraging (Lessons 1–8); Expressing and respecting opinions (Lessons 1, 3, 6, 8)

Values

The importance of learning about past civilisations

Cross-curricular links

Links to Science
Information and Communication Technology

Suggested Arts and Crafts concepts
Contour lines

Key Competences and Key Learning Outcomes

- Name different kinds of messages and communication
- Learn about English words which come from other languages
- Read a message for specific information
- Learn about helping others communicate

Key language

- *advert, blog post, brochure, cartoon, chat message, email, greetings card, leaflet, note, sign, sign language, text message*
- Extension: *chat, design, email (v), post, text (v), type, write*
- *Which language does (hamster) come from? It comes from (German).*

Materials

- Pupil's Book pp50–51; Activity Book p48; Class CD2; Teacher's App on Navio
- Messages and communication flashcards

Optional materials

- Teacher's Resource Bank: Trinity Exams Practice cards (from the Starter Unit and Units 1, 2, 3 and 4)

At a Glance Lesson Plan

Pupil's Book

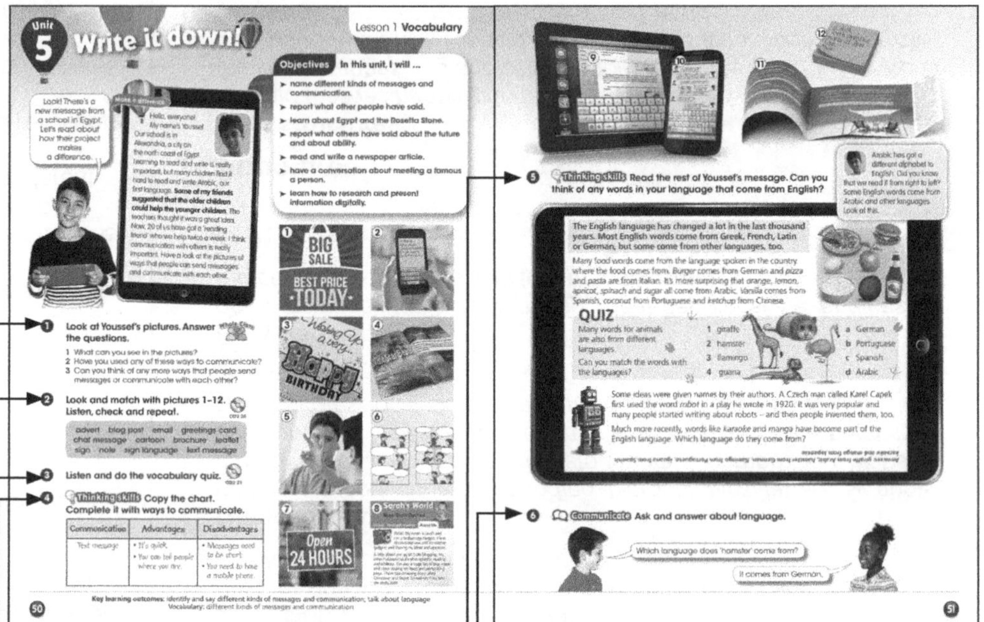

Activity Book

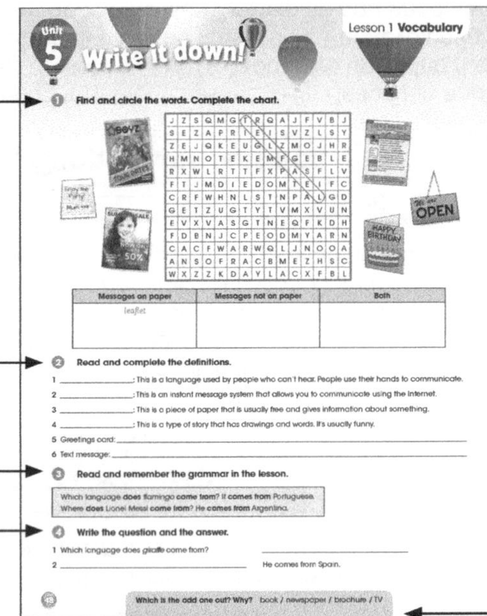

Starting the lesson

- Use the Trinity Exams Practice cards (optional).
- Review languages.
- Set learning outcomes.

Activity 1

- Look at Youssef's pictures.
- Answer the questions.

Vocabulary presentation

- Present the new vocabulary using the messages and communication flashcards.

Activity 2

- Look and match with pictures 1–12.
- Listen, check and repeat.

▶ *CD2 Track 20 p284*

Activity 3

- Listen and do the vocabulary quiz.

▶ *CD2 Track 21 p284*

Activity 4

- Copy the chart.
- Complete it with ways to communicate.

Activity 5

- Read the rest of Youssef's message.
- Can you think of any words in your language that come from English?

Activity 6

- Ask and answer about language.

Go to the Activity Book.

Ending the lesson

- Review the lesson and reflect on learning.

Extra activities

Extension

- Find out about Egypt.

Vocabulary extension

- Present six additional vocabulary items.

Activity Book

Activity 1

- Find and circle the words. Complete the chart.

Activity 2

- Read and complete the definitions.

Activity 3

- Read and remember the grammar in the lesson.

Activity 4

- Write the question and the answer.

Odd one out activity

Digital resources

Teacher's Digital: You can also teach this lesson using the Teacher's App on Navio.

Pupil's Digital: Encourage your pupils to use the Pupil's App on Navio to practise the activities from this lesson.

Powered By NAVIO

Starting the lesson

Use the Trinity Exams Practice cards (optional).

- The pupils practise asking and answering questions.

Review languages.

- Brainstorm different languages. Ask **What languages do you speak?** Write the languages on the board.

Set learning outcomes.

- Say **Today we're going to learn words for the different ways that people use language to communicate.**

Pupil's Book Activity 1

Look at Youssef's pictures. Answer the questions.

- Invite a pupil to read out the speech bubble to find out which school has sent a message. Ask **Do you know where Egypt is?**
- Invite a pupil to read out the message from Youssef. Check understanding.
- Work as a class to answer the questions.

Vocabulary presentation

- Present the new vocabulary using the messages and communication flashcards. Hold up the first flashcard and elicit / say the word or phrase. Ask **When do you see / use this?** Stick the flashcards on the board. Group them according to suggestions from the pupils.

Pupil's Book Activity 2

Look and match with pictures 1–12. Listen, check and repeat.

▶ *CD2 Track 20 p284*

- The pupils look at picture number 1. Ask **What's this?** In pairs, the pupils match 2–12 with the words. Play the CD. The pupils listen and check.
- Play the CD again, pausing after each word for the pupils to repeat. You can find the answers for this activity in the audioscript on page 284.

Pupil's Book Activity 3

Listen and do the vocabulary quiz.

▶ *CD2 Track 21 p284*

- Play the CD. Listen to the first definition, pausing at the beep to allow the pupils to name the item. Play the CD to listen to the answer.
- Repeat the procedure with the other definitions. You can find the answers for this activity in the audioscript on page 284.

Pupil's Book Activity 4

Copy the chart. Complete it with ways to communicate.

- Explain that the pupils are going to think about the advantages and disadvantages of different ways of communicating. The pupils read the example.
- In pairs, they complete the chart. Check answers as a class.

Pupil's Book Activity 5

Read the rest of Youssef's message. Can you think of any words in your language that come from English?

- The pupils read the message and information and share ideas about words in their language that come from English.
- The pupils do the quiz. Check answers as a class.

Pupil's Book Activity 6

Ask and answer about language.

- Invite two pupils to read out the speech bubbles.
- In pairs, the pupils look at the information in Activity 5. They ask and answer questions about the words.

Activity Book

Activity 1

Find and circle the words. Complete the chart.

- The pupils find the words and complete the chart.

Answers: **messages on paper** greetings card, leaflet, sign ***messages not on paper*** blog post **both** advert, note

Activity 2

Read and complete the definitions.

- The pupils complete the definitions.

Answers: **1** sign language **2** email **3** brochure **4** cartoon **5 & 6** Pupils' own answers

Activity 3

Read and remember the grammar in the lesson.

- Invite a pupil to read out the information.

Activity 4

Write the question and the answer.

- The pupils complete the question and the answer.

Answers: **1** It comes from Arabic. **2** Where does he come from?

Odd one out activity

Which is the odd one out? Why?

- The pupils complete the odd one out activity

Answers: TV (It isn't on paper.)

Ending the lesson

Review the lesson and reflect on learning.

- Say **Today we've learnt words for different ways of communicating.**
- Ask **What do you remember?** The pupils do a three-minute review in pairs. (Cooperative Learning Strategies, page 19)

Extra activities

Extension

- The pupils find three interesting facts about Egypt on the Internet or in reference books to present to the class.

Vocabulary extension

- Introduce the words related to communication: *chat, design, post, type, write, text (v), email (v).*
- Use the Vocabulary Booster on NAVIO to practise these new words.

Key Competences and Key Learning Outcomes

- Listen to and read a dialogue
- Learn and practise how to use reported speech
- Identify examples of reported speech in a dialogue
- Learn about helping others to read

Key language

- *characters, letters, look forward to*
- *He said (he was happy with the results). He told me / He said (he liked oranges and apples). She told me / She said (they weren't very good at tennis).*

Materials

- Pupil's Book p52; Activity Book 49; Class CD2; Teacher's App on Navio
- Teacher's Resource Bank: Messages and communication word cards

Optional materials

- Teacher's Resource Bank: Trinity Exams Practice cards (from the Starter Unit and Units 1, 2, 3 and 4)

At a Glance Lesson Plan

Pupil's Book

Starting the lesson

- Use the Trinity Exams Practice cards (optional).
- Review messages and communication vocabulary.
- Set learning outcomes.

Activity 1

- Describe the pictures.
- What do you think Youssef is explaining?
- Read and listen to find out.

▶ *CD2 Track 22 p285*

Activity 2

- Read the dialogue again.
- Then read these sentences.
- Which words change when Youssef tells Callum what his teacher said?

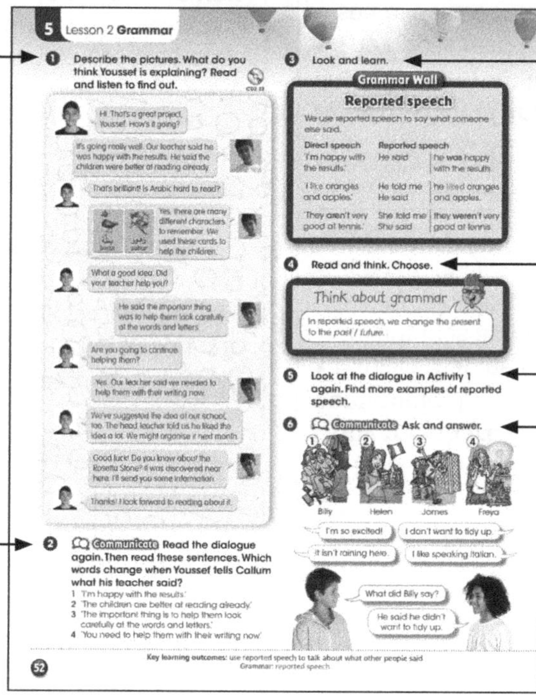

Activity 3

- Look and learn – Grammar wall

Activity 4

- Read and think.
- Choose.

Activity 5

- Look at the dialogue in Activity 1 again.
- Find more examples of reported speech.

Activity 6

- Ask and answer.
- Go to the Activity Book.

Ending the lesson

- Review the lesson and reflect on learning.

Extra activity

Reinforcement

- Play the *What did they say?* game.

Activity Book

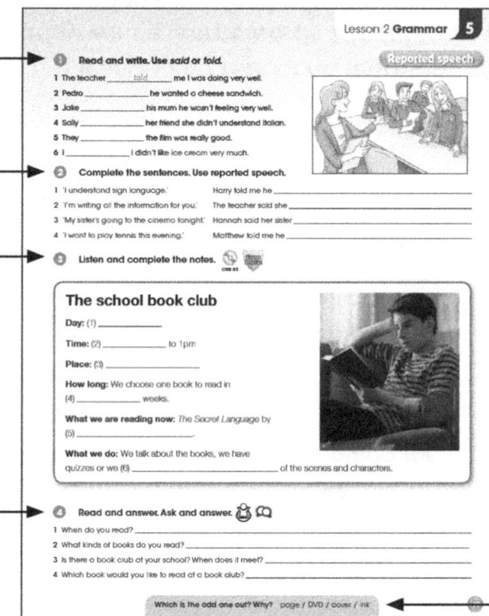

Activity Book

Activity 1

- Read and write. Use *said* or *told.*

Activity 2

- Complete the sentences. Use reported speech.

Activity 3

- Listen and complete the notes.

▶ *CD2 Track 23 p285*

Activity 4

- Read and answer. Ask and answer.

Odd one out activity

Digital resources

Teacher's Digital: You can also teach this lesson using the Teacher's App on Navio.

Pupil's Digital: Encourage your pupils to use the Pupil's App on Navio to practise the activities from this lesson.

Powered By NAVIO

Starting the lesson

Use the Trinity Exams Practice cards (optional).

- The pupils practise asking and answering questions.

Review messages and communication vocabulary.

- Give each group of four a messages and communication word card. The pupils write a definition for that word.
- Groups read out the definitions for the class to guess.

Set learning outcomes.

- Say **Today we're going to learn how to tell others what someone has said. It's called reported speech.**

Pupil's Book Activity 1

Describe the pictures. What do you think Youssef is explaining? Read and listen to find out.

▶ *CD2 Track 22 p285*

- Prompt the pupils to describe the pictures. Ask **Who is using them? What are they used for?**
- Play the CD. The pupils listen and read the dialogue. Confirm that they are word cards that Youssef is using to help teach younger children to read.

Pupil's Book Activity 2

Read the dialogue again. Then read these sentences. Which words change when Youssef tells Callum what his teacher said?

- The pupils read the dialogue. Check understanding.
- The pupils read the sentences. Explain that when someone reports what another person said, some words change. Ask the pupils to identify these words. (*1 I'm – he was 2 are – were 3 is – was 4 You – we, need – needed*)

Pupil's Book Activity 3

Look and learn – Grammar wall

- Read the information on the Grammar wall as a class.
- Encourage the pupils to think about form and identify patterns. Ask **What do '(I)'m' and 'like' change to in reported speech?** (*Was and liked.*)
- Explain that we use 'tell' with a person.

Pupil's Book Activity 4

Read and think. Choose.

- Focus the pupils' attention on the Think about grammar box. Read out the sentence as a class. The pupils discuss and complete the sentence in pairs. (*past*)

Pupil's Book Activity 5

Look at the dialogue in Activity 1 again. Find more examples of reported speech.

- In pairs, the pupils find more examples of reported speech in the dialogue.

Pupil's Book Activity 6

Ask and answer.

- Ask the pupils to describe the pictures. Then invite two pupils to read out the speech bubbles. Explain that the second person is reporting what Billy said.
- In pairs, the pupils ask and answer. Explain that 'here' changes to 'there'.

Activity Book

Activity 1

Read and write. Use *said* or *told*.

- The pupils complete the sentences. Remind them that 'told' is always followed by a person.
- Check answers as a class.

Answers: **1** told **2** said **3** told **4** told **5** said **6** said

Activity 2

Complete the sentences. Use reported speech.

- Ask a pupil to read out the first sentence. As a class change it to reported speech.
- The pupils complete the remaining sentences.

Answers: **1** understood sign language. **2** was writing all the information for me. **3** was going to the cinema tonight / that night. **4** wanted to play football this evening / that evening.

Activity 3

Listen and complete the notes.

▶ *CD2 Track 23 p285*

- Ask the class to read the notes quickly and to think about the kind of words that complete the gaps. Then play the CD. The pupils listen.
- Play the CD again. The pupils complete the notes.

Answers: **1** Wednesday **2** 12.30 **3** the school library **4** three **5** Helen Hawkins **6** draw pictures

Activity 4

Read and answer. Ask and answer.

- The pupils read and answer the questions.
- In pairs, the pupils ask and answer the questions.

Odd one out activity

Which is the odd one out? Why?

- The pupils complete the odd one out activity.

Answers: DVD (The others are all related to books.)

Ending the lesson

Review the lesson and reflect on learning.

- Say **Today we've learnt how to tell other people what someone has said. We used reported speech.** Elicit one or two examples from the pupils.
- Ask **What do you remember?** The pupils do a three-minute review in pairs. (Cooperative Learning Strategies, page 19)

Extra activity

Reinforcement

- Play the *What did they say?* game. Explain that you are going to whisper to a pupil something you like, e.g. **I like playing tennis.** The pupil will then tell the class what you said using reported speech. The other pupils work out the original sentence.
- Then invite two pupils to the front of the class. Ask them to repeat the activity with a different verb. The first pupil whispers to the second and the second pupil reports. Again, the other pupils work out what the first pupil originally said. Repeat the procedure with other pupils.

Key Competences and Key Learning Outcomes
• Read a text with confidence and fluency
• Learn about deciphering hieroglyphic symbols
• Use the Internet to investigate Egypt
• Think about the importance of learning about civilisations from the past
• Learn about ancient Egypt and the Rosetta Stone

Key language

- *ancient Egyptians / Greeks / Romans, code, hieroglyphics, symbols, work it out*
- *It looks like a large piece of boring grey rock.*

Materials

- Pupil's Book p53; Activity Book p50; Class CD2; Teacher's App on Navio

Optional materials

- Teacher's Resource Bank: Trinity Exams Practice cards (from the Starter Unit and Units 1, 2, 3 and 4)

At a Glance Lesson Plan

Pupil's Book

Starting the lesson

- Use the Trinity Exams Practice cards (optional).
- Review words related to communication.
- Set learning outcomes.

Activity 1: Before you read

- Read and discuss.

Activity 2

- Listen and read.

▶ *CD2 Track 24 p285*

Go to the Activity Book.

***Give Me Five!* values**

- Read and discuss.

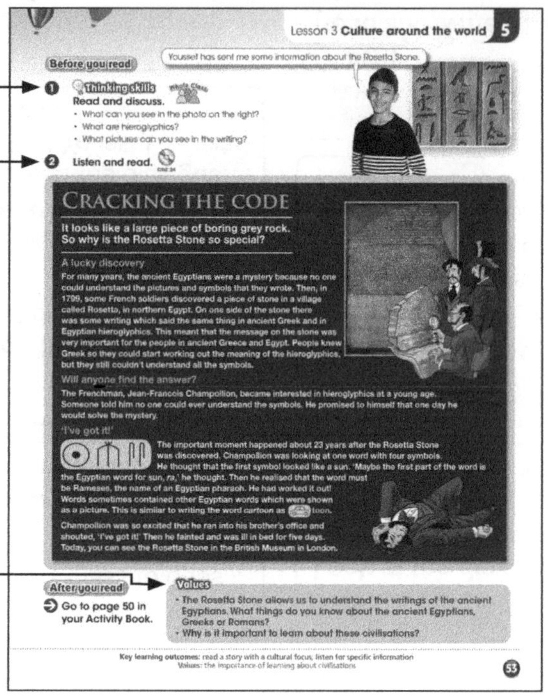

Lesson 3 Culture around the world 5

Before you read

Yousef has sent me some information about the Rosetta Stone.

1 Thinking skills Read and discuss.
- What can you see in the photo on the right?
- What are hieroglyphics?
- What pictures can you see in the writing?

2 Listen and read.

CRACKING THE CODE

It looks like a large piece of boring grey rock. So why is the Rosetta Stone so special?

A lucky discovery

For many years, the ancient Egyptians were a mystery because no one could understand the pictures and symbols that they wrote. Then, in 1799, some French soldiers discovered a piece of stone in a village called Rosetta, in northern Egypt. On one side of the stone there was some writing which said the same thing in ancient Greek and in Egyptian hieroglyphics. This meant that the message on the stone was very important for the people in ancient Greece and Egypt. People knew Greek so they could start working out the meaning of the hieroglyphics, but they still couldn't understand all the symbols.

Will anyone find the answer?

The Frenchman, Jean-François Champollion, became interested in hieroglyphics at a young age. Someone told him no one could ever understand the symbols. He promised to himself that one day he would solve the mystery.

'I've got it!'

The important moment happened about 23 years after the Rosetta Stone was discovered. Champollion was looking at one word with four symbols. He thought that the first symbol looked like a sun. 'Maybe the first part of the word is the Egyptian word for sun, ra,' he thought. Then he realised that the word must be Rameses, the name of an Egyptian pharaoh. He had worked it out! Words sometimes contained other Egyptian words which were shown as a picture. This is similar to writing the word cartoon as [icon] toon.

Champollion was so excited that he ran into his brother's office and shouted, 'I've got it!' Then he fainted and was ill in bed for five days. Today, you can see the Rosetta Stone in the British Museum in London.

After you read

Go to page 50 in your Activity Book.

Values
- The Rosetta Stone allows us to understand the writings of the ancient Egyptians. What things do you know about the ancient Egyptians, Greeks or Romans?
- Why is it important to learn about these civilisations?

53

Ending the lesson

- Review the lesson and reflect on learning.

Extra activity

Extension

- Research the Rosetta Stone.

Activity Book

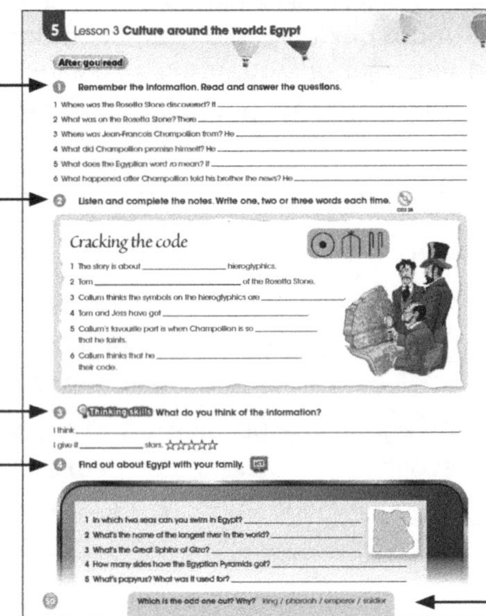

5 Lesson 3 Culture around the world: Egypt

After you read

1 Remember the information. Read and answer the questions.

1 Where was the Rosetta Stone discovered? It
2 What was on the Rosetta Stone? There
3 Where was Jean-François Champollion from? He
4 What did Champollion promise himself? He
5 What does the Egyptian word ra mean? It
6 What happened after Champollion told his brother the news? He

2 Listen and complete the notes. Write one, two or three words each time.

Cracking the code

1 The story is about ______ hieroglyphics.
2 Tom ______ of the Rosetta Stone.
3 Callum thinks the symbols on the hieroglyphics are ______
4 Tom and Jess have got ______
5 Callum's favourite part is when Champollion is so ______ that he faints.
6 Callum thinks that he ______ their code.

3 Thinking skills What do you think of the information?

I think ______

I give it ______ stars. ☆☆☆☆☆

4 Find out about Egypt with your family.

1 In which two seas can you swim in Egypt?
2 What's the name of the longest river in the world?
3 What's the Great Sphinx of Giza?
4 How many sides have the Egyptian Pyramids got?
5 What's papyrus? What was it used for?

Which is the odd one out? Why? king / pharaoh / emperor / soldier

Activity Book: After you read

Activity 1

- Remember the information. Read and answer the questions.

Activity 2

- Listen and complete the notes.

▶ *CD2 Track 25 p285*

- Write one, two or three words each time.

Activity 3

- What do you think of the information?

Activity 4

- Find out about Egypt with your family.

Odd one out activity

Digital resources

Teacher's Digital: You can also teach this lesson using the Teacher's App on Navio.

Pupil's Digital: Encourage your pupils to use the Pupil's App on Navio to practise the activities from this lesson.

Powered By NAVIO

Starting the lesson

Use the Trinity Exams Practice cards (optional).

- The pupils practise asking and answering questions.

Review words related to communication.

- Ask the pupils to imagine that they have a friend in Australia. They would like to tell their friend about an amazing film they have seen. In pairs, the pupils think of seven different ways that they could communicate with their friend.
- The pupils share their ideas with the class, e.g. email, postcard, letter, video call, a long text message, a chat message, a phone call.

Set learning outcomes

- Say **Today we're going to read about a language that used symbols and pictures to write down ideas.**

Pupil's Book Activity 1: Before you read

Read and discuss.

- Read the questions as a class. Encourage the pupils to share their knowledge of the ancient Egyptians and hieroglyphics.

Pupil's Book Activity 2

Listen and read.

▶ *CD2 Track 24 p285*

- Play the CD. The pupils follow in their books.
- Ask questions to check understanding.

Suggested comprehension questions:

- Paragraph 1: **What was on the Rosetta Stone?** (*Writing in ancient Greek and in Egyptian hieroglyphics.*)
- Paragraph 2: **Was Champollion young when he became interested in hieroglyphics?** (*Yes, he was.*)
- Paragraph 3: **What is 'sun' in ancient Egyptian?** (*Ra.*)

Activity Book: After you read

Activity 1

Remember the information. Read and answer the questions.

- The pupils read and answer the questions.

Answers: **1** was discovered in Rosetta in northern Egypt. **2** was some writing in ancient Greek and some Egyptian hieroglyphics. **3** was from France. **4** promised he would solve the mystery. **5** means 'sun'. **6** fainted and was ill for five days.

Activity 2

Listen and complete the notes. Write one, two or three words each time.

▶ *CD2 Track 25 p285*

- Read out the notes as a class. Ask the pupils to guess the missing words.
- Play the CD without pausing. The pupils listen and complete as much information as possible.
- Play the CD again, pausing after each piece of key information to check the answer.

Answers: **1** Egyptian **2** hasn't heard **3** amazing **4** a secret code **5** excited **6** can crack

Activity 3

What do you think of the information?

- The pupils write their opinion and give a rating.
- Invite different pupils to share their opinions.

Activity 4

Find out about Egypt with your family.

- Read out the questions about Egypt. Ask **Where can you find out this information?** (*Internet, library, asking friends and family.*) The pupils complete the activity at home.
- If you prefer to do this activity in the class, connect to a children's website which has information about Egypt, such as www.sciencekids.co.nz/sciencefacts/countries/egypt.html or http://kids.nationalgeographic.com/explore/countries/egypt.
- Read out the questions. The pupils work as a class to find and write the answers.

Answers: **1** Mediterranean Sea, Red Sea **2** the Nile **3** a statue of a lion with a woman's head **4** four **5** paper made from the plant papyrus, used for writing

Odd one out activity

Which is the odd one out? Why?

- The pupils complete the odd one out activity.

Answers: soldier (The other words are all leaders.)

***Give Me Five!* values**

Read and discuss.

- Read out the sentence and questions. Discuss them as a class.
- Explain that we can learn a lot from past civilisations. Some of it is fascinating and helps us understand why things are how they are today. Also, if we understand more about the history of some cultures, we will have more respect for other people who live their lives differently from the way we live our lives.

Ending the lesson

Review the lesson and reflect on learning.

- Say **Today we've read about the discovery of the Rosetta Stone.**
- Ask **What do you remember?** The pupils do a three-minute review in pairs. (Cooperative Learning Strategies, page 19)

Extra activity

Extension

- Ask the pupils to think about what else they would like to know about the Rosetta Stone or the ancient Egyptians, e.g. *What was the text on the Rosetta Stone about?* or *What did ancient Egyptians wear?* In groups or pairs, the pupils write down two or three questions.
- Ask the pupils to read out some questions. Write ten of the questions on the board. Invite the pupils to vote for the five questions that they would most like to answer.
- Then ask the pupils to find out the answers to the questions before the next class. They write sentences in English.

Key Competences and Key Learning Outcomes

- Act out a short dialogue in pairs
- Learn and practise how to use reported speech with 'will / would' and 'can / could'
- Practise saying sentences with 'would' and 'could'
- Think about the different abilities that people have

Key language

- *dance club, do homework, juggle, skate*
- *He said / He told me (it would rain tomorrow). She said / She told me (they could read Arabic).*

Materials

- Pupil's Book p54; Activity Book p51; Class CD2 and CD3; Teacher's App on Navio

Optional materials

- Teacher's Resource Bank: Trinity Exams Practice cards (from the Starter Unit and Units 1, 2, 3 and 4)

At a Glance Lesson Plan

Pupil's Book

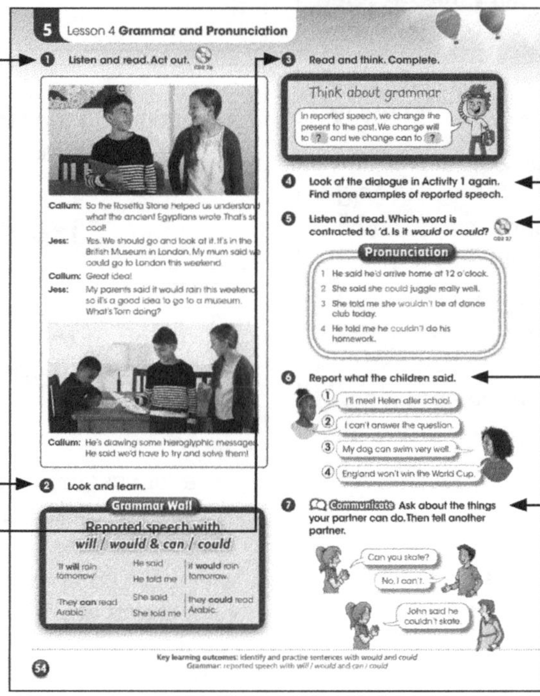

Starting the lesson

- Use the Trinity Exams Practice cards (optional).
- Review the information from Lesson 3.
- Set learning outcomes.

Activity 1

- Listen and read.
- ▶ *CD2 Track 26 p286*
- Act out.

Activity 2

- Look and learn – Grammar wall

Activity 3

- Read and think.
- Complete.

Activity 4

- Look at the dialogue in Activity 1 again.
- Find more examples of reported speech.

Activity 5

- Listen and read.
- ▶ *CD2 Track 27 p286*
- Which word is contracted to '*d*. Is it – *would* or *could*?

Activity 6

- Report what the children said.

Activity 7

- Ask about the things your partner can do.
- Then tell another partner.
- Go to the Activity Book.

Ending the lesson

- Review the lesson and reflect on learning.

Extra activity

Reinforcement

- Do a memory test.

Activity Book

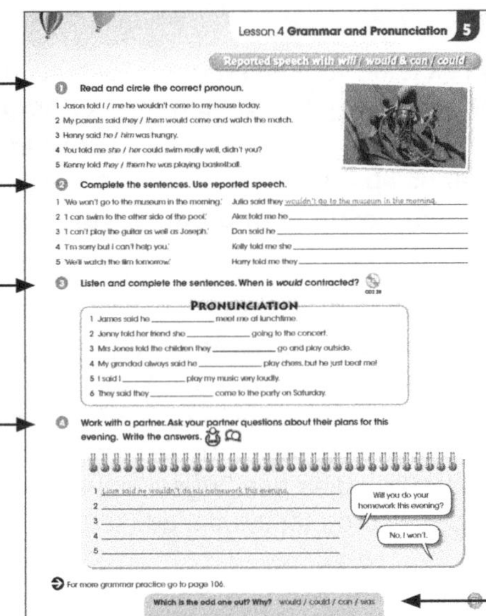

Activity Book

Activity 1

- Read and circle the correct pronoun.

Activity 2

- Complete the sentences. Use reported speech.

Activity 3

- Listen and complete the sentences. When is *would* contracted?

▶ *CD2 Track 28 p286*

Activity 4

- Work with a partner. Ask your partner questions about their plans for this evening. Write the answers.

Odd one out activity

Digital resources

Teacher's Digital: You can also teach this lesson using the Teacher's App on Navio.

Pupil's Digital: Encourage your pupils to use the Pupil's App on Navio to practise the activities from this lesson.

Powered By NAVIO

Starting the lesson

Use the Trinity Exams Practice cards (optional).
- The pupils practise asking and answering questions.

Review the information from Lesson 3.
- Ask yes/no questions about the information from Lesson 3.

Set learning outcomes.
- Say **Today we're going to learn about how we report speech when someone talks about the future or about what they can do.**

Pupil's Book Activity 1

Listen and read. Act out.

▶ *CD2 Track 26 p286*
- The pupils look at the photos. Ask **What are Tom and Jess talking about in photo (1)?**
- Play the CD. The pupils listen and read the dialogue. Check understanding.
- Play the CD again, pausing after each sentence for the pupils to repeat.
- The pupils practise the dialogue in pairs.

Pupil's Book Activity 2

Look and learn – Grammar wall
- Read the information on the Grammar wall as a class.
- Encourage the pupils to think about the difference between the sentences in each pair.

Pupil's Book Activity 3

Read and think. Complete.
- Focus the pupils' attention on the Think about Grammar box. Read out the sentences as a class. The pupils complete the sentences in pairs.
- Check answers as a class. (*would, could*)

Pupil's Book Activity 4

Look at the dialogue in Activity 1 again. Find more examples of reported speech.
- In pairs, the pupils find examples in the dialogue. They then work out what was originally said. Check answers as a class.

Pupil's Book Activity 5

Listen and read. Which word is contracted to *'d*. Is it *would* or *could*?

▶ *CD2 Track 27 p286*
- Play the CD. Elicit that 'would' is contracted to ''d'.
- Play the CD again. The pupils listen, check and repeat.

Pupil's Book Activity 6

Report what the children said.
- Ask four pupils to read out the speech bubbles. In pairs, the pupils report what each child said.
- Check answers as a class.

Pupil's Book Activity 7

Ask about the things your partner can do. Then tell another partner.
- Ask two pupils to read out the speech bubbles. The pupils answer questions in pairs. Then they report to a new partner about their first partner.

Activity Book

Activity 1

Read and circle the correct pronoun.
- The pupils complete the sentences.

Answers: **1** me **2** they **3** he **4** she **5** them

Activity 2

Complete the sentences. Use reported speech.
- The pupils complete the reported speech sentences.

Answers: **1** wouldn't go to the museum in the morning. **2** could swim to the other side of the pool. **3** couldn't play the guitar as well as Joseph. **4** was sorry but she couldn't help me. **5** would watch the film tomorrow.

Activity 3

Listen and complete the sentences. When is *would* contracted?

▶ *CD2 Track 28 p286*
- Play the CD. The pupils listen and complete the sentences.
- The pupils listen again and check their answers.

Answers: **1** 'd **2** wasn't **3** could **4** couldn't **5** wouldn't **6** 'd (Would is contracted in 1 and 6.)

Activity 4

Work with a partner. Ask your partner questions about their plans for this evening. Write the answers.
- In pairs, the pupils ask questions about their partner's plans. They then report their partner's plans.

Odd one out activity

Which is the odd one out? Why?
- The pupils complete the odd one out activity.

Answers: was (It isn't a modal verb.)

Ending the lesson

Review the lesson and reflect on learning.
- Say **Today we've talked about the way we report speech when someone talks about the future or when someone talks about what they can do.**
- Ask **What do you remember?** The pupils do a three-minute review in pairs. (Cooperative Learning Strategies, page 19)

Extra activity

Reinforcement
- Ask ten pupils to think of something that they can do. Then ask the class **Who thinks they've got a good memory?** Choose a pupil who answers yes. That pupil listens while the ten pupils say what they can do. Then the pupil reports as many statements as possible. Repeat with another ten pupils.

Key Competences and Key Learning Outcomes

- Learn words related to news articles
- Practise activity types found in the Cambridge Exams: B1 Preliminary for Schools
- Learn about adjectives with different endings
- Do a communication task

Key language

- *article, caption, fashion section, front page, headline, interview, reporter, review, sports news, world news*
- Extension: *breaking news, celebrity news, comments, local news*
- *What's the name of your new film?*

Materials

- Pupil's Book p55; Activity Book p52; Class CD2; Teacher's App on Navio

Optional materials

- Teacher's Resource Bank: Trinity Exams Practice cards (from the Starter Unit and Units 1, 2, 3 and 4)
- An English-language newspaper

At a Glance Lesson Plan

Pupil's Book

Starting the lesson

- Use the Trinity Exams Practice cards (optional).
- Review reported speech with 'would' and 'could'.
- Set learning outcomes.

Activity 1

- Look and match.
- Listen, check and repeat.
- ▶ ***CD2 Track 29 p286***

Activity 2

- Listen and read.
- ▶ ***CD2 Track 30 p286***
- Which parts of the article are true and which are false?

Activity 3

- Listen again.
- ▶ ***CD2 Track 30 p286***
- Complete the questions and sentences that the interviewer uses.

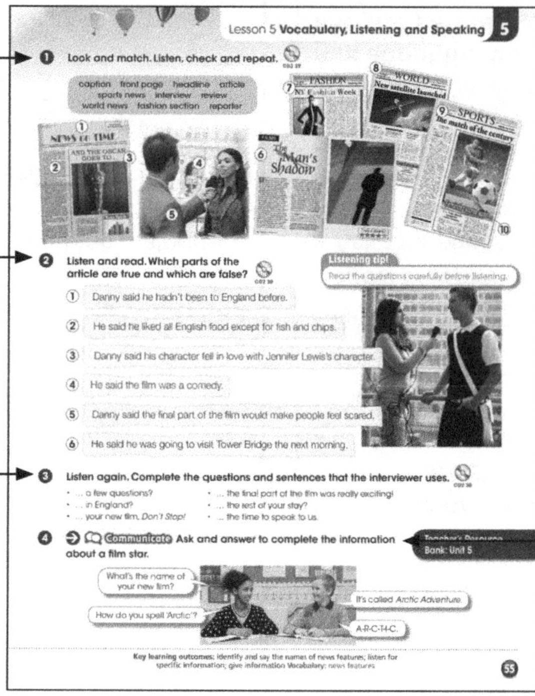

Lesson 5 **Vocabulary, Listening and Speaking** 5

1 Look and match. Listen, check and repeat.

caption front page headline article sports news interview review world news fashion section reporter

2 Listen and read. Which parts of the article are true and which are false?

Listening tip! Read the questions carefully before listening.

1. Danny said he hadn't been to England before.
2. He said he liked all English food except for fish and chips.
3. Danny said his character fell in love with Jennifer Lewis's character.
4. He said the film was a comedy.
5. Danny said the final part of the film would make people feel scared.
6. He said he was going to visit Tower Bridge the next morning.

3 Listen again. Complete the questions and sentences that the interviewer uses.

- … a few questions?
- … in England?
- … your new film, *Don't Stop!*
- … the final part of the film was really exciting!
- … the rest of your stay?
- … the time to speak to us.

4 Communicate Ask and answer to complete the information about a film star.

Teacher's Resource Bank: Unit 5

Key learning outcomes: identify and say the names of news features; listen for specific information; give information Vocabulary: news features

55

Activity 4

- Ask and answer to complete the information about a film star (Teacher's Resource Bank: Unit 5).

Ending the lesson

- Review the lesson and reflect on learning.

Extra activities

Reinforcement

- Look at an English-language newspaper.

Vocabulary extension

- Present four additional vocabulary items.

Activity Book

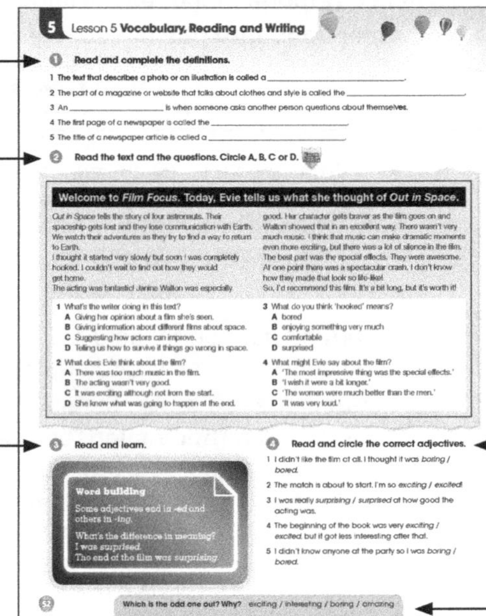

5 Lesson 5 **Vocabulary, Reading and Writing**

1 Read and complete the definitions.

1 The text that describes a photo or an illustration is called a ________.
2 The part of a magazine or website that talks about clothes and style is called the ________.
3 An ________ is when someone asks another person questions about themselves.
4 The first page of a newspaper is called the ________.
5 The title of a newspaper article is called a ________.

2 Read the text and the questions. Circle A, B, C or D.

Welcome to *Film Focus*. Today, Evie tells us what she thought of *Out in Space*.

Out in Space tells the story of four astronauts. Their spaceship gets lost and they lose communication with Earth. We watch their adventures as they try to find a way to return to Earth.
I thought it started very slowly but soon I was completely hooked. I couldn't wait to find out how they would get home.
The acting was fantastic! Janine Walton was especially good. Her character gets braver as the film goes on and Walton showed that in an excellent way. There wasn't very much music. I think that music can make dramatic moments even more exciting, but there was a lot of silence in the film.
The best part was the special effects. They were awesome. At one point there was a spectacular crash. I don't know how they made that look so life-like!
So, I'd recommend this film. It's a bit long, but it's worth it!

1 What's the writer doing in this text?
A Giving her opinion about a film she's seen.
B Giving information about different films about space.
C Suggesting how actors can improve.
D Telling us how to survive if things go wrong in space.

2 What does Evie think about the film?
A There was too much music in the film.
B The acting wasn't very good.
C It was exciting although not from the start.
D She knew what was going to happen at the end.

3 What do you think 'hooked' means?
A bored
B enjoying something very much
C comfortable
D surprised

4 What might Evie say about the film?
A 'The most impressive thing was the special effects.'
B 'I wish it were a bit longer.'
C 'The women were much better than the men.'
D 'It was very loud.'

3 Read and learn.

Word building
Some adjectives end in *-ed* and others in *-ing*.
What's the difference in meaning?
I was *surprised*.
The end of the film was *surprising*.

4 Read and circle the correct adjectives.

1 I didn't like the film at all. I thought it was *boring / bored*.
2 The match is about to start. I'm so *exciting / excited*!
3 I was really *surprising / surprised* at how good the acting was.
4 The beginning of the book was very *exciting / excited* but it got less interesting after that.
5 I didn't know anyone at the party so I was *boring / bored*.

52

Which is the odd one out? Why? exciting / interesting / boring / amazing

Activity Book

Activity 1

- Read and complete the definitions.

Activity 2

- Read the text and the questions. Circle A, B, C or D.

Activity 3

- Read and learn.

Activity 4

- Read and circle the correct adjectives.

Odd one out activity

Digital resources

Teacher's Digital: You can also teach this lesson using the Teacher's App on Navio.

Pupil's Digital: Encourage your pupils to use the Pupil's App on Navio to practise the activities from this lesson.

Powered By NAVIO

Starting the lesson

Use the Trinity Exams Practice cards (optional).

- The pupils practise asking and answering questions.

Review reported speech with 'would' and 'could'.

- Pretend to be a famous person, e.g. Sebastian Vettel. Explain to the pupils that you are going to tell them what you will do this evening. Say five things, e.g**. I will watch some TV.**
- The pupils report back, e.g. *Sebastian Vettel said he would watch some TV.*

Set learning outcomes.

- Say **Today we're going to learn some words and phrases about the news and we're going to do a communication task.**

Pupil's Book Activity 1

Look and match. Listen, check and repeat.

▶ ***CD2 Track 29 p286***

- In pairs, ask the pupils to match the words they know with the pictures.
- Play the CD. The pupils listen and check.
- Play the CD again, pausing after each word or phrase for the pupils to repeat. You can find the answers for this activity in the audioscript on page 286.

Pupil's Book Activity 2

Listen and read. Which parts of the article are true and which are false?

▶ ***CD2 Track 30 p286***

- The pupils listen to the interview. Ask them to find out the film star's name (*Danny*) and the name of his new film (*Don't Stop!*). Read Listening tip! as a class.
- Play the CD. The pupils listen and answer.
- Refer pupils to the Listenining Tip. Then read out the six sentences. Play the CD again. The pupils listen again and say which sentences are true and which are false.
- Check answers as a class.

Answers: **1** True **2** False **3** False **4** False **5** True **6** False

Pupil's Book Activity 3

Listen again. Complete the questions and sentences that the interviewer uses.

▶ ***CD2 Track 30 p286***

- Explain that the pupils are going to listen to the interview again. They should listen to what the interviewer says.
- Read out the sentence halves. In pairs, the pupils think about what the first parts of the sentences might be.
- Play the CD again. The pupils complete the sentences.
- Check answers as a class. Play the CD again if necessary.

Answers: Can I ask you a few questions? Is this your first time in England? Please tell us about your new film, Don't Stop! Someone told me that the final part of the film was really exciting! What are you going to do for the rest of your stay? Thank you for finding the time to speak to us.

Pupil's Book Activity 4

Ask and answer to complete the information about a film star (Teacher's Resource Bank: Unit 5).

- Explain to the pupils that they are going to interview their partner. Invite two pupils to read out the speech bubbles.
- Organise the class into pairs (A and B).
- The pupils complete the questions. They then prepare for the interview. They read the information about themselves.
- Pupil A interviews Pupil B and notes answers to the questions.
- They then swap roles. Pupil B interviews Pupil A.

Activity Book

Activity 1

Read and complete the definitions.

- The pupils read the definitions and complete them.

Answers: **1** caption **2** fashion section **3** interview **4** front page **5** headline

Activity 2

Read the text and the questions. Circle A, B, C or D.

- Read the text as a class. Ask **Did the writer like the film?** (*Yes.*) The pupils answer the questions.
- Check answers as a class.

Answers: **1** A **2** C **3** B **4** A

Activity 3

Read and learn.

- Read the information as a class. Encourage the pupils to give more examples of sentences with 'surprised' and 'surprising'. Then elicit other pairs of adjectives.

Activity 4

Read and circle the correct adjectives.

- The pupils circle the correct adjectives.

Answers: **1** boring **2** excited **3** surprised **4** exciting **5** bored

Odd one out activity

Which is the odd one out? Why?

Answers: boring (The others are positive adjectives.)

Ending the lesson

Review the lesson and reflect on learning.

- Ask **What do you remember about today's lesson?** The pupils do a three-minute review in pairs.

Extra activities

Reinforcement

- Show the pupils an English-language newspaper. Point to the different parts and see if the pupils can name them. Review 'headline', 'front page' and the different sections. You could also introduce other words, e.g. crossword, national news, etc.

Vocabulary Extension

- Present four additional words related to news features: *breaking news, celebrity news, comments, local news.*
- Use the Vocabulary Booster on NAVIO to practise these new words.

Key Competences and Key Learning Outcomes
• Review news vocabulary
• Learn about computer coding
• Do pre-reading tasks to predict content and raise interest • Skim a text for general understanding
• Read a newspaper article

Key language
- *computer coding, keep up, volunteers, website*
- *It was so popular that they started a second group.*

Materials
- Pupil's Book p56; Activity Book p53; Class CD2; Teacher's App on Navio

Optional materials
- Teacher's Resource Bank: Trinity Exams Practice cards (from the Starter Unit and Units 1, 2, 3 and 4)
- Newspapers (one per group of pupils)

At a Glance Lesson Plan

Pupil's Book

Starting the lesson
- Use the Trinity Exams Practice cards (optional).
- Review news vocabulary.
- Set learning outcomes.

Activity 1: Before you read
- Read and discuss.

Activity 2
- Read the article quickly.
- What's it about?

Activity 3: After you read
- What do you think?
- Go to the Activity Book.

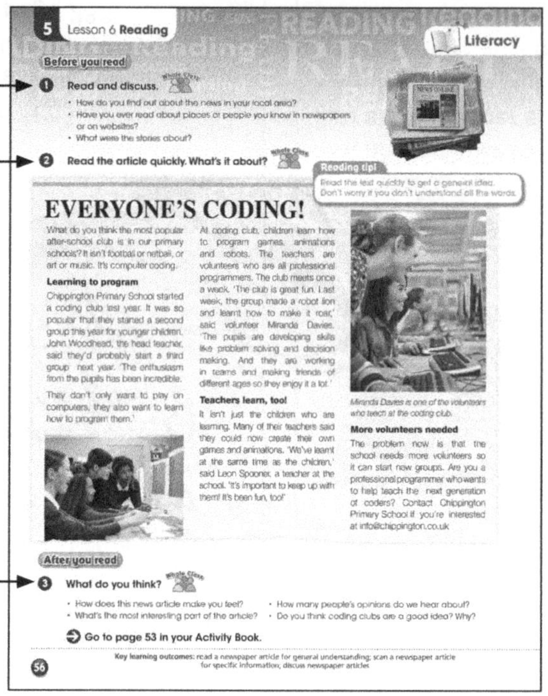
5 Lesson 6 Reading — Literacy

Before you read

1 Read and discuss.

2 Read the article quickly. What's it about?

EVERYONE'S CODING!

After you read

3 What do you think?

Go to page 53 in your Activity Book.

Ending the lesson
- Review the lesson and reflect on learning.

Extra activity

Extension
- Guess the news story.

Activity Book

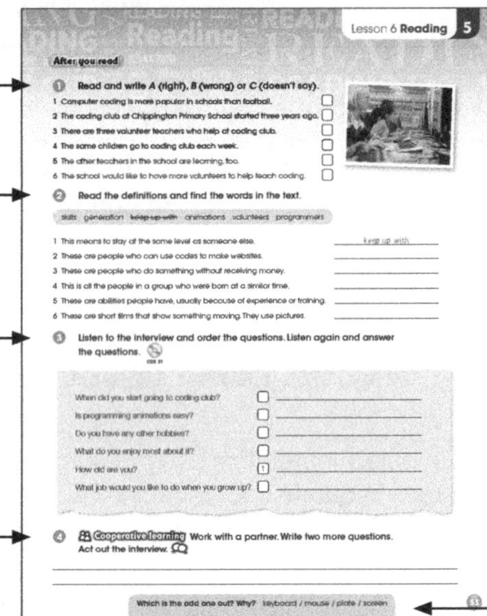
Lesson 6 Reading 5

After you read

1 Read and write A (right), B (wrong) or C (doesn't say).

2 Read the definitions and find the words in the text.

3 Listen to the interview and order the questions. Listen again and answer the questions.

4 Cooperative learning Work with a partner. Write two more questions. Act out the interview.

Which is the odd one out? Why? keyboard / mouse / plate / screen

Activity Book: After you read

Activity 1
- Read and write *A* (right), *B* (wrong) or *C* (doesn't say).

Activity 2
- Read the definitions and find the words in the text.

Activity 3
- Listen to the interview and order the questions. Listen again and answer the questions.

▶ ***CD2 Track 31 p286***

Activity 4
- Work with a partner. Write two more questions. Act out the interview.

Odd one out activity

Digital resources

Teacher's Digital: You can also teach this lesson using the Teacher's App on Navio.

Pupil's Digital: Encourage your pupils to use the Pupil's App on Navio to practise the activities from this lesson.

Powered By NAVIO

Starting the lesson

Use the Trinity Exams Practice cards (optional).

- The pupils practise asking and answering questions.

Review news vocabulary.

- Organise the pupils into small groups. Give each group a newspaper. Say words and phrases from Lesson 5. The pupils find and point to the corresponding sections.

Set learning outcomes.

- Say **Today we're going to read an article from a local newspaper.** Explain that 'local' means that it is a newspaper that tells people the news from the area where they live.

Pupil's Book Activity 1: Before you read

Read and discuss.

- Read the questions as a class. Prompt the pupils to give as many examples as possible.

Pupil's Book Activity 2

Read the article quickly. What's it about?

- Give the pupils one minute to read the article. Explain that they need to look quickly through the article and decide what it is about.
- (Books closed.) The pupils tell you what they think the article is about. Write some ideas on the board.
- (Books open.) Read the article either as a class or individually. Confirm that it is about computer coding classes. Ask **Has anyone done computer coding? Is it difficult? Would you like to do it? Do you think it's an important skill to learn? Why / Why not?**

Pupil's Book Activity 3: After you read

What do you think?

- Read the first question as a class. Encourage the pupils to concentrate on their emotional reaction to the article. Then prompt the pupils to give answers to the other questions. Invite them to explain their answers.

Activity Book: After you read

Activity 1

Read and write *A* (right), *B* (wrong) or *C* (doesn't say).

- Read the sentences as a class. The pupils write the correct letter. Ensure that the pupils understand that 'doesn't say' means that we don't know if the sentence is true or false from reading the article.

Answers: **1** A **2** B **3** C **4** C **5** A **6** A

Activity 2

Read the definitions and find the words in the text.

- The pupils write the words, using the article in the Pupil's Book to help them.

Answers: **1** keep up with **2** programmers **3** volunteers **4** generation **5** skills **6** animations

Activity 3

Listen to the interview and order the questions. Listen again and answer the questions.

▶ *CD2 Track 31 p286*

- Read the questions as a class. Encourage the pupils to predict the answers. Explain that this is an interview with one of the school children.
- Play the CD. The pupils listen and order the questions. They number them from 1 to 6. The pupils check answers with a partner. Then check answers as a class.
- Play the CD again, pausing after each piece of information. The pupils complete the answers to the questions. Then check answers as a class.

Answers: 2 4 6 3 1 5 **2** About three months ago. **3** Programming animations. **4** When you know how to do it, yes. **5** Maybe design websites or computer games. **6** Not really.

Activity 4

Work with a partner. Write two more questions. Act out the interview.

- The pupils write two more questions. In pairs, they then ask the questions from Activity 3 and their questions.
- One pupil asks all the questions and writes down the answers as notes. Then they swap roles.

Odd one out activity

Which is the odd one out? Why?

- The pupils complete the odd one out activity.

Answers: plate (It isn't related to computers.)

Ending the lesson

Review the lesson and reflect on learning.

- Say **Today we've read a newspaper article about a coding club.**
- Ask **What do you remember?** The pupils do a three-minute review in pairs. (Cooperative Learning Strategies, page 19)

Extra activity

Extension

- In pairs, the pupils imagine some local newspaper stories. They only write a headline for the story, e.g. *Everyone's coding!*
- The pupils then read out the headlines. The other pupils guess what the story was about.

Key Competences and Key Learning Outcomes

- Use 'so' to connect sentences
- Review 'Wh-' questions
- Identify the text features of a newspaper article
- Use criteria to check your writing
- Share and discuss your writing with a partner
- Think about reporting news in a local community
- Write a newspaper article

Key language

- *proud, story-writing competition, surprised, thrilled*
- *Darkness has always interested me so I wanted to write about it.*

Materials

- Pupil's Book p57; Activity Book p54; Teacher's App on Navio

Optional materials

- Teacher's Resource Bank: Trinity Exams Practice cards (from the Starter Unit and Units 1, 2, 3 and 4)

At a Glance Lesson Plan

Pupil's Book

Starting the lesson

- Use the Trinity Exams Practice cards (optional).
- Review the newspaper article from Lesson 6.
- Set learning outcomes.

Activity 1: Investigate a text

- Read the title of the article in Activity 2.
- Write six questions you'd like answered by the article using these question words.

Activity 2

- Read the article.
- Does it answer any of your questions?

Activity 3: Discuss a text

- Read the article again.
- Answer the questions.

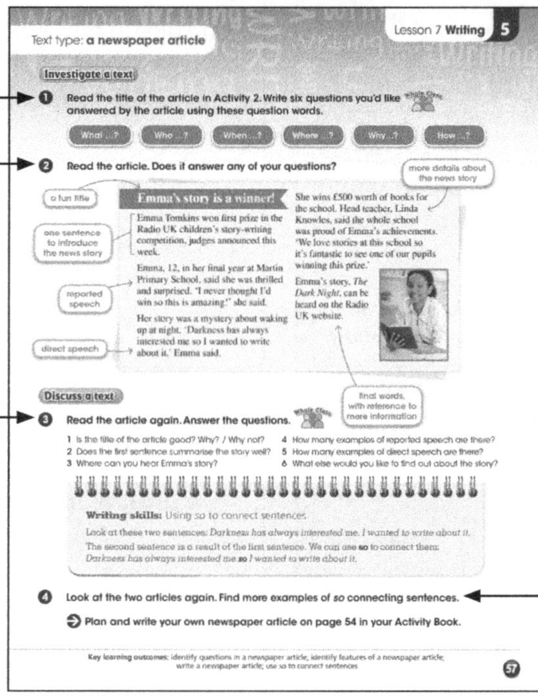

Lesson 7 Writing 5

Text type: **a newspaper article**

Investigate a text

1. **Read the title of the article in Activity 2. Write six questions you'd like answered by the article using these question words.**

What ...? Who ...? When ...? Where ...? Why ...? How ...?

2. **Read the article. Does it answer any of your questions?**

Emma's story is a winner!

Emma Tomkins won first prize in the Radio UK children's story-writing competition, judges announced this week.

Emma, 12, in her final year at Martin Primary School, said she was thrilled and surprised. 'I never thought I'd win so this is amazing!' she said.

Her story was a mystery about waking up at night. 'Darkness has always interested me so I wanted to write about it,' Emma said.

She wins £500 worth of books for the school. Head teacher, Linda Knowles, said the whole school was proud of Emma's achievements. 'We love stories at this school so it's fantastic to see one of our pupils winning this prize.'

Emma's story, *The Dark Night*, can be heard on the Radio UK website.

Discuss a text

3. **Read the article again. Answer the questions.**

1 Is the title of the article good? Why? / Why not?
2 Does the first sentence summarise the story well?
3 Where can you hear Emma's story?
4 How many examples of reported speech are there?
5 How many examples of direct speech are there?
6 What else would you like to find out about the story?

Writing skills: Using *so* to connect sentences

Look at these two sentences: *Darkness has always interested me. I wanted to write about it.*
The second sentence is a result of the first sentence. We can use **so** to connect them:
Darkness has always interested me **so** *I wanted to write about it.*

4. **Look at the two articles again. Find more examples of *so* connecting sentences.**

Plan and write your own newspaper article on page 54 in your Activity Book.

Key learning outcomes: identify questions in a newspaper article; identify features of a newspaper article; write a newspaper article; use so to connect sentences

57

Writing skills

- Using *so* to connect sentences

Activity 4

- Look at the two articles again.
- Find more examples of *so* connecting sentences.
- Plan and write your own newspaper article on page 54 in your Activity Book.

Ending the lesson

- Review the lesson and reflect on learning.

Extra activity

Reinforcement

- Find adjectives in newspaper articles.

Digital resources

Teacher's Digital: You can also teach this lesson using the Teacher's App on Navio.

Pupil's Digital: Encourage your pupils to use the Pupil's App on Navio to practise the activities from this lesson.

Powered By NAVIO

Activity Book

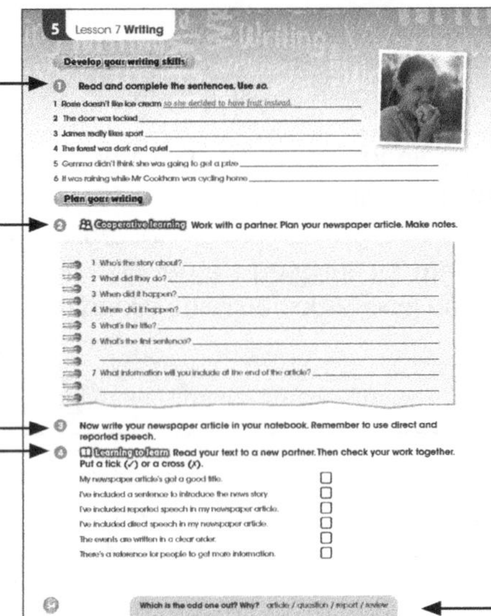

5 Lesson 7 Writing

Develop your writing skills

1. **Read and complete the sentences. Use so.**

1 Rosie doesn't like ice cream *so she decided to have fruit instead.*
2 The door was locked ______
3 James really likes sport ______
4 The forest was dark and quiet ______
5 Gemma didn't think she was going to get a prize ______
6 It was raining while Mr Cookham was cycling home ______

Plan your writing

2. **Cooperative learning Work with a partner. Plan your newspaper article. Make notes.**

1 Who's the story about? ______
2 What did they do? ______
3 When did it happen? ______
4 Where did it happen? ______
5 What's the title? ______
6 What's the first sentence? ______
7 What information will you include at the end of the article? ______

3. **Now write your newspaper article in your notebook. Remember to use direct and reported speech.**

4. **Learning to learn Read your text to a new partner. Then check your work together. Put a tick (✓) or a cross (✗).**

My newspaper article's got a good title. ☐
I've included a sentence to introduce the news story. ☐
I've included reported speech in my newspaper article. ☐
I've included direct speech in my newspaper article. ☐
The events are written in a clear order. ☐
There's a reference for people to get more information. ☐

Which is the odd one out? Why? article / question / report / review

Activity Book

Activity 1: Develop your writing skills

- Read and complete the sentences. Use *so*.

Activity 2: Plan your writing

- Work with a partner. Plan your newspaper article. Make notes.

Activity 3

- Now write your newspaper article in your notebook. Remember to use direct and reported speech.

Activity 4

- Read your text to a new partner. Then check your work together. Put a tick (✓) or a cross (✗).

Odd one out activity

Starting the lesson

Use the Trinity Exams Practice cards (optional).
- The pupils practise asking and answering questions.

Review the newspaper article from Lesson 6.
- On the board, write *What was it about? Who was it about? Why is it interesting?*
- In pairs, the pupils remember the newspaper article from Lesson 6. They answer the questions. Invite some pupils to give their answers.

Set learning outcomes
- Say **Today we're going to read another newspaper article and then write our own article in pairs.**

Pupil's Book Activity 1: Investigate a text

Read the title of the article in Activity 2. Write six questions you'd like answered by the article using these question words.
- Ask the pupils to look at the title of the article. In pairs, they write six questions that they would like answered in the article. They use the question words provided.
- Ask the pupils to share some of their questions. Write a few of the questions on the board.

Pupil's Book Activity 2

Read the article. Does it answer any of your questions?
- The pupils read the article. Then look at the questions on the board. Invite the pupils to answer the questions.
- Ask **Have you ever entered a story-writing competition? Do you like writing stories? Why / Why not?**

Pupil's Book Activity 3: Discuss a text

Read the article again. Answer the questions.
- Read and discuss the questions as a class. Confirm that a good title should be interesting and that the first sentence should summarise the story. Then confirm that the story can be heard on the Radio UK website. Elicit examples of reported and direct speech. The pupils say what else they would like to find out.

Writing skills
- Read the information about using 'so' to connect sentences.

Pupil's Book Activity 4

Look at the two articles again. Find more examples of *so* connecting sentences.
- The pupils look at the text again and identify more examples of sentences connected by 'so'.

Activity Book

Activity 1: Develop your writing skills

Read and complete the sentences. Use *so*.
- The pupils complete the sentences as they wish. Ask some pupils to read their sentences out to the class.

Activity 2: Plan your writing

Work with a partner. Plan your newspaper article. Make notes.
- Read out the questions as a class. Check understanding.
- In pairs, the pupils think of an idea for an article. They complete the questions. Write some prompts on the board to help the pupils, e.g. *people doing unusual things, sports stories, people helping others, school stories, stories about animals*.

Activity 3

Now write your newspaper article in your notebook. Remember to use direct and reported speech.
- The pupils write their newspaper articles in their notebooks. They can find photos or draw pictures to go with the article.

Activity 4

Read your text to a new partner. Then check your work together. Put a tick (✓) or a cross (✗).
- Read through the statements as a class.
- Organise the class into new partners. One pupil reads aloud their text. The other pupil listens. The pupils work together to decide if the text fulfils the criteria and tick the corresponding boxes. The pupils can add, improve or correct the text at this stage.
- The pupils swap roles.

Odd one out activity

Which is the odd one out? Why?
- The pupils complete the odd one out activity.

Answers: question (It isn't a newspaper section.)

Ending the lesson

Review the lesson and reflect on learning.
- Say **Today we've read a newspaper article about a story-writing competition and we've written our own reports.**
- Ask **What do you remember?** The pupils do a three-minute review in pairs. (Cooperative Learning Strategies, page 19)

Extra activity

Reinforcement
- Ask the pupils to find the adjectives used in the newspaper article. On the board, write two column headings *Describing people / Describing things*.
- The pupils categorise the adjectives from the newspaper article.
- Repeat the procedure with the newspaper article on page 58 of the Pupil's Book.
- Check answers as a class. Ensure the pupils understand the meanings of the adjectives.

Key Competences and Key Learning Outcomes

- Review asking questions and describing people, their jobs and their interests
- Prepare and practise speaking activity types found in Cambridge Exams: B1 Preliminary for Schools
- Reflect on learning and progress
- Listen to a text for general and specific information
- Use a concept web to prepare a presentation about a topic
- Learn how to prepare a conversation about meeting a famous person.

Key language

- *excited, friendly, funny, polite, reporter*
- *How did you meet her? What was she like?*

Materials

- Pupil's Book p58; Activity Book pp55–56; Class CD2; Teacher's App on Navio

At a Glance Lesson Plan

Pupil's Book

Starting the lesson

- Review personal description words.
- Set learning outcomes.

Activity 1

- Describe the photos.
- What are these people's jobs?

Activity 2

- Listen to the conversation.
- Who did Leon meet?
- What was her job?

▶ *CD2 Track 32 p286*

Activity 3

- Listen again.
- Complete the five questions that Isabel asks.

Go to the Activity Book.

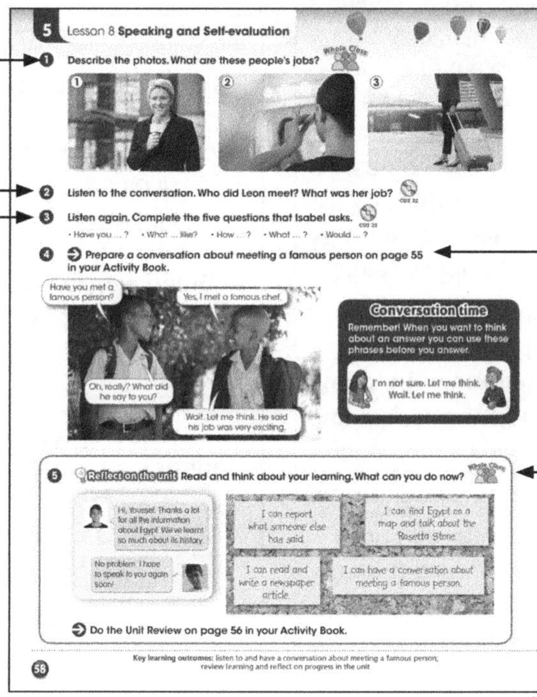

Activity 4

- Prepare a conversation about meeting a famous person on page 55 in your Activity Book.

Go to the Activity Book.

Activity 5

- Read and think about your learning.
- What can you do now?

Ending the lesson

- Review the lesson and reflect on learning.

Activity Book

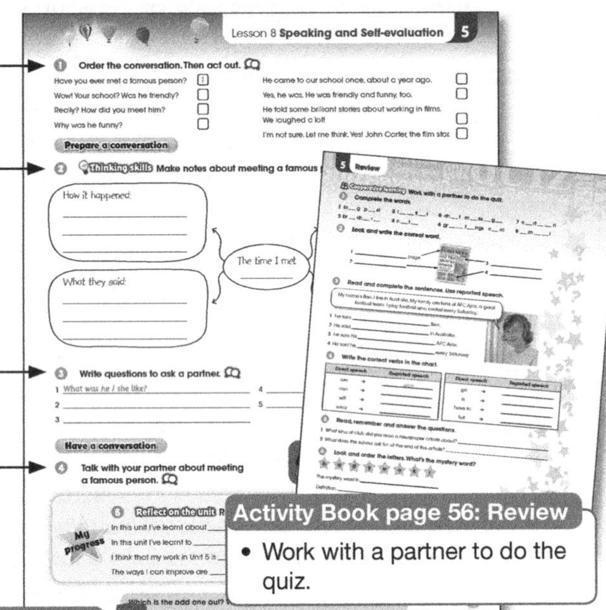

Activity Book page 56: Review

- Work with a partner to do the quiz.

Activity Book

Activity 1

- Order the conversation. Then act out.

Activity 2

- Make notes about meeting a famous person.

Activity 3

- Write questions to ask a partner.

Activity 4

- Talk with your partner about meeting a famous person.

Activity 5

- Read and complete the sentences.

Odd one out activity

Digital resources

Teacher's Digital: You can also teach this lesson using the Teacher's App on Navio.

Powered By NAVIO

Starting the lesson

Review personal description words.

- Choose a pupil in the class. Describe the pupil, using one sentence at a time, e.g. **She's got long, dark hair.** After each sentence, invite the class to guess who you are describing. Continue describing the pupil until the class guesses who it is.
- Then invite a pupil to the front of the class. The pupil chooses someone in the class to describe. The class guesses who it is.

Set learning outcomes.

- Say **Today we're going to listen to and have a conversation about meeting a famous person.**

Pupil's Book Activity 1

Describe the photos. What are these people's jobs?

- The class looks at the photos. The pupils guess the jobs.

Answers: **1** reporter **2** actress / make up artist **3** businesswoman

Pupil's Book Activity 2

Listen to the conversation. Who did Leon meet? What was her job?

▶ ***CD2 Track 32 p286***

- Play the CD. Pupils listen and check their answer with their partner.
- Check answers as a class.

Answers: She was a reporter

Pupil's Book Activity 3

Listen again. Complete the five questions that Isabel asks.

▶ ***CD2 Track 32 p286***

- Play CD again with pauses for pupils to complete the activity.
- Check answers as a class.

Answers: **1** Have you ever met a famous person? **2** What does she look like? **3** How did you meet her? **4** What did you learn about being a reporter? **5** Would you like to be a reporter?

Activity Book

Activity 1

Order the conversation. Then act out.

- After pupils order the conversation in pairs, they act it out. Pupils swap roles.

Answers: 1, 5, 3, 7, 4, 6, 8, 2

Activity 2

Make notes about meeting a famous person.

- Pupils complete the notes individually and show their partners.

Activity 3

Write questions to ask a partner.

- Pupils complete the activity. Remind them to refer to Isabel's questions in the Pupil's Book.

Activity 4

Talk with your partner about meeting a famous person.

- Read the remember box and tell pupils to apply it to their conversations.
- In pairs, the pupils have a discussion. One pupil asks questions and the other replies using their notes from Activity 2 if they wish. Then they swap roles.

Activity 5

Read and complete the sentences.

- Read out the sentences. Encourage the pupils to think of different ways of completing them.
- The pupils complete the sentences.

Odd one out activity

Which is the odd one out? Why?

- The pupils complete the odd one out activity.

Answers: notebook (It isn't a job.)

Pupil's Book Activity 4

Prepare a conversation about meeting a famous person on page 55 in your Activity Book.

- Read the Conversation Time box and the conversation in the Activity. Direct pupils to the Activity Book.

Pupil's Book Activity 5

Read and think about your learning. What can you do now?

- Read the messages as a class. Then look back through the unit and prompt the pupils to identify other things they have learnt / done.

Activity Book page 56: Review

Work with a partner to do the quiz.

- Organise the class into pairs. Set a time limit for the pupils to do this (10–15 minutes). Stress that the pupils are not competing with each other.
- Read out the six tasks that the pupils have to complete. Check understanding. Then say **Ready, steady … Go!**
- The pupils work in their pairs to do the quiz. Ask the pupils who finish quickly to help another pair.
- Correct the answers as a class.

Answers: **1 1** blog post **2** brochure **3** leaflet **4** note **5** chat message **6** greetings card **7** cartoon **8** email **2 1** front **2** caption **3** headline **4** article **3 1** his name was **2** he lived **3** family were fans of **4** played football and cricket **4** were, could, would, wore, went, was, had to, fell **5 1** coding club **2** volunteers **6** keyboard, you use it to type

Ending the lesson

Review the lesson and reflect on learning.

- Say **Today we've learnt and practised how have a conversation about meeting a famous person and we've thought about our learning.**
- Ask **What do you remember?** The pupils do a three-minute review in pairs. (Cooperative Learning Strategies, page 19)

Key Competences and Key Learning Outcomes

- Watch and understand a video about languages
- Understand how to use digital media to research and present information
- Undertake collaborative research about a language with a partner

Key language

- *deaf, sign language, translate, Wales, Welsh*
- *We can listen to people speaking the language online. We can record words using a mobile phone.*

Materials

- Pupil's Book p59; Activity Book p57; Class CD2; Teacher's App on Navio
- Teacher's Resource Bank: Talk cards

Optional materials

- Teacher's Resource Bank: Trinity Exams Practice cards (selected from the Starter Unit)

At a Glance Lesson Plan

Pupil's Book

Starting the lesson

- **Think-Pair-Share.** Review ways of how we can use digital technology to help us research and present information.
- Set learning outcomes and use the talk cards.

Activity 1

- Before you watch.
- Watch the video.
  Unit 5 video p302
- Read and say *true* or *false*.
- Correct the false sentences.

Activity 2

- Watch the video again.
  Unit 5 video
- Match the words to the signs.

Activity 3

- Read, think and answer.

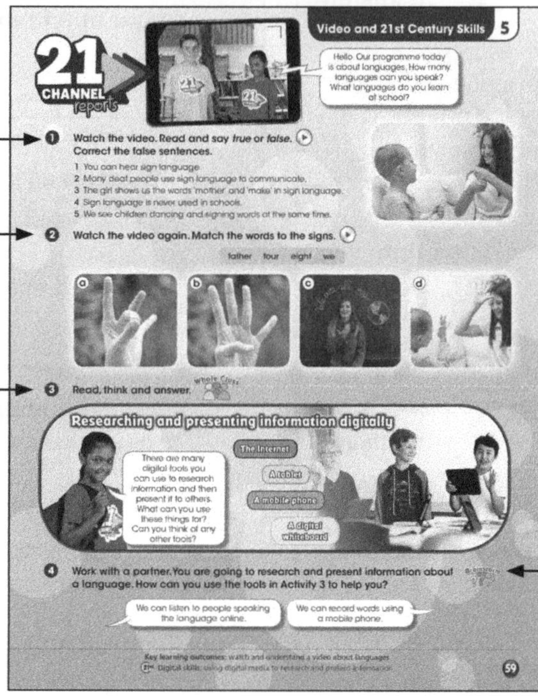

Activity 4

- Work with a partner.
- You are going to research and present information about a language.
- How can you use the tools in Activity 3 to help you?

Go to the Activity Book.

Ending the lesson

- Review the lesson and reflect on learning.

Extra activity

- Research other sign language words and gestures to present to the class.

Activity Book

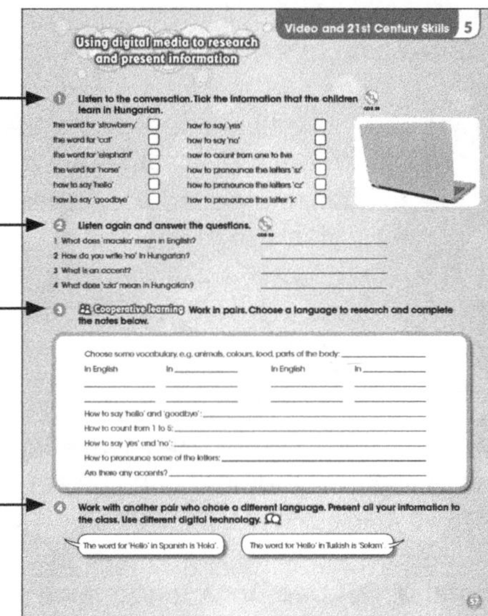

Activity Book

Activity 1 ▶

- Listen to the conversation. Tick the information that the children learn in Hungarian.

▶ *CD2 Track 33 p286*

Activity 2 ▶

- Listen again and answer the questions.

Activity 3

- Work in pairs. Choose a language to research and complete the notes below.

Activity 4

- Work with another pair who chose a different language. Present all your information to the class. Use different digital technology.

Digital resources

Teacher's Digital: You can also teach this lesson using the Teacher's App on Navio.

Pupil's Digital: Encourage your pupils to use the Pupil's App on Navio to practise the activities from this lesson.

Powered By NAVIO

Starting the lesson

Think-Pair-Share. Review ways of how how we can use digital technology to help us research and present information.

- Ask **What do you use to research information for a school project?** Elicit answers and write them on the board.
- Then ask how they can present information digitally and what means they use.
- Pupils work with a Talk Partner to discuss how digital technology helps them research and present information.
- Invite different Talk Partners to tell the class what they discussed with their partners.

Set learning outcomes and use the talk cards.

- Say **Today we're going to watch a video about languages.**
- Ask pupils if they remember who the presenters are (Max and Amy).
- Point to the talk cards to show the pupils the different ways they will be working in the lesson.

Pupil's Book Activity 1

Before you watch

- Read the speech bubble to pupils. Ask how many languages they can speak?
- Ask which languages they would like to learn and why they think language learning is important.

Watch the video. Read and say *true* or *false*. Correct the false sentences. *p302*

- Watch Part 1. Ask if anyone knows sign language. If so, have them demonstrate different words to the class.
- Play Part 2, pausing at each section for pupils to answer. Pupils then work in pairs to answer the questions.

Answers: **1** F **2** T **3** F **4** F **6** F
1 You cannot hear sign language – you can see it.
3 The girl shows 'father' and 'make'.
4 Sign language is shown in schools.
5 We see children singing and signing the language at the same time.

Pupil's Book Activity 2

Watch the video again. Match the words to the signs.

- Ask pupils to tell you what they remember from the video. Ask if they remember what words were presented in sign language.
- Have pupils complete the activity in pairs.
- Play the second part of the video for reinforcement.

Answers: **a** eight **b** four **c** we **d** father

Pupil's Book Activity 3

Read, think and answer.

- Tell pupils that in the last part of the video Amy and Max talk about how they can learn phrases online. Explain that we can research and learn different languages online and with digital equipment.
- Ask pupils if they have ever done this and if so, ask how it helped them.
- Pupils work in pairs to read and think about how each form of digital material can help them learn a foreign language.
- Ask them how they can also use these forms to present their findings.

Pupil's Book Activity 4

Work with a partner. You are going to research and present information about a language. How can you use the tools in Activity 3 to help you?

- Have pupils work with a partner and discuss the different forms mentioned in Activity 3.
- Encourage pupils to add more methods if possible.
- Pupils present their group's notes to the class.

Activity Book

Activity 1

Listen to the conversation. Tick the information that the children learn in Hungarian.

▶ *CD2 Track 33 p286*

- Look at each word in the first list and yes and no from the second list. Ask how pupils say these words in their own language.
- Play the CD and complete the activity.

Answers: Tick: cat, horse, yes, no, hello, goodbye, sz

Activity 2

Listen again and answer the questions.

▶ *CD2 Track 33 p286*

- Have pupils complete the activity and check answers with their partners.
- Extend the activity by asking the pupils to say words in their own language with an accent.

Answers: **1** It means horse. **2** Nem. **3** It stresses a letter in a word. **4** Hello and goodbye.

Activity 3

Work in pairs. Choose a language to research and complete the notes below.

- Pupils complete the activity using available digital resources.

Activity 4

Work with another pair who chose a different language. Present all your information to the class. Use different digital technology.

- In different pairs pupils complete the activity.
- Have pupils present their work to the class.

Ending the lesson

Review the lesson and reflect on learning.

- Say **Today we've watched a video about researching and presenting information digitally. What have we learnt?** Elicit the information from the pupils. The pupils do a three-minute review in pairs. (Cooperative Learning Strategies, page 19)

Extra activity

Reinforcement

- Place pupils in small pairs and ask them to make a list of five words they would like to learn in sign language.
- Explain that they have to research how these words are presented in sign language.
- Pupils then show their words in sign language to the class.

Date: ____________ Unit: ________

1 What did my pupils learn in this unit?

2 How did my pupils work? (✓)

individually ☐ in pairs ☐ in small groups ☐

in large groups ☐ as a class ☐

3 Which key competences did my pupils develop? Give a score from 1 to 5 (5 being the highest).

- Competence in linguistic communication ☐
- Competence in mathematics, science and technology ☐
- Digital competence ☐
- Learning to learn ☐
- Social and civic competences ☐
- Sense of initiative and entrepreneurship ☐
- Cultural awareness and expression ☐

4 Which lessons / activities were the most successful and why?

5 Which lessons / activities did my pupils find the most difficult and why?

6 What did I try in the classroom for the first time? How did it go?

7 Which resources did I find most useful? (including webpages)

8 What could I do differently next time I teach this unit?

Unit 6 Our future

Unit overview

Key competences and learning outcomes

- Review and name different jobs (Lesson 1)
- Learn and practise how to use modal verbs to make predictions (Lesson 2)
- Learn and practise how to use embedded questions (Lesson 4)
- Review and name different life events (Lesson 5)
- Review and practise how to use paragraphs (Lesson 7)
- Watch and understand a video (Video and 21st Century Skills)

- Compare life in the past and today (Lesson 6)

- Use the Pupil's App on Navio
- Investigate Scotland (Lesson 3)

- Identify and practise using rising and falling intonation patterns (Lesson 4)
- Practise sequencing events (Lesson 5)
- Identify the text features of an informal letter (Lesson 7)
- Review learning and reflect on progress in the unit (Lesson 8)
- Practise activity types found in the Cambridge Exams: B1 Preliminary for Schools

- Understand the importance of being positive when there is a challenge (Lesson 3)
- Share hopes for the future (Lesson 8)

- Work in pairs or small groups to practise and reinforce learning (All lessons)
- Do a communication task (Lesson 5)
- Reflect on use of robots in the future (Video and 21st Century Skills)

- Read a story (Lesson 3)
- Learn about Scotland (Lesson 3)
- Read and write an informal letter (Lessons 6 and 7)
- Sing a song (Lesson 8)

Vocabulary

Core vocabulary
archaeologist, businessperson, computer technician, detective, electrician, graphic designer, physiotherapist, plumber, politician, security guard, tour guide, veterinary nurse; get a job, go backpacking, go to university, have children, learn to drive, leave home, start a business

Extension vocabulary (optional)
architect, author, editor, engineer, gardener, surgeon; be born, get married, move house, retire

Other vocabulary
in (one year's) time, in (three months') time, next week, the day after tomorrow, this evening; ambition, challenge, cure, deaf, disease, fingertips, vibrations; arcade game, BMX bike, calculator, cassette, football training, percussion, time capsule, zero-gravity games; frustrated, positive; general description, opinion; deliver, parcels, think outside the box

Recycled vocabulary
accommodation, brochure, entertainment; artist, astronaut, firefighter, musician, teacher; solar-powered

Structures

Core structures
I will definitely be (an archaeologist). I probably won't be (a politician). I may / might / could be (a chemist). Do you think I / you / he / she / we /they will (be famous)?

Other structures
When she was eight, Evelyn began studying the piano. I don't know. I don't think so. I'm not sure. I doubt it. You never know. I don't know the word for it, but (it's used for protecting your eyes). I imagine that life will be very different in the future.

Recycled structures
I've played the (guitar) for (four years). It was buried in (1980). A vet has to have a degree. A vet doesn't have to work at night. Do you (wear a uniform)? I hope that there aren't any wars.

Pronunciation

Rising and falling intonation patterns with modal verbs

Literacy

Text type: an informal letter (information text; writing preparation)
Reading skills: comparing and contrasting information
Writing skills: using paragraphs

Culture ... around the world

The story of Evelyn Glennie, the Scottish musician

21st Century Skills

Ways of thinking: thinking in different ways

Thinking skills

Forming conceptual links and associations (Lesson 1); Logical thinking (Lesson 1); Defining and describing (Lesson 1); Analysing and applying rules and patterns (Lessons 2 and 4); Sequencing (Lessons 5 and Review); Comparing and contrasting (Lesson 6); Spatial thinking (Lesson 8); Evaluating (Lesson 8)

Cooperative learning

Working together (Lessons 1–8); Reflecting and setting goals (Lessons 1–8); Empathising (Lesson 3 and 6); Expressing and respecting opinions (Lesson 3); Collaborative writing (Lesson 7); Peer evaluation (Lesson 7); Showing interest in others (Lessons 2, 4, 5 and 8); Praising and encouraging (Lesson 8)

Values

The importance of being positive when there is a challenge

Cross-curricular links

Links to Science
EU single market

Suggested Arts and Crafts concepts
Perspective

Key Competences and Key Learning Outcomes

- Review and name different jobs
- Form conceptual links and associations between vocabulary items

Key language

- *archaeologist, businessperson, computer technician, detective, electrician, graphic designer, physiotherapist, plumber, politician, security guard, tour guide, veterinary nurse*
- Extension: *architect, author, editor, engineer, gardener, surgeon*
- *Do you (wear a uniform)?*

Materials

- Pupil's Book pp60–61; Activity Book p58; Class CD2; Teacher's App on Navio
- Jobs flashcards

Optional materials:

- Teacher's Resource Bank: Trinity Exams Practice cards (selected from the Starter Unit and Unit 1, 2, 3, 4 and 5)

At a Glance Lesson Plan

Pupil's Book

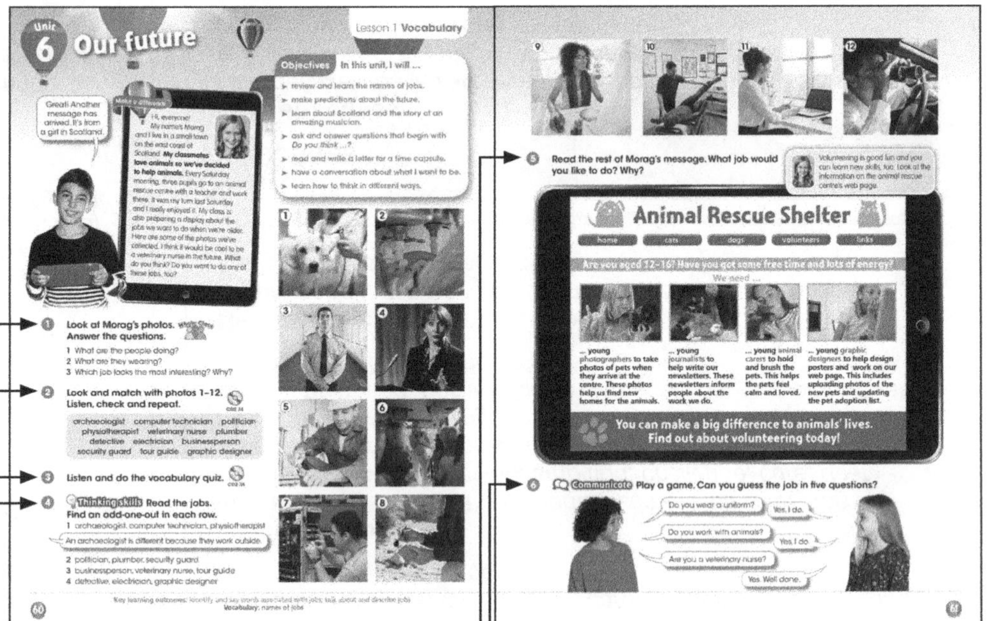

Starting the lesson
- Use the Trinity Exams Practice cards (optional).
- Review jobs.
- Set learning outcomes.

Activity 1
- Look at Morag's photos.
- Answer the questions.

Vocabulary presentation
- Present the new vocabulary using the jobs flashcards.

Activity 2
- Look and match with photos 1–12.
- Listen, check and repeat.

▶ *CD2 Track 34 p287*

Activity 3
- Listen and do the vocabulary quiz.

▶ *CD2 Track 35 p287*

Activity 4
- Read the jobs.
- Find an odd-one-out in each row.

Activity 5
- Read the rest of Morag's message.
- What job would you like to do?
- Why?

Activity 6
- Play a game.
- Can you guess the job in five questions?

Go to the Activity Book.

Ending the lesson
- Review the lesson and reflect on learning.

Extra activities

Extension
- Find out about Scotland.

Vocabulary extension
- Present six additional vocabulary items.

Activity Book

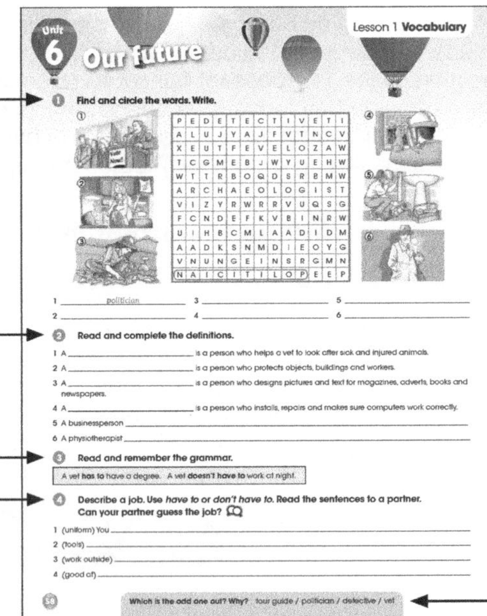

Activity Book

Activity 1
- Find and circle the words. Write.

Activity 2
- Read and complete the definitions.

Activity 3
- Read and remember the grammar.

Activity 4
- Describe a job. Use *have to* or *don't have to*. Read the sentences to a partner. Can your partner guess the job?

Odd one out activity

Digital resources

Teacher's Digital: You can also teach this lesson using the Teacher's App on Navio.

Pupil's Digital: Encourage your pupils to use the Pupil's App on Navio to practise the activities from this lesson.

Powered By NAVIO

Starting the lesson

Use the Trinity Exams Practice cards (optional).
- The pupils practise asking and answering questions.

Review jobs.
- Form groups of three. The groups write the alphabet. They write a job next to as many of the letters as possible. Set a time limit.
- Elicit the jobs and write them on the board.

Set learning outcomes
- Say **Today we're going to learn some more jobs.**

Pupil's Book Activity 1

Look at Morag's photos. Answer the questions.
- Invite a pupil to read out the speech bubble to find out which school has sent a message. Ask **Do you know where Scotland is?**
- Invite a pupil to read out the message from Morag. Check understanding.
- Work as a class to answer the questions.

Vocabulary presentation

- Present the new vocabulary using the jobs flashcards. Hold up the first flashcard so that the class can't see it and give a definition. The pupils name the job. If the pupils don't know the word in English, provide the word. Ask them to repeat it. Stick the flashcard on the board. Repeat with the other jobs.

Pupil's Book Activity 2

Look and match with photos 1–12. Listen, check and repeat.
▶ *CD2 Track 34 p287*
- The class look at photo 1. Ask **Which job is this?** In pairs, the pupils match 2–12 with the words. Play the CD. The pupils listen and check.
- Play the CD again, pausing after each word for the pupils to repeat. You can find the answers for this activity in the audioscript on page 287.

Pupil's Book Activity 3

Listen and do the vocabulary quiz.
▶ *CD2 Track 35 p287*
- Play the CD. Listen to the first definition, pausing at the beep to allow the pupils to name the item. Play the CD to listen to the answer.
- Repeat the procedure with the other definitions. You can find the answers for this activity in the audioscript on page 287.

Pupil's Book Activity 4

Read the jobs. Find the odd-one-out in each row.
- Ask a pupil to read out the speech bubble. Explain that there are several possible answers. In pairs, the pupils identify the odd-one-out words.
- Check answers as a class.

Pupil's Book Activity 5

Read the rest of Morag's message. What job would you like to do? Why?
- Invite a pupil to read out the message.
- The pupils read the information and decide which job they would like to do.
- The pupils share their ideas with the class.

Pupil's Book Activity 6

Play a game. Can you guess the job in five questions?
- Invite two pupils to read out the speech bubbles.
- Demonstrate the game. Think of a job and invite the pupils to ask five questions.
- The pupils play the game in pairs.

Activity Book

Activity 1
Find and circle the words. Write.
- The pupils find and write the jobs.

Answers: **1** politician **2** tour guide **3** archaeologist **4** electrician **5** plumber **6** detective

Activity 2
Read and complete the definitions.
- The pupils complete the definitions.

Answers: **1** veterinary nurse **2** security guard **3** graphic designer **4** computer technician **5 & 6** Pupils' own answers

Activity 3
Read and remember the grammar.
- Invite a pupil to read out the information. Encourage the class to give some examples.

Activity 4
Describe a job. Use *have to* or *don't have to*. Read the sentences to a partner. Can your partner guess the job?
- The pupils work on their own to write their sentences.
- In pairs, they read out their sentences and guess the jobs.

Odd one out activity
Which is the odd one out? Why?
- The pupils complete the odd one out activity.

Answers: detective (It doesn't end in 'ian'.)

Ending the lesson

Review the lesson and reflect on learning.
- Say **Today we've learnt some new jobs.**
- Ask **What do you remember?** The pupils do a three-minute review in pairs. (Cooperative Learning Strategies, page 19)

Extra activities

Extension
- The pupils find three interesting facts about Scotland to present to the class.

Vocabulary extension
- Introduce words related to the topic of jobs: *architect, author, editor, engineer, gardener, surgeon.*
- Use the Vocabulary Booster on NAVIO to practise these new words.

Key Competences and Key Learning Outcomes

- Listen to and read a dialogue
- Learn and practise using modal verbs to make predictions about the future
- Analyse language used for making predictions and apply the rules learnt
- Identify examples of future predictions in the dialogue

Key language

- *artist, astronaut, firefighter, musician, teacher*
- *I will definitely be (an archaeologist). I probably won't be (a politician). I may / might / could be (a chemist).*

Materials

- Pupil's Book p62; Activity Book p59; Class CD2; Teacher's App on Navio
- Teacher's Resource Bank: Jobs word cards

Optional materials

- Teacher's Resource Bank: Trinity Exams Practice cards (selected from the Starter Unit and Units 1, 2, 3, 4 and 5)
- Dice

At a Glance Lesson Plan

Pupil's Book

Starting the lesson

- Use the Trinity Exams Practice cards (optional).
- Review jobs.
- Set learning outcomes.

Activity 1

- Describe the photo.
- What do you need to be good at to be an astronaut?
- Read and listen to find out.

▶ *CD2 Track 36 p287*

Activity 2

- Read the dialogue again.
- Ask and answer.

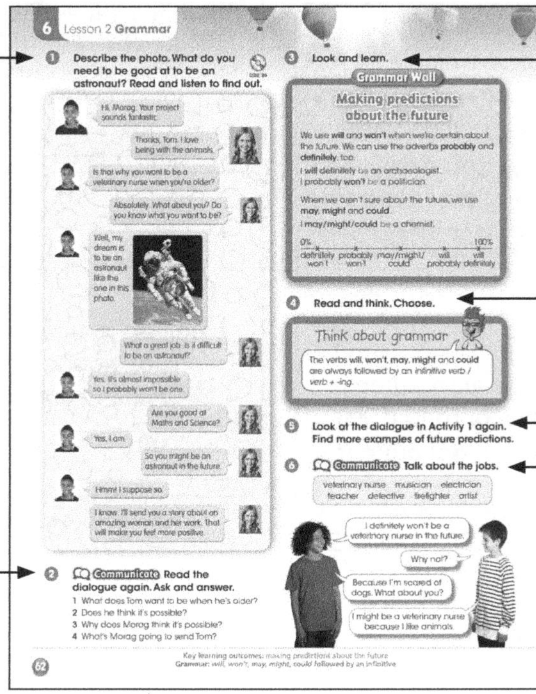
6 Lesson 2 Grammar

1 Describe the photo. What do you need to be good at to be an astronaut? Read and listen to find out.

3 Look and learn.

Grammar Wall

Making predictions about the future

We use **will** and **won't** when we're certain about the future. We can use the adverbs **probably** and **definitely**, too.

I **will definitely** be an archaeologist.

I **probably won't** be a politician.

When we aren't sure about the future, we use **may**, **might** and **could**.

I **may/might/could** be a chemist.

4 Read and think. Choose.

Think about grammar

The verbs **will**, **won't**, **may**, **might** and **could** are always followed by an infinitive verb / verb + -ing.

5 Look at the dialogue in Activity 1 again. Find more examples of future predictions.

6 Communicate Talk about the jobs.

veterinary nurse musician electrician teacher detective firefighter artist

2 Communicate Read the dialogue again. Ask and answer.

1 What does Tom want to be when he's older?
2 Does he think it's possible?
3 Why does Morag think it's possible?
4 What's Morag going to send Tom?

62

Activity 3

- Look and learn – Grammar wall

Activity 4

- Read and think.
- Choose.

Activity 5

- Look at the dialogue in Activity 1 again.
- Find more examples of future predictions.

Activity 6

- Talk about the jobs.
- Go to the Activity Book.

Ending the lesson

- Review the lesson and reflect on learning.

Extra activity

Reinforcement

- Play a true / false game.

Activity Book

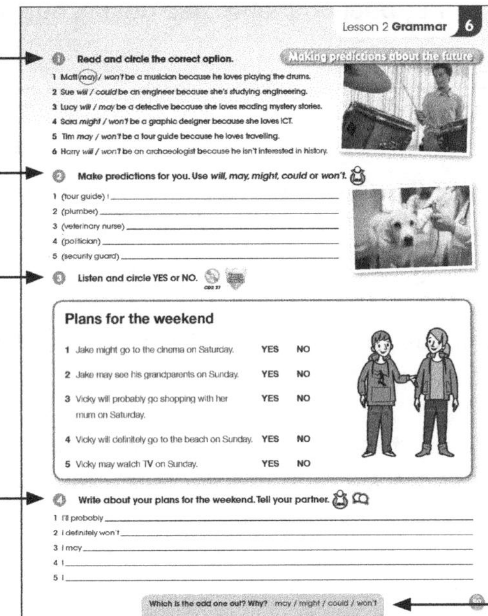
Lesson 2 Grammar 6

Making predictions about the future

1 Read and circle the correct option.

1 Matt (may) / won't be a musician because he loves playing the drums.
2 Sue will / could be an engineer because she's studying engineering.
3 Lucy will / may be a detective because she loves reading mystery stories.
4 Sara might / won't be a graphic designer because she loves ICT.
5 Tim may / won't be a tour guide because he loves travelling.
6 Harry will / won't be an archaeologist because he isn't interested in history.

2 Make predictions for you. Use will, may, might, could or won't.

1 (tour guide) I
2 (plumber)
3 (veterinary nurse)
4 (politician)
5 (security guard)

3 Listen and circle YES or NO.

Plans for the weekend

1	Jake might go to the cinema on Saturday.	YES	NO
2	Jake may see his grandparents on Sunday.	YES	NO
3	Vicky will probably go shopping with her mum on Saturday.	YES	NO
4	Vicky will definitely go to the beach on Sunday.	YES	NO
5	Vicky may watch TV on Sunday.	YES	NO

4 Write about your plans for the weekend. Tell your partner.

1 I'll probably
2 I definitely won't
3 I may
4 I
5 I

Which is the odd one out? Why? may / might / could / won't

Activity Book

Activity 1

- Read and circle the correct option.

Activity 2

- Make predictions for you. Use *will, may, might, could* or *won't.*

Activity 3

- Listen and circle YES or NO.

▶ *CD2 Track 37 p287*

Activity 4

- Write about your plans for the weekend. Tell your partner.

Odd one out activity

Digital resources

Teacher's Digital: You can also teach this lesson using the Teacher's App on Navio.

Pupil's Digital: Encourage your pupils to use the Pupil's App on Navio to practise the activities from this lesson.

Powered By NAVIO

Starting the lesson

Use the Trinity Exams Practice cards (optional).

- The pupils practise asking and answering questions.

Review jobs.

- Place the jobs word cards face down on a desk. Organise the class into groups of three.
- Pupil 1 collects a card and defines the word for the rest of their group. Pupil 2 says the word and Pupil 3 spells it. The pupils change roles. Repeat the procedure with a new word card.

Set learning outcomes.

- Say **Today we're going to talk about the future.**

Pupil's Book Activity 1

Describe the photo. What do you need to be good at to be an astronaut? Read and listen to find out.

▶ *CD2 Track 36 p287*

- Prompt the pupils to describe the photo. Ask **Is it easy to become an astronaut?**
- Play the CD. The pupils listen and read the dialogue. Confirm that it is difficult and you need to be good at Maths and Science.

Pupil's Book Activity 2

Read the dialogue again. Ask and answer.

- In pairs, the pupils read the dialogue again and answer the questions.

Answers: **1** an astronaut **2** no **3** Because he's good at Maths and Science. **4** a story

Pupil's Book Activity 3

Look and learn – Grammar wall

- Read the information on the Grammar wall as a class.
- Encourage the pupils to think about form and identify patterns. Ask **Do we put 'definitely' before or after 'will'? Do we put 'probably' before or after 'won't'?**

Pupil's Book Activity 4

Read and think. Choose.

- Focus the pupils' attention on the Think about grammar box. Read out the sentence as a class. The pupils complete the sentence in pairs.
- Check answers as a class. (*infinitive verb*)

Pupil's Book Activity 5

Look at the dialogue in Activity 1 again. Find more examples of future predictions.

- In pairs, the pupils find examples of future predictions in the dialogue.

Pupil's Book Activity 6

Talk about the jobs.

- Invite two pupils to read out the speech bubbles.
- Ask other pupils to make similar sentences. They give a reason for their prediction each time.
- In pairs, the pupils make predictions about the jobs.

Activity Book

Activity 1

Read and circle the correct option.

- The pupils read the sentences and circle the correct option.

Answers: **1** may **2** will **3** may **4** might **5** won't **6** won't

Activity 2

Make predictions for you.
Use *will, may, might, could* or *won't*.

- Invite different pupils to make predictions. Prompt them to use the modal verbs.
- The pupils write the sentences. They compare answers with a partner.

Activity 3

Listen and circle YES or NO. Exams Practice

▶ *CD2 Track 37 p287*

- Read out the sentences as a class. Focus the pupils on the modal verb in each sentence.
- Play the CD. The pupils listen and circle. They compare answers with a partner.
- Play the CD again, pausing after each piece of key information. The pupils identify and say the answer each time.

Answers: **1** Yes **2** No **3** Yes **4** No **5** Yes

Activity 4

Write about your plans for the weekend. Tell your partner.

- The pupils write about their plans for the weekend.
- In pairs, the pupils tell their partner about their plans.

Odd one out activity

Which is the odd one out? Why?

- The pupils complete the odd one out activity.

Answer: won't (It expresses certainty.)

Ending the lesson

Review the lesson and reflect on learning.

- Say **Today we've made predictions about the future.**
- Ask **What do you remember?** The pupils do a three-minute review in pairs. (Cooperative Learning Strategies, page 19)

Extra activity

Reinforcement

- Choose a pupil to throw a dice. The rest of the class shouldn't see the number on the dice.
- Ask **Will you be (a teacher) in the future?** The pupil answers according to the number on the dice (1–3 = truth, 4–6 = false), e.g. *Yes. I'll definitely be a teacher in the future.* The class listens and decides if the answer is true or false.
- Repeat the procedure with different pupils. Prompt the class to ask questions.

Key Competences and Key Learning Outcomes

- Read a story with confidence and fluency
- Use the Internet to investigate Scotland
- Listen for general and specific information
- Understand the importance of being positive when there is a challenge
- Learn about Scotland
- Express an opinion on a text

Key language

- *ambition, challenge, deaf, fingertips, frustrated, percussion, positive, vibrations*
- *When she was eight, Evelyn began studying the piano.*

Materials

- Pupil's Book p65; Activity Book p60; Class CD 2 and 3; Teacher's App on Navio

Optional materials

- Teacher's Resource Bank: Trinity Exams Practice cards (selected from the Starter Unit and Units 1, 2, 3, 4 and 5)

At a Glance Lesson Plan

Starting the lesson

- Use the Trinity Exams Practice cards (optional).
- Review musical instruments.
- Set learning outcomes.

Activity 1: Before you read

- Read and discuss.

Activity 2

- Listen and read.
- ▶ *CD2 Track 38 p287*
- Go to the Activity Book.

***Give Me Five!* values**

- Read and discuss.

Pupil's Book

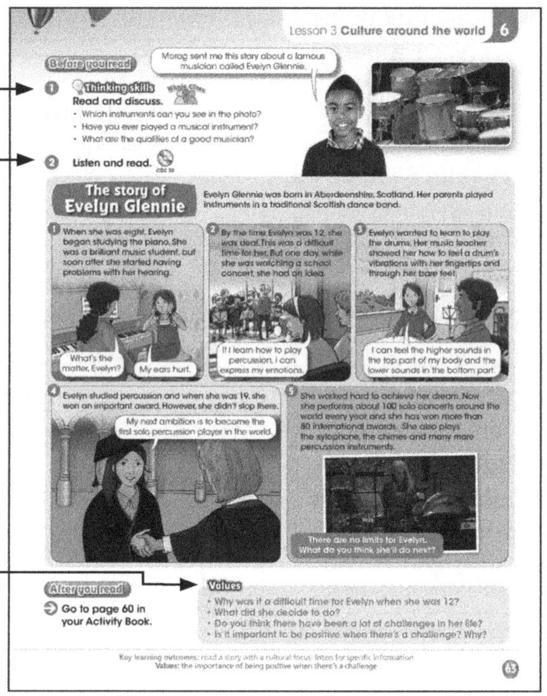

Ending the lesson

- Review the lesson and reflect on learning.

Extra activity

Extension

- Find out about Evelyn Glennie's percussion instruments.

Activity Book

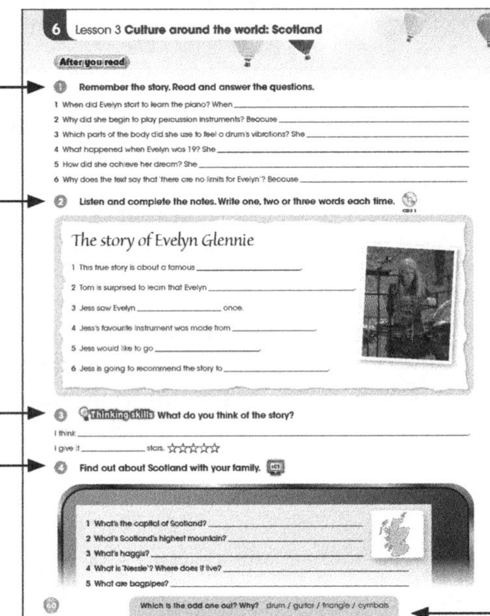

Activity Book: After you read

Activity 1

- Remember the story. Read and answer the questions.

Activity 2

- Listen and complete the notes. Write one, two or three words each time.
- ▶ *CD3 Track 1 p288*

Activity 3

- What do you think of the story?

Activity 4

- Find out about Scotland with your family.

Odd one out activity

Digital resources

Teacher's Digital: You can also teach this lesson using the Teacher's App on Navio.

Pupil's Digital: Encourage your pupils to use the Pupil's App on Navio to practise the activities from this lesson.

Powered By NAVIO

Starting the lesson

Use the Trinity Exams Practice cards (optional).
- The pupils practise asking and answering questions.

Review musical instruments.
- Draw a simple table on the board as follows:

• Wind	• String	• Percussion

- The pupils copy the chart into their notebooks. In pairs, they write musical instruments.
- Elicit the instruments and write them on the board.

Set learning outcomes.
- Say **Today we're going to read a story about a famous musician from Scotland.**

Pupil's Book Activity 1: Before you read

Read and discuss.
- Read the questions as a class. The pupils share information about the instruments and give their opinions.
- **Note:** you can use the Story Tool to present this story.

Pupil's Book Activity 2

Listen and read.

▶ *CD2 Track 38 p287*
- Play the CD. The pupils follow in their books.
- Ask questions to check understanding.

Suggested comprehension questions:
- Frame 1: **When did Evelyn's ears begin to hurt?** (*When she was eight.*)
- Frame 2: **When did she become completely deaf?** (*When she was 12.*)
- Frame 3: **How did she feel the drum's vibrations?** (*With her fingertips and through her bare feet.*)
- Frame 4: **What did Evelyn study?** (*Percussion.*)
- Frame 5: **Where does she perform now?** (*Around the world.*) **How many awards has she won?** (*She's won more than 80 awards.*)
- **Note:** you can use the Story Tool to read and review this story.

Activity Book: After you read

Activity 1

Remember the story. Read and answer the questions.
- Read out the first question. Invite a pupil to answer it.
- The pupils read and answer the remaining questions.

Answers: **1** was eight. **2** she wanted to express her emotions. **3** used her fingertips and her bare feet. **4** won an award. **5** worked hard. **6** she's achieved many things.

Activity 2

Listen and complete the notes. Write one, two or three words each time.

▶ *CD3 Track 1 p288*
- Read out the notes as a class. Ask the pupils to guess the missing words.
- Play the CD without pausing. The pupils listen and complete as much information as possible.
- Play the CD again, pausing after each piece of key information to check the answer.

Answers: **1** musician **2** can't hear **3** on TV **4** an old bed **5** to a concert **6** her sister

Activity 3

What do you think of the story?
- The pupils write their opinion and give a rating.
- Invite different pupils to share their opinions.

Activity 4

Find out about Scotland with your family. ICT
- Read out the questions about Scotland. Ask **Where can you find out this information?** (*Internet, library, asking friends and family.*) The pupils complete the activity at home.
- If you prefer to do this activity in the class, connect to a children's website which has information about Scotland, such as www.sciencekids.co.nz/sciencefacts/countries/scotland.html.
- Read out the questions. The pupils work as a class to find and write the answers.

Answers: **1** Edinburgh **2** Ben Nevis **3** a traditional meat dish **4** the Loch Ness monster, in Loch Ness **5** a wind instrument

Odd one out activity

Which is the odd one out? Why?
- The pupils complete the odd one out activity.

Answers: guitar (It isn't a percussion instrument.)

***Give Me Five!* values**

Read and discuss.
- Read out the questions and discuss them as a class.

Ending the lesson

Review the lesson and reflect on learning.
- Say **Today we've read a story about a famous musician from Scotland.**
- Ask **What do you remember?** The pupils do a three-minute review in pairs. (Cooperative Learning Strategies, page 19)

Extra activity

Extension
- Use the Internet to see and listen to some of Evelyn Glennie's instruments. Encourage the pupils to comment on what they see and hear.

Key Competences and Key Learning Outcomes

- Act out a short dialogue in pairs
- Learn and practise how to use embedded questions to ask about the future
- Review and learn future time expressions

- Analyse and apply rules for forming embedded questions

- Identify and practise using rising and falling intonation patterns to express possibility and certainty

Key language

- *in (one year's) time, in (three months') time, next week, the day after tomorrow, this evening*
- *Do you think I / you / he / she / we / they will (be famous)?*

Materials

- Pupil's Book p64; Activity Book p61; Class CD3; Teacher's App on Navio

Optional materials

- Teacher's Resource Bank: Trinity Exams Practice cards (selected from the Starter Unit and Units 1, 2, 3, 4 and 5)

At a Glance Lesson Plan

Pupil's Book

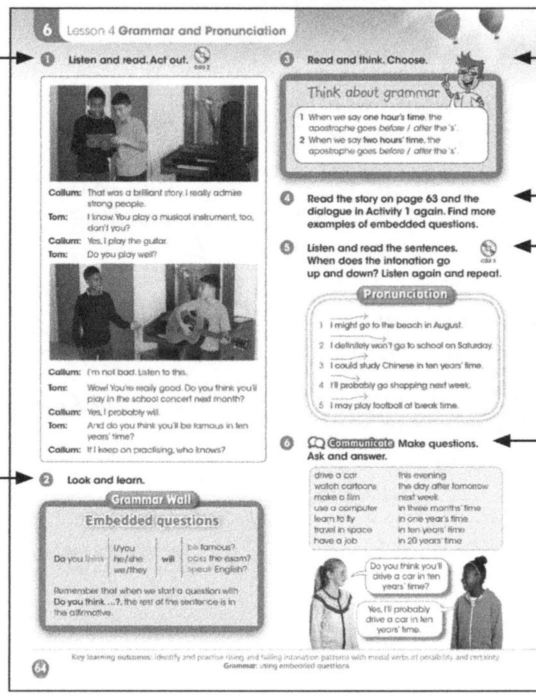

Starting the lesson

- Use the Trinity Exams Practice cards (optional).
- Review past, present and future time references.
- Set learning outcomes.

Activity 1

- Listen and read.
- ▶ *CD3 Track 2 p288*
- Act out.

Activity 2

- Look and learn – Grammar wall

Activity 3

- Read and think.
- Choose.

Activity 4

- Read the story on page 63 and the dialogue in Activity 1 again.
- Find more examples of embedded questions.

Activity 5

- Listen and read the sentences.
- ▶ *CD3 Track 3 p288*
- When does the intonation go up and down?
- Listen again and repeat.

Activity 6

- Make questions.
- Ask and answer.
- Go to the Activity Book.

Ending the lesson

- Review the lesson and reflect on learning.

Extra activity

Reinforcement

- Do a one-question interview.

Activity Book

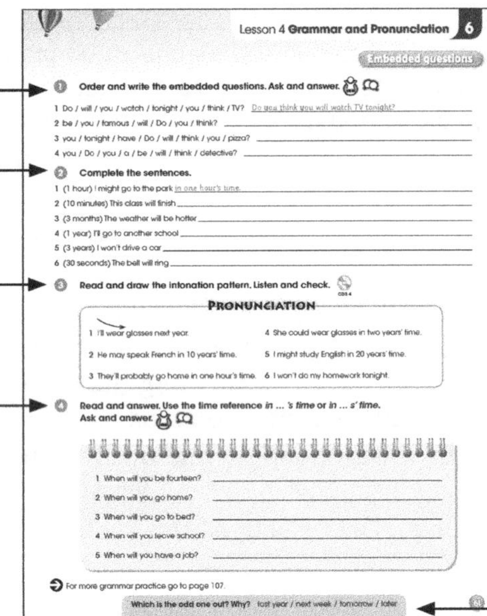

Activity Book

Activity 1

- Order and write the embedded questions. Ask and answer.

Activity 2

- Complete the sentences.

Activity 3

- Read and draw the intonation pattern. Listen and check.

▶ *CD3 Track 4 p288*

Activity 4

- Read and answer. Use the time reference *in …'s time* or *in … s' time*. Ask and answer.

Odd one out activity

Digital resources

Teacher's Digital: You can also teach this lesson using the Teacher's App on Navio.

Pupil's Digital: Encourage your pupils to use the Pupil's App on Navio to practise the activities from this lesson.

Powered By NAVIO

Starting the lesson

Use the Trinity Exams Practice cards (optional).

- The pupils practise asking and answering questions.

Review past, present and future time references.

- Teach these movements: past time point behind, present time point to the floor, future time point in front.
- Say different time references, e.g. **yesterday**. The pupils listen and do the corresponding hand movements.

Set learning outcomes.

- Say **Today we're going to learn some future time references and we're going to learn how to ask embedded questions.**

Pupil's Book Activity 1

Listen and read. Act out.

▶ *CD3 Track 2 p288*

- The pupils look at the photos. Ask **What are Tom and Callum talking about in photo (1)?**
- Play the CD. The pupils listen and read the dialogue. Check understanding.
- Play the CD again, pausing after each sentence for the pupils to repeat.
- The pupils practise the dialogue in pairs.
- **Note:** you can use the Dialogue Tool to present and practise this dialogue.

Pupil's Book Activity 2

Look and learn – Grammar wall

- Read the information on the Grammar wall as a class.
- Focus on the word order. Explain that embedded questions sound more polite than direct questions.

Pupil's Book Activity 3

Read and think. Choose.

- Focus the pupils' attention on the Think about grammar box. The pupils complete the sentences.
- Check answers as a class. (*before, after*)

Pupil's Book Activity 4

Look at the story on page 63 and the dialogue in Activity 1 again. Find more examples of embedded questions.

- In pairs, the pupils find more examples.

Pupil's Book Activity 5

Listen and read the sentences. When does the intonation go up and down? Listen again and repeat.

▶ *CD3 Track 3 p288*

- Play the CD, pausing after each sentence. Elicit that the intonation rises when an action is possible and falls when an action is certain.
- Play the CD again. The pupils listen and repeat.

Pupil's Book Activity 6

Make questions. Ask and answer.

- Invite two pupils to read out the speech bubbles.
- In pairs, the pupils ask and answer.

Activity Book

Activity 1

Order and write the embedded questions. Ask and answer.

- The pupils order and write the questions.
- In pairs, they ask and answer the questions.

Answers: **1** Do you think you will watch TV tonight? **2** Do you think you will be famous? **3** Do you think you will have pizza tonight? **4** Do you think you will be a detective?

Activity 2

Complete the sentences.

- Review the position of the apostrophe in 'one hour's time' and in 'two hours' time'. The pupils complete the sentences with the time references.

Answers: **1** in one hour's time. **2** in ten minutes' time. **3** in three months' time. **4** in one year's time. **5** in three years' time. **6** in thirty seconds' time.

Activity 3

Read and draw the intonation pattern. Listen and check.

▶ *CD3 Track 4 p288*

- In pairs, the pupils draw the intonation patterns.
- Play the CD. The pupils listen and check.

Answers: 1 ↘ 2 ↗ 3 ↘ 4 ↗ 5 ↗ 6 ↘

Activity 4

Read and answer. Use the time reference *in …'s time* or *in … s' time*. Ask and answer.

- The pupils answer the questions. They use an appropriate time reference.
- In pairs, they ask and answer the questions.

Odd one out activity

Which is the odd one out? Why?

- The pupils complete the odd one out activity.

Answers: last year (It isn't a future time reference.)

Ending the lesson

Review the lesson and reflect on learning.

- Say **Today we've learnt some more future time references and how to ask embedded questions.**
- Ask **What do you remember?** The pupils do a three-minute review in pairs. (Cooperative Learning Strategies, page 19)

Extra activity

Extension

- The pupils write a question with *Do you think you will…?* They ask their questions to as many classmates as possible. Set a time limit (3–5 minutes). They record their classmate's name and response. They analyse the responses and write a summary, e.g. *I asked (number) pupils my question. (Number) pupils said (response).*

Key Competences and Key Learning Outcomes

- Review and name different life events
- Practise using expressions to express doubt
- Practise activity types found in the Cambridge Exams: B1 Preliminary for Schools
- Practise sequencing words and events to aid memory
- Listen for gist and specific information
- Do a communication task

Key language

- *get a job, go backpacking, go to university, have children, learn to drive, leave home, start a business*
- Extension: *be born, get married, move house, retire*
- *I don't know. I don't think so. I'm not sure. I doubt it. You never know.*

Materials

- Pupil's Book p65; Activity Book p62; Class CD3; Teacher's App on Navio

Optional materials

- Teacher's Resource Bank: Trinity Exams Practice cards (selected from the Starter Unit and Units 1, 2, 3, 4 and 5)

At a Glance Lesson Plan

Pupil's Book

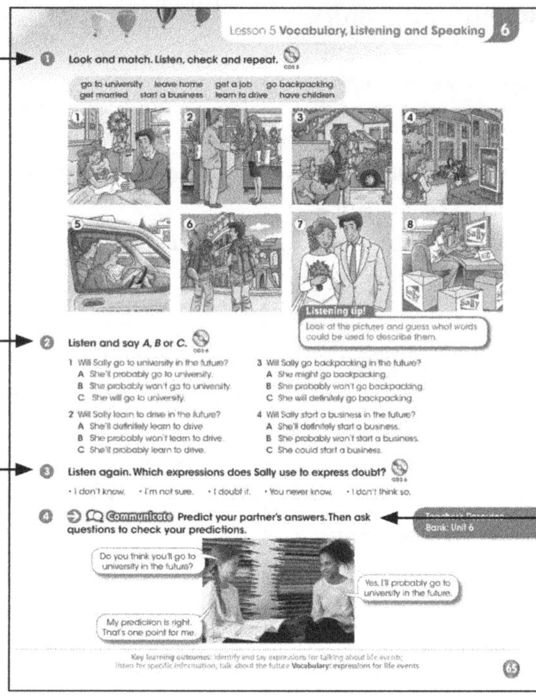

Starting the lesson

- Use the Trinity Exams Practice cards (optional)
- Review future time expressions.
- Set learning outcomes.

Activity 1

- Look and match.
- Listen, check and repeat.

▶ *CD3 Track 5 p288*

Activity 2

- Listen and say *A*, *B* or *C*.

▶ *CD3 Track 6 p288*

Activity 3

- Listen again.

▶ *CD3 Track 6 p288*

- Which expressions does Sally use to express doubt?

Activity 4

- Predict your partner's answers.
- Then ask questions to check your predictions (Teacher's Resource Bank: Unit 6).

Go to the Activity Book.

Ending the lesson

- Review the lesson and reflect on learning.

Extra activities

Extension

- Discuss the advantages and disadvantages of being 16.

Vocabulary extension

- Present four additional vocabulary items.

Activity Book

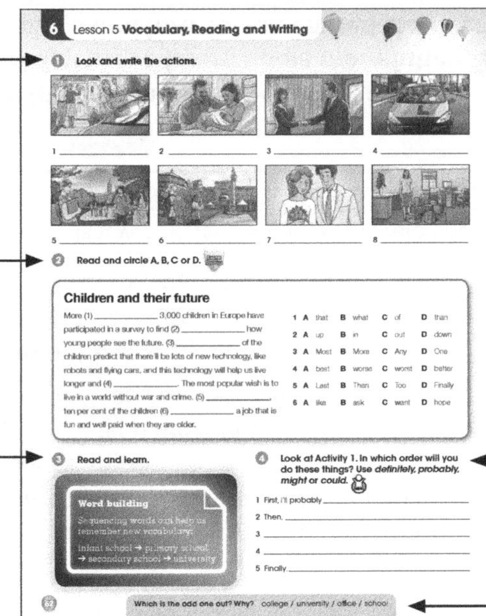

Activity Book

Activity 1

- Look and write the actions.

Activity 2

- Read and circle A, B, C or D.

Activity 3

- Read and learn.

Activity 4

- Look at Activity 1. In which order will you do these things? Use *definitely*, *probably*, *might* or *could*.

Odd one out activity

Digital resources

Teacher's Digital: You can also teach this lesson using the Teacher's App on Navio.

Pupil's Digital: Encourage your pupils to use the Pupil's App on Navio to practise the activities from this lesson.

Powered By NAVIO

Starting the lesson

Use the Trinity Exams Practice cards (optional).
- The pupils practise asking and answering questions.

Review future time expressions.
- On the board, write *five years' time*. Ask **What do you think will happen in five years' time?** The pupils make predictions. Repeat with other expressions.

Set learning outcomes.
- Say **Today we're going to learn the names of some activities you may do in the future.**

Pupil's Book Activity 1

Look and match. Listen, check and repeat.
▶ *CD3 Track 5 p288*
- In pairs, the pupils match the phrases with the pictures.
- Play the CD. The pupils listen and check.
- Play the CD again, pausing after each phrase for the pupils to repeat. You can find the answers for this activity in the audioscript on page 288.

Pupil's Book Activity 2

Listen and say *A, B* or *C*.
▶ *CD3 Track 6 p288*
- Ask a pupil to read out the questions and answers. Read Listening tip! as a class
- Play the CD. The pupils listen and identify the correct answer each time.
- Play the CD another time, pausing to check the pupils' answers.

Answers: **1** A **2** A **3** C **4** C

Pupil's Book Activity 3

Listen again. Which expressions does Sally use to express doubt?
▶ *CD3 Track 6 p288*
- Invite a pupil to read out the expressions.
- Play the CD again. The pupils identify the expressions.

Answers: I don't think so. I'm not sure. I doubt it.

Pupil's Book Activity 4

Predict your partner's answers. Then ask questions to check your predictions (Teacher's Resource Bank: Unit 6).
- Explain to the pupils that they are going to make some predictions about their partner. Invite two pupils to read out the speech bubbles.
- Organise the class into pairs (A and B).
- The pupils work on their own to tick their predictions.
- Invite two pupils to demonstrate the activity. Pupil A asks the first question. Pupil B responds. Encourage them to use the expressions of doubt if appropriate.
- The pupils do the activity in their pairs.

Activity Book

Activity 1
Look and write the actions.
- The pupils label the pictures.

Answers: **1** leave home **2** have children **3** get a job **4** learn to drive **5** go to university **6** go backpacking **7** get married **8** start a business

Activity 2
Read and circle A, B, C or D.
- Read the text aloud. The pupils listen.
- In pairs, the pupils read the text again. They identify the missing words. Remind them to try all four words in the gap before they make their decision.
- They read the completed text silently to check their answers. Check answers as a class.

Answers: **1** D **2** C **3** A **4** D **5** D **6** C

Activity 3
Read and learn.
- Read the information as a class.

Activity 4
Look at Activity 1. In which order will you do these things? Use *definitely*, *probably*, *might* or *could*.
- Read the instructions as a class. Then quickly review other sequencers that the pupils know, e.g. *After that*, *Next*.
- Ask a pupil to complete and read out the first sentence.
- The pupils write the sentences.

Odd one out activity
Which is the odd one out? Why?
- The pupils complete the odd one out activity.

Answers: office (You don't study there.)

Ending the lesson

Review the lesson and reflect on learning.
- Say **Today we've learnt the names of some things you may do in the future.**
- Ask **What do you remember?** The pupils do a three-minute review in pairs. (Cooperative Learning Strategies, page 19)

Extra activities

Extension
- Ask **What are the good things about being 16?** Encourage the class to think of the advantages. Ideas might include getting a mobile phone, going out with friends and staying up later. Then ask the class to think of the disadvantages. Ideas might include more homework, exams and responsibilities.
- Have a class vote to decide if being 12 or 16 is better.

Vocabulary Extension
- Present six additional words related to life events: *be born, get married, move house, retire.*
- Use the Vocabulary Booster on NAVIO to practise these new words.

Key Competences and Key Learning Outcomes

- Review talking about present habits and making future predictions
- Compare life in the past and today
- Do pre-reading tasks to predict content
- Read a text for general understanding
- Guess the meaning of words from context
- Share what you know about this type of text
- Read an informal letter
- Give an opinion on the text

Key language

- *arcade game, BMX bike, calculator, cassette, cure, disease, time capsule*
- *I hope that there aren't any wars.*

Materials

- Pupil's Book p66; Activity Book p63; Class CD3; Teacher's App on Navio

Optional materials

- Teacher's Resource Bank: Trinity Exams Practice cards (selected from the Starter Unit and Units 1, 2, 3, 4 and 5)
- A metal box and items for a time capsule (e.g. maps, photographs, etc.)

At a Glance Lesson Plan

Pupil's Book

Starting the lesson

- Use the Trinity Exams Practice cards (optional).
- Review life events vocabulary.
- Set learning outcomes.

Activity 1: Before you read

- Read and discuss.

Activity 2

- Look at the date on the time capsule letter.
- How long ago was it written?
- Predict what's in the letter.
- Read and find out.

Activity 3: After you read

- What do you think?
- Go to the Activity Book.

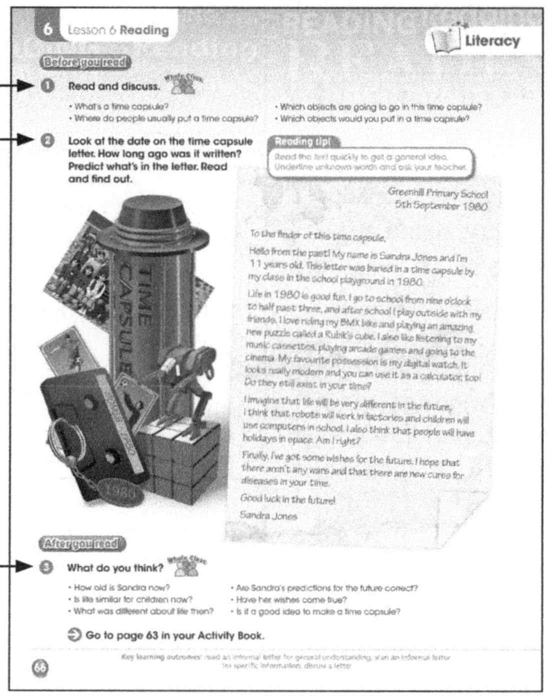

Ending the lesson

- Review the lesson and reflect on learning.

Extra activity

Extension

- Create a class time capsule display.

Activity Book

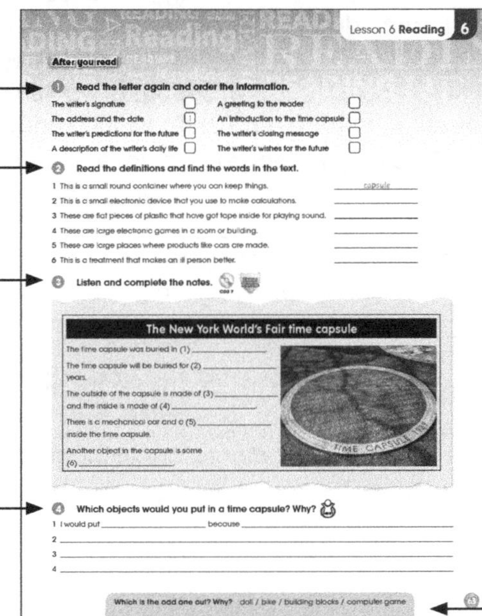

Activity Book: After you read

Activity 1

- Read the letter again and order the information.

Activity 2

- Read the definitions and find the words in the text.

Activity 3

- Listen and complete the notes.

▶ *CD3 Track 7 p288*

Activity 4

- Which objects would you put in a time capsule? Why?

Odd one out activity

Digital resources

Teacher's Digital: You can also teach this lesson using the Teacher's App on Navio.

Pupil's Digital: Encourage your pupils to use the Pupil's App on Navio to practise the activities from this lesson.

Powered By NAVIO

Starting the lesson

Use the Trinity Exams Practice cards (optional).
- The pupils practise asking and answering questions.

Review life events vocabulary.
- Organise the class into pairs. Challenge the pupils to remember the eight life events from Lesson 5.
- Quickly review the events as a class. Ask **Do you think you will (go to university)?**

Set learning outcomes.
- Say **Today we're going to read a letter from the past.**

Pupil's Book Activity 1: Before you read

Read and discuss.
- Read the questions as a class. Prompt the pupils to answer in as much detail as possible.
- Explain that a time capsule is a container that is usually made of metal. People put things from the present time inside the time capsule and then bury it underground. Then, on a certain date in the future (often in 50 years' time), the time capsule is opened.

Pupil's Book Activity 2

Look at the date on the time capsule letter. How long ago was it written? Predict what's in the letter. Read and find out.
- Invite a pupil to read the date on the letter. Ask the pupils to work out how many years ago the letter was written. Then ask them to predict what information will appear in the letter.
- Read the letter as a class. Check if the information appears.

Pupil's Book Activity 3: After you read

What do you think?
- Read and answer the questions as a class. Encourage the pupils to use comparative structures when they compare and contrast life in the past with life today.

Activity Book: After you read

Activity 1

Read the letter again and order the information.
- Invite a pupil to read out the first piece of information. The pupils find the information in the time capsule letter.
- Then ask the pupils to identify and number the next piece of information in the letter.
- In pairs, the pupils order and number the remaining pieces of information, consulting the letter in the Pupil's Book to help them.

Answers: 8, 1, 5, 4, 2, 3, 7, 6

Activity 2

Read the definitions and find the words in the text.
- Invite a pupil to read the first definition and word. The class scans the letter to find the word.
- In pairs, the pupils read the remaining definitions and find the words.
- Check answers as a class.

Answers: **1** capsule **2** calculator **3** cassette **4** arcade games **5** factories **6** cure

Activity 3

Listen and complete the notes.

▶ *CD3 Track 7 p288*
- Read the information as a class. Encourage the pupils to predict the missing words.
- Play the CD. The pupils listen and complete as much of the information as possible. They check their answers with a partner.
- Play the CD again, pausing after each piece of information. The pupils complete and check their answers.

Answers: **1** 1939 / New York **2** 5,000 **3** metal **4** glass **5** doll **6** toothpaste

Activity 4

Which objects would you put in a time capsule? Why?
- Ask the pupils to think of three objects they would put in a time capsule. Remind them that these objects should reflect their interests and their society.
- The pupils write their sentences.
- Ask the pupils to share their answers with a partner. Then invite different pupils to share their answers with the class.

Odd one out activity

Which is the odd one out? Why?
- The pupils complete the odd one out activity.

Answers: computer game (It's an electronic game.)

Ending the lesson

Review the lesson and reflect on learning.
- Say **Today we've read a letter from the past.**
- Ask **What do you remember?** The pupils do a three-minute review in pairs. (Cooperative Learning Strategies, page 19)

Extra activity

Extension
- Create a class time capsule display. Find a metal box and ask the pupils to decide which objects to put in it. The pupils should bring these items from home. Possible items include maps, photos, a shopping receipt or magazines.

Key Competences and Key Learning Outcomes

- Review and practise how to use paragraphs
- Identify the text features of an informal letter
- Use criteria to check your writing
- Share and discuss your writing with a partner
- Write a letter for a time capsule expressing hopes and wishes for the future

Key language

- *football training, solar-powered, zero gravity games*
- *I imagine that life will be very different in the future.*

Materials

- Pupil's Book p67; Activity Book p64; Teacher's App on Navio

Optional materials

- Teacher's Resource Bank: Trinity Exams Practice cards (selected from the Starter Unit and Units 1, 2, 3, 4 and 5)

At a Glance Lesson Plan

Pupil's Book

Starting the lesson

- Use the Trinity Exams Practice cards (optional).
- Review the types of letters that people write.
- Set learning outcomes.

Activity 1: Investigate a text

- Look at the contents of this time capsule.
- What do they tell us about the owner?

Activity 2

- Read the time capsule letter to find out.

Activity 3: Discuss a text

- Read the letter again.
- Answer the questions.

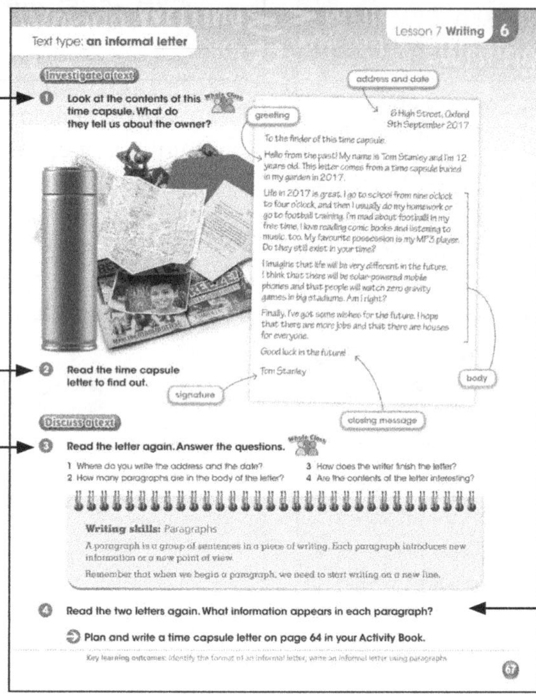

Writing skills

- Read about using paragraphs.

Activity 4

- Read the two letters again.
- What information appears in each paragraph?
- Go to the Activity Book.

Ending the lesson

- Review the lesson and reflect on learning.

Extra activity

Extension

- Share your letters with the class.

Activity Book

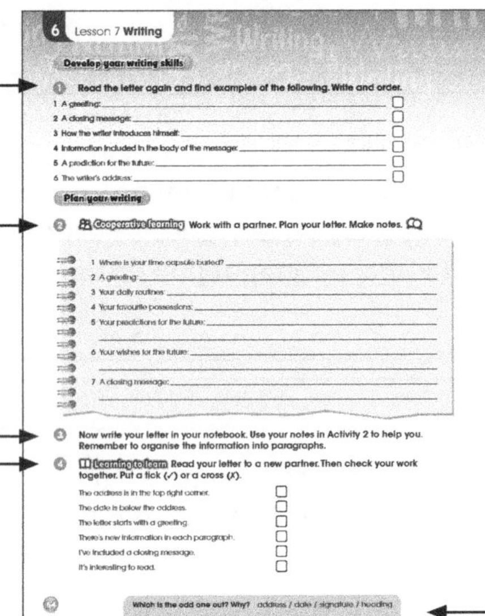

Activity Book

Activity 1: Develop your writing skills

- Read the letter again and find examples of the following. Write and order.

Activity 2: Plan your writing

- Work with a partner. Plan your letter. Make notes.

Activity 3

- Now write your letter in your notebook. Use your notes in Activity 2 to help you. Remember to organise the information into paragraphs.

Activity 4

- Read your letter to a new partner. Then check your work together. Put a tick (✓) or a cross (✗).

Odd one out activity

Digital resources

Teacher's Digital: You can also teach this lesson using the Teacher's App on Navio.

Pupil's Digital: Encourage your pupils to use the Pupil's App on Navio to practise the activities from this lesson.

Powered By NAVIO

Starting the lesson

Use the Trinity Exams Practice cards (optional).

- The pupils practise asking and answering questions.

Review the types of letters that people write.

- Ask **Have you ever received a letter? Have you ever written a letter?** Encourage the pupils to share their experiences.
- Ask **Can you think of any other times people write a letter?** Brainstorm and categorise different formal and informal letters, e.g. Formal: a letter to complain, a letter of application for a job; Informal: an invitation to a friend, a letter to a friend with news.

Set learning outcomes

- Say **Today we're going to read and write an informal letter for a time capsule.**

Pupil's Book Activity 1: Investigate a text

Look at the contents of this time capsule. What do they tell us about the owner?

- Prompt the pupils to describe the photo. Encourage them to make deductions about the owner. Ask **Do you think that the owner is a boy or a girl? Why?**
- **Note:** you could review and practise modal verbs of deduction.

Pupil's Book Activity 2

Read the time capsule letter to find out.

- The pupils read the time capsule letter.
- They then report the information they find out about the time capsule owner.

Pupil's Book Activity 3: Discuss a text

Read the letter again. Answer the questions.

- Read and discuss the questions as a class. Highlight the layout of the letter and how it begins and ends.

Writing skills

- Read about organising information into paragraphs.

Pupil's Book Activity 4

Read the two letters again. What information appears in each paragraph?

- The pupils read the two letters again. They identify the content of the different paragraphs.
- Highlight that each paragraph has a specific purpose, e.g. to introduce the writer, to make some predictions about the future, etc.

Activity Book

Activity 1: Develop your writing skills

Read the letter again and find examples of the following. Write and order.

- Ask the class to find the first piece of information in the letter.
- In pairs, the pupils find the remaining pieces of information. They then order and number the information.

Answers: **1** To the finder of this time capsule. 2 **2** Good luck in the future! 6 **3** My name is Tom Stanley and I'm 12 years old. 3 **4** Life in 2017 is great. 4 **5** there will be solar-powered mobile phones, people will watch zero gravity games in big stadiums 5 **6** 6 High Street, Oxford

Activity 2: Plan your writing

Work with a partner. Plan your letter. Make notes.

- Read out the notes as a class. Check understanding.
- In pairs, the pupils plan their letter.

Activity 3

Now write your letter in your notebook. Use your notes in Activity 2 to help you. Remember to organise the information into paragraphs.

- In pairs, the pupils write their letter in their notebooks.
- Remind the class to use paragraphs.

Activity 4

Read your letter to a new partner. Then check your work together. Put a tick (✓) or a cross (✗).

- Read through the statements as a class.
- Organise the class into new partners. One pupil reads aloud their letter. The other pupil listens. The pupils work together to decide if the letter fulfils the criteria and tick the corresponding boxes. The pupils can add to, improve or correct the letter at this stage.
- The pupils swap roles.

Odd one out activity

Which is the odd one out? Why?

- The pupils complete the odd one out activity.

Answers: heading (It isn't included in a letter.)

Ending the lesson

Review the lesson and reflect on learning.

- Say **Today we've read and written an informal letter.**
- Ask **What do you remember?** The pupils do a three-minute review in pairs. (Cooperative Learning Strategies, page 19)

Extra activity

Extension

- Ask the pupils to leave their notebooks open on their desks. The pupils move around the class, reading the letters. They choose the three letters that they found the most interesting.

Key Competences and Key Learning Outcomes

- Review how to describe photos

- Prepare and practise speaking activity types found in Cambridge Exams: B1 Preliminary for Schools
- Learn and practise how to paraphrase when you don't know a word
- Listen to a text for general and specific information
- Reflect on learning and progress

- Share hopes and expectations for the future

Key language
- *general description, opinion*
- *What do you want to be when you're older?*

Materials
- Pupil's Book p68; Activity Book pp65–66; Class CD3; Teacher's App on Navio

Optional materials
- Teacher's Resource Bank: Trinity Exams Practice cards (selected from the Starter Unit and Units 1, 2, 3, 4 and 5)
- Photos for the class to describe

At a Glance Lesson Plan

Pupil's Book

Starting the lesson
- Use the Trinity Exams Practice cards (optional).
- Review phrases for describing a photo.
- Set learning outcomes.

Activity 1
- Describe the photos.
- What do these people do in their jobs?

Activity 2
- Listen to the conversation.
- What does Eva want to be when she's older?
- ▶ *CD3 Track 8 p288*
- Why?

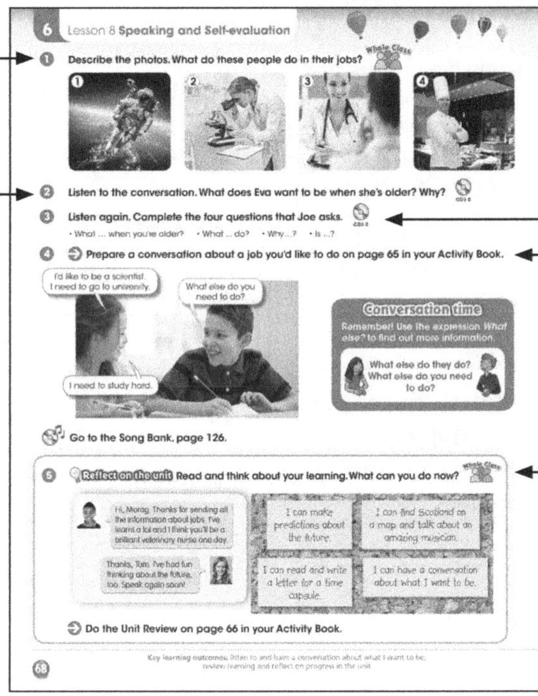

Activity 3
- Listen again.
- ▶ *CD3 Track 8 p288*
- Complete the four questions that Joe asks.
- Go to the Activity Book.

Activity 4
- Prepare a conversation about a job you'd like to do on page 65 in your Activity Book.
- Go to the Activity Book.

Song
- ▶ *CD4 Track 22 p297*
- ▶ *CD4 Track 23 p297 (optional karaoke version)*

Activity 5
- Read and think about your learning.
- What can you do now?

Ending the lesson
- Review the lesson and reflect on learning.

Activity Book

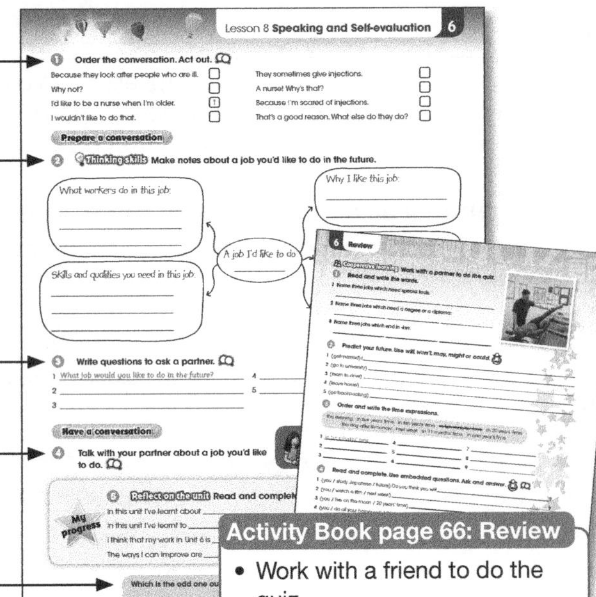

Activity Book page 66: Review
- Work with a friend to do the quiz.

Activity Book

Activity 1
- Order the conversation. Act out.

Activity 2
- Make notes about a job you'd like to do in the future.

Activity 3
- Write questions to ask a partner.

Activity 4
- Talk with your partner about a job you'd like to do.

Activity 5: My progress
- Read and complete the sentences.

Odd one out activity

Digital resources

Teacher's Digital: You can also teach this lesson using the Teacher's App on Navio.

Powered By NAVIO

Starting the lesson

Use the Trinity Exams Practice cards (optional).

- The pupils practise asking and answering questions.

Review phrases for describing a photo.

- Show a photo to the class. Invite the pupils to describe it in as much detail as possible. Highlight and review the phrases for describing photos that they learnt in Unit 4, Lesson 8.

Set learning outcomes.

- Say **Today we're going to listen to and have a conversation about what I want to be and we're going to think about our learning.**

Pupil's Book Activity 1

Describe the photos.
What do these people do in their jobs?

- The pupils describe what they can see in the photos and what the people in the photos do.

Pupil's Book Activity 2

Listen to the conversation. What does Eva want to be when she's older? Why?

▶ *CD3 Track 8 p288*

- Play the CD and prompt answer.
- Ask why Eva wants to be a scientist.(Science is her favourite subject at school.)

Answers: A scientist.

Pupil's Book Activity 3

Listen again. Complete the four questions that Joe asks.

▶ *CD3 Track 8 p288*

- Ask pupils to look at questions and guess how they finish.
- Play CD for pupils to complete activity.
- Check answers as a class.

Answers: What do you want to be when you're older? What do scientists do? Why do you want to be a scientist? Is it difficult to become a scientist?

Pupil's Book Activity 4

Prepare a conversation about a job you'd like to do on page 65 in your Activity Book.

- Pupils read the Conversation time and dialogue and then complete the notes in the Activity Book.

Go to the Activity Book.

Song

Read and discuss the questions.

- Go to the Song Bank on page 126 to do the Pupil's Book activities (see p244).

▶ *CD4 Track 22 p297*

▶ *CD4 Track 23 p297 (optional karaoke version)*

Activity Book

Activity 1

Order the conversation. Act out.

- Pupils order the conversation and check answers as a class.
- Have pupils act out the conversation and swap roles.

Answers: 3, 7, 1, 6, 5, 2, 8, 4

Activity 2

Make notes about a job you'd like to do in the future.

- Pupils work individually to complete the spidergram.
- Ask volunteer students to read some of their sentences to the class.

Activity 3

Write questions to ask a partner.

- Explain that pupils have to make questions for their partners.
- Ask students to say a few questions and write them on the board. Then have pupils complete the activity.

Activity 4

Talk with your partner about a job you'd like to do.

- Refer pupils to the Remember box.
- In pairs, the pupils have a conversation about what they want to be. One pupil asks the questions in Activity 3 and the partner answers. They then swap roles.

Pupil's Book Activity 5

Read and think about your learning. What can you do now?

- Read the messages as a class. Then look back through the unit and prompt the pupils to identify other things they have learnt / done.

Activity Book

Activity 5

Read and complete the sentences.

- Encourage the pupils to think of different ways of completing the sentences.
- The pupils complete the sentences.

Odd one out activity

Which is the odd one out? Why?

Answers: film (It shows people and objects moving.)

Ending the lesson

Review the lesson and reflect on learning.

- Say **Today we've discussed what we want to be in the future and we've thought about our learning.**
- Ask **What do you remember?** The pupils do a three-minute review in pairs.

Activity Book page 66: Review

Work with a partner to do the quiz.

- Organise the class into pairs. Set a time limit for the pupils to do this (10–15 minutes).
- Correct the answers as a class.

Answers: **1 1** Three from: electrician, plumber, archaeologist, computer technician **2** Three from: archaeologist, computer technician, physiotherapist, veterinary nurse, plumber, electrician, graphic designer **3** computer technician, politician, electrician **3 1** in ten minutes' time **2** this evening **3** the day after tomorrow **4** next week **5** in 11 months' time **6** in one year's time **7** in five years' time **8** in ten years' time **9** in 20 years' time **4 1** study Japanese in the future? **2** Do you think you will watch a film next week? **3** Do you think you will live on the moon in 20 years' time? **4** Do you think you will do all your homework this evening? **5** astronaut, someone who travels in space

Key Competences and Key Learning Outcomes

- Watch and understand a video about the future
- Understand how to think outside the box to create new and original ideas
- Reflect on the use of robots in the future

Key language
- *deliver parcels, think outside the box*
- *We can have avocado as a new ingredient for a sandwich. We can have skateboarding as a new subject.*

Materials
- Pupil's Book p69; Activity Book p67; Class CD3; Teacher's App on Navio
- Teacher's Resource Bank: Talk cards

Optional materials
- Teacher's Resource Bank: Trinity Exams Practice cards (selected from the Starter Unit)

At a Glance Lesson Plan

Pupil's Book

Starting the lesson
- **Think-Pair-Share.** Review ways of how we can think outside the box.
- Set learning outcomes and use the talk cards.

Activity 1
- Before you watch.
- Watch the video.
- *Unit 6 video p302*
- Read and answer the questions.

Activity 2
- Watch the video again.
- *Unit 6 video*
- How will these activities change in the future?

Activity 3
- Read, think and answer.

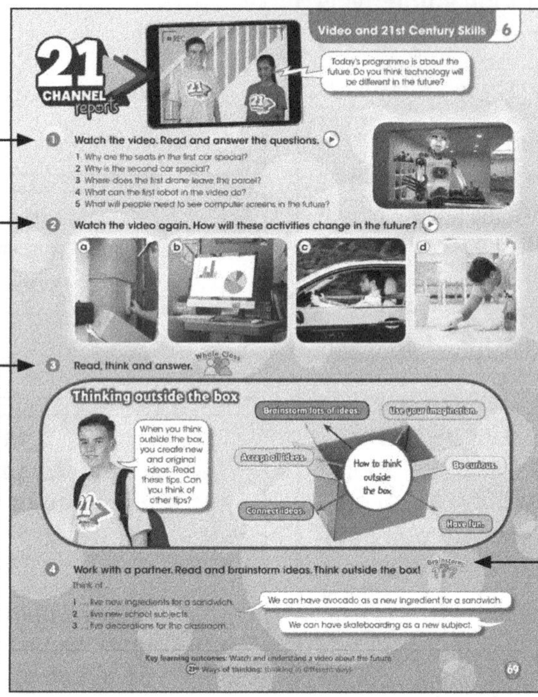

Activity 4
- Work with a partner.
- Read and brainstorm ideas.
- Think outside the box!
- Go to the Activity Book.

Ending the lesson
- Review the lesson and reflect on learning.

Extra activity
- Think about how education will change in the future.

Activity Book

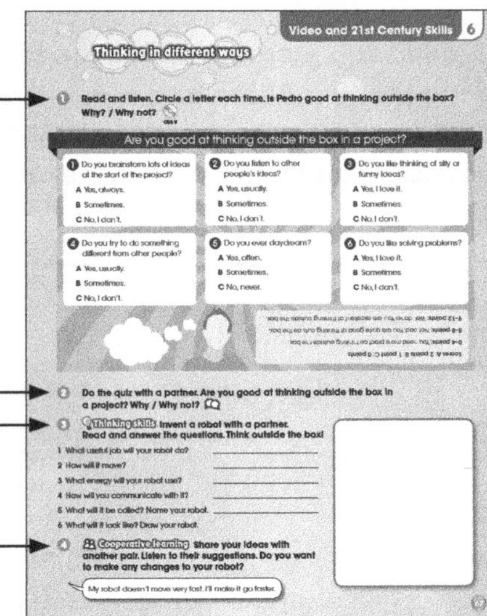

Activity Book

Activity 1
- Read and listen. Circle a letter each time. Is Pedro good at thinking outside the box? Why? / Why not?
- *CD3 Track 9 p289*

Activity 2
- Do the quiz with a partner. Are you good at thinking outside the box in a project? Why / Why not?

Activity 3
- Invent a robot with a partner. Read and answer the questions. Think outside the box!

Activity 4
- Share your ideas with another pair. Listen to their suggestions. Do you want to make any changes to your robot?

Digital resources

Teacher's Digital: You can also teach this lesson using the Teacher's App on Navio.

Pupil's Digital: Encourage your pupils to use the Pupil's App on Navio to practise the activities from this lesson.

Powered By NAVIO

Starting the lesson

Think-Pair-Share. Review ways of how we can think outside the box.

- Explain the term *Think outside the box* (to think openly about a topic and to accept different ideas about it). Ask **How do you think outside the box?** Elicit answers and write them on the board.
- Extend the discussion to talk about why thinking differently about a project or a subject is important and how it can help you.
- Pupils work with a Talk Partner to discuss how to think outside the box.
- Invite different Talk Partners to tell the class what they discussed with their partners.

Set learning outcomes and use the talk cards.

- Say **Today we're going to watch a video about the future.**
- Point to the talk cards to show the pupils the different ways they will be working in the lesson.

Pupil's Book Activity 1

Before you watch

- Ask pupils what they expect to see in today's video. Then ask what they enjoy about the videos in general.
- Read the speech bubble to pupils. Ask what pupils think the future will be like? Will it be better than today? Then ask how they think technology will change in the future. Elicit responses from a number of pupils.

Watch the video. Read and answer the questions. *p302*

- Watch Part 1. Ask pupils if they agree with the opinions presented and say why? / why not?
- Have students read the questions quietly.
- Play Part 2, pausing at each section for pupils to answer. Pupils then work in pairs to check answers.

Answers: **1** They can turn around. **2** It doesn't need a driver. **3** At a person's house. **4** They help with the housework. **5** They'll need special glasses.

Pupil's Book Activity 2

Watch the video again. How will these activities change in the future?

- Ask pupils to tell you what they remember from the video. Ask if they agree with the different things it mentioned and why? / why not?
- Have pupils complete the activity in pairs.
- Play the video for reinforcement.
- Pupils discuss their answers with their partners.

Answers: **a** Drones will deliver parcels **b** We will need special glasses to use computers / they will be in cars. **c** There will be driverless cars. **d** Robots will clean for us.

Pupil's Book Activity 3

Read, think and answer.

- Tell pupils that in the last part of the video Amy and Max talk about how it is important to think outside the box to invent new technology.
- Pupils work in pairs to read and think about the different ways of thinking outside the box.
- Ask them which idea they think is the best and if they can add any more. Note any new methods on the board.

Pupil's Book Activity 4

Work with a partner. Read and brainstorm ideas. Think outside the box!

- Have pupils work with a partner to complete the activity.
- Encourage pupils to add as many ideas as possible.
- Have a class discussion on the different ideas presented for each item. Ask pupils to vote for the best ideas presented.

Activity Book

Activity 1

Read and listen. Circle a letter each time. Is Pedro good at thinking outside the box? Why? Why not?

▸ CD3 Track 9 p289

- Give pupils a little time to read the questions.
- Play the CD and complete the activity.

Answers: **1** A **2** C **3** A **4** B **5** B **6** A

Activity 2

Do the quiz with a partner. Are you good at thinking outside the box in a project? Why / Why not?

- Have pupils complete the activity and check scores with their partners.
- Collect scores from the class and compare them ie how many got 10, 8 etc.
- Ask pupils what they learnt from the quiz and if it has helped them become better outside the box thinkers.

Activity 3

Invent a robot with a partner. Read and answer the questions. Think outside the box!

- Pupils complete the activity with their partners.

Activity 4

Share your ideas with another pair. Listen to their suggestions. Do you want to make any changes to your robot?

- Pupils show other pairs their work.
- Have pairs tell the class what they would change on their robot and why.

Ending the lesson

Review the lesson and reflect on learning.

- Say **Today we've watched a video about the future. What have we learnt?** Elicit the information from the pupils. The pupils do a three-minute review in pairs. (Cooperative Learning Strategies, page 19)

Extra activity

Reinforcement

- Place pupils in small pairs and ask them to think of and discuss ways education might change in the future.
- Have a class discussion on education in the future, encouraging pupils to use the ideas they discussed in groups.

Project 2: Living on Mars

Key Competences and Key Learning Outcomes

- Share information about living conditions on Earth and Mars; Discuss possible solutions to the problems of living on Mars
- Learn about living on Mars
- Research one aspect of living on Mars
- Listen for specific information and complete notes
- Share information with your group

Key language

- *atmosphere, breathe, conditions, energy, grow food, keep warm, melt the ice, oxygen, planets, plants, the Sun, temperature, water*
- *I'm going to find out how we could (breathe on Mars). We need oxygen to breathe.*

Materials

- Pupil's Book p70, Activity Book p68, Class CD3; Teacher's App on Navio

At a Glance Lesson Plan

Pupil's Book

Starting the lesson

- Set learning outcomes.

Activity 1: Share knowlege

- Read and discuss.

Activity 2: Investigate

- Listen and complete the notes about Earth and Mars on page 68 in your Activity Book.

Go to the Activity Book.

Activity 3

- Think about why we can't live on Mars.
- Find out about possible solutions.
- Work in pairs or groups.
- Make notes on page 68 in your Activity Book.

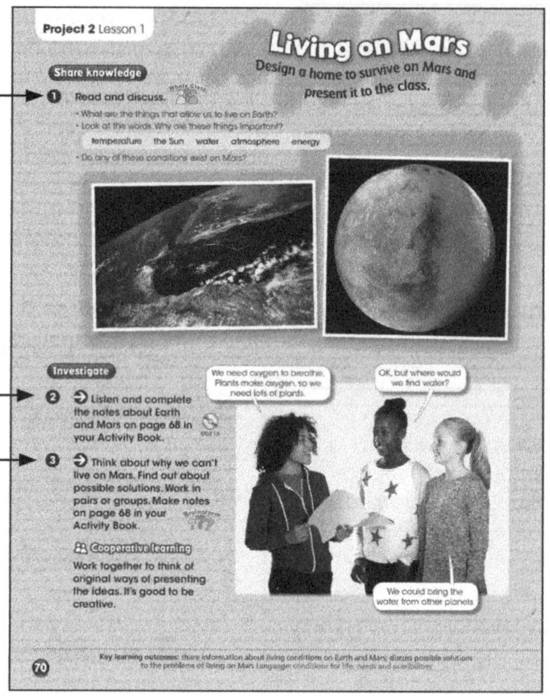

Ending the lesson

- Review the lesson and reflect on learning.

Extension activity

- Do further research on life in space.

Link to Science

- **Life conditions and space:** Future technology

Activity Book

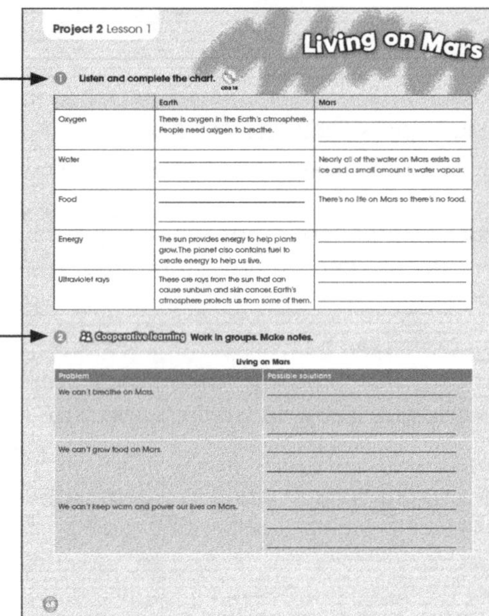

Activity Book

Activity 1

- Listen and complete the chart.

▶ *CD3 Track 10 p289*

Activity 2

- Work in groups. Make notes.

Digital resources

Teacher's Digital: You can also teach this lesson using the Teacher's App on Navio.

Pupil's Digital: Encourage your pupils to use the Pupil's App on Navio to practise the activities from this lesson.

Powered By NAVIO

Starting the lesson

Set learning outcomes.

- Say **Today we're going to begin another project.**
- Have a general class discussion on what pupils know about our solar system.

Pupil's Book Activity 1: Share knowledge

Read and discuss.

- Read the first question and discuss the photos as a class.
- Ask the pupils to read out and explain the words in the word box. Discuss the importance of these conditions to life on Earth.
- Ask the final question. Make notes on the board as the pupils give their thoughts.

Pupil's Book Activity 2: Investigate

Listen and complete the notes about Earth and Mars on page 68 in your Activity Book.

- Explain to the pupils that they are going to hear about the differences between Earth and Mars.

Activity Book

Activity 1

Listen and complete the chart.

▶ *CD3 Track 10 p289*

- Read the information as a class. Explain to the pupils that they should write notes and not full sentences the first time they listen to the CD.
- Play the CD. The pupils listen and complete the chart.
- Play the CD a second time, pausing after each piece of key information. The pupils complete their notes, writing full sentences.
- Play the CD for a third time and stop after each answer.

Answers: **1** There isn't any oxygen on Mars. **2** There is plenty of water on Earth. **3** There are plants and animals on Earth so there is food. **4** There is no oil or gas. There could be solar, wind and nuclear power. **5** There is no protection from ultraviolet rays.

Pupil's Book Activity 3: Investigate

Think about why we can't live on Mars. Find out about possible solutions. Work in pairs or groups. Make notes on page 68 in your Activity Book.

- Read the instructions. Organise the pupils into groups of three.
- Invite three pupils to read out the speech bubbles. Then read the cooperative learning note. Then ask the pupils to open their Activity Books on page 68. The pupils discuss and decide on their tasks. Each pupil in the group focuses on a different problem.

Activity Book

Activity 2

Work in groups. Make notes.

- Explain the three problems. Ask the pupils to investigate possible solutions to these problems. Make it clear that the pupils should make notes and not write full sentences.
- If the pupils have access to the Internet, they can research the information online. Alternatively, they can use reference books.

Ending the lesson

Review the lesson and reflect on learning.

- Say **Today we've learnt about conditions for living on Earth and on Mars.**
- Ask **What do you remember?** The pupils do a three-minute review in pairs. (Cooperative Learning Strategies, page 19)

Extension activity

- In their groups, the pupils use the Internet to find out more information about living in space. This could be on the Moon or in a spacecraft orbiting the Earth. Ask them to find four interesting facts to tell the class.

Link to Science

- If you are studying the Science topic of the solar system, review the different planets in the solar system. Ask the pupils to list some characteristics of the different planets. Then, review what allows us to live on planet Earth and ask the pupils to compare these conditions with those of other planets.

Project 2: Living on Mars

Key Competences and Key Learning Outcomes

- Present your ideas to the class
- Think about designing a house to live in on Mars
- Reflect on what you have learnt and how you have worked together
- Work in a group to plan a presentation

Key language

- *be made of, breathe, cooker, curved, dangerous, electricity, generator, grow food, (to) heat, lights, plastic, protect, spacesuit, ultraviolet rays*
- *What would the house look like? What would the house be made of?*

Materials

- Pupil's Book p71; Activity Book p68; Teacher's App on Navio
- Computer with digital presentation facilities; Poster-making materials (pens, card, etc.)

At a Glance Lesson Plan

Pupil's Book

Starting the lesson

- Set learning outcomes.

Activity 1: Plan and create your project

- Your group is going to design a home on Mars.
- Discuss the questions.
- Write the information on page 69 in your Activity Book.

Go to the Activity Book.

Activity 2

- Prepare a presentation of your design.

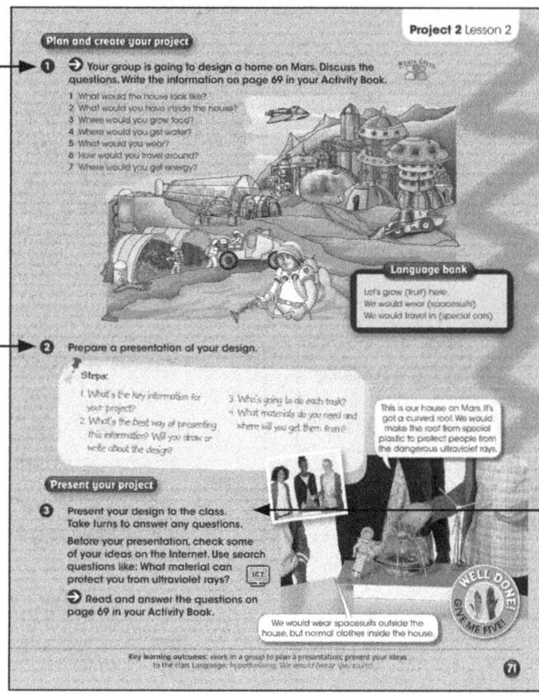
Project 2 Lesson 2

Plan and create your project

1 Your group is going to design a home on Mars. Discuss the questions. Write the information on page 69 in your Activity Book.

1 What would the house look like?
2 What would you have inside the house?
3 Where would you grow food?
4 Where would you get water?
5 What would you wear?
6 How would you travel around?
7 Where would you get energy?

Language bank
Let's grow (fruit) here.
We would wear (spacesuits).
We would travel in (special cars).

2 Prepare a presentation of your design.

Steps:
1 What's the key information for your project?
2 What's the best way of presenting this information? Will you draw or write about the design?
3 Who's going to do each task?
4 What materials do you need and where will you get them from?

This is our house on Mars. It's got a curved roof. We would make the roof from special plastic to protect people from the dangerous ultraviolet rays.

Present your project

3 Present your design to the class. Take turns to answer any questions. Before your presentation, check some of your ideas on the Internet. Use search questions like: What material can protect you from ultraviolet rays?
Read and answer the questions on page 69 in your Activity Book.

We would wear spacesuits outside the house, but normal clothes inside the house.

WELL DONE! GIVE ME FIVE!

71

Activity 3: Present your project

- Present your design to the class.
- Take turns to answer any questions.
- Before your presentation, check some of your ideas on the Internet.
- Use search questions like: What material can protect you from ultraviolet rays?
- Read and answer the questions on page 69 in your Activity Book.

Go to the Activity Book.

Ending the lesson

- Review the lesson and reflect on learning.

Reinforcement activity

- Make a class display of your work.

Activity Book

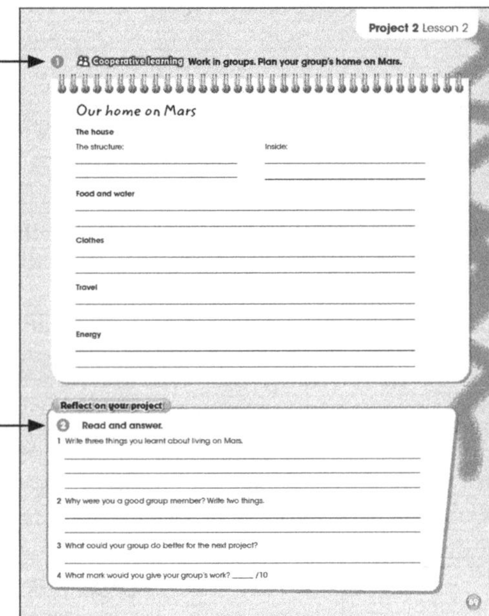
Project 2 Lesson 2

1 Cooperative learning Work in groups. Plan your group's home on Mars.

Our home on Mars

The house
The structure: Inside:
Food and water
Clothes
Travel
Energy

Reflect on your project

2 Read and answer.
1 Write three things you learnt about living on Mars.
2 Why were you a good group member? Write two things.
3 What could your group do better for the next project?
4 What mark would you give your group's work? ___ /10

Activity Book

Activity 1

- Work in groups. Plan your group's home on Mars.

Activity 2

- Read and answer.

Digital resources

Teacher's Digital: You can also teach this lesson using the Teacher's App on Navio.

Pupil's Digital: Encourage your pupils to use the Pupil's App on Navio to practise the activities from this lesson.

Powered By NAVIO

Starting the lesson

Set learning outcomes.

- Say **Today we're going to continue the project.** Prompt the pupils to tell you what they did in the last lesson.
- Highlight that the pupils will be working in small groups again. Prompt the pupils to tell you what they must do when they work in groups: listen, take turns, respect different opinions, etc.

Pupil's Book Activity 1: Plan and create your project

Your group is going to design a home on Mars. Discuss the questions. Write the information on page 69 in your Activity Book.

- Focus the class on the picture. Ask the pupils to describe what they see. Ask **Do you think this is realistic?** Invite the pupils to read out the questions. Ask them to suggest some possible answers for each question using the picture as a prompt.
- Explain that the pupils are going to work in their groups to agree the answers to the questions. This will help them design a place to live in on Mars.
- Focus the pupils on the Language bank. Encourage them to use these sentences to make suggestions to their group.

Activity Book

Activity 1

Work in groups. Plan your group's home on Mars.

- Explain to the pupils that while they are planning their home on Mars, they should make notes. Ask a pupil to read out the sections.
- Ask the groups to complete the task. Go round the groups giving them more ideas and helping them make decisions about their design.

Pupil's Book Activity 2

Prepare a presentation of your design.

- Read out the steps of the presentation plan as a class. Check understanding. Give and elicit examples for each task.
- The groups discuss their presentations and make notes of their decisions. Go round and answer questions. They then prepare the presentation. They can do this as a poster or as a digital presentation, or even present it in a different way if they wish.

Pupil's Book Activity 3: Present your project

Present your design to the class. Take turns to answer any questions. Before your presentation, check some of your ideas on the Internet. Use search questions like: What material can protect you from ultraviolet rays? Read and answer the questions on page 69 in your Activity Book.

- Focus the class on the photo. Encourage the pupils to talk about what they can see. Then ask a pupil to read out the speech bubbles. Ask **What's this group's design like? Do you like it? Is it a successful design?**
- Invite different groups in turn to present their design to the rest of the class. Ensure that each pupil in the group participates in the presentation, but accept that some pupils may contribute more than others. At the end of each presentation, ask the group a question and encourage the rest of the class to think of questions they would like to ask. The group giving the presentation should answer the questions.
- At the end of the activity, you could discuss whether any of the proposals could work together. Ask the pupils what they would change in their own design now that they have looked at other pupils' ideas.

Activity Book

Activity 2

Read and answer.

- The pupils answer the questions on their own or in pairs.

Ending the lesson

Review the lesson and reflect on learning.

- Say **We've done a project about designing a home to live in on Mars.**
- Ask **What do you remember?** The pupils do a three-minute review in pairs. (Cooperative Learning Strategies, page 19)

Reinforcement activity

- Make a display of the pupils' work so that other classes can enjoy and learn from the work. You can use the presentations as they are or you can ask pupils to rework some of their material as a poster. Digital presentations can also be uploaded onto the class or school web page.

Date: ____________ Unit: ____________

1 What did my pupils learn in this unit?

2 How did my pupils work? (✓)

individually ☐ in pairs ☐ in small groups ☐

in large groups ☐ as a class ☐

3 Which key competences did my pupils develop? Give a score from 1 to 5 (5 being the highest).

Competence in linguistic communication ☐

Competence in mathematics, science and technology ☐

Digital competence ☐

Learning to learn ☐

Social and civic competences ☐

Sense of initiative and entrepreneurship ☐

Cultural awareness and expression ☐

4 Which lessons / activities were the most successful and why?

5 Which lessons / activities did my pupils find the most difficult and why?

6 What did I try in the classroom for the first time? How did it go?

7 Which resources did I find most useful? (including webpages)

8 What could I do differently next time I teach this unit?

Unit 7

Buying and selling

Unit overview

Key competences and learning outcomes

- Name words related to money and shopping (Lesson 1)
- Learn and practise how to use comparative forms (Lesson 2)
- Learn and practise how to use the first conditional (Lesson 4)
- Talk about damaged objects (Lesson 5)
- Use alliteration and rhyme to write slogans (Lesson 7)
- Watch and understand a video (Video and 21st Century Skills)

- Compare prices (Lessons 2 and 4)

- Use the Pupil's App on Navio
- Investigate the USA (Lesson 3)

- Practise connected speech: linking words (Lesson 4)
- Learn about adjectives with different endings: *-y*, *-ous*, *-ful* (Lesson 5)
- Identify parts of an advert (Lesson 7)
- Review learning and reflect on progress in the unit (Lesson 8)
- Practise activity types found in the Cambridge Exams: B1 Preliminary for Schools

- Learn about the importance of taking initiative (Lesson 3)
- Practise giving interesting answers in a conversation (Lesson 8)

- Work in pairs or small groups to practise and reinforce learning (All lessons)
- Do a communication task (Lesson 5)
- Think about buying and selling (Video and 21st Century Skills)

- Read a text (Lesson 3)
- Learn about the USA (Lesson 3)
- Read and write an advert (Lessons 6 and 7)
- Sing a song (Lesson 8)

Vocabulary

Core vocabulary
bank notes, cashier, coins, credit card, customer, moneybox, price tag, purse, receipt, save money, spend money, till; bent, cracked, faulty, loose, ripped, scratched, stained

Extension vocabulary (optional)
cents, euros, pence, pounds, yen, yuan; dented, crumpled, shrunken, stretched

Other vocabulary
bargain, business, craftspeople, salesperson, slogan, trade, quote; advertise, compare, complain, encourage, give advice / instructions, raise interest, (to) trade; dime, nickel, quarter; disappointed, fair, superstitious; fibreglass, plastic, polyester; waveboard; alliteration, rhyme, coast, continent, long way away, transport

Recycled vocabulary
big, expensive, old, remote-controlled, tall; boat, cotton, dollar, good / bad luck, kite, online, pocket money; receive

Structures

Core structures
I'm too old to play with teddies now. He isn't old enough to buy a mobile phone. My sister is (not) as tall as her friends. If we buy Fairtrade products, it'll help the workers in poor countries. If I finish my homework early, I'll play games on the computer. If it doesn't rain, we'll play tennis. If you don't buy a ticket, you won't win a prize. What will you do if you miss the bus this afternoon?

Other structures
Can I see your receipt? Would you like your money back?

Recycled structures
Buy one now before we run out! They help them organise their production. How much pocket money does Bella receive? What would you sell at the sale? How much would you sell it for?

Pronunciation

Features of connected speech: linking words

Literacy

Text type: an advert (text to persuade; writing preparation)
Reading skills: skimming text to ascertain meaning
Writing skills: using alliteration and rhyme in slogans

Culture ... around the world

How fair trade started in the USA

21st Century Skills

Living in the world: initiative and entrepreneurial skills

Thinking skills

Defining and describing (Lesson 1); Analysing and applying rules and patterns (Lessons 2 and 4); Giving an opinion on a text (Lesson 3); Organising the ideas in an advert (Lesson 7); Planning, checking and correcting (Lesson 7); Evaluating (Lesson 8)

Cooperative learning

Working together (Lessons 1–8); Reflecting and setting goals (Lessons 1–8); Collaborative speaking (Lesson 5); Collaborative writing (Lesson 7); Peer evaluation and feedback (Lesson 7); Helping and encouraging (Lessons 1–8); Expressing and respecting opinions (Lessons 1, 3, 6 and 8)

Values

The importance of taking initiative

Cross-curricular links

Links to Science
The Eurozone

Suggested Arts and Crafts concepts
Depth in landscapes

Key Competences and Key Learning Outcomes

- Name words related to money and shopping
- Practise using 'would' for imaginary situations
- Read and understand an instruction text
- Learn about saving money and the environment
- Learn about money in the USA

Key language

- *bank notes, cashier, coins, credit card, customer, moneybox, price tag, purse, receipt, save money, spend money, till*
- Extension: *cents, euros, pence, pounds, yen, yuan*
- *What would you sell at the sale? How much would you sell it for?*

Materials

- Pupil's Book pp72–73; Activity Book p70; Class CD3; Teacher's App on Navio
- Money and shopping flashcards

Optional materials

- Teacher's Resource Bank: Trinity Exams Practice cards (from the Starter Unit and Units 1, 2, 3, 4, 5 and 6)

At a Glance Lesson Plan

Pupil's Book

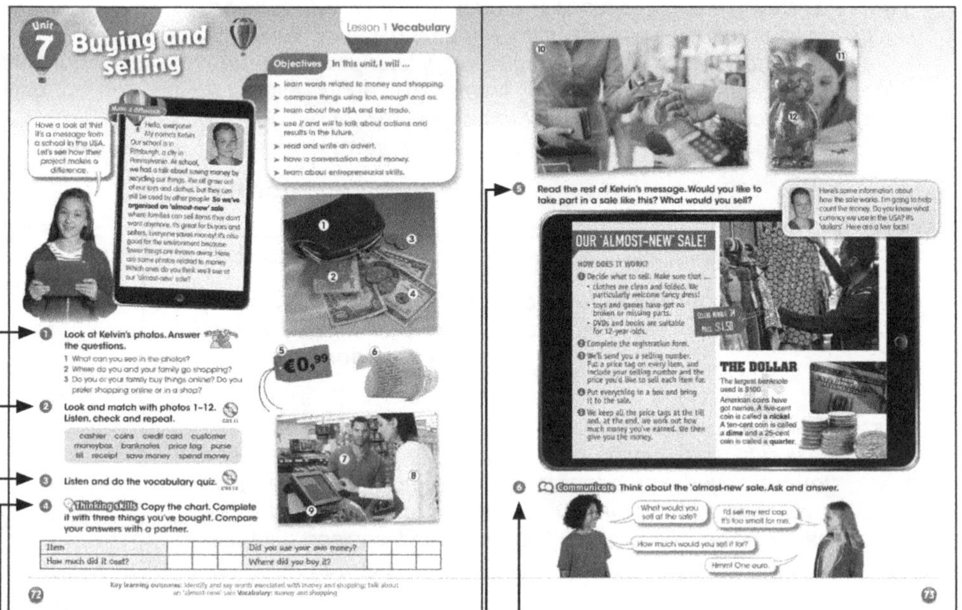

Starting the lesson

- Use the Trinity Exams Practice cards (optional).
- Review different places where you use money.
- Set learning outcomes.

Activity 1

- Look at Kelvin's photos.
- Answer the questions.

Vocabulary presentation

- Present the new vocabulary using the money and shopping flashcards.

Activity 2

- Look and match with photos 1–12.
- Listen, check and repeat.

▶ *CD3 Track 11 p289*

Activity 3

- Listen and do the vocabulary quiz.

▶ *CD3 Track 12 p289*

Activity 4

- Copy the chart.
- Complete it with three things you've bought.
- Compare your answers with a partner.

Activity 5

- Read the rest of Kelvin's message.
- Would you like to take part in a sale like this?
- What would you sell?

Activity 6

- Think about the 'almost-new' sale.
- Ask and answer.

Go to the Activity Book.

Ending the lesson

- Review the lesson and reflect on learning.

Extra activities

Extension

- Find out about the USA.

Vocabulary extension

- Present six additional vocabulary items.

Activity Book

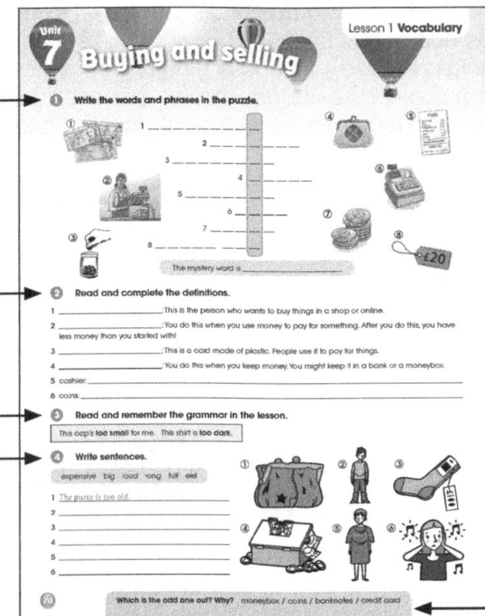

Activity Book

Activity 1

- Write the words and phrases in the puzzle.

Activity 2

- Read and complete the definitions.

Activity 3

- Read and remember the grammar in the lesson.

Activity 4

- Write sentences.

Odd one out activity

Digital resources

Teacher's Digital: You can also teach this lesson using the Teacher's App on Navio.

Pupil's Digital: Encourage your pupils to use the Pupil's App on Navio to practise the activities from this lesson.

Powered By NAVIO

Starting the lesson

Use the Trinity Exams Practice cards (optional).

- The pupils practise asking and answering questions.

Review different places where you use money.

- Ask **Where can you use money?** Elicit shops or places of entertainment, e.g. cinema, theatre, etc.

Set learning outcomes.

- Say **Today we're going to learn words related to money and shopping.**

Pupil's Book Activity 1

Look at Kelvin's photos. Answer the questions.

- Invite a pupil to read out the speech bubble to find out which school has sent a message. Ask **Do you know where Pennsylvania / the USA is?**
- Invite a pupil to read out the message from Kelvin. Check understanding.
- Work as a class to answer the questions.

Vocabulary presentation

- Present the new vocabulary using the money and shopping flashcards. Hold up the first flashcard and elicit / say the word or phrase. Write *people, objects, verbs* on the board. Ask which column each flashcard goes in. Stick the flashcards on the board.

Pupil's Book Activity 2

Look and match with photos 1–12. Listen, check and repeat.

▶ *CD3 Track 11 p289*

- Ask the pupils to look at number 1 in the photo. Ask **What's this?** In pairs, the pupils match 2–12 with the words.
- Play the CD. The pupils listen and check.
- Play the CD again, pausing after each word for the pupils to repeat. You can find the answers for this activity in the audioscript on page 289.

Pupil's Book Activity 3

Listen and do the vocabulary quiz.

▶ *CD3 Track 12 p289*

- Play the CD. Listen to the first definition, pausing at the beep to allow the pupils to name the item. Play the CD to listen to the answer.
- Repeat the procedure with the other definitions. You can find the answers for this activity in the audioscript on page 289.

Pupil's Book Activity 4

Copy the chart. Complete it with three things you've bought. Compare your answers with a partner.

- The pupils think of three things and complete the chart.

Pupil's Book Activity 5

Read the rest of Kelvin's message. Would you like to take part in a sale like this? What would you sell?

- The pupils read the information about how the sale works. The pupils decide if they would like to take part and what they would sell. They then share ideas with the class.
- Read out the text about the dollar. Ask **Have you ever seen any of these coins?**

Pupil's Book Activity 6

Think about the 'almost-new' sale. Ask and answer.

- Invite two pupils to read out the speech bubbles.
- In pairs, the pupils ask and answer questions.

Activity Book

Activity 1

Write the words and phrases in the puzzle.

- The pupils write the words and find the mystery word.

Answers: **1** bank notes **2** cashier **3** moneybox **4** purse **5** receipt **6** till **7** coins **8** price tag Mystery word: shopping

Activity 2

Read and complete the definitions.

- The pupils complete the definitions.

Answers: **1** customer **2** spend money **3** credit card **4** save money **5 & 6** Pupils' own answers

Activity 3

Read and remember the grammar in the lesson.

- Invite a pupil to read out the information. Ask **What kind of word comes after 'too'?** (*Adjective.*)

Activity 4

Write sentences.

- Ask a pupil to read out the first sentence.
- The pupils write the remaining sentences.

Answers: **1** The purse is too old. **2** The trousers are too long. **3** The socks are too expensive. **4** The moneybox is too full. **5** The T-shirt is too big. **6** The music is too loud.

Odd one out activity

Which is the odd one out? Why?

- The pupils write the odd one out activity

Answers: moneybox (You can't shop with it.)

Ending the lesson

Review the lesson and reflect on learning.

- Say **Today we've learnt words related to money and shopping.**
- Ask **What do you remember?** The pupils do a three-minute review in pairs. (Cooperative Learning Strategies, page 19)

Extra activities

Extension

- The pupils find three interesting things about the USA to present to the class.

Vocabulary extension

- Introduce six words related to the topic of money and shopping: *cents, euros, pence, pounds, yen, yuan*.
- Use the Vocabulary Booster on NAVIO to practise these new words.

Key Competences and Key Learning Outcomes

- Listen to and read a dialogue
- Learn and practise how to use comparative forms
- Learn about comparing prices
- Identify examples of comparative forms in a dialogue

Key language

- *big, expensive, old, tall*
- *I'm too old to play with teddies now. He is / isn't old enough to buy a mobile phone. My sister is (not) as tall as her friends.*

Materials

- Pupil's Book p74; Activity Book 71; Class CD3; Teacher's App on Navio
- Teacher's Resource Bank: Money and shopping word cards

Optional materials

- Teacher's Resource Bank: Trinity Exams Practice cards (from the Starter Unit and Units 1, 2, 3, 4, 5 and 6)

At a Glance Lesson Plan

Pupil's Book

Starting the lesson

- Use the Trinity Exams Practice cards (optional).
- Review money and shopping vocabulary.
- Set learning outcomes.

Activity 1

- Describe the photo.
- Why do you think Kelvin has included it?
- Read and listen to find out.

▶ *CD3 Track 13 p290*

Activity 2

- Read and say *true* or *false*.
- Correct the false sentences.

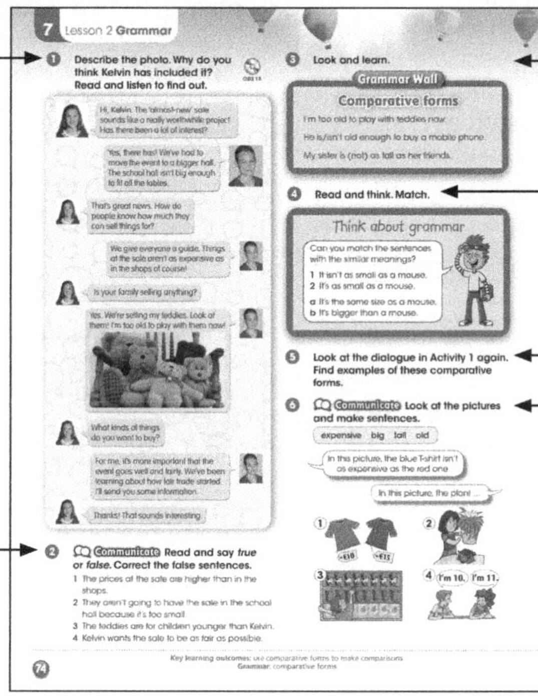

Activity 3

- Look and learn – Grammar wall

Activity 4

- Read and think.
- Match.

Activity 5

- Look at the dialogue in Activity 1 again.
- Find examples of these comparative forms.

Activity 6

- Look at the pictures and make sentences.
- Go to the Activity Book.

Ending the lesson

- Review the lesson and reflect on learning.

Extra activity

Reinforcement

- Compare objects.

Activity Book

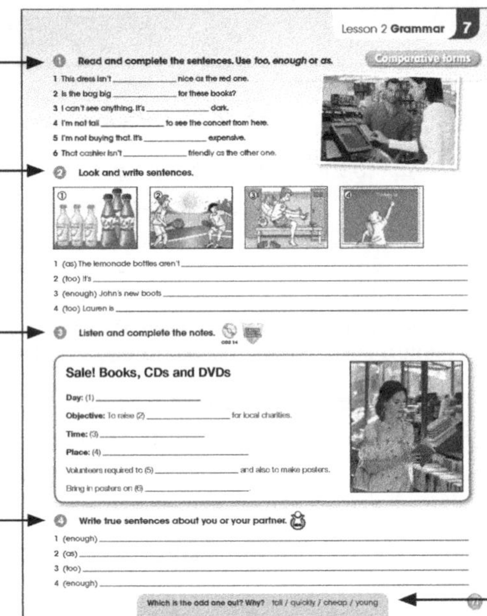

Activity Book

Activity 1

- Read and complete the sentences. Use *too*, *enough* or *as*.

Activity 2

- Look and write sentences.

Activity 3

- Listen and complete the notes.

▶ *CD3 Track 14 p290*

Activity 4

- Write true sentences about you or your partner.

Odd one out activity

Digital resources

Teacher's Digital: You can also teach this lesson using the Teacher's App on Navio.

Pupil's Digital: Encourage your pupils to use the Pupil's App on Navio to practise the activities from this lesson.

Powered By NAVIO

Starting the lesson

Use the Trinity Exams Practice cards (optional).

- The pupils practise asking and answering questions.

Review money and shopping vocabulary.

- Give each group of four a money and shopping word card. The pupils write a definition for that word or phrase.
- Groups read out the definitions for the class to guess. They win an extra point for spelling the word or phrase correctly.

Set learning outcomes.

- Say **Today we're going to learn some ways of comparing things using 'too', 'enough' and 'as'.**

Pupil's Book Activity 1

Describe the photo. Why do you think Kelvin has included it? Read and listen to find out.

▶ *CD3 Track 13 p290*

- Ask the pupils to describe the photo.
- Play the CD. The pupils listen and read the dialogue. Confirm that Kelvin included this photo because he is selling the teddies at the sale.

Pupil's Book Activity 2

Read and say *true* or *false*. Correct the false sentences.

- Read the dialogue and the sentences as a class. The pupils decide if the sentences are true or false. They correct the false sentences.
- Check answers as a class. Ask the pupils which sentences gave them the answers. These sentences focus on the new grammar so don't expect all the pupils to identify them.

Answers: **1** False. The prices at the sale are lower than in the shops. **2** True **3** True **4** True

Pupil's Book Activity 3

Look and learn – Grammar wall

- Read the information on the Grammar wall as a class.
- Ask questions to encourage the pupils to think about the meaning of the sentences.
- Then ask about the form. Ask **Which word comes after the adjective, 'too' or 'enough'?**

Pupil's Book Activity 4

Read and think. Match.

- Focus the pupils' attention on the Think about grammar box. Read out the sentences as a class. In pairs, the pupils match the sentences.
- Check answers as a class.

Answers: **1** b **2** a

Pupil's Book Activity 5

Look at the dialogue in Activity 1 again. Find examples of these comparative forms.

- In pairs, the pupils find examples of the comparative forms in the dialogue. Check answers as a class.

Pupil's Book Activity 6

Look at the pictures and make sentences.

- Ask two pupils to read out the speech bubbles.
- In pairs, the pupils take turns describing a picture with a comparative form. Their partner points to the correct picture.

Activity Book

Activity 1

Read and complete the sentences. Use *too*, *enough* or *as*.

- The pupils complete the sentences.

Answers: **1** as **2** enough **3** too **4** enough **5** too **6** as

Activity 2

Look and write sentences.

- The pupils look at the pictures and write sentences with the words in brackets.
- Check answers as a class.

Answers: **1** as big as the cola bottles. **2** too hot to play tennis. **3** aren't big enough (for him). **4** too short to write on the board.

Activity 3

Listen and complete the notes.

▶ *CD3 Track 14 p290*

- Ask the class to quickly read the notes. They think about the kind of words that would go in the gaps. Then play the CD. The pupils listen.
- Play the CD again. The pupils complete the notes.

Answers: **1** Friday **2** money **3** 3.45 **4** school hall **5** set up **6** Wednesday

Activity 4

Write true sentences about you or your partner.

- In pairs, the pupils write sentences using the words in brackets.
- Ask some pupils to read their sentences to the class.

Odd one out activity

Which is the odd one out? Why?

- The pupils complete the odd one out activity.

Answers: quickly (It's an adverb not an adjective.)

Ending the lesson

Review the lesson and reflect on learning.

- Say **Today we've learnt how to use some comparative forms.** Elicit one or two examples.
- Ask **What do you remember?** The pupils do a three-minute review in pairs. (Cooperative Learning Strategies, page 19)

Extra activity

Reinforcement

- In pairs, the pupils write sentences comparing their school objects.

Key Competences and Key Learning Outcomes

- Read a text with confidence and fluency
- Use the Internet to investigate the USA
- Learn about starting a business and looking for business opportunities
- Learn about trading fairly with others
- Learn about the importance of taking initiative
- Learn about the USA

Key language

- *business, craftspeople, fair, salesperson, trade*
- *They help them organise their production.*

Materials

- Pupil's Book p75; Activity Book p72; Class CD3; Teacher's App on Navio

Optional materials

- Teacher's Resource Bank: Trinity Exams Practice cards (from the Starter Unit and Units 1, 2, 3, 4, 5 and 6)

At a Glance Lesson Plan

Pupil's Book

Starting the lesson

- Use the Trinity Exams Practice cards (optional).
- Review words related to money.
- Set learning outcomes.

Activity 1: Before you read

- Read and discuss.

Activity 2

- Listen and read.

▶ *CD3 Track 15 p290*

Go to the Activity Book.

***Give Me Five!* values**

- Read and discuss.

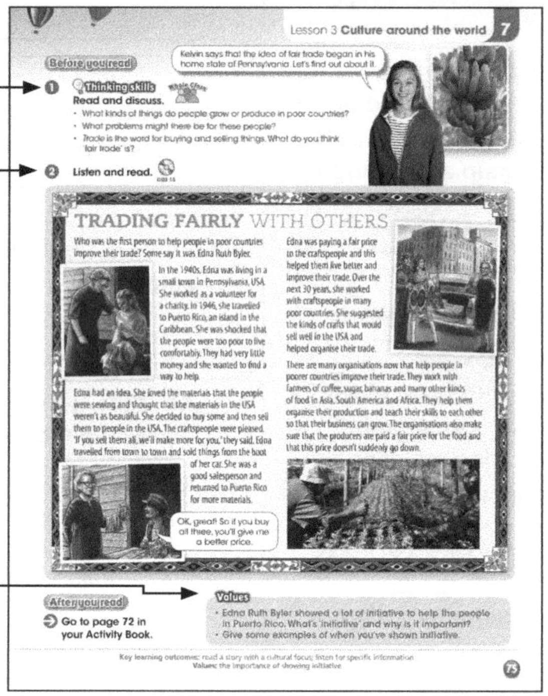

Ending the lesson

- Review the lesson and reflect on learning.

Extra activity

Extension

- Find out more about fair trade.

Activity Book

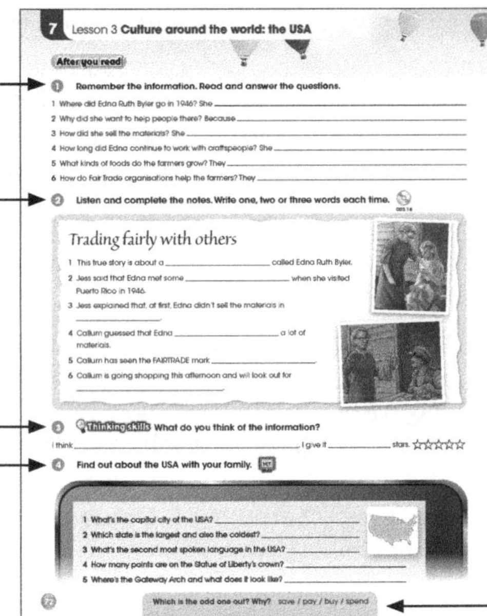

Activity Book: After you read

Activity 1

- Remember the information. Read and answer the questions.

Activity 2

- Listen and complete the notes. Write one, two or three words each time.

▶ *CD3 Track 16 p290*

Activity 3

- What do you think of the information?

Activity 4

- Find out about the USA with your family.

Odd one out activity

Digital resources

Teacher's Digital: You can also teach this lesson using the Teacher's App on Navio.

Pupil's Digital: Encourage your pupils to use the Pupil's App on Navio to practise the activities from this lesson.

Powered By NAVIO

Starting the lesson

Use the Trinity Exams Practice cards (optional).

- The pupils practise asking and answering questions.

Review words related to money.

- On the board, write *buy, sell, spend, save*. In pairs, the pupils discuss the meaning of the words and the differences between them. (*People spend or save money and they buy or sell things.*) Then explain the phrase 'to trade with someone'. (*To buy and sell things with someone.*)

Set learning outcomes.

- Say **Today we're going to read about a woman in the USA who helped people in Puerto Rico.**

Pupil's Book Activity 1: Before you read

Read and discuss.

- Read the questions as a class. Invite the pupils to share their knowledge of the kind of things that people produce in poorer countries. Then encourage them to explain what fair trade might be.

Pupil's Book Activity 2

Listen and read.

▶ *CD3 Track 15 p290*

- Play the CD. The pupils follow in their books.
- Ask questions to check understanding.

Suggested comprehension questions:

- Paragraph 1: **Are we sure that Edna Ruth Byler was the first person to help people in poor countries improve their trade?** (*No.*)
- Paragraph 2: **What was Edna's job?** (*A volunteer for a charity.*) **Why was she shocked when she went to Puerto Rico?** (*Because people had very little money.*)
- Paragraph 3: **What did Edna like in Puerto Rico?** (*The materials that people were sewing.*) **Was she good at selling things?** (*Yes, she was.*)
- Paragraph 4: **For how long did Edna help the craftspeople in Puerto Rico?** (*For 30 years.*)
- Paragraph 5: **What do fair trade organisations do?** (*They help farmers organise their production and they also teach them new skills.*)

Activity Book: After you read

Activity 1

Remember the information. Read and answer the questions.

- Read out the first question. Invite a pupil to answer it. The pupils read and answer the remaining questions.

Answers: **1** went to Puerto Rico. **2** they had very little money. **3** drove from town to town with the materials in the boot of her car. **4** worked with them for 30 years. **5** grow coffee, sugar, bananas and many kinds of food. **6** help them organise their production, teach skills and make sure the producers are paid a fair price.

Activity 2

Listen and complete the notes. Write one, two or three words each time.

▶ *CD3 Track 16 p290*

- Read out the notes as a class. Ask the pupils to guess the missing words. Play the CD. The pupils listen and complete as much information as possible.
- Play the CD again, pausing after each piece of key information to check the answer.

Answers: **1** volunteer **2** craftspeople **3** a shop **4** sold **5** in the supermarket **6** fair trade products

Activity 3

What do you think of the information?

- The pupils write their opinion and give a rating.
- Invite different pupils to share their opinions.

Activity 4

Find out about the USA with your family. ICT

- Read out the questions about the USA. Ask **Where can you find out this information?** (*Internet, library, asking friends and family.*) The pupils complete the activity at home.
- If you prefer to do this activity in the class, connect to a children's website which has information about the USA, such as www.sciencekids.co.nz/sciencefacts/countries/unitedstates.html.
- Read out the questions. The pupils work as a class to find and write the answers.

Answers: **1** Washington DC **2** Alaska **3** Spanish **4** seven **5** St Louis, Missouri, it's an enormous curved arch

Odd one out activity

Which is the odd one out? Why?

- The pupils complete the odd one out activity.

Answers: save (The others result in having less money.)

Give Me Five! values

Read and discuss.

- Read out the question and discuss it as a class.
- Explain that taking initiative means thinking for oneself, realising what is important and then taking action. Many people don't do things until they are asked to.

Ending the lesson

Review the lesson and reflect on learning.

- Say **Today we've read about Edna Ruth Byler and fair trade.**
- Ask **What do you remember?** The pupils do a three-minute review in pairs. (Cooperative Learning Strategies, page 19)

Extra activity

Extension

- Ask the pupils to think about what else they would like to find out about fair trade. In pairs, the pupils write some questions, e.g. *What fair trade products can you buy?*
- The pupils share their questions with the class. Then compile the most popular questions on the board.
- In groups, the pupils research the answers. They then present the information to the class.

Key Competences and Key Learning Outcomes

- Act out a short dialogue in pairs
- Learn and practise how to use the first conditional
- Learn about comparing prices
- Practise connected speech: linking sounds
- Learn about superstitious beliefs

Key language

- *cotton, good / bad luck, superstitious, (to) trade*
- *If we buy Fairtrade products, it'll help the workers in poor countries. If I finish my homework early, I'll play games on the computer. If it doesn't rain, we'll play tennis. If you don't buy a ticket, you won't win a prize. What will you do if you miss the bus this afternoon?*

Materials

- Pupil's Book p76; Activity Book p73; Class CD3; Teacher's App on Navio

Optional materials

- Teacher's Resource Bank: Trinity Exams Practice cards (from the Starter Unit and Units 1, 2, 3, 4, 5 and 6)

At a Glance Lesson Plan

Pupil's Book

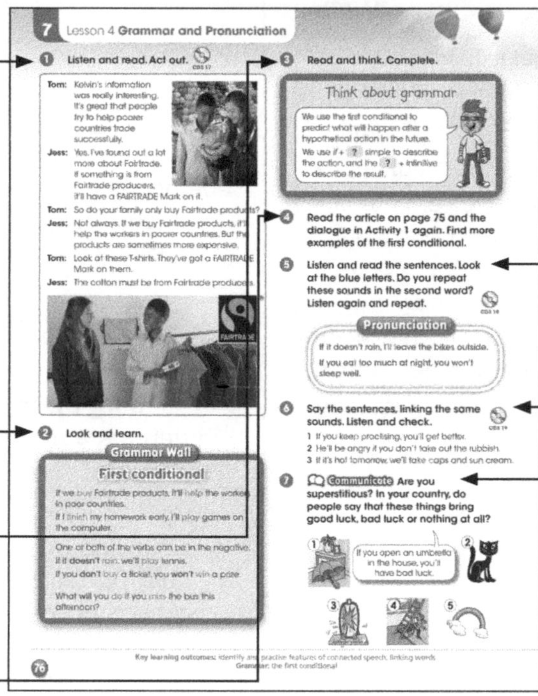

Starting the lesson

- Use the Trinity Exams Practice cards (optional).
- Review the information from Lesson 3.
- Set learning outcomes.

Activity 1

- Listen and read.
- ▶ *CD3 Track 17 p290*
- Act out.

Activity 2

- Look and learn – Grammar wall

Activity 3

- Read and think.
- Complete.

Activity 4

- Read the article on page 75 and the dialogue in Activity 1 again.
- Find more examples of the first conditional.

Activity 5

- Listen and read the sentences.
- ▶ *CD3 Track 18 p290*
- Look at the blue letters.
- Do you repeat these sounds in the second word?
- Listen again and repeat.

Activity 6

- Say the sentences, linking the same sounds.
- Listen and check.
- ▶ *CD3 Track 19 p290*

Activity 7

- Are you superstitious?
- In your country, do people say that these things bring good luck, bad luck or nothing at all?

Go to the Activity Book.

Ending the lesson

- Review the lesson and reflect on learning.

Extra activity

Reinforcement

- Write about superstitions.

Activity Book

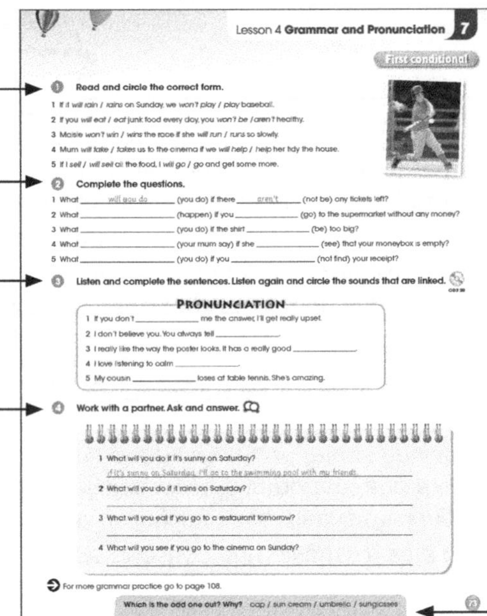

Activity Book

Activity 1

- Read and circle the correct form.

Activity 2

- Complete the questions.

Activity 3

- Listen and complete the sentences. Listen again and circle the sounds that are linked.

▶ *CD3 Track 20 p290*

Activity 4

- Work with a partner. Ask and answer.

Odd one out activity

Digital resources

Teacher's Digital: You can also teach this lesson using the Teacher's App on Navio.

Pupil's Digital: Encourage your pupils to use the Pupil's App on Navio to practise the activities from this lesson.

Powered By NAVIO

Starting the lesson

Use the Trinity Exams Practice cards (optional).
- The pupils practise asking and answering questions.

Review the article in Lesson 3.
- Say true/false sentences about the article in Lesson 3. The pupils guess the true sentences and correct the false ones.

Set learning outcomes.
- Say **Today we're going to learn to make predictions about what will happen after an action takes place. It's called the first conditional.**

Pupil's Book Activity 1

Listen and read. Act out.

▶ *CD3 Track 17 p290*
- The pupils look at the photo. Ask **What do you think Tom and Jess are talking about in photo (1)?**
- Play the CD. The pupils listen and read the dialogue. Check understanding.
- Play the CD again, pausing after each sentence for the pupils to repeat.
- The pupils practise the dialogue in pairs.
- **Note:** you can use the Dialogue Tool to present and practise this dialogue.

Pupil's Book Activity 2

Look and learn – Grammar wall
- Read the information on the Grammar wall as a class.
- The pupils look at the sentence halves. Ask **Are 'if' and 'will' in the same sentence half?** Explain that the verbs can be negative or affirmative.

Pupil's Book Activity 3

Read and think. Complete.
- Focus the pupils' attention on the Think about Grammar box. The pupils discuss and complete the sentence in pairs. Check answers as a class. (*present, future with will*)

Pupil's Book Activity 4

Read the article on page 75 and the dialogue in Activity 1 again. Find more examples of the first conditional.
- In pairs, the pupils find examples. Check answers as a class.

Pupil's Book Activity 5

Listen and read the sentences. Look at the blue letters. Do you repeat these sounds in the second word? Listen again and repeat.

▶ *CD3 Track 18 p290*
- Play the CD. The pupils listen and read the sentences. Explain that the sounds aren't repeated, but are linked.
- Play the CD again. The pupils listen and repeat.

Pupil's Book Activity 6

Say the sentences, linking the same sounds. Listen and check.

▶ *CD3 Track 19 p290*
- In pairs, the pupils practise reading the sentences, linking the same sounds. Ask some pupils to demonstrate.
- Play the CD. The pupils listen and check.

Pupil's Book Activity 7

Are you superstitious? In your country, do people say that these things bring good luck, bad luck or nothing at all?
- Ask the pupils to explain the word 'superstitious'.
- Invite a pupil to read the speech bubble. Ask the pupils if they agree. In pairs, the pupils make sentences with the first conditional.

Activity Book

Activity 1

Read and circle the correct form.
- Ask a pupil to read and complete the first sentence.
- The pupils complete the remaining sentences.

Answers: **1** rains, won't play **2** eat, won't be **3** won't win, runs **4** will take, help **5** sell, will go

Activity 2

Complete the questions.
- The pupils complete the questions.

Answers: **1** will you do, aren't **2** will happen, go **3** will you do, is **4** will your mum say, sees **5** will you do, don't find

Activity 3

Listen and complete the sentences. Listen again and circle the sounds that are linked.

▶ *CD3 Track 20 p290*
- Play the CD. The pupils complete the sentences. They then circle the linked sounds.
- Play the CD again. The pupils listen, check and repeat.

Answers: **1** tell, t'tell **2** lies, l'lies **3** design, d'design **4** music, m'music **5** never, n'never

Activity 4

Work with a partner. Ask and answer.
- In pairs, the pupils ask the questions. They write their partner's response.

Odd one out activity

Which is the odd one out? Why?
- The pupils complete the odd one out activity.

Answer: umbrella (The others are for sunny weather.)

Ending the lesson

Review the lesson and reflect on learning.
- Say **Today we've learnt to make predictions with the first conditional.**
- Ask **What do you remember?** The pupils do a three-minute review in pairs. (Cooperative Learning Strategies, page 19)

Extra activity

Reinforcement
- In groups, the pupils write some superstitions from their country using the first conditional.

Key Competences and Key Learning Outcomes

- Learn words related to damaged objects
- Learn to talk about taking damaged items back to shops
- Practise activity types found in the Cambridge Exams: B1 Preliminary for Schools
- Learn about adjectives with different endings: *-y, -ous, -ful*
- Do a communication task

Key language

- *bent, cracked, faulty, loose, ripped, scratched, stained*
- Extension: *crumpled, dented, shrunken, stretched*
- *Can I see your receipt? Would you like your money back?*

Materials

- Pupil's Book p77; Activity Book p74, Class CD3; Teacher's App on Navio

Optional materials

- Teacher's Resource Bank: Trinity Exams Practice cards (from the Starter Unit and Units 1, 2, 3, 4, 5 and 6)
- Damaged items or descriptions of damaged items

At a Glance Lesson Plan

Pupil's Book

Starting the lesson

- Use the Trinity Exams Practice cards (optional).
- Review first conditional sentences.
- Set learning outcomes.

Activity 1

- Look and match.
- Listen, check and repeat.

▶ *CD3 Track 21 p291*

Activity 2

- Listen and say *A*, *B* or *C*.

▶ *CD3 Track 22 p291*

Activity 3

- Listen to the conversation in the camping shop.

▶ *CD3 Track 23 p291*

- What happens in the end?

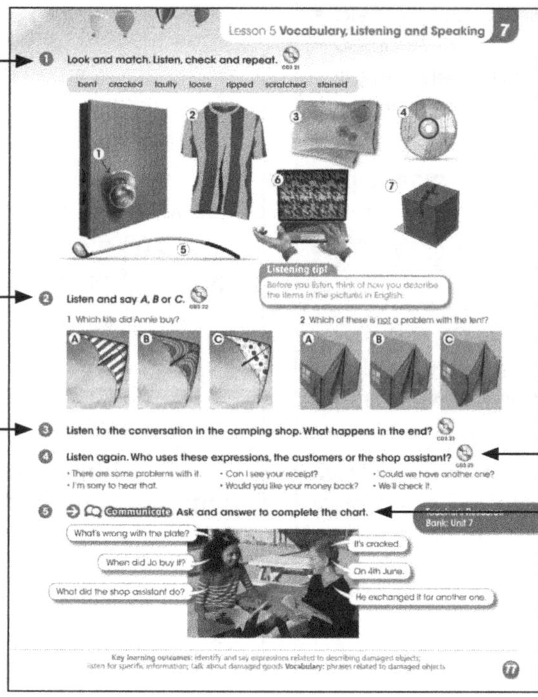

Activity 4

- Listen again.

▶ *CD3 Track 23 p291*

- Who uses these expressions, the customers or the shop assistant?

Activity 5

- Ask and answer to complete the chart (Teacher's Resource Bank: Unit 7).

Go to the Activity Book.

Ending the lesson

- Review the lesson and reflect on learning.

Extra activities

Reinforcement

- Role play a dialogue.

Vocabulary Extension

- Present four additional vocabulary items.

Activity Book

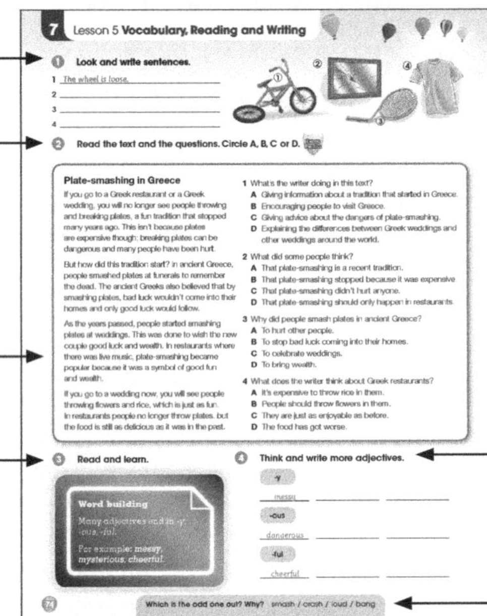

Activity Book

Activity 1

- Look and write sentences.

Activity 2

- Read the text and the questions. Circle A, B, C or D.

Activity 3

- Read and learn.

Activity 4

- Think and write more adjectives.

Odd one out activity

Digital resources

Teacher's Digital: You can also teach this lesson using the Teacher's App on Navio.

Pupil's Digital: Encourage your pupils to use the Pupil's App on Navio to practise the activities from this lesson.

Powered By NAVIO

Starting the lesson

Use the Trinity Exams Practice cards (optional).
- The pupils practise asking and answering questions.

Review first conditional sentences.
- On the board, write *If we go to the shopping centre / sports centre on Saturday…* In pairs, the pupils complete the sentences using the first conditional.

Set learning outcomes.
- Say **Today we're going to learn some words about how things can be damaged and what to say when we bring things back to the shops.**

Pupil's Book Activity 1

Look and match. Listen, check and repeat.
▶ *CD3 Track 21 p291*
- In pairs, ask the pupils to match the words they know with the pictures.
- Play the CD. The pupils listen and check.
- Play the CD again, pausing after each word for the pupils to repeat. You can find the answers for this activity in the audioscript on page 291.

Pupil's Book Activity 2

Listen and say *A*, *B* or *C*.
▶ *CD3 Track 22 p291*
- Invite a pupil to describe the first three pictures.
- Read the Listening tip as a class.
- Play the CD. The pupils listen and identify the correct picture. Repeat the procedure with the second set of pictures.

Answers: **1** C **2** A

Pupil's Book Activity 3

Listen to the conversation in the camping shop. What happens in the end?
▶ *CD3 Track 23 p291*
- Play the CD. The pupils decide what happened. (*They exchanged the tent.*)

Pupil's Book Activity 4

Listen again. Who uses these expressions, the customers or the shop assistant?
▶ *CD3 Track 23 p291*
- Read out the expressions. Check understanding.
- Play the CD. The pupils listen and make a note of who uses each expression.

Answers: Customer: There are some problems with it. Shop assistant: I'm sorry to hear that. Shop assistant: Can I see your receipt? Shop assistant: Would you like your money back? Customers: Could we have another one? Shop assistant: We'll check it.

Pupil's Book Activity 5

Ask and answer to complete the chart (Teacher's Resource Bank: Unit 7).
- Explain to the pupils that they are going to complete a chart in pairs. Each pupil has some information about something bought at a shop. The pupils ask questions to complete the information.
- Invite two pupils to read the speech bubbles. Explain that they will use these questions.
- Organise the class into pairs (A and B).
- Ask the pupils to do the activity in their pairs.

Activity Book

Activity 1
Look and write sentences.
- The pupils look at the pictures and write sentences.

Activity 2 Exams Practice
Read the text and the questions. Circle A, B, C or D.
- The pupils read the text and answer the questions. Check answers as a class.

Answers: **1** A **2** C **3** B **4** C

Activity 3
Read and learn.
- Read the information as a class.

Activity 4
Think and write more adjectives.
- The pupils write two more adjectives for each ending. They could also write sentences in their notebooks using the adjectives.
- Check answers as a class.

Odd one out activity
Which is the odd one out? Why?
- The pupils complete the odd one out activity.

Answers: loud (It isn't an onomatopoeic word.)

Ending the lesson

Review the lesson and reflect on learning.
- Say **Today we've learnt some words about how things can be damaged and what to say when we bring things back to the shops.**
- Ask **What do you remember?** The pupils do a three-minute review in pairs. (Cooperative Learning Strategies, page 19)

Extra activities

Reinforcement
- Give each group of three one of the damaged items that you have brought in or a description of a damaged item.
- The pupils prepare a dialogue between a shopkeeper and two customers.
- Invite groups to act out their dialogues for the class.

Vocabulary extension
- Practise and present additional words related to describing damaged objects: *crumpled, dented, shrunken, stretched.*
- Use the Vocabulary Booster on NAVIO.

Key Competences and Key Learning Outcomes

- Review the language of advertising
- Do pre-reading tasks to predict content and raise interest
- Skim a text for general understanding
- Learn about using language to persuade others
- Read an advert

Key language

- *boat, fibreglass, kite, plastic, polyester, remote-controlled, waveboard*
- *Buy one now before we run out!*

Materials

- Pupil's Book p78; Activity Book p75; Class CD3; Teacher's App on Navio

Optional materials

- Teacher's Resource Bank: Trinity Exams Practice cards (from the Starter Unit and Units 1, 2, 3, 4, 5 and 6)
- Adverts from English-language newspapers

At a Glance Lesson Plan

Pupil's Book

Starting the lesson

- Use the Trinity Exams Practice cards (optional).
- Review talking about damaged objects.
- Set learning outcomes.

Activity 1: Before you read

- Read and discuss.

Activity 2

- Look at the photos.
- Which would you most like to try?
- Read and see if you still feel the same way.

Activity 3: After you read

- What do you think?
- Go to the Activity Book.

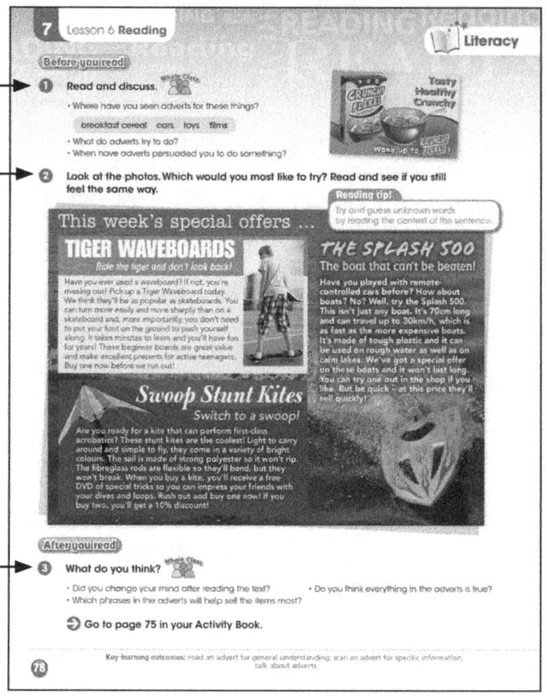

Ending the lesson

- Review the lesson and reflect on learning.

Extra activity

Extension

- Decide what makes a good advert.

Activity Book

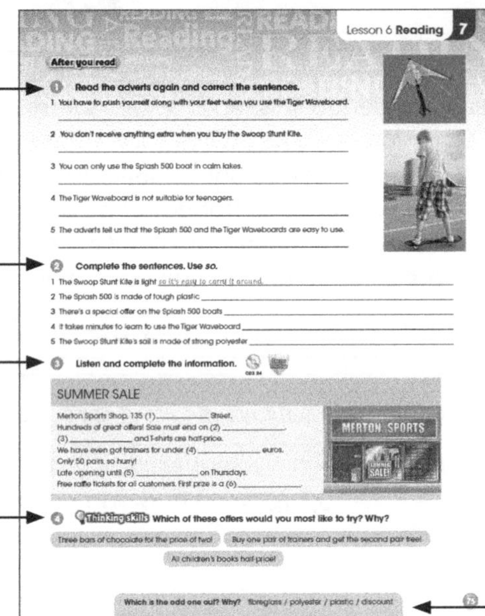

Activity Book: After you read

Activity 1

- Read the adverts again and correct the sentences.

Activity 2

- Complete the sentences. Use *so*.

Activity 3

- Listen and complete the information.

▶ *CD3 Track 24 p291*

Activity 4

- Which of these offers would you most like to try? Why?

Odd one out activity

Digital resources

Teacher's Digital: You can also teach this lesson using the Teacher's App on Navio.

Pupil's Digital: Encourage your pupils to use the Pupil's App on Navio to practise the activities from this lesson.

Powered By NAVIO

Starting the lesson

Use the Trinity Exams Practice cards (optional).

- The pupils practise asking and answering questions.

Review talking about damaged objects.

- Organise the pupils into seven groups. Give each group one of the adjectives from Lesson 5.
- Each group has to write ten objects that can be described with that adjective, e.g. *cracked mirror / plate / window*, etc.
- Invite groups to read out their lists. Other pupils can give their opinions and make corrections.

Set learning outcomes.

- Say **Today we're going to read some adverts.**

Pupil's Book Activity 1: Before you read

Read and discuss.

- Ask **What's an advert? Where do you see adverts?**
- Then read the questions as a class. Prompt the pupils to answer in as much detail as possible.

Pupil's Book Activity 2

Look at the photos. Which would you most like to try? Read and see if you still feel the same way.

- Ask the pupils to look at the three photos. In pairs, they decide which they would most like to try. As a class, decide which is the most popular item and which is the least popular.
- Read the text either as a class or individually. Check understanding. Ask the pupils to explain 'tough', 'calm', 'bright', 'rush' and 'run out'.

Pupil's Book Activity 3: After you read

What do you think?

- Read the first question as a class. Encourage the pupils to think about why they changed their minds, or why they didn't change their minds.
- In pairs, the pupils discuss the other two questions. Then share ideas as a class. Encourage the pupils to give their opinions.

Activity Book: After you read

Activity 1

Read the adverts again and correct the sentences.

- Read the sentences as a class. The pupils work on their own to look at the adverts and correct them.

Answers: **1** You don't have to push yourself along with your feet when you use the Tiger Waveboard. **2** You receive a free DVD when you buy the Swoop Stunt Kite. **3** You can use the Splash 500 boat in rough and calm lakes. **4** The Tiger Waveboard is suitable for teenagers. **5** The adverts tell us that the Swoop Stunt Kite and the Tiger Waveboards are easy to use.

Activity 2

Complete the sentences. Use *so*.

- The pupils work with a partner or on their own to complete the sentences. Remind the pupils that 'so' is a connective word that lets you put two sentences together to make one.

Answers: **2** … so it can be used on rough water. **3** … so they'll sell quickly. **4** … so you'll have fun for years. **5** … so it won't rip.

Activity 3

Listen and complete the information.

▸ *CD3 Track 24 p291*

- Look at the advert as a class. Ask **What kind of shop is it? What time of year is it?** (*A sports shop. It's summer.*)
- Explain that the pupils will hear a conversation about the sale. They need to complete the information.
- Play the CD. The pupils listen and complete.
- Play the CD again, pausing after each piece of information. The pupils correct and complete the information.

Answers: **1** Queen **2** Friday (evening) **3** Tracksuits **4** ten **5** 8.00 **6** tent

Activity 4

Which of these offers would you most like to try? Why?

- In pairs, the pupils decide which offer they would most like to try. They have to think of some reasons for their decisions.
- Ask the pupils to share their ideas with the class.

Odd one out activity

Which is the odd one out? Why?

- The pupils complete the odd one out activity.

Answers: discount (It isn't a material.)

Ending the lesson

Review the lesson and reflect on learning.

- Say **Today we've read three adverts.**
- Ask **What do you remember?** The pupils do a three-minute review in pairs. (Cooperative Learning Strategies, page 19)

Extra activity

Extension

- Hand out some of the adverts you have brought in. Then write these questions on the board *What is the advert for? Is it a good advert? Why / Why not?*
- In groups, the pupils answer the questions. Invite different groups to present their ideas to the class.

Key Competences and Key Learning Outcomes

- Use alliteration and rhyme to write slogans in advertising
- Identify the text features of an advert
- Use criteria to check your writing
- Learn about using language to persuade others
- Share and discuss your writing with a partner
- Write an advert

Key language

- *alliteration, bargain, encourage, quote, raise interest, rhyme, slogan*

Materials

- Pupil's Book p79; Activity Book p76; Teacher's App on Navio
- Teacher's Resource Bank: Talk Cards

Optional materials

- Teacher's Resource Bank: Trinity Exams Practice cards (from the Starter Unit and Units 1, 2, 3, 4, 5 and 6)

At a Glance Lesson Plan

Pupil's Book

Starting the lesson

- Use the Trinity Exams Practice cards (optional).
- Review the adverts from Lesson 6.
- Set learning outcomes.

Activity 1: Investigate a text

- Match the words and their definitions.

Activity 2

- Read the advert to check your answers.

Activity 3: Discuss a text

- Read the advert again. Answer the questions.

Writing skills

- Read about writing a slogan.

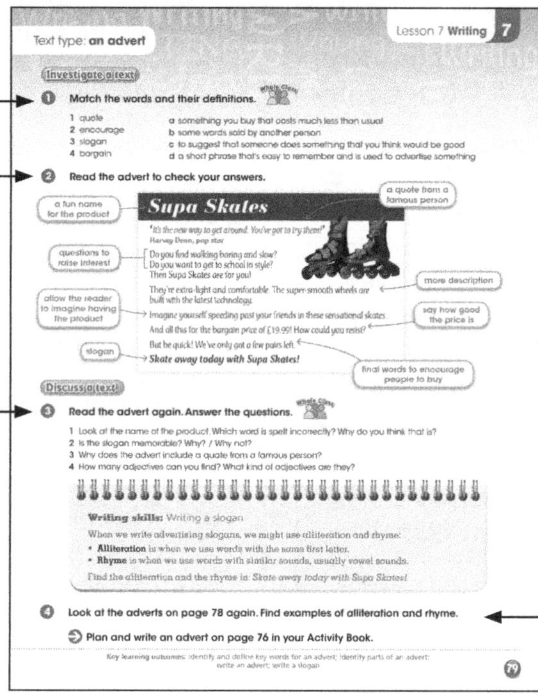

Activity 4

- Look at the adverts on page 78 again.
- Find examples of alliteration and rhyme.

Go to the Activity Book.

Ending the lesson

- Review the lesson and reflect on learning.

Extra activity

Reinforcement

- Do a slogan competition.

Activity Book

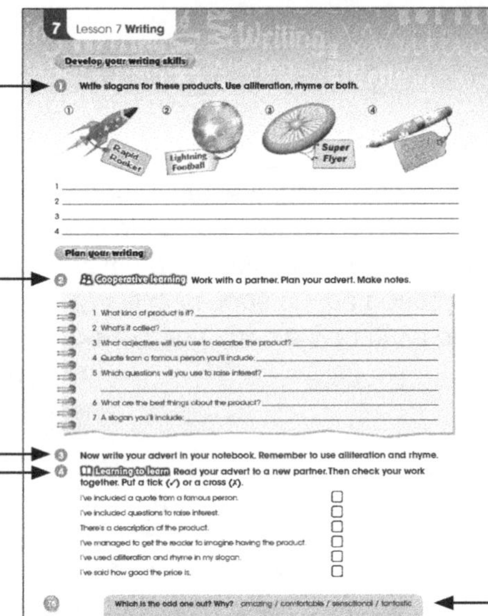

Activity Book

Activity 1: Develop your writing skills

- Write slogans for these products. Use alliteration, rhyme or both.

Activity 2: Plan your writing

- Work with a partner. Plan your advert. Make notes.

Activity 3

- Now write your advert in your notebook. Remember to use alliteration and rhyme.

Activity 4

- Read your advert to a new partner. Then check your work together. Put a tick (✓) or a cross (✗).

Odd one out activity

Digital resources

Teacher's Digital: You can also teach this lesson using the Teacher's App on Navio.

Pupil's Digital: Encourage your pupils to use the Pupil's App on Navio to practise the activities from this lesson.

Powered By NAVIO

Starting the lesson

Use the Trinity Exams Practice cards (optional).

- The pupils practise asking and answering questions.

Review the adverts from Lesson 6.

- Write on the board the three objects from the adverts on Pupil's Book page 82.
- Organise the pupils into three groups. Each group has a turn to say something that they remember about one of the objects from the advert.
- Continue until the pupils find it hard to remember more information.
- If the class remembers more about one object than another, ask **Why did we remember more about this object? Was that advert better?**

Set learning outcomes

- Say **Today we're going to read another advert and then write our own adverts.**

Pupil's Book Activity 1: Investigate a text

Match the words and their definitions.

- Read the words and the definitions as a class. On their own or in pairs, the pupils should match the words and definitions.

Pupil's Book Activity 2

Read the advert to check your answers.

- The pupils read the advert and check their answers.
- Check answers as a class.

Answers: **1** b **2** c **3** d **4** a

Pupil's Book Activity 3: Discuss a text

Read the advert again. Answer the questions.

- Read and answer the questions as a class. Confirm that 'super' is misspelt as 'supa' to make the object seem more fun and that the slogan is memorable because the words start with the same sound. Explain that a quote encourages the readers to believe the advert. Then ask the pupils to find the adjectives in the advert and confirm that some of them are extreme adjectives.

Writing skills

Read the information.

- Read about writing slogans. Use more examples to make it clear what alliteration and rhyme mean.

Pupil's Book Activity 4

Look at the adverts on page 78 again. Find examples of alliteration and rhyme.

- The pupils look at the adverts on page 82 and identify examples. (*Ride the tiger, Switch to a swoop, The boat that can't be beaten!*)

Activity Book

Activity 1: Develop your writing skills

Write slogans for these products. Use alliteration, rhyme or both.

- The pupils work on their own or in pairs to complete the slogans. Invite some pupils to read their slogans to the class.

Activity 2: Plan your writing

Work with a partner. Plan your advert. Make notes.

- Read out the questions as a class. Check understanding.
- In pairs, the pupils think of an idea for a product to advertise and answer the questions. If necessary, brainstorm some product ideas with the class first. Make sure the pupils are not all writing about the same product.

Activity 3

Now write your advert in your notebook. Remember to use alliteration and rhyme.

- The pupils write their adverts in their notebooks. They can find photos or draw pictures to go with the advert. They can also think about the design and look of the advert.

Activity 4

Read your advert to a new partner. Then check your work together. Put a tick (✓) or a cross (✗).

- Read through the statements as a class.
- Organise the class into new partners. One pupil reads aloud their advert. The other pupil listens. The pupils work together to decide if the advert fulfils the criteria and tick the corresponding boxes. The pupils can add, improve or correct the advert at this stage.
- The pupils swap roles.

Odd one out activity

Which is the odd one out? Why?

- The pupils complete the odd one out activity.

Answers: comfortable (It isn't an extreme adjective.)

Ending the lesson

Review the lesson and reflect on learning.

- Say **Today we've read an advert for some skates and written our own adverts.**
- Ask **What do you remember?** The pupils do a three-minute review in pairs. (Cooperative Learning Strategies, page 19)

Extra activity

Reinforcement

- Have a quick slogan competition. Organise the pupils into groups of three or four. Give an idea for a product, e.g. an underwater camera, a special pen, a modern scooter, a football computer game.
- The pupils have three minutes to think of a good slogan for it. They present their slogans to the class.
- The pupils vote on the best slogan. Then ask that group to think of the next product idea. The groups again have three minutes to think of a slogan. Repeat as many times as you wish.

Key Competences and Key Learning Outcomes

- Review talking about money and shopping
- Prepare and practise speaking activity types found in Cambridge Exams: B1 Preliminary for Schools
- Reflect on learning and progress
- Listen to a text for general and specific information
- Make notes to prepare a conversation
- Practise giving interesting answers in conversation
- Plan and prepare for a short conversation

Key language

- *online, pocket money, receive*
- *Do your parents give you pocket money?*

Materials

- Pupil's Book p80; Activity Book pp77–78; Class CD3 and CD4; Teacher's App on Navio

At a Glance Lesson Plan

Pupil's Book

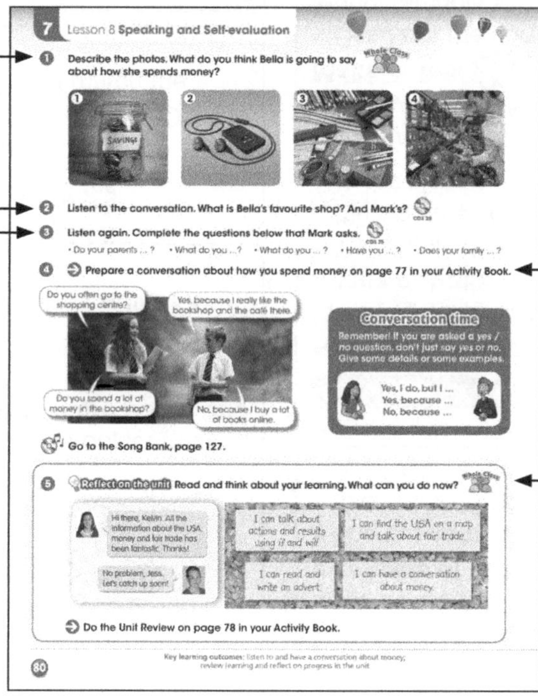

Starting the lesson

- Review words related to money and shopping.
- Set learning outcomes.

Activity 1

- Describe the photos.
- What do you think Bella is going to say about how she spends money?

Activity 2

- Listen to the conversation.
- ▶ *CD3 Track 25 p291*
- What is Bella's favourite shop?
- And Mark's?

Activity 3

- Listen again.
- ▶ *CD 3 Track 25 p291*
- Complete the questions below that Mark asks.

Activity 4

- Prepare a conversation about how you spend money on page 77 in your Activity Book.

Go to the Activity Book.

Song

- ▶ *CD4 Track 24 p297*
- ▶ *CD4 Track 25 p297 (optional karaoke version)*

Activity 5

- Read and think about your learning.
- What can you do now?

Ending the lesson

- Review the lesson and reflect on learning.

Activity Book

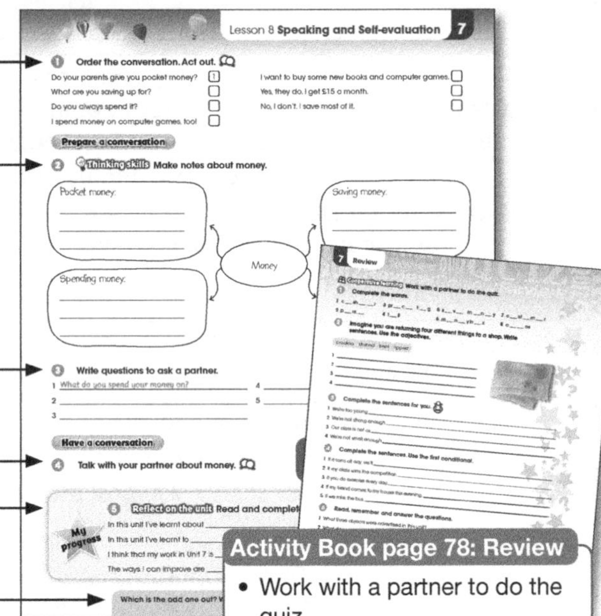

Activity Book page 78: Review

- Work with a partner to do the quiz.

Activity Book

Activity 1
- Order the conversation. Act out.

Activity 2
- Make notes about money.

Activity 3
- Write questions to ask a partner.

Activity 4
- Talk with your partner about money.

Activity 5
- Read and complete the sentences.

Odd one out activity

Digital resources

Teacher's Digital: You can also teach this lesson using the Teacher's App on Navio.

Powered By NAVIO

Starting the lesson

Review words related to money and shopping.

- Play a word chain around the class. The topic is money and shopping. One pupil says a word related to the topic. The next pupil says a word connected to that word and so on. Other pupils can challenge if they feel the word is not connected.

Set learning outcomes.

- Say **Today we're going to listen to and have a conversation about money and we're going to think about our learning.**

Pupil's Book Activity 1

Describe the photos. What do you think Bella is going to say about how she spends money?

- Pupils look at photos and make predictions.
- Ask pupils if they spend or save their pocket money.

Pupil's Book Activity 2

Listen to the conversation. What is Bella's favourite shop? And Mark's?

▶ ***CD3 Track 25 p291***

- Play CD and then check answers as a class.

Answers: Clara's favourite shop is an art shop. Mark's is a book store.

Pupil's Book Activity 3

Listen again. Complete the questions below that Mark asks.

▶ ***CD3 Track 25 p192***

- Have pupils guess how the questions will finish.
- Play CD and check answers as a class.
- Invite pupils to think of other questions they could ask Bella and Mark.

Answers: Do your parents give you pocket money? What do you have to do? What do you do with your money? Have you got any favourite shops? Does your family do their food shopping online?

Pupil's Book Activity 4

Prepare a conversation about how you spend money on page 77 in your Activity Book.

- Pupils read the Conversation time box and the dialogue.
- Direct pupils to the Activity Book.

Song

Read and discuss the questions.

- Go to the Song Bank on page 127 to do the Pupil's Book activities (see p245).

▶ ***CD4 Track 24 p297***

▶ ***CD4 Track 25 p297 (optional karaoke version)***

Activity Book

Activity 1

Order the conversation. Act out.

- After pupils order the conversation in pairs, they act it out.
- Pupils swap roles.

Answers: 1, 5, 3, 7, 6, 2, 4

Activity 2

Make notes about money.

- Pupils complete the notes individually and show their partners.

Activity 3

Write questions to ask a partner.

- Pupils complete the activity. Remind them to refer to Mark's questions in the Pupil's Book.

Activity 4

Talk with your partner about money.

- Refer pupils to the Remember box. Remind them to use the tips in their conversation.
- In pairs, the pupils have a conversation about money. One pupil asks the questions in Activity 3 and the partner answers. They then swap roles.

Pupil's Book Activity 5

Read and think about your learning. What can you do now?

- Read the messages as a class. Then look back through the unit and prompt the pupils to identify other things they have learnt / done.

Activity Book

Activity 5

Read and complete the sentences.

- Read out the sentences. Encourage the pupils to think of different ways of completing them.

Odd one out activity

Which is the odd one out? Why?

- The pupils complete the odd one out activity.

Answers: bank (It doesn't sell objects.)

Ending the lesson

Review the lesson and reflect on learning.

- Say **Today we've learnt and practised how to have a conversation about money and we've thought about our learning in this unit.**
- Ask **What do you remember?** The pupils do a three-minute review in pairs.

Activity Book page 78: Review

Work with a partner to do the quiz.

- Organise the class into pairs. Explain that they are going to work together to do a quiz. Set a time limit for the pupils to do this (10–15 minutes).
- Read out the six tasks that the pupils have to complete. Check understanding. Then say **Ready, steady … Go!**
- The pupils work in their pairs to do the quiz. Ask the pupils who finish quickly to help another pair.

Answers: **1** **1** cashier **2** purse **3** price tag **4** till **5** save money **6** moneybox **7** customer **8** coins **5** **1** a kite, a boat, a waveboard **2** a slogan / an advert **6** receipt, a piece of paper you are given in a shop when you buy something that says how much you spent

Key Competences and Key Learning Outcomes

- Watch and understand a video about buying and selling
- Calculate the cost of making smoothies and what the price will be
- Think about buying and selling

Key language

- *long way away, continent, coast, transport*
- *We could make biscuits. We need flour, butter, sugar and chocolate.*

Materials

- Pupil's Book p81; Activity Book p79; Class CD 3; Teacher's App on Navio
- Teacher's Resource Bank: Talk cards

At a Glance Lesson Plan

Pupil's Book

Starting the lesson

- **Think-Pair-Share**. Review different ways we buy and sell.
- Set learning outcomes and use the talk cards.

Activity 1

- Before you watch.
- Watch the video.
- *Unit 7 video p303*
- Read and say *true* or *false*.
- Correct the false sentences.

Activity 2

- Watch the video again.
- *Unit 7 video*
- What do the pictures show?
- Put them in order.

Activity 3

- Read, think and answer.

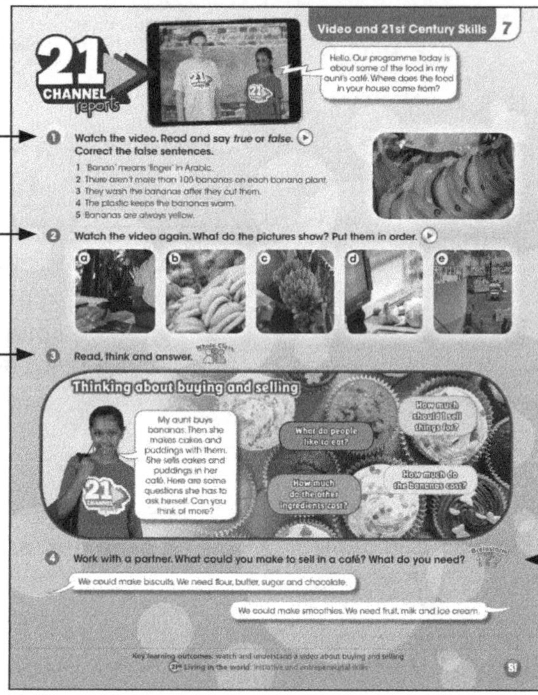

Activity 4

- Work with a partner.
- What could you make to sell in a café?
- What do you need?
- Go to the Activity Book.

Ending the lesson

- Review the lesson and reflect on learning.

Extra activity

- Think about what kind of shops they would like to open in the future and think about buying and selling there.

Activity Book

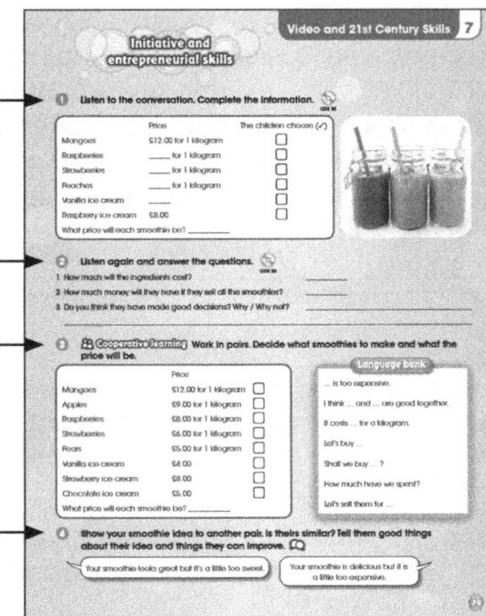

Activity Book

Activity 1
- Listen to the conversation. Complete the information.
- *CD3 Track 26 p291*

Activity 2
- Listen again and answer the questions.
- *CD3 Track 26 p291*

Activity 3
- Work in pairs.
- Decide what smoothies to make and what the price will be.

Activity 4
- Show your smoothie idea to another pair. Is theirs similar? Tell them good things about their idea and things they can improve.

Digital resources

Teacher's Digital: You can also teach this lesson using the Teacher's App on Navio.

Pupil's Digital: Encourage your pupils to use the Pupil's App on Navio to practise the activities from this lesson.

Powered By NAVIO

Starting the lesson

Think-Pair-Share. Review different ways we buy and sell.

- Ask pupils about the different shops or places they shop at. Ask **What different ways can we buy things and how?** Elicit answers and write them on the board. Encourage pupils to think about buying things online, in markets, small shops and malls.
- Extend the discussion to talk about the people who work in shops and what kind of things they do apart from selling items. Write ideas on the board.
- Pupils work with a Talk Partner to discuss different ways of buying and selling.

Set learning outcomes and use the talk cards.

- Say **Today we're going to watch a video about buying and selling.**
- Point to the talk cards to show the pupils the different ways they will be working in the lesson.

Pupil's Book Activity 1

Before you watch

- Ask pupils to look at the pictures in Activity 2 and tell you what they think the video will be about.
- Read the speech bubble to pupils. Ask pupils to tell you where they usually buy food in their homes from.
- Ask if they ever buy from farms or local producers. Then ask why supermarkets are popular and how often they shop there.

Watch the video. Read and say *true* or *false*. Correct the false sentences. *p303*

- Watch Part 1. Ask pupils if they have ever thought about where bread, cakes, and other types of food comes from. Are they surprised by what Aunt May says?
- Have students read the questions quietly.
- Play Part 2, pausing at each section for pupils to answer. Pupils then work in pairs to check answers.

Answers: **1** T **2** F **3** T **4** F **5** F
2 They can have 200 bananas on them.
4 It protects them from the insects and rain.
5 They are green.

Pupil's Book Activity 2

Watch the video again. What do the pictures show? Put them in order.

- Ask pupils to tell you what they remember from the video.
- Have pupils complete the activity in pairs.
- Play the second part of the video for pupils to check their answers.
- Have a class discussion on what they found interesting about the video.

Answers: **a** 1 **b** 3 **c** 2 **d** 5 **e** 4

Pupil's Book Activity 3

Read, think and answer.

- Tell pupils that in the last part of the video Amy and Max talk about buying and selling.
- Ask pupils why the prices increase along the way and why Max and Amy say it's fair.
- Explain that Aunt May, and all shop owners, have to think about what they put in their shops. Ask if they can add to Amy's ideas in the box.
- Note any new ideas on the board.

Pupil's Book Activity 4

Work with a partner. What could you make to sell in a café? What do you need?

- Have pupils work with a partner to complete the activity.
- Encourage pupils to think about different items and ingredients for their shops. Remind them to also think if their items will sell.
- Ask pairs to present their work to the class.
- Have a class discussion on the different ideas presented by each pair.

Activity Book

Activity 1

Listen to the conversation. Complete the information.

▶ *CD3 Track 26 p291*

- Give pupils a little time to read contents in the box and explain any unknown words.
- Play the CD and complete the activity.

Answers: Rasberries: 8 pounds, Strawberries 6 pounds, Peaches 7 pounds, Vanilla ice cream 4 pounds, price of each smoothie: 2 pounds each
Children choose: raspberries, peaches, vanilla ice cream

Activity 2

Listen again and answer the questions.

▶ *CD3 Track 26 p291*

- Have pupils complete the activity and check answers with their partners.

Answers: **1** 19 pounds **2** 40 pounds **3** Pupils' own answers.

Activity 3

Work in pairs. Decide what smoothies to make and what the price will be.

- Direct pupils to the Language bank and explain that they should use this language in their discussion.
- Pupils complete the activity with their partners.

Activity 4

Show your smoothie idea to another pair. Is theirs similar? Tell them good things about their idea and things they can improve.

- Pupils show other pairs their work.
- Have pairs tell the class how they can improve their product.

Ending the lesson

Review the lesson and reflect on learning.

- Say **Today we've watched a video about buying and selling. What have we learnt?** Elicit the information from the pupils. The pupils do a three-minute review in pairs. (Cooperative Learning Strategies, page 19)

Extra activity

Reinforcement

- Pupils work in groups to think of and discuss what kind of shops they would like to open in the future.
- Ask what they would buy and sell there.
- Have a class discussion on buying and selling, encouraging pupils to use the ideas they discussed in groups.

Date: ____________________ Unit: __________

1 What did my pupils learn in this unit?

____
____
____
____

2 How did my pupils work? (✓)

individually ☐ in pairs ☐ in small groups ☐

in large groups ☐ as a class ☐

3 Which key competences did my pupils develop? Give a score from 1 to 5 (5 being the highest).

- Competence in linguistic communication ☐
- Competence in mathematics, science and technology ☐
- Digital competence ☐
- Learning to learn ☐
- Social and civic competences ☐
- Sense of initiative and entrepreneurship ☐
- Cultural awareness and expression ☐

4 Which lessons / activities were the most successful and why?

____
____
____
____

5 Which lessons / activities did my pupils find the most difficult and why?

____
____
____
____

6 What did I try in the classroom for the first time? How did it go?

____
____
____
____

7 Which resources did I find most useful? (including webpages)

____
____
____
____
____
____

8 What could I do differently next time I teach this unit?

____
____
____
____

Unit 8

Let's dream

Unit overview

Key competences and learning outcomes

- Name different activities on a tropical island (Lesson 1)
- Use the second conditional to talk about unlikely situations (Lessons 2 and 4)
- Review and name unreal or unlikely experiences (Lesson 5)
- Use personal pronouns and possessive adjectives (Lesson 7)
- Watch and understand a video (Video and 21st Century Skills)

- Analyse and apply rules for forming and using the second conditional (Lesson 2)
- Sequence events (Lesson 6)

- Use the Pupil's App on Navio
- Investigate Ecuador (Lesson 3)

- Listen for specific information (Lesson 3)
- Identify contracted forms of 'would' (Lesson 4)
- Identify text features of a diary extract (Lesson 7)
- Review learning and reflect on progress in the unit (Lesson 8)
- Practise activity types found in the Cambridge Exams: B1 Preliminary for Schools

- Understand the importance of encouraging in groups (Lesson 3)
- Practise agreeing and disagreeing with an opinion (Lesson 8)

- Work in pairs or small groups to practise and reinforce learning (All lessons)
- Do a communication task (Lesson 5)
- Work as a team (Video and 21st Century Skills)

- Read a story (Lesson 3)
- Learn about Ecuador (Lesson 3)
- Read and write a diary extract (Lessons 6 and 7)

Vocabulary

Core vocabulary
coral, boogie boarding, giant tortoise, hammock, have a nap, palm tree, sea kayaking, sea lion, scuba diving, shore, tropical fish, wildlife spotting; be invisible, be the president, get lost, have three wishes, meet a famous person, travel in space, travel back in time, win the lottery

Extension vocabulary (optional)
dock, lagoon, reef, rock pool, sand dune, tide; find a wallet, lose your phone, see a robbery

Other vocabulary
go sailing, climb a volcano, rescue; matches, stream, sun cream, tent, whale; lifeboat, shelter, sink, sunburnt, yacht; autobiographical, fictional, heading, reflection; anyone, anywhere, anything, shelter, poisonous, sand

Recycled vocabulary
clean a beach, find, lose, meet, visit, win; adventure holiday, compass, desert island, environment, thirsty, hungry, weak; I, me, my, mine, our, ours, we, us

Structures

Core structures
If I lived in the Galapagos Islands, I would go wildlife spotting. If I lived in the Galapagos Islands, I wouldn't climb a volcano. I would go wildlife spotting if I lived in the Galapagos Islands. Would you take water if you abandoned a boat? Yes, I would. No, I wouldn't. What would you do if you were lost at sea? If I was lost at sea, I would make a sail for my boat.

Other structures
I doubt it. It's very unlikely. You never know. I think the (tent) would be a good idea. That's a good point. I see what you mean.

Recycled structures
I wonder if I'll find a better place to live tomorrow. Milo and I love our cave. Would you like to visit the giant tortoise reserve? If I go shopping, I'll buy a T-shirt. While they were sailing towards the Galapagos Islands, their luck changed.

Pronunciation

Contracted forms: 'would'

Literacy

Text type: a diary extract (chronological account; writing preparation)
Reading skills: predicting content
Writing skills: using personal pronouns and possessive adjectives

Culture ... around the world

How a couple were lost at sea for 117 days near the Galapagos Islands

21st Century Skills

Ways of working: working as a team

Thinking skills

Listing and grouping vocabulary items (Lesson 1); Defining and describing (Lesson 1); Analysing and applying rules and patterns (Lessons 2 and 4); Predicting (Lesson 7 and Review); Problem solving (Lesson 8); Evaluating (Lesson 8)

Cooperative learning

Working together (Lessons 1–8); Reflecting and setting goals (Lessons 1–8); Encouraging (Lesson 5); Empathising (Lesson 6); Collaborative writing (Lesson 7); Peer evaluation (Lesson 7); Expressing and respecting opinions (Lessons 3, 6, 8); Initiating a conversation (Lesson 8)

Values

The importance of encouragement in groups

Cross-curricular links

Links to Science
Physical Georgraphy of Spain and Europe

Suggested Arts and Crafts concepts
Analogous colours

Key Competences and Key Learning Outcomes

- Name different activities on a tropical island
- Practise using 'would like' to talk about a desire

- List and group vocabulary items

Key language

- *coral, boogie boarding, giant tortoise, hammock, have a nap, palm tree, sea kayaking, sea lion, scuba diving, shore, tropical fish, wildlife spotting*
- Extension: *dock, lagoon, reef, rock pool, sand dune, tide*
- *Would you like to visit the giant tortoise reserve?*

Materials

- Pupil's Book pp82–83; Activity Book p80; Class CD3; Teacher's App on Navio
- Activities on a tropical island flashcards

Optional materials

- Teacher's Resource Bank: Trinity Exams Practice cards (selected from the Starter Unit and Unit 1, 2, 3, 4, 5, 6 and 7)

At a Glance Lesson Plan

Pupil's Book

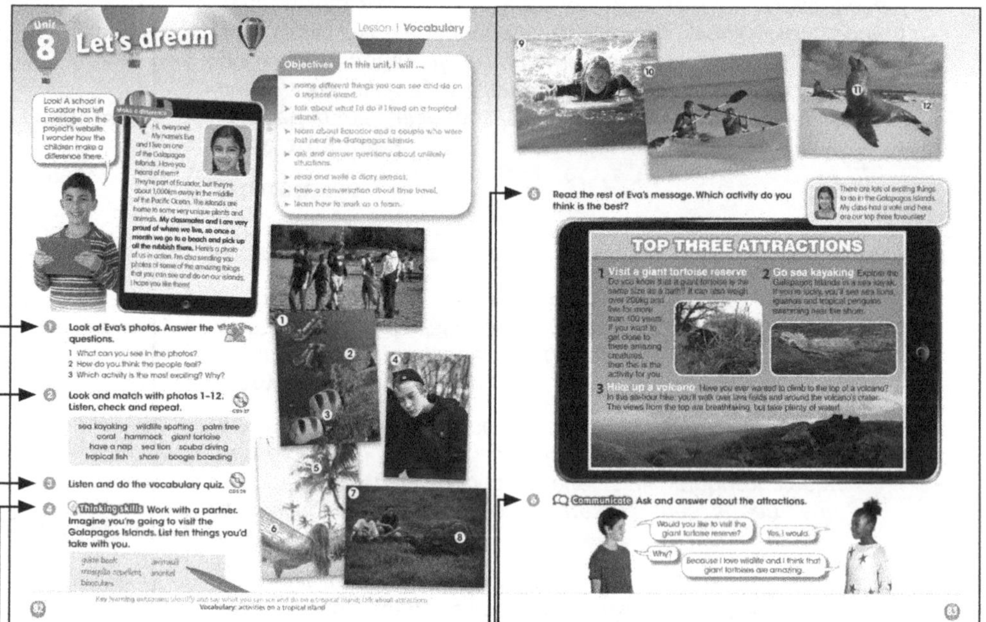

Starting the lesson

- Use the Trinity Exams Practice cards (optional).
- Review beautiful places.
- Set learning outcomes.

Activity 1

- Look at Eva's photos.
- Answer the questions.

Vocabulary presentation

- Present the new vocabulary using the activities on the tropical island flashcards.

Activity 2

- Look and match with photos 1–12.
- Listen, check and repeat.

▶ *CD3 Track 27 p291*

Activity 3

- Listen and do the vocabulary quiz.

▶ *CD3 Track 28 p292*

Activity 4

- Work with a partner.
- Imagine you're going to visit the Galapagos Islands.
- List ten things you'd take with you.

Activity 5

- Read the rest of Eva's message.
- Which activity do you think is the best?

Activity 6

- Ask and answer about the attractions.

Go to the Activity Book.

Ending the lesson

- Review the lesson and reflect on learning.

Extra activities

Extension

- Find out about Ecuador.

Vocabulary extension

- Present six additional vocabulary items.

Activity Book

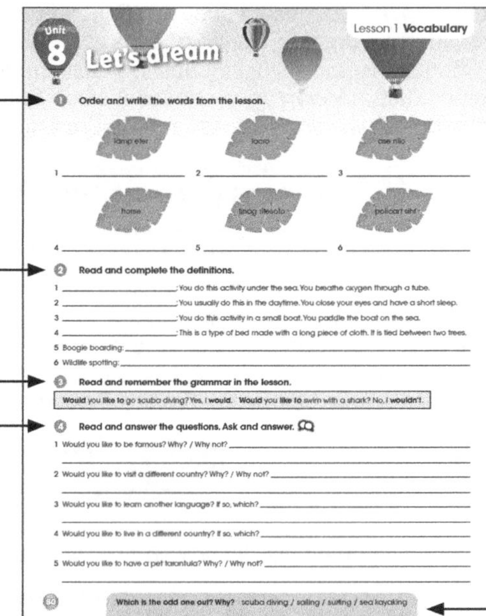

Activity Book

Activity 1

- Order and write the words from the lesson.

Activity 2

- Read and complete the definitions.

Activity 3

- Read and remember the grammar in the lesson.

Activity 4

- Read and answer the questions. Ask and answer.

Odd one out activity

Digital resources

Teacher's Digital: You can also teach this lesson using the Teacher's App on Navio.

Pupil's Digital: Encourage your pupils to use the Pupil's App on Navio to practise the activities from this lesson.

Powered By NAVIO

Starting the lesson

Use the Trinity Exams Practice cards (optional).
- The pupils practise asking and answering questions.

Review beautiful places.
- The pupils think of a beautiful place they have visited. Ask **Where was it? What did you see / do there?**

Set learning outcomes.
- Say **Today we're going to learn the names of activities on a tropical island.**

Pupil's Book Activity 1

Look at Eva's photos. Answer the questions.
- Invite a pupil to read out the speech bubble to find out which school has sent a message. Ask **Do you know where Ecuador is?**
- Invite a pupil to read out the message from Eva. Check understanding.
- Work as a class to answer the questions.

Vocabulary presentation

- Present the new vocabulary using the activities on a tropical island flashcards. Hold up the first flashcard so that the class can't see it. Give a definition. The pupils name the item. If the pupils don't know the word in English, provide the word and ask them to repeat it. Stick the flashcard on the board. Repeat with the other flashcards.

Pupil's Book Activity 2

Look and match with photos 1–12. Listen, check and repeat.

▶ *CD3 Track 27 p291*
- Ask the pupils to look at photo number 1. Ask **What's this?** In pairs, the pupils match 2–12 with the words.
- Play the CD. The pupils listen and check. Play the CD again, pausing after each word for the pupils to repeat. You can find the answers for this activity in the audioscript on page 291.

Pupil's Book Activity 3

Listen and do the vocabulary quiz.

▶ *CD3 Track 28 p292*
- Play the CD. Listen to the first definition, pausing at the beep to allow the pupils to name the item. Play the CD to listen to the answer.
- Repeat the procedure with the other definitions. You can find the answers for this activity in the audioscript on page 292.

Pupil's Book Activity 4

Work with a partner. Imagine you're going to visit the Galapagos Islands.
List ten things you'd take with you.
- In pairs, the pupils negotiate a combined list of ten items.

Pupil's Book Activity 5

Read the rest of Eva's message. Which activity do you think is the best?
- Invite a pupil to read out the message.
- The pupils read the information. They choose the best activity.
- Invite the pupils to share their choices with the class.

Pupil's Book Activity 6

Ask and answer about the attractions.
- Invite two pupils to read out the speech bubbles.
- In pairs, the pupils ask and answer questions about the attractions.

Activity Book

Activity 1

Order and write the words from the lesson.
- The pupils order the letters and write the words.

Answers: **1** palm tree **2** coral **3** sea lion **4** shore **5** giant tortoise **6** tropical fish

Activity 2

Read and complete the definitions.
- The pupils complete the definitions.

Answers: **1** scuba diving **2** have a nap **3** sea kayaking **4** hammock **5 & 6** Pupils' own answers

Activity 3

Read and remember the grammar in the lesson.
- Invite a pupil to read out the information.

Activity 4

Read and answer the questions. Ask and answer.
- The pupils read and answer the questions.
- They then ask and answer the questions with a partner.

Odd one out activity

Which is the odd one out? Why?
- The pupils complete the odd one out activity

Answers: scuba diving (It's an underwater activity.)

Ending the lesson

Review the lesson and reflect on learning.
- Say **Today we've learnt the names of activities on a tropical island.**
- Ask **What do you remember?** The pupils do a three-minute review in pairs. (Cooperative Learning Strategies, page 19).

Extra activities

Extension
- The pupils find three interesting facts about Ecuador to present to the class.

Vocabulary extension
- Introduce six words related to activities on a tropical island: *dock, lagoon, reef, rock pool, sand dune, tide.*
- Use the Vocabulary Booster on NAVIO to practise these new words.

Key Competences and Key Learning Outcomes

- Listen to and read a dialogue
- Learn and practise how to use the second conditional to talk about unlikely situations

- Analyse and apply rules for forming and using the second conditional
- Compare and contrast the first and the second conditional

- Identify examples of the second conditional in the dialogue

Key language

- *clean a beach, go boogie boarding / sailing / scuba diving / sea kayaking / wildlife spotting, climb a volcano*
- *If I lived in the Galapagos Islands, I would go wildlife spotting. If I lived in the Galapagos Islands, I wouldn't climb a volcano. I would go wildlife spotting if I lived in the Galapagos Islands.*

Materials

- Pupil's Book p84; Activity Book p81; Class CD3; Teacher's App on Navio
- Teacher's Resource Bank: Activities on a tropical island word cards

Optional materials

- Teacher's Resource Bank: Trinity Exams Practice cards (selected from the Starter Unit and Units 1, 2 3, 4, 5, 6 and 7)

At a Glance Lesson Plan

Pupil's Book

Starting the lesson

- Use the Trinity Exams Practice cards (optional).
- Review activities on a tropical island.
- Set learning outcomes.

Activity 1

- Describe the photo.
- What do you think Eva did there?
- Read and listen to find out.

▶ *CD3 Track 29 p292*

Activity 2

- Read and say *true* or *false*.
- Correct the false sentences.

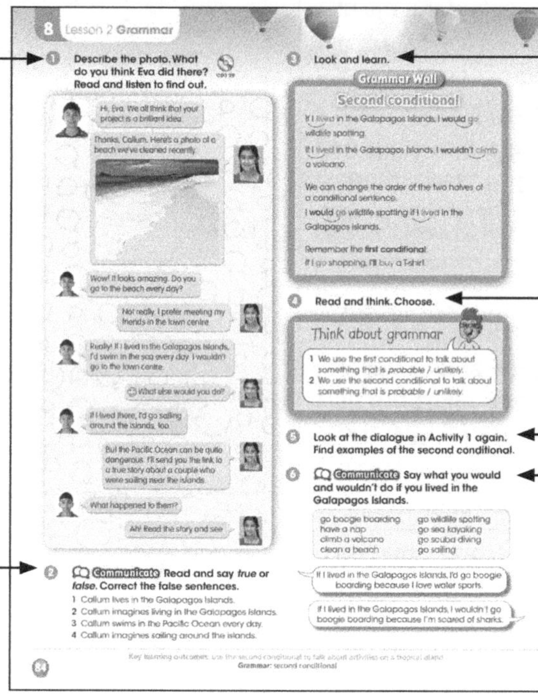

Activity 3

- Look and learn – Grammar wall

Activity 4

- Read and think.
- Choose.

Activity 5

- Look at the dialogue in Activity 1 again.
- Find examples of the second conditional.

Activity 6

- Say what you would and wouldn't do if you lived in the Galapagos Islands.

Go to the Activity Book.

Ending the lesson

- Review the lesson and reflect on learning.

Extra activity

Reinforcement

- Create consequence chains.

Activity Book

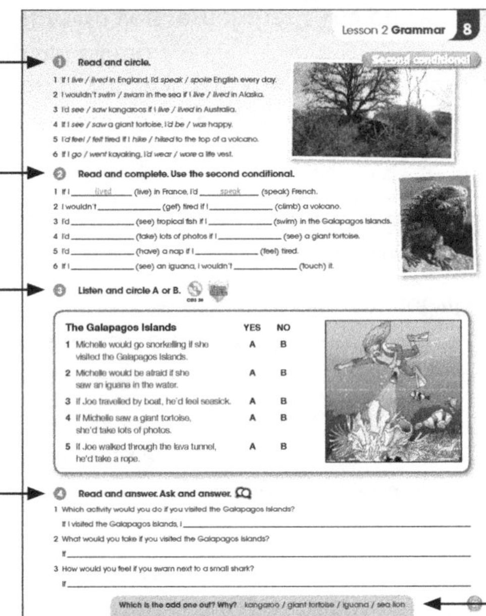

Activity Book

Activity 1

- Read and circle.

Activity 2

- Read and complete. Use the second conditional.

Activity 3

- Listen and circle A or B.

▶ *CD3 Track 30 p292*

Activity 4

- Read and answer. Ask and answer.

Odd one out activity

Digital resources

Teacher's Digital: You can also teach this lesson using the Teacher's App on Navio.

Pupil's Digital: Encourage your pupils to use the Pupil's App on Navio to practise the activities from this lesson.

Powered By NAVIO

Starting the lesson

Use the Trinity Exams Practice cards (optional).

- The pupils practise asking and answering questions.

Review activities on a tropical island.

- Place the activities on a tropical island word cards face down on a desk at the front of the class.
- Organise the class into groups of three. Pupil 1 collects a word card. The pupil defines the word to their group. Pupil 2 says the word and Pupil 3 spells it. The pupils swap roles. Repeat with new word cards.

Set learning outcomes

- Say **Today we're going to learn a new conditional form.**

Pupil's Book Activity 1

Describe the photo. What do you think Eva did there? Read and listen to find out.

▶ *CD3 Track 29 p292*

- Ask the pupils to describe the photo. Then ask **What do you think Eva did at the beach?**
- Play the CD. The pupils listen and read the dialogue. Confirm that she cleaned the beach.

Pupil's Book Activity 2

Read and say *true* or *false*.
Correct the false sentences.

- In pairs, the pupils read the dialogue again. They decide if the sentences are true or false. They correct the false sentences. Check answers as a class. (*1 False. Eva lives in the Galapagos Islands. 2 True 3 False. Callum doesn't swim in the Pacific Ocean every day. 4 True*)

Pupil's Book Activity 3

Look and learn – Grammar wall

- Read the information on the Grammar wall as a class.
- Encourage the pupils to think about form and identify patterns. Say **Second conditional sentences have two halves.** Ask **What tense do we use with 'if'?** (*Past simple.*) **What verbs do we use in the other half?** (*Would + infinitive.*)

Pupil's Book Activity 4

Read and think. Choose.

- Focus the pupils' attention on the Think about grammar box. Read out the sentences as a class. The pupils complete the sentences in pairs. Check answers as a class. *(1 probable 2 unlikely)*
- Discuss the difference in meaning between first and second conditional sentences. Write examples on the board and identify the differences in form.

Pupil's Book Activity 5

Look at the dialogue in Activity 1 again. Find examples of the second conditional.

- In pairs, the pupils find examples of the second conditional in the dialogue.
- Check answers as a class.

Pupil's Book Activity 6

Say what you would and wouldn't do if you lived in the Galapagos Islands.

- Invite two pupils to read out the speech bubbles.
- Then ask other pupils to make similar true sentences.
- In pairs, the pupils tell each other what they would and wouldn't do if they lived in the Galapagos Islands.

Activity Book

Activity 1

Read and circle.

- The pupils read and circle the correct form of the verb.

Answers: **1** lived, speak **2** swim, lived **3** see, lived **4** saw, 'd be **5** 'd feel, hiked **6** went, 'd wear

Activity 2

Read and complete. Use the second conditional.

- The pupils complete the sentences.

Answers: **1** lived, speak **2** get, climbed **3** see, swam **4** take, saw **5** have, felt **6** saw, touch

Activity 3

Listen and circle A or B.

▶ *CD3 Track 30 p292*

- Read the sentences as a class. Play the CD. The pupils listen and circle as many of the answers as possible.
- The pupils compare their answers with a partner.
- Play the CD again, pausing after each piece of key information. The pupils identify and say the answer each time.

Answers: **1** A **2** B **3** A **4** A **5** B

Activity 4

Read and answer. Ask and answer.

- The pupils read the questions and write their answers.
- In pairs, the pupils ask and answer the questions.

Odd one out activity

Which is the odd one out? Why?

- The pupils complete the odd one out activity.

Answers: kangaroo (You can't find it on the Galapagos Islands.)

Ending the lesson

Review the lesson and reflect on learning.

- Say **Today we've learnt a new conditional form.**
- Ask **What do you remember?** The pupils do a three-minute review in pairs. (Cooperative Learning Strategies, page 19)

Extra activity

Reinforcement

- Create a second conditional consequence chain as a class. Start the chain by saying **If I went to the Galapagos Islands, I'd go swimming.** Continue the chain by saying **If I went swimming, ...** Prompt the class to finish the sentence. Elicit more sentences in the chain.
- In pairs, the pupils make similar chains.

Key Competences and Key Learning Outcomes

- Read a story with confidence and fluency
- Use the Internet to investigate Ecuador
- Listen for general and specific information
- Understand the importance of encouragement in groups
- Learn about Ecuador
- Express an opinion on a text

Key language

- *compass, hungry, lifeboat, rainwater, yacht, sink, sunburnt, thirsty, whale*
- *While they were sailing towards the Galapagos Islands, their luck changed.*

Materials

- Pupil's Book p85; Activity Book p82; Class CD3; Teacher's App on Navio

Optional materials

- Teacher's Resource Bank: Trinity Exams Practice cards (selected from the Starter Unit and Units 1, 2, 3, 4, 5, 6 and 7)

At a Glance Lesson Plan

Pupil's Book

Starting the lesson

- Use the Trinity Exams Practice cards (optional).
- Review second conditional sentences.
- Set learning outcomes.

Activity 1: Before you read

- Read and discuss.

Activity 2

- Listen and read.

▶ *CD3 Track 31 p292*

Go to the Activity Book.

***Give Me Five!* values**

- Read and discuss.

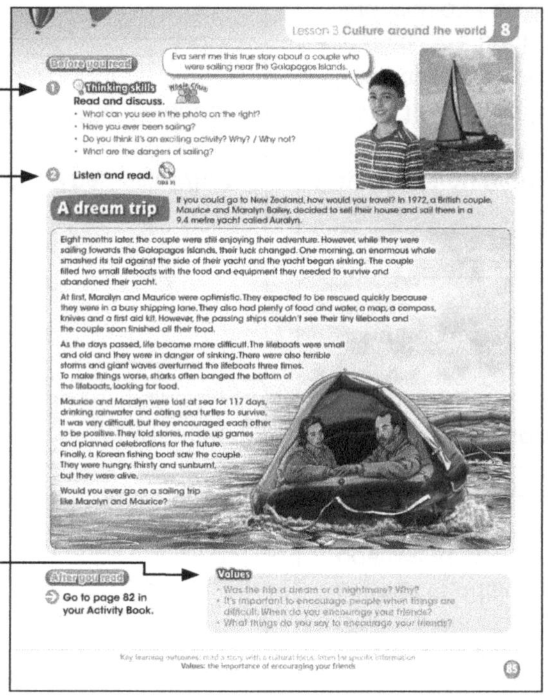

Lesson 3 Culture around the world 8

A dream trip

Ending the lesson

- Review the lesson and reflect on learning.

Extra activity

Extension

- Do a survival problem-solving task.

Activity Book

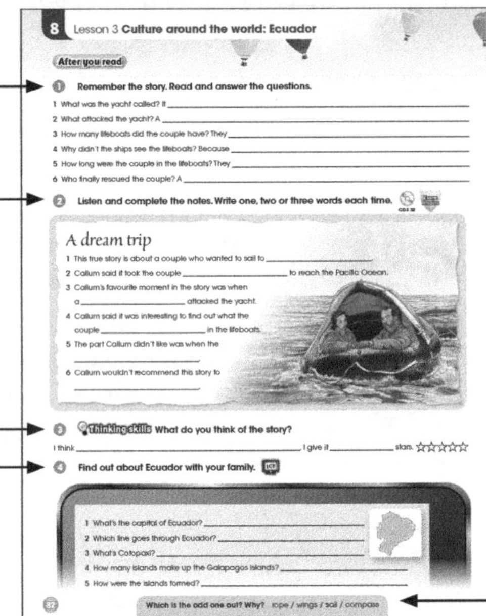

8 Lesson 3 Culture around the world: Ecuador

A dream trip

Activity Book: After you read

▶ *CD3 Track 32 p292*

Activity 1

- Remember the story. Read and answer the questions.

Activity 2

- Listen and complete the notes. Write one, two or three words each time.

Activity 3

- What do you think of the story?

Activity 4

- Find out about Ecuador with your family.

Odd one out activity

Digital resources

Teacher's Digital: You can also teach this lesson using the Teacher's App on Navio.

Pupil's Digital: Encourage your pupils to use the Pupil's App on Navio to practise the activities from this lesson.

Powered By NAVIO

Starting the lesson

Use the Trinity Exams Practice cards (optional).

- The pupils practise asking and answering questions.

Review second conditional sentences.

- On the board, write *If I sailed around the world, …* Prompt the pupils to finish the second conditional sentence in as many ways as possible.

Set learning outcomes.

- Say **Today we're going to read a true story about a couple who wanted to sail to New Zealand.**

Pupil's Book Activity 1: Before you read

Read and discuss.

- Read the questions as a class. Encourage the pupils to share experiences about sailing and to think about the dangers of this sport.

Pupil's Book Activity 2

Listen and read.

▶ *CD3 Track 31 p292*

- Play the CD. The pupils follow in their books.
- Ask questions to check understanding.

Suggested comprehension questions:

- Introduction: **Where did Maurice and Maralyn live before?** (*In Britain.*)
- Paragraph 1: **Why did the yacht start sinking?** (*A whale smashed its tail against the yacht.*)
- Paragraph 2: **Did the passing ships see them?** (*No.*)
- Paragraph 3: **How many times did the lifeboats overturn?** (*Three times.*)
- Paragraph 4: **What did they eat and drink?** (*They ate sea turtles and drank rainwater.*)

Activity Book: After you read

Activity 1

Remember the story. Read and answer the questions.

- Read out the first question. Invite a pupil to answer it.
- The pupils read and answer the remaining questions.

Answers: **1** was called Auralyn. **2** whale attacked the yacht. **3** had two lifeboats. **4** the lifeboats were tiny. **5** were in the lifeboat for 117 days. **6** Korean fishing boat rescued them.

Activity 2

Listen and complete the notes. Write one, two or three words each time.

▶ *CD3 Track 32 p292*

- Read out the notes as a class. Ask the pupils to guess the missing words.
- Play the CD without pausing. The pupils listen and complete as much information as possible.
- Play the CD again, pausing after each piece of key information to check the answer.

Answers: **1** New Zealand **2** eight months **3** whale **4** ate and drank **5** sharks appeared **6** small children

Activity 3

What do you think of the story?

- The pupils write their opinion and give a rating.
- Invite different pupils to share their opinions.

Activity 4

Find out about Ecuador with your family. ICT

- Read out the questions about Ecuador. Ask **Where can you find out this information?** (*Internet, library, asking friends and family.*) The pupils complete the activity at home.
- If you prefer to do this activity in the class, connect to a children's website which has information about Ecuador, such as http://kids.nationalgeographic.com/explore/countries/ecuador.html or www.kidsdiscover.com/spotlight/galapagos-for-kids.
- Read out the questions. The pupils work as a class to find and write the answers.

Answers: **1** Quito **2** the Equator **3** a volcano **4** 14 major islands and many smaller islands **5** by volcanic activity

Odd one out activity

Which is the odd one out? Why?

- The pupils complete the odd one out activity.

Answers: wings (You don't use them in sailing.)

***Give Me Five!* values**

Read and discuss.

- Read out the questions and discuss them as a class.
- Invite the pupils to think about the things they can say to encourage each other.

Ending the lesson

Review the lesson and reflect on learning.

- Say **Today we've read some information about a couple who wanted to sail to New Zealand.**
- Ask **What do you remember?** The pupils do a three-minute review in pairs. (Cooperative Learning Strategies, page 19)

Extra activity

Extension

- Write a list of objects on the board, e.g. *a watch, an axe, a book, a tent, a torch, a guitar, a magnifying glass, a camera, matches, a mobile phone*.
- Organise the pupils into small groups. Explain that they are in a sinking boat and they only have time to get one item each. The group discuss and agree on one item each from those listed on the board.
- Discuss the groups' decisions as a class.

Key Competences and Key Learning Outcomes

- Learn and practise how to ask questions using the second conditional
- Analyse and apply rules for forming and using the second conditional question.
- Practise saying the contracted form of 'would'

Key language

- *find, lose, meet, visit, win*
- *Would you take water if you abandoned a boat? Yes, I would. No, I wouldn't. What would you do if you were lost at sea? If I was lost at sea, I would make a sail for my boat.*

Materials

- Pupil's Book p86; Activity Book p83; Class CD3; Teacher's App on Navio

Optional materials

- Teacher's Resource Bank: Trinity Exams Practice cards (selected from the Starter Unit and Units 1, 2, 3, 4, 5, 6 and 7)

At a Glance Lesson Plan

Pupil's Book

Starting the lesson

- Use the Trinity Exams Practice cards (optional).
- Review the story from Lesson 3.
- Set learning outcomes.

Activity 1

- Listen and read.
- ▶ *CD3 Track 33 p293*
- Act out.

Activity 2

- Look and learn – Grammar wall

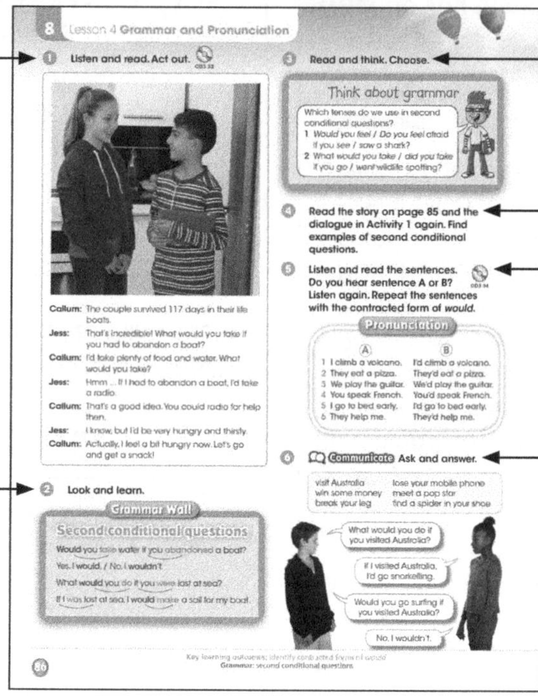

Activity 3

- Read and think.
- Choose.

Activity 4

- Read the story on page 85 and the dialogue in Activity 1 again.
- Find examples of second conditional questions.

Activity 5

- Listen and read the sentences.
- ▶ *CD3 Track 34 p293*
- Do you hear sentence A or B?
- Listen again.
- Repeat the sentences with the contracted form of *would*.

Activity 6

- Ask and answer.
- Go to the Activity Book.

Ending the lesson

- Review the lesson and reflect on learning.

Extra activity

Reinforcement

- Do a one-question interview.

Activity Book

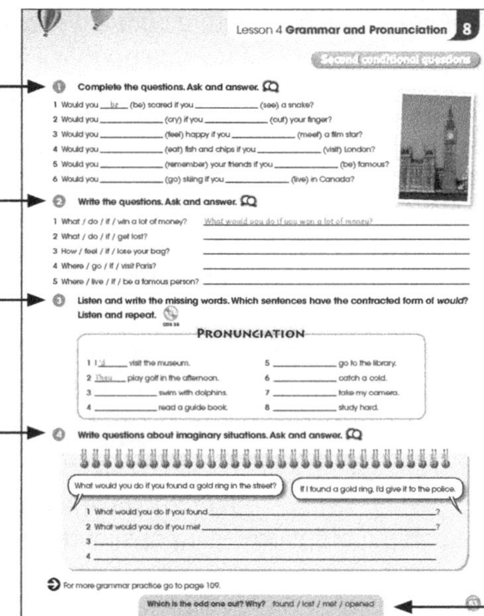

Activity Book

Activity 1

- Complete the questions. Ask and answer.

Activity 2

- Write the questions. Ask and answer.

Activity 3

- Listen and write the missing words. Which sentences have the contracted form of *would*? Listen and repeat.
- ▶ *CD3 Track 35 p293*

Activity 4

- Write questions about imaginary situations. Ask and answer.

Odd one out activity

Digital resources

Teacher's Digital: You can also teach this lesson using the Teacher's App on Navio.

Pupil's Digital: Encourage your pupils to use the Pupil's App on Navio to practise the activities from this lesson.

Powered By NAVIO

Starting the lesson

Use the Trinity Exams Practice cards (optional).

- The pupils practise asking and answering questions.

Review the story from Lesson 3.

- Ask **Do you remember the story that you read in Lesson 3?** In pairs, the pupils recall the story.

Set learning outcomes.

- Say **Today we're going to learn to ask questions using the second conditional and we're going to practise using the contracted form of 'would'.**

Pupil's Book Activity 1

Listen and read. Act out.

▶ *CD3 Track 33 p293*

- The pupils look at the photo. Ask **What are Jess and Callum talking about in the photo?**
- Play the CD. The pupils listen and read the dialogue. Check understanding.
- Play the CD again, pausing after each sentence for the pupils to repeat.
- The pupils practise the dialogue in pairs.
- **Note:** you can use the Dialogue Tool to present and practise this dialogue.

Pupil's Book Activity 2

Look and learn – Grammar wall

- Read the information on the Grammar wall as a class.

Pupil's Book Activity 3

Read and think. Choose.

- Focus the pupils' attention on the Think about Grammar box. The pupils complete the sentences in pairs. Check answers as a class. (*1 Would you feel, saw 2 would you take, went*)

Pupil's Book Activity 4

Read the story on page 85 and the dialogue in Activity 1 again. Find examples of second conditional questions.

- In pairs, the pupils find examples of second conditional questions.

Pupil's Book Activity 5

Listen and read the sentences. Do you hear sentence A or B? Listen again. Repeat the sentences with the contracted form of *would*.

▶ *CD3 Track 34 p293*

- Elicit 'I'd' as the contracted form of 'I would'.
- Play the CD, pausing after the first sentence. The pupils choose A or B. Repeat with the other sentences.
- Play the CD again. The pupils listen and repeat.

Answers: **1** B **2** A **3** B **4** B **5** A **6** B

Pupil's Book Activity 6

Ask and answer.

- Invite two pupils to read out the speech bubbles.
- In pairs, the pupils ask and answer questions.

Activity Book

Activity 1

Complete the questions. Ask and answer.

- The pupils complete the questions.
- In pairs, they ask and answer the questions.

Answers: **1** be, saw **2** cry, cut **3** feel, met **4** eat, visited **5** remember, were **6** go, lived

Activity 2

Write the questions. Ask and answer.

- The pupils write the questions.
- In pairs, they ask and answer the questions.

Answers: **1** What would you do if you won a lot of money? **2** What would you do if you got lost? **3** How would you feel if you lost your bag? **4** Where would you go if you visited Paris? **5** Where would you live if you were a famous person?

Activity 3

Listen and write the missing words. Which sentences have the contracted form of *would*? Listen and repeat.

▶ *CD3 Track 35 p293*

- Play the CD, pausing after the first two sentences. The pupils read the examples.
- Repeat the procedure with the other sentences. The pupils write the missing words. They then identify the contracted form.

Answers: **1** I'd **2** They **3** We'd **4** You **5** We **6** They'd **7** I'd **8** You'd

Activity 4

Write questions about imaginary situations. Ask and answer.

- Invite two pupils to read out the speech bubbles.
- The pupils write their questions. They ask and answer the questions in pairs.

Odd one out activity

Which is the odd one out? Why?

- The pupils complete the odd one out activity.

Answer: opened (It's a regular past participle.)

Ending the lesson

Review the lesson and reflect on learning.

- Say **Today we've learnt to ask questions using the second conditional and practised using the contracted form of 'would'.**
- Ask **What do you remember?** The pupils do a three-minute review in pairs.

Extra activity

Reinforcement

- The pupils write a question with *What would you do if …?*
- They ask their questions to as many classmates as possible in three minutes. The pupils record the name of the classmate and the response.
- Finally, they write a summary of their findings.

Key Competences and Key Learning Outcomes

- Review and name unreal or unlikely experiences
- Learn and practise how to use 'anyone', 'anywhere' and 'anything' in second conditional questions
- Review and practise how to use expressions to express uncertainty

- Practise activity types found in the Cambridge Exams: B1 Preliminary for Schools
- Listen for gist and specific information

- Do a communication task

Key language
- *be invisible, be the president, get lost, have three wishes, meet a famous person, travel in space, travel back in time, win the lottery; anyone, anything, anywhere*
- Extension: *lose your phone, find a wallet, see a robbery*
- *I doubt it. It's very unlikely. You never know.*

Materials
- Pupil's Book p87; Activity Book p84; Class CD3; Teacher's App on Navio

Optional materials
- Teacher's Resource Bank: Trinity Exams Practice cards (selected from the Starter Unit and Units 1, 2, 3, 4, 5, 6 and 7)
- A class set of dice (one per group of four pupils)

At a Glance Lesson Plan

Pupil's Book

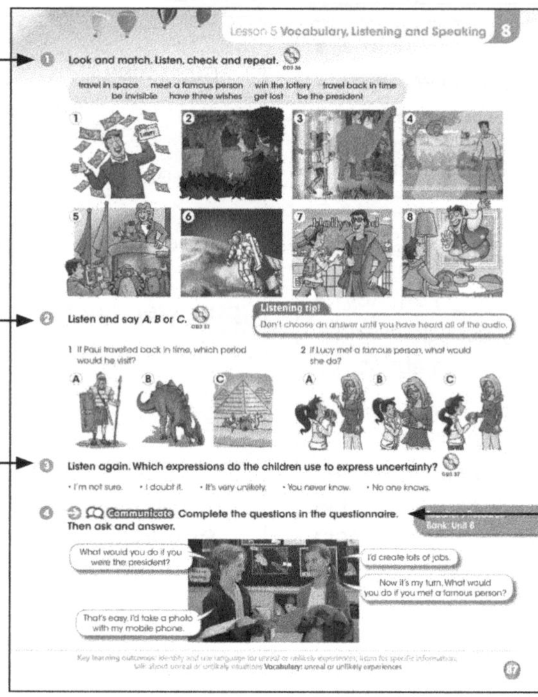

Starting the lesson
- Use the Trinity Exams Practice cards (optional).
- Review talking about probable and unlikely activities.
- Set learning outcomes.

Activity 1
- Look and match.
- Listen, check and repeat.
- ▶ *CD3 Track 36 p293*

Activity 2
- Listen and say *A*, *B* or *C*.
- ▶ *CD3 Track 37 p293*

Activity 3
- Listen again.
- ▶ *CD3 Track 37 p293*
- Which expressions do the children use to express uncertainty?

Activity 4
- Complete the questions in the questionnaire.
- Then ask and answer (Teacher's Resource Bank: Unit 8).

Go to the Activity Book.

Ending the lesson
- Review the lesson and reflect on learning.

Extra activities

Extension
- Play a game with dice.

Vocabulary extension
- Present four additional vocabulary items.

Activity Book

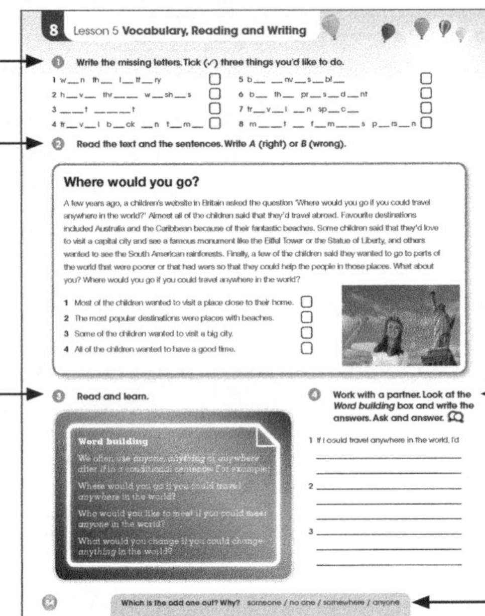

Activity Book

Activity 1
- Write the missing letters. Tick (✓) three things you'd like to do.

Activity 2
- Read the text and the sentences. Write *A* (right) or *B* (wrong).

Activity 3
- Read and learn.

Activity 4
- Work with a partner. Look at the *Word building* box and write the answers. Ask and answer.

Odd one out activity

Digital resources

Teacher's Digital: You can also teach this lesson using the Teacher's App on Navio.

Pupil's Digital: Encourage your pupils to use the Pupil's App on Navio to practise the activities from this lesson.

Powered By NAVIO

Starting the lesson

Use the Trinity Exams Practice cards (optional).

- The pupils practise asking and answering questions.

Review talking about probable and unlikely activities.

- Draw a line on the board. Write *Possible* at one end and *Impossible* at the other.
- Then say different actions, e.g. **Go to the cinema today.** Ask different pupils to draw a cross on the line to show how possible or impossible the actions are for them.
- Ask **When an action is unlikely do we use the first or the second conditional?** (*Second conditional.*) **When do we use the first conditional?** (*When an activity is probable.*)

Set learning outcomes.

- Say **Today we're going to learn the names of some unlikely or impossible activities.**

Pupil's Book Activity 1

Look and match. Listen, check and repeat.

▶ *CD3 Track 36 p293*

- In pairs, ask the pupils to match the words they know with the pictures.
- Play the CD. The pupils listen and check.
- Play the CD again, pausing after each word or phrase for the pupils to repeat. You can find the answers for this activity in the audioscript on page 293.

Pupil's Book Activity 2

Listen and say *A*, *B* or *C*.

▶ *CD3 Track 37 p293*

- Invite a pupil to read out the first question and name the three periods in the pictures. Read Listening tip! as a class
- Play the CD, pausing after the first dialogue. The pupils listen and identify the correct picture.
- Repeat the procedure with the second question.

Answers: **1** C **2** B

Pupil's Book Activity 3

Listen again. Which expressions do the children use to express uncertainty?

▶ *CD3 Track 37 p293*

- Invite a pupil to read out the expressions.
- Play the CD again. The pupils listen and identify the expressions that the children use.
- Quickly review other expressions that the pupils have seen in earlier units. (*I haven't got a clue. I've got no idea. I'm not certain.*)

Answers: I'm not sure. I doubt it. It's very unlikely. You never know.

Pupil's Book Activity 4

Complete the questions in the questionnaire. Then ask and answer (Teacher's Resource Bank: Unit 8).

- Explain to the pupils that they are going to complete a questionnaire.
- Invite two pupils to read out the speech bubbles.
- Organise the class into pairs (A and B). The pupils complete their questions. If a pupil needs more support, ask him / her to work with a pupil who is preparing the same questions.
- Check answers as a class. Then invite two pupils to demonstrate the activity by asking and answering the first question. Encourage them to use the expressions of uncertainty if appropriate.
- Ask the pupils to do the activity in their pairs.

Activity Book

Activity 1

Write the missing letters. Tick (✓) three things you'd like to do.

- The pupils write the missing vowels in the gaps.
- They then tick the three things they would like to do.
- Check answers as a class.

Answers: **1** win the lottery **2** have three wishes **3** get lost **4** travel back in time **5** be invisible **6** be the president **7** travel in space **8** meet a famous person

Activity 2

Read the text and the sentences. Write *A* (right) or *B* (wrong).

- Read the text as a class. In pairs, the pupils decide if the sentences are correct (A) or incorrect (B).

Answers: **1** B **2** A **3** A **4** B

Activity 3

Read and learn.

- Read the information as a class. Highlight that the words mean 'one of many people / things / places' and that they are used in questions and negative sentences.

Activity 4

Work with a partner. Look at the *Word building* box and write the answers. Ask and answer.

- The pupils write their answers.
- In pairs, they ask and answer the questions.

Odd one out activity

Which is the odd one out? Why?

Answers: somewhere (It refers to a place, not people.)

Ending the lesson

Review the lesson and reflect on learning.

- Say **Today we've learnt the names of some more unlikely or impossible activities.**
- Ask **What do you remember?** The pupils do a three-minute review in pairs.

Extra activities

Extension

- Choose a pupil to throw a dice. The class shouldn't see the number. Ask **What would you do if you found some money?** Even number is Truth, odd is False. The class decides if the answer is true or false. Prompt the pupils to ask questions.

Vocabulary Extension

- Present four additional words related to unreal or unlikely experiences: *find a wallet, get lost, lose your phone, see a robbery.*
- Use the Vocabulary Booster on NAVIO to practise these new words.

Key Competences and Key Learning Outcomes

- Review talking about past events
- Sequence the main events in the diary extracts
- Do pre-reading tasks to predict content and raise interest
- Read a text for general understanding
- Read a diary extract
- Express an opinion on the text

Key language

- *autobiographical, desert island, fictional, rescue, shelter*
- *I wonder if I'll find a better place to live tomorrow.*

Materials

- Pupil's Book p88; Activity Book p85; Class CD3; Teacher's App on Navio

Optional materials

- Teacher's Resource Bank: Trinity Exams Practice cards (selected from the Starter Unit and Units 1, 2, 3, 4, 5, 6 and 7)

At a Glance Lesson Plan

Pupil's Book

Starting the lesson

- Use the Trinity Exams Practice cards (optional).
- Review unlikely or impossible activities.
- Set learning outcomes.

Activity 1: Before you read

- Read and discuss.

Activity 2

- Look at the sketches in the diary.
- Where do you think the writer is?
- Read and find out.

Activity 3: After you read

- What do you think?
- Go to the Activity Book.

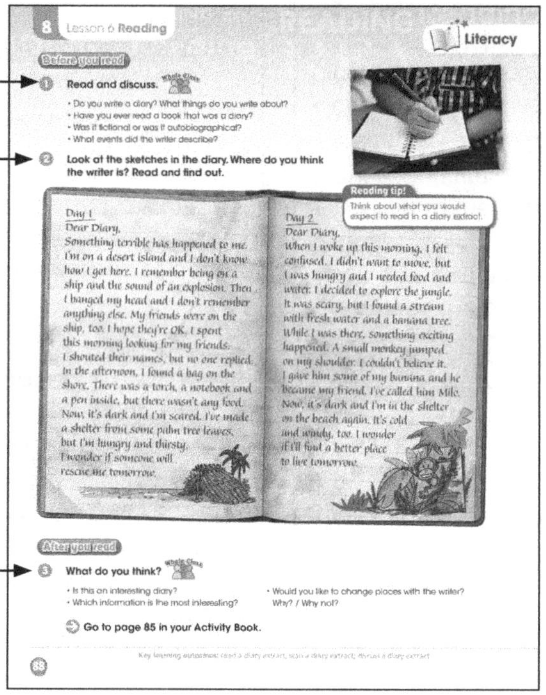
8 Lesson 6 Reading

Literacy

Before you read

1 Read and discuss.

- Do you write a diary? What things do you write about?
- Have you ever read a book that was a diary?
- Was it fictional or was it autobiographical?
- What events did the writer describe?

2 Look at the sketches in the diary. Where do you think the writer is? Read and find out.

Reading tip! Think about what you would expect to read in a diary extract.

Day 1

Dear Diary,

Something terrible has happened to me. I'm on a desert island and I don't know how I got here. I remember being on a ship and the sound of an explosion. Then I banged my head and I don't remember anything else. My friends were on the ship, too. I hope they're OK. I spent this morning looking for my friends. I shouted their names, but no one replied. In the afternoon, I found a bag on the shore. There was a torch, a notebook and a pen inside, but there wasn't any food. Now, it's dark and I'm scared. I've made a shelter from some palm tree leaves, but I'm hungry and thirsty. I wonder if someone will rescue me tomorrow.

Day 2

Dear Diary,

When I woke up this morning, I felt confused. I didn't want to move, but I was hungry and I needed food and water. I decided to explore the jungle. It was scary, but I found a stream with fresh water and a banana tree. While I was there, something exciting happened. A small monkey jumped on my shoulder. I couldn't believe it. I gave him some of my banana and he became my friend. I've called him Milo. Now, it's dark and I'm in the shelter on the beach again. It's cold and windy, too. I wonder if I'll find a better place to live tomorrow.

After you read

3 What do you think?

- Is this an interesting diary?
- Which information is the most interesting?
- Would you like to change places with the writer? Why? / Why not?

Go to page 85 in your Activity Book.

88

Ending the lesson

- Review the lesson and reflect on learning.

Extra activity

Extension

- Role play an interview with the writer of the diary.

Activity Book

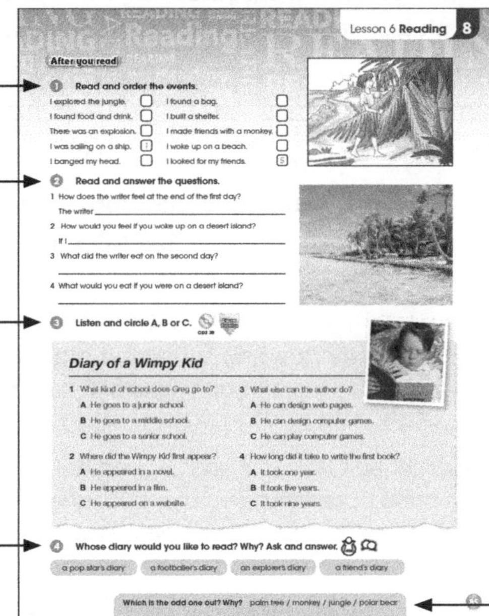
Lesson 6 Reading 8

After you read

1 Read and order the events.

I explored the jungle.		I found a bag.	
I found food and drink.		I built a shelter.	
There was an explosion.		I made friends with a monkey.	
I was sailing on a ship.		I woke up on a beach.	
I banged my head.		I looked for my friends.	5

2 Read and answer the questions.

1 How does the writer feel at the end of the first day?

The writer

2 How would you feel if you woke up on a desert island?

If I

3 What did the writer eat on the second day?

4 What would you eat if you were on a desert island?

3 Listen and circle A, B or C.

Diary of a Wimpy Kid

1 What kind of school does Greg go to?
A He goes to a junior school.
B He goes to a middle school.
C He goes to a senior school.

2 When did the Wimpy Kid first appear?
A He appeared in a novel.
B He appeared in a film.
C He appeared on a website.

3 What else can the author do?
A He can design web pages.
B He can design computer games.
C He can play computer games.

4 How long did it take to write the first book?
A It took one year.
B It took five years.
C It took nine years.

4 Whose diary would you like to read? Why? Ask and answer.

a pop star's diary | a footballer's diary | an explorer's diary | a friend's diary

Which is the odd one out? Why? palm tree / monkey / jungle / polar bear

Activity Book: After you read

Activity 1

- Read and order the events.

Activity 2

- Read and answer the questions.

Activity 3

- Listen and circle A, B or C.

▶ *CD3 Track 38 p293*

Activity 4

- Whose diary would you like to read? Why? Ask and answer.

Odd one out activity

Digital resources

Teacher's Digital: You can also teach this lesson using the Teacher's App on Navio.

Pupil's Digital: Encourage your pupils to use the Pupil's App on Navio to practise the activities from this lesson.

Powered By NAVIO

Starting the lesson

Use the Trinity Exams Practice cards (optional).

- The pupils practise asking and answering questions.

Review unlikely or impossible activities.

- Organise the pupils into pairs. Challenge them to remember the eight unlikely and impossible activities from Lesson 5.
- Quickly review the events as a class. Ask individual pupils a question each time, e.g. **What would you do if you (were invisible)?**

Set learning outcomes.

- Say **Today we're going to read a diary extract.**

Pupil's Book Activity 1: Before you read

Read and discuss.

- Read the questions as a class. Prompt the pupils to talk about their experiences writing and reading diaries.

Pupil's Book Activity 2

Look at the sketches in the diary. Where do you think the writer is? Read and find out.

- Ask the pupils to describe the sketches.
- Then ask the class to predict where the writer of the diary is.
- Read the diary entries as a class to find out. Confirm that the writer is on a desert island.

Pupil's Book Activity 3: After you read

What do you think?

- Read the questions as a class.
- In pairs, the pupils answer the questions. They should explain and justify their opinions each time.
- Check answers as a class.

Activity Book: After you read

Activity 1

Read and order the events.

- Invite a pupil to read out the first sentence. Then ask the class to identify and number what happens next.
- In pairs, the pupils order and number the remaining sentences. They refer to the diary extract in the Pupil's Book to help them.

Answers: 8, 9, 2, 1, 3, 6, 7, 10, 4, 5

Activity 2

Read and answer the questions.

- Invite a pupil to read and answer the first question.
- The pupils answer the remaining questions. They refer to the diary extracts in the Pupil's Book to help them.

Answers: **1** felt scared at the end of the first day.
3 The writer ate bananas on the second day.

Activity 3

Listen and circle A, B or C. Exams Practice

▶ *CD3 Track 38 p293*

- Ask the pupils if they have ever read any of the *Wimpy Kid* books. If they have, encourage the pupils to tell you about the main character, Greg, and what the character writes about in his diaries.
- Read the questions as a class. Encourage the pupils to predict the answer each time.
- Play the CD. The pupils listen and circle the answers.
- Play the CD again, pausing after each piece of information. The pupils check their answers.

Answers: **1** B **2** C **3** B **4** C

Activity 4

Whose diary would you like to read? Why? Ask and answer.

- Read the diary types as a class.
- In pairs, the pupils ask and answer about the different people's diaries.
- Invite different pairs to share their answers with the class.

Odd one out activity

Which is the odd one out? Why?

- The pupils complete the odd one out activity.

Answers: polar bear (You don't find it on tropical islands.)

Ending the lesson

Review the lesson and reflect on learning.

- Say **Today we've read a diary extract.**
- Ask **What do you remember?** The pupils do a three-minute review in pairs. (Cooperative Learning Strategies, page 19)

Extra activity

Extension

- Organise the class into pairs. Explain that one pupil is a journalist and the other is the writer of the diary extract in the Pupil's Book. The journalist is interviewing the writer about the experience of living on the desert island.
- Elicit questions that a journalist might ask. If necessary, write the questions on the board.
- The pupils role play the interview in pairs.

Key Competences and Key Learning Outcomes

- Review and practise how to use personal pronouns and possessive adjectives
- Reflect on existing knowledge to predict content
- Identify the text features of a diary extract
- Use criteria to check your writing
- Share and discuss your writing with a partner
- Write a diary extract

Key language

- *heading, reflection; I, me, mine, my, our, ours, we, us*
- *Milo and I love our cave.*

Materials

- Pupil's Book p89; Activity Book p86; Teacher's App on Navio

Optional materials

- Teacher's Resource Bank: Trinity Exams Practice cards (selected from the Starter Unit and Units 1, 2, 3, 4, 5, 6 and 7)

At a Glance Lesson Plan

Pupil's Book

Starting the lesson

- Use the Trinity Exams Practice cards (optional).
- Review the diary extract from Lesson 6.
- Set learning outcomes.

Activity 1: Investigate a text

- Read and answer.

Activity 2

- Read the diary extract to check your answers.

Activity 3: Discuss a text

- Read the diary extract again.
- Find the following.

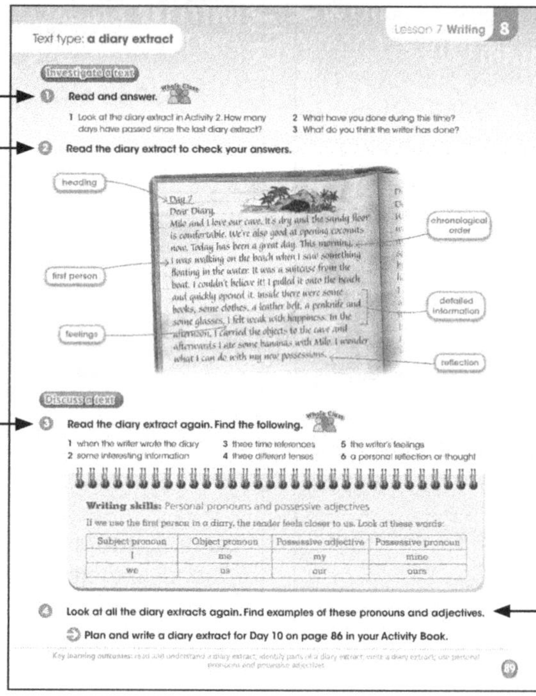
Text type: a diary extract

Investigate a text

1 Read and answer.

2 Read the diary extract to check your answers.

Discuss a text

3 Read the diary extract again. Find the following.

4 Look at all the diary extracts again. Find examples of these pronouns and adjectives.

Plan and write a diary extract for Day 10 on page 86 in your Activity Book.

Writing skills

- Read about personal pronouns and possessive adjectives.

Activity 4

- Look at all the diary extracts again.
- Find examples of these pronouns and adjectives.
- Go to the Activity Book.

Ending the lesson

- Review the lesson and reflect on learning.

Extra activity

Extension

- Share your diary extract with the rest of the class.

Activity Book

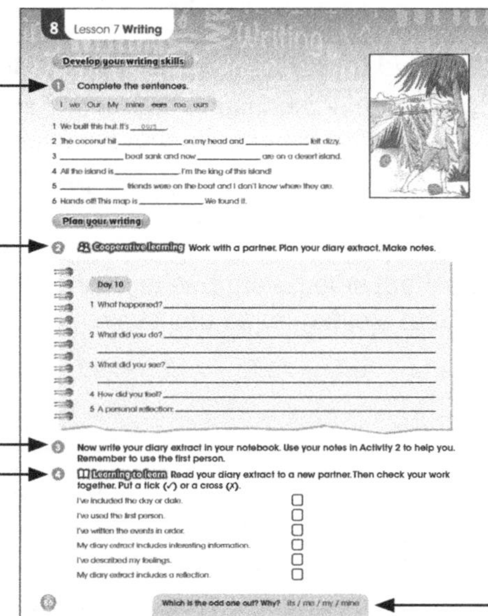
Lesson 7 Writing

Develop your writing skills

1 Complete the sentences.

Plan your writing

2 Cooperative learning Work with a partner. Plan your diary extract. Make notes.

3 Now write your diary extract in your notebook. Use your notes in Activity 2 to help you. Remember to use the first person.

4 Learning to learn Read your diary extract to a new partner. Then check your work together. Put a tick (✓) or a cross (✗).

Which is the odd one out? Why?

Activity Book

Activity 1: Develop your writing skills

- Complete the sentences.

Activity 2: Plan your writing

- Work with a partner. Plan your diary extract. Make notes.

Activity 3

- Now write your diary extract in your notebook. Use your notes in Activity 2 to help you. Remember to use the first person.

Activity 4

- Read your diary extract to a new partner. Then check your work together. Put a tick (✓) or a cross (✗).

Odd one out activity

Digital resources

Teacher's Digital: You can also teach this lesson using the Teacher's App on Navio.

Pupil's Digital: Encourage your pupils to use the Pupil's App on Navio to practise the activities from this lesson.

Powered By NAVIO

Detailed Lesson Plan

Starting the lesson

Use the Trinity Exams Practice cards (optional).

- The pupils practise asking and answering questions.

Review the diary extract from Lesson 6.

- Ask **Do you remember the diary extract in the last lesson? What happened to the writer?** The pupils think for 30 seconds.
- Organise the pupils into pairs. They work together to reconstruct what happened.
- Then quickly review the main events in chronological order as a class.

Set learning outcomes.

- Say **Today we're going to read another diary extract and you're going to write your own diary extract.**

Pupil's Book Activity 1: Investigate a text

Read and answer.

- Read and answer the questions as a class.
- Encourage the pupils to make different predictions about what the writer has done.

Pupil's Book Activity 2

Read the diary extract to check your answers.

- The pupils read the diary extract to find out what has happened.
- Check answers as a class.

Pupil's Book Activity 3: Discuss a text

Read the diary extract again. Find the following.

- Read the information as a class. The pupils find the information in the diary extract.
- Highlight that information in a diary is in (chronological) order and the time references help to organise this information. Also highlight that diaries have personal information, such as how the writer is feeling and personal reflections or thoughts.

Answers: **1** Day 7 **3** now, today, this morning, in the afternoon, afterwards **4** present simple, present continuous, past simple, past continuous, present perfect

Writing skills

- Read about personal pronouns and possessive adjectives.

Pupil's Book Activity 4

Look at all the diary extracts again. Find examples of these pronouns and adjectives.

- The pupils look at the diary extracts in Lessons 6 and 7. They identify examples of personal pronouns and possessive adjectives.

Activity Book

Activity 1: Develop your writing skills

Complete the sentences.

- The pupils complete the sentences with the personal pronouns and possessive adjectives.
- Check answers as a class.

Answers: **1** ours **2** me, I **3** Our, we **4** mine **5** My **6** ours

Activity 2: Plan your writing

Work with a partner. Plan your diary extract. Make notes.

- Read out the notes as a class. Check understanding.
- The pupils work in pairs to plan their diary extract.

Activity 3

Now write your diary extract in your notebook. Use your notes in Activity 2 to help you. Remember to use the first person.

- The pupils work with a partner to write their diary extract in their notebooks.
- Remind the class to use the first person.

Activity 4

Read your diary extract to a new partner. Then check your work together. Put a tick (✓) or a cross (✗).

- Read through the statements as a class.
- Organise the class into new partners. One pupil reads aloud their diary extract. The other pupil listens. The pupils work together to decide if the diary extract fulfils the criteria and tick the corresponding boxes. The pupils can add, improve or correct the diary extract at this stage.
- The pupils swap roles.

Odd one out activity

Which is the odd one out? Why?

- The pupils complete the odd one out activity.

Answers: its (It refers to third person.)

Ending the lesson

Review the lesson and reflect on learning.

- Say **Today we've read and written a diary extract.**
- Ask **What do you remember?** The pupils do a three-minute review in pairs. (Cooperative Learning Strategies, page 19)

Extra activity

Extension

- Ask the pupils to leave their notebooks on their desks so that other pupils can read their diary extracts. The pupils move around the class, reading the texts. Each pupil should make a note of three diary extracts that they found the most exciting.

Key Competences and Key Learning Outcomes

- Review describing objects
- Listen to a text for general and specific information

- Prepare and practise speaking activity types found in Cambridge Exams: B1 Preliminary for Schools
- Reflect on learning and progress

- Work together to discuss and solve a problem

- Practise agreeing and disagreeing with an opinion

Key language

- *dinosaurs, prehistoric age*
- *Would you go to the future or the past?*

Materials

- Pupil's Book p90; Activity Book pp87–88; Class CD3; Teacher's App on Navio

Optional materials

- Teacher's Resource Bank: Trinity Exams Practice cards (selected from the Starter Unit and Units 1, 2, 3, 4, 5, 6 and 7)
- Eight copies of a photo of a deserted island

At a Glance Lesson Plan

Pupil's Book

Starting the lesson

- Use the Trinity Exams Practice cards (optional).
- Review describing scenes.
- Set learning outcomes.

Activity 1

- Describe the photos.
- Do they show the past, the present or the future?

Activity 2

- Listen to the conversation.

▶ *CD3 Track 39 p293*

- What would Sam do if he could travel in time?

Activity 3

- Listen again.

▶ *CD3 Track 39 p293*

- Complete the four questions that Ben asks.

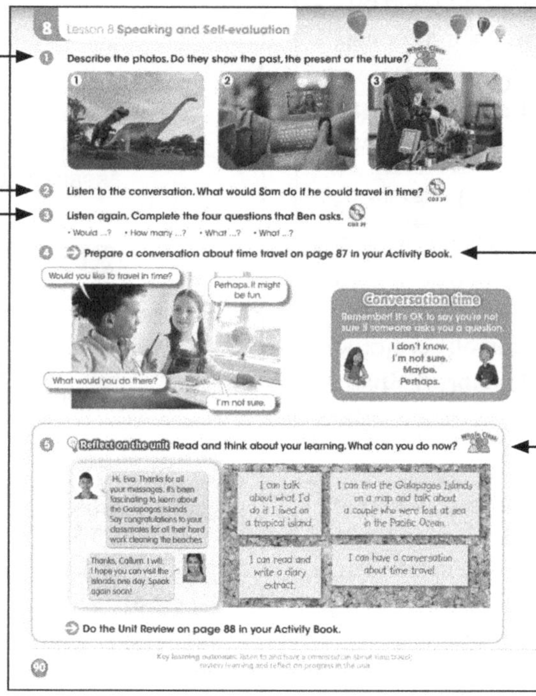

Activity 4

- Prepare a conversation about time travel on page 87 in your Activity Book.

Go to the Activity Book.

Activity 5

- Read and think about your learning.
- What can you do now?

Ending the lesson

- Review the lesson and reflect on learning.

Activity Book

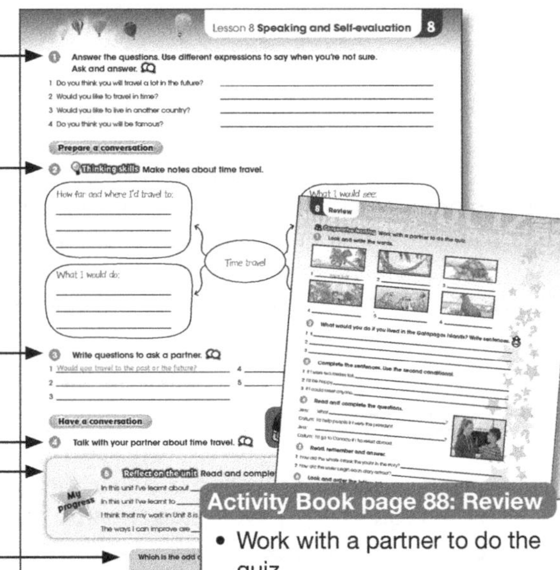

Activity Book page 88: Review

- Work with a partner to do the quiz.

Activity Book

Activity 1

- Answer the questions. Use different expressions to say when you're not sure. Ask and answer.

Activity 2

- Make notes about time travel.

Activity 3

- Write questions to ask a partner.

Activity 4

- Talk with your partner about time travel.

Activity 5

- Read and complete the sentences.

Odd one out activity

Digital resources

Teacher's Digital: You can also teach this lesson using the Teacher's App on Navio.

Powered By NAVIO

Starting the lesson

Use the Trinity Exams Practice cards (optional).

- The pupils practise asking and answering questions.

Review describing scenes.

- Organise the class into eight groups. Explain that one person in each group is going to describe a photo. The other group members listen and draw the scene they hear described. They can ask questions for clarification.
- Give one copy of the photo of a desert island to each group.
- Quickly review phrases for describing a photo, e.g. in the background, on the left, in the centre, etc.
- The pupils work for 3–5 minutes. At the end of that time, they compare their drawing with the original photo.

Set learning outcomes.

- Say **Today we're going to listen to and have a conversation about time travel and we're going to think about our learning.**

Pupil's Book Activity 1

Describe the photos. Do they show the past, the present or the future?

- Pupils describe the photos in pairs.
- Invite pupils to share what they discussed in their conversation with the class.

Pupil's Book Activity 2

Listen to the conversation. What would Sam do if he could travel in time?

▶ *CD3 Track 39 p293*

- Play CD and elicit answer.
- Ask pupils where they would travel in time.

Answers: He would travel to the past.

Pupil's Book Activity 3

Listen again. Complete the four questions that Ben asks.

▶ *CD3 Track 39 p293*

- Have pupils read questions and guess how they are completed.
- Play CD and check answers as a class.

Answers: Would you like to travel in time? / Would you go to the future or the past? How many years would you travel? What would you see there? What would you do? / What would you do if a dinosaur saw you?

Pupil's Book Activity 4

Prepare a conversation about time travel on page 23 in your Activity Book.

- Pupils read the Conversation time box and the dialogue.
- Direct pupils to the Activity Book.

Pupil's Book Activity 5

Read and think about your learning. What can you do now?

- Read the messages as a class. Then look back through the unit and prompt the pupils to identify other things they have learnt / done.

Activity Book

Activity 1

Answer the questions. Use different expressions to say when you're not sure. Ask and answer.

- Pupils complete the activity individually and then show partners their work.
- Invite pupils to share their answers with the class.

Activity 2

Make notes about time travel.

- Pupils complete the notes individually and show their partners.
- Invite pupils to share their notes with the class.

Activity 3

Write questions to ask a partner.

- Pupils complete the activity. Remind them to refer to Ben's questions in the Pupil's Book.

Activity 4

Talk with your partner about time travel.

- Refer pupils to the Remember box.
- In pairs, the pupils have a conversation about what they want to be. One pupil asks the questions in Activity 3 and the partner answers. They then swap roles.

Activity 5: My progress

Read and complete the sentences.

- Read out the sentences. Encourage the pupils to think of different ways of completing them.
- The pupils complete the sentences.

Odd one out activity

Which is the odd one out? Why?

- The pupils complete the odd one out activity.

Answers: statue (It isn't a natural feature.)

Ending the lesson

Review the lesson and reflect on learning.

- Say **Today we've had a conversation about time travel and we've thought about our learning.**
- Ask **What do you remember?** The pupils do a three-minute review in pairs. (Cooperative Learning Strategies, page 19)

Activity Book page 88: Review

Work with a partner to do the quiz.

- Organise the class into pairs. Explain that they are going to work together to do a quiz. Set a time limit for the pupils to do this (10–15 minutes). Stress that the pupils are not competing with each other.
- Read out the six tasks that the pupils have to complete. Check understanding. Then say **Ready, steady ... Go!**
- The pupils work in their pairs to do the quiz. Ask the pupils who finish quickly to help another pair.
- Correct the answers as a class.

Answers: **1 1** palm tree **2** hammock **3** giant tortoise **4** coral **5** tropical fish **6** sea lion **4** would you do if you were the president? Where would you go if you travelled abroad? **5 1** It smashed its tail against the yacht. **2** The writer began with 'Dear diary'. **6** compass, an instrument which shows North, South, East, West

Key Competences and Key Learning Outcomes

- Watch and understand a video about desert island survival
- Understand the best ways to work in a group
- Work as a team to decide on the best objects to take to the desert island

Key language

- *escape, shelter, survival, poisonous*
- *I prefer doing projects in a group. Why? Because it's faster. We can share the work.*

Materials

- Pupil's Book p91; Activity Book p89; Class CD 3; Teacher's App on Navio
- Teacher's Resource Bank: Talk cards

Optional materials

- Teacher's Resource Bank: Trinity Exams Practice cards (selected from the Starter Unit)

At a Glance Lesson Plan

Pupil's Book

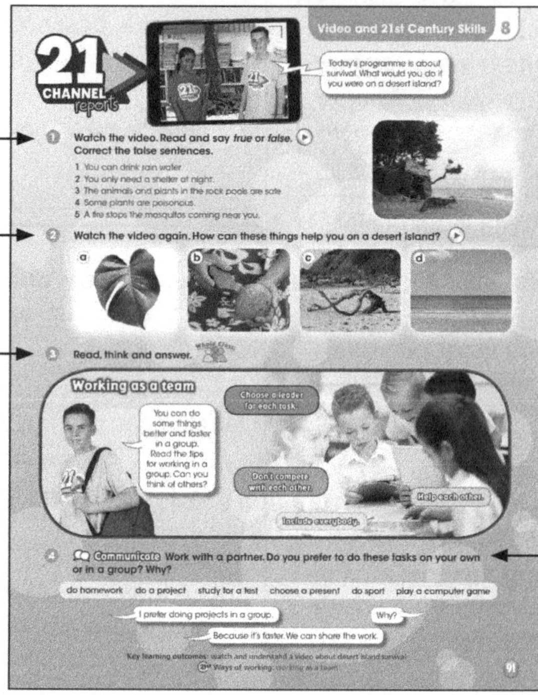

Starting the lesson

- **Think-Pair-Share**. Review different ways and reasons why we should work as a team.
- Set learning outcomes and use the talk cards.

Activity 1

- Before you watch.
- Watch the video.
- *Unit 8 video p303*
- Read and say *true* or *false*.
- Correct the false sentences.

Activity 2

- Watch the video again.
- *Unit 8 video*
- How can these things help you on a desert island?

Activity 3

- Read, think and answer.

Activity 4

- Work with a partner.
- Do you prefer to do these tasks on your own or in a group?
- Why?
- Go to the Activity Book.

Ending the lesson

- Review the lesson and reflect on learning.

Extra activity

- Think about when people should work as a team.

Activity Book

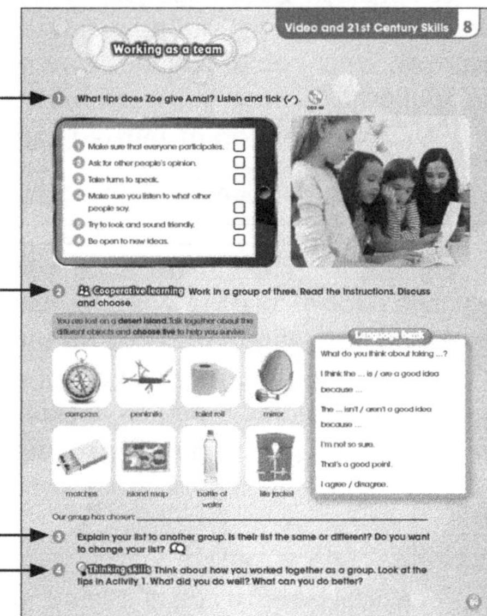

Activity Book

Activity 1

- What tips does Zoe give Amal? Listen and tick (✓).
- *CD3 Track 40 p293*

Activity 2

- Work in a group of three. Read the instructions. Discuss and choose.

Activity 3

- Explain your list to another group. Is their list the same or different? Do you want to change your list?

Activity 4

- Think about how you worked together as a group. Look at the tips in Activity 1. What did you do well? What can you do better?

Digital resources

Teacher's Digital: You can also teach this lesson using the Teacher's App on Navio.

Pupil's Digital: Encourage your pupils to use the Pupil's App on Navio to practise the activities from this lesson.

Powered By NAVIO

Starting the lesson

Think-Pair-Share. Review different ways and reasons why we should work as a team.

- Ask pupils how and when they have worked as a team and if they enjoyed it.

Ask Why should we work in teams? Elicit answers and write them on the board.

- Extend the discussion to talk about different ways people can work in teams, what they do in each team and why it is a positive way of working. Write ideas on the board.
- Pupils work with a Talk Partner to discuss different ways and reasons why we should work as a team.
- Invite different Talk Partners to tell the class what they discussed with their partners.

Set learning outcomes and use the talk cards.

- Say **Today we're going to watch a video about desert island survival.**
- Point to the talk cards to show the pupils the different ways they will be working in the lesson.

Pupil's Book Activity 1

Before you watch

- Ask pupils to imagine they are stranded on a desert island and tell you how they feel.
- Ask if they know of any survival methods and where they learnt them.
- Then ask what type of survival methods are important to know and when one can use them.

Watch the video. Read and say *true* or *false*. Correct the false sentences. *p303*

- Watch Part 1. Ask pupils if they agreed with what the adults in the video say and why? or why not?
- Have pupils read the statements.
- Play Part 2, pausing at each section for pupils to answer. Pupils then work in pairs to check answers.

Answers: **1** T **2** F **3** F **4** T **5** F
2 You need a shelter to protect you from the sun and rain.
3 Animals and plants can be poisonous.
4 A fire stops snakes coming near you.

Pupil's Book Activity 2

Watch the video again. How can these things help you on a desert island?

- Ask pupils to tell you what they remember from the video.
- Have pupils complete the activity in pairs.
- Play the second part of the video for pupils to check their answers.
- Have a class discussion on what they found interesting about the video.

Answers: **a** Leaf can collect water for you to drink. **b** Coconut can give you milk and food. **c** Sticks can help you make shelters and fire. **d** Sand can help you make a help signal.

Pupil's Book Activity 3

Read, think and answer.

- Tell pupils that in the last part of the video Amy and Max talk about how you need to help and trust each other in difficult situations.
- Ask pupils why this is important.
- Have pupils discuss the ideas in the box and to add any more if possible.
- Note any new ideas on the board.

Pupil's Book Activity 4

Work with a partner. Do you prefer to do these tasks on your own or in a group? Why?

- Have pupils work with a partner to complete the activity.
- Encourage pupils to explain the reason behind their opinions.
- Ask pairs to present their work to the class.
- Have a class discussion on the different ideas presented by each pair.

Activity Book

Activity 1

What tips does Zoe give Amal? Listen and tick (✓).

▶ *CD3 Track 40 p293*

- Give pupils a little time to read contents in the box. Have them say which ideas they think they will tick.
- Play the CD and complete the activity.
- Have pupils say which points they think are more important when working in groups. Ask them if they can add to the list.

Answers: Tick: 1, 2, 3, 4, 6

Activity 2

Work in a group of three. Read the instructions. Discuss and choose.

- Direct pupils to the Language bank and explain that they should use this language in their discussion.
- Have pupils complete the activity in small groups.

Activity 3

Explain your list to another group. Is their list the same or different? Do you want to change your list?

- Pupils complete the activity in groups.

Activity 4

Think about how you worked together as a group. Look at the tips in Activity 1. What did you do well? What can you do better?

- Tell pupils that being honest and accepting about how you work helps you become a better team worker.
- Have a class discussion and write notes on the board.

Ending the lesson

Review the lesson and reflect on learning.

- Say **Today we've watched a video about desert island survival. What have we learnt?** Elicit the information from the pupils. The pupils do a three-minute review in pairs. (Cooperative Learning Strategies, page 19)

Extra activity

Reinforcement

- Place pupils in small pairs and ask them to think about when people should work as a team.
- Have a class discussion, encouraging pupils to use the ideas they discussed in groups.

Date: ______________ Unit: ________

1 What did my pupils learn in this unit?

____

____

____

____

2 How did my pupils work? (✓)

individually ☐ in pairs ☐ in small groups ☐

in large groups ☐ as a class ☐

3 Which key competences did my pupils develop? Give a score from 1 to 5 (5 being the highest).

- Competence in linguistic communication ☐
- Competence in mathematics, science and technology ☐
- Digital competence ☐
- Learning to learn ☐
- Social and civic competences ☐
- Sense of initiative and entrepreneurship ☐
- Cultural awareness and expression ☐

4 Which lessons / activities were the most successful and why?

____

____

____

____

5 Which lessons / activities did my pupils find the most difficult and why?

____

____

____

____

6 What did I try in the classroom for the first time? How did it go?

____

____

____

____

7 Which resources did I find most useful? (including webpages)

____

____

____

____

____

____

8 What could I do differently next time I teach this unit?

____

____

____

____

Unit 9

School: past and future

Unit overview

Key competences and learning outcomes

- Name school equipment from the past and present (Lesson 1)
- Use 'used to' to talk about past habits (Lesson 2)
- Compare and practise how to use 'will' and 'going to' for the future (Lesson 4)
- Review and name secondary school subjects and equipment (Lesson 5)
- Use 'so' and 'because' (Lesson 7)
- Watch and understand a video (Video and 21st Century Skills)

- Use a Venn diagram to classify vocabulary (Lesson 1)
- Read about science and technology (Lessons 1 and 3)

- Use the Pupil's App on Navio
- Investigate Sweden (Lesson 3)

- Identify and practise features of connected speech (Lesson 4)
- Identify the text features of an advice column (Lesson 7)
- Review learning and reflect on progress in the unit (Lesson 8)
- Practise activity types found in the Cambridge Exams: B1 Preliminary for Schools

- Understand the universal right to have an education (Lesson 3)
- Listen to and have a conversation about school (Lesson 8)

- Work in pairs or small groups to practise and reinforce learning (All lessons)
- Do a communication task (Lesson 5)
- Analyse types of strong feelings (Video and 21st Century Skills)

- Read a story (Lesson 3)
- Learn about Sweden (Lesson 3)
- Read and write an advice column (Lessons 6 and 7)
- Sing a song (Lesson 8)

Vocabulary

Core vocabulary
blackboard, canvas, chalk, easel, goggles, headphones, interactive whiteboard, laboratory, laptop, oil paints, overall, rows of desks; Chemistry, geometry set, Literature, locker, musical instrument, Physics, sports kit, timetable

Extension vocabulary (optional)
absent, certificate, grades, present, register, report card; folder, highlighter pen, pendrive, stapler

Other vocabulary
(to) award, be strict, carry rucksacks, impress, punish pupils, sit in rows, stay organised, work in silence; agony aunt column, ceremony, dynamite, Nobel Prize, obituary, performing arts; anxious, bossy, sympathetic; corridors, goggles, lockers, overalls

Recycled vocabulary
go shopping / to my grandparent's house; dream / secondary school, tips; active, adventurous, boring, brave, friendly, helpful, important, shy

Structures

Core structures
I / You / He / She / We / They used to (study History). I / You / He / She / We / They didn't use to (play computer games). Did I / you / he / she / we / they use to (have the Internet)? Yes, I / you / he / she / we / they did. No, I / you / he / she / we / they didn't. I'm going to have lunch at two o'clock. I'll answer the telephone. I think he'll pass the exam.

Other structures
I'm nervous about / I'm excited about / I'm looking forward to / I'm worried about (going to secondary school). He feels (excited) about going to secondary school. Starting a new school is a big change.

Recycled structures
Alfred Nobel was born in 1833. It's important to read your timetable. Gina is interested in making things. She isn't keen on very modern music. What's your favourite subject at school?

Pronunciation

Features of connected speech: weak form of 'going to'

Literacy

Text type: an advice column (text to advise; writing preparation)
Reading skills: scanning for specific information
Writing skills: using 'so' and 'because' to talk about results and reasons

Culture ... around the world

The creation of the Nobel Prizes in Sweden

21st Century Skills

Living in the world: managing strong feelings

Thinking skills

Forming conceptual links and associations (Lessons 1 and 8); Defining and describing (Lesson 1); Comparing and contrasting (Lesson 2); Analysing and applying rules and patterns (Lessons 2 and 4); Expressing cause and effect (Lesson 7); Problem solving (Lesson 8); Evaluating (Lesson 8)

Cooperative learning

Working together (Lessons 1–8); Reflecting and setting goals (Lessons 1–8); Expressing and respecting opinions (Lessons 3 and 6); Collaborative writing (Lesson 7); Peer evaluation (Lesson 7); Showing interest in others (Lessons 1, 5, 8); Praising and encouraging (Lesson 8)

Values

The universal right for all children to an education

Cross-curricular links

Links to Science
Virtual museum: past and present

Suggested Arts and Crafts concepts
Volume

Key Competences and Key Learning Outcomes

- Name school equipment from the past and present
- Review and practise how to use the present perfect with 'for' and 'since'

- Use a Venn diagram to classify vocabulary
- Read about science and technology

- Create a topic concept map

Key language

- *blackboard, canvas, chalk, easel, goggles, headphones, interactive whiteboard, laboratory, laptop, oil paints, overall, rows of desks*
- Extension: *absent, certificate, grades, present, register, report card*
- *What's your favourite subject at school?*

Materials

- Pupil's Book pp92–93; Activity Book p90; Class CD3; Teacher's App on Navio
- School equipment flashcards

Optional materials

- Teacher's Resource Bank: Trinity Exams Practice cards (selected from the Starter Unit and Units 1, 2, 3, 4, 5, 6, 7 and 8)

At a Glance Lesson Plan

Pupil's Book

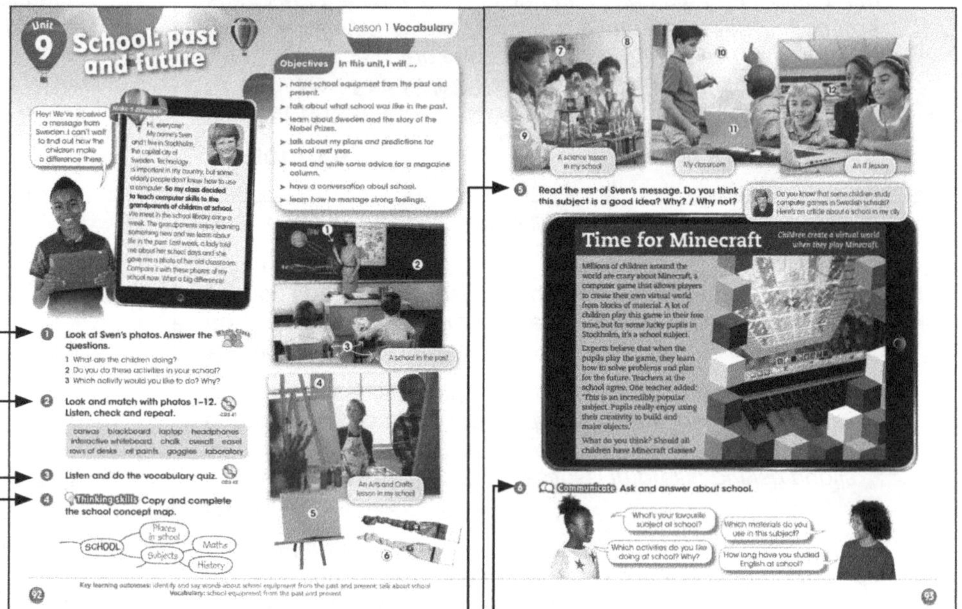

Starting the lesson

- Use the Trinity Exams Practice cards (optional).
- Review school subjects.
- Set learning outcomes.

Activity 1

- Look at Sven's photos.
- Answer the questions.

Vocabulary presentation

- Present the new vocabulary using the school equipment flashcards

Activity 2

- Look and match with photos 1–12.
- Listen, check and repeat.

▶ *CD3 Track 41 p294*

Activity 3

- Listen and do the vocabulary quiz.

▶ *CD3 Track 42 p294*

Activity 4

- Copy and complete the school concept map.

Activity 5

- Read the rest of Sven's message.
- Do you think this subject is a good idea?
- Why? / Why not?

Activity 6

- Ask and answer about school.

Go to the Activity Book.

Ending the lesson

- Review the lesson and reflect on learning.

Extra activities

Extension

- Find out about Sweden.

Vocabulary extension

- Present six additional vocabulary items.

Activity Book

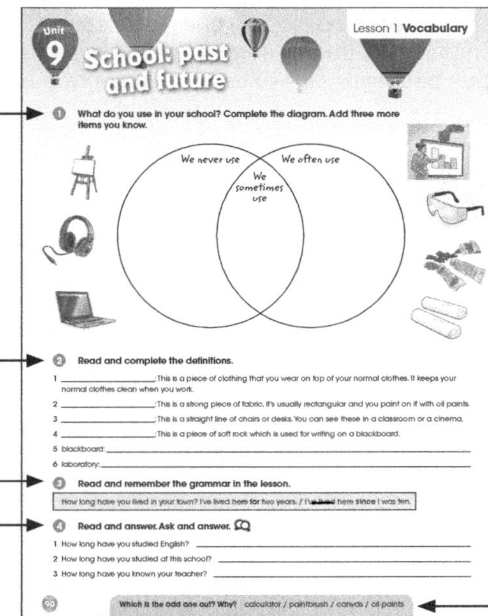

Activity Book

Activity 1

- What do you use in your school? Complete the diagram. Add three more items you know.

Activity 2

- Read and complete the definitions.

Activity 3

- Read and remember the grammar in the lesson.

Activity 4

- Read and answer. Ask and answer.

Odd one out activity

Digital resources

Teacher's Digital: You can also teach this lesson using the Teacher's App on Navio.

Pupil's Digital: Encourage your pupils to use the Pupil's App on Navio to practise the activities from this lesson.

Powered By NAVIO

Starting the lesson

Use the Trinity Exams Practice cards (optional).

- The pupils practise asking and answering questions.

Review school subjects.

- In pairs, the pupils list eight different school subjects.
- They order the school subjects from the easiest to the most difficult. Ask different pupils to share their ideas.

Set learning outcomes.

- Say **Today we're going to learn the names of school equipment from the past and present.**

Pupil's Book Activity 1

Look at Sven's photos. Answer the questions.

- Invite a pupil to read out the speech bubble. Ask **Do you know where Sweden is?**
- Invite a pupil to read out the message from Sven. Check understanding.
- Work as a class to answer the questions.

Vocabulary presentation

- Present the new vocabulary using the school equipment flashcards. Hold up the first flashcard so that the class can't see it. Give a definition of the object or place. The pupils listen and say the word. If the pupils don't know the word in English, provide the word and ask them to repeat it. Stick the flashcard on the board. Repeat with the other flashcards.

Pupil's Book Activity 2

Look and match with photos 1–12 . Listen, check and repeat.

▶ *CD3 Track 41 p294*

- The class look at item 1 in the photo. Ask **What's this?** The pupils match 2–12 with the words. Play the CD. The pupils listen and check.
- Play the CD again, pausing after each word for the pupils to repeat. You can find the answers for this activity in the audioscript on page 294.

Pupil's Book Activity 3

Listen and do the vocabulary quiz.

▶ *CD3 Track 42 p294*

- Play the CD. Listen to the first definition, pausing at the beep to allow the pupils to say the word. Play the CD to listen to the answer.
- Repeat the procedure with the other definitions. You can find the answers for this activity in the audioscript on page 294.

Pupil's Book Activity 4

Copy and complete the school concept map.

- In pairs, the pupils copy and complete the concept map. Set a time limit (4–5 minutes).
- Ask pairs to share their maps with the class.

Pupil's Book Activity 5

Read the rest of Sven's message. Do you think this subject is a good idea? Why? / Why not?

- Invite a pupil to read out the message. The pupils read the information on their own. Check understanding.
- In pairs, ask the pupils to decide if this subject is a good idea or not.
- The pupils report their opinions to the class.

Pupil's Book Activity 6

Ask and answer about school.

- Invite two pupils to read out the speech bubbles.
- In pairs, the pupils ask and answer questions about school.

Activity Book

Activity 1

What do you use in your school? Complete the diagram. Add three more items you know.

- In pairs, the pupils write the objects in the correct section of the diagram. They add three more items.
- Check answers as a class.

Activity 2

Read and complete the definitions.

- The pupils complete the definitions.

Answers: **1** overall **2** canvas **3** row of desks **4** chalk

Activity 3

Read and remember the grammar in the lesson.

- Invite a pupil to read out the information.

Activity 4

Read and answer. Ask and answer.

- The pupils answer the questions.
- In pairs, they ask and answer the questions.

Odd one out activity

Which is the odd one out? Why?

- The pupils complete the odd one out activity

Answers: calculator (You don't use it in Art.)

Ending the lesson

Review the lesson and reflect on learning.

- Say **Today we've learnt the names of school equipment from the past and present.**
- Ask **What do you remember?** The pupils do a three-minute review in pairs. (Cooperative Learning Strategies, page 19)

Extra activities

Extension

- The pupils find three interesting facts about Sweden to present to their class.

Vocabulary extension

- Introduce six words related to school equipment: *absent, certificate, grades, present, register, report card*.
- Use the Vocabulary Booster on NAVIO to practise these new words.

Key Competences and Key Learning Outcomes

- Listen to and read a dialogue
- Learn and practise how to use 'used to' to talk about past habits
- Analyse and apply rules for forming and using 'used to'
- Compare and contrast education in the past with the present
- Identify examples of 'used to' in the dialogue

Key language

- *be strict, carry rucksacks, punish pupils, sit in rows, work in silence*
- *I / You / He / She / We / They used to (study History).*
- *I / You / He / She / We / They didn't use to (play computer games). Did I / you / he / she / we / they use to (have the Internet)? Yes, I / you / he / she / we / they did. No, I / you / he / she / we / they didn't.*

Materials

- Pupil's Book p94; Activity Book p91; Class CD4; Teacher's App on Navio
- Teacher's Resource Bank: School equipment word cards

Optional materials

- Teacher's Resource Bank: Trinity Exams Practice cards (selected from the Starter Unit and Units 1, 2, 3, 4, 5, 6, 7 and 8)

At a Glance Lesson Plan

Pupil's Book

Starting the lesson
- Use the Trinity Exams Practice cards (optional).
- Review school equipment.
- Set learning outcomes.

Activity 1
- Describe the photo.
- What is it?
- Read and listen to find out.

▶ *CD4 Track 1 p294*

Activity 2
- Read the dialogue again.
- Ask and answer.

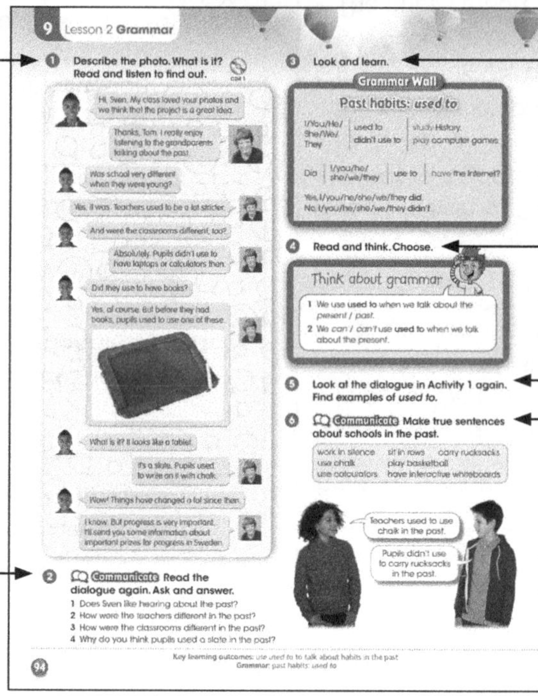

Activity 3
- Look and learn – Grammar wall

Activity 4
- Read and think.
- Choose.

Activity 5
- Look at the dialogue in Activity 1 again.
- Find examples of *used to.*

Activity 6
- Make true sentences about schools in the past.

Go to the Activity Book.

Ending the lesson
- Review the lesson and reflect on learning.

Extra activity

Reinforcement
- Write about infant school.

Activity Book

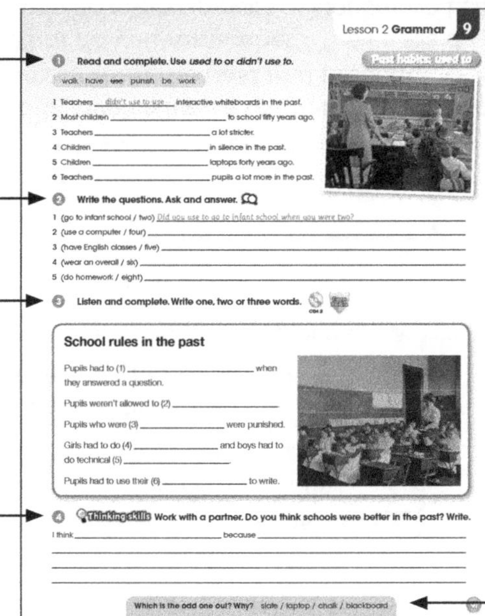

Activity Book

Activity 1
- Read and complete. Use *used to* or *didn't use to.*

Activity 2
- Write the questions. Ask and answer.

Activity 3
- Listen and complete. Write one, two or three words.

▶ *CD4 Track 2 p294*

Activity 4
- Work with a partner. Do you think schools were better in the past? Write.

Odd one out activity

Digital resources

Teacher's Digital: You can also teach this lesson using the Teacher's App on Navio.

Pupil's Digital: Encourage your pupils to use the Pupil's App on Navio to practise the activities from this lesson.

Powered By NAVIO

Starting the lesson

Use the Trinity Exams Practice cards (optional).

- The pupils practise asking and answering questions.

Review school equipment.

- Place the school equipment word cards face down on a desk. Organise the class into groups of three.
- Pupil 1 collects a card and defines the word for the group. Pupil 2 says the word and Pupil 3 spells it.
- The pupils change roles. They repeat the procedure with a new word card.

Set learning outcomes.

- Say **Today we're going to talk about schools in the past.**

Pupil's Book Activity 1

Describe the photo. What is it? Read and listen to find out.

▶ *CD4 Track 1 p294*

- Prompt the pupils to describe the photo. Invite them to guess what the object is.
- Play the CD. The pupils listen and read the dialogue. Confirm that the object is a slate and it was used for writing on in the past.

Pupil's Book Activity 2

Read the dialogue again. Ask and answer.

- In pairs, the pupils read the dialogue again. They ask and answer the questions. They can do this orally or in their notebooks.

Answers: **1** Yes, he does. **2** They were a lot stricter. **3** There weren't any laptops or calculators.

Pupil's Book Activity 3

Look and learn – Grammar wall

- Read the information on the Grammar wall as a class.
- Highlight that we use 'used to' in the affirmative, but we use 'use to' with the auxiliary 'did' in the negative and question form.

Pupil's Book Activity 4

Read and think. Choose.

- Focus the pupils' attention on the Think about grammar box. Read out the sentences as a class. The pupils discuss and complete the sentences in pairs.
- Confirm that we use 'used to' for an action that happened regularly in the past, but doesn't happen now. For an action that happens regularly now, we use a verb in the present simple with an adverb of frequency or a time phrase.

Pupil's Book Activity 5

Look at the dialogue in Activity 1 again. Find examples of *used to*.

- In pairs, the pupils find examples of 'used to'.

Pupil's Book Activity 6

Make true sentences about schools in the past.

- Invite two pupils to read out the speech bubbles.
- In pairs, the pupils make more true sentences about schools in the past.

Activity Book

Activity 1

Read and complete. Use *used to* or *didn't use to*.

- The pupils work in pairs to complete the sentences.

Answers: **1** didn't use to use **2** used to walk **3** used to be **4** used to work **5** didn't use to have **6** used to punish

Activity 2

Write the questions. Ask and answer.

- The pupils write the questions.
- In pairs, the pupils ask and answer the questions.

Answers: **1** Did you use to go to infant school when you were two? **2** Did you use to use a computer when you were four? **3** Did you use to have English classes when you were five? **4** Did you use to wear an overall when you were six? **5** Did you use to do homework when you were eight?

Activity 3

Listen and complete.

Write one, two or three words.

▶ *CD4 Track 2 p294*

- Read the sentences as a class. Play the CD. The pupils listen and complete as many of the answers as possible.
- The pupils compare their answers with a partner.
- Play the CD again, pausing after each piece of key information. The pupils identify and say the answer each time.

Answers: **1** stand up **2** ask questions **3** late **4** needlework **5** drawing **6** right hand

Activity 4

Work with a partner. Do you think schools were better in the past? Write.

- In pairs, the pupils answer the question.

Odd one out activity

Which is the odd one out? Why?

- The pupils complete the odd one out activity.

Answers: laptop (It wasn't used in schools in the past.)

Ending the lesson

Review the lesson and reflect on learning.

- Say **Today we've talked about schools in the past.**
- Ask **What do you remember?** The pupils do a three-minute review in pairs. (Cooperative Learning Strategies, page 19)

Extra activity

Reinforcement

- Ask the pupils to think about when they were in infant school. Ask **Was school different then?**
- The pupils write sentences about five things that they used to do or didn't use to do in infant school.
- They then share their sentences in pairs.

Key Competences and Key Learning Outcomes

- Read a story with confidence and fluency
- Read about science and technology
- Use the Internet to investigate Sweden
- Understand the universal right of children to receive an education
- Learn about Sweden and the creation of the Nobel Prizes
- Express an opinion on a text

Key language

(to) award, dynamite, Nobel Prize, obituary

- *Alfred Nobel was born in 1833.*
- *I think it'll change the world.*
- *I'm going to use my money to create prizes.*

Materials

- Pupil's Book p95; Activity Book p92; Class CD4; Teacher's App on Navio

Optional materials

- Teacher's Resource Bank: Trinity Exams Practice cards (selected from the Starter Unit and Units 1, 2, 3, 4, 5, 6, 7 and 8)

At a Glance Lesson Plan

Pupil's Book

Starting the lesson

- Use the Trinity Exams Practice cards (optional).
- Review past activities.
- Set learning outcomes.

Activity 1: Before you read

- Read and discuss.

Activity 2

- Listen and read.

▶ *CD4 Track 3 p294*

Go to the Activity Book.

Give Me Five! values

- Read and discuss.

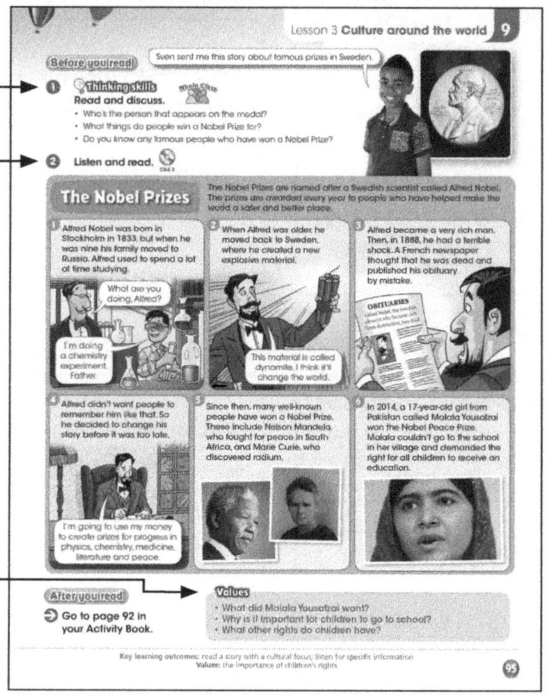

Ending the lesson

- Review the lesson and reflect on learning.

Extra activity

Extension

- Research a Nobel Prize winner.

Activity Book

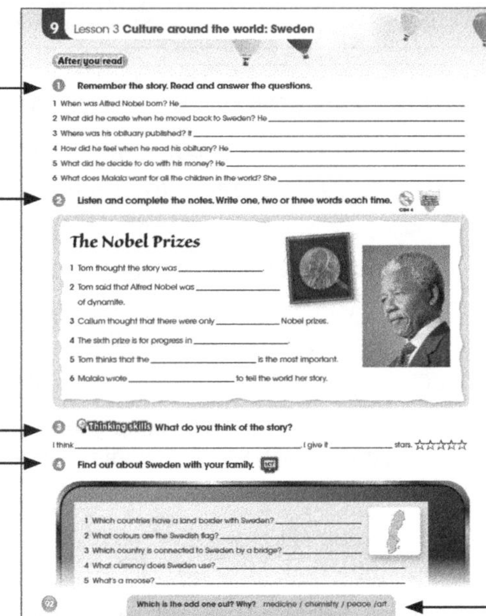

Activity Book: After you read

▶ *CD4 Track 4 p294*

Activity 1

- Remember the story. Read and answer the questions.

Activity 2

- Listen and complete the notes. Write one, two or three words each time.

Activity 3

- What do you think of the story?

Activity 4

- Find out about Sweden with your family.

Odd one out activity

Digital resources

Teacher's Digital: You can also teach this lesson using the Teacher's App on Navio.

Pupil's Digital: Encourage your pupils to use the Pupil's App on Navio to practise the activities from this lesson.

Powered By NAVIO

Starting the lesson

Use the Trinity Exams Practice cards (optional).

- The pupils practise asking and answering questions.

Review past activities.

- The pupils draw an outline of a hand. They write five toys that they used to play with when they were five. They write one object on each finger.
- In pairs, they ask and answer questions, e.g. *Did you use to play with (Lego)?*
- Invite different pupils to share answers with the class.

Set learning outcomes.

- Say **Today we're going to read a true story about a famous prize.**

Pupil's Book Activity 1: Before you read

Read and discuss.

- Read the questions as a class. The pupils share information they know about the Nobel Prizes.

Pupil's Book Activity 2

Listen and read.

▶ *CD4 Track 3 p294*

- Play the CD. The pupils follow in their books.
- Ask questions to check understanding.

Suggested comprehension questions:

- Introduction: **Who are Nobel Prizes awarded to?** (*To people who have helped make the world a safer and better place.*)
- Frame 1: **Where did Alfred live when he was younger?** (*In Russia.*)
- Frame 2: **What did Alfred invent when he was older?** (*Dynamite.*)
- Frame 3: **Why did Alfred have a terrible shock?** (*Because he read his obituary.*)
- Frame 4: **Was Alfred happy with his obituary?** (*No.*)
- Frames 5 and 6: **Who has won a Nobel Prize in the past?** (*Nelson Mandela, Marie Curie, Malala Yousafzai.*)

Activity Book: After you read

Activity 1

Remember the story. Read and answer the questions.

- Read out the first question. Invite a pupil to answer it.
- The pupils answer the remaining questions.

Answers: **1** was born in 1833. **2** created dynamite. **3** was published in France. **4** had a terrible shock. **5** decided to create prizes for progress (in physics, chemistry, medicine, literature and peace). **6** wants all children to receive an education.

Activity 2

Listen and complete the notes.
Write one, two or three words each time.

▶ *CD4 Track 4 p294*

- Read out the notes. The pupils guess the missing words each time.
- Play the CD without pausing. The pupils listen and complete as much information as possible.
- Play the CD again, pausing after each piece of key information to check the answer.

Answers: **1** interesting **2** the inventor **3** five **4** Economics **5** Peace Prize **6** a blog

Activity 3

What do you think of the story?

- The pupils write their opinion and give a rating.
- Invite different pupils to share their opinions.

Activity 4

Find out about Sweden with your family.

- Read out the questions about Sweden. Ask **Where can you find out this information?** (*Internet, library, asking friends and family.*) The pupils complete the activity at home.
- If you prefer to do this activity in class, connect to a children's website which has information about Sweden, such as www.sciencekids.co.nz/sciencefacts/countries/sweden.html.
- Read out the questions. The pupils work as a class to find and write the answers.

Answers: **1** Finland and Norway **2** blue and yellow **3** Denmark **4** krona **5** a very large mammal

Odd one out activity

Which is the odd one out? Why?

- The pupils complete the odd one out activity.

Answers: art (There isn't a Nobel Prize for art.)

***Give Me Five!* values**

Read and discuss.

- Read out the questions and discuss them as a class.
- Encourage the pupils to consider how education can help their personal and professional life in the future and how it can help society.
- Prompt the pupils to think of other rights that children have.

Ending the lesson

Review the lesson and reflect on learning.

- Say **Today we've read a true story about the Nobel Prizes.**
- Ask **What do you remember?** The pupils do a three-minute review in pairs. (Cooperative Learning Strategies, page 19)

Extra activity

Extension

- In groups, ask the pupils to investigate a past Nobel Prize winner. The groups find out why the winner was awarded the prize and some background information about the person's life.
- The groups present their findings to the class.

Key Competences and Key Learning Outcomes

- Compare and practise how to use 'going to' and 'will' to talk about the future
- Act out a short dialogue in pairs

- Identify and practise features of connected speech: the weak form of 'going to'

Key language

- *ceremony, go shopping / to my grandparent's house*
- *I'm going to have lunch at two o'clock. I'll answer the telephone. I think he'll pass the exam.*

Materials

- Pupil's Book p96; Activity Book p93; Class CD4; Teacher's App on Navio

Optional materials

- Teacher's Resource Bank: Trinity Exams Practice cards (selected from the Starter Unit and Units 1, 2, 3, 4, 5, 6, 7 and 8)
- Eight cards with future plans

At a Glance Lesson Plan

Pupil's Book

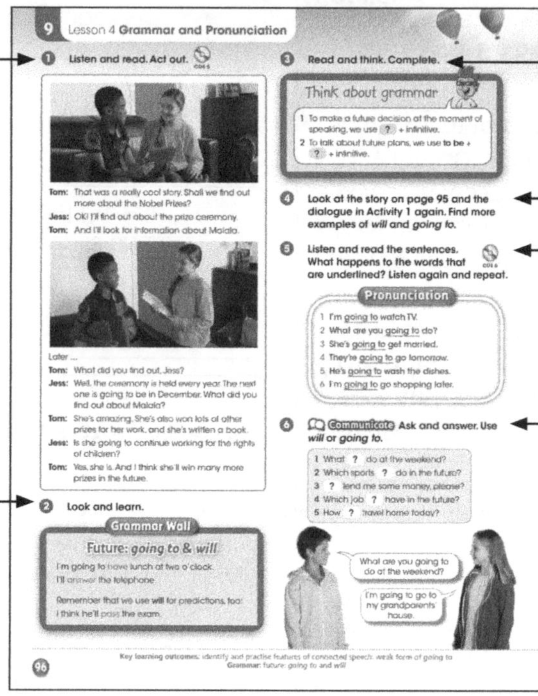

Starting the lesson
- Use the Trinity Exams Practice cards (optional).
- Review the story from Lesson 3.
- Set learning outcomes.

Activity 1
- Listen and read.
- ▶ *CD4 Track 5 p295*
- Act out.

Activity 2
- Look and learn – Grammar wall

Activity 3
- Read and think.
- Complete.

Activity 4
- Look at the story on page 95 and the dialogue in Activity 1 again.
- Find more examples of *will* and *going to*.

Activity 5
- Listen and read the sentences.
- ▶ *CD4 Track 6 p295*
- What happens to the words that are underlined?
- Listen again and repeat.

Activity 6
- Ask and answer. Use *will* or *going to*.
- Go to the Activity Book.

Ending the lesson
- Review the lesson and reflect on learning.

Extra activity

Reinforcement
- Play a predictions game.

Activity Book

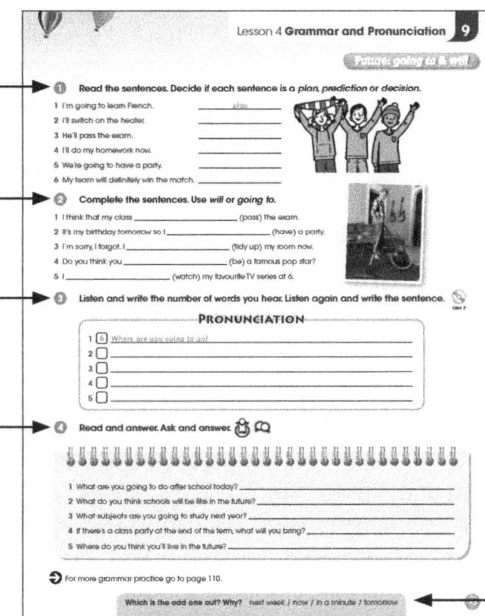

Activity Book

Activity 1
- Read the sentences. Decide if each sentence is a *plan*, *prediction* or *decision*.

Activity 2
- Complete the sentences. Use *will* or *going to*.

Activity 3
- Listen and write the number of words you hear. Listen again and write the sentence.
- ▶ *CD4 Track 7 p295*

Activity 4
- Read and answer. Ask and answer.

Odd one out activity

Digital resources

Teacher's Digital: You can also teach this lesson using the Teacher's App on Navio.

Pupil's Digital: Encourage your pupils to use the Pupil's App on Navio to practise the activities from this lesson.

Powered By NAVIO

Starting the lesson

Use the Trinity Exams Practice cards (optional).
- The pupils practise asking and answering questions.

Review the story from Lesson 3.
- Ask **Do you remember the story in Lesson 3?**
- In pairs, the pupils recall the story in as much detail as possible.

Set learning outcomes.
- Say **Today we're going to compare different ways of talking about the future.**

Pupil's Book Activity 1

Listen and read. Act out.

▶ *CD4 Track 5 p295*
- The pupils look at the photos. Ask **What are Jess and Tom talking about in the photos?**
- Play the CD. The pupils listen and read the dialogue. Check understanding. Ask **What did the children find out about Malala?**
- Play the CD again, pausing after each sentence for the pupils to repeat.
- The pupils practise the dialogue in pairs.

Pupil's Book Activity 2

Look and learn – Grammar wall
- Read the information on the Grammar wall as a class.
- Review the affirmative, negative and question forms of 'to be + going to' and 'will'.

Pupil's Book Activity 3

Read and think. Complete.
- Focus the pupils' attention on the Think about Grammar box. The pupils complete the sentences in pairs.
- Check answers as a class. (*1 will 2 going to*)

Pupil's Book Activity 4

Look at the story on page 95 and the dialogue in Activity 1 again. Find more examples of *will* and *going to*.
- In pairs, the pupils find more examples of 'going to' and 'will'.

Pupil's Book Activity 5

Listen and read the sentences. What happens to the words that are underlined? Listen again and repeat.

▶ *CD4 Track 6 p295*
- Play the CD, pausing after each sentence. Highlight that the 'g' sound at the end of 'going' isn't pronounced and that the 'o' sound in 'to' has a weak form.
- Play the CD again. The pupils listen and repeat.

Pupil's Book Activity 6

Ask and answer. Use *will* or *going to*.
- Invite two pupils to read out the speech bubbles.
- Read the prompts as a class and decide if each question is a plan, prediction or decision.
- In pairs, the pupils ask and answer questions. They use 'will' or 'going to'.

Activity Book

Activity 1

Read the sentences. Decide if each sentence is a *plan*, *prediction* or *decision*.
- Quickly review that we use 'going to' for plans and 'will' for predictions or spontaneous decisions.
- In pairs, the pupils identify the purpose of each sentence.

Answers: **1** plan **2** decision **3** prediction **4** decision **5** plan **6** prediction

Activity 2

Complete the sentences. Use *will* or *going to*.
- The pupils complete the sentences.

Answers: **1** will pass **2** 'm going to have **3** 'll tidy up **4** 'll be **5** 'm going to watch

Activity 3

Listen and write the number of words you hear. Listen again and write the sentence.

▶ *CD4 Track 7 p295*
- Explain that it can be difficult to understand English because sounds disappear or we use weak forms.
- Play the CD, pausing after the first sentence. The pupils count the words. In contracted forms they count each word (e.g. I'm = two). They write the sentence.
- Repeat with the other sentences.
- Play the CD again. The pupils check their answers.

Answers: **1** 6, Where are you going to go? **2** 7, They're going to do their homework. **3** 7, Are you going to ride your bike? **4** 7, He's going to wash the dishes. **5** 9, They aren't going to go to the cinema.

Activity 4

Read and answer. Ask and answer.
- The pupils write their answers.
- In pairs, they ask and answer the questions.

Odd one out activity

Which is the odd one out? Why?
- The pupils complete the odd one out activity.

Answers: now (It isn't in the future.)

Ending the lesson

Review the lesson and reflect on learning.
- Say **Today we've compared different ways of talking about the future.**
- Ask **What do you remember?** The pupils do a three-minute review in pairs. (Cooperative Learning Strategies, page 19)

Extra activity

Reinforcement
- Place eight cards with future plans face down on a desk, e.g. *I'm going to visit Australia*.
- Invite a pupil to pick a card. The pupil reads out the plan. The class makes predictions, e.g. *You'll see lots of kangaroos*.
- Repeat with different pupils and the remaining cards.

Key Competences and Key Learning Outcomes
• Review and name secondary school subjects and equipment • Identify and practise how to form compound nouns
• Practise activity types found in the Cambridge Exams: B1 Preliminary for Schools • Listen for gist and specific information
• Practise expressions for talking about feelings
• Do a communication task

Key language
- *Chemistry, geometry set, Literature, locker, musical instrument, Physics, sports kit, timetable*
- Extension: *highlighter pen, folder, pendrive, stapler*
- *I'm nervous about / I'm excited about / I'm looking forward to / I'm worried about (going to secondary school)*
- *Do you think you'll make new friends there?*

Materials
- Pupil's Book p97; Activity Book p94; Class CD4; Teacher's App on Navio

Optional materials
- Teacher's Resource Bank: Trinity Exams Practice cards (selected from the Starter Unit and Units 1, 2, 3, 4, 5, 6, 7 and 8)

At a Glance Lesson Plan

Pupil's Book

Starting the lesson
- Use the Trinity Exams Practice cards (optional).
- Brainstorm ideas about secondary school.
- Set learning outcomes.

Activity 1
- Look and match.
- Listen, check and repeat.
- ▶ *CD4 Track 8 p295*

Activity 2
- Listen and say *A, B* or *C*.
- ▶ *CD4 Track 9 p295*

Activity 3
- Listen again.
- ▶ *CD4 Track 9 p295*
- Which expressions does Anna use to say how she feels?

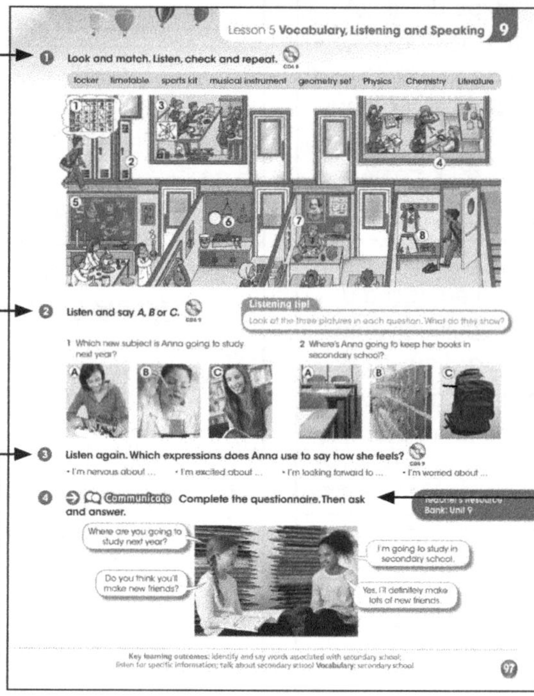

Activity 4
- Complete the questionnaire.
- Then ask and answer (Teacher's Resource Bank: Unit 9).

Go to the Activity Book.

Ending the lesson
- Review the lesson and reflect on learning.

Extra activities

Extension
- Brainstorm questions about secondary school.

Vocabulary extension
- Present four additional vocabulary items.

Activity Book

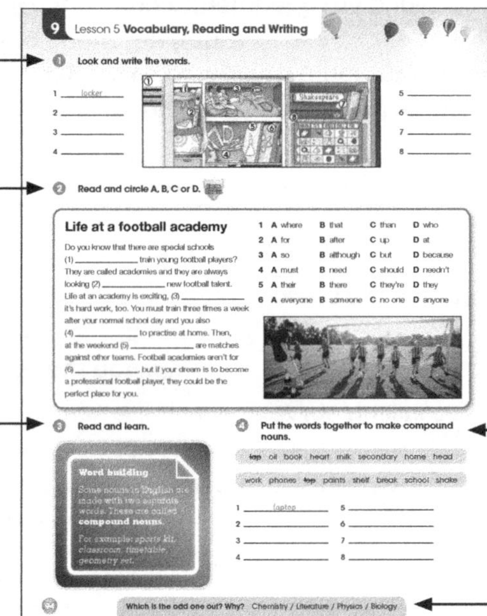

Activity Book

Activity 1
- Look and write the words.

Activity 2
- Read and circle A, B, C or D.

Activity 3 Word building activity
- Read and learn.

Activity 4
- Put the words together to make compound nouns.

Odd one out activity

Digital resources

Teacher's Digital: You can also teach this lesson using the Teacher's App on Navio.

Pupil's Digital: Encourage your pupils to use the Pupil's App on Navio to practise the activities from this lesson.

Powered By NAVIO

Starting the lesson

Use the Trinity Exams Practice cards (optional).

- The pupils practise asking and answering questions.

Brainstorm ideas about secondary school.

- Say **You're going to start secondary school soon**.
- In pairs, the pupils list some good and bad things about secondary school. Discuss their ideas as a class.

Set learning outcomes.

- Say **Today we're going to learn the names of some secondary school subjects and equipment.**

Pupil's Book Activity 1

Look and match. Listen, check and repeat.

▶ *CD4 Track 8 p295*

- In pairs, ask the pupils to match the words they know with 1–8.
- Play the CD. The pupils listen and check.
- Play the CD again, pausing after each word or phrase for the pupils to repeat. You can find the answers for this activity in the audioscript on page 295.

Pupil's Book Activity 2

Listen and say *A*, *B* or *C*.

▶ *CD4 Track 9 p295*

- Invite a pupil to read out the first question and identify the school subjects.
- Read Listening tip! as a class
- Play the CD, pausing after the first dialogue. The pupils listen and identify the correct photo.
- Repeat the procedure with the second question.

Answers: **1** C **2** B

Pupil's Book Activity 3

Listen again. Which expressions does Anna use to say how she feels?

▶ *CD4 Track 9 p295*

- Invite a pupil to read out the expressions.
- Play the CD again. The pupils identify the expressions.

Answers: I'm looking forward to … I'm excited about …

Pupil's Book Activity 4

Complete the questionnaire. Then ask and answer (Teacher's Resource Bank: Unit 9).

- Explain that the pupils are going to prepare and do a questionnaire. Invite two pupils to read out the speech bubbles.
- Organise the class into pairs (A and B).
- The pupils complete their questions. If a pupil needs more support, ask him / her to work with a pupil who is preparing the same questions.
- Check the questions as a class. Then invite two pupils to demonstrate the activity.
- Ask the pupils to do the activity in their pairs.

Activity Book

Activity 1

Look and write the words.

- The pupils look at the picture and write the words.

Answers: **1** locker **2** rucksack **3** sports kit **4** geometry set **5** Chemistry **6** Physics **7** Literature **8** timetable

Activity 2

Read and circle A, B, C or D. Exams Practice

- Ask **What do you know about football academies**?
- Read the text aloud, pausing slightly at each gap.
- In pairs, the pupils read the four options for each gap. They decide which one is best.
- The pupils read the completed text silently to check that it makes sense. Check answers as class.

Answers: **1** B **2** A **3** C **4** B **5** B **6** A

Activity 3

Read and learn.

- Read the information as a class. Elicit other examples of compound nouns.

Activity 4

Put the words together to make compound nouns.

- The pupils work on their own or in pairs to make the compound nouns.

Answers: **1** laptop **2** oil paints **3** bookshelf **4** heartbreak **5** milkshake **6** secondary school **7** homework **8** headphones

Odd one out activity

Which is the odd one out? Why?

- The pupils complete the odd one out activity.

Answers: Literature (It isn't a Science school subject.)

Ending the lesson

Review the lesson and reflect on learning.

- Say **Today we've learnt the names of subjects and equipment in secondary school.**
- Ask **What do you remember?** The pupils do a three-minute review in pairs. (Cooperative Learning Strategies, page 19)

Extra activities

Extension

- In pairs, the pupils write three questions they have about secondary school. If necessary, write prompts on the board, e.g. *Where do I go when …? What do I do if …? What happens if …?*
- Discuss and answer the questions as a class.

Vocabulary extension

- Present additional words related to secondary schools: *highlighter pen, folder, pendrive, stapler.*
- Use the Vocabulary Booster on NAVIO to practise these words.

Key Competences and Key Learning Outcomes

- Review language for giving advice
- Do pre-reading tasks to predict content and raise interest
- Read a text for general understanding
- Read a magazine advice column
- Express an opinion on the text

Key language

- *agony aunt column, shy, tips*
- *Starting a new school is a big change.*

Materials

- Pupil's Book p98; Activity Book p95; Class CD4; Teacher's App on Navio

Optional materials

- Teacher's Resource Bank: Trinity Exams Practice cards (selected from the Starter Unit and Units 1, 2, 3, 4, 5, 6, 7 and 8)

At a Glance Lesson Plan

Starting the lesson

- Use the Trinity Exams Practice cards (optional).
- Review school subjects and equipment from Lesson 5.
- Set learning outcomes.

Activity 1: Before you read

- Read and discuss.

Activity 2

- Read the title and the introduction.
- Predict what the writer is worried about.
- Read and find out.

Activity 3: After you read

- What do you think?
- Go to the Activity Book.

Pupil's Book

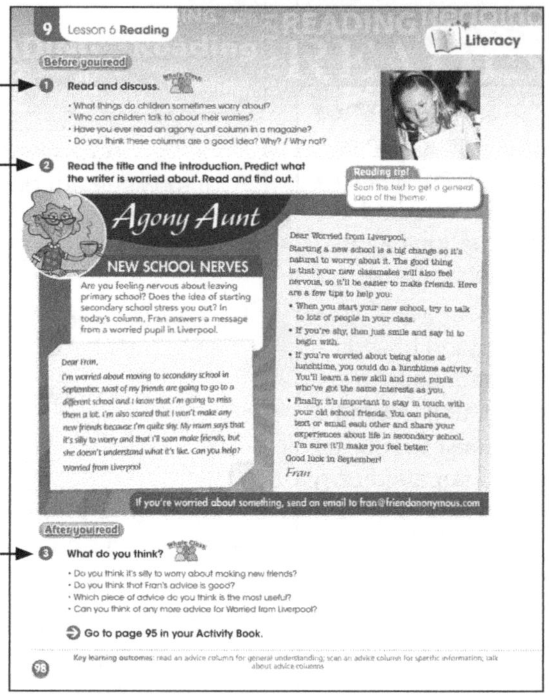

9 Lesson 6 Reading — Literacy

Before you read

1 Read and discuss.
- What things do children sometimes worry about?
- Who can children talk to about their worries?
- Have you ever read an agony aunt column in a magazine?
- Do you think these columns are a good idea? Why? / Why not?

2 Read the title and the introduction. Predict what the writer is worried about. Read and find out.

Reading tip! Scan the text to get a general idea of the theme.

Agony Aunt

NEW SCHOOL NERVES

Are you feeling nervous about leaving primary school? Does the idea of starting secondary school stress you out? In today's column, Fran answers a message from a worried pupil in Liverpool.

Dear Fran,
I'm worried about moving to secondary school in September. Most of my friends are going to go to a different school and I know that I'm going to miss them a lot. I'm also scared that I won't make any new friends because I'm quite shy. My mum says that it's silly to worry and that I'll soon make friends, but she doesn't understand what it's like. Can you help?
Worried from Liverpool

Dear Worried from Liverpool,
Starting a new school is a big change so it's natural to worry about it. The good thing is that your new classmates will also feel nervous, so it'll be easier to make friends. Here are a few tips to help you:
- When you start your new school, try to talk to lots of people in your class.
- If you're shy, then just smile and say hi to begin with.
- If you're worried about being alone at lunchtime, you could do a lunchtime activity. You'll learn a new skill and meet pupils who've got the same interests as you.
- Finally, it's important to stay in touch with your old school friends. You can phone, text or email each other and share your experiences about life in secondary school. I'm sure it'll make you feel better.

Good luck in September!
Fran

If you're worried about something, send an email to fran@friendanonymous.com

After you read

3 What do you think?
- Do you think it's silly to worry about making new friends?
- Do you think that Fran's advice is good?
- Which piece of advice do you think is the most useful?
- Can you think of any more advice for Worried from Liverpool?

Go to page 95 in your Activity Book.

Key learning outcomes: read an advice column for general understanding; scan an advice column for specific information; talk about advice columns

98

Ending the lesson

- Review the lesson and reflect on learning.

Extra activity

Extension

- Play a guessing game.

Activity Book

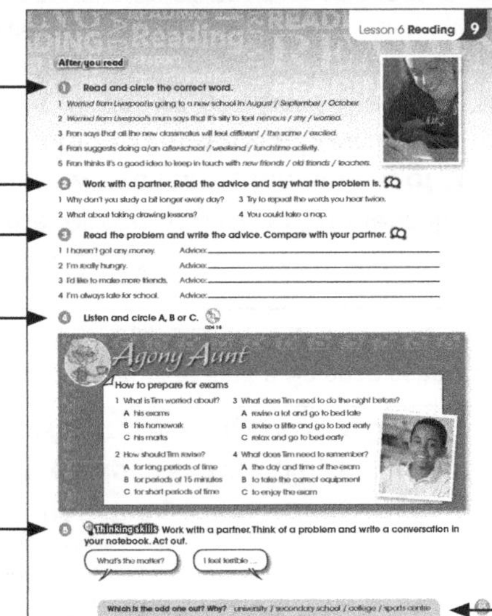

Lesson 6 Reading 9

After you read

1 Read and circle the correct word.
1 Worried from Liverpool is going to a new school in August / September / October.
2 Worried from Liverpool's mum says that it's silly to feel nervous / shy / worried.
3 Fran says that all the new classmates will feel different / the same / excited.
4 Fran suggests doing a/an afterschool / weekend / lunchtime activity.
5 Fran thinks it's a good idea to keep in touch with new friends / old friends / teachers.

2 Work with a partner. Read the advice and say what the problem is.
1 Why don't you study a bit longer every day?
2 What about taking drawing lessons?
3 Try to repeat the words you hear twice.
4 You could take a nap.

3 Read the problem and write the advice. Compare with your partner.
1 I haven't got any money. Advice: ______
2 I'm really hungry. Advice: ______
3 I'd like to make more friends. Advice: ______
4 I'm always late for school. Advice: ______

4 Listen and circle A, B or C.

Agony Aunt

How to prepare for exams
1 What is Tim worried about? A his exams B his homework C his marks
2 How should Tim revise? A for long periods of time B for periods of 15 minutes C for short periods of time
3 What does Tim need to do the night before? A revise a lot and go to bed late B revise a little and go to bed early C relax and go to bed early
4 What does Tim need to remember? A the day and time of the exam B to take the correct equipment C to enjoy the exam

5 Thinking skills Work with a partner. Think of a problem and write a conversation in your notebook. Act out.
What's the matter? / I feel terrible ...

Which is the odd one out? Why? university / secondary school / college / sports centre

Activity Book: After you read

Activity 1

- Read and circle the correct word.

Activity 2

- Work with a partner. Read the advice and say what the problem is.

Activity 3

- Read the problem and write the advice. Compare with your partner.

Activity 4

- Listen and circle A, B or C.

▶ *CD4 Track 10 p295*

Activity 5

- Work with a partner. Think of a problem and write a conversation in your notebook. Act out.

Odd one out activity

Digital resources

Teacher's Digital: You can also teach this lesson using the Teacher's App on Navio.

Pupil's Digital: Encourage your pupils to use the Pupil's App on Navio to practise the activities from this lesson.

Powered By NAVIO

Starting the lesson

Use the Trinity Exams Practice cards (optional).
- The pupils practise asking and answering questions.

Review school subjects and equipment from Lesson 5.
- Organise the class into pairs. Challenge them to remember the school subjects and equipment from Lesson 5.
- Quickly review the words as a class. Ask individual pupils a question each time, e.g. **Do you think you will have a locker? Do you think you will enjoy studying Physics?**

Set learning outcomes.
- Say **Today we're going to read some letters in a magazine.**

Pupil's Book Activity 1: Before you read

Read and discuss.
- Read the questions as a class. Prompt the pupils to talk about the agony aunt columns they have read.

Pupil's Book Activity 2

Read the title and the introduction. Predict what the writer is worried about. Read and find out.
- Ask the pupils to read the title and the introduction to the column.
- Invite the pupils to make predictions about what the writer is worried about.
- Read out the advice column as a class. Confirm the writer is worried about starting secondary school.

Pupil's Book Activity 3: After you read

What do you think?
- In pairs, the pupils answer the questions. The pupils should explain and justify their opinions each time.
- Discuss the questions as a class.

Activity Book: After you read

Activity 1

Read and circle the correct word.
- Invite a pupil to read out the first sentence. The class scans the agony aunt column in the Pupil's Book to find the correct information.
- In pairs, the pupils read the other sentences. They circle the correct word.

Answers: **1** September **2** worried **3** the same **4** lunchtime **5** old friends

Activity 2

Work with a partner. Read the advice and say what the problem is.
- Organise the class into pairs. One pupil reads a sentence. The other pupil listens and identifies the problem.
- The pupils swap roles. They repeat the procedure.

Activity 3

Read the problem and write the advice. Compare with your partner.
- Invite a pupil to read the first problem. Ask the pupils to suggest some advice. Repeat the procedure with the other problems. Highlight that the pupils need to use the infinitive or the gerund form each time.
- The pupils write their advice. They compare answers with a partner.

Activity 4

Listen and circle A, B or C.

▶ *CD4 Track 10 p295*
- Read out the questions as a class. Encourage the pupils to predict the answer each time.
- Play the CD. The pupils listen and circle the answers.
- Play the CD again, pausing after each piece of information. The pupils check their answers.

Answers: **1** A **2** C **3** B **4** B

Activity 5

Work with a partner. Think of a problem and write a conversation in your notebook. Act out.
- Read out the question. Invite different pupils to complete the answer.
- In pairs, the pupils think or a problem. They write a dialogue. They then act it out.
- Invite different pupils to act out their dialogue for the class.

Odd one out activity

Which is the odd one out? Why?
- The pupils complete the odd one out activity.

Answers: sports centre (You don't study there.)

Ending the lesson

Review the lesson and reflect on learning.
- Say **Today we've read an agony aunt column in a magazine.**
- Ask **What do you remember?** The pupils do a three-minute review in pairs. (Cooperative Learning Strategies, page 19)

Extra activity

Extension
- Play a guessing game. Invite a pupil to sit at the front of the class facing the pupils. Explain that the pupil has got a problem. Write the problem on the board behind the pupil. The class reads the problem.
- In turns, different pupils give a piece of advice. The pupil at the front listens and tries to identify the problem.
- Once the pupil guesses the problem, repeat the game with another pupil.
- **Note:** take care to choose problems that will not cause offense. Possible problems are *You've lost your mobile. You can't sleep. You spend too long on the computer. You haven't done your homework.*

Key Competences and Key Learning Outcomes

- Practise using 'so' and 'because' to talk about cause and effect
- Identify the text features of an advice column
- Use criteria to check your writing
- Understand the importance of talking about worries
- Share and discuss your writing with a partner
- Write an advice column for a magazine

Key language

- *anxious, boring, bossy, friendly, helpful, stay organised, sympathetic*
- *It's important to read your timetable.*

Materials

- Pupil's Book p99; Activity Book p96; Teacher's App on Navio

Optional materials

- Teacher's Resource Bank: Trinity Exams Practice cards (selected from the Starter Unit and Units 1, 2, 3, 4, 5, 6, 7 and 8)

At a Glance Lesson Plan

Pupil's Book

Starting the lesson

- Use the Trinity Exams Practice cards (optional).
- Review agony aunt letters.
- Set learning outcomes.

Activity 1: Investigate a text

- Read and discuss.
- Complete the sentences.

Activity 2

- Read the advice.
- What do you think Messy from Manchester was worried about?

Activity 3: Discuss a text

- Read the advice again.
- Find the following.

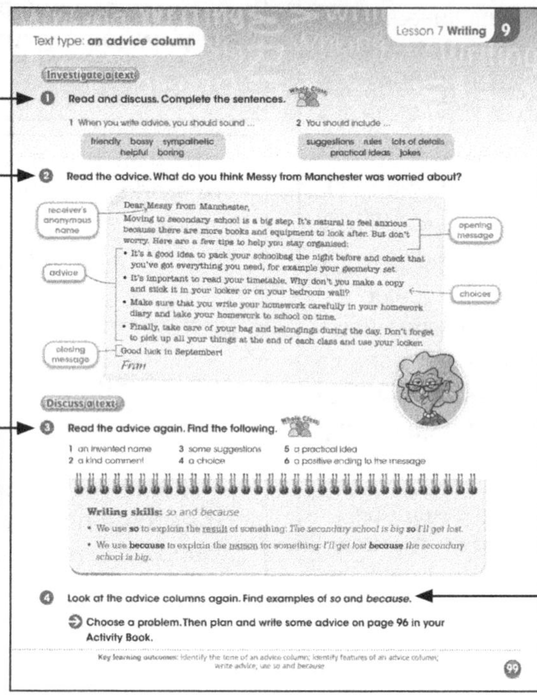

Writing skills

- Read about how to use '*so*' and '*because*'.

Activity 4

- Look at the advice columns again.
- Find examples of *so* and *because*.

Go to the Activity Book.

Ending the lesson

- Review the lesson and reflect on learning.

Extra activity

Extension

- Share letters of advice.

Activity Book

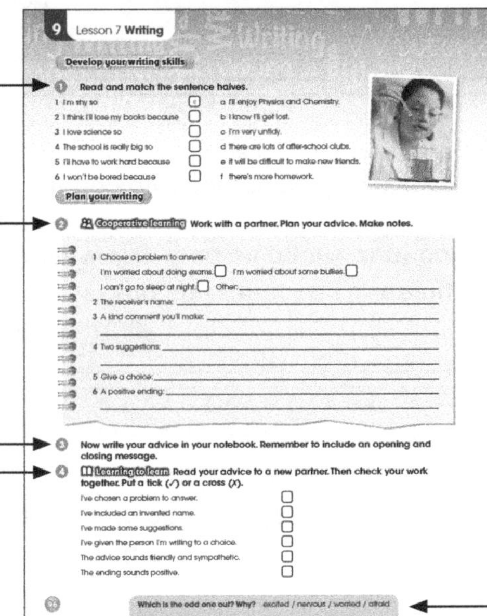

Activity Book

Activity 1: Develop your writing skills

- Read and match the sentence halves.

Activity 2: Plan your writing

- Work with a partner. Plan your advice. Make notes.

Activity 3

- Now write your advice in your notebook. Remember to include an opening and closing message.

Activity 4

- Read your advice to a new partner. Then check your work together. Put a tick (✓) or a cross (✗).

Odd one out activity

Digital resources

Teacher's Digital: You can also teach this lesson using the Teacher's App on Navio.

Pupil's Digital: Encourage your pupils to use the Pupil's App on Navio to practise the activities from this lesson.

Powered By NAVIO

Starting the lesson

Use the Trinity Exams Practice cards (optional).

- The pupils practise asking and answering questions.

Review agony aunt letters.

- Quickly review agony aunt letters. Ask **Who can people write to when they've got a problem? What did Worried from Liverpool write about? What advice did the agony aunt give?**

Set learning outcomes.

- Say **Today we're going to read another letter from an agony aunt and you're going to write some advice for a problem.**

Pupil's Book Activity 1: Investigate a text

Read and discuss. Complete the sentences.

- Complete the sentences as a class. Highlight that the tone of a letter of advice is very important. The writer should sound friendly, sympathetic and helpful. A letter of advice should also make suggestions and give practical ideas.

Pupil's Book Activity 2

Read the advice. What do you think Messy from Manchester was worried about?

- The pupils read the advice as a class.
- In pairs, the pupils discuss what they think the writer's problem is.
- Check answers as a class. Confirm that the writer is worried about losing things or being disorganised.

Pupil's Book Activity 3: Discuss a text

Read the advice again. Find the following.

- Read the information as a class. The pupils find the information in the letter.
- Highlight that the letter starts with a kind, sympathetic comment and that the suggestions are simple and practical. The letter finishes with a positive message.

Writing skills

- Read about using 'so' and 'because' to explain the result of something and the reason for something.

Pupil's Book Activity 4

Look at the advice columns again. Find examples of *so* and *because*.

- The pupils look at the magazine columns in Lessons 6 and 7. They identify examples of 'so' and 'because'.

Activity Book

Activity 1: Develop your writing skills

Read and match the sentence halves.

- The pupils work on their own or in pairs to read and match the sentence halves.
- Check answers as a class.

Answers: **1** e **2** c **3** a **4** b **5** f **6** d

Activity 2: Plan your writing

Work with a partner. Plan your advice. Make notes.

- Read out the notes as a class. Check understanding.
- In pairs, the pupils choose a problem. They then discuss and complete the notes.

Activity 3

Now write your advice in your notebook. Remember to include an opening and closing message.

- The pupils work with a partner to write their advice in their notebooks.

Activity 4

Read your advice to a new partner. Then check your work together. Put a tick (✓) or a cross (✗).

- Read through the statements as a class.
- Organise the class into new partners. One pupil reads aloud their advice. The other pupil listens. The pupils work together to decide if the advice fulfils the criteria and tick the corresponding boxes. The pupils can add, improve or correct the advice at this stage.
- The pupils swap roles.

Odd one out activity

Which is the odd one out? Why?

- The pupils complete the odd one out activity.

Answers: afraid (It's followed by 'of'.)

Ending the lesson

Review the lesson and reflect on learning.

- Say **Today we've read and written some advice for a problem.**
- Ask **What do you remember?** The pupils do a three-minute review in pairs. (Cooperative Learning Strategies, page 19)

Extra activity

Extension

- Ask the pupils to leave their notebooks open on their desk. The pupils move around the class, reading the advice. Each pupil should make a note of the three letters of advice that they found most helpful.

Key Competences and Key Learning Outcomes

- Review talking about school
- Use a spidergram to prepare a conversation about a topic
- Prepare and practise speaking activity types found in Cambridge Exams: B1 Preliminary for Schools
- Listen to a text for general and specific information
- Reflect on learning and progress
- Learn a simple tip for speaking about a topic in a speaking test

Key language
- *nursery school, primary school, secondary school, overalls, university*
- *Did you go to nursery school, Lucy?*

Materials
- Pupil's Book p100; Activity Book pp97–98; Class CD4; Teacher's App on Navio

At a Glance Lesson Plan

Pupil's Book

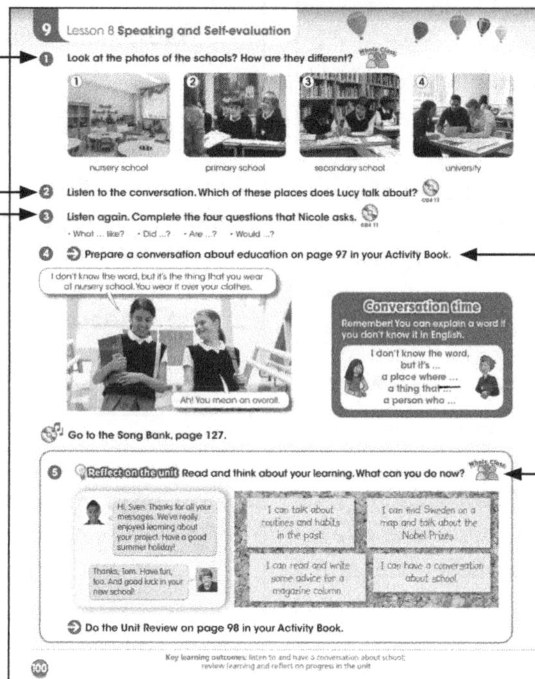

Starting the lesson
- Review school vocabulary.
- Set learning outcomes.

Activity 1
- Look at the photos of the schools.
- How are they different?

Activity 2
- Listen to the conversation.
- ▶ *CD 4 Track 11 p295*
- Which of these places does Lucy talk about?

Activity 3
- Listen again.
- ▶ *CD4 Track 11 p295*
- Complete the four questions that Nicole asks.

Activity 4
- Prepare a conversation about education on page 97 in your Activity Book.
- Go to the Activity Book.

Song
- ▶ *CD4 Track 26 p297*
- ▶ *CD4 Track 27 p297 (optional karaoke version)*

Activity 5
- Read and think about your learning.
- What can you do now?

Ending the lesson
- Review the lesson and reflect on learning.

Activity Book

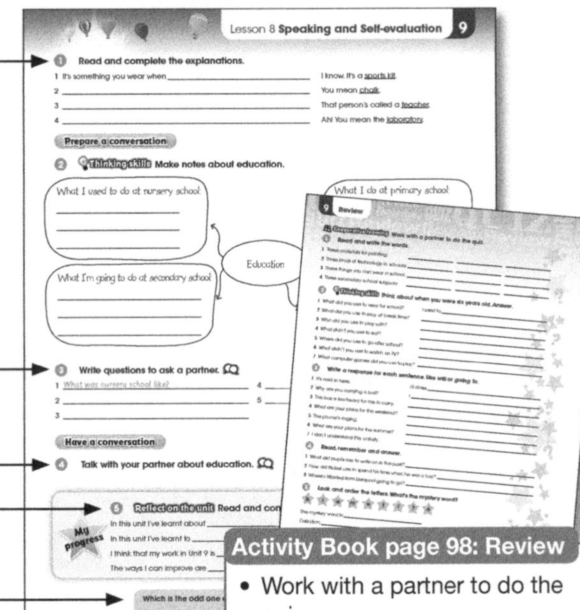

Activity Book page 98: Review
- Work with a partner to do the quiz.

Activity Book

Activity 1
- Read and complete the explanations.

Activity 2
- Make notes about education.

Activity 3
- Write questions to ask a partner.

Activity 4
- Talk with your partner about education.

Activity 5
- Read and complete the sentences.

Odd one out activity

Digital resources

Teacher's Digital: You can also teach this lesson using the Teacher's App on Navio.

Powered By NAVIO

Detailed Lesson Plan

Starting the lesson

Review school vocabulary.

- Explain to the pupils that they are going to play Bingo.
- Ask the pupils to draw a grid (2 × 6). They write six words or phrases in the grid. They choose from the vocabulary items in Lessons 1 and 5.
- Give definitions of the different items of vocabulary. The pupils listen and identify the word or phrase. If the word appears in their grid, they cross it out.
- The first pupil to cross out all six words, calls out *Bingo*. Check their answers.

Set learning outcomes.

- Say **Today we're going to prepare and have a conversation about a topic and we're going to think about our learning.**

Pupil's Book Activity 1

Look at the photos of the schools. How are they different?

- Pupils describe the photos and as a class discuss their differences.

Pupil's Book Activity 2

Listen to the conversation. Which of these places does Lucy talk about?

▶ *CD4 Track 11 p295*

- Play the CD. Elicit answer.
- Confirm that Mike talks about all the discussion points.

Answer: Nursery school, secondary school, university

Pupil's Book Activity 3

Listen again. Complete the four questions that Nicole asks.

▶ *CD4 Track 11 p295*

- Play the CD with pauses for pupils to complete the activity and elicit answers as a class.

Answers: What was it like? Did you go to nursery school, Lucy? / Did you use to wear a ..? Are you going to go to secondary school? Would you like to go to university in the future?

Pupil's Book Activity 4

Prepare a conversation about education on page 97 in your Activity Book.

- Ask pupils what type of questions they would ask their friends about education.
- Refer pupils to the Conversation time box.
- Have pupils read the dialogue.
- Refer pupils to the Activity Book.

Song

Read and discuss the questions.

- Go to the Song Bank on page 245.

▶ *CD4 Track 26 p297*

▶ *CD4 Track 27 p297 (optional karaoke version)*

Activity Book

Activity 1

Read and complete the explanations.

- The pupils work on their own to complete the activity and then show answers to their partners.

Activity 2

Make notes about education.

- Pupils work individually to complete the spidergram.
- Ask volunteer students to read some of their sentences to the class.

Activity 3

Write questions to ask a partner.

- Ask pupils what types of questions they'd like to ask.

Activity 4

Talk with your partner about education.

- Refer pupils to the Remember box.
- In pairs, the pupils have a conversation about education.

Pupil's Book Activity 5

Read and think about your learning. What can you do now?

- Read the messages as a class. Then look back through the unit and prompt the pupils to identify other things they have learnt / done.

Activity Book

Activity 5

Think about your work in this unit. Read and complete the sentences.

- Read out the sentences. Encourage the pupils to think of different ways of completing them.
- The pupils complete the sentences.

Odd one out activity

Which is the odd one out? Why?

- The pupils complete the odd one out activity.

Answers: ropes (You don't use them at the beach.)

Activity Book page 98: Review

Work with a partner to do the quiz.

- Organise the class into pairs. Set a time limit for the pupils to do this (10–15 minutes).
- Read out the five tasks and check understanding. Then say **Ready, steady … Go!**
- Correct the answers as a class.

Answers: **1 1** oil paints, canvas, easel **2** interactive whiteboard, laptop, headphones **3** overall, goggles, sports kit **4** Physics, Chemistry, Literature **4 1** They used to write on a slate. **2** He used to spend his time studying. **3** He's / She's going to go to secondary school. **5** timetable, a plan of your school subjects and times

Ending the lesson

Review the lesson and reflect on learning.

- Say **Today we've prepared and had a conversation about education and we've thought about our learning.**
- Ask **What do you remember?** The pupils do a three-minute review in pairs. (Cooperative Learning Strategies, page 19)

Key Competences and Key Learning Outcomes

- Watch and understand a video about secondary school
- Understand how to manage strong feelings and control your emotions
- Analyse types of strong feelings

Key language

- *corridors, goggles, lockers, overalls*
- *We're going to a new school after the summer. What was your secondary school like? It was nice. I used to do a lot of sport. What did you use to study at secondary school, grandad? I used to study lots of subjects, but I didn't study ICT.*

Materials

- Pupil's Book p101; Activity Book p99; Class CD 4; Teacher's App on Navio
- Teacher's Resource Bank: Talk cards

Optional materials

- Teacher's Resource Bank: Trinity Exams Practice cards (selected from the Starter Unit)

At a Glance Lesson Plan

Pupil's Book

Starting the lesson

- **Think-Pair-Share.** Review different types of schools and the importance of education.
- Set learning outcomes and use the talk cards.

Activity 1

- Before you watch.
- Watch the video.
- *Unit 9 video p304*
- Read and say *true* or *false*.
- Correct the false sentences.

Activity 2

- Watch the video again.
- *Unit 9 video*
- When do students use these objects?

Activity 3

- Read, think and answer.

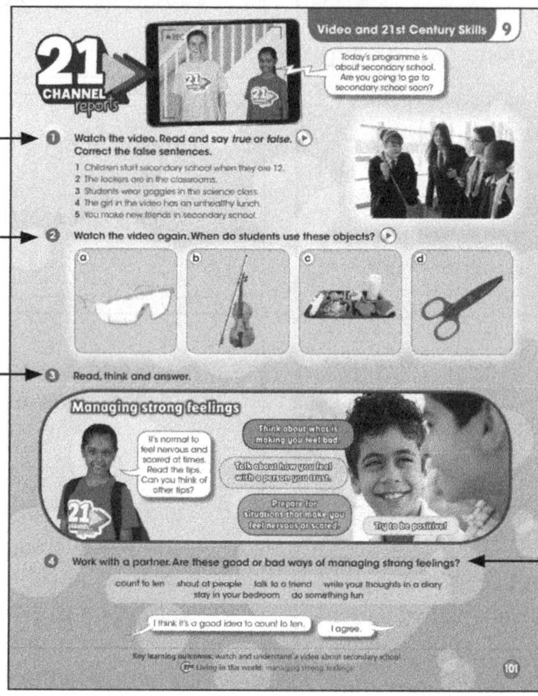

Activity 4

- Work with a partner.
- Are these good or bad ways of managing strong feelings?
- Go to the Activity Book.

Ending the lesson

- Review the lesson and reflect on learning.

Extra activity

- Think about how school changes as we get older.

Activity Book

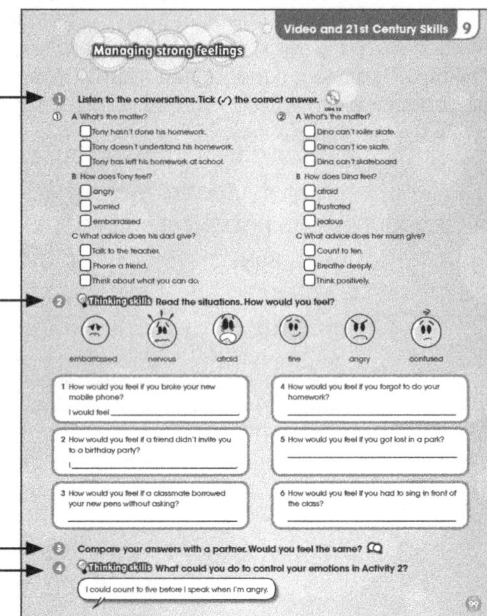

Activity Book

Activity 1 ▶

- Listen to the conversations. Tick (✓) the correct answer.

▶ *CD4 Track 12 p295*

Activity 2

- Read the situations. How would you feel?

Activity 3

- Compare your answers with a partner. Would you feel the same?

Activity 4

- What could you do to control your emotions in Activity 2?

Digital resources

Teacher's Digital: You can also teach this lesson using the Teacher's App on Navio.

Pupil's Digital: Encourage your pupils to use the Pupil's App on Navio to practise the activities from this lesson.

Powered By NAVIO

Starting the lesson

Think-Pair-Share. Review different types of schools and the importance of education.

- Ask pupils to talk about the different types of schools and how old they are to go to each one.
- Ask **Why is it important to get an education?** Write ideas on the board.
- Pupils work with a Talk Partner to discuss different types of schools and why education is important.
- Invite different Talk Partners to tell the class what they discussed with their partners.

Set learning outcomes and use the talk cards.

- Say **Today we're going to watch a video about secondary school.**
- Point to the talk cards to show the pupils the different ways they will be working in the lesson.

Pupil's Book Activity 1

Before you watch

- Ask pupils to express how they feel about going to secondary school.
- Have them tell you what they expect from secondary school and what they think they will experience there.

Watch the video. Read and say *true* or *false*. Correct the false sentences. *p304*

- Watch Part 1. Ask pupils if they what their parents did in secondary school.
- Ask how secondary school has changed in the past compared to today.
- Have pupils read the statements.
- Play Part 2, pausing at each section for pupils to answer. Pupils then work in pairs to check answers.
- Ask pupils what they liked about the secondary school in the video.

Answers: **1** F **2** F **3** T **4** F **5** T
1 You start when you are 11.
2 They are in the corridors.
4 The lunch is healthy.

Pupil's Book Activity 2

Watch the video again. When do students use these objects?

- Ask pupils to name the items and of they have ever used them.
- Have pupils complete the activity in pairs.
- Play the second part of the video for pupils to check their answers.

Answers: **a** You can use goggles in a Science lab. **b** A violin is used in music lessons. **c** The lunch tray is used in the canteen. **d** Scissors are used in art classes.

Pupil's Book Activity 3

Read, think and answer.

- Tell pupils that in the last part of the video Amy and Max talk about how going to secondary school could make you feel nervous but this is something normal.
- Ask pupils what they do to control their feelings when they feel nervous.
- Have pupils discuss the ideas in the box and to add any more if possible.
- Note any new ideas on the board.

Pupil's Book Activity 4

Work with a partner. Are these good or bad ways of managing strong feelings?

- Have pupils work with a partner to complete the activity.
- Encourage pupils to explain the reason behind their opinions.
- Have pupils add any more ideas of positive ways of dealing with strong feelings.
- Ask pairs to present their work to the class.

Activity Book

Activity 1

Listen to the conversations. Tick (✓) the correct answers.

▶ *CD4 Track 12 p295*

- Give pupils a little time to read the questions and answers.
- Play the CD and complete the activity.
- Have pupils check answers with their partners.

Answers: **1 A** Tony has left his homework at school. **B** worried **C** Think about what you can do. **2 A** Dina can't ice skate. **B** Frustrated **C** Count to ten.

Activity 2

Read the situations. How would you feel?

- Go through the icons and ask pupils in what situations they would feel like each one.
- Have pupils complete the activity individually.

Activity 3

Compare your answers with a partner. Would you feel the same?

- Encourage pupils to explain why they would feel the same or different.

Activity 4

What could you do to control your emotions in Activity 2?

- Have pupils complete the activity in groups. Encourage them to use as many ideas as possible.
- Ask groups to share their ideas with the class.

Ending the lesson

Review the lesson and reflect on learning.

- Say **Today we've watched a video about secondary school. What have we learnt?** Elicit the information from the pupils. The pupils do a three-minute review in pairs. (Cooperative Learning Strategies, page 19)

Extra activity

Reinforcement

- Place pupils in small pairs and ask them to think about how school changes as we get older.
- Have a class discussion, encouraging pupils to use the ideas they discussed in groups.

Project 3: Life in the past

Key Competences and Key Learning Outcomes

- Write questions to find out about how people lived in the past
- Research aspects of living in the past
- Listen for specific information and complete notes
- Share knowledge about how people lived in the past
- Share information with your group
- Learn about everyday life in the past

Key language

- *classroom, community, elderly, food, past, relative, travel*
- *I'm going to write questions about (schools) in the past. That's a good question. What / How about this?*

Materials

- Pupil's Book p102; Activity Book p100; Class CD4; Teacher's App on Navio

At a Glance Lesson Plan

Pupil's Book

Starting the lesson

- Set learning outcomes.

Activity 1: Share knowlege

- Read and discuss.

Activity 2: Investigate

- Listen to Joan's experience of life in the 1950s. Complete the notes on page 100 in your Activity Book.

Go to the Activity Book.

Activity 3

- Work in a group. You're going to collect information about life in the time of your grandparents.
- Write questions you'd like to find the answers to on page 100 in your Activity Book.

Go to the Activity Book.

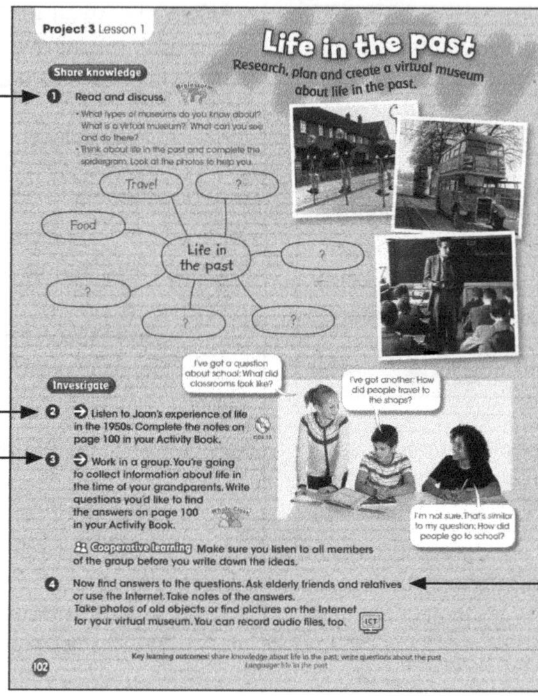
Project 3 Lesson 1
Life in the past
Research, plan and create a virtual museum about life in the past.
Share knowledge
1 Read and discuss.
Investigate
2 Listen to Joan's experience of life in the 1950s. Complete the notes on page 100 in your Activity Book.
3 Work in a group. You're going to collect information about life in the time of your grandparents. Write questions you'd like to find the answers on page 100 in your Activity Book.
Cooperative learning Make sure you listen to all members of the group before you write down the ideas.
4 Now find answers to the questions. Ask elderly friends and relatives or use the Internet. Take notes of the answers. Take photos of old objects or find pictures on the Internet for your virtual museum. You can record audio files, too.
102

Activity 4

- Now find answers to the questions.
- Ask elderly friends and relatives or use the Internet.
- Take notes of the answers.
- Take photos of old objects or find pictures on the Internet for your virtual museum.
- You can record audio files, too.

Ending the lesson

- Review the lesson and reflect on learning.

Extension activity

- Do further research on life in the 1950s.

Link to Science

- **Local history:** Life in the 20th Century

Activity Book

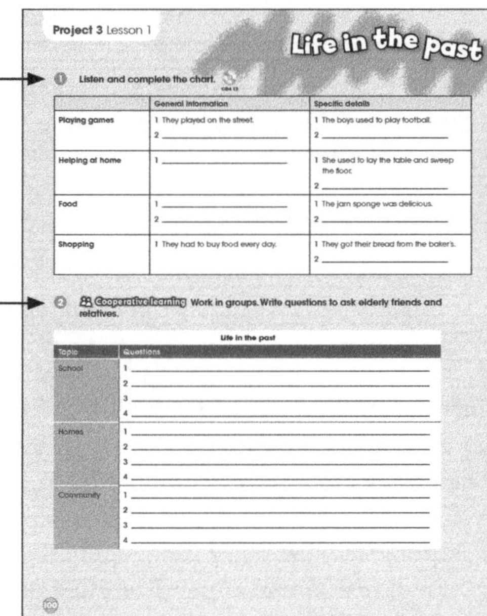
Project 3 Lesson 1
Life in the past
1 Listen and complete the chart.
2 Cooperative learning Work in groups. Write questions to ask elderly friends and relatives.
100

Activity Book

Activity 1

- Listen and complete the chart.

▶ ***CD4 Track 13 p296***

Activity 2

- Work in groups. Write questions to ask elderly friends and relatives.

Digital resources

Teacher's Digital: You can also teach this lesson using the Teacher's App on Navio.

Pupil's Digital: Encourage your pupils to use the Pupil's App on Navio to practise the activities from this lesson.

Powered By NAVIO

Starting the lesson

Set learning outcomes.

- Say **Today we're going to begin another project.**
- Have a brief class discussion on what pupils know about the past.

Pupil's Book Activity 1: Share knowledge

Read and discuss.

- Read and discuss the photos and the first question as a class.
- Ask the pupils to draw a spidergram in their notebooks. They then complete it in pairs.
- Draw a spidergram on the board. Elicit ideas.

Pupil's Book Activity 2: Investigate

Listen to Joan's experience of life in the 1950s. Complete the notes on page 100 in your Activity Book.

- Explain that the pupils are going to hear an interview with a woman about life in the 1950s. Ask **What do you already know about life in the 1950s?**

Activity Book

Activity 1

Listen and complete the chart.

▶ *CD4 Track 13 p296*

- Read the information as a class. Check that the pupils understand the difference between general and specific information.
- Play the CD. The pupils listen and complete the notes.
- Play the CD a second time, pausing after each piece of key information. The pupils complete their notes.
- Play the CD a third time. Check answers as a class.

Answers: **1 Playing games:** (general) They all played together. (specific) The girls used to play with skipping ropes. **2 Helping at home:** (general) Joan and her sister had their own jobs to do. (specific) Her sister had to hang the washing / fold the dry clothes. **3 Food:** (general) They had lunch at school. They usually had meat, potatoes, vegetables and pudding. The fruit came from the UK. (specific) There were no bananas. There were strawberries for a few months in summer. **4 Shopping:** (specific) They got meat from the butcher's / vegetables from the greengrocer's.

Pupil's Book Activity 3

Work in a group. You're going to collect information about life in the time of your grandparents. Write questions you'd like to find the answers to on page 100 in your Activity Book.

- Read the instructions. Organise the pupils into groups.
- Invite three pupils to read out the speech bubbles.
- Read the Cooperative Learning tip as a class. Remind pupils to implement it in this activity.
- The pupils open their Activity Books on page 100. They discuss and decide on their tasks. Each pupil in the group writes questions on a different topic.

Activity Book

Activity 2

Work in groups. Write questions to ask elderly friends and relatives.

- Explain the sections. Make it clear that pupils only write questions in their chosen topic area. They write complete questions.

Pupil's Book Activity 4 ICT

Now find answers to the questions. Ask elderly friends and relatives or use the Internet. Take notes of the answers. Take photos of old objects or find pictures on the Internet for your virtual museum. You can record audio files, too.

- Invite three pupils to read out the speech bubbles.
- Then focus the class on the Language bank. Read out the words as a class. Encourage the pupils to use this language as they discuss the questions.
- In groups, the pupils agree on the questions that they are going to ask in their interviews.

Ending the lesson

Review the lesson and reflect on learning.

- Say **Today we've learnt about life in the 1950s.**
- Ask **What do you remember?** The pupils do a three-minute review in pairs. (Cooperative Learning Strategies, page 19)

Extension activity

- In their groups, the pupils use the Internet to find out more information about what life was like in the 1950s. Ask the pupils to choose three interesting facts that they discover to share with the class.

Link to Science

- If you are studying the Science topic of The Contemporary Age, review the events of the 20th century in your country. What changed during that period? Talk about major historical events and things that have contributed to progress. Ask **Is life better now than in the past?**

Project 3: Life in the past

Key Competences and Key Learning Outcomes

- Present your virtual museum to the class
- Reflect on what you have learnt and how you have worked together
- Work in groups to plan a virtual museum
- Find out about life in the past

Key language

- *cricket, football, leapfrog, skipping ropes*
- *What did he say about the games children used to play?*

Materials

- Pupil's Book p103; Activity Book p101; Teacher's App on Navio
- Computer with digital presentation facilities; Poster-making materials (pens, card, etc.)

At a Glance Lesson Plan

Pupil's Book

Starting the lesson

- Set learning outcomes.

Activity 1: Plan and create your project

- Share the information you have with your group.
- Choose the topic you'd like to include in the virtual museum.
- Find an object to put in the museum, too.
- Write the information on page 101 in your Activity Book.

Go to the Activity Book.

Activity 2

- Prepare your information for the virtual museum.

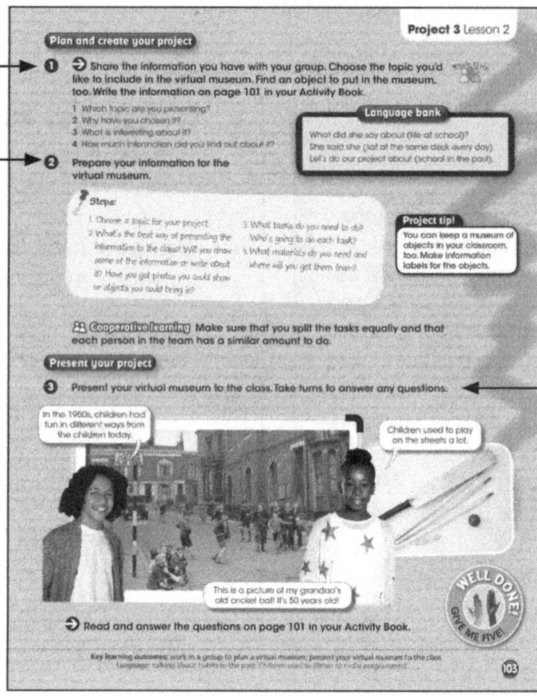

Activity 3: Present your project

- Present your virtual museum to the class.
- Take turns to answer any questions.

Ending the lesson

- Review the lesson and reflect on learning.

Reinforcement activity

- Create a play about life in the past.

Activity Book

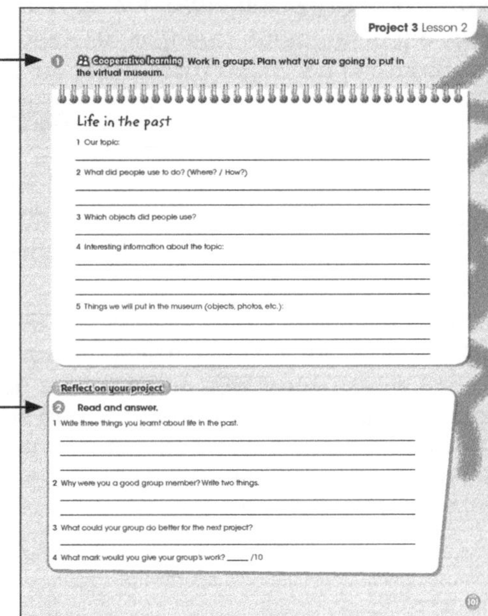

Activity Book

Activity 1

- Work in groups. Plan what you are going to put in the virtual museum.

Activity 2

- Read and answer.

Digital resources

Teacher's Digital: You can also teach this lesson using the Teacher's App on Navio.

Pupil's Digital: Encourage your pupils to use the Pupil's App on Navio to practise the activities from this lesson.

Powered By NAVIO

Starting the lesson

Set learning outcomes.

- Say **Today we're going to continue the project.** Prompt the pupils to tell you what they did in the last lesson.
- Highlight that the pupils will be working in small groups again. Prompt the pupils to tell you what they must do when they work in groups: listen, take turns, respect different opinions, etc.

Pupil's Book Activity 1: Plan and create your project

Share the information you have with your group. Choose the topic you'd like to include in the virtual museum. Find an object to put in the museum, too. Write the information on page 101 in your Activity Book.

- Check that the pupils have collected information from elderly friends and relatives about life in the past.
- Give the pupils some time to make sure that they have the key phrases of what they have found out. Make it clear that they do not need to explain everything they have discovered. They can choose the parts that they can explain in English. This will be a challenging task for the pupils so you may need to help them.
- Explain that the pupils need to share their information with their group. They then choose the most interesting topics for their presentation.

Pupil's Book Activity 2

Prepare your information for the virtual museum.

- Read out the steps of the presentation plan as a class. Check understanding. Give and elicit examples for each task.
- Focus the pupils on the Cooperative learning. Encourage them to be fair in the way they divide up the tasks.
- Then focus the pupils on the Language bank. Invite different pupils to read out the sentences. Encourage the pupils to use this language when they are making suggestions to each other.

Activity Book

Activity 1

Work in groups. Plan what you are going to put in the virtual museum.

- Explain to the pupils that while they are discussing the questions, they should make notes. Ask a pupil to read out the sections.
- Ask the groups to complete the task. Go round the groups giving them more ideas and helping them make decisions about their presentations.

Pupil's Book Activity 3: Present your project

Present your virtual museum to the class. Take turns to answer any questions.

- Focus the class on the photo. Encourage the pupils to talk about what they can see. Then ask three pupils to read out the speech bubbles. Ask **What's this group's presentation about? Is it an interesting presentation?**
- Invite different groups in turn to present to the rest of the class. Ensure that each pupil in the group participates in the presentation, but accept that some pupils may contribute more than others. At the end of each presentation, ask the group a question and encourage the rest of the class to think of questions they would like to ask. The group giving the presentation should answer the questions.
- At the end of the activity, the pupils decide on the most interesting things they learnt about the past.

Read and answer the questions on page 101 in your Activity Book.

- The pupils answer the questions in the Activity Book.

Activity Book

Activity 2

Read and answer.

- The pupils answer the questions on their own or in pairs.

Ending the lesson

Review the lesson and reflect on learning.

- Say **We've done a project about life in the past.**
- Ask **What do you remember?** The pupils do a three-minute review in pairs. (Cooperative Learning Strategies, page 19)

Reinforcement activity

- In new groups, the pupils create a short play of about three minutes. The play should demonstrate some of the activities from the past that the pupils have discovered in this project. Invite different groups to act out their plays.

Thanksgiving Day

Key Competences and Key Learning Outcomes

- Write about different festival food in your country
- Listen to and perform a poem about Thanksgiving
- Learn about Thanksgiving Day in America
- Learn about Thanksgiving food traditions around the world

Key language

- *celebrate, marching bands, marshmallows, parade, pecan nuts, seeds, stuffing, squash*
- *What special food do you eat during festivals?*

Materials

- Pupil's Book p104; Teacher's Resource Bank: Festivals worksheets; Class CD4; Teacher's App on Navio

Optional materials

- Teacher's Resource Bank: Trinity Exams Practice cards (selected from Starter Unit and Units 1, 2 and 3)

At a Glance Lesson Plan

Starting the lesson

- Use the Trinity Exams Practice cards (optional).
- Set learning outcomes.

Activity 1

- What's the weather like in November in your country?
- What season is it?
- Read and find out about a November festival in the USA.

Activity 2

- Read the text again.
- Answer the questions.

Activity 3

- What is the most important meal in the year for your family?
- What do you eat?
- Read about the Thanksgiving meal.
- Match the red words with the letters.

Pupil's Book

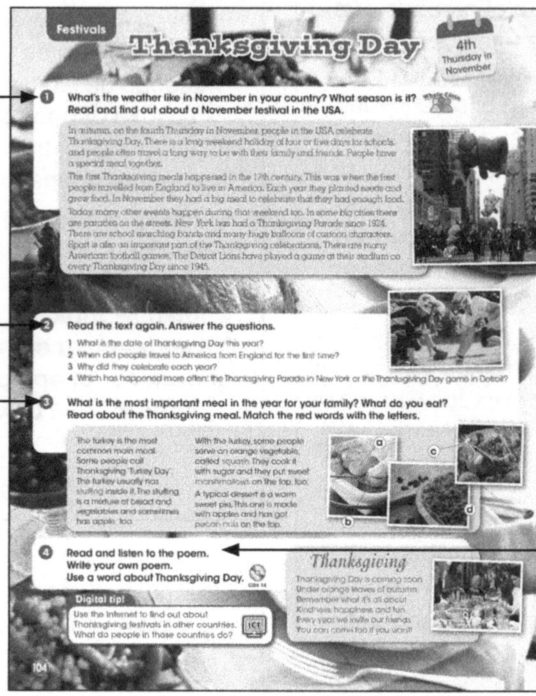

Activity 4

- Read and listen to the poem.
- ▶ ***CD4 Track 14 p296***
- Write your own poem.
- Read about the Thanksgiving meal.
- Use a word about Thanksgiving Day.

Ending the lesson

- Review the lesson and reflect on learning.

Extra activity

Extension

- Write about traditional food in your country.

Digital resources

Teacher's Digital: You can also teach this lesson using the Teacher's App on Navio.

Pupil's Digital: Encourage your pupils to use the Pupil's App on Navio to practise the activities from this lesson.

Powered By NAVIO

Starting the lesson

Use the Trinity Exams Practice cards (optional).

- The pupils practise asking and answering questions.

Set learning outcomes.

- Say **Today we're going to learn about how people celebrate Thanksgiving around the world.**

Pupil's Book Activity 1

What's the weather like in November in your country? What season is it? Read and find out about a November festival in the USA.

- Ask **What's the weather like in November in your country? What's it like in America? Do you have any important festivals in November?**
- Discuss any festivals.
- Explain that in America there is a big festival which gives thanks to for all the food and good people have in their lives.
- Read the text as a class. Ask what the festival is called.
- Then ask the pupils to describe the photo.

Pupil's Book Activity 2

Read the text again. Answer the questions.

- Ask the pupils to read the text again.
- The pupils answer the questions.
- Check answers as a class.

Answers: **1** It's the fourth Thursday in November. **2** In the 17th century. **3** To give thanks for all the food they had. **4** The parade in New York.

Pupil's Book Activity 3

What is the most important meal in the year for your family? What do you eat? Read about the Thanksgiving meal. Match the red words with the letters.

- Ask pupils what the most important meal in their family is and what they eat.
- Ask pupils why meals are an important part of family life.
- Have pupils read the text and explain any unknown words.
- Pupils complete the activity and check answers with their partners.

Answers: **a** marshmallows **b** squash **c** stuffing **d** pecan nuts

Pupil's Book Activity 4

Read and listen to the poem. Write your own poem. Use a word about Thanksgiving Day.

▸ *CD4 Track 14 p296*

- Play the CD and ask pupils what the poem is about.
- Put the word PECAN on the board and invite pupils to help you write a poem using the first letter of the word. Do the activity on the board.
- Place pupils in pairs and have them complete the activity.
- Direct pupils to the ICT box and have them research different countries that celebrate Thanksgiving.
- Explain that they will use the information in the Activity Book.

Ending the lesson

Review the lesson and reflect on learning.

- Say **Today we've learnt about Thanksgiving around the world.**
- Ask **What do you remember?** The pupils do a three-minute review in pairs. (Cooperative Learning Strategies, page 19)

Extra activity

Extension

- Ask the pupils to write a short paragraph about traditional foods in their countries.

Endangered Species Day

Key Competences and Key Learning Outcomes

- Complete a reading and listening task
- Learn about endangered species
- Think about how people can help endangered species
- Learn about Endangered Species Day

Key language

- *aquarium, block rivers, botanical gardens, build houses, climate change, destroy, disappear, endangered species, extinct, habitat, hunt, orang-utan, polar bears, pollute water, protect, survive, vaquita, wildlife refuge, zoo*
- *These are animals and plants that are in danger of disappearing completely from the world.*

Materials

- Pupil's Book p105; Teacher's Resource Bank: Festivals worksheets; Class CD4; Teacher's App on Navio

Optional materials

- Teacher's Resource Bank: Trinity Exams Practice cards (selected from Starter Unit and Units 1, 2, 3, 4, 5, 6, 7, 8 and 9)

At a Glance Lesson Plan

Pupil's Book

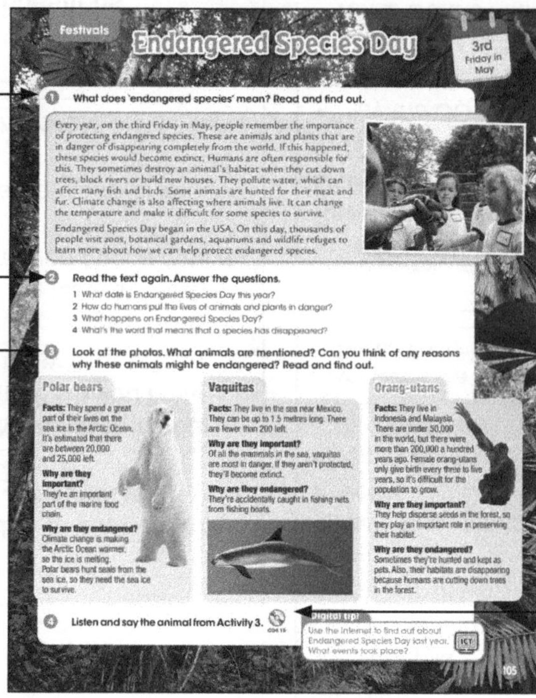

Starting the lesson

- Use the Trinity Exams Practice cards (optional).
- Set learning outcomes.

Activity 1

- What does 'endangered species' mean?
- Read and find out.

Activity 2

- Read the text again.
- Answer the questions.

Activity 3

- Look at the photos.
- What animals are mentioned?
- Can you think of any reasons why these animals might be endangered?
- Read and find out.

Activity 4

- Listen and say the animal from Activity 3.

▶ *CD4 Track 15 p296*

Ending the lesson

- Review the lesson and reflect on learning.

Extra activity

Extension

- Make a poster for Endangered Species Day.

Digital resources

Teacher's Digital: You can also teach this lesson using the Teacher's App on Navio.

Pupil's Digital: Encourage your pupils to use the Pupil's App on Navio to practise the activities from this lesson.

Powered By NAVIO

Starting the lesson

Use the Trinity Exams Practice cards (optional).

- The pupils practise asking and answering questions.

Set learning outcomes.

- Say **Today we're going to learn about Endangered Species Day.**

Pupil's Book Activity 1

What does 'endangered species' mean? Read and find out.

- Ask **What does 'endangered species' mean?**
- Then ask the pupils to read the text quickly. Confirm that endangered species are animals and plants that are in danger of disappearing completely. Ask if they know any endangered species.
- Ask the pupils to describe the photo. Ask **What animal is in the photo?** (*A snake.*)

Pupil's Book Activity 2

Read the text again. Answer the questions.

- Ask the pupils to read the text again. They then read the four questions.
- The pupils work on their own or in pairs to answer the questions.
- Check answers as a class.

Answers: **1** The date varies from year to year. It is the third Friday in May. **2** They cut down trees, block rivers, build new houses, pollute water and hunt animals. **3** People visit zoos, botanical gardens, aquariums and wildlife refuges and learn more about endangered species. **4** extinct

Pupil's Book Activity 3

Look at the photos. What animals are mentioned? Can you think of any reasons why these animals might be endangered? Read and find out.

- Ask the pupils to look at the photos. Ask **What do you know about each of the animals? Why might these animals be endangered?**
- Explain to the pupils that they are going to find out more information about the animals. Say **Let's see if you are right about why they are endangered.**
- The pupils read the text as a class or on their own. Check their answers. Then check understanding. Ask **Which animal gives birth every three to five years?** (*Orang-utans.*) **Which animal gets caught in fishing nets?** (*Vaquitas.*) **Which animal hunts seals?** (*Polar bears.*)

Pupil's Book Activity 4

Listen and say the animal from Activity 3.

▶ ***CD4 Track 15 p296***

- Play the CD. The pupils listen to the sentences and point to the correct animal.
- Play the CD again. The pupils say the animal.

Answers: **1** orang-utan **2** polar bear **3** vaquita **4** orang-utan **5** vaquita **6** orang-utan

Use the Internet to find out about Endangered Species Day last year. What events took place? ICT

- Read the instructions at the bottom of the page. The pupils find out the information on the Internet or as a homework activity. Refer the pupils to the Endangered Species Day website, www.endangered.org.

Ending the lesson

Review the lesson and reflect on learning.

- Say **Today we've learnt about Endangered Species Day.**
- Ask **What do you remember?** The pupils do a three-minute review in pairs. (Cooperative Learning Strategies, page 19)

Extra activity

Extension

- Ask the pupils to design a poster for an event on Endangered Species Day. In groups of three, they think of an event. They research and design the poster together. Encourage the pupils to use facts about endangered animals. Ask them to think about the kind of language that they should use on an information poster, e.g. *Did you know that …? Help to … Save the … Come to … on …*

Date: ______________________ Unit: __________

1 What did my pupils learn in this unit?

____

____

____

____

2 How did my pupils work? (✓)

individually ☐ in pairs ☐ in small groups ☐

in large groups ☐ as a class ☐

3 Which key competences did my pupils develop? Give a score from 1 to 5 (5 being the highest).

Competence in linguistic communication ☐

Competence in mathematics, science and technology ☐

Digital competence ☐

Learning to learn ☐

Social and civic competences ☐

Sense of initiative and entrepreneurship ☐

Cultural awareness and expression ☐

4 Which lessons / activities were the most successful and why?

____

____

____

____

5 Which lessons / activities did my pupils find the most difficult and why?

____

____

____

____

6 What did I try in the classroom for the first time? How did it go?

____

____

____

____

7 Which resources did I find most useful? (including webpages)

____

____

____

____

____

____

8 What could I do differently next time I teach this unit?

____

____

____

____

Unit 1 Song

Pupil's Book Song Bank Unit 1 (page 125)

Activity 1

Read and discuss the questions.

- Work as a class to answer the questions about travelling by plane.

Activity 2

Listen and sing *It's delayed!*

▶ *CD4 Track 16 p296*

▶ *CD4 Track 17 p296 (optional karaoke version)*

- Explain to the pupils that they are going to listen to a song called *It's delayed!*
- The pupils look at the photos and predict what happens. Ask **Is the singer happy?**
- Play the CD. The pupils listen and read the song in their book. Confirm that the singer is happy to be going on holiday, but gets bored when the flight is delayed.
- Play the CD again. The pupils sing along with the recording.
- When the pupils are familiar with the song, you can use the karaoke version to practise it.

Extension activity

- Imagine that your flight was delayed. What did you do while you waited?
- Elicit examples of all the things you can do at the airport.
- Make sure the pupils use the structure *While I was waiting, I …*
- The pupils work on their own or in pairs to write the sentences.
- Invite different pupils to read out their sentences to the rest of the class.

Unit 3 Song

Pupil's Book Song Bank Unit 3 (page 125)

Activity 1

Read and discuss the questions.

- Work as a class to answer the questions about growing vegetables and fruit.

Activity 2

Listen and sing *I want to grow some vegetables*.

▶ *CD4 Track 18 p296*

▶ *CD4 Track 19 p296 (optional karaoke version)*

- Explain to the pupils that they are going to listen to a song called *I want to grow some vegetables.*
- Ask **What fruit and vegetables do you think the singer grows?**
- Play the CD. The pupils listen and read the song in their book. Confirm that the singer grows some tomatoes, but also peas and beans.
- Play the CD again. The pupils sing along with the recording.
- When the pupils are familiar with the song, you can use the karaoke version to practise it.

Extension activity

Plan your vegetable garden.
What will you plant? Write.

- Elicit examples of fruit and vegetables the pupils like.
- The pupils work on their own or in pairs to write their sentences.
- Invite different pupils to read out their sentences to the rest of the class.

Detailed Lesson Plan

Unit 4 Song

Pupil's Book Song Bank Unit 4 (page 126)

Activity 1

Read and discuss the questions.

- Work as a class to answer the questions about quiz competitions.

Activity 2

Listen and sing *The quiz*.

▶ *CD4 Track 20 p297*

▶ *CD4 Track 21 p297 (optional karaoke version)*

- Explain to the pupils that they are going to listen to a song called *The quiz.*
- Ask **What subjects do you think the quizmaster asks about?**
- Play the CD. The pupils listen and read the song in their book. List the subjects (science, music, films).
- Play the CD again. The pupils sing along with the recording.
- When the pupils are familiar with the song, you can use the karaoke version to practise it.

Extension activity

Choose a subject and write some questions. Ask and answer.

- Ask **What other subjects could be interesting for a quiz? What questions could you ask?**
- The pupils work in small groups to write their questions and answers.
- Invite one person to come and ask the questions for their group to the rest of the class. The pupils from the other groups answer.
- Then a pupil from another group asks their questions.
- The group that answers the most questions correctly wins the quiz.

Unit 6 Song

Pupil's Book Song Bank Unit 6 (page 126)

Activity 1

Read and discuss the questions.

- Work as a class to answer the questions about future jobs.

Activity 2

Listen and sing *The future is far away*.

▶ *CD4 Track 22 p297*

▶ *CD4 Track 23 p297 (optional karaoke version)*

- Explain to the pupils that they are going to listen to a song called *The future is far away.*
- Say **Look at the photos. Predict what jobs are mentioned in the song.**
- Play the CD. The pupils listen and read the song in their book. Confirm that the following jobs are mentioned: vet, researcher, photographer, singer, sports star.
- Play the CD again. The pupils sing along with the recording.
- When the pupils are familiar with the song, you can use the karaoke version to practise it.

Extension activity

Think about three jobs you might like to do in the future. Write. Compare with your partner.

- Elicit examples of different ways of completing the first sentence.
- The pupils can use the jobs in Activity 1 or think of different jobs.
- The pupils work on their own to write their sentences. Then they read their sentences to their partner and discuss the jobs.
- Invite different pupils to share their sentences with the rest of the class.

Unit 7 Song

Pupil's Book Song Bank Unit 7 (page 127)

Activity 1

Read and discuss the questions.

- Work as a class to answer the questions about window shopping.

Activity 2

Listen and sing *Window shopping*.

▶ *CD4 Track 24 p297*

▶ *CD4 Track 25 p297 (optional karaoke version)*

- Explain to the pupils that they are going to listen to a song called *Window shopping.*
- Ask **What do you think the singer sees when he's window shopping? What would he like to buy?**
- Play the CD. The pupils listen and read the song in their book. Confirm that the singer would like to buy an airblast rocket, a jacket and a guitar.
- Play the CD again. The pupils sing along with the recording.
- When the pupils are familiar with the song, you can use the karaoke version to practise it.

Extension activity

What have you bought recently. Write two true sentences and a false one.

- Ask a pupil **What is the last thing you bought? Are you happy you bought it?**
- The pupils then work on their own to write their true and false sentences.

Read the sentences to your partner. Which is the false one?

- Organise the class into pairs.
- The pupils read their sentences out and their partner tries to identify the false information each time.

Unit 9 Song

Pupil's Book Song Bank Unit 9 (page 127)

Activity 1

Read and discuss the questions.

- Work as a class to answer the questions about life in the past.

Activity 2

Listen and sing *Life was very different*.

▶ *CD4 Track 26 p297*

▶ *CD4 Track 27 p297 (optional karaoke version)*

- Explain to the pupils that they are going to listen to a song called *Life was very different.*
- Say **Look at the photos. What aspects of the past do you think this song is about?**
- Play the CD. The pupils listen and read the song in their book.
- Play the CD again. The pupils sing along with the recording.
- When the pupils are familiar with the song, you can use the karaoke version to practise it.

Extension activity

Write about life in the past. Draw.

- Explain that you want the pupils to think about how people used to live in the past.
- The pupils work on their own to write the sentences and draw a picture of life in the past.
- Invite different pupils to share their sentences with the rest of the class.

Key Competences and Key Learning Outcomes

- Introduce and practise Preliminary for Schools exam tasks Reading Part 1; Listening Part 2; Writing Part 3; Speaking Parts 1, 3 and 4
- Learn to work out an answer before looking at answer options
- Learn to listen for specific information

- Learn about interpreting signs in various locations
- Write a short story with a prompt
- Talk about travel

Key language

- *bus journey, crash, sign, stairs*
- *You can't catch a bus here.*

Materials

- Pupil's Book p115; Activity Book pp 120 and 129, 5; Class CD4; Teacher's App on Navio

At a Glance Lesson Plan

Pupil's Book

Starting the lesson

- Review different types of signs.
- Set learning outcomes.

Activity 1

- Read the sign.
- Where do you think it is?
- Who do you think it is for?

Activity 2

- Read the sentences about the sign.
- Which one is true?
- Which words in the sign helped you?

Activity 3

- Read the short texts.
- What kind of texts are they and who are they for?
- Choose the correct answer for each one.

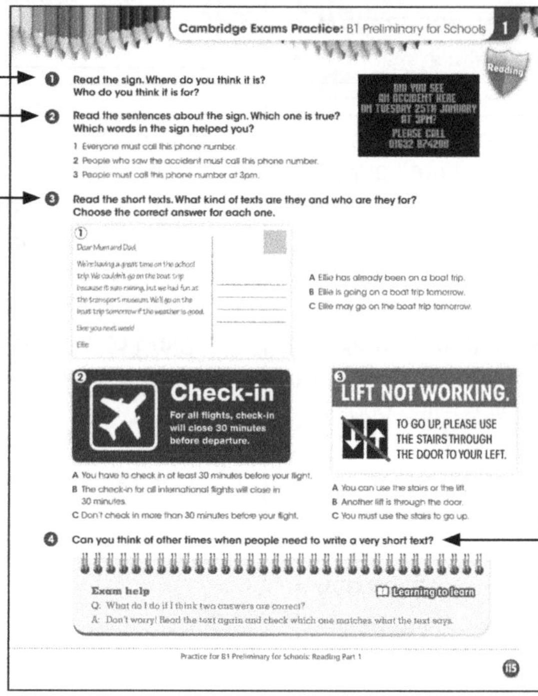

Activity 4

- Can you think of other times when people need to write a very short text?

Ending the lesson

- Review the lesson and reflect on learning.

Extra activity

Extension

- Write your own signs.

External Exams Videos

Additional Cambridge Exams Practice Video: B1 Preliminary for Schools

- Additional external exams preparation material, including videos, worksheets and practice tests, can be found in the Teacher's Resource Bank on Navio.

Digital resources

Teacher's Digital: You can also teach this lesson using the Teacher's App on Navio.

Pupil's Digital: Encourage your pupils to use the Pupil's App on Navio to practise the activities from this lesson.

Powered By NAVIO

Activity Book

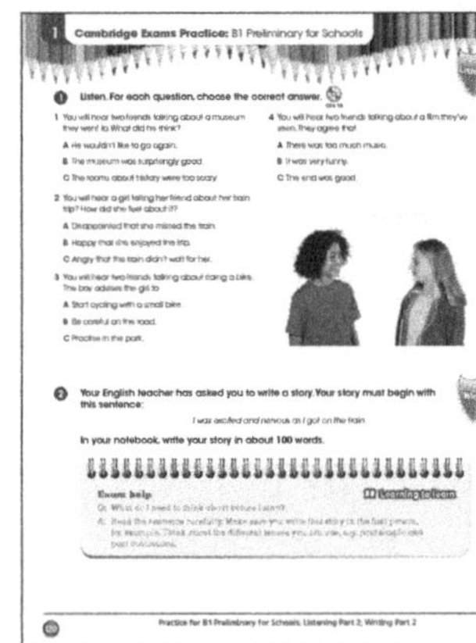

Activity Book page 120: Cambridge Exams Practice

Activity 1

- Listen. For each question, choose the correct answer.
▶ *CD4 Track 28 p298*

Activity 2

- Your English teacher has asked you to write a story. Your story must begin with this sentence: *I was excited and nervous as I got on the train.* In your notebook, write your story in about 100 words.

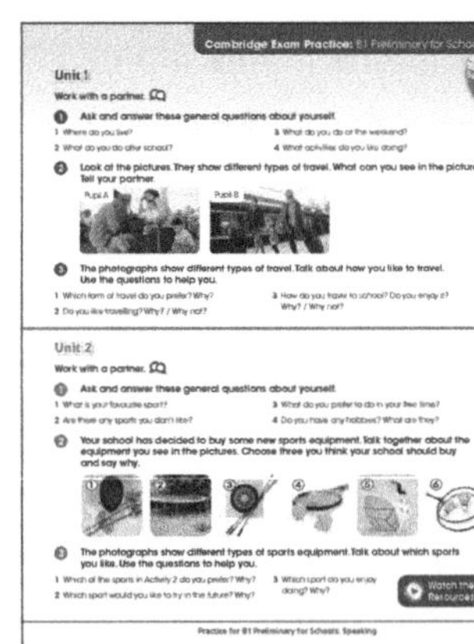

Activity Book page 129: Cambridge Exams Practice

Activity 1

- Work with a partner. Ask and answer these general questions about yourself.

Activity 2

- Look at the pictures. They show different types of travel. What can you see in the pictures? Tell your partner.

Activity 3

- The photographs show different types of travel. Talk about how you like to travel. Use the questions to help you.

Starting the lesson

Review facts about the Titanic.

- Ask **Do you remember the Titanic?** Prompt the class to tell you what they remember about what happened.

Set learning outcomes.

- Say **Today we're going to read some signs and practice more exam activities.**

Pupil's Book Activity 1

Read the sign. Where do you think it is? Who do you think it is for?

- Pupils look and decide where they would see the sign.

Possible answer: At the scene of the accident.

Pupil's Book Activity 2

Read the sentences about the sign. Which one is true? Which words in the sign helped you?

- In pairs, the pupils read the sentences as they refer to the signs. Check answers as a class.

Answers: 2 - Sign asks if they saw the accident to call the number given.

Pupil's Book Activity 3

Read the short texts. What kind of texts are they and who are they for? Choose the correct answer for each one.

- Pupils work individually to complete the activity. Ask why each sentence can / can't be correct.

Answers: **1** B **2** A **3** C

Exam help

- Read the Remember! box as a class.

Pupil's Book Activity 4

Can you think of other times when people need to write a very short text?

- Elicit answers and write a few ideas on the board.

External Exams Videos

Additional Cambridge Exams Practice Video: B1 Preliminary for Schools

- Additional external exams preparation material, including videos, worksheets and practice tests, can be found in the Teacher's Resource Bank on Navio.

Activity Book page 120: Cambridge Exams Practice

Activity 1

Listen. For each question, choose the correct answer.

▶ *CD4 Track 28 p298*

- Play the CD for pupils to complete the activity.
- Play the CD again, pausing after each piece of information. The pupils complete and check their answers.

Answers: **1** B **2** A **3** C **4** C

Exam help

- Refer pupils to the Exam help box.

Activity Book page 120: Cambridge Exams Practice

Activity 2

Your English teacher has asked you to write a story. Your story must begin with this sentence: *I was excited and nervos as I got on the train.*

In your notebooks, write your story in about 100 words.

- Ask pupils why they would feel nervous and excited before getting on a train.
- Ask what adjectives they would use to describe how they feel. Write them on the board.
- Tell pupils they should explain why they felt nervous and excited in their story and why they were getting on the train.
- Pupils read their stories to the class or partners.

Answers: **1** B **2** A **3** A **4** B **5** C

Activity Book page 129: Cambridge Exam Practice

Activity 1

Work with a partner. Ask and answer these general questions about yourself.

- In pairs, have pupils complete the activity.
- Bring volunteer pairs to the front of the class to act out the questions and answers.

Activity 2

Look at the pictures. They show different types of travel. What can you see in the pictures? Tell your partner.

- Invite pupils to give you descriptive words for each picture. Write them on the board.
- In pairs, have pupils complete the activity.
- Bring volunteer pairs to the front of the class to act out the questions and answers.

Activity 3

The photographs show different types of travel. Talk about how you like to travel. Use the questions to help you.

- Lead a class discussion on how pupils like to travel, using the questions in Activity 3. Write keywords on the board.
- In pairs, have pupils complete the activity.
- Bring volunteer pairs to the front of the class to act out their dialogue.

Ending the lesson

Review the lesson and reflect on learning.

- Say **Today we've looked at understanding signs and practised more exam activities.**
- Ask **What do you remember?** The pupils do a three-minute review in pairs.

Extra activity

Extension

- Ask the pupils to draw three or four signs of their own. They need to imagine that they are real signs that they would see in an English-speaking country. In groups, ask the pupils to guess where they would see each sign.

Key Competences and Key Learning Outcomes

- Read and understand a text about fencing
- Introduce and practise Preliminary for Schools exam tasks: Reading Part 3, Listening Part 4, Writing Part 2, Speaking Parts 1, 2 and 4.
- Learn a simple strategy for choosing the correct answer
- Read for specific information
- Learn about a famous gymnast

Key language

- *Internet access, online games, social networking sites*
- *I'd really recommend it as a sport for young people.*

Materials

- Pupil's Book p116; Activity Book pp121 and 129; Class CD4; Teacher's App on Navio

At a Glance Lesson Plan

Pupil's Book

Starting the lesson

- Review information about Gisela Pulido from Lesson 6.
- Set learning outcomes.

Activity 1

- Read the text quickly.
- Then answer the questions.

Activity 2

- Read the text again and answer the questions.
- For each question, choose A, B, C or D.

Exam help

- Read the Exam help boxes.

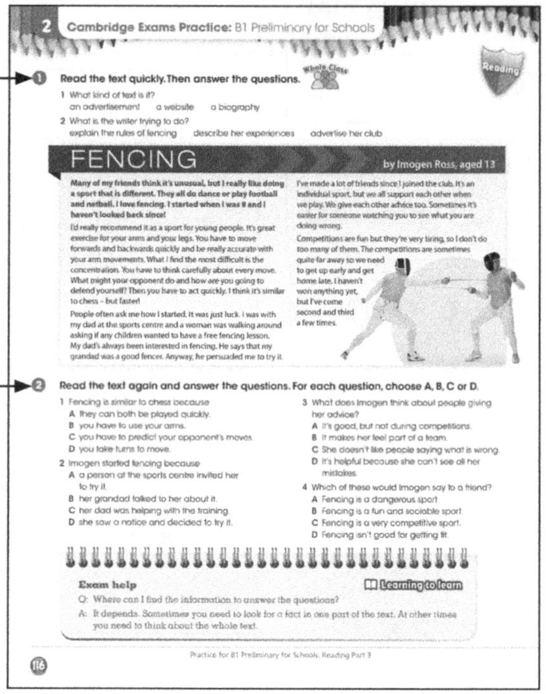

Ending the lesson

- Review the lesson and reflect on learning.

Extra activity

Reinforcement

- Write a paragraph about a hobby and two questions for it.

External Exams Videos

Additional Cambridge Exams Practice Video: B1 Preliminary for Schools

- Additional external exams preparation material, including videos, worksheets and practice tests, can be found in the Teacher's Resource Bank on Navio.

Digital resources

Teacher's Digital: You can also teach this lesson using the Teacher's App on Navio.

Pupil's Digital: Encourage your pupils to use the Pupil's App on Navio to practise the activities from this lesson.

Powered By NAVIO

Activity Book

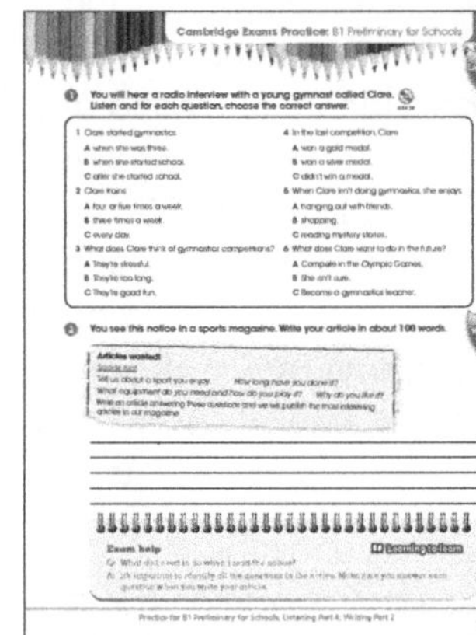

Activity Book page 121: Cambridge Exams Practice

Activity 1

- You will hear a radio interview with a young gymnast called Clare. Listen and for each question, choose the correct answer.

▶ *CD4 Track 29 p298*

Activity 2

- You see this notice in a sports magazine. Write your article in about 100 words.

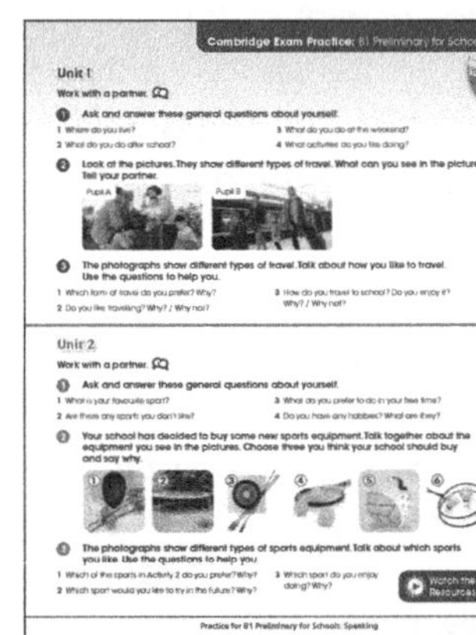

Activity Book page 129: Cambridge Exams Practice

Activity 1

- Work with a partner. Ask and answer these general questions about yourself.

Activity 2

- Your school has decided to buy some new sport equipment. Talk together about the equipment you see in the pictures. Choose three you think your school should buy and say why.

Activity 3

- The photographs show different types of sports equipment. Talk about which sports you like. Use the questions to help you.

Starting the lesson

Review information about Gisela Pulido from Lesson 6.

- Ask **Do you remember who Gisela Pulido is?** Prompt the pupils to tell you what they remember about this sports woman.

Set learning outcomes.

- Say **Today we're going to read about Imogen Ross, a pupil who does fencing in his free time.**

Pupil's Book Activity 1

Read the text quickly. Then answer the questions.

- Read out the title and look at the photo. Encourage the pupils to predict what they will read in the text.
- The pupils read the text to confirm if their predictions were correct.
- Read the first question as a class. Ask pupils what kind of text they think they will read and why.
- In pairs, the pupils complete the activity, referring back to the text as they do so.

Answers: **1** a website **2** describe her experiences

Exam help

- Read the Exam help box as a class.

Pupil's Book Activity 2

Read the text again and answer the questions. For each question, choose A, B, C or D.

- Read through the questions and ask pupils to note their answers in their notebooks from memory.
- The pupils read the text to complete the activity.
- Elicit answers. In pairs, pupils look at the answers they gave in their notebooks and check how many they had guessed correctly.

Answers: **1** C **2** A **3** D **4** B

External Exams Videos

Additional Cambridge Exams Practice Video: B1 Preliminary for Schools

- Additional external exams preparation material, including videos, worksheets and practice tests, can be found in the Teacher's Resource Bank on Navio.

Activity Book page 121: Cambridge Exams Practice

Activity 1

You will hear a radio interview with a young gymnast called Clare. Listen and for each question, choose the correct answer.

▶ *CD4 Track 29 p298*

- Read the questions as a class.
- Play the CD. The pupils listen and complete as much of the information as possible. They check their answers with a partner.
- Play the CD again, pausing after each piece of information. The pupils complete and check their answers.

Answers: **1** C **2** A **3** A **4** B **5** A **6** B

Exam help

- Read the Exam help box as a class.

Activity Book page 121: Cambridge Exams Practice

Activity 2

You see this notice in a sports magazine. Write your article in about 100 words.

- Ask pupils how many words they should write and what kind of text they have been asked to write.
- Go through each point and ask pupils what words they can use, e.g. for three years, since I was eight, bow and arrow, ball, racket, fun, I keep fit, I enjoy playing with others.
- Pupils complete the activity and read their article to their partners.

Activity Book page 129: Cambridge Exams Practice

Activity 1

Work with a partner. Ask and answer these general questions about yourself.

- In pairs, have pupils complete the activity.
- Bring volunteer pairs to the front of the class to act out the questions and answers.

Activity 2

Your school has decided to buy some new sport equipment. Talk together about the equipment you see in the pictures. Choose three you think your school should buy and say why.

- Invite pupils to tell you why each of these pieces of equipment is useful.
- In pairs, have pupils complete the activity.
- Bring volunteer pairs to the front of the class to act out the questions and answers.

Activity 3

The photographs show different types of sports equipment. Talk about which sports you like. Use the questions to help you.

- Lead a class discussion on what sports children like using the questions in Activity 3. Write keywords on the board.
- In pairs, have pupils complete the activity.
- Bring volunteer pairs to the front of the class to act out their dialogues.

Ending the lesson

Review the lesson and reflect on learning.

- Say **Today we've read about fencing and what is needed to do it.**
- Ask **What do you remember?** The pupils do a three-minute review in pairs.

Extra activity

Reinforcement

- Ask the pupils to write a paragraph about a hobby and two questions with four multiple choice options.
- Have pupils exchange paragraphs with their partners for them to find the answers.

Key Competences and Key Learning Outcomes

- Introduce and practise Preliminary for Schools exam tasks: Reading Part 6, Listening Part 3, Writing Part 1, Speaking Parts 1, 3 and 4
- Learn to take notes and check spelling

- Learn about reading email texts
- Learn to interpret restaurant menus

Key language

- *address, attach, invite, meeting time, phone number*
- *The table is reserved for 1pm.*

Materials

- Pupil's Book p117; Activity Book pp122 and 130; Class CD4; Teacher's App on Navio

At a Glance Lesson Plan

Pupil's Book

Starting the lesson

- Review healthy lifestyles.
- Set learning outcomes.
- Go to the Activity Book page 34: Review.

Activity 1

- Read and correct the mistakes.

Activity 2

- Read the email with the missing words.
- Answer the questions.

Activity 3

- Write the seven missing words in your notebook. Compare with a friend. Try to explain why you chose each word.

Activity 4

- Write sentences with missing words. Test your friend.

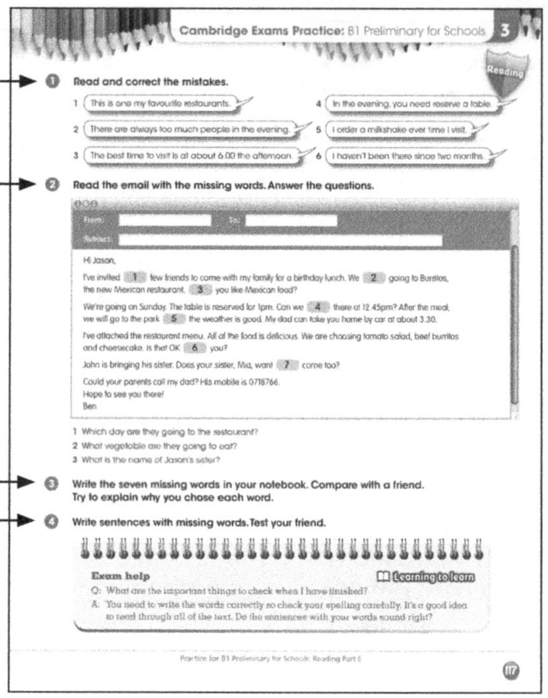

Exam help

- Read the Exam help box.

Ending the lesson

- Review the lesson and reflect on learning.

Extra activity

Extension

- Write incorrect sentences for your partner to correct

External Exams Videos

Additional Cambridge Exams Practice Video: B1 Preliminary for Schools

- Additional external exams preparation material, including videos, worksheets and practice tests, can be found in the Teacher's Resource Bank on Navio.

Digital resources

Teacher's Digital: You can also teach this lesson using the Teacher's App on Navio.

Pupil's Digital: Encourage your pupils to use the Pupil's App on Navio to practise the activities from this lesson.

Powered By NAVIO

Activity Book

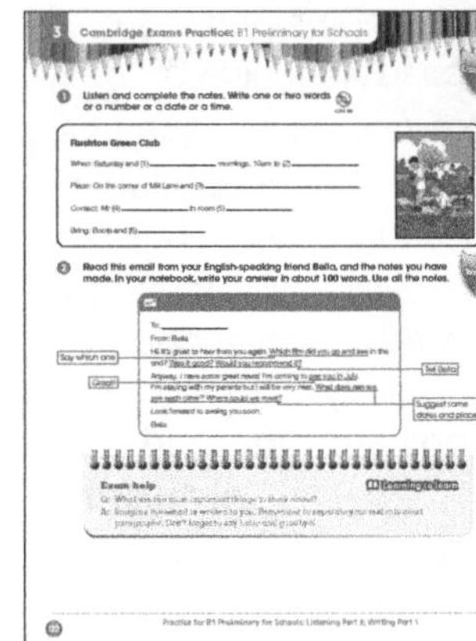

Activity Book page 122: Cambridge Exams Practice

Activity 1

- Listen and complete the notes. Write one or two words or a number or a date or a time.

▶ *CD4 Track 30 p298*

Activity 2

- Read this email from your English-speaking friend Bella, and the notes you have made. In your notebooks, write your answer in about 100 words. Use all the notes.

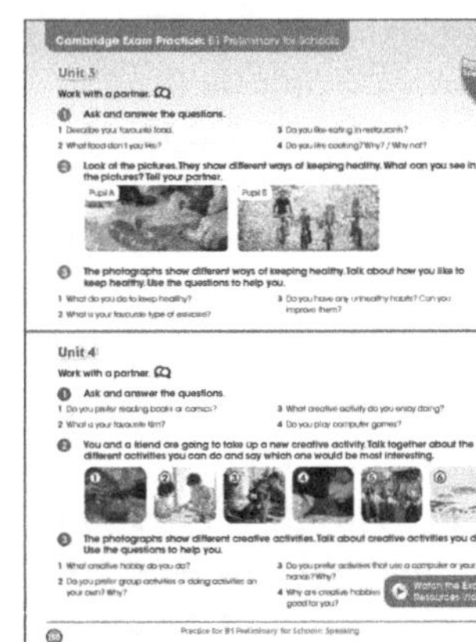

Activity Book page 130: Cambridge Exams Practice

Activity 1

- Work with a partner. Ask and answer the questions.

Activity 2

- Look at the pictures. They show different ways of keeping healthy. What can you see in the pictures? Tell your partner.

Activity 3

- The photographs show different ways of keeping healthy. Talk about how you like to keep healthy. Use the questions to help you.

Starting the lesson

Review healthy lifestyles.

- Ask **What can we do to have a healthy lifestyle?** Prompt the class to tell you about food and exercise.

Set learning outcomes.

- Say **Today we're going to read an email and find its missing words.**

Pupil's Book Activity 1

Read and correct the mistakes.

- Explain that in this lesson they have to correct the sentences.
- Pupils complete the activity individually. Check answers as a class.

Answers: **1** This is one of my favourite restaurants. **2** There are always too many people in the evening. **3** The best time to visit is at about 6.00 in the afternoon. **4** In the evening, you need to reserve a table. **5** I order a milkshake every time I visit. **6** I haven't been there for two months.

Pupil's Book Activity 2

Read the email with the missing words. Answer the questions.

- Give pupils a little time to read the email and answer the questions. Check answers as a class.

Answers: **1** Sunday **2** tomato **3** Mia

Pupil's Book Activity 3

Write the seven missing words in your notebook. Compare with a friend.

Try to explain why you chose each word.

- Look at the first item and complete it with the class.
- Pupils complete the activity individually and then check answers with their partners.

Answers: **1** a **2** are **3** Do **4** be /get **5** if **6** with **7** to

Exam help

- Read the Exam help box as a class.

Pupil's Book Activity 4

Write sentences with missing words. Test your friend.

- Write three sentences on the board with missing words. Ask pupils to find the missing words.
- Have pupils write their own sentences with missing words and swap papers with their partners.

External Exams Videos

Additional Cambridge Exams Practice Video: B1 Preliminary for Schools

- Additional external exams preparation material, including videos, worksheets and practice tests, can be found in the Teacher's Resource Bank on Navio.

Activity Book page 122: Cambridge Exams Practice

Activity 1

Listen and complete the notes. Write one or two words or a number or a date or a time.

▶ *CD4 Track 30 p298*

- Play the CD. The pupils listen and complete the poster.
- Play the CD again, pausing after each piece of information. The pupils complete and check their answers.

Answers: **1** Sunday **2** midday **3** Bridge Street **3** Webber **4** Webber **5** 291

Activity Book page 122: Cambridge Exams Practice

Activity 2

Read this email from your English-speaking friend Bella, and the notes you have made. In your notebooks, write your answer in about 100 words. Use all the notes.

- Explain to the pupils that they are going to read another email. This time they will need to reply. Read the email together as a class. Ask **How many questions will you need to answer in your reply?** (*Four*)
- The pupils write an email to Bella. Remind them that they must write about 100 words.

Activity Book page 130: Cambridge Exams Practice

Activity 1

Work with a partner. Ask and answer the questions.

- In pairs, have pupils complete the activity.
- Bring volunteer pairs to the front of the class to act out the questions and answers.

Activity 2

Look at the pictures. They show different ways of keeping healthy. What can you see in the pictures? Tell your partner.

- Ask pupils what activities they see.
- Invite pupils to give you descriptive words for each picture. Write them on the board.
- In pairs, have pupils complete the activity.
- Bring volunteer pairs to the front of the class to act out the questions and answers.

Activity 3

The photographs show different ways of keeping healthy. Talk about how you like to keep healthy. Use the questions to help you.

- Ask pupils to make notes on how they like to keep healthy.
- Lead a class discussion on how pupils like to keep healthy. Tell pupils they can use their notes. Write keywords on the board.
- Pupils complete the activity in pairs then bring volunteer pairs to the front of the class to act out their dialogues.

Ending the lesson

Review the lesson and reflect on learning.

- Say **Today we've read and written short emails.**
- Ask **What do you remember?** The pupils do a three-minute review in pairs.

Extra activity

Extension

- Ask the pupils to write a restaurant menu in groups. It can be any style of restaurant they wish. The menu should include prices. They can use the menu in the Pupil's Book as a model.

Key Competences and Key Learning Outcomes

- Introduce and practise Preliminary for Schools exam tasks: Reading Part 5, Listening Part 1, Writing Part 2, Speaking Parts 1, 2 and 4
- Learn a simple strategy for choosing the best meaning of a text

Key language

- *concert, musical, play, exhibition, stage school*
- *My ambition is to appear in a film.*

Materials

- Pupil's Book p118; Activity Book pp123–130; Class CD4; Teacher's App on Navio

At a Glance Lesson Plan

Pupil's Book

Starting the lesson

- Review different forms of entertainment.
- Set learning outcomes.
- Go to the Activity Book page 46: Review.

Activity 1

- Read and discuss.
- How are these words different?

Activity 2

- Read the text with the missing words.
- What do you learn about stage schools?

Activity 3

- Read the text again.
- Choose the correct word for each space.

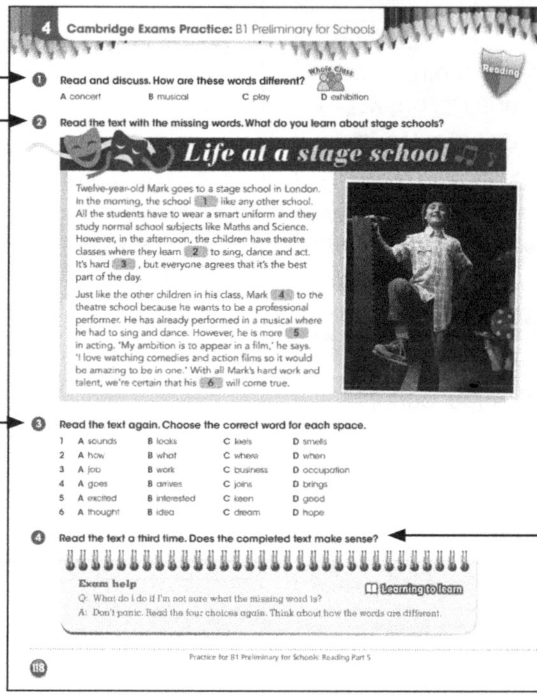

4 Cambridge Exams Practice: B1 Preliminary for Schools

1 Read and discuss. How are these words different?
A concert B musical C play D exhibition

2 Read the text with the missing words. What do you learn about stage schools?

Life at a stage school

Twelve-year-old Mark goes to a stage school in London. In the morning, the school (1) like any other school. All the students have to wear a smart uniform and they study normal school subjects like Maths and Science. However, in the afternoon, the children have theatre classes where they learn (2) to sing, dance and act. It's hard (3), but everyone agrees that it's the best part of the day.

Just like the other children in his class, Mark (4) to the theatre school because he wants to be a professional performer. He has already performed in a musical where he had to sing and dance. However, he is more (5) in acting. 'My ambition is to appear in a film,' he says. 'I love watching comedies and action films so it would be amazing to be in one.' With all Mark's hard work and talent, we're certain that his (6) will come true.

3 Read the text again. Choose the correct word for each space.

	A	B	C	D
1	sounds	looks	feels	smells
2	how	what	where	when
3	job	work	business	occupation
4	goes	arrives	joins	brings
5	excited	interested	keen	good
6	thought	idea	dream	hope

4 Read the text a third time. Does the completed text make sense?

Exam help
Q: What do I do if I'm not sure what the missing word is?
A: Don't panic. Read the four choices again. Think about how the words are different.

118 Practice for B1 Preliminary for Schools: Reading Part 5

Activity 4

- Read the text a third time.
- Does the completed text make sense?

Exam help

- Read the Exam help.

Ending the lesson

- Review the lesson and reflect on learning.

Extra activity

Reinforcement

- Write your own short texts.

External Exams Videos

Additional Cambridge Exams Practice Video: B1 Preliminary for Schools

- Additional external exams preparation material, including videos, worksheets and practice tests, can be found in the Teacher's Resource Bank on Navio.

Activity Book

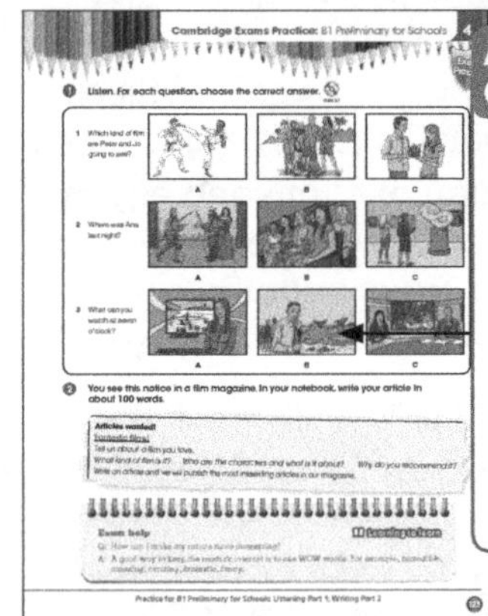

Activity Book page 123: Cambridge Exams Practice

Activity 1

- Listen. For each question, choose the correct answer.

▶ *CD4 Track 31 p298*

Activity 2

- You see this notice in a film magazine. In your notebook, write your article in about 100 words.

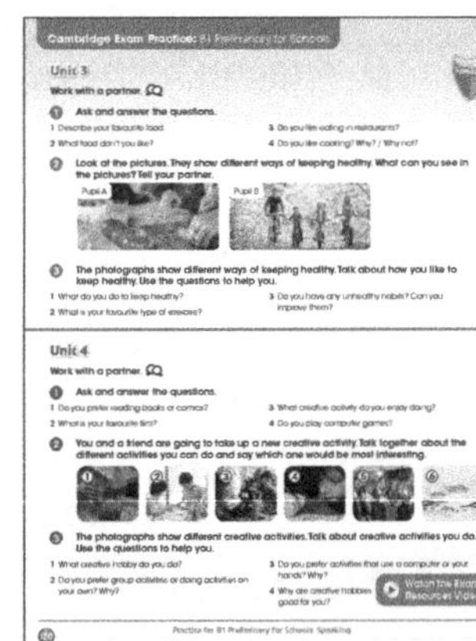

Activity Book page 130: Cambridge Exams Practice

Activity 1

- Work with a partner. Ask and answer the questions.

Activity 2

- You and a friend are going to take up a new creative activity. Talk together about the different activities you can do and say which one would be most interesting.

Activity 3

- The photographs show different creative activities. Talk about creative activities you do. Use the questions to help you.

Digital resources

Teacher's Digital: You can also teach this lesson using the Teacher's App on Navio.

Pupil's Digital: Encourage your pupils to use the Pupil's App on Navio to practise the activities from this lesson.

Powered By NAVIO

Detailed Lesson Plan

Starting the lesson

Review different forms of entertainment.

- Write the word *entertainment* in the middle of the board. Prompt the pupils to name different forms of entertaiment. Write the forms around the central word.
- Ask **Which forms of entertainment do you enjoy the most? Why?**

Set learning outcomes

- Say **Today we're going to read some short texts and find the missing words.**

Pupil's Book Activity 1

Read and discuss. How are these words different?

- Read the words as a class. Encourage different pupils to explain the differences between the words.

Answer: **A** people go there to listen to a group or musician **B** a theatrical play or film with singing and dancing **C** what we see at the theatre **D** a series of objects on display for people to see.

Pupil's Book Activity 2

Read the text with the missing words. What do you learn about stage schools?

- Read the text as a class.
- Ask pupils what they learnt about the stage school and if they found it interesting.

Pupil's Book Activity 3

Read the text again. Choose the correct word for each space.

- Go through random words from the items and ask pupils to make sentences (sounds – It sounds like a bird. job – I got a job in a bakery etc.)
- Pupils complete the activity. Do not check answers at this stage.

Answers: **1** B **2** A **3** B **4** A **5** B **6** C

Pupil's Book Activity 4

Read the text a third time. Does the completed text make sense?

- Have pupils read the text with the words they chose.
- Check answers as a class.

Exam help

- Read the Exam help box as a class.

External Exams Videos

Additional Cambridge Exams Practice Video: B1 Preliminary for Schools

- Additional external exams preparation material, including videos, worksheets and practice tests, can be found in the Teacher's Resource Bank on Navio.

Activity Book page 123: Cambridge Exams Practice

Activity 1

Listen. For each question, choose the correct answer.

▶ *CD4 Track 31 p286*

- Read the first question. Invite a pupil to describe the three pictures. Ask pupils what words they expect to hear for each picture.
- Play the CD. The pupils listen and identify the correct answer.
- Repeat the procedure with the other questions.

Answers: **1** A **2** C **3** B

Activity Book page 123: Cambridge Exams Practice

Activity 2

You see this notice in a film magazine. In your notebook, write your article in about 100 words.

- Ask pupils to give words that describe a fantastic film. Write them on the board.
- Tell pupils that they should say what film the saw and explain why they think the film was fascinating.
- Pupils complete the activity.

Activity Book page 130: Cambridge Exams Practice

Activity 1

Work with a partner. Ask and answer the questions.

- In pairs, have pupils complete the activity.
- Bring volunteer pairs to the front of the class to act out the questions and answers.

Activity 2

You and a friend are going to take up a new creative activity. Talk together about the different activities you can do and say which one would be most interesting.

- Invite pupils to describe each picture. Write descriptive adjectives on the board.
- In pairs, have pupils complete the activity.
- Bring volunteer pairs to the front of the class to act out the questions and answers.

Activity 3

The photographs show different creative activities. Talk about creative activities you do. Use the questions to help you.

- Lead a class discussion on what type of creative activities pupils do, using the questions in Activity 3.
- In pairs, have pupils complete the activity.
- Bring volunteer pairs to the front of the class to act out their dialogues.

Ending the lesson

Review the lesson and reflect on learning.

- Say **Today we've read a short text about a stage school.**
- Ask **What do you remember?** The pupils do a three-minute review in pairs.

Extra activity

Reinforcement

- On the board write *Life at my school* In pairs, the pupils choose one of the headings. They write a short text of 40 words.

Key Competences and Key Learning Outcomes

- Introduce and practise Preliminary for Schools exam tasks: Reading part 2, Listening Part 1, Writing Part 2, Speaking Parts 1, 3 and 4
- Learn to read large amounts of text in an organised way

- Appreciate people who are blind

Key language

- *active, current affairs, engines, film set, keep a blog*
- *If you want to be a journalist, this is for you.*

Materials

- Pupil's Book p119; Activity Book pp124–131; Class CD4; Teacher's App on Navio

At a Glance Lesson Plan

Pupil's Book

Starting the lesson

- Review learning in Unit 5.
- Set learning outcomes.

Go to the Activity Book page 56: Review.

Activity 1

- Read about these four teenagers.
- Then answer the questions.

Activity 2

- The teenagers are going to do some work experience this summer.
- Read and decide which place would be most suitable for each teenager.
- There will be one place left over.

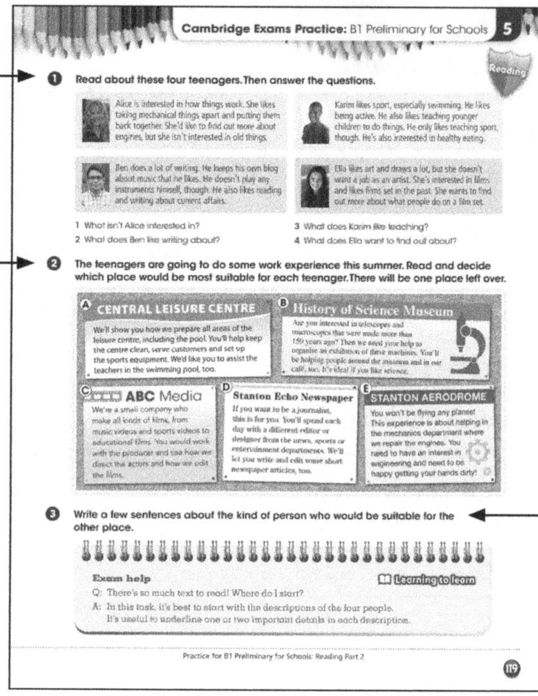

Cambridge Exams Practice: B1 Preliminary for Schools 5

1 Read about these four teenagers. Then answer the questions.

1 What isn't Alice interested in?
2 What does Ben like writing about?
3 What does Karim like teaching?
4 What does Ella want to find out about?

2 The teenagers are going to do some work experience this summer. Read and decide which place would be most suitable for each teenager. There will be one place left over.

A CENTRAL LEISURE CENTRE
B History of Science Museum
C ABC Media
D Stanton Echo Newspaper
E STANTON AERODROME

3 Write a few sentences about the kind of person who would be suitable for the other place.

Exam help

Q: There's so much text to read! Where do I start?
A: In this task, it's best to start with the descriptions of the four people. It's useful to underline one or two important details in each description.

Practice for B1 Preliminary for Schools: Reading Part 2 119

Activity 3

- Write a few sentences about the kind of person who would be suitable for the other place.

Go to the Activity Book.

Exam help

- Read the Exam help.

Ending the lesson

- Review the lesson and reflect on learning.

Extra activity

Extension

- Invent short interviews.

External Exams Videos

Additional Cambridge Exams Practice Video: B1 Preliminary for Schools

- Additional external exams preparation material, including videos, worksheets and practice tests, can be found in the Teacher's Resource Bank on Navio.

Activity Book

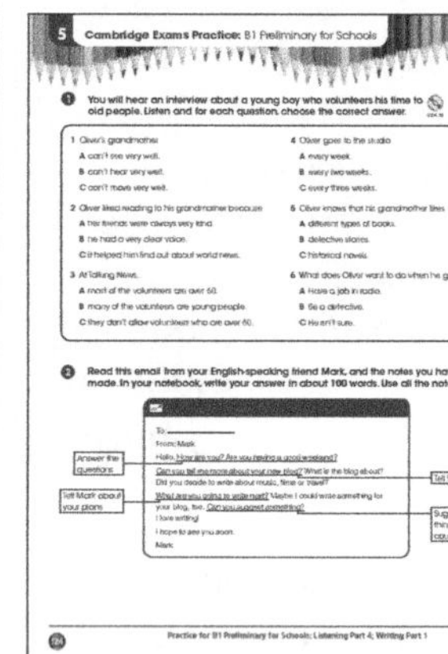

Activity Book page 124: Cambridge Exams Practice

Activity 1

- You will hear an interview about a young boy who volunteers his time to old people. Listen and for each question, choose the correct answer.

▶ *CD4 Track 32 p286*

Activity 2

- Read this email from your English-speaking friend Mark, and the notes you have made. In your notebook, write your answer in about 100 words. Use all the notes.

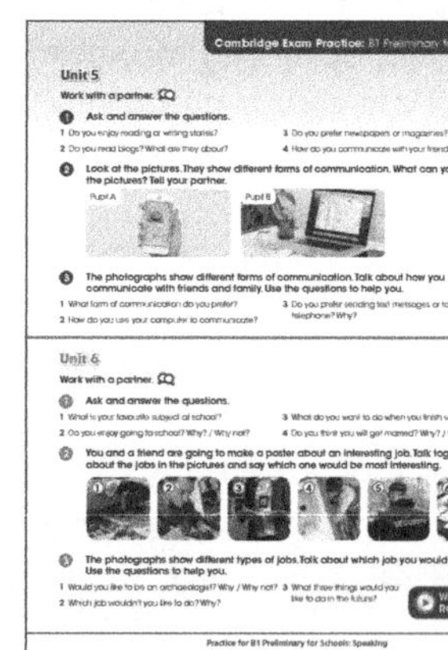

Activity Book page 131: Cambridge Exams Practice

Activity 1

- Work with a partner. Ask and answer the questions.

Activity 2:

- Look at the pictures. They show different forms of communication. What can you see in the pictures? Tell your partner.

Activity 3

- The photographs show different forms of communication. Talk about how you communicate with friends and family. Use the questions to help you.

Digital resources

Teacher's Digital: You can also teach this lesson using the Teacher's App on Navio.

Pupil's Digital: Encourage your pupils to use the Pupil's App on Navio to practise the activities from this lesson.

Powered By NAVIO

Starting the lesson

Review learning in Unit 5.

- Ask **What do you remember most about this unit?** Prompt the class to tell you about the Rosetta Stone, newspaper articles, etc.

Set learning outcomes.

- Say **Today we're going to do a reading task and a listening task.**

Pupil's Book Activity 1

Read about these four teenagers. Then answer the questions.

- Ask the pupils to read about the four teenagers. They then answer the questions.

Answers: **1** old things **2** current affairs **3** teaching younger children sport **4** what people do on a film set

Pupil's Book Activity 2

The teenagers are going to do some work experience this summer. Read and decide which place would be most suitable for each teenager. There will be one place left over.

- Ask the pupils to explain what 'work experience' is. (*Helping at a place of work as a volunteer to get some experience of a particular job.*)
- The pupils read about five different work places. They decide which place is most suitable for each person in Activity 1.
- Check answers as a class.

Answers: **Alice** E **Ben** D **Karim** A **Ella** C

Pupil's Book Activity 3

Write a few sentences about the kind of person who would be suitable for the other place.

- The pupils look at the History of Science Museum text. In pairs, they write a few sentences to describe the kind of person who would be suitable to do work experience there.
- Invite different pupils to read out their suggestions.

Exam help

- Read the Exam help box as a class. Ask the pupils to suggest other strategies that they used when they read the texts.

External Exams Videos

Additional Cambridge Exams Practice Video: B1 Preliminary for Schools

- Additional external exams preparation material, including videos, worksheets and practice tests, can be found in the Teacher's Resource Bank on Navio.

Activity Book page 124: Cambridge Exams Practice

Activity 1

You will hear an interview about a young boy who volunteers his time to old people. Listen and for each question, choose the correct answer.

▶ *CD4 Track 32 p286*

- Read the questions as a class.
- Play the CD. The pupils listen and choose the correct answers.
- Play the CD again, pausing after each piece of information. The pupils complete and check their answers. Ask **Would you like to volunteer for Talking News?**

Answers: **1** A **2** C **3** A **4** C **5** B **6** C

Activity 2

Read this email from your English-speaking friend Mark, and the notes you have made. In your notebook, write your answer in about 100 words. Use all the notes.

- The pupils read the instructions about an email they have to write. Check they understand that they must include all the information that the question asks.
- The pupils complete the writing task. They compare their work in pairs.
- Invite a few pupils to read out their emails.

Activity Book page 131: Cambridge Exams Practice

Activity 1

Work with a partner. Ask and answer the questions.

- In pairs, have pupils complete the activity.
- Bring volunteer pairs to the front of the class to act out the questions and answers.

Activity 2

Look at the pictures. They show different forms of communication. What can you see in the pictures? Tell your partner.

- Invite pupils to give you descriptive words for each picture. Write them on the board.
- In pairs, have pupils complete the activity.

Activity 3

The photographs show different forms of communication. Talk about how you communicate with friends and family. Use the questions to help you.

- Lead a class discussion on how pupils communicate with their family and friends, using the questions in Activity 3. Write keywords on the board.
- Bring volunteer pairs to the front of the class to act out their dialogues.

Ending the lesson

Review the lesson and reflect on learning.

- Say **Today we've done a reading task and a listening task.**
- Ask **What do you remember?** The pupils do a three-minute review in pairs.

Extra activity

Extension

- Ask the pupils to imagine a job interview between Alice, Ben, Karim or Ella (Pupil's Book Activity 1) and someone from a work experience place in Pupil's Book Activity 2.
- In pairs, the pupils choose a teenager and a place, e.g. Alice and the Stanton Aerodrome. They think of questions to ask. They then act out the short interview.
- Ask some pupils to act out the interview for the class.

Key Competences and Key Learning Outcomes

LEARN

- Introduce and practise Preliminary for Schools exam tasks: Reading Part 4, Listening Part 3, Writing Part 2, Speaking Parts 1, 2 and 4
- Learn a simple strategy for dealing with unknown words in a text

Key language

- *accommodation, brochure, entertainment*
- *This holiday is for people who enjoy doing new things.*

Materials

- Pupil's Book p120; Activity Book pp125 and 130; Class CD4; Teacher's App on Navio

At a Glance Lesson Plan

Pupil's Book

Starting the lesson

- Play a word game.
- Set learning outcomes.

Activity 1

- Read the title and predict what the text is about.

Activity 2

- Quickly read the text to find out.
- Then answer the questions.

Activity 3

- Read the eight sentences carefully.
- Which part of the text do you think each sentence comes from?

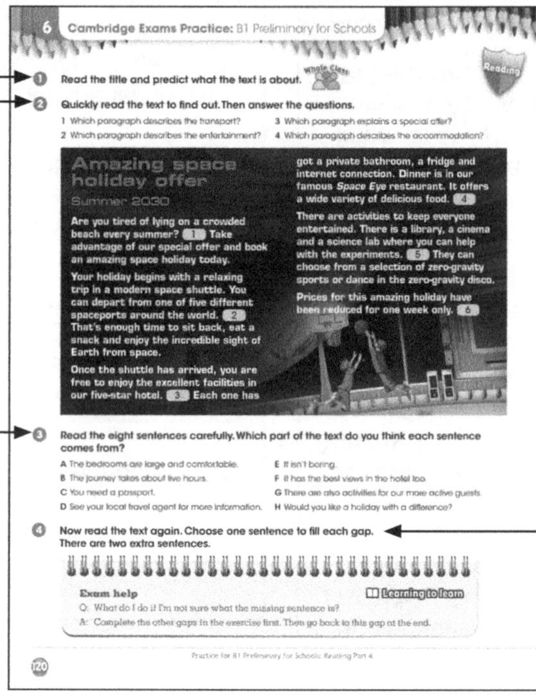

6 Cambridge Exams Practice: B1 Preliminary for Schools

1 Read the title and predict what the text is about.

2 Quickly read the text to find out. Then answer the questions.

1 Which paragraph describes the transport? 3 Which paragraph explains a special offer?
2 Which paragraph describes the entertainment? 4 Which paragraph describes the accommodation?

Amazing space holiday offer

Summer 2030

Are you tired of lying on a crowded beach every summer? 1 Take advantage of our special offer and book an amazing space holiday today.

Your holiday begins with a relaxing trip in a modern space shuttle. You can depart from one of five different spaceports around the world. 2 That's enough time to sit back, eat a snack and enjoy the incredible sight of Earth from space.

Once the shuttle has arrived, you are free to enjoy the excellent facilities in our five-star hotel. 3 Each one has got a private bathroom, a fridge and internet connection. Dinner is in our famous *Space Eye* restaurant. It offers a wide variety of delicious food. 4

There are activities to keep everyone entertained. There is a library, a cinema and a science lab where you can help with the experiments. 5 They can choose from a selection of zero-gravity sports or dance in the zero-gravity disco.

Prices for this amazing holiday have been reduced for one week only. 6

3 Read the eight sentences carefully. Which part of the text do you think each sentence comes from?

A The bedrooms are large and comfortable.
B The journey takes about two hours.
C You need a passport.
D See your local travel agent for more information.
E It isn't boring.
F It has the best views in the hotel too.
G There are also activities for our more active guests.
H Would you like a holiday with a difference?

4 Now read the text again. Choose one sentence to fill each gap. There are two extra sentences.

Exam help — Learning to learn
Q: What do I do if I'm not sure what the missing sentence is?
A: Complete the other gaps in the exercise first. Then go back to this gap at the end.

120 Practice for B1 Preliminary for Schools: Reading Part 4

Activity 4

- Now read the text again.
- Choose one sentence to fill each gap.
- There are two extra sentences.

Exam help

- Read the Exam help.

Ending the lesson

- Review the lesson and reflect on learning.

Extra activity

Reinforcement

- Play a true / false game.

External Exams Videos

Additional Cambridge Exams Practice Video: B1 Preliminary for Schools

- Additional external exams preparation material, including videos, worksheets and practice tests, can be found in the Teacher's Resource Bank on Navio.

Digital resources

Teacher's Digital: You can also teach this lesson using the Teacher's App on Navio.

Pupil's Digital: Encourage your pupils to use the Pupil's App on Navio to practise the activities from this lesson.

Powered By NAVIO

Activity Book

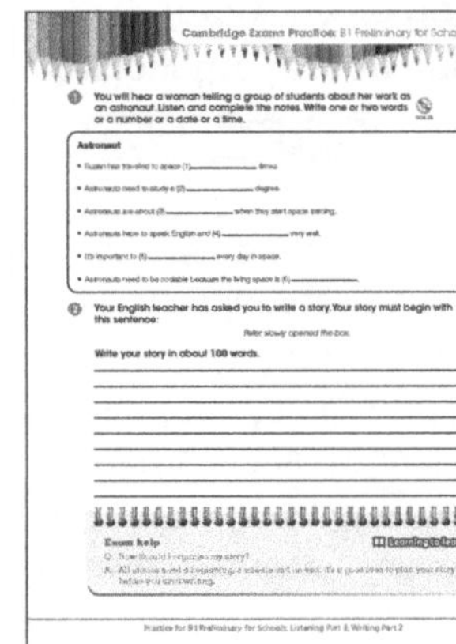

Activity Book page 125: Cambridge Exams Practice

Activity 1

- You will hear a woman telling a group of students about her work as an astronaut. Listen and complete the notes. Write one or two words or a number or a date or a time.

▶ *CD4 Track 33 p299*

Activity 2

- Your English teacher has asked you to write a story. Your story must begin with this sentence: *Peter slowly opened the box.* Write your story in about 100 words.

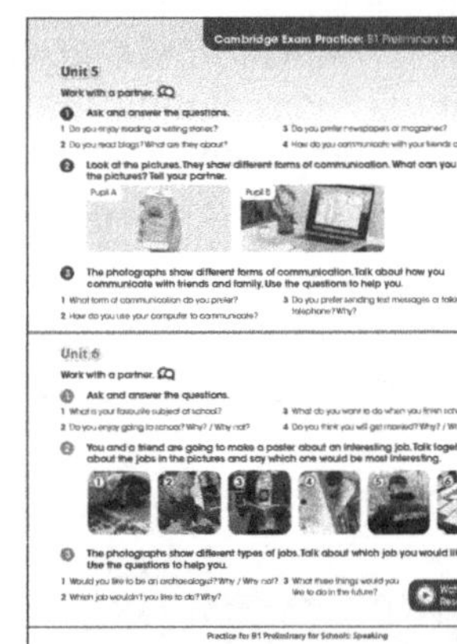

Activity Book page 131: Cambridge Exams Practice

Activity 1

- Work with a partner. Ask and answer the questions.

Activity 2

- You and a friend are going to make a poster about an interesting job. Talk together about the jobs in the pictures and say which one would be most interesting.

Activity 3

- The photographs show different types of jobs. Talk about which job you would like to do. Use the questions to help you.

Starting the lesson

Play a word game.

- Draw eight dashes on the board, one per letter in the mystery word (BROCHURE).
- Invite a pupil to say a letter. If the letter appears in the word, write it on the corresponding line. If it doesn't appear, write it on the side of the board.
- After six letters, the pupils attempt to guess the word.

Set learning outcomes.

- Say **Today we're going to read a holiday brochure.**

Pupil's Book Activity 1

Read the title and predict what the text is about.

- The pupils read the title and predict what the text is about.

Answers: **1** a brochure about a holiday in space

Pupil's Book Activity 2

Quickly read the text to find out. Then answer the questions.

- Read the questions as a class. Explain that this activity will help them locate the correct answer in the next activity.

Answers: **1** 2 **2** 4 **3** 5 **4** 3

Pupil's Book Activity 3

Read the eight sentences carefully. Which part of the text do you think each sentence comes from?

- The pupils read the sentences. In pairs, they decide where the sentences belong.

Pupil's Book Activity 4

Now read the text again. Choose one sentence to fill each gap. There are two extra sentences.

- Pupils complete the activity individually and check answers as a class.
- Ask why the two remaining sentences cannot be used.

Answers: **1** H **2** B **3** A **4** F **5** G **6** D

Exam help

- Read the Exam help as a class.

External Exams Videos

Additional Cambridge Exams Practice Video: B1 Preliminary for Schools

- Additional external exams preparation material, including videos, worksheets and practice tests, can be found in the Teacher's Resource Bank on Navio.

Activity Book page 125: Cambridge Exams Practice

Activity 1

You will hear a woman telling a group of students about her work as an astronaut. Listen and complete the notes. Write one or two words or a number or a date or a time.

▶ *CD4 Track 33 p299*

- Read the information as a class. Encourage the pupils to predict the missing words each time.
- Play the CD. The pupils listen and complete as much of the information as possible. They check their answers with a partner.
- Play the CD again, pausing after each piece of information. The pupils complete and check their answers.

Answers: **1** five **2** scientific **3** thirty **4** Russian **5** exercise **6** small

Activity 2

Your English teacher has asked you to write a story. Your story must begin with this sentence:

Peter slowly opened the box.

Write your story in about 100 words.

- Read the instructions as a class.
- In pairs, the pupils brainstorm ideas on what to write in the story.
- Quickly review how to start and finish a story. The pupils then write the story.

Exam help

- Ask pupils why it's important to plan and organise a story before writing it.

Activity Book page 131: Cambridge Exams Practice

Activity 1

Work with a partner. Ask and answer the questions.

- In pairs, have pupils complete the activity.
- Bring volunteer pairs to the front of the class to act out the questions and answers.

Activity 2

You and a friend are going to make a poster about an interesting job. Talk together about the jobs in the pictures and say which one would be most interesting.

- Invite pupils to give you descriptive words for each picture and say what job it is. Write them on the board.
- In pairs, have pupils complete the activity.
- Bring volunteer pairs to the front of the class to act out the questions and answers.

Activity 3

The photographs show different types of jobs. Talk about which job you would like to do. Use the questions to help you.

- Lead a class discussion on jobs pupils would like to do and why. Write keywords on the board.
- In pairs, have pupils complete the activity.
- Bring volunteer pairs to the front of the class to act out their dialogues.

Ending the lesson

Review the lesson and reflect on learning.

- Say **Today we've read a holiday brochure.**
- Ask **What do you remember?** The pupils do a three-minute review in pairs. (Cooperative Learning Strategies, page 19)

Extra activity

Reinforcement

- The pupils write three sentences about the 'Amazing space holiday offer'. The sentences can be true or false.
- In pairs, the pupils read out their sentences. Their partner decides if the sentence is true or false.

Key Competences and Key Learning Outcomes

- Learn to identify a writer's intentions
- Introduce and practise Preliminary for Schools exam tasks: Reading Part 3, Listening Part 2, Writing Part 2, Speaking Parts 1, 2 and 4
- Learn to read texts carefully and thoroughly
- Learn about shopping at a market

Key language

- *advertise, disappointed, compare, complain, give advice / instructions*

Materials

- Pupil's Book p121; Activity Book pp126 and 132; Class CD4; Teacher's App on Navio

At a Glance Lesson Plan

Pupil's Book

Starting the lesson

- Review learning in Unit 7.
- Set learning outcomes.

Activity 1

- Read these short texts.
- Where might you see them?
- Match them to the sentences on the right.

Activity 2

- Read the article and the questions.
- For each question, choose A, B, C or D.

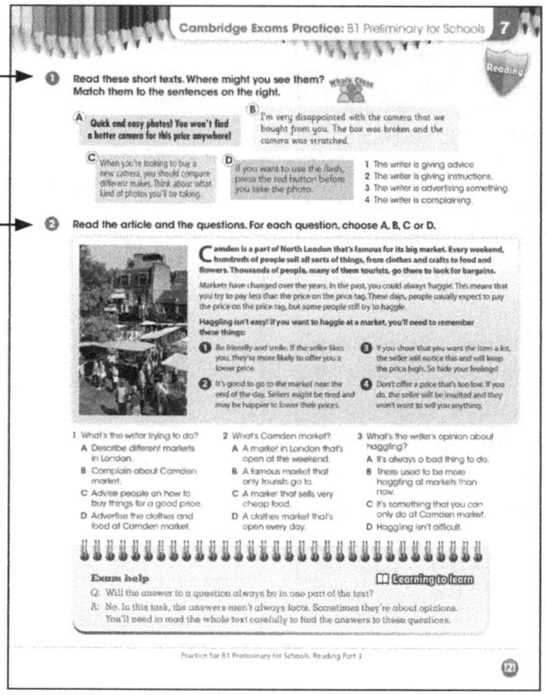

External Exams Videos

Additional Cambridge Exams Practice Video: B1 Preliminary for Schools

- Additional external exams preparation material, including videos, worksheets and practice tests, can be found in the Teacher's Resource Bank on Navio.

Ending the lesson

- Review the lesson and reflect on learning.

Extra activity

Extension

- Role play haggling at a market stall.

Exam help

- Read the Exam help.

Digital resources

Teacher's Digital: You can also teach this lesson using the Teacher's App on Navio.

Pupil's Digital: Encourage your pupils to use the Pupil's App on Navio to practise the activities from this lesson.

Powered By NAVIO

Activity Book

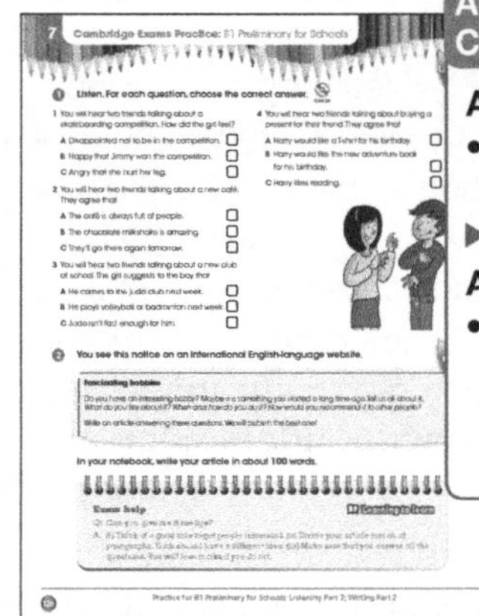

Activity Book page 126: Cambridge Exams Practice

Activity 1

- Listen. For each question, choose the correct answer.

▶ *CD4 Track 34 p299*

Activity 2

- You see this notice on an international English-language website. In your notebook, write your article in about 100 words.

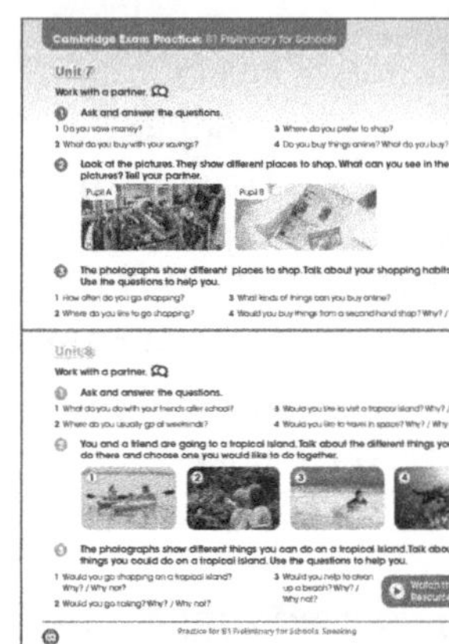

Activity Book page 132: Cambridge Exams Practice

Activity 1

- Work with partner. Ask and answer the questions.

Activity 2

- Look at the pictures. They show different places to shop. What can you see in the pictures? Tell your partner.

Activity 3

- The photographs show different places to shop. Talk about your shopping habits. Use the questions to help you.

Starting the lesson

Review learning in Unit 7.

- Ask **What do you remember most about this unit?** Prompt the class to tell you about Edna Ruth Byler, the adverts, etc.

Set learning outcomes.

- Say **Today we're going to do a reading task and a listening task.**

Pupil's Book Activity 1

Read these short texts. Where might you see them? Match them to the sentences on the right.

- Ask the pupils to read the four texts and say where they would see them.
- The pupils then match the texts with the sentences.
- Check the answers. Encourage the pupils to give another example of each of the types of text (advice, complaint, advert, instruction).

Answers: **1** C **2** D **3** A **4** B

Pupil's Book Activity 2

Read the article and the questions. For each question, choose A, B, C or D.

- Ask the pupils if they have bought things in markets before. Ask **Is there always a price on the objects? Can you ask to pay less?**
- The pupils look at the photo. Explain that this is a famous market in London.
- The pupils then read the text and find the answers.
- Check answers as a class.

Answers: **1** C **2** A **3** B

Exam help

- Read the Exam help as a class.

External Exams Videos

Additional Cambridge Exams Practice Video: B1 Preliminary for Schools

- Additional external exams preparation material, including videos, worksheets and practice tests, can be found in the Teacher's Resource Bank on Navio.

Activity Book page 126: Cambridge Exams Practice

Activity 1

Listen. For each question, choose the correct answer.

▸ *CD4 Track 34 p299*

- Explain that the pupils will hear a different situation each time.
- Read the questions as a class.
- Play the CD. The pupils listen and choose the correct answers.
- Play the CD again, pausing after each piece of information. The pupils complete and check their answers.

Answers: **1** A **2** B **3** B **4** C

Activity 2

You see this notice on an international English-language website.

In your notebook, write your article in about 100 words.

- Read the instructions as a class.
- Ask what type of hobbies they would like to write about.
- Ask pupils to give you different adjectives to describe them. Write them on the board.
- Pupils complete the activity and show their work to their partners.
- Have volunteer pupils read their work to the class.

Exam help

- Read the exam tip and ask how it will help pupils do better in the actual exams.

Activity Book page 132: Cambridge Exams Practice

Activity 1

Work with a partner. Ask and answer the questions.

- In pairs, have pupils complete the activity.
- Bring volunteer pairs to the front of the class to act out the questions and answers.

Activity 2

Look at the pictures. They show different places to shop. What can you see in the pictures? Tell your partner.

- Invite pupils to give you descriptive words for each picture. Write them on the board.
- In pairs, have pupils complete the activity.
- Bring volunteer pairs to the front of the class to act out the questions and answers.

Activity 3

The photographs show different places to shop. Talk about your shopping habits. Use the questions to help you.

- Lead a class discussion on what pupils like to buy and how often they go shopping.
- In pairs, have pupils complete the activity.
- Bring volunteer pairs to the front of the class to act out their dialogues.

Ending the lesson

Review the lesson and reflect on learning.

- Say **Today we've done a reading task about shopping in a market.**
- Ask **What do you remember?** The pupils do a three-minute review in pairs.

Extra activity

Extension

- In pairs, the pupils plan a conversation between a market trader and a customer. The customer sees an item, asks how much it is and haggles for a lower price. The market trader negotiates on the price.
- Invite two pupils to act out their conversation for the class. Focus on the language that the customer uses to get a cheaper price. Repeat with another pair.

Key Competences and Key Learning Outcomes

- Introduce and practise Preliminary for Schools exam tasks: Reading Part 5, Listening Part 3, Writing Part 5, Speaking Parts 1, 2 and 4
- Learn a simple strategy for choosing the correct word to complete a gapped text

Key language

- *document, environment, leaders, manifesto, parliament, peace*
- *The document was sent to the United Nations.*

Materials

- Pupil's Book p122; Activity Book pp127 and 132; Class CD4; Teacher's App on Navio

At a Glance Lesson Plan

Pupil's Book

Starting the lesson

- Play a word game.
- Set learning outcomes.

Activity 1

- Read the title.
- Predict what you are going to find out in the text.

Activity 2

- Quickly read the text and find out.

Activity 3

- Read the text again and choose the correct word for each space.

Activity 4

- Read the text again.
- Check that it makes sense.

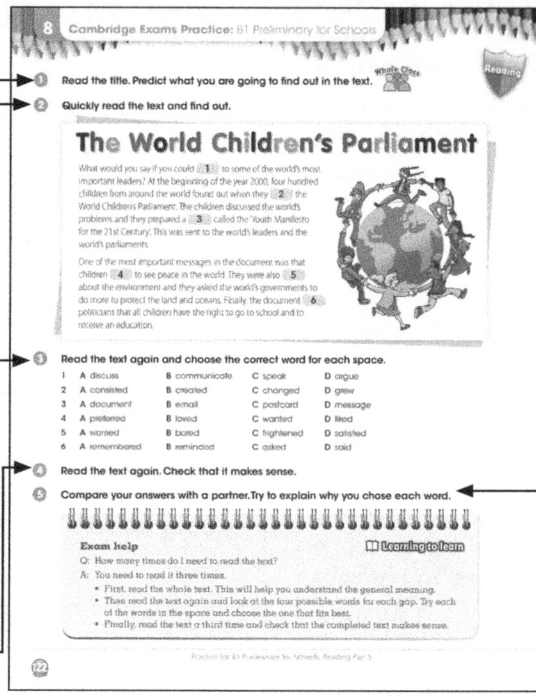

Activity 5

- Compare your answers with a partner.
- Try to explain why you chose each word.

Exam help

- Read the Exam help.

Ending the lesson

- Review the lesson and reflect on learning.

Extra activity

Reinforcement

- Prepare a Children's Parliament manifesto.

External Exams Videos

Additional Cambridge Exams Practice Video: B1 Preliminary for Schools

- Additional external exams preparation material, including videos, worksheets and practice tests, can be found in the Teacher's Resource Bank on Navio.

Activity Book

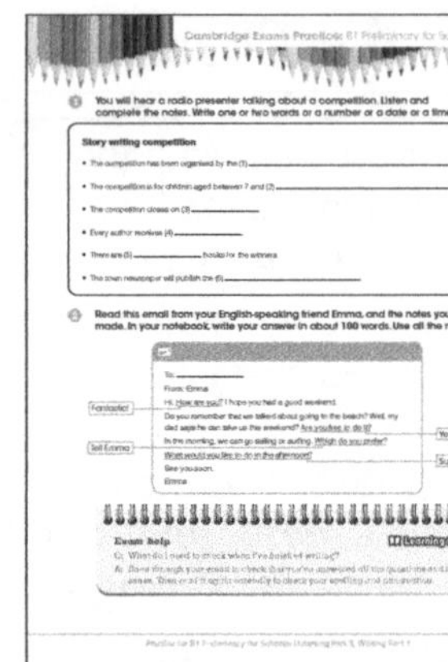

Activity Book page 127: Cambridge Exams Practice

Activity 1

- You will hear a radio presenter talking about a competition. Listen and complete the notes. Write one or two words or a number or a date or a time.

▶ *CD4 Track 35 p299*

Activity 2

- Read this email from your English-speaking friend Emma, and the notes you have made. In your notebook, write your answer in about 100 words. Use all the notes.

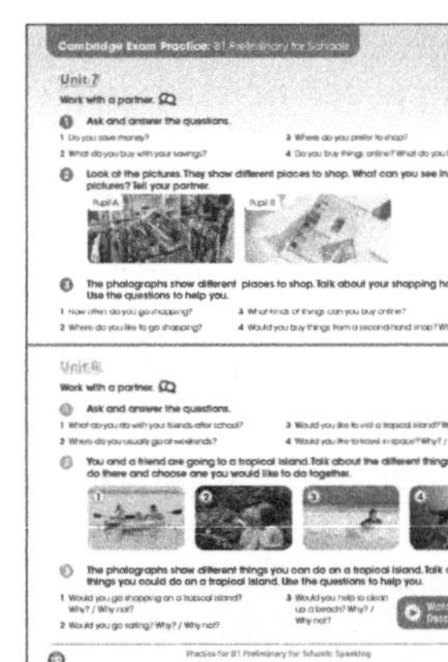

Activity Book page 132: Cambridge Exams Practice

Activity 1

- Work with a partner. Ask and answer the questions.

Activity 2

- You and a friend are going to a tropical island. Talk about the different tropical island. Talk about the different things you can do there and choose one you would like to do together.

Activity 3

- The photographs show different things you can do on a tropical island. Talk about other things you could do on a tropical island. Use the questions to help you.

Digital resources

Teacher's Digital: You can also teach this lesson using the Teacher's App on Navio.

Pupil's Digital: Encourage your pupils to use the Pupil's App on Navio to practise the activities from this lesson.

Powered By NAVIO

Starting the lesson

Play a word game.

- Draw ten dashes on the board, one per letter in the mystery word (PARLIAMENT).
- Invite a pupil to say a letter. If the letter appears in the word, write it on the corresponding line. If it doesn't appear, write it on the side of the board.
- After ten letters, the pupils attempt to guess the word.

Set learning outcomes.

- Say **Today we're going to read about the World Children's Parliament.**

Pupil's Book Activity 1

Read the title. Predict what you are going to find out in the text.

- Read the title as a class.
- The pupils predict what information they will find out.

Pupil's Book Activity 2

Quickly read the text and find out.

- Explain to the pupils that the text has some missing words. However, even without these words they will be able to understand the main ideas in the text.
- Read the text as a class. The pupils decide if their predictions were correct.

Pupil's Book Activity 3

Read the text again and choose the correct word for each space.

- In pairs, the pupils read the text again. They identify the missing words. The clues below the four options will support more analytical thinking.

Pupil's Book Activity 4

Read the text again. Check that it makes sense.

- The pupils read the completed text. They check that it makes sense.
- Check answers as a class. The pupils explain their answer each time.

Answers: **1** B **2** A **3** D **4** B **5** A **6** B **7** A **8** C

Pupil's Book Activity 5

Compare your answers with a partner. Try to explain why you chose each word.

- Have pupils complete the activity with their partners.

Exam help

- Read the Exam help as a class.

External Exams Videos

Additional Cambridge Exams Practice Video: B1 Preliminary for Schools

- Additional external exams preparation material, including videos, worksheets and practice tests, can be found in the Teacher's Resource Bank on Navio.

Activity Book page 127: Cambridge Exams Practice

Activity 1

You will hear a radio presenter talking about a competition. Listen and complete the notes. Write one or two words or a number or a date or a time.

CD4 Track 35 p299

- Read the information as a class.
- Play the CD. The pupils listen and complete the gaps.
- Play the CD again, pausing after each piece of information for pupils to check their answers.

Answers: **1** town library **2** 16 **3** 1st of June **4** T-shirt **5** 100 **6** best stories

Activity 2

Read this email from your English-speaking friend Emma, and the notes you have made. In your notebook, write your answer in about 100 words. Use all the notes.

- Read the information as a class.
- In pairs, the pupils brainstorm key information.
- Quickly review how to start and finish an informal letter before pupils write the letter.

Exam help

- Remind pupils to use Exam help box as a check box after they've complete the letter.

Activity Book page 132: Cambridge Exams Practice

Activity 1

Work with a partner. Ask and answer the questions.

- In pairs, have pupils complete the activity.
- Bring volunteer pairs to the front of the class to act out the questions and answers.

Activity 2

You and a friend are going to a tropical island. Talk about the different things you can do there and choose one you would like to do together.

- Invite pupils to give you describe what is happening in each picture.
- In pairs, have pupils complete the activity.
- Bring volunteer pairs to the front of the class to act out the questions and answers.

Activity 2

The photographs show different things you can do on a tropical island. Talk about other things you could do on a tropical island. Use the questions to help you.

- Lead a class discussion on what pupils would do if they were on a tropical islandusing the questions in Activity 3. Write keywords on the board.
- In pairs, have pupils complete the activity. Bring volunteer pairs to the front of the class to act out their dialogues.

Ending the lesson

Review the lesson and reflect on learning.

- Say **Today we've read about the World Children's Parliament.**
- Ask **What do you remember?** The pupils do a three-minute review in pairs.

Extra activity

Reinforcement

- Ask **What would you say to the world leaders if you were a member of the Children's Parliament?**
- The pupils discuss the ideas as a class.
- In pairs or small groups, they prepare their Children's Parliament manifesto.

Key Competences and Key Learning Outcomes

- Introduce and practise Preliminary for Schools exam tasks: Reading Part 2, Listening Part 1, Writing Part 2, Speaking Parts 1, 2, 3 and 4
- Learn a simple strategy for dealing with confusing answers

Key language

- *active, adventurous, brave, impress, performing arts*
- *Gina is interested in making things. She isn't keen on very modern music.*

Materials

- Pupil's Book p123; Activity Book pp128 and 133; Class CD4; Teacher's App on Navio

At a Glance Lesson Plan

Pupil's Book

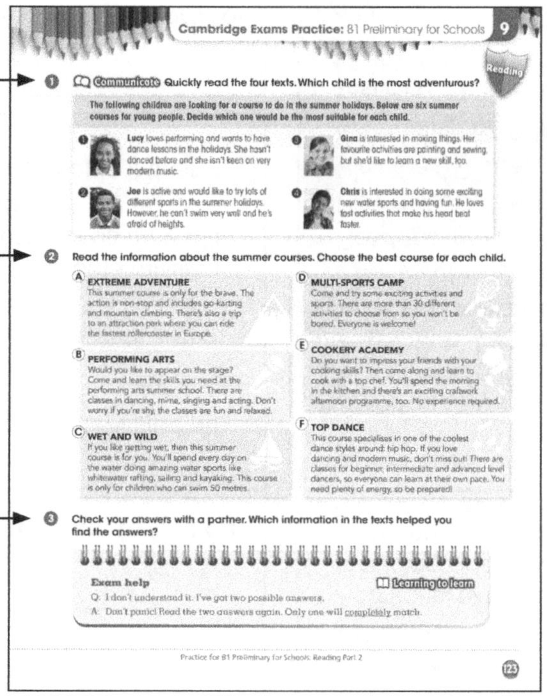

Starting the lesson

- Share information about summer camps and activities.
- Set learning outcomes.

Activity 1

- Quickly read the four texts.
- Which child is the most adventurous?

Activity 2

- Read the information about the summer courses.
- Choose the best course for each child.

Activity 3

- Check your answers with a partner.
- Which information in the text helped you find the answers?

Exam help

- Read the Exam help.

Ending the lesson

- Review the lesson and reflect on learning.

Extra activity

Extension

- Prepare a class summer camp.

External Exams Videos

Additional Cambridge Exams Practice Video: B1 Preliminary for Schools

- Additional external exams preparation material, including videos, worksheets and practice tests, can be found in the Teacher's Resource Bank on Navio.

Activity Book

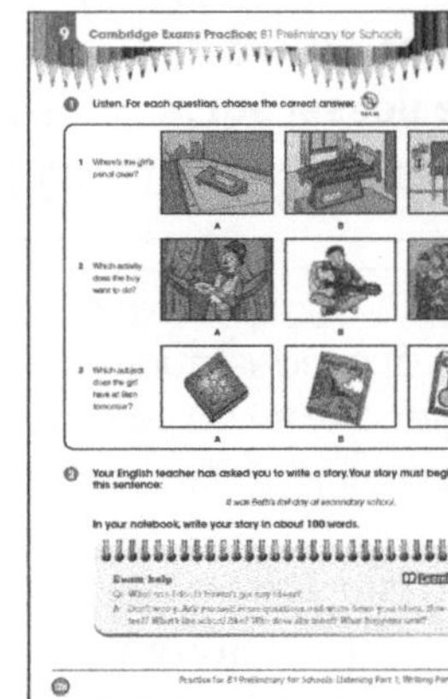

Activity Book page 128: Cambridge Exams Practice

Activity 1

- Listen. For each question, choose the correct answer.

▶ *CD4 Track 36 p299*

Activity 2

- Your English teacher has asked you to write a story. Your story must begin with this sentence: *It was Beth's first day at secondary school.* In your notebook, write your story in about 100 words.

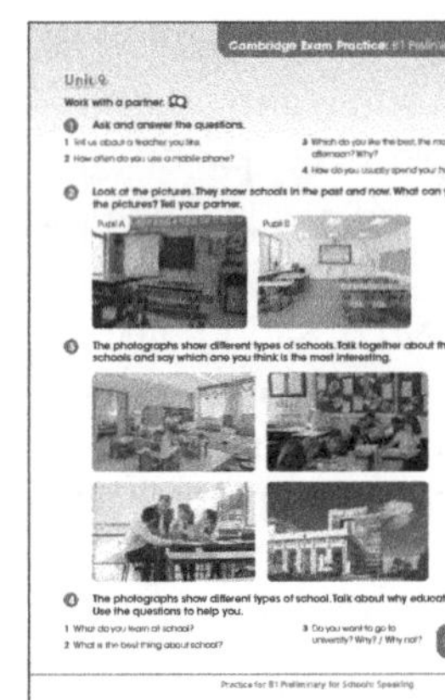

Activity Book page 133: Cambridge Exams Practice

Activity 1

- Work with a partner. Ask and answer the questions.

Activity 2

- Look at the pictures. They show schools in the past and now. What can you see in the pictures? Tell your partner.

Activity 3

- The photographs show different types of schools. Talk together about the different schools and say which one you think is the most interesting.

Activity 4

- The photographs show different types of school. Talk about why education is important. Use the questions to help you.

Digital resources

Teacher's Digital: You can also teach this lesson using the Teacher's App on Navio.

Pupil's Digital: Encourage your pupils to use the Pupil's App on Navio to practise the activities from this lesson.

Powered By NAVIO

Starting the lesson

Share information about summer camps and activities.

- Ask **What are you going to do this summer holiday? Have you ever been to a summer camp or done a summer course? What was it like? Which activities did you do?**
- Invite different pupils to share their plans and experiences with the class.

Set learning outcomes.

- Say **Today we're going to read about different summer courses.**

Pupil's Book Activity 1

Quickly read the four texts. Which child is the most adventurous?

- The pupils read the texts. In pairs, they decide which child is the most adventurous.
- Check answers as a class. Confirm that Chris is the most adventurous.

Pupil's Book Activity 2

Read the information about the summer courses. Choose the best course for each child.

- The pupils read the texts. They choose a course for each child.
- Remind the class to check that the summer course matches all the information about each child.

Pupil's Book Activity 3

Check your answers with a partner. Which information in the text helped you find the answers?

- In pairs, the pupils compare their answers. They look back at the text to identify the relevant information each time.
- Check answers as a class.

Answers: **1** B **2** D **3** E **4** A

Exam help

- Read the Exam help as a class.

External Exams Videos

Additional Cambridge Exams Practice Video: B1 Preliminary for Schools

- Additional external exams preparation material, including videos, worksheets and practice tests, can be found in the Teacher's Resource Bank on Navio.

Activity Book page 128: Cambridge Exams Practice

Activity 1

Listen. For each question, choose the correct answer.

▶ *CD4 Track 36 p299*

- Invite a pupil to read out the first question and describe the three drawings.
- Play the CD, pausing after the first dialogue. The pupils listen and identify the correct picture.
- Repeat the procedure with the other questions.

Answers: **1** C **2** A **3** C

Activity 2

Your English teacher has asked you to write a story. Your story must begin with this sentence:

It was Beth's first day at secondary school.

In your notebook, write your story in about 100 words.

- Read out the instructions as a class.
- In pairs, the pupils brainstorm the key information and write their notes.
- The pupils then write their stories. Remind them to begin with the opening sentence. Refer pupils to Exam help box for guidance.
- Organise the pupils into new pairs. The pupils read their stories to their partner.

Activity Book page 133: Cambridge Exams Practice

Activity 1

Work with a partner. Ask and answer the questions.

- In pairs, have pupils complete the activity.
- Bring volunteer pairs to the front of the class to act out the questions.

Activity 2

Look at the pictures. They show schools in the past and now. What can you see in the pictures? Tell your partner.

- Invite pupils to give you descriptive words for each picture. Write them on the board.
- In pairs, have pupils complete the activity.
- Bring volunteer pairs to the front of the class to act out the questions and answers.

Activity 3

The photographs show different types of schools. Talk together about the different schools and say which one you think is the most interesting.

- Look at the photos and ask pupils what schools are shown (pre-school, primary, secondary and university).
- In pairs, have pupils complete the activity.
- Bring volunteer pairs to the front of the class to act out the questions and answers.

Activity 4

The photograph shows different types of school. Talk about why education is important. Use the questions to help you.

- Lead a class discussion on why education is important. Write key words and expressions on the board.
- Bring volunteer pairs to the front of the class to act out their dialogues.

Ending the lesson

Review the lesson and reflect on learning.

- Say **Today we've read about different summer courses.**
- Ask **What do you remember?** The pupils do a three-minute review in pairs.

Extra activity

Reinforcement

- Organise the class into small groups. The pupils work together to plan a class summer camp, deciding on a location, accommodation, activities and a price.
- Invite the groups to present their proposals.
- The pupils vote on their favourite class summer camp.

Grammar and Vocabulary Practice answers

Unit 1 Grammar

AB page 102 Activity 1

1 was listening, dropped **2** fell off, was riding **3** were sleeping, blew **4** arrived, was watching **5** began, were having

AB page 102 Activity 2

1 The doorbell rang while I was watching TV. **2** While the children were walking home, it began to rain. **3** While Tim was swimming, he saw a starfish. **4** Sue dropped a plate while she was doing the washing up.

AB page 102 Activity 3

1 playing tennis **2** to carry **3** to be **4** visiting

AB page 102 Activity 4

Pupils' own answers

Unit 1 Vocabulary

AB page 102 Activity 5

1 passenger **2** trolley **3** Departures **4** runway **5** check-in desk

AB page 102 Activity 6

1 ticket office **2** receptionist **3** backpacker **4** guard **5** tourist information centre

Unit 2 Grammar

AB page 103 Activity 1

1 met **2** done **3** Have you ever used **4** Have you ever been **5** Have you ever played

AB page 103 Activity 2

Have you ever met, met, did you meet, met, haven't met

AB page 103 Activity 3

1 for six months **2** They have played volleyball since they were 10. **3** He has made models since last year. **4** I've known my best friend for a long time.

AB page 103 Activity 4

Pupils' own answers

Unit 2 Vocabulary

AB page 103 Activity 5

1 racket **2** hoop **3** crash mat **4** rope **5** net

AB page 103 Activity 6

1 done photography **2** go to drama class **3** done needlework **4** making models **5** sing in a choir

Unit 3 Grammar

AB page 104 Activity 1

1 any **2** much **3** a little **4** is **5** many **6** some **7** any

AB page 104 Activity 2

1 is too much **2** aren't enough **3** isn't enough **4** are too many **5** is too much **6** isn't enough

AB page 104 Activity 3

1 mustn't **2** need to **3** need to **4** need to **5** needn't **6** mustn't

AB page 104 Activity 4

Pupils' own answers

Unit 3 Vocabulary

AB page 104 Activity 5

1 avocado **2** lime **3** Peanuts **4** chilli pepper **5** Garlic

AB page 104 Activity 6

1 fizzy drinks **2** junk food **3** rest **4** spend on the computer **5** do exercise

Unit 4 Grammar

AB page 105 Activity 1

1 was performed **2** weren't written **3** was built **4** wasn't painted

AB page 105 Activity 2

1 Donald Duck and Mickey Mouse were created by Walt Disney. **2** *Sunflowers* was painted by Van Gogh (in 1888). **3** *The Lord of the Rings* wasn't directed by James Cameron. **4** *The Hunger Games* wasn't written by J.K. Rowling.

AB page 105 Activity 3

1 Who was your favourite book written by? **2** Where was your favourite film made? **3** Where was your favourite video game created?

AB page 105 Activity 4

Pupils' own answers

Unit 4 Vocabulary

AB page 105 Activity 5

1 Clay **2** stage **3** costume **4** Beads **5** puppet

AB page 105 Activity 6

1 fashion designer **2** graffiti artist **3** sound engineer **4** novelist **5** film director

Unit 5 Grammar

AB page 106 Activity 1

1 he loved reading cartoons. **2** there was a note on the fridge. **3** Tim told me he was writing an email to his cousin. **4** Tim told me the leaflet had lots of interesting information.

AB page 106 Activity 2

1 Lily said Emma could speak three languages. **2** Lily said Peter would win the competition. **3** Lily said Sam wouldn't help her. **4** Lily said she thought she would pass the exam.

AB page 106 Activity 3

said, could, could, said, would

AB page 106 Activity 4

Pupils' own answers

Unit 5 Vocabulary

AB page 106 Activity 5

1 interview **2** sports news **3** article **4** fashion section **5** front page

Unit 6 Grammar

AB page 107 Activity 1

Pupils' own answers

AB page 107 Activity 2

Pupils' own answers

AB page 107 Activity 3

1 be famous in the future? **2** Do you think you will be a politician in the future? **3** Do you think you will get married in the future? **4** Do you think you will be a millionaire in the future? **5** Do you think you will write a book in the future? **6** Do you think you will learn Chinese in the future?

AB page 107 Activity 4

Pupils' own answers

Unit 6 Vocabulary

AB page 107 Activity 5

1 politician **2** plumber **3** electrician **4** archaeologist **5** detective

AB page 107 Activity 6

1 learn to drive **2** leave home **3** start a business **4** go to university **5** go backpacking

Unit 7 Grammar

AB page 108 Activity 1

1 old enough **2** too short **3** strong enough **4** too expensive **5** too young **6** fashionable enough

AB page 108 Activity 2

1 expensive as the car. **2** old as the motorbike. **3** The car is as fast as the motorbike. **4** The car isn't as easy to park as the motorbike.

AB page 108 Activity 3

1 share, will save **2** will save, compare **3** do, will earn **4** won't save, buy

AB page 108 Activity 4

Pupils' own answers

Unit 7 Vocabulary

AB page 108 Activity 5

1 credit card **2** purse **3** till **4** customer

AB page 108 Activity 6

1 ripped **2** stained **3** cracked

Unit 8 Grammar

AB page 109 Activity 1

1 lived, would swim **2** would take, visited **3** wouldn't touch, went **4** saw, wouldn't be **5** didn't have, would eat

AB page 109 Activity 2

1 Would you be scared if you saw a tarantula? **2** Would you be happy if you won a competition? **3** Would you say hello if you met a pop star? **4** Would you be worried if you were lost?

AB page 109 Activity 3

Pupils' own answers

AB page 109 Activity 4

Pupils' own answers

Unit 8 Vocabulary

AB page 109 Activity 5

1 shore **2** sea lion **3** hammock **4** Coral **5** palm tree

AB page 109 Activity 6

1 travel in space **2** travel back in time **3** were (the) president **4** won the lottery

Unit 9 Grammar

AB page 110 Activity 1

Pupils' own answers

AB page 110 Activity 2

1 What did you use to watch on TV? **2** What time did you use to go to bed? **3** Which songs did you use to sing? **4** Which stories did you use to listen to?

AB page 110 Activity 3

'm going to go, 'll, is going to, 'll

AB page 110 Activity 4

Pupils' own answers

Unit 9 Vocabulary

AB page 110 Activity 5

1 overall **2** Chalk **3** laptop **4** Headphones **5** easel

AB page 110 Activity 6

1 musical instrument **2** sports kit **3** locker **4** geometry set **5** Literature

1 Study skills: extending your vocabulary

Key Competences and Key Learning Outcomes
- Use word webs to collect information
- Learn how to extend your vocabulary

Key language
- *amazing, attractive, entertaining, excited, nice, personality, tasty*

Materials
- Activity Book p111, Teacher's App on Navio

Optional materials
- Teacher's Resource Bank: Trinity Exams Practice cards (selected from Unit 1)

Detailed Lesson Plan

Starting the lesson

Use the Trinity Exams Practice cards (optional).
- The pupils practise asking and answering questions.

Set Learning objectives
- Say **Today we are going to learn how to extend our vocabulary.**

Activity 1

Read and discuss.
- Write the following sentences on the board: *This is a nice skirt. He is a nice person.*
- Explain that the word *nice* can mean pretty or good, depending on the context.
- Ask a pupil to read the first question and hold a class discussion.
- Repeat with the second question and note on the board adjectives pupils mention.
- In pairs, pupils make sentences with adjectives from the board and then present them to the class.

Activity 2

Complete the word web with these words. Words can go in more than one place.
- Go through the adjectives and explain new words.
- Pupils work on their own to complete the word web.
- Check as a class by having different pupils read parts of the word web.

Answers: A book or film: exciting, entertaining, brilliant, helpful, What someone looks like: beautiful, attractive, confident, pretty. Food: delicious, healthy, tasty. How you feel: confident, healthy, excited, amzing. Someone's personality: beautiful, kind

Activity Book

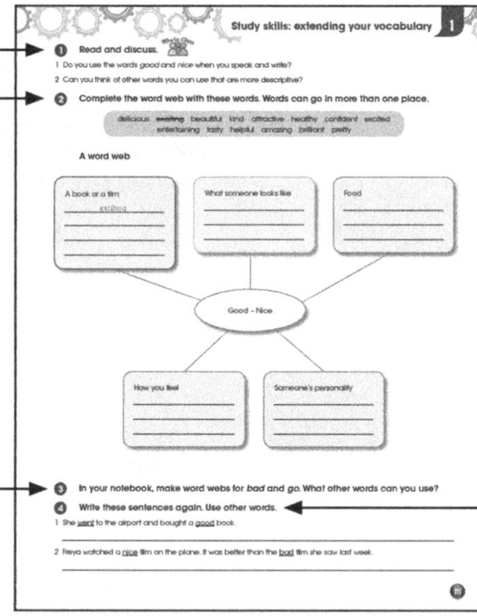

Activity 3

In your notebook, make word webs for *bad* and *go*. What other words can you use?
- Ask pupils to complete the activity in pairs.
- Have pairs read out their adjectives to the class. Write a few on the board.
- Have pupils write sentences using adjectives from the board and present them to the class.

Activity 4

Write these sentences again. Use other words.
- Pupils complete the activity individually and read their sentences to their partners.

Suggested answers: **1** She went to the airport and bought interesting / exciting / serious / funny books.
2 Freay watched a good / interesting / brilliant / funny film on the plane. It was better than the boring / serious film she saw last week.

Ending the lesson

Review the lesson and reflect on learning.
- Say **Today we've learnt how to extend our vocabulary.**
- Ask **Which was your favourite activity today? Which activity was easy / difficult?**

Extra activity

Reinforcement
- Ask pupils how the word web in Activity 2 helped them learn new words.
- On the board write *clothes, restaurants, hobbies, the Internet*.
- Place pupils in small groups and have them make their own word webs for one of the topics from the board.
- Pupils present their work to the class.

Key Competences and Key Learning Outcomes

- Read definitions to learn new vocabulary
- Learn what type of learner you are

Key language

- *image, logic, self, strategy*
- *I'm Image Smart because photos and graphs help me learn and understand a lesson better. I'm also People Smart because I like working in groups and sharing ideas.*

Materials

- Activity Book p112, Teacher's App on Navio

Optional materials

- Teacher's Resource Bank: Trinity Exams Practice cards (selected from Units 1 and 2)

Detailed Lesson Plan

Starting the lesson

Use the Trinity Exams Practice cards (optional).

- The pupils practise asking and answering questions.

Set Learning objectives

- Say **Today we are going to learn about different ways of learning.**

Activity 1

Read and discuss.

- Ask pupils to read the discussion question and explain any unknown words.
- Have pupils work in small groups to discuss the question.
- Have a class discussion, noting on the board new ideas and methods of learning pupils enjoy.

Activity 2

Read the different ways people like to learn. Match them to the type of intelligence they have.

- Go through the different ways of learning, a-h and ask pupils what they think they mean.
- Have pupils complete the activity in pairs and check answers as a class.
- Ask pupils if they had ever thought that there could be so many different ways of learning.

Answers: **1** c **2** e **3** a **4** g **5** b **6** d **7** h **8** i

Activity Book

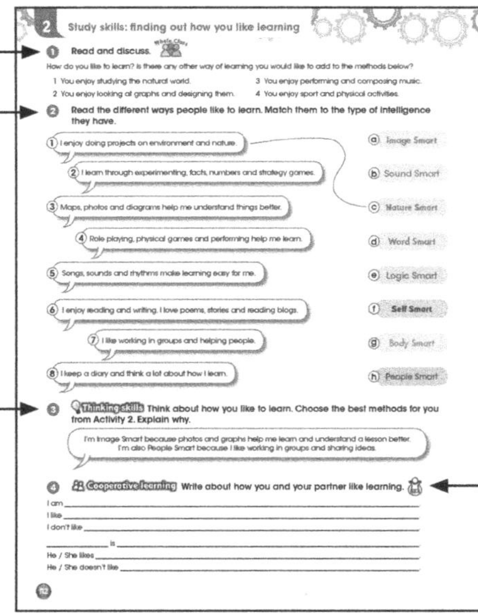

2 Study skills: finding out how you like learning

1 Read and discuss.

How do you like to learn? Is there any other way of learning you would like to add to the methods below?

1 You enjoy studying the natural world.
2 You enjoy looking at graphs and designing them.
3 You enjoy performing and composing music.
4 You enjoy sport and physical activities.

2 Read the different ways people like to learn. Match them to the type of intelligence they have.

1 I enjoy doing projects on environment and nature.
2 I learn through experimenting, facts, numbers and strategy games.
3 Maps, photos and diagrams help me understand things better.
4 Role playing, physical games and performing help me learn.
5 Songs, sounds and rhythms make learning easy for me.
6 I enjoy reading and writing. I love poems, stories and reading blogs.
7 I like working in groups and helping people.
8 I keep a diary and think a lot about how I learn.

a Image Smart
b Sound Smart
c Nature Smart
d Word Smart
e Logic Smart
f Self Smart
g Body Smart
h People Smart

3 Thinking skills Think about how you like to learn. Choose the best methods for you from Activity 2. Explain why.

I'm Image Smart because photos and graphs help me learn and understand a lesson better. I'm also People Smart because I like working in groups and sharing ideas.

4 Cooperative learning Write about how you and your partner like learning.

I am ____
I like ____
I don't like ____
____ is ____
He / She likes ____
He / She doesn't like ____

112

Activity 3

Think about how you like to learn. Choose the best methods for you from Activity 2. Explain why.

- Pupils complete the activity individually. Explain that they could have two or more ways of learning.
- Have pupils discuss their answers in small groups.
- Have a few pupils tell the class what type of learners they are.

Activity 4

Write about how you and your partner like learning.

- Pupils complete the activity individually. Explain they can use the ideas they discussed in Activity 3 with their groups.
- Pupils then read their sentences to their partners.

Ending the lesson

Review the lesson and reflect on learning.

- Say **Today we've learnt about different ways of learning.**
- Ask **What did you find interesting about today's lesson? Why was that part interesting?**

Extra activity

Reinforcement

- Ask pupils to make a poster for homework, showing how they learn.
- Explain that they are to give examples and to illustrate it as well.
- Tell pupils that they also have to present one method of learning they would like to try, again explaining why, e.g. *I want to try to be more people smart because I think working in groups will help me have a more balanced view.*

3 Study skills: helping yourself

Key Competences and Key Learning Outcomes

- Learn how to help yourself when you have a problem with work
- Learn how to understand and help your partner with a problem

Key language

- *concentrate, messy, nervous, pay attention*
- *When I have a test, I will talk to my teacher about how to study for it.*

Materials

- Activity Book p113, Teacher's App on Navio

Optional materials

- Teacher's Resource Bank: Trinity Exams Practice cards (selected from Units 1, 2 and 3)

Detailed Lesson Plan

Starting the lesson

Use the Trinity Exams Practice cards (optional).

- The pupils practise asking and answering questions.

Set Learning objectives

- Say **Today we are going to learn about helping ourselves when we have a problem.**

Activity 1

Read and discuss.

- Ask pupils to read the discussion questions and to think about them.
- In pairs, pupils discuss the questions.
- Have a class discussion, writing on the board the different problems pupils mention that they have with work.
- Ask how they feel knowing that other pupils also have problems with their work.

Activity 2

Look at the pictures and match them with the problems.

- Have pupils look at the pictures and suggest what they could be presenting.
- Pupils complete the activity in pairs. Check answers as a class.
- Ask pupils if they have any of the problems in the activity and what they do about it.
- Have a class discussion on what the person in each of the situations presented in the activity should do to help themselves.

Answers: **1** c **2** e **3** d **4** f **5** a **6** b

Activity Book

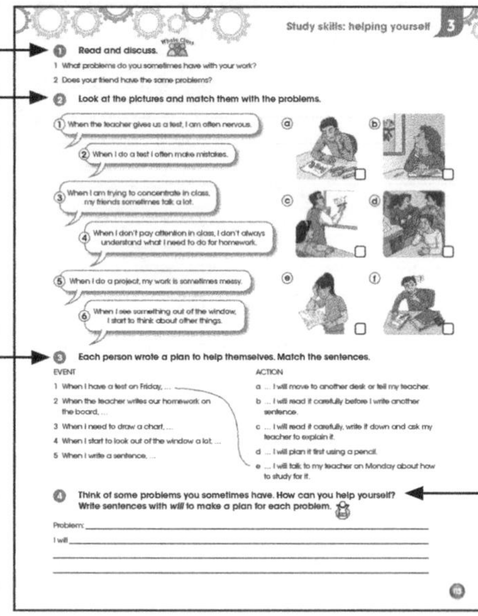
Study skills: helping yourself 3

1 Read and discuss.

1 What problems do you sometimes have with your work?

2 Does your friend have the same problems?

2 Look at the pictures and match them with the problems.

1 When the teacher gives us a test, I am often nervous.

2 When I do a test I often make mistakes.

3 When I am trying to concentrate in class, my friends sometimes talk a lot.

4 When I don't pay attention in class, I don't always understand what I need to do for homework.

5 When I do a project, my work is sometimes messy.

6 When I see something out of the window, I start to think about other things.

3 Each person wrote a plan to help themselves. Match the sentences.

4 Think of some problems you sometimes have. How can you help yourself? Write sentences with *will* to make a plan for each problem.

Activity 3

Each person wrote a plan to help themselves. Match the sentences.

- Pupils complete the activity individually.
- Check answers as a class. Ask if any of the actions were the same as the ones they discussed in Activity 2.

Answers: **1** e **2** c **3** d **4** a **5** b

Activity 4

Think of some problems you sometimes have. How can you help yourself? Write sentences with *will* to make a plan for each problem.

- Pupils complete the activity individually. Explain they can use the ideas they discussed in Activity 2.
- Pupils form small groups and read their sentences.
- Have pupils compare their answers and decide if their actions will help them with their problems.

Ending the lesson

Review the lesson and reflect on learning.

- Say **Today we've learnt about helping ourselves when we have problems.**
- Ask **What did you learn about yourself in today's lesson? Has it helped you learn how you can help yourself? How?**

Extra activity

Reinforcement

- Ask pupils to make a list of other problems they encounter at school.
- Place pupils in pairs and have them read their problems to each other. Explain that they should offer advice on how to action the problems presented.
- Have a few pupils role play their discussion in front of the class.

Key Competences and Key Learning Outcomes

- Use the Internet to find information
- Learn how to take notes

Key language

- *research, skyscraper, subway, taking notes*

Materials

- Activity Book p114, Teacher's App on Navio

Optional materials

- Teacher's Resource Bank: Trinity Exams Practice cards (selected from Units 1, 2, 3 and 4)

Detailed Lesson Plan

Starting the lesson

Use the Trinity Exams Practice cards (optional).

- The pupils practise asking and answering questions.

Set Learning objectives

- Say **Today we are going to learn about how to take notes when doing research.**

Activity 1

Read and discuss.

- Ask pupils to read the discussion questions and to think about them.
- In pairs, pupils discuss the questions.
- Have a class discussion, writing on the board the different ways pupils take notes.

Activity 2

Read Harry's homework. Then look at Harry's first notes from his research. What are the differences?

- Have pupils work individually.
- Elicit the answer from a pupil.
- Ask why it is important to make notes when we are researching.
- Ask if pupils take notes like Harry.

Answers: The difference is that the notes are very brief.

Activity Book

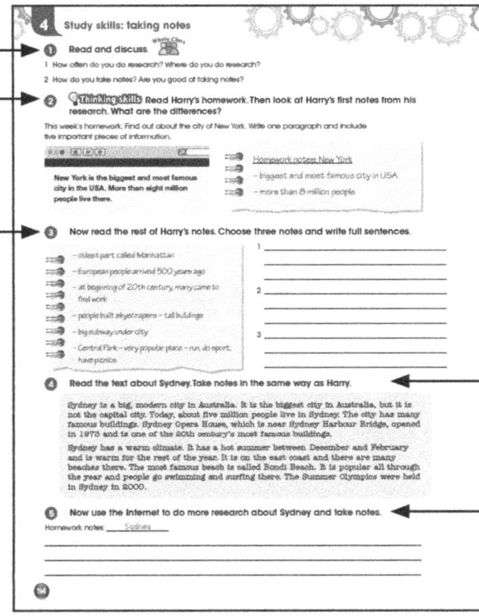

4 Study skills: taking notes

1 Read and discuss. Whole Class

1 How often do you do research? Where do you do research?

2 How do you take notes? Are you good at taking notes?

2 Thinking skills Read Harry's homework. Then look at Harry's first notes from his research. What are the differences?

This week's homework: Find out about the city of New York. Write one paragraph and include five important pieces of information.

New York is the biggest and most famous city in the USA. More than eight million people live there.

Homework notes: New York
- biggest and most famous city in USA
- more than 8 million people

3 Now read the rest of Harry's notes. Choose three notes and write full sentences.

- oldest part called Manhattan
- European people arrived 500 years ago
- at beginning of 20th century, many came to find work
- people built skyscrapers – tall buildings
- big subway under city
- Central Park – very popular place – run, do sport, have picnics

1 ______

2 ______

3 ______

4 Read the text about Sydney. Take notes in the same way as Harry.

Sydney is a big, modern city in Australia. It is the biggest city in Australia, but it is not the capital city. Today, about five million people live in Sydney. The city has many famous buildings. Sydney Opera House, which is near Sydney Harbour Bridge, opened in 1973 and is one of the 20th century's most famous buildings.

Sydney has a warm climate. It has a hot summer between December and February and is warm for the rest of the year. It is on the east coast and there are many beaches there. The most famous beach is called Bondi Beach. It is popular all through the year and people go swimming and surfing there. The Summer Olympics were held in Sydney in 2000.

5 Now use the Internet to do more research about Sydney and take notes.

Homework notes: Sydney

114

Activity 3

Now read the rest of Harry's notes. Choose three notes and write full sentences.

- Pupils complete the activity individually and then check answers with a partner.
- Elicit answers from different pupils and write a few on the board.

Suggested answers: The oldest part of New York is called Manhattan. European people first arrived in New York more than 500 years ago. At the beginning of 20th century, many people came to New York to find work. People built skyscrapers, which are tall buildings, and a big subway under the city for people to travel. Central Park is a very big and popular place where people run, do sports and have picnics.

Activity 4

Read the text about Sydney. Take notes in the same way as Harry.

- Pupils complete the activity individually. Explain they should refer to Activity 3 for guidance.
- Have pupils compare their answers with a partner.

Activity 5

Now use the Internet to do more research about Sydney and take notes.

- Pupils work in pairs to complete the activity. If there is no Internet connection in class, have pupils complete the activity for homework.

Ending the lesson

Review the lesson and reflect on learning.

- Say **Today we've learnt about taking notes when we do research.**
- Ask **Which was your favourite activity today? Which activity was easy / difficult?**

Extra activity

Reinforcement

- Give pupils other topics to research and make notes on. Topics can include hobbies, music, famous people and so forth.
- Pupils work in groups to make notes.

5 Study skills: presenting information

Key Competences and Key Learning Outcomes

- Use charts, graphs and tables to collect and present information
- Learn how to present information

Key language
- *spider diagram, Venn diagram*

Materials
- Activity Book p115, Teacher's App on Navio

Optional materials
- Different types of infographics
- Sheets of A4 paper, enough for the whole class
- Teacher's Resource Bank: Trinity Exams Practice cards (selected from Units 1, 2, 3, 4 and 5)

Detailed Lesson Plan

Starting the lesson

Use the Trinity Exams Practice cards (optional).
- The pupils practise asking and answering questions.

Set Learning objectives
- Say **Today we are going to learn how to present information.**

Activity 1

Look at these different ways of presenting information. Can you add more information to each one?
- On the board write *Venn diagram, spider diagram, table*.
- Ask pupils to look at the different charts and name them, using the words from the board (spider diagram, table, Venn diagram).
- Ask pupils what information each diagram is presenting (ways of communicating, words from other languages used in English and aspects of TV and magazines).
- Explain that in the Venn diagram, the middle part, where the two circles overlap, shows things TV and magazines have in common.
- Have pupils work in pairs to add more information to each diagram.
- Check answer as a class.

Answers: Pupils' own answers.

Activity Book

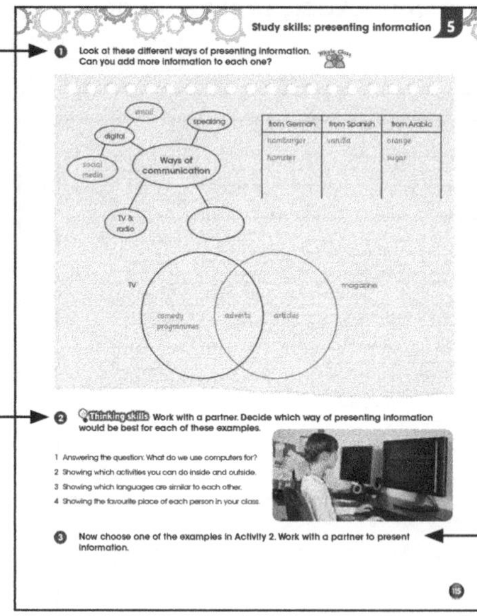
Study skills: presenting information 5

1 Look at these different ways of presenting information. Can you add more information to each one?

2 Thinking skills Work with a partner. Decide which way of presenting information would be best for each of these examples.

1 Answering the question: What do we use computers for?
2 Showing which activities you can do inside and outside.
3 Showing which languages are similar to each other.
4 Showing the favourite place of each person in your class.

3 Now choose one of the examples in Activity 2. Work with a partner to present information.

Activity 2

Work with a partner. Decide which way of presenting information would be best for each of these examples.
- Show pupils the different types of infographics. Explain that pictures are also a good way of presenting information.
- Ask pupils which methods of presenting information they like best and why.
- Have pupils complete the activity.
- Elicit answers from pairs.

Activity 3

Now choose one of the examples in Activity 2. Work with a partner to present information.
- Pupils complete the activity in pairs in their notebooks or sheets of A4 paper.
- Elicit answers from different pupils and write a few on the board.

Ending the lesson

Review the lesson and reflect on learning.
- Say **Today we've learnt about presenting information.**
- Ask **Which was your favourite activity today? Which activity was easy / difficult?**

Extra activity

Reinforcement
- Hold a class vote on which presentation was the best and why. Then ask pupils to look at their presentations again and try to use another method to present the same information.
- Pupils present their work to the class.

Key Competences and Key Learning Outcomes

- Learn how to set and accomplish goals
- Help a partner improve their goals

Key language

- *goal, intonation, improve*

Materials

- Activity Book p116, Teacher's App on Navio

Optional materials

- Teacher's Resource Bank: Trinity Exams Practice cards (selected from Units 1, 2, 3, 4, 5 and 6)

Detailed Lesson Plan

Starting the lesson

Use the Trinity Exams Practice cards (optional).

- The pupils practise asking and answering questions.

Set Learning objectives

- Say **Today we are going to learn about setting goals and achieving them.**

Activity 1

Read and discuss.

- Ask pupils to read the discussion questions and to think about them.
- In pairs, pupils discuss the questions.
- Have a class discussion, writing on the board the different ways pupils set goals and what learning goals pupils have.

Activity 2

Look at these goals. Find this information.

- Explain pupils have to read the graphics to find the answers to the questions. Have pupils work individually.
- Check answers as a class.
- Ask pupils if they have any other ideas as to how the goals can be achieved.

Answers: **Goal 1: 1** improve intonation, **2** this month **3** listen carefully in class, concentrate when they repeat, always try again when they say something wrong. **4** teacher will understand 90% of their English, teacher will say their intonation is improving. **Goal 2: 1** finish homework on time **2** this month **3** start homework when arrive home, won't look out of the window, will look at the clock. **4** I will give teacher homework on time all month.

Activity Book

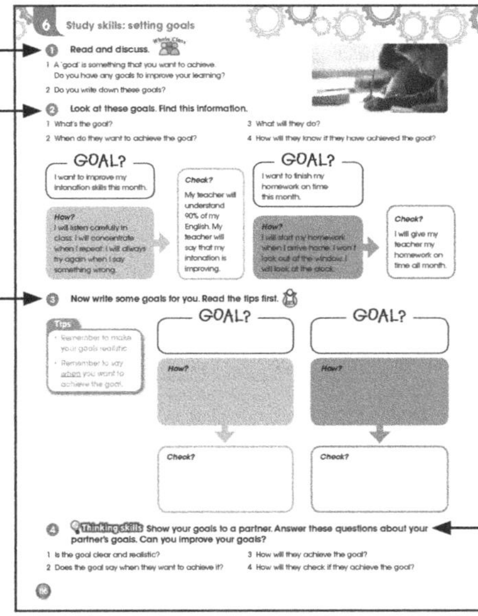
6 Study skills: setting goals

1 Read and discuss.

1 A 'goal' is something that you want to achieve. Do you have any goals to improve your learning?
2 Do you write down these goals?

2 Look at these goals. Find this information.

1 What's the goal?
2 When do they want to achieve the goal?
3 What will they do?
4 How will they know if they have achieved the goal?

GOAL? I want to improve my intonation skills this month.
How? I will listen carefully in class. I will concentrate when I repeat. I will always try again when I say something wrong.
Check? My teacher will understand 90% of my English. My teacher will say that my intonation is improving.

GOAL? I want to finish my homework on time this month.
How? I will start my homework when I arrive home. I won't look out of the window. I will look at the clock.
Check? I will give my teacher my homework on time all month.

3 Now write some goals for you. Read the tips first.

Tips
- Remember to make your goals realistic.
- Remember to say when you want to achieve the goal.

GOAL? How? Check?
GOAL? How? Check?

4 Thinking skills Show your goals to a partner. Answer these questions about your partner's goals. Can you improve your goals?

1 Is the goal clear and realistic?
2 Does the goal say when they want to achieve it?
3 How will they achieve the goal?
4 How will they check if they achieve the goal?

Activity 3

Now write some goals for you. Read the tips first.

- Read the tip box to the class. Explain that setting impossible goals will make them feel disappointed when they cannot achieve them. This is why it is important to set goals that can be achieved.
- Have pupils complete the activity individually. Remind them to check their work against the Tips to make sure they have completed the activities.

Activity 4

Show your goals to a partner. Answer these questions about your partner's goals. Can you improve your goals?

- Pupils work in pairs to discuss their goals.
- Have volunteer pupils role play their discussion in front of the class.

Ending the lesson

Review the lesson and reflect on learning.

- Say **Today we've learnt about setting and accomplishing goals.**
- Ask **Do you think this lesson has helped you understand more about yourself and setting goals? Why? / Why not?**

Extra activity

Reinforcement

- Ask pupils to tell you some of the goals they have set and write them on the board.
- Then ask for other goals they have where school is concerned. Write these on the board as well.
- Invite pupils to give advice on how to achieve each goal on the board. Continue activity as a class.

7 Study skills: checking information on the Internet

Key Competences and Key Learning Outcomes

- Use the Internet for fact checking
- Learn how to check information on the Internet

Key language

- *click, scroll down, valuable, worth*

Materials

- Activity Book p117, Teacher's App on Navio

Optional materials

- Teacher's Resource Bank: Trinity Exams Practice cards (selected from Units 1, 2, 3, 4, 5, 6 and 7)

Detailed Lesson Plan

Starting the lesson

Use the Trinity Exams Practice cards (optional).

- The pupils practise asking and answering questions.

Set Learning objectives

- Say **Today we are going to learn checking information on the Internet.**

Activity 1

Read and discuss.

- Ask pupils what kind of things they search the Internet for and if they think the information they find is always correct.
- Ask pupils to read the discussion questions and to think about them.
- In pairs, pupils discuss the questions.
- Have a class discussion.

Activity 2

Find the answers to these questions on the Internet.

- Have pupils work in pairs.
- Ask pupils what keywords they used to find the answers in the search engines.

Answers: **1** 2,598km **2** India **3** depends in exchange rate of day **4** Winston Churchill

Activity Book

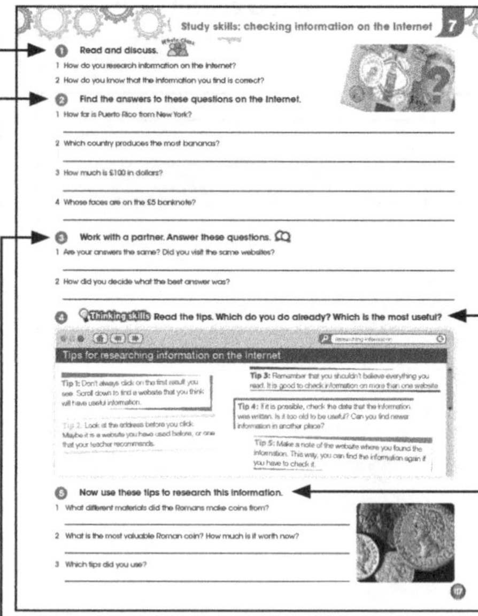

Activity 3

Work with a partner.
Answer these questions.

- Discuss questions as a class.

Activity 4

Read the tips. Which do you do already? Which is the most useful?

- Have pupils complete the activity in pairs first. Explain they have to rate the tips from 1 to 5, 1 being the best tip, 5 the worst. Tell pupils there is no correct answer.
- As a class have a vote on which point is the best, second best, etc.
- Ask pupils why they think their tip is the most / least important.

Activity 5

Now use these tips to research this information.

- Pupils work in pairs to complete the activity.
- Have pupils present their work to the class.

Ending the lesson

Review the lesson and reflect on learning.

- Say **Today we've learnt about checking facts when we do research.**
- Ask **What is the most important thing you learnt in today's lesson? Why?**

Extra activity

Reinforcement

- Have pupils research a topic of their choice and present five facts about it. Tell pupils to intentionally present one false fact.
- Pupils swap facts with partners, who have to research the topic and correct the false fact.
- Ask pupils to explain how they proved there was one false fact.

Key Competences and Key Learning Outcomes

- Discuss with a partner time management methods
- Learn how to manage your time

Key language

- *be honest, keep a record, manage, priority list, task calendar, urgent*
- *What did I want to do, but I didn't have time? When could I do it?*

Materials

- Activity Book p118, Teacher's App on Navio

Optional materials

- Teacher's Resource Bank: Trinity Exams Practice cards (selected from Units 1, 2, 3, 4, 5, 6, 7, and 8)

Detailed Lesson Plan

Starting the lesson

Use the Trinity Exams Practice cards (optional).

- The pupils practise asking and answering questions.

Set Learning objectives

- Say **Today we are going to learn how to manage our time.**

Activity 1

Read and discuss.

- Explain the term time management (making sure you have enough time to complete activities).
- Ask pupils to read the discussion questions and to think about them.
- In pairs, pupils discuss the questions.
- Have a class discussion, writing on the board the different ways children manage their time.

Activity 2

Look at how you use your time.
Then compare your record with a partner's.

- Have pupils make a record of their day so far and how they plan to spend the rest of it.
- Ask, what kind of things they will make room for on their calendar.
- Have pupils look at the calendar and be as honest as they can about how they have managed their time and how they can improve it.
- Pupils compare their diaries with their partners.
- Have a class discussion on how well the pupils have or haven't managed their time.

Activity Book

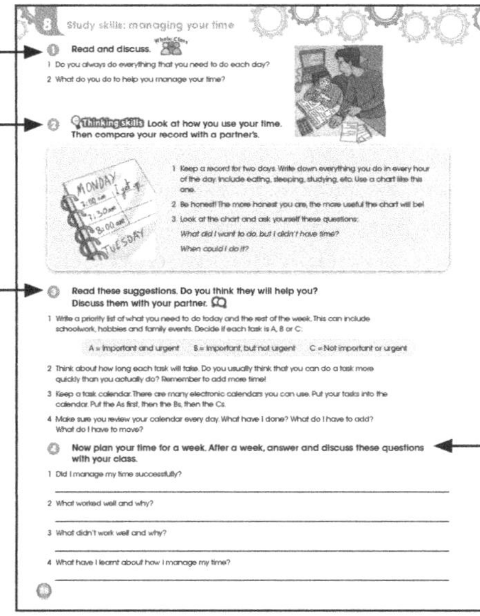

Activity 3

Read these suggestions. Do you think they will help you? Discuss them with your partner.

- Have pupils read through the suggestions and explain any unknown words. Explain that a priority is something that we must do before anything else, e.g homework is a priority over playing video games.
- Pupils complete the activity in pairs.
- Have pupils tell the class what they discussed with their partners.

Activity 4

Now plan your time for a week. After a week, answer and discuss these questions with your class.

- Explain to pupils that for a week they have to keep a record of their time management.
- When you come back to this activity, have pupils share their answers as honestly as possible.
- Have a class discussion encouraging pupils to discuss how they did or didn't succeed with their time management.

Ending the lesson

Review the lesson and reflect on learning.

- Say **Today we've learnt about managing our time better.**
- Ask **Has this lesson helped you become a better time manager? Why? / Why not?**

Extra activity

Reinforcement

- Have pupils tell you where they failed with time management and to explain why they think this happened. Explain to pupils that it is OK to fail because we learn from it.
- Write a few things they mention on the board.
- Then have a class discussion on how the things they have mentioned can be improved.

9 Study skills: managing stress

Key Competences and Key Learning Outcomes
- Learn how to manage stress
- Help a partner with a plan to manage stress

Key language
- *bad mood, stress, upset, worried*

Materials
- Activity Book p119, Teacher's App on Navio

Optional materials
- Teacher's Resource Bank: Trinity Exams Practice cards (selected from Units 1, 2, 3, 4, 5, 6, 7, 8 and 9)

Detailed Lesson Plan

Starting the lesson

Use the Trinity Exams Practice cards (optional).
- The pupils practise asking and answering questions.

Set Learning objectives
- Say **Today we are going to learn how to manage stress.**

Activity 1

Read and discuss.
- Explain the term stress to pupils (feeling anxious or worried about something). Ask why they think stress can be bad for them.
- Ask pupils what kind of things they stress about.
- Using the questions, have a class discussion.

Activity 2

Look at these pictures. How often do these things happen when you have important things to do? Read and answer.
- Pupils complete the activity individually and then show their answers to their partners.
- Have class vote on which of the symptoms in the activity are the most common.
- Ask pupils how these syptoms can affect their school work and their social relationships.
- Have pupils tell you how often in a week they feel stressed and what type of things they do to stop it.

Activity Book

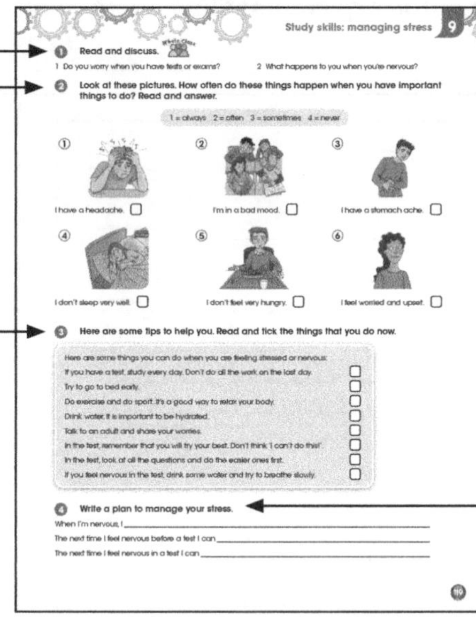
Study skills: managing stress 9

1 Read and discuss.

1 Do you worry when you have tests or exams? 2 What happens to you when you're nervous?

2 Look at these pictures. How often do these things happen when you have important things to do? Read and answer.

1 = always 2 = often 3 = sometimes 4 = never

① I have a headache. ☐ ② I'm in a bad mood. ☐ ③ I have a stomach ache. ☐
④ I don't sleep very well. ☐ ⑤ I don't feel very hungry. ☐ ⑥ I feel worried and upset. ☐

3 Here are some tips to help you. Read and tick the things that you do now.

Here are some things you can do when you are feeling stressed or nervous:
- If you have a test, study every day. Don't do all the work on the last day. ☐
- Try to go to bed early. ☐
- Do exercise and do sport. It's a good way to relax your body. ☐
- Drink water. It is important to be hydrated. ☐
- Talk to an adult and share your worries. ☐
- In the test, remember that you will try your best. Don't think 'I can't do this!'. ☐
- In the test, look at all the questions and do the easier ones first. ☐
- If you feel nervous in the test, drink some water and try to breathe slowly. ☐

4 Write a plan to manage your stress.

When I'm nervous, I ___
The next time I feel nervous before a test I can ___
The next time I feel nervous in a test I can ___

119

Activity 3

Here are some tips to help you. Read and tick the things that you do now.
- Pupils complete the activity individually.
- Then go through each point and ask pupils to raise their hand if they ticked it.
- Stop at each tip and ask how it can help them with stress.

Activity 4

Write a plan to manage your stress.
- Have pupils complete the sentences individually and then share answers with their partners.
- Tell pupils to tell their partners if they think their plans will work, and if not how to improve them.
- Have pupils share their ideas with the class.

Ending the lesson

Review the lesson and reflect on learning.
- Say **Today we've learnt about helping ourselves when we are stressed.**
- Ask **Has this lesson helped you understand why it is important not to stress? Has it taught you how to deal with stress? Why? / Why not?**

Extra activity

Reinforcement
- Have pupils research the effects of stress and present their ideas to the class.
- Lead a class discussion on why it is important not to stress about school. Explain that not getting top marks in a test is fine because what matters is working hard and trying.

Starter Unit Lesson 1

Pupil's Book

CD1 Track 1

PB page 4 Activity 3

Pilot: Hi, everyone. What are your names?
Tom: I'm Tom. These are my friends, Callum and Jess.
Pilot: Which school do you go to?
Tom: We go to Bluebell Primary School.
Pilot: Really? How old are you?
Callum: I'm 12 and they're 11.
Pilot: Oh dear. You aren't old enough to have a ride on your own.
Jess: Don't worry. My dad is here, too.
Pilot: Great! Are you ready then?
Jess: Absolutely!

Starter Unit Lesson 1

Pupil's Book

CD1 Track 2

PB page 4 Activity 4

Pilot: Ok everyone. We're now 150 metres off the ground.
Callum: The views are amazing up here.
Jess: I know. You can see the whole town.
Callum: Can you see your house, Tom?
Tom: Let me see … It should be easy to find. There's an enormous stadium in front of it.
Jess: The stadium is over there. Look!
Tom: Oh yes. I can see my house now. And look! There's a skate park nearby. I didn't know that was there.
Jess: Can you help me find my house? It's in a square in the centre of the town.
Callum: There's a square over there with a statue in the middle. Is that it?
Jess: Yes, it is. My house is the one with the blue front door. It looks tiny!
Tom: What about you, Callum? Have you found your block of flats yet?
Callum: Not yet.
Tom: I think I can see it. Is it near a bridge?
Callum: Yes, it is. It's white and grey.
Tom: Then it's over there. Look!
Callum: Oh, yes. I can see my bedroom window on the fifth floor. That's amazing!

Starter Unit Lesson 2

Pupil's Book

CD1 Track 3

PB page 5 Activity 2

1
Girl: This person usually wears a football kit on Saturday morning because he goes to football training. However, today he's waiting in the queue to have a ride in the hot-air balloon and he's wearing a pair of baggy trousers and a striped sweater.
2
Boy: This person usually does her homework on Saturday morning. But now she's standing at the front of the queue with her friends. She's carrying a pair of binoculars so she can see things that are far away.
3
Girl: This person usually tidies his bedroom on Saturday morning. However, now he's standing in the queue. He's carrying a bag on his back and he's talking to Emma and smiling. He looks excited.
4
Boy: This person usually watches TV on Saturday morning. But now he's waiting to have a ride in the hot-air balloon. He's near the front of the queue and looks nervous.
5
Girl: This person usually goes swimming on Saturday morning. However, now she's standing near the back of the queue. She's taking a photo of the hot-air balloon with her mobile phone.

Starter Unit Lesson 3

Pupil's Book

CD1 Track 4

PB page 6 Activity 1

Teacher: What did you do at the weekend, Jess?
Jess: I had a hot-air balloon ride in the park.
Teacher: Really? Was there a special reason for the ride?
Jess: Yes, the money from the hot-air balloon rides is going to be used to protect wild birds.
Tom: It's a great project. We'd like to find out how other people help in their communities.
Teacher: I know about a global project called 'Make a difference'. Schoolchildren from different countries write and share their ideas about helping in the community. Their logo is a hot-air balloon. Why don't you join?
Callum: It sounds amazing! And we can learn about life in other countries, too.

Unit 1 Lesson 1

Pupil's Book

CD1 Track 5

PB page 8 Activity 2

1 arrivals
2 departures
3 queue
4 boarding pass
5 hand luggage
6 passenger
7 check-in desk
8 trolley
9 take off
10 flight attendant
11 land
12 runway

Unit 1 Lesson 1

Pupil's Book

CD1 Track 6

PB page 8 Activity 3

1
Girl: This is the place that you go to first when you arrive at the airport. The people there take your suitcase, look at your passport and give you a boarding pass.
Boy: check-in desk
2
Girl: This is a line of people who are waiting for something. When someone gets to the front of the line, it's his or her turn.
Boy: queue
3
Girl: A plane does this when it leaves the ground. It usually travels very fast along the ground before doing this.
Boy: take off
4
Girl: You use this when you've got a lot of luggage. You use it to push your luggage from one place to another place.
Boy: trolley
5
Girl: People come here after their flight has landed. Other people may come to meet them here.
Boy: arrivals
6
Girl: This person works on a plane. He or she helps the passengers during the flight.
Boy: flight attendant
7
Girl: This is a long piece of road that planes move along. They take off and land here.
Boy: runway
8
Girl: Passengers have to show their boarding passes and passports when they come to this part of the airport. Then they wait here until they get on their flight.
Boy: departures
9
Girl: A plane does this when it comes back down to the ground. It does this on a runway at the airport.
Boy: land
10
Girl: This is a person who has a ticket and is going to travel on a plane.
Boy: passenger
11
Girl: You're given this at the check-in desk. It's a piece of paper that allows you to get on the plane.
Boy: boarding pass
12
Girl: This is the bag that you take onto the plane with you. It doesn't include the suitcases that you give in at the check-in desk.
Boy: hand luggage

Unit 1 Lesson 2

Pupil's Book

CD1 Track 7

PB page 10 Activity 1

Jess: Hi, Julie. Your project is brilliant. Have you decided which poster to do yet?
Julie: Thanks, Jess. No, not yet.
Jess: Did you enjoy your trip to the airport?
Julie: Yes, we did. It was really interesting. And it gave us lots of ideas.
Jess: That's great.

Audioscript

Julie: And guess what? While we were walking around the airport, we saw a player from the Belgian football team!
Jess: Lucky you!
Julie: And while I was taking photos, he agreed to sign a football and bring it to our school!
Jess: Brilliant. Will you post photos when you've got the ball?
Julie: Of course. While I was at the airport, I discovered something else, too. I learnt about a solar-powered plane that landed here in Belgium. I'll send you some information about it.
Jess: A solar-powered plane? That sounds interesting.

Unit 1 Lesson 2

Activity Book

CD1 Track 8

AB page 7 Activity 3

Harriet: Hi, Carl. Have you got any plans for this weekend?
Carl: Yes, I'll be spending the weekend with my cousins. They arrived from Canada yesterday.
Harriet: Really? I didn't know you had cousins in Canada!
Carl: I went with my Dad to meet them at the airport. We had a really bad journey there, though.
Harriet: What happened?
Carl: Well, we left home on time and there was no traffic at all. We were listening to some great music in the car when Dad went the wrong way and we got lost!
Harriet: Oh dear! Did you arrive late at the airport?
Carl: Yes, we did. My cousins were waiting in a café when we arrived.
Harriet: How old are they?
Carl: Well, Luke's 17 and Greg's 15. They've got a younger sister who's 10. She's called Kelly, but she hasn't come with them this time.
Harriet: Have you ever been to Canada?
Carl: No, but I'd love to go one day. While we were driving home, Luke and Greg told us about all the sports they do there. They go hiking in the summer and play ice hockey and go skiing in the winter! They've never played cricket though, so we're all going to play tomorrow.

Unit 1 Lesson 3

Pupil's Book

CD1 Track 9

PB page 11 Activity 2

A plane that could fly forever
Name: Bertrand Piccard
Born: 1958
Explorers in the family: his grandfather was a balloonist and his father was an undersea explorer.
First famous achievement: he flew around the world in a hot-air balloon without stopping.
Flying without fuel
After his balloon flight in 1999, Bertrand Piccard promised to fly around the world without using any fuel. He started building a plane that only used energy from the sun. The plane had to be very light and needed long wings covered with solar panels. It took many years to build this new plane. He called the plane *Solar Impulse*.
The record-breaking flight
In May 2011, the plane was ready to fly from Switzerland to Belgium, its first international flight. André Borschberg, Piccard's colleague, was the pilot. While Borschberg was flying the plane, Piccard's team and a large crowd of people arrived at Brussels Airport. It was a long, nervous wait. After 13 hours, the plane came into sight. While it was moving towards the runway, the weather became windy and Borschberg had to turn the plane around. They decided to use a different runway and the plane landed safely. Crowds of people cheered.
A fuel-free future?
Piccard's plane took off from Switzerland with little energy in the batteries. During the flight, the batteries were charging. The plane landed with more energy than when it took off! In 2016, Piccard flew the Solar Impulse 2, and completed the first round-the-world flight. The journey took 505 days, but only used solar power. Can you imagine flying without fuel in the future?

Unit 1 Lesson 3

Activity Book

CD1 Track 10

AB page 8 Activity 2

Callum: What are you looking at, Jess?
Jess: I'm reading about Bertrand Piccard. He's a French explorer who's travelled around the world in a hot-air balloon. Now, he's building planes that use energy from the sun. They use solar power.
Callum: That sounds interesting!
Jess: It's a great story because he's trying to fly planes without using any fuel!
Callum: Is he going to fly around the world without any fuel?
Jess: Yes, that's his plan. I was reading about his first international flight. The best part is when the pilot's trying to land in Belgium.
Callum: What happened?
Jess: A lot of people were waiting at the airport. The weather was too windy, so the pilot had to land on a different runway. I think everyone was very nervous.
Callum: I'm not surprised. Is the plane big?
Jess: I think so. You should have a look at these photos. They are amazing. The plane's very light and the wings are really long. And look! They're covered with solar panels.
Callum: I'd like to find out more about what it looks like. I'm sure I can find some videos online. So, the plane can fly only if it's sunny?
Jess: Well, it's better if it's sunny. They only take off if the weather's good. While the plane's flying, it gets energy from the sun. One of the most interesting things is that the plane had more energy when it landed than when it took off.
Callum: So, do you think that all planes will use solar power in the future?
Jess: That would be great. Planes use a lot of the world's energy in fuel.
Callum: What's Piccard's next plan?
Jess: Well, they have flown across the USA, too and soon they will fly around the world!
Callum: Wow! And without any fuel!
Jess: I think Tom would find this interesting. He loves articles about science and technology.
Callum: I think you're right.

Unit 1 Lesson 4

Pupil's Book

CD1 Track 11

PB page 12 Activity 1

Jess: I enjoyed reading about Bertrand Piccard.
Tom: It's amazing that a plane can fly without any fuel.
Jess: Yes. Piccard suggested using the technology for other forms of transport, too.
Tom: Really? But the plane goes very slowly.
Jess: That's true, but Piccard promised to make his plane faster next time.
Tom: Did you know that our school is going to use solar energy, too?
Jess: Really?
Tom: Yes. They've agreed to put solar panels on the school roof to save energy.

Unit 1 Lesson 4

Pupil's Book

CD1 Track 12

PB page 12 Activity 5

enjoyed
suggested
promised
imagined
decided
started
stopped
agreed
liked
tried

Unit 1 Lesson 4

Activity Book

CD1 Track 13

AB page 9 Activity 3

1 liked
2 stopped
3 enjoyed
4 suggested
5 promised

Unit 1 Lesson 5

Pupil's Book

CD1 Track 14

PB page 13 Activity 1

1 guard
2 backpacker
3 platform
4 tourist information centre
5 ticket office
6 receptionist
7 reception
8 guest
9 lift

Unit 1 Lesson 5

Pupil's Book

CD1 Track 15

PB page 13 Activity 2

1 Where did Amy's family leave the passports?
Boy: Hi, Amy. I heard about your trip. It sounds terrible.
Girl: Yes. First of all there was a really long queue at the check-in desk.
Boy: Your mum said you lost your passports.
Girl: We did. But that was later. We showed them at the desk but we didn't leave them there.
Boy: So then you went through to departures?
Girl: Yes, we did. We had something to drink in the café.
Boy: Then what happened?
Girl: Well, when we were getting on the plane, we couldn't find our passports – none of them. The plane had to go without us!
Boy: Where were the passports?
Girl: After we left the café, Dad dropped them near a lift.
2 What was happening at the station?
Boy: I went to London with my Mum yesterday.
Girl: Really? What did you do?
Boy: Well actually, the best thing happened at the end of the train journey.
Girl: Really? At the station? What was happening?
Boy: Well - a guard was walking along the platform and he suddenly started singing! Then a man came out of the ticket office and sang with him.
Girl: Were they playing instruments – or just singing?
Boy: They didn't have any instruments. They were singing and lots of people on the platform started dancing, too.
Girl: What happened next?
Boy: We saw some TV cameras and we realised it was a trick for a TV programme.

Unit 1 Lesson 6

Activity Book

CD1 Track 16

AB page 11 Activity 3

Boy: I'm working on a project about the sinking of the Titanic in 1912. It's really interesting. I didn't know very much about it.
Girl: What have you found out?
Boy: Well, the first thing is how big the Titanic was. When it was built, it was the biggest object ever made by humans. It was 269 metres long.
Girl: It was travelling from Britain to the United States, wasn't it?
Boy: That's right. It was the ship's first journey. It stopped in France first, then in Ireland and then continued on its way to the United States.
Girl: Why did the Titanic hit an iceberg?
Boy: Well, the crew saw the iceberg and tried to turn the ship. But they hit the iceberg 37 seconds later.
Girl: And then it started sinking.
Boy: Yes. It sank really quickly, too. The ship was completely underwater in less than three hours. Nobody thought the ship could sink. And there weren't enough lifeboats for everybody.
Girl: So how did they decide who went in the lifeboats?
Boy: Women and children went into the lifeboats first. There were about 2,200 people on the ship and more than 1,500 people died. So about 700 people, and two dogs, survived.
Girl: That's terrible.
Boy: Yes. That's why nowadays ships must always have enough lifeboats for everyone.

Unit 1 Lesson 8

Pupil's Book

CD1 Track 17

PB page 16 Activity 2

Ella: Do you like travelling, Alec?
Alec: Yes, I do.
Ella: Have you ever been abroad?
Alec: Yes, I've been to Scotland and I've been to France too.
Ella: Really? Which is the most interesting place you've visited?
Alec: went to Paris last year and I really loved it!
Ella: That's fantastic! I'd love to go to Paris. How did you get there?
Alec: We went by train from London.
Ella: That's so cool. Lucky you! Are you going anywhere this summer?
Alec: We aren't going abroad. We're going by train to the coast.
Ella: Are you camping or staying in a hotel?
Alec: We're camping. Have you ever been camping?
Ella: Yes, and I've stayed in a caravan too.
Alec: Really? That's great! I want to do that one day.
Ella: Yes. It's a lot of fun.

Unit 1 Video and 21st Century Skills

Activity Book

CD 1 Track 18

AB page 15 Activity 1

1
Woman: Think about what would be a good transport system in our town. Work in pairs. Tom and Ella – you can work together.
Boy: OK. What do you think, Ella?
Girl: Let's think about something new and exciting – a cable car system.
Boy: OK. Why is it a good thing?
Girl: There's a big hill in our town. Many people live at the top.
Boy: Yes, so it's easier to travel home after work or after school.
Girl: There aren't any traffic problems, so people always arrive on time.
Boy: Yes, and fewer people will use the roads. That's a good thing.
Girl: But there are some negative things too.
Boy: Yes. I think it would be very expensive to build!
Girl: So the tickets might be expensive too!
Boy: Maybe people won't use it!
Girl: I agree. Many people like walking up the hill!
2
Boy: I think bicycles are the best kind of transport.
Girl: Really? Why?
Boy: They help you to keep fit and they are good for the environment too.
Girl: But it isn't very safe in our town. There are lots of cars.
Boy: I agree. But it is usually quicker to travel by bike than by car.
Girl: Do you think so?
Boy: Yes, there are too many cars on the roads.
Girl: I like cycling, but not when it's raining!
Boy: Ah yes, I agree. It isn't very nice cycling in bad weather.
Girl: And for some people, it isn't easy to ride a bike.
Boy: Hmmm, yes.

Unit 2 Lesson 1

Pupil's Book

CD1 Track 19

PB page 18 Activity 2

1 fencing
2 trampolining
3 archery
4 hoop
5 rope
6 crash mat
7 gymnastics
8 athletics
9 martial arts
10 net
11 racket
12 water polo

Audioscript

Unit 2 Lesson 1

Pupil's Book

CD1 Track 20

PB page 18 Activity 3

1
Boy: This is an object that's used for hitting a ball. It's got strings in the middle. You hold it in your hand when you play a game of tennis or badminton.
Girl: racket
2
Boy: People usually wear white clothes when they do this sport. They also wear masks to protect their faces and gloves to protect their hands. They fight with long, thin swords.
Girl: fencing
3
Boy: This piece of equipment is soft and flat. You put it on the floor when you do martial arts or a sport like gymnastics. It protects your body if you fall over.
Girl: crash mat
4
Boy: People usually wear white clothes and a belt when they do this. Judo is one of these sports.
Girl: martial arts
5
Boy: This piece of equipment is round and has got a hole in the middle. You score a point if you throw the ball through it when you play basketball.
Girl: hoop
6
Boy: This is a team sport which is played in a swimming pool. The players need to throw a ball into a net to score a goal.
Girl: water polo
7
Boy: This piece of equipment is long and thin. You use it for skipping or when you go climbing.
Girl: rope
8
Boy: People shoot arrows at a target when they do this sport. The arrows have got a sharp point at the end so you need to be careful.
Girl: archery
9
Boy: This is a sport in which people jump on a large piece of material. They bounce up and down.
Girl: trampolining
10
Boy: This is an indoor sport in which people do different physical exercises. They need to be strong, flexible and have very good balance.
Girl: gymnastics
11
Boy: Players have to hit the ball over this when they play a game of tennis or table tennis.
Girl: net
12
Boy: In this sport people do different physical exercises outdoors. They need to run, jump and throw objects.
Girl: athletics

Unit 2 Lesson 2

Pupil's Book

CD1 Track 21

PB page 20 Activity 1

Callum: Hi, Mei. Your project sounds amazing.
Mei: Thanks, Callum. I'm sure the school will be happy with the sports equipment.
Callum: Will the children use the rope for skipping?
Mei: No. They'll use it to play tug-of-war. It's a traditional sport in China. Look!
Callum: That looks great fun. Have you ever played tug-of-war?
Mei: Yes, of course.
Callum: Really. When did you play it?
Mei: I played it at a camp last summer. My team lost, but we didn't mind.
Callum: What other traditional Chinese sports and games have you tried?
Mei: I've played chess and I've done kung fu, too.
Callum: Kung fu! But that's a violent sport, isn't it?
Mei: Not at all. There's some information about kung fu on my class wiki. I'll send it to you.

Unit 2 Lesson 2

Activity Book

CD1 Track 22

AB page 17 Activity 3

Tim: Hi, Sally. Have you got any plans for the weekend?
Sally: I have actually. I'm going sailing with my uncle. There's a lake near where he lives.
Tim: That sounds cool. Have you been sailing before?
Sally: Yes, I have. I went sailing with him last year.
Tim: Lucky you! Have you done any other sports?
Sally: Well, I've been horse riding. I went horse riding with my mum a couple of years ago. I play volleyball quite often, too. In fact, I played a game with my brother yesterday.
Tim: What about adventure sports? Have you ever been rock climbing?
Sally: Yes, I have.
Tim: Really? When did you go?
Sally: My dad took me last summer. I have to admit it was a bit scary, but we had our own safety equipment, so it was quite safe.
Tim: What is the most exciting activity you've done?
Sally: It's archery! I tried it two months ago for the first time. It was brilliant. Oh, that's my mum! I have to go.

Unit 2 Lesson 3

Pupil's Book

CD1 Track 23

PB page 21 Activity 2

Kung fu
Kung means 'skill' and *fu* means 'man'. When we put these words together it means skill achieved through hard work.
History
About 1,500 years ago, Chinese monks started using kung fu for self-defence and to protect their temples. The most famous monks lived in the Shaolin Temple where they trained their bodies and minds to help people and to understand the world around them. Nowadays, Shaolin monks travel all around the world to demonstrate their kung fu skills. They have also appeared on television and millions of people have seen their amazing strength and flexibility.
Styles
Shaolin monks divide kung fu into five styles, which are based on the movements of animals. The most powerful and energetic style is the dragon. The tiger style helps develop strength and the leopard style develops power and speed. The snake style develops flexibility and the crane style develops balance and fast foot movement. All five styles develop discipline and self-control.
Training
Children can begin training with the Shaolin monks when they're about six years old. They get up at five o'clock in the morning to exercise and go to bed at nine o'clock in the evening. Trainee monks aren't allowed to play computer games and their diet is only rice and vegetables. However, they can play football in their free time and they're brilliant players.

Unit 2 Lesson 3

Activity Book

CD1 Track 24

AB page 18 Activity 2

Jess: Hi, Callum. What are you reading?
Callum: It's a text about kung fu.
Jess: Is it any good?
Callum: Yes, it's really interesting. Have you ever heard of the Shaolin monks?
Jess: Yes, I have. I saw them last year. They were amazing. What does the text say about them?
Callum: It talks about the monks' five styles of kung fu. Did you know that each style copies the movement of an animal?
Jess: No, I didn't. Which animals do they copy?
Callum: The dragon, the tiger, the leopard, the snake and the crane.
Jess: What's a crane? I've never heard of that animal before.
Callum: It's a bird that's got long legs. You can find them in China.
Jess: And which kung fu style do you like the best?
Callum: I'm not sure. I suppose the dragon style is the coolest because it's powerful and energetic.
Jess: Would you like to train to be a Shaolin monk?

Callum: Hmm … I don't think so.
Jess: Why not?
Callum: Because their life is very hard and I hate getting up early!

Unit 2 Lesson 4

Pupil's Book

CD1 Track 25

PB page 22 Activity 1

Callum: Are you interested in martial arts, Tom?
Tom: Yes, I am. I do karate twice a week.
Callum: I didn't know that. Do you like it?
Tom: Yes, it's good fun. I get fit and it helps me concentrate, too.
Callum: How long have you done karate?
Tom: I've done it since I was eight. I've got an orange belt now.
Callum: Really? How long have you had your orange belt?
Tom: I've had it for six months. If I work hard, I'll get a green belt next.
Callum: Can you show me a karate move?
Tom: Yes, of course. Watch this!

Unit 2 Lesson 4

Pupil's Book

CD1 Track 26

PB page 22 Activity 5

1 How long have you played the piano?
2 I've played the piano for three years.
3 How long have you worn glasses?
4 I've worn glasses since I was six.
5 How long has she lived next door?
6 She's lived next door for a long time.

Unit 2 Lesson 4

Activity Book

CD1 Track 27

AB page 19 Activity 3

1 I've played the violin for two years.
2 How long have they studied English?
3 She's been ill since Saturday.
4 He's worn glasses for six months.
5 I've had a dog since last year.
6 How long has she known her friend?

Unit 2 Lesson 5

Pupil's Book

CD1 Track 28

PB page 23 Activity 1

1 sing in a choir
2 go to drama class
3 belong to a sports club
4 do circus skills
5 do photography
6 do needlework
7 make models
8 collect cards

Unit 2 Lesson 5

Pupil's Book

CD1 Track 29

PB page 23 Activity 2

1 What does Sophie enjoy collecting?
Girl 1: Hi, Sophie. What have you got there?
Girl 2: It's an album. It's where I stick my stamp collection.
Girl 1: I didn't know you collected stamps. How long have you done that?
Girl 2: I've collected them for ages. I've got more than 3,000 now.
Girl 1: Have you ever collected anything else?
Girl 2: Yes. I collected key rings when I was little, but I stopped a few years ago. I got bored.
Girl 1: What about cards? A lot of people collect them.
Girl 2: I know, but I'd rather collect stamps than cards. They're more interesting.

2 What's Sue's hobby?
Girl 2: Have you got a hobby, Sue?
Girl 1: Yes, I have. I love making things.
Girl 2: Really? What sort of things do you make?
Girl 1: I make boats and planes and then I paint them.
Girl 2: You did a lot of needlework before, didn't you?
Girl 1: Yes, but I prefer making models now, it's more interesting and you can make lots of different things.

Unit 2 Lesson 6

Activity Book

CD1 Track 30

AB page 21 Activity 3

Instructor: Hello, everybody. Welcome to our kitesurfing school. Before we start the lesson I want to explain some very important safety rules. First, you need the correct equipment. You must always wear a helmet, a lifejacket and a quick release harness when you go out on the water. Is that clear?
Children: Yes.
Instructor: Good. Another thing you have to do is to look after your equipment. You need to check it regularly and repair any damage. You also need to check that you've got a knife in the pocket of your lifejacket. Does anybody know why you need to carry a knife?
Girl: Is it so that you can cut the strings of the kite if there's a problem?
Instructor: That's right. Another important thing is the weather. You must always check the weather before you ride. If it's too windy or stormy, you mustn't go out. Has anybody got any questions?
Boy: Can we ride anywhere on the water?
Instructor: Absolutely not. You must never ride too far from the shore and you must never practise jumping next to the beach. Finally, you must never kitesurf in a swimming area. That's really important.

Unit 2 Lesson 8

Pupil's Book

CD1 Track 31

PB page 26 Activity 2

James: Are you sporty, Anna?
Anna: Yeah, I think so. I enjoy doing sport. What about you?
James: I love sport.
Anna exclaiming: James! Can you speak more slowly, please?
James: Oh sorry. I said 'I love sport'.
Anna: What sports do you do?
James: I play water polo.
Anna: Oh yes, that's right. How often do you play it?
James: I train three times a week and then I have a match on Saturday mornings.
Anna: That IS a lot. Do you ever watch any sport?
James: Absolutely. I watch football matches on TV. My team's doing really well at the moment.
Anna: Who's your favourite sports person?
James: It's Lionel Messi. He's an amazing footballer.
Anna: I agree. He plays really well. What about in the future? Would you like to try a new sport?
James: Yes, I'd love to try athletics.
Anna: Sorry. I didn't catch that. Can you speak more loudly, please?
James: Yes, of course. I said 'I'd love to try athletics'.
Anna: Ah. Yes. I'd like to try athletics too. It looks fun.

Unit 2 Video and 21st Century Skills

Activity Book

CD1 Track 32

AB page 25 Activity 1

1
Male adult: Are you ready for the football game,Tony?
Boy: I suppose so…
Male adult: Are you sure? You don't sound very happy.
Boy: Well…
Male adult: What's the matter?
Boy: I want to give up football classes.
Male adult: Really? That's a surprise! Why?
Boy: Because I'm not very good.
Male adult: Why do you say that?
Boy: I don't score a lot of goals.
Male adult: That's true, but the other players are bigger and older than you. You need to be patient. I'm sure you will score lots of goals in the future.
Boy: Really?
Male adult: Yes, of course. So - do you want to play in the football game today?
Boy: Yes. Yes, I do.

Audioscript

2
Female adult: Are you ready for your drawing class, Dina?
Girl: No, not really…
Female adult: What's the matter?
Girl: I want to give up drawing classes.
Female adult: Oh! Why's that?
Girl: Because my drawings are rubbish. I always make lots of mistakes.
Female adult: But that's normal.
Girl: What do you mean?
Female adult: Everybody makes mistakes when they begin a new hobby. The important thing is to learn from your mistakes.
Girl: Really?
Female adult: Of course. You need to think why you made the mistake and how you can do it better next time.
Girl: Ah!
Female adult: So, do you want to go to your drawing class today?
Girl: Yes, I do. Thanks, Mum.

Unit 3 Lesson 1

Pupil's Book

CD1 Track 33

PB page 28 Activity 2

1 an avocado
2 an onion
3 a lime
4 a chilli pepper
5 prawns
6 corn
7 turkey
8 beans
9 beef
10 cinnamon
11 garlic
12 peanuts

Unit 3 Lesson 1

Pupil's Book

CD1 Track 34

PB page 28 Activity 3

1
Girl: These are creatures that live in the sea. They're small and pink once they've been cooked.
Boy: prawns
2
Girl: This is a yellow vegetable that grows in large fields. People cook the vegetable to eat it, or they make flour from it.
Boy: corn
3
Girl: This is red meat that you get from cows. People sometimes make burgers using this meat.
Boy: beef
4
Girl: This is a green vegetable that is the same shape as a pear. There's a big stone in the middle of it.
Boy: an avocado
5
Girl: This is a round vegetable that grows in the ground and it can be red, white or yellow. People often chop it and cook it, and then add it to savoury food.
Boy: an onion
6
Girl: This is a hard brown spice. It's ground into a powder and then added to savoury food or sweet food.
Boy: cinnamon
7
Girl: This vegetable can be red, yellow, orange or green. It's long and thin and it's usually hot and spicy.
Boy: a chilli pepper
8
Girl: This is meat from a bird. The bird is bigger than a chicken. People often eat this meat at Christmas.
Boy: turkey
9
Girl: These are nuts that grow underground. People often roast them and eat them with salt.
Boy: peanuts
10
Girl: These are seeds of plants that are cooked and eaten. There are many different kinds and they're often white, red, brown or black.
Boy: beans
11
Girl: This is a small white vegetable that grows underground. It's usually cut into small pieces, cooked, and then added to savoury food. It's got a strong smell.
Boy: garlic
12
Girl: This is a fruit and it's small and green. Its juice is used in cooking. It isn't usually eaten on its own.
Boy: a lime

Unit 3 Lesson 2

Pupil's Book

CD1 Track 35

PB page 30 Activity 1

Tom: Hi, Gabriela. Your community garden sounds fantastic.
Gabriela: Thanks, Tom. Here's a photo of the tomatoes we collected this morning. I think we might have too many tomatoes this year! Many families are going to make tomato sauce to keep in jars.
Tom: Wow! That's a lot of tomatoes!
Gabriela: We want to plant some more vegetables, but there aren't enough volunteers here for us to do everything.
Tom: Do you grow food all year round?
Gabriela: Yes, but from June to September there's too much rain, so we cover parts of the garden. From November to February there isn't enough rain, so we have to water the plants a lot.
Tom: Well, I'm sure it's worth it.
Gabriela: It is! Did you know that another famous food comes from Mexico? I'll send you some information about it.
Tom: I wonder what it is. Thanks!

Unit 3 Lesson 2

Activity Book

CD1 Track 36

AB page 27 Activity 3

Teacher: Hello, everyone. Listen carefully. I've got some information about a new school club. It's the cookery club. Quiet please. We planned to have the club on Wednesday, but I'm afraid the kitchen isn't free that day. So, we'll have the club on Friday after school. When school finishes, please come to Room 30. The cookery club will start at 3:15. Unfortunately, there aren't enough cookers for everybody. We've got eight cookers in Room 30, so you'll work in groups of three. This means there'll be only 24 places in the club. Let me know if you are interested in joining. Are there any questions? Yes, Harry.
Harry: What styles of cookery will we do? Will we cook Spanish food?
Teacher: Ah, good question. I'm afraid we won't cook any Spanish food. We'll start with some Italian and Chinese dishes. Any more questions?

Unit 3 Lesson 3

Pupil's Book

CD1 Track 37

PB page 31 Activity 2

The food of the gods
Narrator: The story of chocolate started over 2,000 years ago, in a part of Central America which later became Mexico, when farmers discovered the fruit, or pods, of the cocoa tree.
Narrator: They noticed a delicious smell coming from the pods. They took the beans from the pods and dried them. Then they roasted and ground them.
Narrator: They mixed the powder with water and spices to make a cold drink. The chocolate was so good that people believed it was a miracle food.
Narrator: More than a thousand years later, the Spanish explorer, Hernán Cortés, tried the drink. It was very bitter, but he liked it.
Narrator: He brought some beans back to Spain. The King liked the drink, too. Cortés suggested adding sugar, vanilla and cinnamon.
Hernán Cortés: You needn't drink it cold. You can drink it warm, too.
Narrator: The sweet hot chocolate became a big success. People enjoyed sharing it in groups and drinking it on special occasions. However, it was too expensive for poorer people.
Woman: This is delicious!
Narrator: Chocolate facts
It took until 1847 before people began making chocolate bars. Soon, eating chocolate became much more popular than drinking chocolate! The cocoa tree can only be grown in warm climates near the equator. A large percentage of the world's cocoa beans grow in Ivory Coast in Africa.

Unit 3 Lesson 3

Activity Book

CD1 Track 38

AB page 28 Activity 2

Callum: What are you reading about?
Tom: I'm reading a text about where chocolate came from.
Callum: Oh, right. It came from South America, didn't it?
Tom: Well, not exactly. It started with the discovery of cocoa pods by the Mayan farmers in Central America. They noticed a delicious smell coming from the pods. Then they realized there were beans inside these pods.
Callum: And did they make these into chocolate bars?
Tom: Chocolate bars came much later. They're only about 150 years old. The Mayans lived about 2,000 years ago.
Callum: What did they do with the beans then?
Tom: They dried them, roasted them and then ground them into powder. They put this powder into cold water to make a drink.
Callum: Did it taste good?
Tom: Yes, that's what they thought. It was so good they thought it was given to them by the gods. I think it's interesting that when Cortés arrived in Central America from Spain, he thought it was too bitter. When he took the beans back to Spain, he suggested adding sugar. Now most people like chocolate with sugar.
Callum: So did the people in Spain like it?
Tom: Oh yes. Rich people drank chocolate in special shops. They had it on special occasions too.
Callum: Was chocolate expensive?
Tom: Well, I suppose it was. Do you know where half of the world's cocoa beans grow?
Callum: Do you mean in which country?
Tom: Yes.
Callum: Is it Mexico?
Tom: No, it isn't. It's Ivory Coast.
Callum: Oh really? I didn't know!
Tom: But chocolate is made in factories all over the world.
Callum: This is all very interesting. But, guess what? I don't like chocolate at all!
Tom: How strange. I love chocolate!

Unit 3 Lesson 4

Pupil's Book

CD1 Track 39

PB page 32 Activity 1

Tom: You need to read this, Jess. It's about the discovery of chocolate in Mexico. They drank chocolate without sugar.
Jess: I can't imagine having chocolate without sugar. It would taste so bitter.
Tom: It was probably healthier to drink chocolate without sugar. Eating too much sugar is bad for you.
Jess: That's true, but you needn't stop eating sugar completely.
Tom: Well, you shouldn't eat too many chocolate bars. Callum needn't worry, he doesn't like chocolate.
Jess: Really? That reminds me, we need to make a cake for Callum's birthday.
Tom: What kind of cake shall we make?
Jess: Well, we mustn't make a chocolate one!

Unit 3 Lesson 4

Pupil's Book

CD1 Track 40

PB page 32 Activity 5

1 You shouldn't go to bed without brushing your teeth.
2 You needn't put lemonade in the fridge.
3 You mustn't heat chocolate in a pan.

Unit 3 Lesson 4

Activity Book

CD1 Track 41

AB page 29 Activity 3

1 wouldn't
2 listen
3 island
4 white
5 whistle
6 plumber
7 guest
8 knife
9 mustn't
10 answer

Unit 3 Lesson 5

Pupil's Book

CD1 Track 42

PB page 33 Activity 1

1 do exercise
2 eat junk food
3 go for walks
4 drink fizzy drinks
5 eat fruit and vegetables
6 drink water
7 rest
8 spend time on the computer

Unit 3 Lesson 5

Pupil's Book

CD2 Track 1

PB page 33 Activity 2

1 What does Jane not do every day?
Boy: OK. I've got some questions here for you, Jane. They're to see how healthy your lifestyle is. First question. How often do you do exercise?
Girl: Well, I go for walks every day and I sometimes go swimming. Oh, and I play hockey for a team every weekend.
Boy: OK. How often do you eat fruit and vegetables?
Girl: With every meal! I have at least three or four pieces of fruit every day.
Boy: How often do you drink fizzy drinks?
Girl: I probably drink fizzy drinks twice a day. I often drink fizzy drinks after sport, too.
Boy: How often do you eat junk food?
Girl: I eat chips every day but I don't eat any other junk food, like burgers or pizza. Maybe just once a month.
Boy: How much sleep do you have?
Girl: I usually watch TV until quite late. I go to sleep at half past eleven every night and wake up at 7.30 when I have to go to school.

2 What advice does Alfie give to Jane?
Boy: Right. Well, I think you do enough exercise and eat enough fruit and vegetables.
Girl: OK. That's good.
Boy: But you drink too many fizzy drinks and eat too many chips.
Girl: Oh.
Boy: And you should go to bed earlier. You don't have enough rest.

Unit 3 Lesson 6

Activity Book

CD2 Track 2

AB page 31 Activity 3

Boy: Hi, Leah. Can I ask you some questions about fast food?
Girl: Sure …
Boy: How often do you eat food from a fast food restaurant?
Girl: Hmm … Probably about once every two weeks.
Boy: Would you say between one and two weeks or between two and three weeks?
Girl: I'd say between two and three weeks.
Boy: And what kind of fast food do you normally eat?
Girl: Well, it depends. Sometimes I have a burger. Other times I have a sandwich or a salad. The only thing that I don't really like is pizza.
Boy: What do you like about fast food?
Girl: I like that it's quick – just like the name "fast food"! I also think it tastes good.
Boy: Where do you eat it?
Girl: Where do I eat it? Well, if the weather's good I sometimes eat in the park. Sometimes we have it at home, too. We always take the food away, we don't eat it in the restaurant.
Boy: Do you think fast food is bad for you?
Girl: No, Not really … Well, maybe sometimes I guess. I think it's important to have a varied diet and fast food can be part of that.

Unit 3 Lesson 8

Pupil's Book

CD2 Track 3

PB page 36 Activity 2

Charlotte: Hi Finn. What are you eating?
Finn: It's a chocolate bar. Do you want one?
Charlotte: No, I've just eaten an apple. It's much healthier.
Finn: Hmmm. You're right. Do you think you're healthy?
Charlotte: Yes, I think so.
Finn: What do you do to keep healthy?
Charlotte: I do a lot of sports. I go swimming twice a week and I also ride my bike to school every day.
Finn: Yes, I do too. Do you get enough rest?

Audioscript

Charlotte: Yes, although I go to bed late and sometimes I feel tired in the morning.
Finn: Do you usually eat healthily?
Charlotte: We usually eat fruit and vegetables with every meal.
Finn: Really? We don't always have fruit.
Charlotte: I don't have fizzy drinks.
Finn: No, I don't either. They have a lot of sugar in them.
Charlotte: But you sometimes eat chocolate?
Finn: Er, yes. But not every day.
Charlotte: That's the same as me. I eat chocolate about twice a week.

Unit 3 Video and 21st Century Skills

Activity Book

CD 2 Track 4

AB page 35 Activity 1

Male adult: Talk about your exercise routines in pairs. Try and organize a routine for each other.
Boy: Tell me about your routine, Maddie. Do you do much exercise?
Girl: I do some exercise. But I would like to do more.
Boy: What exercise do you do?
Girl: I go to football training once a week.
Boy: On which day?
Girl: On Wednesday afternoon.
Boy: Let's put that on the calendar. OK. Anything else?
Girl: Well I sometimes ride my bike on Saturdays.
Boy: OK. Do you go running?
Girl: No, I don't like running.
Boy: You could go swimming. Are you good at swimming?
Girl: Yes. That's a good idea. Put swimming in the calendar for Monday afternoon.
Boy: OK. And you could go cycling every Saturday morning for an hour. We can go together.
Girl: OK. Let's look at your exercise calendar now, Tom.
Boy: I love running. I go running with my older sister on Sunday morning at the park. And on Thursday afternoon too.
Girl: You go running twice a week? That's good. Let's write that in the calendar. Do you do anything else?
Boy: I do PE at school of course. But nothing else.
Girl: Why don't you try another sport?
Boy: I might start playing tennis soon, but there's too much rain at the moment. That's on Tuesday afternoon.
Girl: OK. I'll put that in the calendar too.
Boy: Oh, and I'm going to go cycling with you on Saturday mornings too.
Girl: Of course!

Project 1 Lesson 1

Activity Book

CD2 Track 5

AB page 36 Activity 1

Radio presenter: Hi, everyone and welcome to Hands On!, the radio show about science. Today we're talking about energy. We've got Julia Adams here from the Environmental Institute to explain a few things. Morning, Julia.
Julia: Hello, Peter.
Radio presenter: We want to explain to the listeners a bit about renewable energy. So, first of all, what is renewable energy?
Julia: Renewable energy is energy that comes from a source that isn't running out. In other words, it isn't disappearing as you use it. So gas isn't renewable because when we use it, less of it is left behind.
Radio presenter: So, give us some examples of renewable energy.
Julia: Well, there are a few different kinds but let's look at three examples. We can use the sun, the wind and water from rivers.
Radio presenter: So, shall we start with the sun?
Julia: Yes, that's called solar energy. You can use large, flat solar panels to collect energy from the sun.
Radio presenter: And what happens to that energy?
Julia: We can use it to heat water.
Radio presenter: So you can only use solar energy to heat water?
Julia: No. You can use solar cells, too. They can also collect energy from the sun. These cells can change solar energy directly into electricity.
Radio presenter: OK, great. And what about the wind?
Julia: Well, you've seen tall wind turbines before, haven't you? They're usually white and have got three long blades.
Radio presenter: Yes, I've seen them many times.
Julia: Well, the wind turns the blades and the turbine creates power that produces electricity.
Radio presenter: OK. And finally, what about water?
Julia: This is called hydroelectric energy. This uses the energy from the water in a river. People build a wall, also called a dam, to change the direction of the water. The water falls over the wall and turns a turbine. Like the wind turbine, this produces electricity.
Radio presenter: OK, great. Thanks for this, Julia.

Unit 4 Lesson 1

Pupil's Book

CD2 Track 6

PB page 40 Activity 2

1 puppet
2 do origami
3 do ceramics
4 clay
5 create an animation
6 perform a play
7 costume
8 stage
9 make jewellery
10 beads
11 make a film
12 do traditional dancing

Unit 4 Lesson 1

Pupil's Book

CD2 Track 7

PB page 40 Activity 3

1
Boy: When you do this activity, you record a moving image and create a story. You need a video camera and some actors.
Girl: make a film
2
Boy: When you do this activity, you fold paper to make a model. You can make models of animals, people and objects.
Girl: do origami
3
Boy: These are clothes that are typical of a place or a region. Actors also wear these clothes when they perform on a stage.
Girl: costume
4
Boy: When you do this activity, you stand on a stage and act out a story. You usually wear a costume and you need to speak loudly and clearly.
Girl: perform a play
5
Boy: When you do this activity, you make rings, bracelets and necklaces. You can use materials like cotton and leather or gold and silver.
Girl: make jewellery
6
Boy: When you do this activity, you do a dance that is typical of your country or your region. You usually wear a costume, too.
Girl: do traditional dancing
7
Boy: When you do this activity, you make pictures of animals and people and they appear to move. In the past, people drew the pictures on paper, but now they are made digitally.
Girl: create an animation
8
Boy: This is a character made from wood, material or paper which you can use to tell a story.
Girl: puppet
9
Boy: When you do this activity, you use your hands to make plates and cups from clay. This activity is messy, but good fun.
Girl: do ceramics
10
Boy: This is the platform at the front of the theatre. The actors stand on it when they perform a play.
Girl: stage
11
Boy: These are small, round, colourful objects that are used for making jewellery. They're often made of glass or clay and they look beautiful.
Girl: beads
12
Boy: This is a natural material that you use to do ceramics. It's soft and wet, but it becomes hard when you put it in the oven.
Girl: clay

Unit 4 Lesson 2

Pupil's Book

CD2 Track 8

PB page 42 Activity 1

Jess: Hi, Kenji. Thanks for the photos. Your puppet looks great, but why is it painted black?
Kenji: Because it's a shadow puppet. We're going to perform a shadow puppet show at the hospital.
Jess: That sounds cool. What do you have to do?
Kenji: We have to shine a light behind a screen and then use sticks to move the puppets. Look! Here's a photo of how it works.
Jess: Wow! It looks amazing. Do shadow puppets come from Japan?
Kenji: No, they don't. The first shadow puppets were made in China, but they quickly appeared in Japan, too.
Jess: And are shadow puppets very old?
Kenji: Absolutely. The first shadow puppets were created over one thousand years ago.
Jess: That's incredible. Do you like them?
Kenji: Yes, of course. But I prefer more modern Japanese art. I'll send you some information about that.

Unit 4 Lesson 2

Activity Book

CD2 Track 9

AB page 39 Activity 3

Mark: What are you doing, Josh?
Josh: I'm writing a book report for school.
Mark: Which book are you writing about?
Josh: *The Hobbit*, it's my favourite book. Have you ever read it?
Mark: No, I haven't. Who's the author?
Josh: It was written by a man called Tolkien.
Mark: That's a very unusual name. How do you spell it?
Josh: T-O-L-K-I-E-N.
Mark: And when did he write the book?
Josh: I'm not sure, let's see … There's some information on the back cover. It says that it took Tolkien 12 years to write the book and that it was published in 1937.
Mark: That's a bit old, don't you think?
Josh: The book is really good. Have you seen the films they made about the book?
Mark: No, I haven't.
Josh: I don't believe it! I've seen the films and I've also got the DVDs. Look! This is the first one.
Mark: What a cool cover! When was this film released?
Josh: Let me have a look. It says it was released in 2012.
Mark: What else does it say?
Josh: It says that *The Hobbit* was filmed in New Zealand and that nearly 11 million people in North America watched the film in the first weekend.
Mark: Wow!

Unit 4 Lesson 3

Pupil's Book

CD2 Track 10

PB page 43 Activity 2

Manga magic

Man means 'amusing' and *ga* means 'picture'. When we put these words together it means amusing picture.
What is manga?
Manga is a style of art that was originally created by Katsushika Hokusai in Japan more than 200 years ago. Nowadays, manga drawings are like comics that tell stories with pictures and words. When you read manga, you start at the back of the comic and finish at the front. You also read the story frames from right to left.
What is manga style?
Manga style is easy to recognise because the characters aren't very realistic. They've usually got large eyes, small mouths and tiny noses. Manga characters exaggerate their emotions. When they cry, tears run out of their eyes like water from a tap. When they're angry, they go very red and steam appears around their bodies. Patterns, lines and shapes in the background also help express a character's mood.
What is anime?
When a manga comic book series is very popular, it can be made into an animated series. This is called anime. There are anime films, too. The most famous anime film is called *Spirited Away* and it was made by Studio Ghibli. It won an Oscar in 2003 for the best animated feature film and millions of people around the world have seen it. Another famous anime film is Your Name. In 2016, it won best anime film at the Los Angeles Film Critics.

Unit 4 Lesson 3

Activity Book

CD2 Track 11

AB page 40 Activity 2

Callum: Hi, Jess. What are you reading?
Jess: It's a text about Manga and animated films. Kenji sent it to me.
Callum: Is it any good?
Jess: Yes, it is. There's lots of really interesting information. Did you know that Manga was created more than 200 years ago?
Callum: No, I didn't.
Jess: Do you like Manga, Callum?
Callum: Not very much.
Jess: Really? Why not?
Callum: Because the drawings look strange. I don't like the characters' big eyes. What about you?
Jess: I love the way they look. I enjoy drawing Manga in my free time.
Callum: I know, I've seen some of your drawings. They're very good.
Jess: Thanks!
Callum: Another thing I don't like is that you have to read the comics from right to left.
Jess: Interesting … I don't mind doing that. What about anime? Do you watch any of the series on TV?
Callum: Yes, I quite like watching Dragon Ball. I've watched it for three years.
Jess: Dragon Ball's my favourite!

Unit 4 Lesson 4

Pupil's Book

CD2 Track 12

PB page 44 Activity 1

Tom: Have you ever read a manga comic book, Jess?
Jess: Yes, I've read lots of them. I collect some manga comics called *Dragon Ball*. Wait a minute, I've got one in my bag.
Tom: It looks really exciting. Who was it written by?
Jess: It was written by Akira Toriyama.
Tom: And when was it published?
Jess: It was first published in 1984.
Tom: That's really old!
Jess: I know, but it's still cool.

Unit 4 Lesson 4

Pupil's Book

CD2 Track 13

PB page 44 Activity 5

1 When was *Diary of a Wimpy Kid* written?
2 Who was *The Sword in the Stone* written by?
3 Where were the two films made?

Unit 4 Lesson 4

Activity Book

CD2 Track 14

AB page 41 Activity 3

1 *Alice in Wonderland* was written by Lewis Carroll.
2 There were two wrong answers in the exam.
3 *The Sword in the Stone* was written in 1938.
4 The woman twisted her wrist twice.
5 William ate two whole watermelons.

Unit 4 Lesson 5

Pupil's Book

CD2 Track 15

PB page 45 Activity 1

1 composer
2 novelist
3 fashion designer
4 photographer
5 actor
6 sound engineer
7 graffiti artist
8 film director

Audioscript

Unit 4 Lesson 5

Pupil's Book

CD2 Track 16

PB page 45 Activity 2

Girl: Hi, Sam. Do you want to do a quiz with me? It's all about creative people.
Boy: Yeah, OK.
Girl: Great. Here's the first question. Who was the Eiffel Tower built by? Was it built by A) Gustave Eiffel, B) Thomas Eiffel or C) Leonardo da Vinci?
Boy: I haven't got a clue. Was it built by Gustave Eiffel?
Girl: Yes, it was. Well done. Number 2: Who was Avatar directed by? Was it directed by A) Steven Spielberg, B) George Lucas or C) James Cameron?
Boy: I'm not certain about this one. Was it George Lucas?
Girl: No, it wasn't. It was James Cameron. Never mind. Number 3: Was Best Song Ever sung by A) The Beatles, B) One Direction or C) Rihanna?
Boy: I definitely know this one. It was sung by One Direction.
Girl: That's right! Number 4: Who was The Hunger Games written by? Was it written by A) Stephenie Meyer, B) Suzanne Collins, or C) J.K. Rowling?
Boy: I'm sure I know the answer. The Hunger Games was written by Suzanne Collins.
Girl: That's right – brilliant! Now, here's the last question. Number 5: Who was the role of Belle in the film Beauty and the Beast performed by? Was it A) Kristen Stewart, B) Emma Watson or C) Jennifer Lawrence?
Boy: I've got no idea so I'm going to make a guess. Was it performed by Emma Watson?
Girl: Yes, it was. Well done! You've got four out of five.

Unit 4 Lesson 6

Activity Book

CD2 Track 17

AB page 43 Activity 3

Radio presenter: Good morning! You're listening to Radio FM. Today, I've got Mrs Evans on the phone. She's the local librarian and she's got news about a great new competition for children. So, can you tell us all about this competition?
Mrs Evans: Well, comics are always very popular with children so we've decided to have a comic drawing competition. The topic is superheroes. The children can invent their own superhero!
Radio presenter: What an exciting idea!
Mrs Evans: Thank you. There are a couple of rules to follow, though. Firstly, the comics can't be too long. They must only have six frames. Secondly, they mustn't have any fighting or weapons. We really don't want to see blood.
Radio presenter: And when is the competition exactly?
Mrs Evans: It's next Saturday. The children need to bring their comics to the library at 10. There are two age groups. The first is for children who are between eight and 12 and the second is for children between the ages of 13 and 17.
Radio presenter: Are there any prizes for the winners?
Mrs Evans: Yes, of course. In each age group, the children who are second and third will receive a new art set. The winners will receive an amazing collection of comic books and DVDs.
Radio presenter: What fantastic prizes!

Unit 4 Lesson 8

Pupil's Book

CD2 Track 18

PB page 48 Activity 2

Sarah: Hey, Lucas. Do you think you're creative?
Lucas: Not really.
Sarah: Are you sure? The doodles in your notebooks are amazing. They're really creative.
Lucas: Yeah, I suppose they are. What creative activities do you do?
Sarah: Well, some of the games I play on the computer are creative. My favourite is Minecraft. I build virtual worlds in that game.
Lucas: Really? What sort of things do you build?
Sarah: I usually build houses. They've got windows and lights. They've even got furniture.
Lucas: That sounds cool.
Sarah: It is.
Lucas: How often do you play Minecraft?
Sarah: I usually play when I've finished my homework. I'd like to play more, but my mum says I can't.
Lucas: And what's the best thing you've built?
Sarah: That's easy. I built a water park last year.
Lucas: Wow! I'm impressed. Well done!

Unit 4 Video and 21st Century Skills

Activity Book

CD 2 Track 19

AB page 47 Activity 1

Boy: Hi, Sarah, What are you doing?
Girl: I'm looking at this online catalogue. It's got some really cool digital technology.
Boy: It IS cool! Have you ever used any of it?
Girl: Yes, I have. I've used a laptop a lot. In fact, I used one yesterday to create a digital presentation for school. I took some photos with my mobile phone and put those in the presentation, too.
Boy: Excellent! What about a digital camera? Have you ever used one of those?
Girl: Yes. I used one last summer to create an animation with my friends. It was brilliant! What about you? What digital technology have you used?
Boy: Well, I've used a graphics tablet.
Girl: Really? What for?
Boy: I used it to design a birthday card for my mum. Then I printed the card out on my printer.
Girl: Nice. Have you used anything else?
Boy: Yes, I've used a scanner and a microphone to create a digital story. I recorded myself reading the story and I scanned my drawings.
Girl: Wow! That sounds amazing. Is that the best thing you've created?
Boy: No. The best thing was a musical video. I used a video camera to film me and my friends singing and dancing.
Girl: You ARE creative.
Boy: Thanks. Do you want to see the music video?
Girl: Yes, please.

Unit 5 Lesson 1

Pupil's Book

CD2 Track 20

PB page 50 Activity 2

1 advert
2 text message
3 greetings card
4 brochure
5 sign language
6 cartoon
7 sign
8 blog post
9 email
10 chat message
11 leaflet
12 note

Unit 5 Lesson 1

Pupil's Book

CD2 Track 21

PB page 50 Activity 3

1
Girl: This is a message that you type on your mobile phone to send to someone. It's usually a short message.
Boy: text message
2
Girl: This is a short message that you usually write on paper. You might write it when you want to make a list or remind someone to do something.
Boy: note
3
Girl: You can look at this to find things to buy or places to go on holiday. It's usually a thin book with photos of things.
Boy: brochure
4
Girl: You write this as a part of an online diary. You might write something interesting that you'd like others to read.
Boy: blog post
5
Girl: This is something you give to a friend or a family member. It's to wish someone a happy birthday or to congratulate them on an achievement, for example.
Boy: greetings card

6
Girl: This is a language used by people who cannot hear. It uses movements of the hands to communicate things.
Boy: sign language
7
Girl: You can find this in a newspaper, online, on TV or on the street. It's a message that tells people about an event, or is trying to sell something.
Boy: advert
8
Girl: This is a way of having a conversation with someone online. You can send these messages from a computer or sometimes from a mobile phone.
Boy: chat message
9
Girl: This is like a story with drawings and sometimes words. It's usually funny and you can find it in newspapers and magazines.
Boy: cartoon
10
Girl: This is a piece of paper or card that gives information about something. It might be about museums and galleries, special offers in shops or many other things.
Boy: leaflet
11
Girl: This is a message that you type on the computer and then send to someone. You can attach photos or other documents to it.
Boy: email
12
Girl: This is usually a short message that you see outside or inside buildings. It usually gives some useful information about what to do in that place.
Boy: sign

Unit 5 Lesson 2

Pupil's Book

CD2 Track 22

PB page 52 Activity 1

Callum: Hi. That's a great project, Youssef. How's it going?
Youssef: It's going really well. Our teacher said he was happy with the results. He said the children were better at reading already.
Callum: That's brilliant! Is Arabic hard to read?
Youssef: Yes, there are many different characters to remember. We used these cards to help the children.
Callum: What a good idea. Did your teacher help you?
Youssef: He said the important thing was to help them look carefully at the words and letters.
Callum: Are you going to continue helping them?
Youssef: Yes. Our teacher said we needed to help them with their writing now.
Callum: We've suggested the idea at our school, too. The head teacher told us he liked the idea a lot. We might organise it next month.
Youssef: Good luck! Do you know about the Rosetta Stone? It was discovered near here. I'll send you some information.
Callum: Thanks! I look forward to reading about it.

Unit 5 Lesson 2

Activity Book

CD2 Track 23

AB page 49 Activity 3

Mark: I've just started going to the school book club.
Josh: Oh, really? Do you meet every week?
Mark: Yes, we meet every Wednesday at 12:30 for half an hour.
Josh: So where do you meet?
Mark: We meet in the school library.
Josh: And can you choose which book to read?
Mark: Well, at the beginning of term the teacher brings us a choice of about ten books and we decide which one we are going to read. We all read the same book. Every week the teacher gives us a page number that we have to read up to. We read one book in three weeks. Then we choose another book.
Josh: What are you reading now?
Mark: Our first book is called *The Secret Language* by Helen Hawkins.
Josh: Helen Hawkins? I don't know her. How do you spell her surname?
Mark: H-A-W-K-I-N-S
Josh: Is it good?
Mark: Yes, it's a mystery book. It's about two brothers who discover some messages which they can't understand, so they try to find out which unknown language they are written in.
Josh: That sounds interesting. So what do you do when you meet?
Mark: We talk about the book, we have quizzes or draw pictures of the scenes and characters.
Josh: Can I join the club?
Mark: I think it's full, but maybe you should try for next term.
Josh: Oh, that's a shame, but I will!

Unit 5 Lesson 3

Pupil's Book

CD2 Track 24

PB page 53 Activity 2

Cracking the code
It looks like a large piece of boring grey rock. So why is the Rosetta Stone so special?
A lucky discovery
For many years, the ancient Egyptians were a mystery because no one could understand the pictures and symbols that they wrote. Then, in 1799, some French soldiers discovered a piece of stone in a village called Rosetta, in northern Egypt.
On one side of the stone there was some writing which said the same thing in ancient Greek and in Egyptian hieroglyphics. This meant that the message on the stone was very important for the people in ancient Greece and Egypt. People knew Greek so they could start working out the meaning of the hieroglyphics, but they still couldn't understand all the symbols.
Will anyone find the answer?
The Frenchman, Jean-Francois Champollion, became interested in hieroglyphics at a young age. Someone told him no one could ever understand the symbols. He promised to himself that one day he would solve the mystery.
'I've got it!'
The important moment happened about 23 years after the Rosetta Stone was discovered. Champollion was looking at one word with four symbols.
He thought that the first symbol looked like a sun. 'Maybe the first part of the word is the Egyptian word for sun, *ra*,' he thought. Then he realised that the word must be Rameses, the name of an Egyptian pharaoh. He had worked it out! Words sometimes contained other Egyptian words which were shown as a picture. This is similar to writing the word *cartoon* as 'car' (with a picture of a car), and 'toon'.
Champollion was so excited that he ran into his brother's office and shouted, 'I've got it!' Then he fainted and was ill in bed for five days. Today, you can see the Rosetta stone in the British Museum in London.

Unit 5 Lesson 3

Activity Book

CD2 Track 25

AB page 50 Activity 2

Tom: Hi, Callum. What are you reading?
Callum: It's a story about Egyptian hieroglyphics and how people started to understand them. Youssef sent it to me.
Tom: Is it interesting?
Callum: Yes. Have you heard of the Rosetta Stone? It's in the British Museum.
Tom: No, I haven't.
Callum: It's got Egyptian hieroglyphics on it. People used it to work out what the symbols mean. Look at this photo of the stone. I think the symbols are amazing. Don't you think so?
Tom: Oh, yes. Can you understand any of it?
Callum: No, but I'd like to find out what some symbols mean.
Tom: Me too. I like writing secret codes so I think this is very interesting.
Callum: Really?
Tom: Jess and I have got a secret code. I'll show you later. It's really difficult to crack it!
Callum: OK!
Tom: So what's your favourite part of the story?
Callum: Actually, I really like the end of the story. Champollion, a Frenchman, finally worked out what the symbols of the hieroglyphics meant. He was so excited that he fainted and was ill in bed for five days!
Tom: (laughs)
Callum: Right, let's see your code now! I'm sure I can crack it.
Tom: We'll see …

Audioscript

Unit 5 Lesson 4

Pupil's Book

CD2 Track 26

PB page 54 Activity 1

Callum: So the Rosetta Stone helped us understand what the ancient Egyptians wrote. That's so cool!
Jess: Yes. We should go and look at it. It's in the British Museum in London. My mum said we could go to London this weekend.
Callum: Great idea!
Jess: My parents said it would rain this weekend, so it's a good idea to go to a museum.
Jess: What's Tom doing?
Callum: He's drawing some hieroglyphic messages. He said we'd have to try and solve them!

Unit 5 Lesson 4

Pupil's Book

CD2 Track 27

PB page 54 Activity 5

1 He said he'd arrive home at 12 o'clock.
2 She said she could juggle really well.
3 She told me she wouldn't be at dance club today.
4 He told me he couldn't do his homework.

Unit 5 Lesson 4

Activity Book

CD2 Track 28

AB page 51 Activity 3

1 James said he'd meet me at lunchtime.
2 Jenny told her friend she wasn't going to the concert.
3 Mrs Jones told the children they could go and play outside.
4 My grandad always said he couldn't play chess, but he just beat me!
5 I said I wouldn't play my music very loudly.
6 They said they'd come to the party on Saturday.

Unit 5 Lesson 5

Pupil's Book

CD2 Track 29

PB page 55 Activity 1

1 front page
2 article
3 headline
4 interview
5 reporter
6 review
7 fashion section
8 world news
9 sports news
10 caption

Unit 5 Lesson 5

Pupil's Book

CD2 Track 30

PB page 55 Activity 2

Woman: Excuse me … hello. Hi! My name's Rachel Jones from the London Globe. Can I ask you a few questions?
Man: Yes, of course.
Woman: Is this your first time in England?
Man: Yes, it is. I love it. I've met so many nice people. The food here is great, too. Fish and chips are much more delicious than I expected!
Woman: Please tell us about your new film, *Don't Stop!*
Man: Well, it's an adventure film about some criminals who steal some paintings from a museum. An ordinary police officer, that's me, discovers the clues to help solve the crime.
Woman: And Jennifer Lewis is in the film too, isn't she? Do you fall in love?
Man: I'm not going to tell you that! You'll have to go and see the film! But she's a wonderful actress, and she's very funny, too!
Woman: Is the film a comedy?
Man: Well, it isn't a comedy, but there are some funny bits and some good jokes.
Woman: Someone told me the final part of the film was really exciting! It happens on a speeding train, doesn't it?
Man: Oh yes. It's amazing! The train gets faster and faster. I think it'll make people feel scared, but excited, too.
Woman: Is it a sad ending?
Man: I can't say too much, but I think people will leave the cinema happy, not sad!
Woman: OK. Well, I hope you enjoy your time in London. What are you going to do for the rest of your stay?
Man: I'm going to do some sightseeing this afternoon. I haven't seen Tower Bridge or Big Ben yet!
Woman: Thank you for taking the time to speak to us.

Unit 5 Lesson 6

Activity Book

CD2 Track 31

AB page 53 Activity 3

Journalist: Hello, I'm a reporter from the Chippington Gazette. Your teacher said you'd be happy to answer a few questions.
Girl: No problem. What's it about?
Journalist: It's about your school coding club.
Girl: Oh yes, I love it!
Journalist: Let's see … First, how old are you?
Girl: I'm 11.
Journalist: And when did you start going to coding club?
Girl: About three months ago. I wanted to start earlier, but there were many people who also wanted to do it.
Journalist: What do you enjoy most about it?
Girl: Well, we do lots of different things but the thing I enjoy the most is programming animations. It's so much fun!
Journalist: Is programming animations easy?
Girl: When you know how to do it, yes! I didn't think it would be easy but now I can make simple games.
Journalist: What job would you like to do when you grow up?
Girl: Well, I really like designing and creating things. Maybe I'll design websites or computer games.
Journalist: Do you have any other hobbies?
Girl: Hmm … not really. I play lots of sports, but on the computer.
Journalist: Oh dear. Maybe you're spending too much time on the computer!

Unit 5 Lesson 8

Pupil's Book

CD2 Track 32

PB page 58 Activity 2

Isabel: Hi Leon. Have you ever met a famous person?
Leon: I'm not sure. Let me think. Well, do you watch The Now Show on TV?
Isabel: Yes, sometimes.
Leon: I met a reporter from that show. She's called Sandra Scott.
Isabel: Oh really? What does she look like?
Leon: She's tall with long, curly black hair.
Isabel: How did you meet her?
Leon: My cousin is a good friend of Sandra Scott's daughter. So, we met at my cousin's birthday party. I wanted to ask her some questions about her job.
Isabel: Was she friendly?
Leon: Yes, she was really friendly. She answered all my questions and asked me about my life, too.
Isabel: That's nice of her. What did you learn about being a reporter?
Leon: She said it was great fun. She has to travel a lot and she meets different people every day. It is hard work and she gets up very early most days.
Isabel: Would you like to be a reporter?
Leon: Wait. Let me think. I wasn't sure before I met Sandra Scott. But now I think I would like to be a reporter. Would you?
Isabel: No I wouldn't. I'd like to be a teacher.

Unit 5 Video and 21st Century Skills

Activity Book

CD 2 Track 33

AB page 57 Activity 1

Male adult: I want you to work in pairs. Choose a language to research. Look at the questions and research the information.
Boy: So, Lara, what language shall we choose?
Girl: My dad went to Hungary last year.
Boy: Hungary? That's in Europe, isn't it? What do they speak there?
Girl: Yes, it's in the centre of Europe. They speak Hungarian. My dad told me it was a very difficult language to learn.

Boy: OK. Let's see. We need to choose some vocabulary to research. How about fruit or animals or school subjects?
Girl: "Animals" is a good idea. This online dictionary is useful. Let's try "cat" or "dog".
Boy: Look. This dictionary has "cat". You can listen to it in Hungarian.
Girl: Macska. That's a nice word. Look, this is "horse".
Boy: It has an accent on the "o".
Girl: What's an accent?
Boy: It's a line on top of the letter. Look.
Girl: I want to know how to say "yes" and "no"
Boy: OK.
Girl: "Yes" is … igen. And "no" is …
Boy: Nem. N-e-m. That's easy to say. Nem.
Girl: And listen to this. What do you think that means?
Boy: I don't know.
Girl: It means hello and it means goodbye too!
Boy: Oh OK. Szía.
Girl: You spell it s-z-i-a. There's an accent on the "i". In Hungarian, an "s" and a "z" together is a "s" sound.
Boy: That's interesting. Let's get ready to present the information to the class. How shall we do it?

Unit 6 Lesson 1

Pupil's Book

CD2 Track 34

PB page 60 Activity 2

1 veterinary nurse
2 plumber
3 security guard
4 politician
5 electrician
6 tour guide
7 computer technician
8 archaeologist
9 graphic designer
10 physiotherapist
11 businessperson
12 detective

Unit 6 Lesson 1

Pupil's Book

CD2 Track 35

PB page 60 Activity 3

1
Boy: This is a person who fits and repairs pipes. These pipes are used for carrying water indoors and outdoors.
Girl: plumber
2
Boy: This is a person who helps people when their muscles or joints hurt. This person uses special exercises to help the patient move their muscles and joints.
Girl: physiotherapist
3
Boy: This is a person who helps a vet look after animals that are injured or sick. This person usually wears a white overall to protect their clothes.
Girl: veterinary nurse
4
Boy: This is a person who fits and repairs wires. These wires transport electricity indoors and outdoors.
Girl: electrician
5
Boy: This is a person who protects buildings, objects or people. This person usually wears a uniform.
Girl: security guard
6
Boy: This is a person who investigates a crime. This person can be a police officer or can work on their own.
Girl: detective
7
Boy: This is a person who studies how people lived in the past. This person looks for ancient objects in the ground.
Girl: archaeologist
8
Boy: This is a person who uses a computer to create pictures. This person designs things like magazines, posters and adverts.
Girl: graphic designer
9
Boy: This is a person who works in the government. This person debates and creates laws to help make our society better.
Girl: politician
10
Boy: This is a person who takes tourists to a new place. This person gives the tourists information and answers their questions.
Girl: tour guide
11
Boy: This is a person who repairs computers and makes sure that a computer system operates correctly.
Girl: computer technician
12
Boy: This is a person who works in an office or a bank. This person has meetings and has to make important decisions.
Girl: businessperson

Unit 6 Lesson 2

Pupil's Book

CD2 Track 36

PB page 62 Activity 1

Tom: Hi, Morag. Your project sounds fantastic.
Morag: Thanks, Tom. I love being with the animals.
Tom: Is that why you want to be a veterinary nurse when you're older?
Morag: Absolutely. What about you? Do you know what you want to be?
Tom: Well, my dream is to be an astronaut like the one in this photo.
Morag: What a great job. Is it difficult to be an astronaut?
Tom: Yes. It's almost impossible so I probably won't be one.
Morag: Are you good at Maths and Science?
Tom: Yes, I am.
Morag: So you might be an astronaut in the future.
Tom: Hmm! I suppose so.
Morag: I know. I'll send you a story about an amazing woman and her work. That will make you feel more positive.

Unit 6 Lesson 2

Activity Book

CD2 Track 37

AB page 59 Activity 3

Vicky: Have you got any plans for the weekend, Jake?
Jake: Not really. I might go to the cinema with my dad on Saturday, but it depends on what's on. We'll definitely go if there's an action film, but if there isn't, we'll do something else.
Vicky: What about on Sunday?
Jake: We usually have lunch with my grandparents on Sunday, but this weekend they're on holiday, so we'll probably stay at home. Do you have any plans for Saturday?
Vicky: I'm not sure. I'll do my homework and I need some new school shoes, so I'll probably go shopping with my mum.
Jake: Are you going to do anything on Sunday?
Vicky: We don't know yet. We might go to the beach, but it depends on the weather. If it's bad, we'll stay at home and watch TV.

Unit 6 Lesson 3

Pupil's Book

CD2 Track 38

PB page 63 Activity 2

The story of Evelyn Glennie
Narrator: Evelyn Glennie was born in Aberdeenshire, Scotland. Her parents played instruments in a traditional Scottish dance band.
Narrator: When she was eight, Evelyn began studying the piano. She was a brilliant music student, but soon after she started having problems with her hearing.
Evelyn's Mum: What's the matter, Evelyn?
Evelyn: My ears hurt.
Narrator: By the time Evelyn was 12, she was deaf. This was a difficult time for her. But one day, while she was watching a school concert, she had an idea.
Evelyn: If I learn how to play percussion, I can express my emotions.
Narrator: Evelyn wanted to learn to play the drums. Her music teacher showed her how to feel a drum's vibrations with her fingertips and through her bare feet.

Audioscript

Evelyn: I can feel the higher sounds in the top part of my body and the lower sounds in the bottom part.
Narrator: Evelyn studied percussion and when she was 19 she won an important award. However, she didn't stop there.
Evelyn: My next ambition is to become the first solo percussion player in the world.
Narrator: She worked hard to achieve her dream. Now she performs about 100 solo concerts around the world every year and she has won more than 80 international awards. She also plays the xylophone, the chimes and many more percussion instruments. There are no limits for Evelyn. What do you think she'll do next?

Unit 6 Lesson 3

Activity Book

CD3 Track 1

AB page 60 Activity 2

Jess: Hi, Tom. What are you reading?
Tom: It's a true story that Morag sent to me from Scotland.
Jess: What's it about?
Tom: It's about a famous musician called Evelyn Glennie.
Jess: She's a percussionist, isn't she?
Tom: That's right. The surprising thing is that Evelyn can't hear.
Jess: Really? I didn't know that.
Tom: She lost her hearing when she was twelve. It was a difficult time for her at first, but then she learnt how to play the drums and that helped her.
Jess: That's amazing.
Tom: I know.
Jess: I saw Evelyn on TV once. She made instruments out of different objects and then played them. My favourite was one that she made from an old bed.
Tom: An old bed! How funny! Thinking about it, would you like to go to a concert this weekend?
Jess: Yes, I'd love to!
Tom: And would you recommend this story?
Jess: Absolutely. In fact, I'm going to recommend it to my sister.
Tom: Why?
Jess: Because she plays the piano and I think it'll help her practise more.

Unit 6 Lesson 4

Pupil's Book

CD3 Track 2

PB page 64 Activity 1

Callum: That was a brilliant story.
Tom: I know. You play a musical instrument, too, don't you?
Callum: Yes, I play the guitar.
Tom: Do you play well?
Callum: I'm not bad. Listen to this.
Tom: Wow! You're really good. Do you think you'll play in the school concert next month?
Callum: Yes, I probably will.
Tom: And do you think you'll be famous in ten years' time?
Callum: If I keep on practising, who knows?

Unit 6 Lesson 4

Pupil's Book

CD3 Track 3

PB page 64 Activity 5

1 I might go to the beach in August.
2 I definitely won't go to school on Saturday.
3 I could study Chinese in ten years' time.
4 I'll probably go shopping next week.
5 I may play football at break time.

Unit 6 Lesson 4

Activity Book

CD3 Track 4

AB page 61 Activity 3

1 I'll wear glasses next year.
2 He may speak French in ten years' time.
3 They'll probably go home in one hour's time.
4 She could wear glasses in two years' time.
5 I might study English in 20 years' time.
6 I won't do my homework tonight.

Unit 6 Lesson 5

Pupil's Book

CD3 Track 5

PB page 65 Activity 1

1 have children
2 get a job
3 leave home
4 go to university
5 learn to drive
6 go backpacking
7 get married
8 start a business

Unit 6 Lesson 5

Pupil's Book

CD3 Track 6

PB page 65 Activity 2

Boy: Hi, Sally. What are you doing?
Girl: I'm writing an email to my sister. She's studying at university.
Boy: Do you think you'll go to university in the future?
Girl: It's a little difficult but I hope so. I want to be a music teacher when I'm older and you need to go to university to do that.
Boy: What other things will you do in the future?
Girl: Hmm, let me think … Well, I'll definitely learn to drive when I'm 18.
Boy: Why?
Girl: Because it's good to be independent and not rely on others to take you everywhere. I think it's really important to drive a car.
Boy: You're right. What about travelling? Do you think you'll travel a lot?
Girl: Absolutely. I want to travel all around the world.
Boy: How do you think you'll travel? Will you go backpacking?
Girl: No, I don't think so. Backpacking is cheap, but I prefer staying in hotels.
Boy: What about starting a business? Do you think you'll do that?
Girl: I'm not sure. It's difficult to start a business. But I suppose I might do it one day.
Boy: Who knows, you could be a millionaire in the future.
Girl: That's true, but I doubt it.

Unit 6 Lesson 6

Activity Book

CD3 Track 7

AB page 63 Activity 3

Boy: What are you reading, mum?
Mum: It's a newspaper article about a time capsule that was buried in New York a long time ago. It's very interesting.
Boy: When was it buried?
Mum: It was buried in 1939 to celebrate New York's World's fair.
Boy: Are they going to open it soon?
Mum: I'm afraid not. The time capsule's going to be under the ground for 5,000 years.
Boy: Wow! 5,000 years! The world will be totally different then.
Mum: I know.
Boy: What's the time capsule made of?
Mum: The article says that the outside is made of metal, but the inside is made of glass. These materials protect the objects that are inside.
Boy: Are there any toys inside?
Mum: Yes, there are. There's a mechanical car and a doll. These were the typical toys the children played with in the 1930s.
Boy: Is there anything else inside the capsule?
Mum: Well, there's some toothpaste …
Boy: Toothpaste!
Mum: Yes!

Unit 6 Lesson 8

Pupil's Book

CD3 Track 8

PB page 68 Activity 2

Joe: What do you want to be when you're older, Eva?
Eva: I'm not one hundred percent sure. I think I'd like to be a scientist.
Joe: A scientist? That's a cool job.
Eva: I know.
Joe: So what do scientists do?
Eva: They do a lot of experiments.
Joe: I know that. What else do they do?
Eva: Well, they use the experiments to solve problems, for example, to clean the oceans or to invent a new medicine.
Joe: That IS important. Why do you want to be a scientist?
Eva: Because science is my favourite subject at school. Do you like science?
Joe: Not really. I prefer maths. Is it difficult to become a scientist?
Eva: I think so. I need to work really hard at school.
Joe: What else do you need to do?
Eva: I need to go to university when I'm older.
Joe: Don't worry. I'm sure you'll do it.
Eva: Thanks, Joe

Unit 6 Video and 21st Century Skills

Activity Book

CD3 Track 9

AB page 67 Activity 1

Boy: Hi, Maria. What are you reading?
Girl: It's a quiz. Do you want to do it with me?
Boy: What's it about?
Girl: It's about thinking outside the box when you do a project.
Boy: OK. That sounds interesting.
Girl: Great. Here's question number 1: Do you brainstorm lots of ideas at the start of the project?
Boy: Yes, I always do that. I know that the first idea isn't always the best.
Girl: That's true. And do you listen to other people's ideas?
Boy: Not really. I usually think of my own ideas when other people talk.
Girl: Really? Next question. Do you like thinking of silly or funny ideas?
Boy: Absolutely! I love doing that.
Girl: And do you try to do something different from other people?
Boy: It depends. I sometimes try to be original, but not always.
Girl: OK. We're on question 5 now. Do you ever daydream?
Boy: What do you mean?
Girl: Do you think of nice and exciting things instead of paying attention.
Boy: Yes, I sometimes daydream – usually when I'm doing a boring activity.
Girl: Me too. And do you like solving problems?
Boy: Yes, I do. I love solving problems. It's fun.
Girl: Great!
Boy: So, what's my score?
Girl: Let me see … You've got 8 points. Not bad. You are quite good at thinking outside the box.

Project 2 Lesson 1

Activity Book

CD3 Track 10

AB page 68 Activity 1

Radio presenter: Hello. Have you ever thought about how people could live on Mars one day? Will it happen? Maybe it will. But one thing we know is that living on Mars won't be as easy as living on Earth. The things we need to stay alive aren't easy to find on Mars! We have space expert Larry Bishop here to explain. Hi, Larry.
Larry: Hello, Emily.
Radio presenter: So let's start with the simple things. Can we breathe on Mars?
Larry: No. We need oxygen to breathe and there isn't any oxygen on Mars.
Radio presenter: Well that's a bad start!
Larry: Yes. You'd need to create oxygen there, or bring it to Mars.
Radio presenter: We've got plenty of water on Earth, haven't we? And we'd need water to survive on Mars. Is there any?
Larry: Well, there is, but it's all ice. It's very cold on Mars, especially at night, so there isn't any liquid water. There is a little water vapour, though.
Radio presenter: So without water, there can't be any food, I suppose.
Larry: You're right. There's no life of any kind that we know of, so there's nothing to eat there.
Radio presenter: Could you start growing food there?
Larry: Well, there's energy from the Sun, although Mars is much further from the Sun than Earth is. And plants need water and oxygen and carbon dioxide to grow, as on Earth.
Radio presenter: And what about other forms of energy to help us live our lives? Is there any fuel there? Oil or gas, for example?
Larry: There are no fossil fuels, no – so no oil or gas. We'd have to find other ways to produce energy. You could maybe use solar power or wind power – or build a nuclear power plant.
Radio presenter: Is there anything else that we need to know about the atmosphere on Mars?
Larry: As I said, it's very cold. But, strangely, the Sun's rays can be very dangerous. Sunlight has got ultraviolet rays. These are the rays that cause sunburn and skin cancer. Luckily for us here on Earth, the atmosphere protects us from some of these rays.
Radio presenter: OK. And what about on Mars?
Larry: Unfortunately, Mars hasn't got the same atmosphere so there's little protection from the ultraviolet rays. People would need to find a way of protecting themselves.
Radio presenter: Right. Many thanks, Larry. There's a lot to think about there, isn't there.

Unit 7 Lesson 1

Pupil's Book

CD3 Track 11

PB page 72 Activity 2

1 purse
2 credit card
3 coins
4 bank notes
5 price tag
6 receipt
7 customer
8 cashier
9 till
10 spend money
11 save money
12 moneybox

Unit 7 Lesson 1

Pupil's Book

CD3 Track 12

PB page 72 Activity 3

1
Girl: You look at this to see how much something costs. It's usually stuck on the thing you want to buy or attached to it.
Boy: price tag
2
Girl: This is money that's round and made of metal. It's usually for small amounts.
Boy: coins
3
Girl: This is the person who wants to buy something. This person can buy things in a shop or online.
Boy: customer
4
Girl: This is a place where you keep your money. You usually keep it at home because it's too big to carry around with you.
Boy: moneybox
5
Girl: You do this when you use money to pay for something. After you do this, you have less money than you started with!
Boy: spend money
6
Girl: This is something that you put money into. It's usually quite small and fits into your pocket. You can keep coins, bank notes and credit cards in it.
Boy: purse
7
Girl: This is a piece of paper that a shop assistant gives you when you buy something. It's important to keep this safe in case there's a problem or you need to change what you've bought.
Boy: receipt
8
Girl: This is where you pay for your shopping. It's usually got a machine that scans the items you're buying and a place where the money is kept.
Boy: till
9
Girl: This is the person who you pay in a shop. In a supermarket, they usually pass every item through a scanning machine and tell you how much money you have to pay for all your items.
Boy: cashier
10
Girl: This is a small card made of plastic. People use it to pay for something instead of using coins and notes. After they pay, the money comes out of their bank account.
Boy: credit card
11
Girl: You do this when you keep your money. You might keep it in a bank or in a moneybox.
Boy: save money
12
Girl: This is money that's made of a special kind of paper. They've got different values. One may be worth €10 and another may be worth €20.
Boy: bank notes

Audioscript

Unit 7 Lesson 2

Pupil's Book

CD3 Track 13

PB page 74 Activity 1

Jess: Hi, Kelvin. The 'almost-new' sale sounds like a really worthwhile project. Has there been a lot of interest?
Kelvin: Yes, there has! We've had to move the event to a bigger hall. The school hall isn't big enough to fit all the tables.
Jess: That's great news. How do people know how much they can sell things for?
Kelvin: We give everyone a guide. Things at the sale aren't as expensive as in the shops of course!
Jess: Is your family selling anything?
Kelvin: Yes. We're selling my teddies. Look at them! I'm too old to play with them now!
Jess: What kinds of things do you want to buy?
Kelvin: For me, it's more important that the event goes well and fairly. We've been learning about how fair trade started. I'll send you some information.
Jess: Thanks! That sounds interesting.

Unit 7 Lesson 2

Activity Book

CD3 Track 14

AB page 71 Activity 3

Teacher: Before we start today's class I'd like to tell you about an event on Friday after school. I think some of you might already know about it because you'll be helping. It's a book, CD and DVD sale. All the money we raise will go to our local charities for this year. We're hoping to raise more than last year's total of €110. We'd like to raise €150 if we can.
The sale begins at 3:45 in the school hall. We're looking for four or five volunteers to help us set everything up at 3:15. Just let me know at the end of the class if you are interested.
We'd also like some volunteers to make small posters to put up outside the school. These need to include the time and date of the event. You should bring any posters you've made by Tuesday. Actually, let's change it to Wednesday so that you have more time to make them.
And of course encourage your family and friends to come along!
Does anybody have any questions?

Unit 7 Lesson 3

Pupil's Book

CD3 Track 15

PB page 75 Activity 2

Trading fairly with others
Who was the first person to help people in poor countries improve their trade? Some say it was Edna Ruth Byler.
In the 1940s, Edna was living in a small town in Pennsylvania, USA. She worked as a volunteer for a charity. In 1946, she travelled to Puerto Rico, an island in the Caribbean. She was shocked that the people were too poor to live comfortably. They had very little money and she wanted to find a way to help.
Edna had an idea. She loved the materials that the people were sewing, and thought that the materials in the USA weren't as beautiful. She decided to buy some and then sell them to people in the USA. The craftspeople were pleased. 'If you sell them all, we'll make more for you,' they said. Edna travelled from town to town and sold things from the boot of her car. She was a good salesperson and returned to Puerto Rico for more materials.
Edna was paying a fair price to the craftspeople and this helped them live better and improve their trade. Over the next 30 years, she worked with craftspeople in many poor countries. She suggested the kinds of crafts that would sell well in the USA and helped organise their trade.
There are many organisations now that help people in poorer countries improve their trade. They work with farmers of coffee, sugar, bananas and many other kinds of food in Asia, South America and Africa. They help them organise their production and teach their skills to each other so that their business can grow. The organisations also make sure that the producers are paid a fair price for the food and that this price doesn't suddenly go down.

Unit 7 Lesson 3

Activity Book

CD3 Track 16

AB page 72 Activity 2

Callum: Hi, Jess. What's that you're looking at?
Jess: It's a story that Kelvin sent me from Pennsylvania.
Callum: What's it about?
Jess: It's a true story about a volunteer called Edna Ruth Byler.
Callum: And what did she do?
Jess: Well, she was one of the first people to help poorer countries to improve their economy.
Callum: That's interesting. How did she do that?
Jess: She visited Puerto Rico in 1946 and while she was there she met some craftspeople. She bought some of the materials they were sewing. When she got back to the USA, she decided to sell them.
Callum: Did she have a shop?
Jess: Well, not at first. She travelled around from town to town with the materials in her car.
Callum: So, did she sell all the materials and decide to go back to Puerto Rico to buy some more?
Jess: Exactly! In the USA people loved the material. She helped the crafts people in Puerto Rico choose more materials to sell. She paid them a fair price, too, so they could pay more people to work for them.
Callum: Do you know if people still do this nowadays?
Jess: Yes, today there are organisations which work together with farmers to help them improve their lives.
Callum: Ah! I've seen the fair trade mark on some products we bought at the supermarket.
Jess: That means that those products are made by people who are paid a fair price for the food they grow.
Callum: Oh, right. I'm going to look out for those products when we go to the supermarket this afternoon.

Unit 7 Lesson 4

Pupil's Book

CD3 Track 17

PB page 76 Activity 1

Tom: Kelvin's information was really interesting. It's great that people try to help poorer countries trade successfully.
Jess: Yes. I've found out a lot more about fairtrade. If something is from fairtrade producers, it'll have a FAIRTRADE mark on it.
Tom: So do your family only buy fairtrade products?
Jess: Not always. If we buy fairtrade products, it'll help the workers in poorer countries. But the products are sometimes more expensive.
Tom: Look at these T-shirts. They've got a FAIRTRADE mark on them.
Jess: The cotton must be from fairtrade producers.

Unit 7 Lesson 4

Pupil's Book

CD3 Track 18

PB page 76 Activity 5

If it doesn't rain, I'll leave the bikes outside.
If you eat too much at night, you won't sleep well.

Unit 7 Lesson 4

Pupil's Book

CD3 Track 19

PB page 76 Activity 6

1 If you keep practising, you'll get better.
2 He'll be angry if you don't take out the rubbish.
3 If it's hot tomorrow, we'll take caps and sun cream.

Unit 7 Lesson 4

Activity Book

CD3 Track 20

AB page 73 Activity 3

1 If you don't tell me the answer, I'll get really upset.
2 I don't believe you. You always tell lies.

3 I really like the way the poster looks. It has a really good design.
4 I love listening to calm music.
5 My cousin never loses at table tennis. She's amazing.

Unit 7 Lesson 5

Pupil's Book

CD3 Track 21

PB page 77 Activity 1

1 loose
2 ripped
3 stained
4 scratched
5 bent
6 faulty
7 cracked

Unit 7 Lesson 5

Pupil's Book

CD3 Track 22

PB page 77 Activity 2

1 Which kite did Annie buy?
Man: So, Annie. Did you get the kite?
Girl: I did. I can't wait to use it.
Man: Which one did you buy in the end?
Girl: Well, I was going to get the stripy one, wasn't I? But then when I saw it in the shop, I didn't like it very much. And it was too expensive so I couldn't afford it.
Man: What other ones did they have?
Girl: There were two others that I liked: one was multi-coloured and one had blue and yellow spots. They didn't have any of the multi-coloured ones left so I bought the other one. I really like it, though!

2 Which of these is not a problem with the tent?
Woman: Well? Have you put up the new tent, Dylan?
Boy: No. I think we need to take it back to the shop.
Woman: Why? What's wrong with it?
Boy: At first I thought that part of the tent was ripped, but it wasn't. But then I saw that the door was stained – look, can you see? There's a green mark.
Woman: Hmmm, yes. That isn't good. But maybe we can wash it off.
Boy: Possibly, but I don't think so. And look at this! The left tent pole is completely bent.
Woman: Right! Well let's take it back to the shop this afternoon and see what they say.

Unit 7 Lesson 5

Pupil's Book

CD3 Track 23

PB page 77 Activity 3

Man: Hello. Can I help you?
Woman: Yes. I hope so. We bought this tent on Wednesday and there are some problems with it.
Man: Really? I'm sorry to hear that. Let's have a look.
Woman: The door of the tent is stained.
Boy: And look! One of the poles is bent.
Man: I'm really sorry about that. That's very unusual. Can I see your receipt?
Woman: Here you are.
Man: OK. Would you like your money back or would you like me to exchange it for another one?
Woman: Could we have another one, please?
Man: Sure. And we'll check it before you take it away.

Unit 7 Lesson 6

Activity Book

CD3 Track 24

AB page 75 Activity 3

Boy 1: Have you seen the posters? There's a sale on at Merton Sports all week.
Boy 2: Really? Which sports shop is that?
Boy 1: You know, it's the big one at number 135 Queen Street.
Boy 2: Ah, yes. I know where Queen street is. I might go on Saturday then. I need some new trainers.
Boy 1: If you wait until Saturday, you'll miss it. It finishes on Friday evening.
Boy 2: Oh no! I'm not sure I can get there before Saturday. Do you know what kinds of things are on sale?
Boy 1: All football and tennis equipment has a 10 per cent discount. I can't remember everything on the poster, but it said some tracksuits and T-shirts are half-price. You should get your new trainers there. The poster said they had 50 pairs of trainers for under €10!
Boy 2: Is it open late during the week?
Boy 1: Yes, it's open until 8 on Thuarsdays. It's open until 6 during the rest of the week.
Boy 2: That's good. I'll go there on Thursday then. Do you want to come with me?
Boy 1: Yes, why not? We have to remember to collect a free raffle ticket when we enter the shop. I think the first prize is a tent and there are sleeping bags for the second and third prizes.

Unit 7 Lesson 8

Pupil's Book

CD3 Track 25

PB page 80 Activity 2

Mark: Hey, Bella. Do your parents give you pocket money?
Bella: Yes, they do. I get £5 a week, but I have to help around the house.
Mark: What do you have to do?
Bella: I have to clear the table after dinner and keep my bedroom tidy.
Mark: What do you do with your money? Do you save it?
Bella: Yes. I put it in my moneybox.
Mark: Are you saving up for anything at the moment?
Bella: Yes. I want to buy a phone, but I've still got a lot of money to save.
Mark: Have you got any favourite shops?
Bella: I like Clara's. It sells things for doing art, like pencils, paper and paints. I really love art. Do you like Clara's?
Mark: Yes, because I love the posters in there. I like Weston's Books too. I love looking at all the books. I don't like buying them online. Does your family do their food shopping online?
Bella: Sometimes.

Unit 7 Video and 21st Century Skills

Activity Book

CD3 Track 26

AB page 79 Activity 1

Male: I want you to work in pairs. You have to make some smoothies. But you have to make some money for the school too! What will you use for your smoothies? How much will you sell them for?
Boy: OK. Let's look at the prices of the fruit. We need 2 kilograms of fruit. Let's buy some mangoes. I love mangoes.
Girl: But they're very expensive. I know a lot of people who don't like mango.
Boy: OK. Raspberries cost £8 for a kilogram.
Girl: That's good. Strawberries are £6 for a kilogram.
Boy: I think peaches and raspberries are good together. How much are the peaches?
Girl: They are £7. You're right. Let's buy one kilogram of raspberries and one kilogram of peaches.
Boy: Shall we buy some ice-cream too?
Girl: Yes, let's buy one box of vanilla ice cream. It's £4.
Boy: Yes, the raspberry ice cream is too expensive.
Girl: So. How much have we spent?
Boy: I think that's … £19. How many smoothies can we make?
Girl: With 2 kilograms of fruit we can make 20 smoothies.
Boy: So we can sell them for £1 each. That's £20.
Girl: But it costs £19. If we sell all the smoothies we will have £1. That's not enough. And it's a lot of work!
Boy: Good point! Let's sell the smoothies for £2 each.
Girl: OK. That sounds good.
Boy: Let's write this down.

Unit 8 Lesson 1

Pupil's Book

CD3 Track 27

PB page 82 Activity 2

1 scuba diving
2 coral
3 tropical fish
4 have a nap
5 palm tree
6 hammock
7 wildlife spotting
8 giant tortoise
9 boogie boarding
10 sea kayaking
11 sea lion
12 shore

Audioscript

Unit 8 Lesson 1

Pupil's Book

CD3 Track 28

PB page 82 Activity 3

1
Boy: These creatures live in the seas and oceans close to the equator. They're often brightly coloured. Some people like keeping them in tanks as pets.
Girl: tropical fish
2
Boy: This tall plant has got a long narrow trunk and no branches. At the top, there are large wide leaves.
Girl: palm tree
3
Boy: You do this activity in the sea or ocean. You lie down on a small flat board and surf on the waves.
Girl: boogie boarding
4
Boy: This enormous creature is only found on tropical islands like the Galapagos Islands. It's got a large hard shell and claws. It moves very slowly.
Girl: giant tortoise
5
Boy: This is the land that's on the edge of a river, a lake, the sea or the ocean. It can be sandy or rocky.
Girl: shore
6
Boy: You can do this underwater activity in the sea, the ocean, a lake or a swimming pool. You wear a tank on your back and breathe in oxygen through a tube.
Girl: scuba diving
7
Boy: This large marine animal lives in many places around the world. It's a mammal and it's got whiskers and a long nose. It swims very well.
Girl: sea lion
8
Boy: People often do this activity in the middle of the day, after lunch. It's a short sleep.
Girl: have a nap
9
Boy: This is a hard substance that grows in the sea or ocean. It's home to many tropical fish.
Girl: coral
10
Boy: This is a kind of bed. It's made of a large piece of cloth. You tie the cloth to a tree at each end.
Girl: hammock
11
Boy: You do this activity in the sea or ocean. You sit in a small boat and move it with a paddle.
Girl: sea kayaking
12
Boy: You usually need a pair of binoculars to do this activity. You need to move very slowly and quietly so you don't scare the animals.
Girl: wildlife spotting

Unit 8 Lesson 2

Pupil's Book

CD3 Track 29

PB page 84 Activity 1

Callum: Hi, Eva. We all think that your project is a brilliant idea.
Eva: Thanks, Callum. Here's a photo of a beach we've cleaned recently.
Callum: Wow! It looks amazing. Do you go to the beach every day?
Eva: Not really. I prefer meeting my friends in the town centre.
Callum: Really! If I lived in the Galapagos Islands, I'd swim in the sea every day. I wouldn't go to the town centre.
Eva: What else would you do?
Callum: If I lived there, I'd go sailing around the islands, too.
Eva: But the Pacific Ocean can be quite dangerous. I'll send you the link to a true story about a couple who were sailing near the islands.
Callum: What happened to them?
Eva: Ah! Read the story and see.

Unit 8 Lesson 2

Activity Book

CD3 Track 30

AB page 81 Activity 3

Joe: Hi, Michelle. What are you reading?
Michelle: Oh hi, Joe. I'm reading a really interesting magazine article. It's about the Galapagos Islands. I'd definitely go snorkelling if I went there! It would be great to swim next to sea lions and iguanas.
Joe: Iguanas! But I thought that iguanas didn't live on islands!
Michelle: Well, there are some marine iguanas in the Galapagos Islands. There are also dolphins, penguins and lots of tropical fish. The only thing that I wouldn't like to see is a shark. I think I'd be afraid if I saw one!
Joe: Yeah, they're scary. What else have you read in the article?
Michelle: Well, there are eighteen large islands, so lots of tourists travel by boat. It's faster and you can get closer to the animals that way. Would you like to travel by boat if you went there, Joe?
Joe: It's a good idea, but I think I'd feel sea sick if I did that. Which animals can you see on land?
Michelle: The most famous animal is the giant tortoise, of course. You can only find them on the Galapagos Islands. If I saw a giant tortoise, I'd take lots of photos.
Joe: Me too.
Michelle: Another exciting activity you can do is to visit some pirates' caves. You walk through an old lava tunnel underground. Look! Here's a photo. It looks really dark and creepy.
Joe: Cool! I'd definitely take a torch if I did that.
Michelle: It would be fantastic to visit the Galapagos Islands, wouldn't it?
Joe: Yes, it would.

Unit 8 Lesson 3

Pupil's Book

CD3 Track 31

PB page 85 Activity 2

A dream trip

If you could go to New Zealand, how would you travel? In 1972 a British couple, Maurice and Maralyn Bailey, decided to sell their house and sail there in a 9.4 metre yacht called *Auralyn*. Eight months later, the couple were still enjoying their adventure. However, while they were sailing towards the Galapagos Islands, their luck changed. One morning, an enormous whale smashed its tail against the side of their yacht and the yacht began sinking. The couple filled two small lifeboats with the food and equipment they needed to survive and abandoned their yacht.

At first, Maralyn and Maurice were optimistic. They expected to be rescued quickly because they were in a busy shipping lane. They also had plenty of food and water, a map, a compass, knives and a first aid kit. However, the passing ships couldn't see their tiny lifeboats and the couple soon finished all their food.

As the days passed, life became more difficult. The lifeboats were small and old and they were in danger of sinking. There were also terrible storms and giant waves overturned the lifeboats three times. To make things worse, sharks often banged the bottom of the lifeboats, looking for food.

Maurice and Maralyn were lost at sea for 117 days, drinking rainwater and eating sea turtles to survive. It was very difficult, but they encouraged each other to be positive. They told stories, made up games and planned celebrations for the future. Finally, a Korean fishing boat saw the couple. They were hungry, thirsty and sunburnt, but they were alive.

Would you ever go on a sailing trip like Maralyn and Maurice?

Unit 8 Lesson 3

Activity Book

CD3 Track 32

AB page 82 Activity 2

Tom: What are you doing Callum?
Callum: I'm reading a true story about a couple who wanted to sail to New Zealand.
Tom: Sail to New Zealand? How lucky!
Callum: It sounds fantastic, doesn't it? And the trip began well. They left the UK and after about eight months they got to the Pacific Ocean.
Tom: Wow!
Callum: But then, while they were sailing to the Galapagos Islands, disaster struck.
Tom: What happened?
Callum: This is my favourite moment in the story. A whale attacked the yacht and it began sinking.
Tom: Did they have a lifeboat?
Callum: Yes, fortunately they did. They had two lifeboats, but they were very small and old.
Tom: How did they survive?
Callum: Well, they had plenty of food and drink at first. And then, when that was finished, they caught sea turtles to eat. They also drank rainwater. Finding out what the couple ate and drank in the lifeboats was the most interesting part of the story for me.

Tom: Was there anything you didn't like?
Callum: I suppose the part I least liked was when the sharks appeared.
Tom: There were sharks?
Callum: Yes, they were banging the bottom of the lifeboats, looking for food.
Tom: That's terrifying.
Callum: I know. That's why I wouldn't recommend this story to small children. It's too scary.

Unit 8 Lesson 4

Pupil's Book

CD3 Track 33

PB page 86 Activity 1

Callum: The couple survived 117 days in their lifeboats. Would you sell your house and sail around the world?
Jess: No, I wouldn't. What would you take if you had to abandon a boat?
Callum: I'd take plenty of food and water. What would you take?
Jess: Hmm… If I had to abandon a boat, I'd take a radio.
Callum: That's a good idea. You could radio for help then.
Jess: I know, but I'd be very hungry and thirsty.
Callum: Actually, I feel a bit hungry now. Let's go and get a snack!

Unit 8 Lesson 4

Pupil's Book

CD3 Track 34

PB page 86 Activity 5

1 I'd climb a volcano.
2 They eat a pizza.
3 We'd play the guitar.
4 You'd speak French.
5 I go to bed early.
6 They'd help me.

Unit 8 Lesson 4

Activity Book

CD3 Track 35

AB page 83 Activity 3

1 I'd visit the museum.
2 They play golf in the afternoon.
3 We'd swim with dolphins.
4 You read a guide book.
5 We go to the library.
6 They'd catch a cold.
7 I'd take my camera.
8 You'd study hard.

Unit 8 Lesson 5

Pupil's Book

CD3 Track 36

PB page 87 Activity 1

1 win the lottery
2 get lost
3 travel back in time
4 be invisible
5 be the president
6 travel in space
7 meet a famous person
8 have three wishes

Unit 8 Lesson 5

Pupil's Book

CD3 Track 37

PB page 87 Activity 2

1 If Paul travelled back in time, which period would he visit?
Girl: Hi, Paul. What are you doing?
Boy: I'm reading a science fiction novel. It's about a scientist who travels back to the time of the Romans.
Girl: Wow! Would you like to travel back in time?
Boy: Absolutely!
Girl: If you travelled back in time, which period would you visit?
Boy: I'm not sure. I wouldn't go back to the prehistoric period where the dinosaurs lived as that would be too dangerous. I'd probably choose Ancient Egypt. I could visit a pyramid then.
Girl: Do you think people will travel back in time in the future?
Boy: It's very unlikely, but you never know.

2 If Lucy met a famous person, what would she do?
Boy: What are you reading?
Girl: It's a magazine. It's got lots of information about famous actors and singers.
Boy: Have you ever met a famous person?
Girl: No, I haven't.
Boy: What would you do if you met a famous person? Would you ask for a photo or shake their hand?
Girl: I don't think I'd take a photo of them or shake their hand. But I'd ask for an autograph.
Boy: Do you think you'll meet a famous person in the future?
Girl: I doubt it, but you never know.

Unit 8 Lesson 6

Activity Book

CD3 Track 38

AB page 85 Activity 3

Boy: Have you ever read any of the 'Wimpy Kid' books, Emma?
Girl: Yes, I have. I've read them all. They're brilliant.
Boy: What are they about?
Girl: They're about a boy called Greg Heffley. He goes to middle school in the USA .
Boy: Was the Wimpy Kid on TV?
Girl: Hmm … I don't think so. Let's have a look on the Internet. Here's some interesting information. It says that the Wimpy Kid first appeared on a website. Then, it became so popular that the author decided to write a book.
Boy: Who's the author?
Girl: His name is Jeff Kinney and he's American. He draws all the cartoons in the Wimpy Kid books and he designs computer games, too.
Boy: Did it take him long to write the first book?
Girl: Let me see … Oh! Yes, it did. He first had the idea for the book in 1998 and the book was published in 2007. So it took him nine years.

Unit 8 Lesson 8

Pupil's Book

CD3 Track 39

PB page 90 Activity 2

Sam: Hey, Ben. Would you like to travel in time?
Ben: Umm, I'm not sure. What about you?
Sam: Perhaps. I think it would be interesting.
Ben: Really? Would you go to the future or the past?
Sam: Good question. I think I'd go to the past.
Ben: How many years would you travel?
Sam: I'd travel millions of years. I'd go to the prehistoric age.
Ben: Wow! What would you see there?
Sam: I'd see the dinosaurs, of course.
Ben: And what would you do?
Sam: I'd take some photos with my phone. And maybe I'd record a video.
Ben: But what would you do if a dinosaur saw you?
Sam: I don't know … I'd travel back to the present – FAST!

Unit 8 Video and 21st Century Skills

Activity Book

CD 3 Track 40

AB page 89 Activity 1

Older Girl: Where are you going, Amal?
Girl: I'm going to Beth's house. Me, Beth and Emma are doing a science project together.
Older Girl: You don't look very happy.
Girl: It's our first time working together and I'm worried that we'll argue.
Older Girl: Don't worry. Working in a group is cool. You just need to remember a few things.
Girl: Like what?
Older Girl: Well, the most important thing is to make sure everyone participates. It's no fun if some people do all the work and other people do nothing.
Girl: You're right. That's not fair. What can I do if that happens?
Older Girl: You can ask everyone for their opinion. That usually works.
Girl: OK. What else?
Older Girl: It's important to take turns to speak – don't all speak at the same time - and you need to listen carefully to what the others say.
Girl: OK.
Older Girl: Finally, it's important to be open to new ideas.
Girl: What do you mean?
Older Girl: Maybe somebody has got an idea that you haven't thought of. Don't just say no, think about the idea. It might be brilliant.
Girl: You're right. Thanks Zoe.
OlderGirl: You're welcome. Have fun doing the project!

Audioscript

Unit 9 Lesson 1

Pupil's Book

CD3 Track 41

PB page 92 Activity 2

1 chalk
2 blackboard
3 rows of desks
4 easel
5 canvas
6 oil paints
7 goggles
8 laboratory
9 overall
10 interactive whiteboard
11 laptop
12 headphones

Unit 9 Lesson 1

Pupil's Book

CD3 Track 42

PB page 92 Activity 3

1
Girl: This is a soft white rock. It's used for writing or drawing on a blackboard.
Boy: chalk
2
Girl: This is a wooden structure. You put your canvas on it when you're painting a picture.
Boy: easel
3
Girl: This is something that you wear on top of your clothes when you work. It looks like a coat and it keeps your clothes clean.
Boy: overall
4
Girl: This object is flat and rectangular. You usually find it on a classroom wall and you use chalk to write on it.
Boy: blackboard
5
Girl: This is a small flat computer. It's easy to carry from place to place.
Boy: laptop
6
Girl: This is a large board that's connected to a computer in a classroom. You write on it using a special pen.
Boy: interactive whiteboard
7
Girl: This is a line of things that you sit at in a classroom.
Boy: row of desks
8
Girl: You use these when you want to paint on a canvas. They're thick and oily and you need a paintbrush to use them.
Boy: oil paints
9
Girl: This is a place where people do scientific experiments. You need to protect your clothes and your eyes when you work here.
Boy: laboratory
10
Girl: This is a strong piece of fabric that you paint on. It's usually white and square or rectangular.
Boy: canvas
11
Girl: You wear these over your ears. They're used for listening to music or sound.
Boy: headphones
12
Girl: You wear these when you do experiments or when you make things in a workshop. They protect your eyes.
Boy: goggles

Unit 9 Lesson 2

Pupil's Book

CD4 Track 1

PB page 94 Activity 1

Tom: Hi, Sven. My class loved your photos and we think that the project is a great idea.
Sven: Thanks, Tom. I really enjoy listening to the grandparents talking about the past.
Tom: Was school very different when they were young?
Sven: Yes, it was. Teachers used to be a lot stricter.
Tom: And were the classrooms different, too?
Sven: Absolutely. Pupils didn't use to have laptops or calculators then.
Tom: Did they use to have books?
Sven: Yes, of course. But before they had books, pupils used to use one of these.
Tom: What is it? It looks like a tablet.
Sven: It's a slate. Pupils used to write on it with chalk.
Tom: Wow! Things have changed a lot since then.
Sven: I know. But progress is very important. I'll send you some information about important prizes for progress in Sweden.

Unit 9 Lesson 2

Activity Book

CD4 Track 2

AB page 91 Activity 3

Jane: What are you reading, Luke?
Luke: I'm reading some information about schools in the past. It's quite interesting.
Jane: Were schools very different then?
Luke: Absolutely. There used to be lots of rules.
Jane: What kinds of rules?
Luke: Well, for example, the pupils had to stand up when they answered a question.
Jane: Really? What about when the pupils asked a question? Did they stand up then?
Luke: Oh, no. Pupils weren't allowed to ask questions. That was strictly forbidden.
Jane: Really?
Luke: Pupils had to be very punctual, too. If they were late, they were punished.
Jane: That's awful! What other rules were there?
Luke: Well, girls and boys had to study different things. The girls had to do needlework and the boys had to do technical drawing.
Jane: That's not very fair!
Luke: I know. Did you know that pupils weren't allowed to write with their left hand?
Jane: I don't believe it!
Luke: Well, it's true. They had to use their right hand to write.
Jane: Wow!

Unit 9 Lesson 3

Pupil's Book

CD4 Track 3

PB page 95 Activity 2

The Nobel Prizes
Narrator: The Nobel prizes are named after a Swedish scientist called Alfred Nobel. The prizes are awarded every year to people who have helped make the world a safer and better place.
Frame 1
Narrator: Alfred Nobel was born in Stockholm in 1833, but when he was nine his family moved to Russia. Alfred used to spend a lot of time studying.
Alfred's father: What are you doing, Alfred?
Alfred: I'm doing a chemistry experiment, Father.
Frame 2
Narrator: When Alfred was older, he moved back to Sweden where he created a new explosive material.
Alfred: This material is called dynamite. I think it'll change the world.
Frame 3
Narrator: Alfred became a very rich man. Then, in 1888, he had a terrible shock. A French newspaper thought that he was dead and published his obituary by mistake.
Alfred: Alfred Nobel, the Swedish chemist who became rich from destruction, has died.
Frame 4
Narrator: Alfred didn't want people to remember him like that. So he decided to change his story before it was too late.
Alfred:I'm going to use my money to create prizes for progress in physics, chemistry, medicine, literature and peace.
Frame 5
Narrator: Since then, many well-known people have won a Nobel Prize. These include Nelson Mandela, who fought for peace in South Africa, and Marie Curie, who discovered radium.
Frame 6
Narrator: In 2014, a seventeen-year-old girl from Pakistan called Malala Yousafzai won the Nobel Peace Prize. Malala couldn't go to the school in her village and demanded the right for all children to receive an education.

Unit 9 Lesson 3

Activity Book

CD4 Track 4

AB page 92 Activity 2

Tom: Look at this, Callum.
Callum: What is it?
Tom: It's some information about the Nobel prizes. Sven sent it to me.
Callum: Is it interesting?
Tom: It is, actually. Did you know that Alfred Nobel was the inventor of dynamite?
Callum: No, I didn't.
Tom: It made him very rich and he used the money to create the Nobel prizes.
Callum: Oh, I didn't know that.
Tom: And did you know that there are six Nobel prizes?

Callum: No, I didn't. I thought that there were only five. What's the sixth prize for?
Tom: I've just checked on the Internet. It's for progress in Economics.
Callum: Which prize do you think is the most important?
Tom: Hmm … I think the peace prize is definitely the most important.
Callum: Me too. Did you know that a school girl from Pakistan received the Nobel peace prize in 2014?
Tom: Oh, yes! I remember her. Her name is Malala and she was 17 years-old when she won it.
Callum: Why was she given the Nobel peace prize?
Tom: Well, she couldn't go to school so she wrote a blog to tell the world about it. It was a very dangerous thing to do!
Callum: Wow, I think she's really brave!

Unit 9 Lesson 4

Pupil's Book

CD4 Track 5

PB page 96 Activity 1

Tom: That was a really cool story. Shall we find out more about the Nobel Prizes?
Jess: OK! I'll find out about the prize ceremony.
Tom: And I'll look for information about Malala.
Later …
Tom: What did you find out, Jess?
Jess: Well, the ceremony is held every year. The next one is going to be in December. What did you find out about Malala?
Tom: She's amazing. She's also won lots of other prizes for her work, and she's written a book.
Jess: Is she going to continue working for the rights of children?
Tom: Yes, she is. And I think she'll win many more prizes in the future.

Unit 9 Lesson 4

Pupil's Book

CD4 Track 6

PB page 96 Activity 5

1 I'm going to watch TV.
2 What are you going to do?
3 She's going to get married.
4 They're going to go tomorrow.
5 He's going to wash the dishes.
6 I'm going to go shopping later.

Unit 9 Lesson 4

Activity Book

CD4 Track 7

AB page 93 Activity 3

1 Where are you going to go?
2 They're going to do their homework.
3 Are you going to ride your bike?
4 He's going to wash the dishes.
5 They aren't going to go to the cinema.

Unit 9 Lesson 5

Pupil's Book

CD4 Track 8

PB page 97 Activity 1

1 timetable
2 locker
3 Physics
4 geometry set
5 Chemistry
6 musical instrument
7 Literature
8 sports kit

Unit 9 Lesson 5

Pupil's Book

CD4 Track 9

PB page 97 Activity 2

1 Which new subject is Anna going to study next year?
Boy: It's almost the end of the school year.
Girl: I know. I can't believe that we're going to go to secondary school in September.
Boy: How do you feel about going to a new school? Are you worried?
Girl: Not really. My sister goes to secondary school and she says it's great.
Boy: Why?
Girl: Well, you make lots of new friends and there are some new school subjects, too.
Boy: That sounds good.
Girl: Yes. I love reading so I'm looking forward to studying Literature.
Boy: Are we going to study Physics and Chemistry next year, too?
Girl: I'm not sure. I think we'll study those when we're older.

2 Where's Anna going to keep her books in secondary school?
Girl: Do you know that you have to change classrooms a lot in secondary school?
Boy: What do you mean?
Girl: Well, there's a classroom for each subject. And at the end of a lesson, you put all your things in your bag and go to another classroom.
Boy: Uff. Your school bag must get very heavy.
Girl: A bit… but you can have a locker if you want.
Boy: Are you going to have a locker?
Girl: Absolutely. I'm excited about having one. It's better than a school desk because you can decorate it with photos and postcards.

Unit 9 Lesson 6

Activity Book

CD4 Track 10

AB page 95 Activity 4

Radio presenter: You're listening to Radio FM and I'm Peter Goodman. On today's programme we're going to talk to our favourite agony aunt, Fran Waters. Welcome to the show, Fran.
Fran: Thank you. I'm very happy to be here.
Radio presenter: What are you going to talk about today?
Fran: Well, last week I received a letter from an eleven-year-old pupil called Tim. He told me he was very worried about his summer exams. So I'm going to talk about how to prepare for exams.
Radio presenter: What advice have you got? Is it important to revise before an exam?
Fran: Of course it is. But you need to take regular breaks. You should revise for a short period of time, about 45 minutes, and then take a break. After about 15 minutes, you can continue revising.
Radio presenter: Should you study a lot the night before an exam?
Fran: Quite the contrary. It isn't a good idea to revise too much the night before an exam. Remember that you need plenty of sleep! The best thing is to read your notes one last time and then have an early night.
Radio presenter: Is there any more advice you can give us?
Fran: Well, you need to be prepared on the day. Make sure that you have all the things you need, for example, rulers, a calculator or a geometry set.
Radio presenter: Well, I think that's all for today! Thank you very much, Fran.

Unit 9 Lesson 8

Pupil's Book

CD4 Track 11

PB page 100 Activity 2

Nicole: Did you go to nursery school, Lucy?
Lucy: Yes, I did. I went there when I was three.
Nicole: What was it like?
Lucy: I don't remember very much, but I liked it.
Nicole: Did you use to wear a … erm …
Lucy: What?
Nicole: I don't know the word, but it's the thing that you wear at nursery school. You wear it over your clothes.
Lucy: Ah! You mean an overall.
Nicole: Yes, that's right. Did you use to wear an overall?
Lucy: Yes, I did.
Nicole: What about next year? Are you going to go to secondary school?
Lucy: Yes, I am. I'm looking forward to it.
Nicole: What's it like?
Lucy: It's really big and there are hundreds of students, but you can do some cool things.
Nicole: That sounds great. Would you like to go to university in the future?
Lucy: I think so, but I'm not 100% sure. Anyway, what about you?

Unit 9 Video and 21st Century Skills

Activity Book

CD 4 Track 12

AB page 99 Activity 1

1
Male adult: What's up, Tony? You don't look very happy.
Boy: I can't do my homework.
Male adult: Why not?

Audioscript

Boy: Because I've left my books at school. [getting anxious] I'm worried that the teacher will be angry with me.
Male: Calm down – I'm sure there's a solution. Think about what you can do.
Boy: Maybe I could borrow the books from my friend, Tim.
Male adult: That's a good idea.
Boy: I'll phone him now. Thanks dad.
Male: You're welcome.
2
Female adult: Are you OK, Dina?
Girl: No, not really…
Female adult: What's the matter?
Girl: I want to give up ice skating.
Female adult: Oh! Why's that?
Girl: Because I don't do it very well. Mary ice skates much better than me.
Female adult: Do you feel jealous?
[Girl: No, of course not. Mary's my friend.
Female adult: So what's the problem?
Girl: When I try to do a jump, I fall over. I've tried hundreds of times and I can't do it!
Female adult: I know it's frustrating, but you'll do it in the end.
Girl: Really?
Female adult: Of course. Next time you fall down, count to ten and then try again. Don't give up!
Girl: You're right. Thanks Mum.

Project 3 Lesson 1

Activity Book

CD4 Track 13

AB page 100 Activity 1

Radio presenter: Hello and welcome to *Go Back in Time*. Today we talk to Joan Rushton about her experience of life in England in the 1950s. Can you tell us a bit about what growing up in the 50s was like?
Joan: Yes, of course. When I think about growing up, I think about playing out on the street. All the children in the neighbourhood played together. I remember every day after school, the boys used to have a big game of football and the girls used to play with skipping ropes.
Radio presenter: Didn't the girls play football?
Joan: Well, I wanted to sometimes but the boys didn't like it. They didn't think it was a sport for girls!
Radio presenter: That's different today, isn't it? So, you played outside a lot?
Joan: Yes, even when it was quite cold. But we had to come inside to do our chores.
Radio presenter: Ah. So you helped at home?
Joan: Oh yes. My sister and I had our own jobs to do. I used to lay the table for dinner and sweep the floor. My sister had to help my mum hang the washing and fold the dry clothes. We didn't have a washing machine then.
Radio presenter: And what kind of food did you eat?
Joan: We had lunch at school. I think most children did then. It was usually some meat, potatoes and vegetables. We always had a warm pudding – the jam sponge was delicious! Oh, and in those days all our fruit came from the UK, so we didn't have bananas, and we only had strawberries for a few weeks in the summer.
Radio presenter: And not many people had a fridge – is that true?
Joan: Yes, that's absolutely true. Only a few people had a fridge. We had to buy food every day because it was hard to keep it cold.
Radio presenter: So your parents went shopping every day?
Joan: My parents? Well, no – just my mother! In those days, men went to work and women were housewives. And one of the things they had to do was go shopping every day. They got their bread from the bakers, meat from the butchers, vegetables from the greengrocer's. These days people just go to the supermarket for everything.
Radio presenter: That's really interesting …

Festivals

Thanksgiving Day

Pupil's Book

CD4 Track 14

PB page 104 Activity 4

T*hanksgiving Day is coming soon*
U*nder orange leaves of autumn.*
R*emember what it's all about*
K*indness, happiness and fun.*
E*very year we invite our friends*
Y*ou can come too if you want!*

Festivals

Endangered Species Day

Pupil's Book

CD4 Track 15

PB page 105 Activity 4

1 This animal doesn't live in or near the sea.
2 This animal hunts from the sea ice.
3 Humans sometimes catch this animal by accident.
4 This animal lives in Asia.
5 There are fewer than 1,000 of these animals left.
6 A hundred years ago, there were more than 200,000 of these animals.

Song Bank Unit 1

Pupil's Book

CD4 Track 16

PB page 125 Activity 2

It's delayed!
We got to the airport early,
And checked in all our bags.
Our holiday was beginning.
We started to relax.

And then we heard the loudspeaker,
Delay, delay, delay!
Flight 619 to Paris,
It's delayed.

I decided to buy a milkshake,
A comic and a shirt.
We walked around the airport,
Until our feet began to hurt.

And then we heard the loudspeaker,
Delay, delay, delay!
Flight 619 to Paris,
It's delayed.

I suggested playing a board game,
I wanted something to do.
Waiting was getting boring,
I got the airport delay blues!

And then we heard the loudspeaker,
Delay, delay, delay!
Flight 619 to Paris,
It's delayed.

Suddenly we heard a voice say
'Now it's time to board.'
We were on our way to Paris,
Starting our grand tour.

CD4 Track 17

PB page 125 Activity 2

Karaoke version: *It's delayed!* song

Song Bank Unit 3

Pupil's Book

CD4 Track 18

PB page 125 Activity 2

I want to grow some vegetables
I want to grow some vegetables,
I want to grow some fruit.
You will be amazed,
As the seeds turn into shoots.
I want to grow some vegetables.
Get your plates ready, please.
Soon you will be eating my tomatoes and my peas!

The first step is to plant the seeds.
They should be in a row.
Then we wait and see
How many shoots begin to grow.

I need to give them water,
And protect them from the snails.
Then I'll watch as peas
And beans crawl upwards on the rails.

And later, in the summer,
I'll take my basket out
And collect up all the vegetables,
That have grown all around.

I want to grow some vegetables,
I want to grow some fruit.
You will be amazed,
As the seeds turn into shoots.
I want to grow some vegetables.
Get your plates ready, please.
Soon you will be eating my tomatoes and my peas!

CD4 Track 19

PB page 125 Activity 2

Karaoke version: *I want to grow some vegetables* song

Song Bank Unit 4

Pupil's Book

CD4 Track 20

PB page 126 Activity 2

The quiz
Who was it sung by?
When was it made?
Where did it happen first?
How is it played?
It's time to start thinking.
My pencil's ready now.
I love doing quizzes.
I love doing quizzes. Do you?

The first round is science
It's fish and plants and birds.
We work out all the answers.
We write down all the words.

The second round is music.
It's jazz and rock and pop.
We recognise the singer,
Before the song has stopped.

The final round is films.
It's actors, quotes and dates.
Our score is our best ever,
We finish in third place!

Who was it sung by?
When was it made?
Where did it happen first?
How is it played?
It's time to start thinking.
My pencil's ready now.
I love doing quizzes.
I love doing quizzes. Do you?

CD4 Track 21

PB page 126 Activity 2

Karaoke version: *The quiz* song

Song Bank Unit 6

Pupil's Book

CD4 Track 22

PB page 126 Activity 2

The future is far away
Do you think you'll be famous?
Do you think you'll be a star?
Who knows what will happen anyway?
The future is so far away.

I might be an archaeologist,
A politician or a vet.
Or I might be a fisherman,
I haven't decided yet.

I might be a photographer,
Taking photos for the news.
It might be nice to work outside
In theme parks or in zoos.

Do you think you'll be famous?
Do you think you'll be a star?
Who knows what will happen anyway?
The future is so far away.

I might be a researcher,
And find important cures.
Or I could work as a tour guide,
Giving brilliant city tours.

I might be a sports star,
An actor or a singer.
But as long as I'm happy,
I will always be a winner!

Do you think you'll be famous?
Do you think you'll be a star?
Who knows what will happen anyway?
The future is so far away.

CD4 Track 23

PB page 126 Activity 2

Karaoke version: *The future is far away* song

Song Bank Unit 7

Pupil's Book

CD4 Track 24

PB page 127 Activity 2

Window shopping
I'm walking down the high street,
An empty wallet in my pocket.
I know it's too expensive,
But I'd love that airblast rocket.

So for now I'm window shopping,
On the outside looking in.
Window shopping, window shopping.

I'm walking past the clothes shop,
I can see a trendy jacket.
If I save my money wisely,
I'll have enough to get it.

So for now I'm window shopping,
On the outside looking in.
Window shopping, window shopping.

I'm walking past the music shop.
There's a red guitar that rocks!
If I help around the house,
I'll fill my moneybox.

So for now I'm window shopping,
On the outside looking in.
Window shopping, window shopping.

Now it's two months later,
And my wallet's nearly popping!
I'm going to buy my favourite things,
So goodbye to window shopping!

I'm no longer window shopping,
On the outside looking in.
No more window shopping, no more window shopping.

CD4 Track 25

PB page 127 Activity 2

Karaoke version: *Window shopping* song

Song Bank Unit 9

Pupil's Book

CD4 Track 26

PB page 127 Activity 2

Life was very different
I love the first week of the month.
It's the time my granny stays.
We sit on armchairs by the fire,
She talks about the 'good old days.'

And she always says
Life was very different.
No computers or Internet,
Life was very different.
It was all so simple then.

Her stories of how things used to be,
Keep me listening to the end.
She tells me of the games she played,
And the letters she used to send.

And she always says
Life was very different.
No computers or Internet,
Life was very different.
It was all so simple then.

She sometimes plays me records
Of her very favourite tunes.
She used to dance with Grandad,
Round and round the living room.

And she always says
Life was very different.
No computers or Internet,
Life was very different.
It was all so simple then.

She's got hundreds of fading photos,
Of old-fashioned bikes with bells.
I wish I could travel back in time,
And see it for myself.

And she always says
Life was very different.
No computers or Internet,
Life was very different.
It was all so simple then.

CD4 Track 27

PB page 127 Activity 2

Karaoke version: *Life was very different* song

Audioscript

Unit 1

Cambridge Exams Practice

Activity Book

CD4 Track 28

AB page 120 Activity 1

1

M: I'm pleased I agreed to come with you to the museum. It was good fun. I didn't think a museum about transport could be so good.
F: Yes, it's good, isn't it? The room about air travel is amazing. Did you go inside the helicopter?
M: I did. That was interesting. I think I preferred the rooms about the history of travel. Some of the stories were amazing and pretty scary too!
F: Do you want to go again one day?
M: Yes, it's a really big place. There's a lot more I'd like to see there.

2

M: You promised to tell me about your trip to London yesterday. How did it go?
F: I haven't told you because it was a bit of a disaster.
M: Really? What happened?
F: Well, when I was on the bus I realized I didn't have my train ticket. So I had to go home. When I got to the station, the train wasn't there. I missed my train! I had to wait for over an hour for the next train. I was so bored.
M: But did you enjoy being in London?
F: I did, I suppose. But I didn't have much time to do anything. Next time I will remember my ticket!

3

F: I'm finally going to start riding a bike. I can't believe I still don't know how to.
M: I can help you to learn. You'll be fine. You need to make sure the bike is the right size for you and not too small. You need to find a quiet place to practise. There's a place in the park where there are no cars. That's better than starting on the road.
F: OK. Thanks!

4

F: I went to see that film yesterday. I really liked it a lot. I laughed loads!
M: Did you? I liked it but I didn't think it was that funny. The main characters were really interesting I thought. I didn't think they were going to be friends at the end but I was wrong.
F: Yes, that was a clever ending, wasn't it? I was surprised by that too. The music wasn't my kind of thing, though. And there was a lot of it.
M: Really? Did you think so? Some of that music was brilliant, especially in the long scene at the end.

Unit 2

Cambridge Exams Practice

Activity Book

CD4 Track 29

AB page 121 Activity 1

Int: In today's programme we're going to talk to a local gymnast; fourteen year old Clare Evans. Hi, Clare.
Girl: Hi.
Int: When did you start gymnastics? Were you very young?
Girl: Not really. I wanted to start when I was three, but I couldn't because I was too young. I had to wait until I started school two years later.
Int: How often do you do gymnastics now?
Girl: I do it most days. I train on Monday, Wednesday and Friday and then I do competitions at the weekend.
Int: Can you tell us a little bit about the competitions?
Girl: Well, the first thing to say is that they're long, three or four hours, but I think that's ok. Some children get stressed, but I enjoy them. I have fun with my friends and I always learn something new.
Int: And have you ever won a medal?
Girl: Yes, I've won lots of medals. I've won twelve gold medals this year. I didn't win gold in the last competition. I only got a silver medal. But that's ok.
Int: What about when you aren't doing gymnastics? What do you do in your free time?
Girl: I have to do my homework, of course. But I usually find time to meet my friends. We usually chat about films. I love mystery films).
Int: And what about the future?
Girl: I'd love to compete in an international competition, like the Olympic Games. I know it's very difficult, but I've got a fantastic gymnastics teacher and I'm prepared to work hard.
Int: Well, lots of luck and thank you for coming.
Girl: You're welcome.

Unit 3

Cambridge Exams Practice

Activity Book

CD4 Track 30

AB page 122 Activity 1

A lot of people were asking me about the new gardening club. It's called Rushton Green Club. They grow all sorts of things there including tomatoes, peas, beans and strawberries. We've decided to do it at the weekend and not during the school week. So it will be on Saturday and Sunday mornings from 10 o'clock to midday.
Now, the important thing is that it is not going to be at the school. If you turn left out of the school and continue to the end of the road you will see a sign for the club. It's on the corner of Mill Lane and Bridge Street.
If you would like to go, you can just turn up there at 10. You will need to wear boots and it's useful to have gloves too.
The club needs as much help as possible, so ask your brothers, sisters and parents to come along too!
The teacher in charge is Mr Webber. That's the Mr Webber with two Bs! W-E-B-B-E-R. You can ask him if you have any questions. He is usually in room 291 at lunch time.

Unit 4

Cambridge Exams Practice

Activity Book

CD4 Track 31

AB page 123 Activity 1

1 Which kind of film are Peter and Jo going to see?
Peter: Which film shall we see, Jo?
Jo: I don't mind. Anything except a romantic film.
Peter: There's a comedy and an action film. Which do you prefer?
Jo: I like them both, but I saw a comedy on TV last night.
Peter: So let's watch the action film then.

2 Where was Ana last night?
Ben: Hi, Ana. How was the cinema last night?
Ana: We didn't go in the end.
Ben: Why not? You love the cinema.
Ana: I know. But my sister had some tickets for an art exhibition so we went there.
Ben: Was it any good?
Ana: It wasn't as good as the cinema or the theatre, but it was ok.

3 What can you watch at seven o'clock?
TV presenter: If you like basketball, don't miss the big game this evening. Spain's playing France and it starts at 8. Before that, at 7, there's a treat for animal lovers. We're showing the prize winning documentary *Dolphin Spy*. But first, it's 6:30 and time for the national and international news.

Unit 5

Cambridge Exams Practice

Activity Book

CD4 Track 32

AB page 124 Activity 1

Interviewer: Today we're going to speak to Oliver Dennis. He's joined a group that helps people who can't see well. Is that right, Oliver?
Oliver: Yes, that's right.
Interviewer: Can you tell us more about it?
Oliver: Sure. My grandmother has always had difficulty with her eyes. When I visited her after school, she often asked me to read newspaper articles to her. She loved it. She said I had a very clear voice. She even invited a friend of hers to listen to me once!
Interviewer: You were a very popular young man.
Oliver: I actually enjoyed doing it. I learnt a lot about what was happening around the world.
Interviewer: Then what happened?
Oliver: Someone told me there was a group called *Talking News*. This group meets every week to read interesting news articles. They record the articles and put them on CDs and memory sticks. Then they send them to people to listen to. So I became a volunteer. They were pleased to have a younger voice. Most people who volunteer are over 60.

Interviewer: So do you choose which articles to read?
Oliver: Not really. Two people decide which articles we're going to read. They make sure that none of the articles repeat information. Then each week, three people meet to read the articles. It isn't the same people each time. We take turns. For example, I go in every three weeks for two hours. We record them at a radio studio. It's really good fun.
Interviewer: And do you still read the newspaper to your grandmother?
Oliver: Of course. I read books to her, too. I started reading her one of the Harry Potter books, but she didn't like it at all. She prefers detective stories. I might try some historical novels, too, although I don't know if she'll like them.
Interviewer: Maybe it's best to continue with the detective stories. Have you thought about the future? Maybe you'd like a job in radio?
Oliver: I'm not sure about that. It's certainly fun at the moment, but I might find other things I enjoy, too!

Unit 6

Cambridge Exams Practice

Activity Book

CD4 Track 33

AB page 125 Activity 1

Hello, everyone. Thank you for inviting me. My name is Susan Philips and I've been an astronaut for ten years. In this time, I've been on five space expeditions. I know some of you are interested in becoming astronauts, so I'm here to explain what you need to do.
First, you need to study very hard. All astronauts have to go to university to get a scientific degree, for example maths, science or engineering. Lots of astronauts learn how to fly a plane too. For these reasons, astronauts don't usually begin their space training until they are about thirty years old.
Languages are very important. That's because astronauts come from different countries and they need to communicate with each other when they are in space. There are the two international space languages; English and Russian, so you have to speak these very well.
You also need to be fit and healthy. And when you're in space you need to exercise every day or your bones and muscles get weak. Astronauts need to be sociable too. They live and work in a very small space so they must get on together.
You can see that it's a lot of work to become an astronaut, but it's also one of the most exciting jobs in the world. Have you got any questions?

Unit 7

Cambridge Exams Practice

Activity Book

CD4 Track 34

AB page 126 Activity 1

1
Male: Did you go to that skateboarding competition you were talking about the other day?
Female: I decided not to take part because I hurt my leg. But it was great fun watching. Do you know Jimmy from our school? He was there. One of the jumps he did was incredible!
Male: Yes, I know him. I wish I'd seen him skateboarding. Did you feel sad that you couldn't be in the competition?
Female: Yes, I suppose so. But I need to wait until my leg feels better.

2
Male: So have you been to the new café in town yet? You know, the place with the fantastic milkshakes!
Female: Actually yes. I went yesterday. It was so busy, though. There was nowhere to sit. It was really loud in there too.
Male: Really? It was quite quiet and relaxing on Tuesday. Did you try the milkshakes? The chocolate one is amazing.
Female: You're right… it is. I tried that one. My friend had the strawberry flavour which she didn't like that much. We'll definitely go there again one day.

3
Male: I'd like to try a new sport. I play football every week but it would be good to play something else.
Female: There's a new judo club at school. I'm going to go to it.
Male: I'm not sure. I prefer team sports. Judo is too slow for me.
Female: Are you sure? Why don't you come along next week and try it. If you don't like it you can try something else, like volleyball or badminton.
Male: OK. Maybe I'll do that.

4
Female: OK. What are we going to buy Harry? I think we can spend £5.
Male: We can spend more than that. How about £10?
Female: OK. He likes T-shirts. We could get him one from that shop he really likes.
Male: I agree that he likes T-shirts but I don't think he'd like one for his birthday. He's got so many! He likes reading, doesn't he? We could buy him that new adventure book everyone is talking about.
Female: He does like reading a lot. Actually, I saw him looking at a book the other day. He said he wanted to buy it. it was a comedy I think.
Male: Well that sounds like a good idea.

Unit 8

Cambridge Exams Practice

Activity Book

CD4 Track 35

AB page 127 Activity 1

Radio announcer: Good afternoon, everyone. You're listening to Radio FM and I'm Daniel Browne. The town library is organising another story writing competition. This year the topic is 'What would you do if you had a time machine?' The story should be about 500 words long and it can be written by hand or on a computer. There are two categories in the competition. The first is for children who are between 7 and 11 and the second is for children between 12 and 16. If you're interested, you need to get writing straight away as the last day you can hand in your story is the 1st of June. There are some fabulous prizes this year. Every child author will get a T-shirt, and the winners in each category will receive 100 books. Finally, the best stories will appear in the town's newspaper!

Unit 9

Cambridge Exams Practice

Activity Book

CD4 Track 36

AB page 128 Activity 1

1
Where's the girl's pencil case?
Girl: I can't find my pencil case.
Boy: Don't panic. When did you use it last?
Girl: Let me think … I used it to do my homework last night. It was definitely on my desk then.
Boy: Did you put it in your rucksack afterwards?
Girl: Yes, I think so. Oh no! I hope I haven't dropped it on the way to school.
Boy: Have another look in your rucksack.
Girl: OK. Oh, look! Here it is. It was under the desk all the time.

2
Which activity does the boy want to do?
Girl: Do you still enjoy singing Ben?
Boy: Yes, I do. But I don't go to singing classes any more.
Girl: Why not?
Boy: It was on the same day as my guitar lesson and I couldn't do both activities.
Girl: That's a pity.
Boy: It doesn't matter. I'm interested in doing drama classes now. You learn how to sing, dance and act there.

3
Which subject does the girl have at 9am tomorrow?
Boy: Is this your new timetable, May?
Girl: Yes, it is. It's still a bit confusing.
Boy: Which subjects do you have tomorrow morning?
Girl: I've got physics at nine o'clock and then geography after that.
Boy: Are you sure?
Girl: Let me have a look at the timetable again. Sorry! I got it wrong. I've got chemistry first and then geography.

Videoscript

Unit 1

21st Century Video

PB page 17 Activities 1 and 2

Max: Hi everyone. Here we are again! Welcome back to Channel 21. I'm Max.
Amy: And I'm Amy. In these programmes we show you videos about fun and interesting things.
Max: We interview people too.
Amy: Today's programme is about transport.
Amy: We are at Max's dad's office to find out about how people travel around.

Amy: How do you usually go to work in the morning?
Worker 1: I usually go by bike. It isn't far.
Amy: Did you go by bike this morning?
Worker 1: This morning I went by bus. It was raining a lot.
Amy: How do you usually go to work in the morning?
Worker 2: I always drive. I travel with a friend because she lives near me.
Amy: How long does it take?
Worker 2: This morning there was a lot of traffic. It took almost an hour!
Amy: Hi. How do you usually go to work?
Max's dad: I usually walk. If I am late I sometimes go by scooter!
Amy: Really?

Amy: I wanted to find out about some other ways to travel round towns and cities. Here's my video.
We know all about cars, buses, underground trains and bikes. But what other ways are there to travel round a town?
Let's start in the sky in La Paz, Bolivia. These are cable cars. The long cable pulls the cars up to higher parts of the city.
Now we are in San Francisco, a city in the USA. These look like old electric trams, but they are cable cars too! The cable is under the road and it pulls the car. Watch how they turn the cable car round!
Now we are in an Asian city. It's Jakarta in Indonesia. These are called cycle rickshaws. One person cycles and another sits and enjoys the ride! They are a kind of taxi.
This is a city in Germany. It has a monorail to carry people around the city. It is more than a hundred years old.

Max: That was a great video, Amy.
Amy: Thanks, Max.
Max: What do you think would be a good transport system in our town?
Amy: I think the cycle rickshaws are great. They are good for the environment.
Max: But they only carry one or two people.
Amy: Yes, that's true. We need to think about the positive things and the negative things.
Max: Can you think about some positive and some negative things about different transport systems?
Amy: Bye!

Unit 2

21st Century Video

PB page 27 Activities 1 and 2

Amy: Hi everyone. Welcome back to Channel 21.
I'm Amy.
Max: And I'm Max. Today's programme is about hobbies.
Amy: What are your hobbies?
Max: We've come to the library to find out about other people's hobbies.

Max: Have you got a hobby?
Librarian 1: Yes, I play the piano.
Max: How long have you played the piano?
Librarian 1: I've played the piano for ten years. I can play really well now.
Max: Great!
Max: Have you got a hobby?
Librarian 2: Yes, I do photography.
Max: Are you good at it?
Librarian 2: I think so. Some of my photos have won competitions.
Max: Congratulations!
Max: Have you got a hobby?
Librarian 3: Yes, I do judo.
Max: How long have you done it?
Librarian 3: I've done judo for eight years. I've got a black belt now.
Max: Wow!

Max: I wanted to find out what people do to be good at a hobby. Here's my video. I hope you like it!
My brother plays the piano really well. He practises for 15 minutes every day. He even practises when he's tired. He's amazing!
My cousin has had guitar lessons for five years. She says the lessons are difficult, but she keeps going. She's fantastic at playing the guitar!
My friend is very good at tennis. He plays in tournaments and he almost always wins. But when he loses, he says it doesn't matter.
This boy is making model planes with his dad and his grandad. He needs to be very patient with this hobby.
These girls are doing ballet. They have to concentrate on their steps and work very hard. They're very good, aren't they?
This girl plays badminton. It takes a lot of precision and skill to be good at this hobby.
My friend likes team sports. Look at him practising for a football match. He says he runs a lot when he plays football. So he has to keep fit.

Amy: That was a brilliant video, Max.
Max: Thanks, Amy.
Amy: You need to work hard to be very good at an activity.
Max: Yes – you need to keep going when it's difficult too.
Amy: That's right. Keep practising your hobbies everyone.
Max: And don't give up! See you next time.
Amy and Max: Bye!

Unit 3

21st Century Video

PB page 37 Activities 1 and 2

Max: Hi everyone. Welcome back to Channel 21. I'm Max.
Amy: And I'm Amy. Today's programme is about running to keep fit.
Max: Do you like running?
Amy: We've come to my aunt's café to ask people about their running habits!

Amy: Hi. Do you like running Aunt May?
Aunt May: Yes, I love it. I go running four times a week.
Amy: That's a good routine! How far do you run?
Aunt May: I run about four kilometres. And, on Saturday, I run five kilometres.
Amy: That's great!
Amy: Do you like running?
Barista 1: Me? No, I don't like running.
Amy: Do you do any other exercise?
Barista 1: Yes, I go for walks and sometimes I play tennis. But I don't go running!

Amy: I like running. One day, I'd like to run in a long race. Here's what I found out about running!
Amy: These people are running in a long race called a marathon. It is more than forty kilometres. This marathon is in New York. Maybe one day I'll run a marathon.
We do athletics club at school. But that is only in the summer. There is another club called cross-country club. This is for running outside in fields and parks. We run in all weather! It rains a lot sometimes but I love it.
Every Saturday morning, people run in our park. The race is five kilometres and everyone starts at the same time – half past nine. We run through the trees and by the lake. It's a beautiful run.
This is my friend, Katy. She's really fast. She is always one of the first children to finish the race. She started running when she was six years old!
Are you ready to run? Go for it. It's fun and it's good for you too.

Max: That was a great video, Amy. Maybe I'll start running.
Amy: You should, Max. You needn't run very far at first.
Max: Oh good.
Amy: But you need to have a routine and keep a record of your times and distances.
Max: Great idea. I'll think about a routine now!
Amy: Maybe you can have an exercise routine too. See you next time!
Max: Yes, see you soon!

Unit 4

21st Century Video

PB page 49 Activities 1 and 2

Amy: Hi everyone. Welcome back to Channel 21. I'm Amy.
Max: And I'm Max. Today's programme is about being creative with digital technology.
Max: We've come to dad's office to see how people are creative with computers.
Max: Excuse me. What's your job?
Worker 1: I'm a graphic designer.
Max: Do you use the computer to design things?
Worker 1: Yes, of course. Look! This was designed on the computer.
Max: That's great!
Max: Hello. What's your job?
Worker 2: I'm an illustrator.
Max: Do you draw on paper?
Worker 2: Not always. Look! This was drawn on the computer.
Max: Wow! That's amazing!

Max: I wanted to learn more about being creative with digital technology. Here's what I found out!
Fashion designers usually use computers. This fashion designer is designing a dress. Look! She can change the colour of the dress with one click!
Architects use computers when they design buildings. This design is in 3D. You can see the sides, the top … and even the bottom of the building.
Film makers use digital cameras to record. Then they use computers to edit the film.
Graphic designers sometimes use a tablet for drawing. This designer has just drawn a car.
Now the drawing is almost finished. The designer only needs to choose a colour. There are lots of colours to choose from. Which colour do you prefer?
A lot of artists use a tablet for drawing too. The drawing appears on the computer screen.
This artist is creating a comic. Sometimes artists create cartoons. Cartoons are cool!
Working with a computer is fun and there are lots of creative things you can do. But remember! Too much screen time is bad for you.

Amy: I loved that video, Max.
Max: Thanks, Amy.
Amy: I'd like to create a comic on the computer.
Max: And I'd like to design a building. That's really creative! What would you like to do?
Amy: Digital technology is great, but remember - don't spend a long time on the computer.
Max: Enjoy being creative.
Amy: See you next time.
Max: Bye!

Videoscript

Unit 5

21st Century Video

PB page 59 Activities 1 and 2

Max: Hi everyone. Welcome back to Channel 21. I'm Max.
Amy: And I'm Amy. Today's programme is about communication.
Max: What languages are you learning at school?
Amy: We're at the library to ask people some questions about learning languages.

Amy: How many languages can you speak?
Adult 1: I am from Wales so I can speak Welsh. And I can speak English.
Amy: Did you learn another language at school?
Adult 1: I learnt French at school, but I can't remember any of it!

Amy: How many languages can you speak?
Adult 2: I love travelling and learning new languages. I can speak English, Spanish, French, Italian and a bit of Chinese.
Amy: Really?
Adult 2: And I'm learning Russian too!
Max: She said she could speak five languages. That's incredible!
Amy: Yes. But here is a language that she doesn't speak! This video is about sign language.

Amy: This is a language that you can see, but you can't hear. It's sign language. Deaf people use it to communicate. Different countries have different sign languages. It's a good language to learn. It helps you to understand deaf people – and helps them to understand you!
Amy: Do you know any words in sign language?
Amy: This girl is teaching signs to her brother. This means 'father'. Now she is showing her brother the word 'make'.
Amy: Now it's your turn. Let's learn to count. 1, 2, 3, 4, 5, 6, 7, 8, 9 and 10. Can you remember that?

Amy: And here is a message from another girl. What do you think the sign for 'we' is?
Amy: Deaf children learn at school using sign language. Sometimes people translate lessons for deaf people. They do this for TV programmes and plays too.
Amy: Today, many schools teach all their pupils some sign language. This school choir is signing the words as they sing a song.

Max: That's great. I'd like to learn some sign language.
Amy: That's a good idea. It's easy to learn some words and phrases online. Maybe you could try too. Try this.
Max: What does that mean?
Amy: It means "see you later!"
Amy and Max: See you later!

Unit 6

21st Century Video

PB page 69 Activities 1 and 2

Amy: Hi everyone. Welcome back to Channel 21. I'm Amy.
Max: And I'm Max. Today's programme is about the future. We're at my house today. Let's ask my family about their predictions for the future.

Max: What will the future be like?
Max's mum: I think there will be lots of robots in the future.
Max: What will they do?
Max's mum: Robots will do everything!
Max: What will the future be like, Uncle Frank?
Uncle Frank: I think there will be more electric cars in the future so the cities will be cleaner.
Max: Do you think cars will fly?
Uncle Frank: Yes, cars will travel in the air.
Max: For my video, I did some research on future technology. Look what I found out.

Max: Cars in the future will look very different. Look at this design. The seats can turn around. There's a computer too.
Can you imagine travelling in a car with no driver? These amazing cars use cameras and sensors to travel from A to B. They're safer than the cars we have now.
Drones are popular toys at the moment. But in the future they will deliver parcels to your house.
In this amazing design, the drone flies from the van when there is a lot of traffic.
There will definitely be more robots in the future too. These robots will help at home. Maybe they will talk too.
Computers will be probably be very different in the future. People will need special glasses to see the screen.
Look at this idea for the future. It's very original. What do you think?

Amy: Technology can make life easier and safer.
Max: But inventing new technology isn't easy. You need to think of an original idea.
Amy: That's right. You can't follow everyone else's ideas – you need to think outside the box!
Max: Why don't you design some technology for the future?
Amy: Enjoy thinking outside the box!
Max and Amy: Bye!

Unit 7

21st Century Video

PB page 81 Activities 1 and 2

Max: Hi everyone. Welcome back to Channel 21. I'm Max.
Amy: And I'm Amy. We're at my aunt's café today.
Max: We know that food in the supermarket comes from many different countries. We want to find out more about where our food comes from.
Amy: First, I'm going to ask my aunt some questions about the food in her café.
Amy: Hi Aunt May? Where does the rice and the bread from your café come from?
Amy's aunt: The rice usually comes from the United States. But this rice is from India.
Amy: And the bread?
Amy's aunt: Well, we make the bread ourselves in the café.

Amy: And what about this fruit? Where does this come from?
Amy's aunt: These apples, pears and plums come from Britain. But the oranges come from Spain and the bananas from South America.
Amy: South America? That's a long way away.
I wanted to find out more about where bananas come from. Here's my video.

Amy: Do you like bananas? Do you ever think about how they arrive in your supermarket? They usually have a long journey from one continent to another! The word "banana" comes from the Arabic word "banan". It means finger!
Bananas grow on plants in warm, tropical countries. Each plant can have 200 bananas!
These bananas grow in Peru, South America. The farmers cover the bananas with plastic. This protects them from insects and the rain.
The bananas have to travel a long way. Before they travel, the farmers pick them when they are green. They cut them into small bunches. Then they wash them.
The bananas are put into bags. They are then put into big boxes.
The boxes are then taken to the coast. Here, the bananas are put onto a ship.
Soon the bananas are in your supermarket. They are usually yellow and ready to eat.
How do you like to eat your bananas? I sometimes eat them with chocolate sauce and nuts. Yum!

Max: That was a really interesting video, Amy. So, the farmers sell the bananas to the big supermarkets.
Amy: Yes, that's right. The supermarkets transport the bananas to Europe.
Max: And then the supermarkets sell the bananas to us.
Amy: Yes. They sell them to us for a higher price. This helps them to pay for the transport and other things.
Max: And your aunt sells food at a higher price than she buys it for. So, everyone is happy because they've made some money. It's only fair.
Amy: Exactly!
Max: I'm hungry now! Let's say goodbye.
Max and Amy: Bye!

Unit 8

21st Century Video

PB page 91 Activities 1 and 2

Amy: Hi everyone. Welcome back to Channel 21. I'm Amy.
Max: And I'm Max. Today's programme is really exciting. It's about how to survive on a desert island.
Amy: Cool!
Max: We've come back to the library to interview people.

Max: What would you do if you were on a desert island?
Adult 1: If I was on a desert island, I would build a boat and I would try to escape.

Max: If you were on a desert island, what would you do?
Adult 2: I would build a shelter.
Max: Those were interesting answers. Here's my survival video. I hope you like it.
Max: If you were on this island, what would you do? What would you eat and drink? Where would you sleep?
Max: The first thing you need to think about is water. If you don't drink water, you will die. Rainwater is the best. You can use big leaves to catch it.
If there isn't any water, you can drink coconut milk. It's got lots of vitamins. Coconuts are difficult to open but you can use a rock.
Next, you must make a shelter. This will protect you from the sun in the day and tropical storms at night. This shelter is made from an old boat.
Food is important too. Look for tropical fruit on the island. There are crabs in the rock pools too. But be careful – some plants and animals are poisonous!
You need to make a fire so look for wood on the beach. A fire keeps you warm and you can use it for cooking. It stops snakes coming near too.
Finally, it's important to make a big sign in the sand. People will see it when they look for you.

Amy: What a great video. Well done, Max.
Max: Thanks, Amy. I learnt a lot.
Amy: What was the most useful thing you learnt?
Max: The most useful things was, if you are with people, it's important to work in a group. You need to help and trust each other in difficult situations.
Amy: That's true. Working well in a group is very important. Do you work well in a group?
Max: Bye everyone!
Amy: Bye!

Videoscript

Unit 9

21st Century Video

PB page 101 Activities 1 and 2

Max: Hi everyone. I'm Max.
Amy: And I'm Amy. Welcome back to Channel 21 for the last time. We're going to a new school after the summer.
Max: So, we decided to make a programme about secondary school.
Amy: First, let's find out what secondary school was like in the past. We're at Max's house.

Amy: What was your secondary school like?
Max's mum: It was nice. I used to do a lot of sport. My favourite sport was hockey.
Amy: What did you use to study at secondary school?
Max's dad: I used to study lots of subjects, but I didn't study ICT. There weren't many computers when I was at school.

Amy: Here's my video about secondary schools in Britain now. What do you think of them?
Amy: In Britain, students go to secondary school when they are eleven. It's a big change. Secondary schools are bigger than primary schools and there are a lot more students.
In secondary school, the students change classrooms. They can change classroom five or six times in one day.
There are usually lockers in the corridors. The students keep their books and school equipment there.
The science department has got laboratories. Students do cool experiments there. They need to wear overalls and goggles.
There is also a big computer room where students study ICT. They sometimes have design classes there too.
At lunch time, students can eat in the canteen. They choose the food they want and put it on a tray. This girl has got a very healthy lunch!
There are different clubs in secondary school. You can join the school band. Or maybe you prefer being in a sports team. If you're creative, what about joining an art club? School clubs are great, but the best thing about going to secondary school is making lots of new friends.

Max: That was a great video, Amy.
Amy: Thanks Max. I'm really looking forward to going to secondary school. Are you?
Max: No. I'm a bit nervous.
Amy: Don't worry. It's normal to be nervous. But you can learn to control your emotions.
Max: Really?
Amy: Yes. For example, you can take deep breaths when you feel nervous. (Max deep breathing). Can you think of other ways of controlling your emotions?
Max: Have a good holiday everyone!
Amy and Max: Bye!